In *The Genesis of Animal Play*, Gordon Burghardt examines the origins and evolution of play in humans and animals. He asks what play might mean in our understanding of evolution, the brain, behavioral organization, and psychology. Is play essential to development? Is it the driving force behind human and animal behavior? What is the proper place for the study of play in the cognitive, behavioral, and biological sciences?

The engaging nature of play—who does not enjoy watching a kitten attack a ball of yarn?—has made it difficult to study. Some scholars have called play undefinable, nonexistent, or a mystery outside the realm of scientific analysis. Using the comparative perspectives of ethology and psychology, *The Genesis of Animal Play* goes further than other studies in reviewing the evidence of play throughout the animal kingdom, from human babies to animals not usually considered playful. Burghardt finds that although playfulness may have been essential to the origin of much that we consider distinctive in human (and mammalian) behavior, it only develops through a specific set of interactions among developmental, evolutionary, ecological, and physiological processes. Furthermore, play is not always beneficial or adaptive.

Part I offers a detailed discussion of play in placental mammals (including children) and develops an integrative framework called surplus resource theory. The most fascinating and most controversial sections of the book, perhaps, are in the seven chapters in part II in which Burghardt presents evidence of playfulness in such unexpected groups of animals as kangaroos, birds, lizards, and "fish that leap, juggle, and tease." Burghardt concludes by considering the implications of the diversity of play for future research, and suggests that understanding the origin and development of play can shape our view of society and its accomplishments through history.

Gordon Burghardt is Alumni Distinguished Professor in Psychology and Ecology & Evolutionary Biology at the University of Tennessee. He is a coeditor of *The Cognitive Animal* (MIT Press, 2002), past president of the Animal Behavior Society, and editor of the *Journal of Comparative Psychology*.

The Genesis of Animal Play

Mother bonobo ("pygmy chimpanzee," *Pan paniscus*) bouncing her infant by using her feet. This behavior represents the bottom-up approach to play advocated in this book. (Photo by Frans Lanting)

The Genesis of Animal Play

Testing the Limits

Gordon M. Burghardt

A Bradford Book
The MIT Press
Cambridge, Massachusetts
London, England

MIT Press books may be purchased at special quantity discounts for business or sales promotional use. For information, please email special_sales@mitpress.mit.edu or write to Special Sales Department, The MIT Press, 5 Cambridge Center, Cambridge, MA 02142.

This book was set in Stone sans and Stone serif on 3B2 by Asco Typesetters, Hong Kong and was printed and bound in the United States of America.

Library of Congress Cataloging-in-Publication Data

Burghardt, Gordon M., 1941–
The genesis of animal play : testing the limits / Gordon M. Burghardt.
    p.   cm.
"A Bradford book."
Includes bibliographical references (p.   ).
ISBN 0-262-02543-4 (hc. : alk. paper)
1. Play behavior in animals. 2. Play. 3. Behavior evolution. I. Title.
QL763.5.B87   2004
591.56′3—dc21   2002045227

10 9 8 7 6 5 4 3 2 1

For family, friends,
students, and colleagues,
who realize now
that dealing with one
composing a play book
is not very playful for them!

Contents

Foreword

Scholars of all kinds have been seriously at work now for more than one hundred years trying to figure out the meaning of play and its function in animals and humans. The most interesting shift in theoretical opinion over this time has been that the earliest theories emphasized the commonalities of man and animal. Play, it was said, recapitulated the behavior of earlier species and as such was often animal-like, a not very pleasant activity with all its rough contests, its bullying and hazing of the less fortunate, its gross rhymes and joking, its gambling, and its often quite nasty fancifulness. It was also seen as a largely childhood preoccupation which with God's grace could be grown out of during the adolescent years. A century later, however, we are told primarily that play is a voluntary undertaking that reflects the creativity of young children, including their improvisations, their imaginations, and their cognitive, social, and emotional development. Furthermore, even though adults are now seen to spend much of their lives in recreation and entertainments, these activities, it is said, present them with opportunities to discover true play within their own higher level experience of these activities. This "true" or even "pure" play can be characterized in aesthetic terms, or can be seen as a kind of self-actualization, or trance experience that lifts the individual player out of life's usual mediocrity onto a higher religious plane. What seems very clear is that in these advocacies play has become something of a secular consumer luxury—a kind of conspicuous consumption once talked about by Veblen in material terms (as the wealthy playing with their horses and their yachts), but now addressed in more ontological or meditational terms as a luxury of the personal spirit. Unfortunately, those more concerned with the science of play than with these metaphysical properties have found it a continuing bafflement.

In these circumstances we are fortunate to have Gordon Burghardt's *The Genesis of Animal Play* return us once again to consider more carefully our relationship to animals in order to discover more factually who we are in our playing selves. In this he has rendered those who are less familiar with the biological, neural, and evolutionary aspects of play a great service. This is such a comprehensive, careful, and even graceful scholarly coverage that it shines light on the field much as was done by Robert Fagen in his earlier monumental coverage of 1981. Fagen sought to show that the key to play was its flexibility. In my own work I have emphasized play as adaptive potentiation or adaptive variability (1997). But what Burghardt now makes more clear and more specific is that play both originates from and creates *surplus resources*, any or all of which may be used on subsequent occasions. And what he does in the rest of the book is detail what these resources are in a full variety of more ancient creatures—some not hitherto known to be playful. His work now becomes the map within which any scholars who take seriously their own efforts to understand the universality of play have to establish their own probability of being other than a surplus resource.

Brian Sutton-Smith
Professor Emeritus, University of Pennsylvania

Preface

Playing is the most engaging behavior performed by any animal or human being. Watching puppies wrestle and kittens "attack" anything from a wad of paper to a rubber catnip-scented mouse has amused countless children and adults. Parents love watching their offspring play, and look forward to romps with them. Millions of people spend their discretionary hours in fishing, tennis, golf, biking, and hobbies of all types; others watch people play games; engage in make-believe (plays, film, and theater); or sing, dance, and play musical instruments. But then isn't all life really a game? Didn't Shakespeare in *Macbeth* say everyone is but an actor on a stage? When trying to sort out the boundaries of play, one quickly one gets tangled in a web of definitions, controversies, and elusive notions that slip away just when one thinks that they are grasped.

As a boy I spent many happy and frustrating hours trying to capture slimy salamanders and frogs that slithered or leapt free at the moment my hand signaled success. The study and analysis of play has many of the same satisfactions and frustrations as the undertakings of the child herpetologist. Indeed, I find myself wondering if the study of play is itself play. Committed herpetologists are only happy, in my experience, when they have the opportunity, or excuse, to get back to the field and personally collect at least some of their specimens. The dirt, water, sand, heat, muck, cold, thirst, ticks, leeches, wasps, bites, scratches, and foul-smelling feces all are part of the treasured experience—though not if all are encountered in the same expedition! By this point I may have lost readers who are not herpetologists, but I trust that any field biologist will understand what I mean. Returning to the issue at hand: Is playing, then, a completely arbitrary category?

Even eminent scholars have thrown up their hands and considered play more a mystery than a specifiable phenomenon that can be understood through scientific analysis. Others have used the problems of clearly characterizing play to declare that it doesn't really exist. Still others claim that play is so obvious when you see it that it doesn't need definition or careful analysis. It exists. Accept it and move on.

In child-rearing and educational circles, play has had an equally hard time. How should play be incorporated in school activities and curricula? Many educational theorists have stated that education should be made enjoyable and interesting through play; others seem troubled by the notion that a solid, academic preparation for life should or can be can be based on play, which is fun and thus not serious. Are such views the legacy of America's Puritan roots (Mergen, 1982)? Not really, because other cultures and times have shown similar ambiguity toward play (Burton, 1883). Play is indeed ambiguous, as our leading scholar on play has pointed out (Sutton-Smith, 1997) and as I indicate in chapter 1, while in chapter 2 I give an overview of several hundred years of trying to understand and explain play.

Is play in nonhuman animals on a continuum with play in human beings? Is play essential for their well-being? Could play in animals be an artifact of captivity and domestication? If all animals do not play, or play in different ways and to different extents, why is this so? What does play mean for understanding evolution, development, the brain, behavioral organization, psychology, and the meaning of life itself?

The problem of defining play and its role is one of the greatest challenges facing neuroscience, behavioral biology, psychology, education, and the social sciences generally. Alas, it is rarely recognized as such. Although it is not my aim to use new perspectives on play to understand and alleviate social problems or even to address human behavior, I do, on occasion, offer some grounded speculation on the ways in which playful tendencies invade and control many aspects of modern life. In a very real sense, only when we understand the nature of play will we be able to understand how to better shape the destinies of human societies in a mutually dependent world, the future of our species, and perhaps even the fate of the biosphere itself.

Human play is continuous with nonhuman animal play in many respects. To get at the roots of playfulness and the conditions in which it may have evolved, one must take other species seriously. For ease of reference, I will sometimes use terms such as *animal*, *mammal*, or *primate* when referring to nonhuman species in contrast to human beings, and at other times these terms will be meant to include our own species. The context should make the usage clear. This is a compromise between my strong stand on continuity of human and nonhuman existence and the need to avoid the cumbersome "nonhuman primate" or "nonhuman animal." Also, as a terminological aside, note that many of the authors quoted used the masculine pronoun to refer to both males and females, as is still true in many other languages today.

This book is not meant to be a thorough review of play research in animals or people on either a narrow or broad scale. Many writings on play often tell us more about the authors' agendas and perspectives on animals, behavior, psychology, and society than about play itself. A critical reading of any attempt at synthesis and integration, however limited, is always essential. This book is my reflection on the origins and nature of play, ideas emerging from a comparative perspective in ethology and psychology that incorporates recent findings in ecology, evolution, physiology, and neuroscience. I have tried to synthesize diverse information to create a useful, integrative story. This story is based on the view that although playfulness may have been a driving force behind much of what we consider most distinctive about human behavior (and much mammalian behavior in general), playfulness itself could develop only under a special set of biological conditions that led to a most remarkable interaction among developmental, phylogenetic, ecological, and physiological processes.

While I attempt to accurately review our understanding of playfulness, I argue that despite what we may think or wish, much of what play entails may not be as it seems, and that the importance and/or origins of play may not lie in the future-oriented practice and "preparation for life" claims frequently made for it. The truth may lie in other directions, and be much more interesting and important.

While this book does not provide a thorough treatment of scientific studies on the ontogeny, function, and physiology of play, I have made interim statements elsewhere (Burghardt, 2001). Unfortunately, most of this work focuses on just a small number of species of eutherian (placental) mammals, including children. An extensive coverage here would overly enlarge this book, the primary task of which is searching for play in animals that are rarely thought to play. Much fascinating and important descriptive, theoretical, and experimental work on mammalian play is available (Bekoff & Byers, 1998; Power, 2000). If many other animals do play, however, work based only on a few, selected mammals is unnecessarily limiting, if not potentially misleading. The need to integrate the perspectives and methods of those studying play in mammals and the much more extensive literature on play in children is great, however, and so I have devoted some discussion to both literatures in part I.

How and why play has evolved, then, is the topic of this book. Although we need to know more about many aspects of play, I have narrowed my focus in part I to placing the study of play in an ethological context (chapter 1), characterizing how scholars and researchers have tried to explain play (chapter 2), developing a more comprehensive and objective way to define and recognize play (chapter 3), describing the diversity of play in the most playful species (chapter 4), summarizing some of the major research methods and findings on play (chapter 5), and outlining a provisional framework to explain how play could have originated (chapter 6).

In part II, after discussing limitations in the data available for most species of animals (chapter 7), the heart of the book is presented in seven chapters (chapters 8 through 14) based on a search throughout the animate world for play or playlike phenomena. I present these chapters, especially 12 through 14, with some trepidation because senior scientists I respect have told me I will suffer ridicule and highly critical reviews for seriously raising the issue of play in nontraditional animals, especially without strong evidence. Chapter 15 revisits the basic premises of chapter 6 and discusses the implications of the comparative diversity of play for future research on the most playful species, especially humans.

Although the book is meant to tie together many disparate approaches and findings, I hope those interested in the details of how diverse animals play, covered in part II, will at least skim chapters 2 through 6, especially reading chapter 1, the second half of chapter 3, and chapter 4. Similarly, I suggest that those most interested in conceptual and experimental issues in play, or just play in people, should not totally avoid the evolutionary trek in part II because many of the often little-known examples recounted there confront essential issues on the nature and ontology of play.

Finally, perhaps a book on play should not be serious; occasionally you might indeed conclude that I am not being serious. Note, however, that the term *serious* is one that can be opposed to the *trivial* as well as the *humorous* and *playful*. Sigmund Freud once expressed a profound insight evident to every observer of child and animal play: "Every playing child behaves like a poet, in that he creates a world of his own, or more accurately expressed, he transposes things into his own world according to a new arrangement which is to his liking. It would be unfair to believe that he does not take this world seriously; on the contrary, he takes his play very seriously, he spends large amounts of affect on it. The antithesis of play is reality, not seriousness" (Freud, 1959: 174). While this statement may be true for the player, it is not true of play. Play *is* a reality that we have not effectively confronted in science or society. Yet it may lie at the core of who we are and how we came to be.

Acknowledgments

This book had its genesis in an invitation from Peter K. Smith to write a chapter in a book he was editing that expanded on a brief critique of his seminal 1982 *Behavioral and Brain Sciences* article on play in primates. Clearly, a chapter was not enough and Peter, whom I have never met, is somewhat responsible for my resulting long-lasting compulsion to explore the topic of play in depth. The work reported here was partially supported by grants from the National Science Foundation and the Science Alliance and Research Office of the University of Tennessee. Observations at many zoos throughout my life have enriched my knowledge of play. The important role of zoos and aquariums in this book should be obvious. I take full responsibility for any errors in documenting and interpreting the published and unpublished contributions of my colleagues and hope everyone realizes that any book like this is ultimately a series of snapshots. I sincerely acknowledge and thank the following as well as any others inadvertently omitted. Merely listing the names does not, however, adequately thank those special folks who have been deeply involved in this project for a very long time.

For reading and commenting on chapters or sections: Julie Albright, Colin Allen, Paul Andreadis, George Barlow, Ben Beck, Mark Bekoff, Matthew Bealor, Elliott Blass, Ronald Coleman, David Cundall, Daniel Cunningham, David Etnier, Neil Greenberg, Mark Krause, Matthew Lanier, Barbara Manzer, James Murphy, Arthur Myrberg, Sergio Pellis, Irene Pepperberg, Jesus Rivas, Erich Ritter, Steve Siviy, Brian Sutton-Smith, R. Mark Waters, and Duncan Watson.

For translations: Paul Andreadis, William Harris, and C. J. Mellor.

For correspondence, references, suggestions, skepticism, and unpublished observations: Paul Andreadis, George Barlow, Ellis Bacon, Ben Beck, Curtis Bell, Rick Bevins, Maxine Biben, Gerald Borgia, Eli Bryant-Cavazos, Thomas Bugnyar, John Byers, Roy Caldwell, Ray Coppinger, Anne Clark, Ronald Coleman, Seth Coleman, David Croft, David Cundall, Dan Cunningham, Stephanie Day, Allen Dunn, Gerhard von der Emde, Nathan Emery, John Endler, Robert Fagen, Afra Foroud, Susan Foster, Harry Frank, Hans Fricke, Val Geist, Neil Greenberg, Harry Greene, Don Griffin, Jocelyn Crane Griffin, Monique Halloy, Jon Harrison, Ruston Hartdegen, Carl Hopkins, Inge

Illich, Andrew Iwaniuk, Ken Kawata, Erich Klinghammer, Bryan Kolb, Bernd Kramer, Matthew Kramer, Mark Krause, Michael Kuba, J. D. (Skip) Lazell, Kerrie Lewis, Judy Loeven, The Lubee Foundation, Jennifer Manrod, Jennifer Mather, Roger Mellgren, Robert Mitchell, Peter Moller, Allen Moore, Dan Mulcahy, James B. Murphy, Arthur Myrberg, Christine Nalepa, Jennifer Nielsen, Andrew Odum, Jaak Panksepp, Tony Pelligrini, Cheryl Pruitt, Susan Parker, Sergio Pellis, Phil Pister, Daniel Promislow, Erich Ritter, John Robinson, Roger Rosscoe, Nathan Sanders, Barbara Savitsky, Wolfgang Schleidt, Steve Siviy, Merek Spinka, Patrick Stephens, Lori Taylor, Deborah Tegano, Sandy Trautwein, Larissa Trut, John Vandenbergh, Anita Vinson, Harold Voris, Duncan Watson, Paul Weldon, Stim Wilcox, and Kevin Zippel.

To the numerous students who looked up library references, watched animals in the lab and zoo, and did other tasks essential for this book over a more than 15-year period. Listing them here would miss too many. Those helping in the final stages or not mentioned elsewhere include Karen Davis, Kerry Hansknecht, Lauren Kirby, Jennifer Miller, and John Placyk.

To the staffs at the Dallas, Detroit, Knoxville, National (DC), Toledo, Toronto, and other zoos that provided examples, logistic support, and otherwise helped in the observations informing much of this book.

For help with figures and visuals: Kathleen Bennett, Matthew Bealor, Shannon Campbell, Cyndy Frame, Ann Hawthorne, Matthew Kramer, Michael Kuba, Minden Pictures, The Oriental Institute at the University of Chicago, Randy Small, Trooper Walsh, Paul Weldon, and all those authors whose work is depicted in figures and tables.

For typing and help with manuscript preparation: Linda Duffey and Madge Beeler. For editing the entire typescript: Ruth Haas. For proofing and improving the galleys: Jody Greenberg. For checking text references: Virginia Johnstone, Janet Rosenthal, and Ann Zahn. For preparing the subject index: Karen Davis. For preparing the animal and name indexes: Martha Conrad.

To David Houghton, Andy Snider, the volunteers at the Detroit Zoo acknowledged above and their coordinator, Linda Denomme, as well as the staff at the National Amphibian Conservation Center of the Detroit Zoological Institute who made my stay in Detroit just when the page proofs inauspiciously arrived so supportive and productive. The Department of Psychology at the University of Tennessee also aided my efforts throughout the tenure of several department heads.

To the editorial staff at The MIT Press who had considerable patience: Katherine Almeida, Margy Avery, Jessica Lawrence-Hurt, Tom Stone, Sharon Deacon Warne, and David Weininger.

To the Sunday night staff of the probability seminars who kept asking when the book would be done.

And finally, to my wife, Sandra Twardosz, who supported my commitment to this project in so many ways for so many years, and to my daughters, Karin and Liana, who accepted that writing a book on play sometimes interfered with playing with them.

The Path of Life
is a road to nowhere.
It is a balance
between insanity and reason.
It waits for no one.
Promises nothing.
Yet nothing else exists,
except the Path.

—Michael Robinson (1992)

I The Nature of Play

1 Play: Many Meanings, Few Answers

Now in myth and ritual the great instinctive forces of civilized life have their origin: law and order, commerce and profit, craft and art, poetry, wisdom, and science. All are rooted in the primaeval soil of play.
—Huizinga (1955: 5)

1.1 Prologue: Different Visions

Huizinga's claim is certainly strong, but one only more subtly expressed by many other writers (e.g., Dissanayake, 1992; Lorenz, 1981). Following Huizinga's lead, Stephenson developed an influential theory that "mass communication in its play aspects may be the way a society develops its culture—the way it dreams, has its myths, and develops its loyalties" (Stephenson, 1967: 48). My goal in this book is not to evaluate the first part of Huizinga's statement, but to explore the origins and more fundamental legacies of "the primaeval soil of play." Before we start to look for these origins and how they have affected the development of play, some old but enduring ideas about play should be examined.

A satisfactory theory of play is still wanting, and yet a man does not learn through any kind of instruction or study in later life anything like so much as the child learns in the first four years of his careless existence, through the perceptions and ideas acquired in his play.... as I have previously spoken of the experimenting of little children as play, I may now mention the internal resemblance of their procedure to that of the naturalist. (Preyer, 1893: 42)

This charming view of play expressed by one of the first important scientists to study child and infant behavior reflected a progressive, and still prominent, view of play. It reflects the great influence of Charles Darwin, who himself pioneered the study of human children with the tools of the naturalist and comparative biologist.

Now consider a chilling portrayal, written in 1888, of where this all may lead (H. G. Wells, 1934b). To set the stage, a perplexed Time Traveler from the nineteenth century has met some of the inhabitants of a future world, the Eloi:

I had always anticipated that the people of the year Eight Hundred and Two Thousand odd would be incredibly in front of us in knowledge, art, everything. Then one of them suddenly asked me a question that showed him to be on the intellectual level of one of our five-year-old children. (Wells, 1934b: 18)

These sunloving Eloi were delicate, attractive, excitable, and playful. Indeed, they originally viewed the Time Traveler as just another plaything. Perhaps, the Traveler thought, this change in the human species was a result of its success in taming the forces of nature, for "in a state of physical balance and security, power, intellectual as well as physical, would be out of place" (Wells, 1934b: 24) and succeeded by art, eroticism, languor, and decay. Indeed, the artistic impulse had itself almost died away by this time, and the Eloi were reduced to adorning themselves with flowers, dancing, bathing, eating fruit, singing in the sunlight, and "making love in a half-playful fashion.... The too-perfect world of the Upper-worlders had led them to a slow movement of degeneration, to a general dwindling in size, strength, and intelligence" (Wells, 1934b: 25).

Something was amiss, however. For example, how did the Eloi, who did no work, obtain their clothing? The Time Traveler discovered that a subterranean offshoot of humanity, the Morlocks, were responsible for keeping the Eloi provided with life's necessities. More intelligent than the Eloi, Morlocks were ghostlike creatures with bleached skin and big eyes. Unable to stand light, they were nocturnal carnivores and preyed upon the Eloi. They had their own language. Reproductive isolation was complete.

The Time Traveler realized with horror that the "Eloi were mere fatted cattle, which the ant-like Morlocks preserved and then preyed upon." He tried to empathize with the Morlocks, descended from the working class, but the Eloi retained more of our human form and thus claimed his sympathy, try as he might to see them merely as the well-deserved end of a "wretched aristocracy in decay" (Wells, 1934b: 46). "I understood now what all the beauty of the over-world people covered. Very pleasant was their day, as pleasant as the day of the cattle in the field.... And their end was the same" (Wells, 1934b: 56). By striving for a society marked by comfort, ease, security, and permanency, and seemingly attaining it, the human intellect had committed suicide.

It is a law of nature we overlook, that intellectual versatility is the compensation for change, danger, and trouble. An animal perfectly in harmony with its environment is a perfect mechanism. Nature never appeals to intelligence until habit and instinct are useless. There is no intelligence where there is no change and no need of change. Only those animals partake of intelligence that have to meet a huge variety of needs and dangers. (Wells, 1934b: 57)

In the end, neither the mechanically minded Morlocks nor the effete Eloi could escape change, culminating in the macabre drama the Time Traveler beheld.

Of course, this is mere fantasy written more than a hundred years ago. I have devoted space to this story because it represents a pessimistic view of what play means or
where it may lead. The author of *The Time Machine*, H. G. Wells, was enthralled with
Darwinism and was an influential popularizer of science as well as an eminent nov-
elist. As he later wrote about his early science fiction novels, he wanted to provide "a
glimpse of the future that ran counter to the placid assumption of that time that Evolution was a pro-human force making things better and better for mankind" (Wells,
1934a: v).

Accepting Wells's resistance to orthogenesis (the then scientifically popular doctrine
that evolution is inevitably progressive), we might well consider that play, like evolution itself, should not be viewed as a vehicle for transmitting our current cultural
values. Just as evolution was viewed as benignly progressive at the end of the nineteenth century, play, at the end of the twentieth century, was also viewed as a
uniquely positive force by many educators and scholars (e.g., Singer & Singer, 1990).
Wells was correct about evolution. Could he have also been correct in viewing excessive play as degenerate behavior? On the other hand, Preyer's view on play in children
as the origin of experimentation has been reinvented by an eminent engineer who sees
in play the origins of engineering design (Petroski, 2003).

Both Preyer and Wells understood that the roots of human behavior must be sought
in changes over evolutionary time and comparisons with other animals. It is unrealistic
to think we can truly understand human play without understanding the play of dogs,
monkeys, and turtles, although most treatments of human play pay scant attention to
the nonhuman animal literature (e.g., Fromberg & Bergen, 1998). Indeed, when the
subject is the evolution of human behavior, many scientists and scholars draw back
from an objective look at our own behavior (Burghardt, 1985a), seemingly afraid of
what they will see. Being themselves human, there are certain myths and rituals they
find comforting, myths and rituals that Huizinga (1955) might even see as deriving
from play.

Nevertheless, often for political and ideological reasons, science and logic are suddenly found wanting when the evolutionary lens is focused on our own behavior. If
the existence of play is thought to be independent of the pruning shears of natural
selection, then an evolutionary analysis of play, including human play, may also appear suspect. Nonetheless, many scientists increasingly see an evolutionary approach
to virtually all aspects of human behavior as both inevitable and necessary (Barkow,
Cosmides, & Tooby, 1992).

Members of the general public are often disturbed by an evolutionary interpretation
of human behavior for reasons that are only superficially different from those invoked
by intellectuals who hold that only human bodies, not our minds and behavior, have
biological origins (e.g., Gaylin, 1990; Lewontin, 1998). The two groups just have different cultural and religious heritages. Chief among these reasons is the presumed need

to have a rigid theological discontinuity between "the human" and "the animal," lest human dignity (or the human soul) be degraded. Yet these same individuals will readily recount the exploits, joys, fears, and suffering of their pets and are especially fascinated by play. They apply the most endearing but uncritical anthropomorphism in interpreting animal behavior. They are vigorous, though often selective, in condemnation of animal abuse and neglect. Perhaps some day they will be able to follow the lessons and intuitions from their own experiences and resist, without guilt and fear, scientific ignorance that is too often cloaked in righteousness. The biblical quote that follows is as unambiguous as the first two chapters of the book of Genesis are contradictory, and is compatible with evolutionary attitudes informing modern science, as well as many religious traditions.

I said in my heart with regard to human beings that God is testing them to show that they are but animals. For the fate of humans and the fate of animals is the same; as one dies, so dies the other. They all have the same breath, and humans have no advantage over the animals; for all is vanity. All go to one place; all are from the dust, and all turn to dust again. (Ecclesiastes 3:18–21, NRSV)

In short, to understand play we need to examine its genesis without preconceptions; to understand play in human beings, we need to study other playful species and test our ideas; to understand animals that play, we need to study those that do not. Genesis is no help. The study of play is indeed a minefield, and one must be resistant to the paradox and the pun!

1.2 Many Meanings

The study of play has gone through periods of faddish enthusiasm and benign neglect (Fagen, 1995; Power, 2000). Serious scholars typically ignore play; the exceptions also find themselves ignored. This is particularly true of the study of play in nonhuman animals. Scientific journals are filled with studies on obviously important behavior patterns of animals: eating, drinking, mating, parenting, and avoiding predators. How do animals learn? How do they communicate? What kinds of behavior are inherited? How are territories and dominance relationships established and maintained? What are the factors influencing whether a species has a mating system characterized by polygamy or monogamy? How do animals recognize relatives? How do they cooperate and help each other? Play behavior itself is either ignored or assumed to be important in an animal's survival and simply cataloged and described along with other behavior patterns.

The problem with play is that we are unclear as to what it is, what it is good for, how it originated, and how it evolved. We are so confused about play in our own species that it is not surprising that most scientists working on animal behavior shy away from a topic that, as I know from experience, leads to at best amused interest and a shared story about a pet. And in the case of biologists who do not work on behavior, blank stares and brief awkward pauses are more often the norm.

As this book will show, there is much confusion and debate about play in the animal literature. The problem for those wanting to create an "animal model" of human play comparable to animal models of learning, obesity, AIDS, or the behavioral effects of environmental toxins and drugs, is that there is even more confusion about the nature of play in our species than in animals. Consider the following contrasting views, all of which have been stated in the literature (Fagen, 1981; Huizinga, 1955; Lorenz, 1981; Mergen, 1982; J. L. Singer, 1991; Sutton-Smith & Kelly-Byrne, 1984; Turner, 1982).

- Play is the process most conducive to improved motor skills, learning ability, imagination, and educational attainments in infancy and childhood.
- Play underlies all creativity and innovation, including art and science produced by adults.
- Play, like idleness, is not only wasted time, but is also a process leading to the neglect of study and work.
- Play is just fooling around; the start of the slippery slope leading to delinquency, gambling, and even crime.
- Play is freedom.
- Play is the happy and enthusiastic participation in life.
- Play is cruel sport, teasing, and competition.
- Play is an essential respite from the solemn cares of life.
- Play is serious behavior in which the arts of war are learned (think of the Duke of Wellington's remark about the Battle of Waterloo being won on the playing fields of Eton).
- Play is encouraged by the powerful in society to distract the masses from their oppression, or more benignly, their lack of control over decisions affecting them.
- Play must be organized and controlled by governments or other adult institutions to control young people and channel them into responsible adulthood.
- Play has been idealized by manufacturers in order to sell expensive toys to nervous parents rather than their children.
- Play behavior has been exploited by manufacturers so they can produce and sell antisocial or gender-stereotyping toys and violent games that appeal to children, but have no socially redeeming value.
- Play is subversive and undermines the state.
- Play is a bourgeois product of industrialization and was so labeled only after work became estranged from everyday activities.
- Play is the source of the rituals and myths by which we structure our lives. All life is but a game or a stage on which we strut during our allotted time.

If these often contradictory assertions are not sufficient cause for scientific despair, other authorities argue, increasingly in these postmodern days, that play is beyond definition and scientific study. By trying to capture play, we lose it. Huizinga states that play should be "approached historically, not scientifically" (1955: ix). Hyland holds that play needs a "reflective" approach untouched by the concerns of conceptual clarification that mark the "mathematical sciences" (1984: xxii). Even if play could be defined, which he doubts, a definition is not "needful." Play lends itself to being viewed as an ineffable mystery or even as intrinsic to spiritual quests. Even animal play researchers have become enmeshed in this net. Fagen (1993) has claimed that the study of play encroaches upon spiritual territory, a region where scientists have to confront their own goals and humanity and are thus threatened. In child development, however, play is definitely considered to be important and it has been endlessly classified and studied (Berk, 1996; Garvey, 1990), although without any consensus on its nature or role (Power, 2000; P. K. Smith, 1996).

In his recent writings, one of the most prolific and seminal writers on play has focused on these ambiguities in how we characterize play (Sutton-Smith, 1997, 2003b). Such confusion poses dilemmas that we need to resolve before going on to talk about what play is, why it exists, and how it has evolved. Sutton-Smith tries to resolve the ambiguities of play by organizing views of play into seven traditions, each with its own rhetoric and associated with different historical traditions, meanings, forms, players, disciplines, and scholars.

• Progress   Play is viewed as an adaptation, as progressive, and as essential for learning, for acquiring skills and socialization, and for development of the brain, cognition, and emotion. Associated with evolution and enlightenment-era environmentalism, most biological, psychological, and educational notions about play, and their authors, fall into this camp. Juveniles are the prime players.

• Fate   Play is viewed as existential optimism. Play has a dark side associated with animism, divination, magic, chance, chaos, unrealistic expectations, and psychic masochism. Gamblers are the typical players.

• Power   Play is viewed as hegemony. Play involves strategy and skill games, with the ends being victory and enhanced status. From play fighting and teasing in children to athletic contests and deep play (play that has serious consequences to one's life or possessions) in adults, the primary players are in politics and warfare. The disciplines of sociology and history focus on this rhetoric.

• Identity   Play is viewed in a social context. Play involves symbolic interaction, bonding, communal life, and such rituals as parades, festivals, parties, theatrical performances, political gatherings, and religious services. Its origins lie in anthropology and folklore traditions, with the general public the primary players.

• Imaginary   Play is viewed as transformation. In animals, this is reflected in play being fragmentary, exaggerated, reordered, or repetitive. In humans, this rhetoric is manifested in pretense, fantasy, symbolism, creativity, and imagination. Scholars in art and literature emphasize this rhetoric. Its origins lie in romanticism. Actors are typical players.

- Self   Play is viewed as a peak experience. Play involves positive emotions and affect, ecstasy, flow, relaxation, and optimism. It involves leisure, as well as solitary activities and extreme games. This is play as individualism. Players are often avant-garde.
- Frivolity   Play is viewed as the world turned upside down. Here we find inversions and role reversals (e.g., Mardi Gras). This is the world of nonsense and grotesque realism. It derives from, and contrasts with, the work ethic and is studied by the students of popular culture. Typical players include the trickster, the jester, the comedian, and the fool.

Listing these seven rhetorics of play does not solve any real issues about play, and Sutton-Smith accepts them all as legitimate in their own ways. It is interesting that all seven have some counterpart in animal play. The list, however, does suggest how controversies originating in the use of the word *play* may derive from vastly different phenomena. Once this is recognized, it may be possible to address or put aside the real points of difference, as the case may be. The summary I have offered here does not do Sutton-Smith's sophisticated analysis justice, to be sure. It will also not be the last word on how the ambiguities of play should be formalized. Regardless, classification is a necessary first step in any effective analysis, and this one has brought the diverse uses of play concepts into one barn, if not into the same stalls. The rhetorics have power. Sutton-Smith (personal communication, 2000) has told me how the adherents of the progress rhetoric (which to them is truth, not just a point of view), hijacked a public television series on play on which he was working as a major consultant. They rejected any views or findings that questioned play as an unqualified positive force, or that pointed out the complexities of play.

Play, being a protean concept, lends itself to the diverse meanings encapsulated in the seven rhetorics of human play. There are similar confusions infecting the study of animal play, confusions largely clarified only in the past two decades (e.g., P. Martin, 1984a).

1.3   Animals as Players

With all these conflicting concepts and rhetorics about play, the study of play in animals may seem to be not only a minefield but also a quagmire into which no scientist should want to step. If not blown up, he or she may simply sink out of sight. On the contrary, recent work on animal play has begun to open up the field for an effective scientific analysis (Bekoff & Byers, 1998; Power, 2000). Much work remains, but exciting research, carefully and quantitatively performed, is providing new insights at many levels of analysis. That is the good news. The bad news is that play is much more diverse than anticipated, and it is hard to know what can be generalized across various kinds of play and even among closely related species (Pellis, 1993).

Our modern understanding of animal play largely results from new information. This includes descriptions of play in little-known species, as well as experimental studies with traditional laboratory animals such as Norway rats, mice, dogs, cats, and several species of monkeys and apes. Combining this information with the wealth of data on human beings, especially children, provides a more holistic view of play in the more playful and well-studied species, and has been admirably accomplished by Power (2000).

What has also greatly aided in the new generation of play research, as well as the re-interpretation of earlier research, is the application of modern ethological approaches to understanding important aspects of animal play. This allows us to pinpoint what we need to know and helps us discriminate between real controversies and those based on the different rhetorics.

1.4   An Ethological Perspective

Ethology can be defined succinctly as *the naturalistic study of behavior from an evolutionary perspective*. Its modern origins lie in the post-Darwinian synthesis of comparative biology, comparative psychology, and natural history (Burghardt, 1985b; Lorenz, 1981). Ethology was responsible for reawakening interest in the study of instinctive behavior in animals (Burghardt, 1973; Tinbergen, 1951). Initially controversial, such instinctive behavior patterns are now a feature of most current animal behavior study, although the term *instinct* is usually avoided. Some of the conceptual accomplishments of ethology as applied to play will be discussed in later chapters. Here a general methodological description will help in evaluating the theories in the next and later chapters.

The first characteristic of ethology is that it begins with describing behavior. Ideally it is an objective, descriptive catalog of behavior patterns of interest, often called the ethogram. Animals are observed either in nature or in captive environments that provide appropriate settings and stimuli. After acquiring some behavioral knowledge of a species and its natural history background, there are five specific classes of questions that can and should be asked about every type of behavior. The first four of these stem from the four aims of ethological analysis as formalized by Niko Tinbergen (1963), the Nobel Prize-winning ethologist. They roughly map onto the classic four causes of Aristotle (efficient, material, final, and formal) (Killeen, 2001).

The first aim is to study what factors *cause* or *control* behavioral performance (e.g., physiological, sensory, ecological, social, and other processes). This is the realm in which most psychological and biomedical research (and research funding) takes place.

Too often the complexity found here leads to scientists getting stuck in this realm. The second aim focuses inquiry on *ontogeny*, the development of the behavior and its underlying mechanisms, in the life of the individual. This is accomplished by not only describing how behavior changes over the life-span, but also by carrying out experiments on the role of environmental events in altering behavioral paths, and the duration and consequences of such interventions (e.g., early experiences, prenatal effects, learning). The third aim is to study the *adaptive value* of performing the behavior in terms of enhancing fitness at some level (e.g., individual, offspring, or group). The term *function* is often used to refer to the third aim, but it may be confused with the study of how the performance of any given behavior enhances or decreases the successful completion of any activity, regardless of whether that behavior is adaptive in an evolutionary sense. (As an extreme but clarifying example, consider a botched versus a successful suicide attempt!) Adaptive function is perhaps the best description. The fourth aim is to inquire into the evolutionary *origins* and *phyletic radiation* of a behavior and the processes by which this is accomplished or limits the study of the other three aims. This fourfold approach covers almost every aspect of behavior that one should know in order to understand it. It has had a continuing influence on current research. For example, Tinbergen's four aims are used as the conceptual framework in a major review of animal communication (Hauser, 1996).

For ethologists and other students of behavior, none of this is new. In the study of play, however, the application of these aims was not well articulated or stressed until the 1980s (P. Martin, 1984a). Once these aims were applied, however, guidance in formulating research questions at different levels was made possible. In terms of play, the four aims can be framed in the following way: What are the internal and external processes leading to performance of playful behavior? What is the ontogenetic path of play and its development in the life of the individual animal? What are the consequences to an animal of performing a given playful behavior or behavioral variant? How did play evolve from nonplay and what has been its evolutionary history?

In this book, the fourth aim is the central one. The main questions are the following:

- Is play just a trash-can concept for a motley set of behavioral phenomena that share superficial characteristics?
- Do all kinds of play share common causal mechanisms deriving from common ancestors?
- What factors led to play becoming prominent in the lives of so many animals, yet absent in so many others?
- Where does playfulness first appear in animal evolution and did it evolve just once or repeatedly?

The answers to these questions are neither simple nor obvious. They cannot be obtained without considering all four of Tinbergen's ethological aims. By the end of the book, I hope to have provided some answers and helped to inspire the search for better ones.

Notice that the key element of this ethological approach is that the same behavior must be examined from different perspectives. Many current controversies in all areas of behavioral study stem from the view that study of one aim excludes consideration of the others. For example, comparative and experimental psychology developed a strong interest in issues of mechanisms and developmental history, especially learning. Thus they emphasized the first and second aims, often termed proximal causes or factors. Until after the 1960s, most animal psychologists largely ignored what animals actually did in the wild; they also failed to consider the evolutionary history and ecological theater in which behavioral repertoires were shaped. In the 1970s, sociobiologists and behavioral ecologists reacted to the lack of rigorous field studies of behavior and the impact of "selfish gene" theory by ignoring "mere mechanisms," as well as development, and asserting through their research that adaptation and natural selection (aim three) were the primary, if not sole, sources of understanding.[1]

For others, evolution in a broader sense was also important, but aims one and two were downplayed (Alcock, 2001). Ethological aims three and four were thus termed the ultimate causes or factors. Although mechanisms and ontogenies are essential in understanding adaptation and evolution (Burghardt, 1997), a generation of graduate students and faculty were taught that these were unnecessary and an integrated ethology was not needed. This attitude unfortunately alienated psychologists and physiologists on the other side of the "proximal"–"ultimate" split. The exchange between Alcock and Sherman (1994) and Dewsbury (1994) provides an illuminating glimpse of these issues.

The heavy emphasis on studying behavior from a largely adaptive perspective had baleful consequences for the study of play, since 20 years ago the empirical basis for claims of the adaptive value of any kind of play was virtually nonexistent. Nonetheless, the adaptive value or "function" of play was viewed as its most important feature because of the great confidence that behavioral ecologists had in the power of natural selection to modify behavioral phenotypes rapidly in natural conditions.[2]

Consequently, since empirical evidence was lacking, support for the adaptive evolution of play was sought in mathematical modeling that was often divorced from any detailed behavioral knowledge. Fagen's early writings (Fagen, 1974, 1981), created in the early, heady days of sociobiology under the influence of E. O. Wilson (1975), epit-

---

1. For a recent impassioned statement that aim three trumps all others and that "causal pluralism" reflects "fuzzy thinking," see Reeve (2001).

2. There is a striking parallel here with the excessive confidence shown two decades earlier in psychologists' ability to control and predict behavior with conditioning methods and reinforcement schedules.

omized this view: "Analysis of play using hypothetico-deductive evolutionary theory may offend ethologists and comparative psychologists who prefer data to mathematical models and physiological metaphors to evolutionary logic" (Fagen, 1981: 480). Despite this rhetoric, mathematical modeling largely failed to provide new insights and research direction (Burghardt, 1984), a judgment that Fagen himself seemed to reach only later (Fagen, 1993). In retrospect, these efforts were premature. We just did not know enough about the details of play to generate any predictions that were both novel and general. As we gain more information on the actual rates, costs, and behavioral details of play, mathematical modeling of play will have a revival.

Today there is a growing realization in both biology and psychology that Tinbergen was indeed correct. We need to approach behavioral problems from a multifocused perspective (Burghardt, 1997). Tinbergen viewed the division of ethology into the four aims as a useful analytical and methodological framework, but information gained by work on each aim needed to be carried out with some understanding of the behavior from the other perspectives and integrated into a complex dialectic. Tinbergen never meant them to stand alone. He merely felt that it was important for students of behavior to stand back and recognize that to understand any behavioral phenomenon, all four classes of questions must be asked.

Why was this seemingly obvious point such a major contribution? The basic approach of understanding phenomena from different perspectives was not original with Tinbergen, of course, even in biology. As noted earlier, Aristotle's four causes captured comparable themes in a preevolutionary context. Nonetheless, researchers and scholars repeatedly failed to recognize such pluralities as they pushed their pet views or favorite approaches. Heated controversies over early theories on play, which are reviewed in the next chapter, occurred in large part because the protagonists confused the aims and how to test ideas about them. For example, it should be apparent from the four aims that a hypothesis on the effects of nutritional levels on the frequency of play can be neither proved nor disproved by showing that play does or does not aid in survival or fitness.

Play was somewhat of an enigma to Tinbergen himself, for he claimed that play has "subjectivist, anthropomorphic undertones" and might never be able to be "satisfactorily defined objectively" (Tinbergen, 1963: 413). This book takes on both of these challenges (chapter 3).

Tinbergen left out one group of phenomena in his four aims: the emotional, experiential, or phenomenological aspects of behavior. He did so because he was trying to gain the acceptance of ethology in a behavioristic *Zeitgeist* (spirit of the times) in American and British academic psychology and animal behavior (Burghardt, 1985a). When he was writing his creative early work (e.g., Tinbergen, 1951), some schools of animal behavior, especially in Europe, were still highly teleological and vitalistic (Bierens de Haan, 1947). Behavior was a product of purposeful striving and mental causes that could never be understood through the analysis of an animal's physical features, including the brain. In order to clearly protect ethology from being tainted by such views, one of the most distinctive attributes claimed for play, that it is fun or pleasurable, could not be validly investigated. Why? Because it involved "subjective" phenomena that Tinbergen felt were beyond scientific study (Tinbergen, 1951) and opened the door to pure speculation. Behaviorists also avoided such labels, despite accepting expressions such as "positively reinforcing" or "self-rewarding." These latter terms described behavior derived from primary drive reducers such as food, water, copulation, or pain avoidance. Any attributions of emotion, consciousness, or awareness to animals were highly suspect.

The denial of subjective factors did not have an immediately detrimental effect on most ethological research and probably was salutary: There was so much basic work to be done in describing and analyzing the myriad behavior patterns and diversity in courtship, predation, and social organization. One outcome, however, was to ensure that play remained a topic largely neglected by researchers who wanted to be considered "hard" rather than "soft" scientists.

Many persons studying play in animals, as well as in human beings, viewed play as containing a subjective component. Indeed, for many the defining characteristic of play was "having fun," and this is still true today (Spinka, Newberry, & Bekoff, 2001). Since traditional behaviorists and evolutionary biologists think fun is impossible to study in animals, especially "lower ones" such as rodents and birds, the basic premise of studying play was thus highly dubious from the start (Burghardt, 2003). I never realized the extent of this bias until I started writing this book and had to deal with skeptical colleagues. Since for many other researchers the essence of play is that observers must be able to recognize and appreciate the phenomenology or experience of play, play research has suffered.

Certainly we must have empirically verifiable data before accepting the statement that a behavior is enjoyable to any animal, but this caveat is as true for our understanding of play in people, including babies and children, as it is for animals. It is also true for the study of emotions in general (Panksepp, 1998a). As we will see in chapter 3, using a subjective component as a criterion for recognizing play, in isolation from other criteria, fails for numerous reasons. Nevertheless, in the study of play, more than any other area, the experience of the playing animal cannot be ignored.

In order to rectify the omission of an animal's "private experience" in the study of behavior, I have promoted a fifth aim to supplement Tinbergen's four aims (Burghardt, 1997). The case for doing this is not repeated here, but new methods, including brain imaging, neuroendocrinology, neurochemistry and pharmacology, virtual reality, computer simulations, and molecular genetics have led to a greater need to incorporate such issues into ethology and psychology. Table 1.1 shows each of the five aims with its application to play.

Table 1.1
The five ethological aims as applied to play behavior

Name	Related Terms	Description	Application to Play
Control	Causation, mechanism	Internal and external factors underlying behavioral performance	Do animals play more at high temperatures? Is the neocortex of the brain essential for play?
Adaptive function	Adaptiveness, function, survival value	Contributions of behavior patterns to individual, group, reproductive, and inclusive fitness	Do animals that play fight more in their youth fight better as adults? Do animals that play fight more have more offspring?
Development	Ontogeny	Patterns and processes in behavioral change during individual lifetimes	How does play fighting change in frequency between juvenile and adult stages?
Evolution	Phylogeny, genetic and cultural inheritance	Historical patterns and processes in behavioral change across generations and taxa	Did pretend object play evolve independently in cats and apes?
Private experience	Personal world, phenomenal world, subjective experience, heterophenomenology	Patterns and processes in life as experienced	Is all play accompanied by a few specific emotions or one?

1.5   Applying the Perspective: Horsing Around

People have kept, bred, raised, trained, worked, ridden, raced, and studied horses (*Equus caballus*) for millennia. Horses are surprisingly playful animals and engage in all the major kinds of play.[3] Exaggerated movements involving running, jumping, bucking, and related patterns of behavior performed by horses, alone or in groups, characterize locomotor play. This is particularly prominent in foals (figure 1.1a). Manipulative play with objects is also common (figure 1.1b). Social play is characterized by chasing, nipping, mounting, rearing, striking, circling, and other behavior patterns that can be classified as either play fighting or precocious sexual play (figure 1.2). Thus, a large series of prominent activities involving elements derived from locomotor, grooming, feeding, fighting, and sexual behavior patterns constitute play in horses. If we go through the five aims, the information available or needed for understanding each and how they often overlap or complement each other, can be illustrated. What is apparent is how little we really know.

3. Unless indicated otherwise, the following information on horses is derived from George Waring's book on horse behavior (Waring, 1983).

Figure 1.1
Young horses playing. (*a*) Locomotor play. (*b*) Play with objects. (From Waring, 1983)

Figure 1.2
Social play in young male horses. (From Waring, 1983)

1.5.1 Aim 1—Control

The amount of information needed to understand this aim is enormous and includes the roles of the senses and motor abilities; the environmental (space, structures, micro-climate), temporal, and social contexts; the role of internal mechanisms, including health, physiology, motivation (e.g., arousal), cognition (e.g., prior conditioning), and nutritional condition; and genetic factors. These issues alone warrant a lifetime of work and involve studies at different levels of analysis, from the molecular to the eco-logical. Needless to say, we have little of this information, even for a domesticated species as well studied as horses. Recent evidence suggests that differences in play among individual foals of the same breed on the same farm have a genetic basis (Wolff & Hausberger, 1994). The presence of other horses and their age and sex influence the kinds and amount of play performed. Approach and other behavior patterns seen in play fighting apparently serve as indicators that the interaction is playful and not serious.

1.5.2 Aim 2—Development

Horses are born with functioning senses and motor abilities. They are thus classified as a precocial species. In fact, foals can be observed playing within 2 hours after birth

(Waring, 1983). Exaggerated galloping play may occur. Play with the mother that involves nipping and biting various parts of the mother's body also takes place the first day. Foals also mouth objects such as hay, twigs, and grass, although they do not eat solid food for some time, not even being able to graze while standing. Changes occur rather quickly. After a few weeks, locomotor play occurs over greater distances and also when the foal is separated from its mother. Social play with the mother declines as other foals are sought out as play partners. However, play with the mother is now more of a mutual rather than a one-sided affair and the foal inhibits its initially rough biting.

After a month, the play behavior of male horses (colts) begins to differ from that of female horses (fillies). Colts play aggressively with each other for long periods. They may also play with yearlings. Generally, however, they pair off and partners do not interact with other colts except when chasing. Sometimes a colt and filly will pair and become play partners, but play fights are less rough than in colt pairs. Filly pairs engage in less social play than colt pairs. Filly pair play is also often characterized by frisky galloping side by side. In addition, play partners also perform quieter affiliative behavior with each other, such as mutual grooming.

Sexual behavior, including mounting and erections, is seen in young colts. Colts mount almost any object, including their own mother. Puberty and dispersal from the maternal band are not seen until the second year, at which time fillies have their first estrus and serious sexual encounters take place. Waring (1983) repeats the suggestion made by Tyler, in an unpublished dissertation on sex differences in behavior, that the more frequent play fighting in colt pairs than in colt-filly or filly-filly pairs is due to the precocious sexual behavior found in colts.

Adult play is rare in horses. Budiansky (1997) quotes observations that Przewalski's horses (an ancient and nearly extinct breed) in a zoo played less than 0.2 percent of the time.

1.5.3 Aim 3—Adaptive Function

The significance of play in horses is little known, which is true of play in all animals (P. Martin & Caro, 1985). How the different play elements function in the performance of play bouts or sequences can be inferred from careful description (Pellis & Pellis, 1998b). We could even try to relate the performance of different behavior patterns to physiological changes in heart rate, arousal, and the brain. Having a play partner may aid in later social competition for mates or harems. Perhaps a horse that plays more will be healthier and live longer. Almost all the vigorous exercise a foal has occurs during play (Fagen & George, 1977). As far as I am aware, there is no unequivocal information on any of these supposed benefits of play in horses except, perhaps, how discrete play elements function in bouts. The methods that need to be used to rigorously establish the adaptive value of play are systematically discussed in chapter 5.

1.5.4   Aim 4—Evolution

Horses are members of the mammalian order Perissodactyla, which includes close relatives such as zebras and asses, as well as the more distantly related tapirs and rhinoceroses. Play throughout the order appears rather similar in both the kinds observed and their developmental pacing (Fagen, 1981). This suggests that play in this order is a plesiomorphic (ancient universal) trait that shows only minor variation across species. However, detailed comparative observational studies are not available, so at this point little more can be said about the evolution of horse play, or even how it differs from play in other orders of mammals. Budiansky (1997) states that horse breeds that are more foal-like in appearance (such as having proportionately longer legs) seem more juvenile in behavior than Przewalski's horse and ponies, and thus may play more as adults. We also need to know more about the source of play behaviors in their "serious" counterparts and the possible links among play elements and their quantitative expression.

1.5.5   Aim 5—Private Experience

Play in horses is often described as exuberant, spontaneous, and intense. Appropriate partners and environments facilitating play are sought out by the animals. Beyond this, it may seem difficult to infer anything useful about what play means to the playing horse. Waring (1983), however, does provide a detailed description of lip, head, eye, nostril, and ear movements that, along with sounds, indicate "sensual pleasure." These are most often observed when the horse is groomed, scratched, or rubbed by others or by itself. Measurements of pleasurable states during play have not yet been carried out. However, heart rate, which is a measure of emotional and temperament variability, has been measured in young horses in response to presentation of a novel object (an open blue umbrella) suddenly lowered into an arena. The horses were allowed to investigate it (Visser et al., 2002). Not only did their heart rate increase when they were confronted with the novel stimulus, but variabilty in the heart rate declined, which is often found when an animal's attention is focused. Heart rate changes were consistent over time and differed among horses, with those deemed more "emotional" showing higher heart rates. Studying heart rate changes during free play sessions might be useful in assessing the experience of horses when they play.

As with humans, many animals can be described as shy or bold (Wilson et al., 1994). Human personality, it is generally agreed today, can be described by five factors generally labelled Neurotocism, conscientiousness, extraversion, openness to experience, and agreeableness. These personality characteristics are now being applied to other animals with considerable success, horses in particular. Positive scores on the last three factors may be associated with playfulness. In a careful study, nine stable workers independently evaluated ten horses using questions derived from human personality tests and achieved remarkable agreement on all five factors (Morris, Gale, & Duffy,

2002). Thus, although horses cannot fill out their own questionnaires, they, like us, can be reliably judged by those that know them.

There is clearly much that is not known about the play of horses; the kinds of information needed to address the ethological aims are diverse and extensive. All five ethological aims need to be kept conceptually distinct when examining early, but still useful, ideas about play in the next chapter, and when the defining characteristics of play are derived in chapter 3. Indeed, I have cheated a bit here. Why, a skeptic might wonder, should any of this horseplay be called play?

2 Footprints in the Sand: The Origins and Radiation of Play Theory

I sit alone,
by my fire,
Surrounded by these lonely men,
Who like me,
Passed this spot
On the back of the Serpent's tail.
—Robinson (1992: 11)

2.1 Introduction

This book is about what we can learn from what has gone before. This statement may seem obvious when we talk about the origins or genesis of any phenomenon, and here my goal is to trace the evolutionary origins of playfulness. However, there is another sense in which we learn from the past, from the history of our attempts at understanding nature. Thus, at the epistemological heart of this volume is the conviction that when we deal with something as complex and enigmatic as play, the efforts and ideas of prior laborers in the sand dunes of play must be considered and evaluated with respect. This is not just dusty scholarship; the effort is critical in facilitating our study of play so that we (1) do not spend efforts arriving at concepts already formulated and somewhat worked out, (2) build on and extend the promising leads of the past and (3) avoid dead ends already encountered. In short, we should not ignore the often surprisingly sophisticated conceptualizations of different eras that could enrich our toolkit of ideas in areas where improved theory is urgently needed (Fagen, 1981).

Many scientists view the footprints of scientists from previous generations as being left in sand. They seem to think that their predecessors left imprints too indistinct and unreliable for us to examine for direction, size, and pattern, let alone follow them. Besides, we have new tools that they did not have. Can we not go straight to the goal and forget the footprints entirely? Yet, to me, the early struggles to understand difficult issues are as important to the progress of science as understanding the fossil-ized footprints left by dinosaurs in the Cretaceous mudflats 100 million years ago (mya). They might once have been left in sand, but now are enduring clues to an ancient era that laid the foundations for the present world.

There are all kinds of footprints, and a useful starting point is to consider some of those left by our intellectual forebears in the attempt to understand play. The views summarized here are best appreciated in the original sources, but the edited books of selected excerpts by Bruner, Jolly, and Sylva (1976) and Müller-Schwarze (1978) are useful. I summarize the most influential and enduring older views of play here, often in the authors' original wording, because current textbook summaries are often too cursory to be useful, and often appear derived from secondary sources that are them-selves erroneous or misleading. Unfortunately, working scientists in an area may ig-nore prior work because of faulty textbooks, or because graduate program curricula (and Web sites) downplay the importance of reading original material that is more than a decade or two old.

A comprehensive survey of all theories of play is not possible here. I do attempt to provide a framework in which a careful reader could situate the most similar older views and thus identify what is new. More important, I hope to motivate the reader to dip into some of the early writings by those who struggled to make sense of play, especially its origins, adaptiveness, and evolution.

My goal in this chapter, then, is to encourage readers to go behind current fashions and recognize that what is new is often recycled, and that what is novel is often a matter of emphasis. Care is needed in winnowing claims, those in this book included!

2.2 Play and Animal Play

The English word *play* has many meanings. According to the great eleventh edition (1911) of the *Encyclopaedia Britannica*, play originated as a term with the primary meaning of exercise or active movement. *Play* can refer to the play of light and color on a surface, the play of flames in a fireplace, the play of an axle in a wheel, or the play of thoughts or ideas. However, these uses may derive from the more specific meaning "of the free movement of parts of a mechanism on each other, of a joint or limb, & c" (Vol. 21: 830). Thus, playing a musical instrument referred to the movement of the fingers on or across it. Indeed, until the eighteenth century one used the word *play* with the name of the instrument, as in "to play on a recorder." The use of play as a noun to refer to a dramatic production is also an early use, as was the use of the term to refer to active recreational sports or amusements.

Play, broadly considered then, incorporates more than what is generally meant in psychology and education today by the play of animals and children: engaging in nonserious amusement. Play may mean something other than amusement to the performer; the amusement is transferred to the audience. Thus we have theatrical productions, concerts, and sporting events in which the performers may be playing in terms of the original meaning, but the modern derived meaning that play is spirited, voluntary, and fun, may not apply. For the audience, however, attendance at such events may involve all three aspects. Today, the same issue is posed by professional sports stars and coaches who may earn enormous salaries for "playing a game" that most people engage in "just for fun." Thus, the seeds are planted for the innumerable controversies in conceptualizing what play really is and what it is for, even in animals. Brian Sutton-Smith's seven rhetorics of play listed in chapter 1 incorporate some of these broader conceptions of play.

Play is not only a word that has meant different things throughout the years in English-speaking cultures. Words in any language can always mean more or less than the phenomenon to be captured. For example, other languages often do not have any word at all that captures what we casually mean by play in English (Bax, 1977). Consequently, developing a set of criteria for identifying "play" in a scientific sense should not be held hostage to the various ways in which the English word is used (Sutton-Smith, 1997).

An attempt to break some new ground in defining play that goes beyond the English word *play* to the underlying behavioral concept more amenable to rigorous analysis is delayed until the next chapter. Here I trace the different views of play that grew out of Darwin's attempt to have us look at all organic life as a product of evolutionary change and differentiation, largely based on natural selection. These new approaches to understanding the diversity of life led, in the late nineteenth century, to much interest in mental and behavioral similarities across all species, including humans (Richards, 1987). It is not surprising that the first enduring attempts to construct a theory of play occurred in the years of the late nineteenth century.

Writers on animal and child play generally recognize that the views of play contentiously debated a century ago have elements that are found in most modern theories as well. These early views are important because they set the stage for the kinds of ideas and phenomena that theorists have tried to deal with as more data accumulated. The power of any integrative approach is measured by the success with which it can accommodate the valid points of conflicting theories. It turns out that the positive points at the core of many of these theories are much more on target than the criticisms their proponents made of competing views.

The discussion that follows is an extension of an earlier exploration of this literature (Burghardt, 1984). Here I describe (1) what aspects of play various theories addressed, (2) some of the examples used, and especially (3) points relating to the evolution and origins of play.

2.3   An Early Description of Animal Play

Play, sports, games, amusements, and recreation have been important components of human behavior in all known cultures throughout history (Avedon & Sutton-Smith, 1971). For example, Janssen and Janssen (1990) describe how the activities of children in ancient Egypt included ball games; tug-of-war; gymnastics and acrobatics; pretend games; and the use of many toys, including balls, dolls, moveable figures and animals, tops, puppets, and model boats. Lancy (1996), who extensively observed play in an African village, is representative of many ethnographers who have described play in nonwestern cultures. Games from various cultures are being used in modern classrooms and schools (Clements, 1995).

Play has also long been recognized as occurring in animals, especially in common companion animals such as dogs and cats. Consider the entry on playfulness in a 150-year-old "encyclopedia" of comparative psychology and animal behavior by Edward Thompson (1851) titled *The Passions of Animals*. The first sentences convey the way that play in animals was viewed then and in many respects now.

In the waking hours the influence of the imagination manifests itself by a playfulness of manner, and an exhuberance of animal spirits. The animal in its sportive moments abandons itself to a feeling in which its whole being seems to be concentrated in the performance of one of its passions, whether of joy or mischief, defiance or fear. (E. P. Thompson, 1851: 61)

Thompson then provides a series of examples, many of which would be accepted by play researchers today. His first example, oddly, is of crabs that "play with little round stones, and empty shells, as cats do with a cork or small ball" (1851: 62). However, this is quickly followed by examples that are more familiar.

Dogs, particularly young ones, are carried away with the impulse, rolling over and chasing each other in circles, seizing and shaking objects as if in anger, and enticing even their masters to join in their games. Horses in freedom, gallop hither and thither, snort and paw the air, advance to their groom, stop suddenly short, and again dash off at speed. A horse belonging to one of the large brewing establishments in London, at which a great number of pigs were kept, used frequently to scatter the grains on the ground with his mouth, and as soon as a pig came within his reach, he would seize it without injury and plunge it into the water-trough. The hare will gambol round in circles, tumble over, and fly here and there.... Whales, as described by Scoresby, are extremely frolicsome, and in their play leap twenty feet out of the water. (E. P. Thompson, 1851: 62)

After these examples, Thompson adds several more in an attempt to systematize and generalize the kinds of play.

Deer often engage in a sham battle, or a trial of strength, by twisting their horns together, and pushing for the mastery. All animals that pretend violence in their play, stop short of exercising it; the dog takes the greatest precaution not to injure by his bite, and the ourang outang, in wrestling with his keeper, attempts to throw him, and makes feints of biting him. Some animals carry out in their play the semblance of catching their prey; young cats, for instance, leap after every small and moving object, even to the leaves, strewed by the autumn wind; they crouch, and steal forward ready for the spring, the body quivering and the tail vibrating with emotion, they bound on the moving leaf, and again watch, and again spring forward at another. Renegger saw young jaguars and cuguars [sic] playing with round substances like kittens.

Young lambs collect together on the little hillocks and eminences in their pastures, racing and sporting with each other in the most interesting manner. Birds of the Pie kind, are the analogues of the monkeys, full of mischief, play and mimicry. There is a story told of a tame magpie, which was seen busily employed in a garden, gathering pebbles, and with much solemnity, and a studied air, dropping them in a hole, about 18 inches deep, made to receive a post. After dropping each stone, it cried, Currack! triumphantly, and set off for another. On examining the spot a poor toad was found in the hole, which the magpie was stoning for his amusement. (E. P. Thompson, 1851: 63)

In these few short paragraphs Thompson gives examples that encompass the range of play as described today. An admirable diversity of species and play types are mentioned: locomotor play; object play; play with prey or prey substitutes; and social play, including play chasing, wrestling, fighting, and dominance contests. Play is linked with exploratory behavior, energetic activity, and the realization that it is often most evident in young animals (kittens, puppies, lambs). We see the inhibition of behavior, biting, for example, which is a frequently noted characteristic of social and predatory play (but note the touch of cruelty to the toad). The view that play involves pretense (semblance) is evident, as is the recognition that there are play-soliciting signals that even other species can recognize. Indeed, play with humans is cited several times. By current standards the comparison of some birds (magpies) with primates in their level of curiosity (mischief) and play is prescient. The development of games by animals that are not exclusively the product of instinctive or genetically controlled behavior is also mentioned. In short, virtually every behavioral aspect of animal play commonly studied today is listed.

However, Thompson was not a modern student of play in animals. These were the days before experiments on animal behavior were either formalized or developed. Even post-Darwinian authors such as Romanes (1883), Lindsay (1879), and Büchner (1880) relied heavily on anecdotes, often by reliable observers, but too often not. The last example quoted from Thompson (1851), although certainly compatible with what we know about the behavior of corvids, including magpies, reads like an oft-told tale. Thompson also was hampered by the limited knowledge of the natural history of the animals described. Thus, he did not get everything right by current lights. For example, he apparently confused courtship rituals in cranes with social play. On the other hand, courtship can have its playful, gamelike aspects in humans, and we might want to keep open this possibility in other species as well.

2.4   The Early Darwinian Legacy

The aftermath of the publication of *On the Origin of Species* was an intense search for commonalities between the behavior of human and nonhuman animals. Darwin contributed to this search with two important books that emphasized the links between us and other species in terms of social behavior, intelligence, and emotional expression (Darwin, 1871, 1872). Darwin discussed play, but did not add any new theoretical substance:

... the lower animals, like man, manifestly feel pleasure and pain, happiness and misery. Happiness is never better exhibited than by young animals, such as puppies, kittens, lambs, &c., when playing together, like our own children. Even insects play together, as has been described by that excellent observer, P. Huber, who saw ants chasing and pretending to bite each other, like so many puppies. (Darwin 1877: 68)

It is worth noting that for Darwin, like Thompson and other writers in the nineteenth century, play was not limited to vertebrates or even mammals, although the majority of examples always came from eutherian (placental) mammals.

In actuality, during the nineteenth century not much progress was made in our detailed knowledge of animal play. Lindsay (1879) recounted many examples, again anecdotal, on play in animals in chapters on "deception" and "practical jokes." He went beyond Thompson in drawing out some further characteristics of play. For example, he noted the limits to the distinction between serious and nonserious activities or, as he wrote, "the perception of the distinction between *jest and earnest*. Unfortunately, just as in children, there is the same tendency in the mimic fights of young cocks or sporting dogs for jest and sport to pass into earnest. And the consequences of such a transition are sometimes quite as serious or sad in other animals as in man" (Lindsay, 1879: 530). The fact that internal or motivational factors as well as the topography of the playful acts (what they look like) are both relevant is integral to this distinction. Nonetheless, Lindsay's attribution of pretense, humor, and make-believe to the behavior of animals was wildly and uncritically anthropomorphic, assuming a level of consciousness and intentionality (Bekoff & Allen, 1998) that would be rejected today without much better evidence. The early search for the evolutionary roots of human psychology too often led to similar overreaching (Lorenz, 1985).

Although the collection of more data on play lagged, after Darwin the emphasis switched to developing a theory that would explain why play occurred and how it evolved among species and developed in individuals. This was important because play, if viewed as not serious or not important to survival or reproduction, posed a problem for evolutionists (see Rosenberg, 1990, for a more recent critique). How can we explain through natural selection the occurrence of something that did not seem important, just fun? This challenge to viewing play as a product of evolution was recognized by neither Darwin nor the early post-Darwinian writers such as Romanes (1883). In the early days of Darwinian theory, trying to explain the evolution of the vertebrate eye and sterile castes in social insects seemed much more urgent difficulties to attend to. Nonetheless, by the turn of the century, several views of human and animal play were formalized and competition among them was intense.

The theories that were to eventually dominate discussion for much of the twentieth century were summarized in the entry on play in the seminal *Dictionary of Philosophy and Psychology* edited by the founder of developmental evolutionary psychology, James Mark Baldwin (1902b). Baldwin wrote the essay on play and provides a good benchmark for evaluating where we are today a century later.

Baldwin grouped the theories of play into two camps: the biological and the psychological. From the biological perspective, he listed the "surplus energy" theory developed by Herbert Spencer and the "instinct practice" theory of Groos. A third view mentioned by Baldwin was "recuperation" theory. On the psychological side, Baldwin listed the "semblance" theory and "autotelic" theories. Another major theory of the time, not mentioned by Baldwin, was the "recapitulation" theory of G. Stanley Hall, which did not become widely known until shortly after Baldwin's dictionary appeared.

The three main contending theories are described here with their original labels: surplus energy, instinct practice, and recapitulation. This is risky since names alone can foster premature dismissal of good ideas. Energy, instinct, and recapitulation were all to be eventually, and authoritatively, flung on the ash heap of science by leading scientists. Harlow (1971: 33) dismissed these theories of play as "quaint and curious," as they were based on anecdotes and outmoded ideas about physiology and evolution. The phenomenal reality underlying these terms was forgotten in attacks on various weaknesses of each theory, problems that limited their scope to be sure, but which in retrospect did not discredit them completely. It is interesting that the biological bases of all three terms have been resurrected, albeit in altered form, by modern scientific methods that would have been inconceivable to the critics![4] The lesson to be learned is that if one goes beyond the rhetoric, one finds a core of commonsense ideas at the root of these views. The problem is that the theories often addressed different levels and domains of explanation. This is where analytical application of the five ethological aims plays a critical role.

In the following section these three main contending early theories on animal play (Müller-Schwarze, 1978) are presented and are followed by some others listed by Baldwin (1902a) and Carr (1902) that presaged later influential approaches to human as well as animal play.

---

4. I have discussed some of this history elsewhere (Burghardt, 1973, 1984, 1985a,b, 1998b).

2.5   Three Major Sources of Modern Play Theory

2.5.1   Surplus Energy Theory

In the early nineteenth century, Friedrich Schiller wrote a series of influential letters on aesthetic education (F. Schiller, 1967, original 1795). A major German playwright and poet, he developed a complex theory of beauty that is still promoting debate and clarification. For Schiller, civilized society began with "a propensity for ornamentation and play" (F. Schiller, 1967: 193). Now what are the conditions in which this happens? Schiller makes the following case in his twenty-seventh letter.

It is true that Nature has given even to creatures without reason more than the bare necessities of existence, and shed a glimmer of freedom even into the darkness of animal life. When the lion is not gnawed by hunger, nor provoked to battle by any beast of prey, his idle strength creates an object for itself: he fills the echoing desert with a roaring that speaks defiance, and his exuberant energy enjoys its *self* in purposeless display. With what enjoyment of life do insects swarm in the sunbeam; and it is certainly not the cry of desire that we hear in the melodious warbling of the songbird. Without doubt there is freedom in these activities; but not freedom from compulsion altogether, merely from a certain kind of compulsion, compulsion from without. An animal may be said to be at work, when the stimulus to activity is some lack; it may be said to be at play, when the stimulus is sheer plenitude of vitality, when superabundance of life is its own incentive to action. (F. Schiller, 1967: 207)

Putting aside Schiller's lack of modern understanding of insect swarming and bird song, the point is clear that play occurs only when the animal is not under compulsion from external demands. And in this he also sees the essence of true human freedom. He not only makes a link to animal play as in the quotation, but goes even further to include trees that put forth more buds, roots, branches, and leaves than are needed for survival, suggesting the linkage of play with the essence of life itself.

Although Schiller may be the original framer of a surplus energy view of play and its origins, the theory discussed and dismissed first in almost all reviews of play is Herbert Spencer's (1872) surplus energy theory. It is found in the second edition of his *Principles of Psychology*, in the very last chapter (of seventy-five) titled "Aesthetic sentiments." In a compact six-page discussion, Spencer builds on something he had read by a "forgotten German author," undoubtedly Friedrich Schiller (Elias, 1973), that artistic endeavors "originate from the play-impulse" (Spencer, 1872: 627). He proceeds brilliantly to show how this might have occurred, but first he shows how play itself originated and domesticates Schiller's wilder prose.

Spencer begins by noting that unlike most other bodily functions and behavior patterns, artistic and play activities are not necessary for life. "The activities we call play are united with the aesthetic activities, by the trait that neither subserve, in any direct way, the processes conducive to life" (1872: 627). This view is embedded in the then-fashionable "faculty psychology": "From the primary action of a faculty there results the immediate normal gratification, *plus* the maintained or increased ability due to exercise, *plus* the objective end achieved or requirement fulfilled" (Spencer, 1872: 628). Play and art only satisfy the first two objectives, not the third, which for Spencer is limited to "proximate ends that imply ulterior benefits." Notice that the second objective asserts that play *does* have a function of producing "increased ability due to exercise," even if benefits such as eating, mating, or accessing other resources are not attained.

How did play originate? Spencer provided an insightful but ultimately flawed answer.

Inferior kinds of animals have in common the trait, that all their forces are expended in fulfilling functions essential to the maintenance of life. They are unceasingly occupied in searching for food, in escaping from enemies, in forming places of shelter, and in making preparations for progeny. But as we ascend to animals of high types having faculties more efficient and more numerous, we begin to find that time and strength are not wholly absorbed in providing for immediate needs. Better nutrition, gained by superiority, occasionally yields a surplus of vigour. The appetites being satisfied, there is no craving which directs the overflowing energies to the pursuit of more prey, or to the satisfaction of some pressing want.... When there have been developed many powers adjusted to many requirements, they cannot all act at once: now the circumstances call these into exercise and now those; and some of them occasionally remain unexercised for considerable periods. Thus there happens that in the more-evolved creatures, there often recurs an energy somewhat in excess of immediate needs, and there comes also such rest, now of this faculty and now of that, as permits the bringing of it up to a state of high efficiency by the repair which follows waste. (Spencer, 1872: 628–629)

In brief, Spencer proposed that play originates in "higher" animals (mammals), which have more efficient and more numerous ways of obtaining food, avoiding enemies, and solving other day-to-day problems. Better nutrition may give rise to a surplus of energy or vigor and at the same time certain behavioral faculties are not used for some time. This leads to lowered thresholds for both behavior patterns and their associated motivations and emotions ("desires"). The latter idea derived from the neurophysiological model that Spencer developed to explain what was going on inside the animal's brain (this in the days when neurophysiology hardly existed!). His theory of nerve centers held that those parts of the nervous system that are undischarged through behavior become "unusually ready to undergo change, to yield up molecular motion" (1872: 629). His views are remarkably prescient of Lorenz's model of action-specific energy (Lorenz, 1981), one of the first useful models developed by the ethologists (see chapter 5).

Spencer also viewed play as on a continuum with nonplay. For example, rats have incisors that continue to grow and are normally worn down throughout life; in captivity rats will gnaw anything available to keep their incisors worn. Similarly, house cats, deprived of the opportunity to hunt, will claw at chair coverings or tree bark to stretch and exercise their limbs. This captivity-induced activity, "which hardly rises to what we call play, passes into play ordinarily so called where there is a more manifest union of feeling with the action. Play is equally an artificial exercise of powers, which in default of their natural exercise, become so ready to discharge that they relieve themselves by simulated actions in place of real actions" (1872: 630). This feeling or affect can be interpreted as pleasurable or fun.

An important aspect of Spencer's view is that play is often a simulation and reflects a species' characteristic behavioral repertoire. Thus predatory dogs have chasing and fighting games, kittens pounce after cotton balls, and boys chase and wrestle with one another and thus "gratify in a partial way the predatory instincts." Children play with dolls, give tea parties, and show other "dramatizings of adult activities" (1872: 631). Child and adult games of skill are all based on achieving victory, and this can extend to chess, conversation and repartee, and wit combat in general. "That is to say, this activity of the intellectual faculties in which they are not used for purposes of guidance in the business of life, is carried on partly for the sake of the pleasure of the activity itself, and partly for the accompanying satisfaction of certain egoistic feelings which find for the moment no other sphere" (1872: 631).

Remarkably, Spencer's theory was on the surface able to cover all aspects of play, and was quite successful in postulating a satisfactory understanding of how playful activities evolved from nonplayful ones. It contains the seed of the theory advanced in this book. If the psychologist reader thinks that Spencer's reliance on a nineteenth-century faculty psychology renders his views suspect, this may be too harsh; while the original nineteenth-century faculty psychology has not come round again, the approach has resurfaced as "modularity of mind" theory (Fodor, 1983) and has become increasingly popular in evolutionary, psychological, and neurophysiological circles (Barkow, Cosmides, & Tooby, 1992; Restak, 1994; Shettleworth, 1998).

2.5.2 Instinct-Practice Theory

Already in Spencer we see that the forms of play seen in animals were related to the characteristic and instinctive activities the species performed "seriously." Lindsay was one of the first to explicitly state that "playfulness, sportiveness, or friskiness in the young" were instincts (Lindsay, 1879: 131). Indeed, he advances what is today a major interpretation of play that is gaining support (K. V. Thompson, 1998): that through play animals master skills and assess their abilities.

Self-tuition includes systematic muscular exercise.... The play of all young animals is to be regarded as an important part of physical *education*, as a means of imparting or developing that bodily agility which is so necessary in the struggle for life. Hence their mimic fights and races, their gambols, games, sports, pastimes of all kinds, have a high educational value, as well as an important relation to health, mental and bodily. (Lindsay, 1879: 280)

Here we see a shift that was soon to cause much confusion, that from the proximate causes of play behavior to the survival value or functions of play. The main protagonist in this shift was Karl Groos, a philosopher who wrote two highly influential books. His book on the play of animals (Groos, 1898)[5] was until Fagen (1981) the only comprehensive treatment of the topic. A later volume on human play (Groos, 1901) was the first thorough treatment of that topic as well.

Groos argued, in quite modern fashion, that most behavior patterns, including song learning in birds, are a combination of instinct and experience. When a tiger cub is first confronted with prey it must capture alone, any "hereditary impulse" to creep up to, leap on, and seize prey would not be very successful unless such maneuvers had been practiced earlier. That is, the instinctive mechanisms would have to be near perfect. Groos considered such innate mastery impossible in more intelligent animals. "In the very moment when advancing evolution has gone so far that intellect alone can accomplish more than instinct, hereditary mechanism tends to lose its perfection, and the 'chiseling out of brain predispositions' by means of individual experience becomes more and more prominent. And it is by the play of children and animals alone that this carving out can be properly and perfectly accomplished" (Groos, 1898: 74). As support for this view, Groos notes that playful versions of necessary activities appear earlier in an animal's life than when they are needed seriously. His very long book can be summed up in this famous quotation:

Animals can not be said to play because they are young and frolicsome, *but rather they have a period of youth in order to play*; for only by so doing can they supplement the insufficient hereditary endowment with individual experience in view of the coming tasks in life. (Groos, 1898: 75)

Thus play is founded on instinct, play perfects instinct, and play is necessary for the adequate development of mind and body. A large role is claimed for play in these few words. Fagen (1981), though critical of many specifics, largely endorsed the functional approach of Groos.

A problem Groos faced was play in adult animals. An adult should have no need for practice once instinctive behaviors are perfected. Groos uses the proximate pleasures of play to explain play in adult animals. ("A creature that once knows the pleasure of play will derive satisfaction from it even when youth is gone" Groos, 1898: 81.) The Baldwins (J. D. Baldwin & Baldwin, 1977) unwittingly rediscovered this explanation in their application of reinforcement theory to the retention of play in adult monkeys. Groos also pointed out that that "preservation of the species is advanced by exercise of the mind and body even in later years" (Groos, 1898: 81).

5. The original German edition was published in 1895. The English translation by Mark Baldwin's wife, Elizabeth, omits some text and otherwise alters the original and must be treated as a somewhat different edition.

Groos devoted a long chapter to the weaknesses of surplus energy theory. He summarized the theory as follows (1898: 6):

1. The higher animals being able to provide themselves with better nourishment than the lower,
their time and strength are no longer exclusively occupied in their own maintenance, hence they
acquire a superabundance of vigour.
2. The overflow of energy will be favored in those cases where the higher animals have need for
more diversified activities, for while they are occupied with one, the other special powers can find
rest and reintegration.
3. When in this manner, the overflow of energy has reached a certain pitch, it tends to discharge.
4. If there is no occasion at the moment for the correlative activity to be seriously exercised, simply imitative activity is substituted, and this is play.

Groos (1898) states that although the surplus energy theory is plausible, it is easily
shown to be inadequate. He criticizes each main aspect, primarily by pointing out
exceptions. Although young well-fed animals in comfortable surroundings may be exuberant, he points out that tired animals may play, as when a kitten chases a leaf that
blows past "even if it has been exercising for hours and its superfluous energies entirely
disposed of" (1898: 19).

Furthermore, the "physical and mental overflow of energy" cannot be the main
process since "it does not explain how it happens that all the individuals of a species
manifest exactly the specific kind of play expression which prevails with their species,
but differs from every other" (1898: 12). For Groos, the answer lies in instinct, not
surplus energy or imitation.

Finally, the imitative process in point 4 cannot apply to the first occurrences of play
in young animals and children. Imitation is learning details of behavior by observing
another animal perform the behavior. As Groos states, such forms of play "at the very
outset ... are not imitative repetitions, but rather preparatory efforts. They come before
any serious activity, and evidently aim at preparing the young creature for it and making him familiar with it" (1898: 7).

It is at this point that Groos's critique of Spencer collapses, for Groos's assertion that
imitation is at the heart of Spencer's theory is based on a quotation from someone
else (or a translator) who apparently confused imitation with "simulation," the word
Spencer actually used. Simulation is not imitation, but is Spencer's word to indicate
that the behaviors were not functional but "as if" (see the discussion on semblance
theory in the next section).[6] Furthermore, Spencer clearly tied the type of play animals
perform to their specific instinctive activities. In addition, the fact that animals that
appear to be exhausted still manage to engage in another round of vigorous play will
not be surprising to any parent of a 3-year-old child.

6. Schiller clearly does use imitation in his theory, and this could be a source of the confusion as
well.

Why was Groos so set on discrediting Spencer, and why was James Mark Baldwin such a supporter, a disciple more doctrinaire than the prophet? (According to J. M. Baldwin's preface to the English translation, Groos's criticisms of surplus energy theory "put this theory permanently out of court" [Groos, 1898: iii].) My surmise is that to enthusiastic evolutionists such as Baldwin, Spencer's theory did not sufficiently address the "biological significance of play," which obviously had to be practice of adult behavior! As Groos eloquently states:

Can a phenomenon that is of so great, so incalculable value possibly be simply a convenient method of dissipating superfluous accumulations of energy? In all this there seems nothing to hinder the assumption that the instincts operative in play, like so many other phenomena of heredity, first appear when the animal really needs them. Where, then, would be the play of the young? It would not be provoked either by overflowing nervous energy or by the need for recreation. Yet the early appearance of this instinct is of inestimable importance. Without it the adult animal would be but poorly equipped for the tasks of his life. He would have far less than the requisite amount of practice in running and leaping, in springing on his prey, in seizing and strangling his victim, in fleeing from his enemies, in fighting his opponents, etc. The muscular system would not be sufficiently developed and trained for all these tasks. Moreover, much would be wanting in the structure of his skeleton, much that must be supplied by functional adaptation during the life of each individual, even in the period of growth. The thought presents itself here that it must be the iron hand of natural selection that brings into bold relief without too compelling insistence and apparently without serious motive—namely by means of play—what will later be so necessary.... A condition of superabundant nervous force is always, I must again emphatically reiterate, a favorable one for play, but it is not the motive cause, nor, as I believe, a necessary condition for its existence. Instinct is the real foundation of it. Foundation, I say, because all play is not purely instinctive activity. On the contrary, the higher we ascend in the scale of existence the richer and finer become the psychological phenomena that supplement the mere natural impulse, ennobling it, elevating it, and tending to conceal it under added detail. (Groos, 1898: 23–24)

Groos and Spencer were both correct in many respects, and their controversy was largely due to trying to understand different aspects of play: origins, mechanisms, and functions. Issues of energy and instinctive behavior are both crucial for understanding the origins of play.

In his subsequent book on human play (Groos, 1901) Groos altered his views. Whereas in animals play is derived from instinct, for humans instinct is not an appropriate concept. Likewise, while he earlier viewed imitation as a process separate from instinct, now "Imitation is the connecting link between instinctive and intelligent conduct" (Groos, 1901: 281). Writers at this time were not aware of the ways in which social experience could influence the performance of behavior patterns typically labeled as instinctive. Thus Groos's dilemma: Is imitation a social process (by which one animal repeats movements or sounds performed by another), a substitute or replacement for instinct, or is it a kind of instinct itself? This problem would not be resolved by ethologists and comparative ethologists for another 70 years (cf. Lorenz, 1969 and Galef, 1998). Now we know that social learning processes (song learning, food preferences, language acquisition) are themselves rooted in evolved ("instinctive") adaptations, although the exact mechanisms are still controversial (Zentall, 2003).

Harvey Carr, a thoughtful comparative psychologist of the early twentieth century and in the 1920s a president of the American Psychological Association, wrote a balanced review of both surplus energy theory and Groos's two efforts (Carr, 1902).

In conclusion it will be noticed that if Groos limits the qualities of instability and forceful reactibility to hereditary impulse alone—those based upon instinct—his position is open to all the objections urged against the pure instinct conception of play, while the essential characteristic of his final position is really identical with Spencer's surplus energy theory which he attempts to overthrow. (Carr, 1902: 10)

Most early treatments of animal behavior such as those by Morgan (1920), Alverdes (1927), and Hornaday (1922), repeated the views of these two primary competing theories: surplus energy and instinct practice. Today, however, surplus energy is generally given little attention.

2.5.3 Recapitulation Theory

The last of the three major theories is most associated with G. Stanley Hall, a major figure in American psychology, especially human developmental psychology. His two-volume opus on adolescence (G. S. Hall, 1904) is still cited in textbooks today (e.g., Berk, 1996). Hall strongly disagreed with Groos that play has its origins in the need to anticipate and prepare for the future needs of life. He viewed play in people, especially children, as the residue of behavior once necessary in the life of primitive humans, but now not needed in a serious manner. Play is not to be understood in terms of the needs of the future, but in the evolutionary past.

The view of Groos that play is practise for future adult activities is very partial, superficial, and perverse. It ignores the past where lie the keys to all play activities. True play never practises what is phyletically new, and this, industrial life often calls for. It exercises many atavistic and rudimentary functions, a number of which will abort before maturity, but which live themselves out in play like the tadpoles [sic] tail, that must be developed and used as stimulus to the growth of legs which will otherwise never mature. In place of this mistaken and misleading view, I regard play as the motor habits and spirit of the past of the race, persisting in the present, as rudimentary functions sometimes of and always akin to rudimentary organs. The best index and guide to the stated activities of adults in past ages is found in the instinctive, untaught, and non-imitative plays of children which are the most spontaneous and exact expressions of their motor needs. (G. S. Hall 1904: 202)

Play, for Hall, as for Groos and Spencer, is based on instinct. Hall noted the prevalence of play fighting in many animals and the many human games involving throwing, kicking, hitting, running, and dodging. These were once crucial activities: "The
power to throw with accuracy and speed was once pivotal for survival, and non-
throwers were eliminated. Those who throw unusually well best overcame enemies,
killed game, and sheltered family.... running and dodging with speed and endurance,
and hitting with a club, were also basal to hunting and fighting" (G. S. Hall, 1904:
206). Nevertheless, it is important to note that Hall did not conclude that play had no
role in life, being mere atavistic remnants. On the contrary, although play behaviors
are now "less urgent for utilitarian needs, they are still necessary for perfecting the
organism" (1904: 206).

Hall did not neglect less aggressive kinds of play. His discussion of dolls in Hall
(1904) is elaborated in Ellis and Hall (1921), originally published in 1896. Dolls are not
just played with by girls, nor should they be. Boys are more likely to play with adult
and animal dolls than baby dolls. Likewise, even for girls "before puberty dolls were
more likely to be adults; after puberty they are almost always children or babies" (G. S.
Hall, 1904: 209). Hall claimed that it was doubtful if girls who played most with dolls
would "make the best mothers later, or if it has any value as preliminary practise of
motherhood" (1904: 209). Hall is somewhat inconsistent, however, because Ellis and
Hall (1921) "are convinced that, on the whole, more play with girl dolls by boys would
tend to make them more sympathetic with girls as children, if not more tender with
their wives and with women later" (Ellis & Hall, 1921: 190).

Since play reflects the evolutionary past, Hall (1904: 202) is skeptical about the value
of the content of play in current times. What is important is that we enjoy these
activities, for even in our modern (circa 1900!) urban life, they "touch and revive the
deep basic emotions of the race." Universal human play activities should be encouraged as they provide "*interest*, zest, and spontaneity" (1904: 207). The dreary confor-
mity and regularity of much industrialized societal life leads to the urge for fatigue,
to play till one drops. Even a "hunger for fatigue" is a basic human trait separate from
urges for activity or achievement, and is most prevalent during youth. Thus, Hall
counters one of Groos's main objections to surplus energy theory.

Hall's views concerning the order of the unfolding of the play types in ontogeny
have been most controversial and cannot be sustained, as is true of recapitulation
views in embryology. This does not mean that development does not proceed through
some stages that reflect limits established by earlier evolutionary history. Many terrestrial vertebrate embryos go through a gill slit stage that can only be there because of an
aquatic ancestry.

The earliest recapitulation view that I have found predates most of Hall's writings
and explicitly derives lessons for childhood education. Here play is more than just enjoyment for the jaded adult.

Science has shown that the embryonic period of physical development is a masquerade of long-vanished forms of life. In like manner the children of each new generation seek instinctively to revive the life that is behind them and in their favorite occupations and amusements re-enact the prehistoric experiences of mankind. All children crave living pets, build sand houses, and make caves in the earth; are fond of intertwining bits of straw, paper, or other pliable material; delight in shaping bowls and cups and saucers out of mud; and are inveterate diggers in the ground, even when, as in city streets and alleys, such digging is wholly without result. Can we fail to recognize in these universal cravings the soul echoes of that forgotten past when man began the subjugation of Nature by the taming of wild beasts, the erection of rude shelters, the weaving of garments, and the manufacture of pottery? Can we doubt that the order of history should be the order of education, and that before we teach the child to read and write we should aid his efforts to repeat in outline the earlier stages of human development. (Blow, 1894: 125–126)

Given this early statement in a prominent education text, it is unclear why Groos, Baldwin, and Carr all ignored recapitulation. It was not ignored, although heavily criticized, after the 1904 discussion by Hall. Recapitulation ideas still reverberate today in the writings of major evolutionary biologists (e.g., Mayr, 1994). Calvin's (1983, 1993) ballistic theory of human intelligence is based on the need for throwing accuracy in our early hominid history. S. T. Parker and Gibson (1979) and Parker (1996) use an explicit recapitulationist model of mental development in tracing cognitive stages in primate evolution, a thesis exhaustively blended with Piagetian stages of cognitive ontogeny in S. T. Parker and McKinney (1999).

2.6   Additional Early Views

2.6.1   Recuperation Theory
Play in animals, as in people, might be a time for recuperation from serious and stressful occupations, allowing exercise of bodily functions neglected during serious activities and work, but with less strain and effort. Carr (1902) postulated that circulatory and muscular reactions during play could remove toxic substances that build up in response to physical or mental work. One of the main theories, then as now, for the function of sleep, was to allow time for exhausted systems to recuperate. Play, like sleep, was a pleasurable means to accomplish this need.

2.6.2   Recreation Theory
In the late nineteenth century, the industrial revolution in the western world was only a few decades old. Large numbers of workers, including children, were undereducated, ill used, poorly paid, and worked to the limits of endurance. Recreation and play were now seen as not only opposites of work and labor, but also as remedies for the desperate plight of the exploited working class. Play involved a subset of recreational activities and diversions separated from work at the same time that work itself be-

came sharply delimited from other activities. Perhaps more important, in the rising industrial environment others controlled one's work schedule. Before this, the farmer, trader, shop owner, and artisan were more independent and able to schedule their work activities themselves. Enjoyable, even playful, elements could be incorporated into one's work, much as they are today by artists, craftspersons, scientists, and even teachers when they are not overburdened. Marxists and socialists were among the first to recognize the deterioration of communal and recreational life caused by industrialization.

Darwin's protege, George John Romanes (1897, original in 1877), himself a wealthy man, saw the plight of the working class and realized that recreation was as important for them as for the more refined (and delicate) upper classes. Recreation, as Romanes emphasizes, is "re-creation." If appropriate recreation is provided, the worker will be renewed and more fit for work.

... what our forefathers saw in recreation was not so much play, pastime, or pleasantry, as that of the restoration of enfeebled powers of work.... Recreation is, *or ought to be*, not a pastime entered upon for the sake of pleasure which it affords, but an act of duty undertaken for the sake of the subsequent power which it generates, and the subsequent profit which it ensures. (Romanes, 1897: 166–167)

Romanes takes a less crassly utilitarian, or capitalistic, bottom-line approach as his lengthy essay proceeds, although he never once mentions evolution. He does incorporate recuperation, both psychologically and physiologically, in his analysis, but notes that it is change and variety of activity, rather than the actual activities engaged in, that provide the recuperative function. This is another idea newly "discovered" in recent years.

G. S. Hall (1904) argued that the popularity of sport fishing is derived from a response to our ancestors who fished, resulting in a "fishing instinct." Thus today people fish who have no need of fish to eat, and hunt for game they do not need for survival. For more than 30 years I have participated in a poker group; one of our members is a professor who spends 10 weeks or so every summer on a remote island fishing and then smoking the captured fish. He keeps track of the days he does *not* fish at least once. Another member, a wealthy business school professor, eats virtually no meat, but is an avid deer hunter, often using only bow and arrows. He gives the meat to friends and family, but his financial status and investment acumen is such that buying even expensive steaks would be more prudent (and perhaps less risky). The little meat he does eat is from the animals that he kills himself.

Changes in recreational activities occur that may not be due merely to fads. When I grew up in the Midwest, hunting was highly popular and fishing even more so. Even a decade or so ago fishing was labeled the most popular sport in the United States. Today this does not seem to be the case. Fishing, especially lazy still fishing from a pier or an anchored rowboat, does not seem quite as popular in the country today when population increases are taken into account. Could it be that fishing was a more popular recreation when most men worked at hard manual labor and fishing was a rather quiet, sedentary activity serving a recuperative function? The growth of bass fishing, fly fishing, and deep-sea fishing, with their attendant technology, may reflect a need for more active participation. Similarly, in games today, fewer American children appear to play baseball compared to their engagement in the more active sports of basketball, football, tennis, and soccer.

The extreme games (X games), mountain biking, rock climbing, and whitewater sports all challenge the individual in extreme environments. Hall might argue that this change in popular pastimes is due at least in part to an increased need to engage in vigorous activity as labor, youth, and life itself grow more sedentary. Of course, the availability of more resources and opportunities may also play a role in shifting play priorities. Against this line of thought would be the popularity of golf. Courses are sprouting up everywhere and golf does not have the energy costs of football. Still, golf frequently involves walking and being outdoors in parklike surroundings, however domesticated. Hall's ideas might be tested by looking at the kinds of recreational activities employed by cultures over time and different subsets of those cultures (Avedon & Sutton-Smith, 1971).

2.6.3 Diversion Theory

Diversion theory (Carr, 1902) is related to the closely linked recuperation and recreation theories. Play is a pastime: literally it is performed to pass the time. The movement to establish urban playgrounds in the United States started in the late nineteenth century as a way of diverting the behavior of uneducated immigrant children from delinquent and socially disruptive activities (viewed with some fear by middle-class and socially progressive citizens) that flourished in boring, impoverished communities (Mergen, 1982). In fact, play often does appear to be primarily a product of boredom, but may often, especially in the elderly, provide some mental stimulation, as in playing cards with a group (which also provides socialization) or alone (including the computer variant of solitaire). It might appear that these pastimes are not practice for anything at all, except perhaps to play a game better. However, Microsoft originally added solitaire to its operating system so computer novices could obtain practice using a computer mouse.

Theories concerning recuperation, recreation, and diversion can be traced back to the ancients, as in the writings of Plato. Thus modern conditions of life, although they may influence the specific forms of some kinds of play activities, are not the cause or origin of playfulness. Indeed, it has long been known that play can be therapeutic for adult humans. Burton (1883, original 1652) was quite positive about this in his section on the cures for melancholy, which we currently label depression.

Of these labours, exercises, and recreations, which are likewise included, some properly belong to the body, some to the mind, some more easy, some hard, some with delight, some without, some within doors, some natural, some are artificial. Amongst bodily exercises, Galen commends *ludum parvae pilae*, to play at ball, be it with the hand or racket, in tennis-courts or otherwise, it exerciseth each part of the body, and doth much good, so that they sweat not too much. (Burton, 1883: 309)

The role of physical exercise in treating depression is increasingly recognized today, and it may be superior to both psychotherapy and drug treatment; it is certainly a good adjunct to them. Burton treated at length different kinds of activities, not just physically energetic ones, as useful in distracting and refreshing people. These included sports, hunting, hiking, traveling, wildlife observation, reading, playing chess, dancing, singing, feasting, puppetry, and playing with children and pets.

This which I aim at, is for such as are *fracti animis*, troubled in mind, to ease them, over-toiled on the one part, to refresh: over idle on the other, to keep themselves busied. And to this purpose, as any labour or employment will serve to the one, any honest recreation will conduce to the other, so that it be moderate and sparing, as the use of meat and drink; not to spend all their life in gaming, playing, and pastimes, as too many gentlemen do; but to revive our bodies and recreate our souls with honest sports. (Burton, 1883: 317)

But unlike some of the more recent writings that idealize play (cf. P. K. Smith, 1996), Burton also found much evidence that play, especially when tied to gambling, was too seductive a diversion.

They labour most part not to pass the time in honest disport, but for filthy lucre, and covetousness of money.... that which was once their livelihood, and should have maintained wife, children, family, is now spent and gone.... So good things may be abused, and that which was first invented to refresh men's weary spirits, when they come from other labours and studies to exhilarate the mind, to entertain time and company, tedious otherwise in those long solitary winter nights, and keep them from worse matters, an honest exercise is contrarily perverted. (Burton, 1883: 315)

With the increase in legalized gambling almost everywhere, including throughout the United States, this addiction is now recognized as a psychological disorder that is due to the very problems that Burton wrote about 350 years ago. Play can take many forms and have many consequences.

2.6.4   Semblance Theory

In semblance theory, the essence of play is its quality of make-believe, "as if," pretend, or pretense. It includes what today we call sociodramatic play or role playing, as well as the play of animals with inanimate objects as if they were prey. It was a key aspect of the view of Schiller, who stated: "And as soon as the play-drive begins to stir, with its pleasure in semblance, it will be followed by the shaping spirit of imitation, which treats semblance as something autonomous" (F. Schiller, 1967: 195). Although listed by J. M. Baldwin (1902a) as a separate psychological theory of play, semblance is better viewed as a characteristic of much, although not all, play. This aspect of play is the focus of much research in child behavior and is often incorporated in kindergarten and daycare settings (Power, 2000). True pretend play is often limited to the great apes and humans (S. T. Parker & McKinney, 1999), an issue I will return to later.

Psychoanalytic theory, as construed by Freud (1959, original 1931), Wälder (1978, original 1933), Winnicott (1971), and others is largely a variant of semblance theory. For example, young children play "doctor" so that they can deal with their own pain and anxiety resulting from visits to the doctor. By actively reliving unpleasant experiences in a safe and playful manner, children gain experience in "mastering the outside world" (Freud, 1959: 264). Play also involves wish fulfillment and oedipal conflicts (Marans & Cohen, 1991). Such views constitute the rationale behind much of the play therapy movement in child psychotherapy (Coppolillo, 1991). Play therapy may involve scribbling, modeling clay, and playing with dolls, as well as "innocent" games meant to relax the child and increase rapport with the therapist. As Winnicott states: "the child does not usually possess the command of language that can convey the infinite subtleties to be found in play" (1971: 39). Play therapy is frequently applied, using realistic dolls and other props, in the exploration and treatment of sexual abuse in children (Webb, 1991). Play may indeed have beneficial effects in these contexts, but such work takes us too far from the origins of play in normal animals.

2.6.5 Autotelic Theory

Autotelic theory derives from the view that all play is done for its own sake. As Spencer noted, the play performance is its own gratification, not the putative end or goal. Thus, autotelic means that the goal (*telos*) of the behavior is itself (*auto*). By itself, this characteristic of play, which Groos acknowledges is universal, is not a theory at all. Furthermore, not all behavior patterns performed in this manner would be considered play, as Spencer realized in his play continuum process. Lorenz (1981) also made this point in his theory of instinctive behavior. From the animal's point of view, the goal of instinctive (consummatory) acts was the behavioral performance itself. This performance, not the nourishment from eating food, the offspring resulting from copulation, or the increased survival of offspring that was due to having built a nest, was both goal and reward. Lorenz's view was explicitly derived from the distinction made by Wallace Craig between appetitive behavior and consummatory acts that terminate behavioral sequences (Craig, 1918). This seems the best explanation, at the causal or control level (see chapter 1), for the rewarding effect of unsuccessful predatory attacks. For example, it is known that newborn gartersnakes (*Thamnophis sirtalis*) will attack cotton swabs rubbed on prey the species normally eats, such as earthworms. If snakes have struck at such swabs but never have eaten, they later strike more at earthworm swabs than they would have without such unsuccessful attacks (Burghardt, 1990). Rather than being deterred (habituated) by stimuli that lead to no conventional reward, the animal's performance of a behavior in the presence of certain stimuli appears to be rewarding in some way. Bühler's (1930) *"Funktionslust"* theory, in which play is maintained by the sheer pleasure of performing it, is another later variant of autotelic theory. More recently, R. W. Mitchell (1990) has advanced an explicitly autotelic theory of play (chapter 4).

2.6.6 Exercise Theory

The view that motor and perceptual development is facilitated by, if not dependent upon, play is perhaps the most popular current theory (cf. Byers, 1998; Fagen, 1981). The modern version of the theory is generally credited to Brownlee's (1954) writings on cattle, but it had already been described by Carr (1902) and was implicit and even explicit in some of the earlier views I quoted. Carr was able to cite experiments showing that both sensory stimulation and motor activity are needed for proper development. Both the motor and neural systems need such stimulation; such systems then become linked and associations are formed that enhance later intellectual development. Carr advocated the use of different modes of providing such stimulation for children, noting that through free play young animals and children spontaneously and naturally aided their own development. Could nonplay activities be as effective as playful ones in obtaining this stimulation? Perhaps, but Carr thought that play involved specific parts of the brain associated with important natural behavior and thus could be uniquely valuable in development. For example, physically active free play, rather than rote gymnastics, should be encouraged in educational settings.

2.6.7 Cognitive Theories

Going well beyond the instinct-practice view, Carr (1902) also discussed the role of play in the transmission of ideas and anticipated Huizinga (1955). Important aspects of culture, such as traditions, customs, religion, ideals, and history, can be conveyed through legends, myths, poetry, songs, and dance. These are all-important features of preliterate societies. Just as active play is more effective than rote gymnastics, so too is play important in cognitive development. Carr noted favorably that "Arithmetic is being taught under cover of the play reaction. The dramatic method of reading aims to secure a more vivid and lasting association between the idea and the symbol" (Carr, 1902: 24). Mental play was important.

Chess and mental puzzles organize neural associations. Myths, fairy stories, daydreams, etc., are plays among ideas, plays of the imagination, which physiologically are nothing but reactions involving new associations. Reveries to some extent are the play periods of the intellect; they stimulate growth and new associations and lay out lines for voluntary thought. (Carr, 1902: 24)

The role of play in cognitive development has been explored in a most influential manner by Piaget (1962), who credits James Mark Baldwin as a major influence on him (Richards, 1987). Imagination as play has been explored by many (see J. L. Singer, 1991), the book by D. J. Singer and J. L. Singer (1990) being perhaps most well known.

2.6.8   Socialization Theory

The possibility that social play is important in establishing one's role in a group or in learning social skills became very popular in the 1970s (Fagen, 1981). Carr also recognized these types of theories. Group games, such as football, involve the development of "the habits of emotional control, of co-operation, subordination and obedience to authority" (Carr, 1902: 23).

In addition to discussing the role of play in helping an individual function effectively in a group, Carr also included a lengthy section on the role of play in unifying groups or cultures, especially if they later needed to act as a cohesive society against an external threat. The low visibility of play is reflected in the fact that this role is not included in the recent debates on possible mechanisms of group selection in human behavior (D. S. Wilson & Sober, 1994; Sober & D. S. Wilson, 1998).

The rediscovery of writings by Vygotsky in the 1930s (e.g., Vygotsky, 1967; Vygotsky & Luria, 1993), has reinvigorated the study of social and cultural factors in play and child development, areas rather neglected by Piaget. However, these ideas, too, were far from being new, even in the period between the two world wars.

2.7   Conclusion

This survey illustrates that many of the most seminal ideas about the causal bases for play, its origin, its development, and its possible adaptive value had already been outlined a century ago. Most, except for the surplus energy, instinct practice, and recapitulation theories, focused on the possible functions of play in enhancing an animal's life, not on play's genesis in ontogeny and phylogeny. Unfortunately, limited data were available for testing any of these ideas and sorting through the many conflicting claims. The conceptual tools needed to evaluate them in terms of the differing ethological aims were not available to clarify sources of confusion and, perhaps for that reason, none of the early theories were developed in any depth or evaluated with extensive data for many decades to come.

Carr (1902) wisely noted that theories proposed for the function of play, such as the exercise, cognitive, and socialization theories, were neither exhaustive nor mutually exclusive. There was no necessary reason to hold that play *had* to serve these functions; other more serious activities might do as well. He did, however, advance five "special utilities of play," suggesting that play might be a superior mode of achieving certain ends.

• Ease of the reaction   By this, Carr means that playful reactions are readily performed. The requisite motor, sensory, neural, and regulatory processes are already in place. Insofar as they lead to adaptive ends, they would be selected for and thus survive.

• Increased activity   Play is a process encouraging activity that, as we have seen, is valuable in exercising body and mind. "In work there is precision and definiteness of certain continually recurring reactions. Whim and caprice—change in the reacting centres—is reduced to a minimum; all is constraint and drear monotony. Thus fatigue is easily engendered and rest is a necessity. Play with its change and continual variability in reacting centres allows time for rest and recuperation and thus tends to a more continued activity" (Carr, 1902: 28).

• Greater intensity of reaction, including emotions   Play involves attention and concentration: "The attentiveness and self-absorbtion of children at play is remarkable. Players in games involving a decided vaso-motor reaction are characterized by an energetic whole-souled attitude" (Carr, 1902: 29). Carr contrasts the college grind with the healthy active athlete.

• Greater stimulation to growth and development   Carr presents many aspects of the physiology of young animals in which stimulation is critical to proper development. Play, by involving so many aspects of the organism, is particularly valuable in this respect.

• Increased variability of reactions and ideas   This is probably the most prescient of Carr's suggestions and is again being advocated (e.g., Sutton-Smith, 1997), but itself derives from Spencer's view that play is the source of artistic creativity.

Read without prejudice, almost the entire body of modern play research in both animals and humans can be seen as working on the themes listed above and throughout this chapter. Recognizing the footprints left a century ago takes a bit of practice and pays off in increased insight and humility. Science suffers if we fail to appropriately identify the truly new and novel, place it in context, and give priority and credit where they belong.

Some recent developments of these early theories have been mentioned in passing here and will be discussed more fully in later chapters. Today we know much more about biology and the nature of animal diversity, and play researchers are clarifying and testing these and other ideas with increasing rigor. Much of the state of the art on animals' play can be read in detail in Bekoff and Byers (1998) and Power (2000). Similarly, J. E. Johnson, Christie, and Yawkey (1999); Frost, Wortham, and Reifel (2001) and Pellegrini and Smith (1998) are good sources for updates on child play theory.

Unfortunately, as at the end of chapter 1, the issue of what play *is* and how to recognize it, has still not been addressed. It is time.

3   Defining Play: Can We Stop Playing Around?

The very ambiguity of the term "play," the uncertainty as to just how different behaviors may be to still qualify as "play," will constantly work to divide and confuse all who do not first consider and communicate their personal definitions of the term. And if research on theories of play is to be carried out, a satisfactory dependent measure of play will have to be devised.

—J. Barnard Gilmore (1966: 342–343)

No behavioral concept has proven more ill-defined, elusive, controversial, and even unfashionable.

—E. O. Wilson (1975: 164)

Play is the hobgoblin of animal behavior, mischievously tempting us to succeed in what, judging from the number of failed attempts, seems a futile task: defining play.

—Robert Mitchell (1990: 197)

3.1   Why We Need General Criteria for Recognizing Play

In his landmark book on animal play, Robert Fagen (1981) thoroughly examined many definitions of play, providing appendices with representative lists of criteria or definitions drawn from the literature. Fagen considered philosophical issues in how behavior patterns are labeled, including the ways in which categories of behavior are developed and used by ethologists and psychologists. He was often insightful, as well as scathing, in his characterizations of previous definitions of play, and he analyzed the problems involved in using descriptive, motivational, and functional criteria of play. After his intensive analysis, which consumes upward of fifty pages, he finally ventured the following definition:

I view play as behavior that functions to develop, practice, or maintain physical or cognitive abilities and social relationships, including both tactics and strategies, by varying, repeating, and/ or recombining already functional subsequences of behavior outside their primary context. It is a matter of taste whether behaviors that do not simultaneously satisfy the structural, causal—

contextual, functional, and developmental criteria of this definition are to be called play.[7] (Fagen, 1981: 65)

This definition is based, foremost, on function. Yet Fagen hedged by underscoring the arbitrariness in the kinds or number of criteria that need to be satisfied in any instance of play. He clearly leaned toward a functional definition of play, as opposed to a "structural" definition based on how the behavior looks (topography). However, he was well aware of the paucity of research at that time that could experimentally demonstrate any function for animal play, and he realized that a purely functional definition was too restrictive. In any event, his definition is difficult to apply. Indeed, the appeal to one's "taste" may have inadvertently reinforced the notion that play research was not yet ready for scientific prime time.

As Fagen's dilemma and the opening quotes illustrate, the problems in defining play are legendary. The most recent comprehensive treatment of play in nonhuman mammals and children ends on the pessimistic note that "Given its elusive nature, it is unlikely that researchers will ever come up with a satisfactory definition of play" (Power, 2000: 391). Gilmore's warning that opened this chapter is still valid today. Theoretical advances require adequate working definitions and measures. There are lessons to be learned from previous attempts to conceptualize play, however, and this chapter touches on some of these lessons before proposing a solution. Readers who are not interested in the problems of identifying play may want to skip to section 3.7 to see the way play will be recognized throughout the rest of this book.

Why should time be spent trying to provide a definition? We instantly recognize play, do we not? Well, no, actually; we may often fail to recognize play, or may classify as play behavior patterns, which, when more is known, would not be considered play at all, such as serious fighting (Aldis, 1975).[8] The latter has happened repeatedly in claims for the occurrence of play in ants, birds, fish, and in some mammals as well, owing to a combination of insufficient data and inadequate criteria for recognizing play. The former will continue to be a problem with unfamiliar species, but what can be addressed

---

7. Although "casual" appeared in the original, my suspicion that "causal" was meant has been confirmed (Fagen, personal communication, July 1998).

8. As mentioned in chapter 1, in the realm of human behavior some authors do consider serious competition as play. Here the consequences of play (e.g., losing a game) can be humiliation or death (Sutton-Smith & Kelly-Byrne, 1984). Including serious competition under the rubric of play may have led to the poor reputation of play as a meaningful category of behavior in animals and children. This is not to say that war games in the military cannot be both playful and serious, nor that generals, politicians, bosses, coaches, and spouses may not be engaging in play (e.g., teasing) when they deal with subordinates or even peers. However, those at the receiving end or the pawns in this kind of play may not see it as play at all, and for them it is *not* play. As with the black bears (*Ursus americanus*) I studied, play wrestling bouts can also very quickly turn serious (Burghardt & Burghardt, 1972). An adequate characterization of play has to deal with many issues.

is the lack of general objective criteria, which hinders recognition of the diverse ways in which play can be expressed. Unrecognized and unarticulated biases color many claims for what is or is not play; to accept the definition that play is what play researchers study (Power, 2000) is not helpful beyond the closed group of these researchers.

Speculation on the role of play in the lives of animals (including humans) has outstripped convincing evidence (P. Martin & Caro, 1985; Power, 2000). This speculation has had consequences. Many authors render play as an important but enigmatic category of behavior when they present overviews for both professional (e.g., Eisenberg, 1981) and student (e.g., Drickamer, Vessey, & Meikle, 1996) audiences. Owing to the lack of consensus on what play is and why it exists, the tendency is to briefly acknowledge play's existence and possible role, generally in the context of mammalian behavior and ontogeny. If a textbook author is not a researcher on vertebrate animals, play might even be completely ignored (Alcock, 2001).[9] Play has been treated variously as nonexistent, as an anthropocentric conceit, as impossible to characterize and study, as enigmatic and mysterious although possibly important, and as something critical to all "higher" behavioral processes. The lack of a clear conception of what should be included under the rubric of play has contributed to this confusion.

In those commonly studied animals that are generally considered to be very playful (dogs, cats, monkeys), there may often be agreement on what constitutes play. This agreement is especially true when the focus is limited to young animals engaging in a specific kind of play, such as chasing each other or manipulating objects (toys), even if the origin, control, motivation, and adaptive function of the behavior are unclear. For example, when behavior patterns are being described and quantified, labeling a behavior as play usually involves clear contextual and structural features that allow useful scientific data to be obtained. The specific behavior patterns are often organized in a behavioral catalog (ethogram) and grouped into functional categories of behavior, such as feeding, body maintenance, courtship, and fighting. When such "play" behavior constitutes a substantial amount of the activity budget, especially in young mammals, some observers cannot help but conclude that play is a rather ubiquitous type of behavior that is essential for proper behavioral development. They may go on to assert that play has been ignored only because it is considered frivolous by those who are too unimaginative to appreciate its critical importance in the lives of animals (cf. Fagen, 1981; Gandelman, 1992; Hoyenga & Hoyenga, 1984). Skeptics, however, are more likely to be impressed by data than by assertions about adaptive function that have proved difficult to sustain when they are actually tested.

9. In a major college textbook, Grier (1984) broke ranks and included a fine and balanced chapter on animal play. In the second edition (Grier & Burk, 1992), criticisms by reviewers and editors led to animal play being demoted to a subsection of the chapter on development, although play was still much more extensively treated than in other animal behavior texts (James Grier, personal communication, 1991). Encouragingly, Dugatkin's recent text (2004) has a play chapter.

Sometimes play researchers, themselves frustrated by their inability to provide a sat-isfactory definition, appear defensive in their response to critics. Alternatively, they may avoid the issue by restricting their attention to a specific type of behavior they label play (Gandelman, 1992). This is actually a valid, if narrowly focused, strategy, as discussed in section 3.3. Nonetheless, eventually shared commonalities among various "play" activities must be addressed in a conceptual framework (Fagen, 1981; Thompson, 1998).

3.2 Overly Rigid Concepts and the Search for Scientific Truth: Consciousness, Learning, and Parental Care

William James, the premier American psychologist of the nineteenth century, wrote concerning consciousness that "Its meaning we know so long as no one asks us to define it" (James, 1890: 225). When Donald Griffin (1976) advocated a return to the study of animal awareness and cognition, he faced much criticism from experimental and comparative psychologists for failing to provide strict operational definitions and conceptual clarity. Even so, some early critics now recognize that Griffin was raising issues that once were, and should have remained, integral to comparative psychology, if not psychology in general (e.g., Wasserman, 1997). However, progress has not been easy. More than a century after James, Damasio wrote "for those who wish to under-stand the biological underpinnings of the mind, consciousness is generally regarded as the towering problem, in spite of the fact that the definition of the problem may vary considerably from investigator to investigator. If elucidating mind is the last frontier of the life sciences, consciousness often seems like the last mystery in the elucidation of the mind. Some regard it as insoluble" (Damasio, 1999: 4).

As the criteria and methods for evaluating complex animal behavior and cognitive processes have been refined through empirical analysis (Roitblat, 1987; Wasserman, 1997) and philosophical reflection (Allen & Bekoff, 1997), carefully delineated research questions have led to considerable progress in even these difficult areas of study in nonhuman animals (see almost any issue of the *Journal of Comparative Psychology*) and people (e.g., Damasio, 1999). In short, seemingly intractable problems of long standing have yielded to modern science, partly because researchers asked questions that the "smart" money said were impossible, if not fruitless, to address.[10]

10. Eminent psychologists have written or told me that none of the following phenomena can be scientifically studied because they will never be formulated sufficiently clearly: emotion, awareness, instinct, innate behavior, consciousness, intelligence, mind, motivation, cognition, biological gender differences, and of course play. These assertions are based on a confusion of a finalistic "truth"-based definition with a pragmatic scientific definition.

Good working knowledge exists on diverse broad topics of behavioral study, such as ingestion, learning, communication, courtship, parental care, and antipredator defense. In each of these areas there is much greater agreement on what behaviors should be included than in the area of play. However, unlike consciousness and cognition, play behavior can be directly observed. Thus with all the research and study on play in animals and people available today, we should finally be able to characterize what play is about in a sufficiently cogent manner to allow us to identify play in taxa where it has not yet been described, and to compare and analyze different kinds of putative play and the repertoires of different species. This must be done if we are ever to reach an integrative understanding of what play is, how it works, how it is experienced, what it is good for, and how it develops and evolves.

At a certain point in the development of any science, further progress depends on careful analysis of the basic phenomena being linked together. For example, as animal welfare laws begin to mandate the reduction of unnecessary pain and suffering of animals used in research, concepts such as "distress" need to be made much more precise (Holden, 2000). The aim of this chapter is to provide the tools needed to identify play across wide ranges of species and behavior.

The challenge is in finding a balance between a conception of play that aids research without being so vague that nothing is eliminated or so rigid that relevant phenomena are excluded. Clarifying our conceptions and definitions of cooperation, altruism, kin selection, and group selection has been important in both resolving and creating controversies in these areas, and the same will, I believe, prove true in animal play.

In the search for truth, the knowledge gained by scientists consists of approximations with varying degrees of certainty. Such provisional truth can be highly useful, as the progress and limitations of medical knowledge well exemplify. From a scientific standpoint, the main role of approximations in reducing uncertainty is to help pose the next questions to be asked. Similarly, the role of definitions in science is not to capture *the* truth, but to help us progress toward a more complete understanding of the natural world. Thus, a scientific definition should be pragmatic, specifying those characteristics of a concept that are essential for distinguishing it from other concepts in the light of current knowledge. It is within this framework combining realism and instrumentalism (Cacioppo, Semin, & Berntson, 2004) that we should develop a workable definition of play.

The importance of having a working definition that is neither so broad that it is loose and vague, nor so precise that it excludes relevant novel phenomena, is shown in the study of animal learning by experimental psychologists. Fifty years ago, there were several competing grand models of learning that dominated much of psychology and biological studies of learning (Osgood, 1953). For most scientists, all learning in all animals was reduced to the operation of either Pavlovian (classical association) or instrumental (operant) conditioning; there were heated debates over whether even these two could be reduced to one unitary process explaining all behavioral change. The competition among schools of learning theory for the most parsimonious and operational formulation of learning led to studying a few model systems (maze running, lever pressing, shuttle boxes, pecking) in a few species. Whatever its merits, this narrow focus hindered the rise of comparative cognition, field and laboratory studies of naturalistic learning phenomena, studies of behavioral plasticity (flexibility) in evolution, investigations of learning in individual nerve cells, and neural net and connectionist modeling in computers. For example, learning theorists resisted accepting imprinting (Hess, 1973) and delayed illness-induced aversions (Garcia, Hankins, & Rusniak, 1976) as important learning phenomena because these behaviors did not meet the mandated criteria of what conditioning must entail.[11] Thus the history of the traditional area of animal learning studies shows the stultifying effects of excessively strict conceptions of a phenomenon. Perhaps this historical scenario will be repeated if we try to prematurely develop too rigid a conception of play.

A rather different approach to defining play is to argue that play is always defined as nonfunctional, nonadaptive, or nonserious behavior. However, since we know so little about the functions of behavior, or how behavior develops, or what is really "serious," we are essentially defining play by exclusion.[12] In this view, until we know much more

11. In filial imprinting (Hess, 1973), ducklings and chicks rapidly learn the characteristics of their mother, or a model such as a moving basketball, only if the mother or object is available during a critical or sensitive period within the first day of life. Not only is there an age dependence that is not incorporated into the classical learning models, but the animal follows and directs filial behaviors toward a stimulus that provides none of the primary reinforcements (food, water, warmth, etc.) that were once held to be essential for learning to occur (Osgood, 1953).

In illness-induced aversions, two other assumptions were violated. The learning occurred even if there was a long (20 minutes or more) interval between the presentation of the conditioned stimulus (CS, such as taste of a novel food) and the unconditioned stimulus (UCS, such as feeling ill or nauseous). Furthermore, not all possible CS and UCS pairings led to the same degree of learning. In rats, chemical cues associated with food could be readily associated with digestive system illness, but visual cues could not be. However, in birds, which rely on vision for food selection more than rats do, visual cues were far more salient than chemosensory ones (Wilcoxon, Dragoin, & Kral, 1971).

12. This is a variant of an argument put forth by Frank Beach, an eminent figure in comparative psychology and the author of a seminal article on play (Beach, 1945). He was one of the participants in the famous "instinct" wars of the 1950s and 1960s (Burghardt, 1973). Beach (1955), commenting on the resurgence of interest and research on instinct and innate behavior advanced the following paraphrased syllogistic argument: (a) In practice innate or instinctive behavior patterns are defined as "unlearned." (b) We do not yet know everything about learning. (c) Therefore, "it is logically indefensible to categorize any behavior as unlearned unless the characteristics of learned behavior have been thoroughly explored and are well known" (Beach, 1955: 406). One

about the natural behavior patterns of animals, how they develop, and their role in fitness, no behavior should be labeled play. For these reasons, developmentalists of the once influential school led by the late T. C. Schneirla (1965) are among those skeptics who find little of value in play as a category (Lazar & Beckhorn, 1974; Welker, 1971). Thus there is a regression from rigid definitions that inhibit study of a wide range of species and behavioral systems, to an "I know it when I see it" approach, to the view that the phenomenon (i.e., play) does not even exist!

Definitions are often problematic for behavioral phenomena that might seem less difficult to characterize than play. One example is communication (Burghardt, 1970); another is parental care, which is worth further scrutiny. A deservedly highly praised book on parental care (Clutton-Brock, 1991) begins by recognizing the need to define parental care before subdividing it and analyzing the costs and benefits of parental investment. The definition offered of parental care is deceptively simple: "Any form of parental behavior that appears likely to increase the fitness of a parent's offspring" (Clutton-Brock 1991: 8). Not only is this definition tautological (what does "care" mean if it is not directed at benefiting the target), but the phrase "appears likely" is vague to the point of being useless. Appears likely to whom? Is this essentially an anthropomorphic conception delimited by a crude guess at a probable function? Probably. However, such a definition has some value if we keep open the possibility that future work may demonstrate that even nonobvious behaviors increase the fitness of offspring. What *is* a problem is Clutton-Brock's assertion that parental care, as he defines it, is purely "a descriptive term" with no functional implications. It is not hard to envision, especially with human beings, examples of misdirected parental care that results in offspring being less fit and competitive in life: feeding offspring diets that make them too fat, or providing care past the period when offspring would be better off without it. How do we decide if spanking (or any kind of punishment) of children is parental care? Thousands of studies on parenting have not led to clear answers in even one species, our own. What confidence should we have in "appearances" in other species? Actually, Clutton-Brock would have been better advised to just define parental behavior and keep any considerations of its fitness consequences separate.[13]

---

of the several fallacies here can be exposed by simply arguing the reverse: (a) In practice, learning is essentially defined as behavior modified from preexisting unconditioned, innate, or instinctive responses. (b) We do not yet know everything about the provenance of genetic, unconditioned, and innate influences on behavior. (c) Therefore, until we know everything about how genetics and innate processes influence behavior, we should not consider labeling any behavior as environmentally controlled, conditioned, or "learned." Obviously neither Beach nor anyone else would seriously accept the second syllogism! The main error is in proposition a in the first syllogism. Another problem is the simplistic and misleading dichotomy of instinct and learning.

13. After writing this, I discovered that a similar analysis of Clutton-Brock's definition was made earlier (Gowaty, 1996).

Recalling Tinbergen (1963), he should have kept description separated from issues of control, adaptive function, evolution, and ontogeny. Similarly, it is *play behavior* that concerns us, a large enough task. It is useful to retain the lessons of defining parental care as play definitions are probed more deeply.

3.3   When General Definitions Are Not Essential

Fortunately, the lack of a clear, generally accepted conceptual and comparative understanding of play has not been detrimental in collecting fundamental information on species-typical playfulness, just as a similar lack has not hampered research on parental care. Current knowledge of play derives from studies in three major categories: (1) descriptive ethograms of wild or captive animals, (2) detailed observational studies focusing primarily on specific play phenotypes, and (3) experimental studies on a specific aspect or consequence of play. Here are some examples of each of these types of studies, all of which also raise issues to which we will return later.

First are studies that incorporate play as one category among many others. Investigators may decide to include play, or types of play, in constructing or utilizing an ethogram or behavior pattern profile. Typically, many behavioral measures that can be reliably observed are recorded. For example, Hoff, Forthman, and Maple (1994) compared the behavior of lowland gorillas (*Gorilla gorilla gorilla*) in an outdoor zoo enclosure and an indoor holding pen. The group of six animals included two mothers, two infants, a silverback male, and a juvenile female. They had access to a relatively large (1500-m²) naturalistic exhibit by day and were held in much smaller indoor areas (50 m²) at night. Their caretakers reported informally that social play among infants was seen in the indoor area, but not outdoors. This report led to a systematic observational study over several weeks in which thirty different carefully defined behavioral measures of adult and infant behavior were recorded in a focal subject design with 30-minute samples.[14] Among the behaviors recorded were solitary play, social play, and object examination (exploration and manipulation). Both solitary play and object examination were found at significantly higher rates in the outdoor enclosure. It is interesting that social play occurred at statistically equivalent very low rates in both enclosures. Although the importance given to these findings may vary with the interpretation of play, it is not a conceptually troubling issue in the study by Hoff and co-workers. No speculations were made about the nature of play in gorillas, nor were extrapolations made to different gorillas. We could call the behavior patterns labeled as play "x," "y," and "z" without losing content.

14. Focal animal sampling is described in Altmann (1974) and consists of watching one individual at a time for a specified period and recording only behavior performed by the focal subject or those animals interacting with the focal subject. It is considered one of the most powerful and reliable observational methods for obtaining unbiased systematic behavior records for animals in groups.

In the second category are studies that observationally investigate a certain type of behavior in detail. For example, Biben (1986) looked carefully at individual and sex differences in two different types of wrestling play in a captive group of young squirrel monkeys (*Saimiri sciureus*). She called wrestling play on a flat surface, where one animal was on top, directional play. Wrestling play where both monkeys hung from a perch and grappled with their forelimbs was categorized as nondirectional play. She followed the behavior of five male and five female monkeys for several months using 5-minute focal subject sampling.

One of the many interesting findings was that animals initiated directional play if they were likely to dominate, but were more likely to initiate nondirectional play when the targeted partners were of equal ability. Males initiated play bouts more often than females, and chose males as partners more often. Males were also more successful in these initiations than were females. Female monkeys initiated play more often with other females, but their success rate was about equal with both sexes. This study involved clear, objective, observational categories that would hold even if someone later showed that these behavior patterns were sexual or aggressive behaviors and not play. The type of sex differences seen here are commonly, but not always, found in the mammalian social play literature. The recognition that the behavior category "play wrestling" can be usefully subdivided illustrates the level of sophistication informing much of the best current research.

An example of the third category, an experimental study, examined play fighting in laboratory rats (Panksepp & Beatty, 1980). Play fighting in rats and other rodents has developed into one of the most active areas of play research (Pellis & Pellis, 1998a). One of the still hotly contested issues is whether social play is based on an intrinsic motivational process, as are behavior patterns such as feeding, drinking, and copulation. Depriving an animal of only the opportunity to play is, as we will discuss later, much more difficult than depriving an animal of the opportunity to eat, drink, or mate.

Panksepp and Beatty (1980) reported on three experiments that compared various measures of play fighting and associated social responses in paired same-sex social- and isolate-housed rats. In one study rats were weaned at 18 days of age; half were kept in social groups, and half were housed in individual cages. At day 21, rats from both housing conditions were paired with same-sex rats for 5 minutes. Previously isolated rats engaged in play fighting 90 percent of the time, but socially housed rats interacted only about 30 percent of the time. The rate of various combined play measures such as pouncing, charging, mounting, and boxing was much higher in the isolates. A second experiment with a different strain of rats and a more refined category system had comparable results. However, in this case, videotaped records were obtained and only 24 hours of social isolation were imposed. In a complex third experiment, rats were socially deprived for 0, 8, or 24 hours at both 18 and 28 days of age. At both ages, play

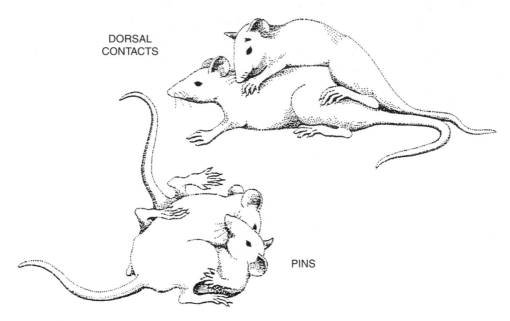

DORSAL
CONTACTS

PINS

Figure 3.1
Social play wrestling in laboratory rats showing dorsal contacts and pinning. (From Panksepp, 1998a)

increased monotonically with social deprivation. However, both baseline (0 hour) and deprivation play levels were much higher at 28 than at 18 days of age. Thus we see that some ontogenetic variable is interacting with the social deprivation process and social play. Sex differences were not found.

There is another aspect of this study worth noting. To Panksepp and Beatty, play fighting in rats is vigorous, easily recognized, and involves many behavior patterns, although "most are difficult to categorize and operationalize" (1980: 198). Thus they were also testing the usefulness and reliability of a single marker behavior, pinning, that might substitute for the tedious recording and analysis that requires extensively trained observers. Pinning occurs when one animal lies on its back with the other on top (figure 3.1). All three experiments supported the value of pinning frequency as a reliable, easily quantified measure that correlates highly with other measures of play fighting. Can pinning behavior in this and related species be used as a measure of playfulness, much as the numbers of bites of food, licks of water, and copulations can be used as reliable measures of hunger, thirst, and lust?

These analyses show how the study of play can progress even if researchers lack both a consensus definition and a conception of what play is all about. Today we have a growing literature on comparable studies of many species in laboratories, zoos, and field settings around the world. In order, then, to effectively integrate and compare them, place them in a modern evolutionary context, and suggest how to frame future research, we need some tools.

3.4   Additional Problems with Existing Definitions

As noted earlier, the primary function of a scientific definition is to separate as unambiguously as possible phenomena that are included in a concept from those that are excluded. The difficulties in doing so have been well recognized. The same year that Fagen's definition of play was published, an influential authoritative handbook included a short treatment of play that underlined the conceptual and definitional problems in play (Millar in McFarland, 1981) while avoiding an actual definition. Millar did state that the common view that play "refers to all activities that have no use or FUNCTION, and appear to be undertaken for pleasure" utilizes "unworkable criteria" (McFarland, 1981: 457). However, also in 1981, a definition more concise and objective than Fagen's that omitted any suggestion of the adaptive value or function of play was formulated by Bekoff and Byers in an influential review of the ethology of play:

Play is all motor activity performed postnatally that appears to be purposeless in which motor patterns from other contexts may often be used in modified form and altered temporal sequencing. (Bekoff & Byers, 1981: 300)

A few years later, in P. Martin and Caro's seminal review of the possible functions of play, they modified this definition to read:

Play is all locomotor activity performed postnatally that *appears* to an observer to have no obvious immediate benefits for the player, in which motor patterns resembling those used in serious functional contexts may be used in modified form. The motor acts constituting play have some or all of the following structural characteristics: exaggeration of movements, repetition of motor acts, and fragmentation or disordering of sequences of motor acts. (1985: 65)

These last two definitions of play are probably the ones most commonly cited today. They have served admirably and I have relied on them myself (Burghardt, 1984, 1988b, 1998b). However, while these two definitions are useful in characterizing play as we generally understand it, they have some drawbacks. The primary problem is that the use of the word *may* in both versions limits our ability to apply the definition to phenomena that we do not already consider play. In actuality, the apparent lack of purpose in the observed behavior is the central and essential component of each definition.

A more recent definition of animal play presents similar and additional difficulties.

A free and creative form of individual or social behaviour, in which many motor and role patterns may be mixed in a graceful manner, often occurring without obvious external provocation. (Kortmulder, 1998: 157)

Not only are *may* and *often* the operative words, but the assessment of a behavior as "free," "creative," and "graceful" is left unexplained. Regardless, most persons who have studied play would allow that some basic truths about play underlie these definitions, and that they eventually will need to be accommodated. Kortmulder, in fact, develops a theory of play in which the "graceful" takes center stage. However, note that Kortmulder, like Bekoff and Byers (1981) and P. Martin and Caro (1985), omits any functional components from his definition. Fagen (1984) has also emphasized the creative side of animal play. A more recent definition of play by Fagen avoids vague words like *may*, and although it includes some suspect terms such as *skilled* and *improvised*, it also incorporates elements that will later prove important.

Play is improvised performance, with variations, of skilled motor and communicative actions in a context separate from the environment in which behavior including these actions proximately increases reproductive success. (Fagen, 1993: 182)

Nevertheless, no recent treatments of animal play have solved the problem of how to objectively recognize play in nontraditional contexts. In fact, in the secondary animal behavior literature, the attitude toward definitions of play seems to have actually regressed in recent years. Play behavior is defined simply as a "behavior performed without the 'serious point' that such behavior has in its normal context" (Immelmann & Beer, 1989: 223), or "as activity that imitates elements of goal-directed behavior but does not lead to an immediate goal" (R. Maier, 1998: 63).

This discrepancy is reminiscent of the problem in communication between Spencer and Groos, namely, the opposition between causal mechanism and adaptive function as the proper "explanation." A further wrench is thrown in by Rosenberg (1990), who argued against the possibility of any physiological or evolutionary approach to play, or even its definition, because play must be "intentional" in the rather precise sense of philosophers of mind (Bekoff & Allen, 1998) and thus is not open to scientific study at all!

A completely different approach would be to avoid behavioral, motivational, affective, and other criteria completely by having play defined as involving brain and neurotransmitter processes that underlie play behavior; however, as Gandelman (1992) points out, this does not help us understand what should be subsumed under the traditional concept of play, and would preclude the study of play in animals that neuroscientists have not yet studied. In short, it seems the problems in characterizing play are indeed insolvable. Other pitfalls await.

3.5 Perplexing Phenomena That Must Not Be Equated with Play

Two classes of behavior have often been confused with play: exploratory behavior and stereotyped behavior. Both have some characteristics in common with play, and most definitions do not effectively exclude them. However, any comprehensive definition of play needs to limit their inclusion in play activities. A third phenomenon often linked to play is tool use (Power, 2000), but this should be resolved by testing whether such tool use is playful or not. For example, African elephants (*Loxodonta africana*) throw objects at interfering animals such as rhinos (e.g., Wickler & Seibt, 1997); studies of young animals and other contexts could reveal a play version.

3.5.1 Exploration, Curiosity, and Stimulation Seeking

Most animals approach and investigate new objects that appear in their environment. Rats sniff out potential food; monkeys hesitantly approach and jab at a toy snake; and dogs approach each other mutually, perhaps rapidly, size each other up and bark, growl, or play bow at each other. Ants and cockroaches are experts at locating sources of food through chemical exploration. Snakes and iguanas tongue flick repeatedly when they are put into novel environments. In general, animals placed in a new cage or moved to a new habitat may spend much time wandering around or checking things out before settling down into a regular routine. Such exploration and curiosity are major topics in psychology and are often linked with play (Weisler & McCall, 1976), as is stimulation seeking in general (Hoyenga & Hoyenga, 1984). Yet, play seems different from "mere" exploration and curiosity, although it often involves activity and new or varied stimulation.

In the influential treatment by Berlyne, exploratory behavior consists of all processes that "affect the nature of stimulation reaching the sense organs" (Berlyne, 1960: 78). The function of exploratory responses is "to afford access to environmental information that was not previously available" and to "enable stimuli not at present acting on receptors to be placed in command of behavior" (Berlyne, 1960: 79).

Berlyne (1960) posits three categories of exploration. These involve orienting responses in which the animal changes posture or sense organ state (e.g., turning to gaze, cocking a head or ear, sniffing), locomotor exploration in which the animal moves his or her body in space (e.g., walking to patches of food resources), and investigatory responses in which, through manipulation, the animal makes changes in external objects. The latter may also be termed curiosity (e.g., turning over a rock to see what is under it).

Berlyne makes many distinctions among these kinds of exploratory behaviors and the nature of both intrinsic (internal) and extrinsic (external environmental) determinants. Relevant here are stimulus intensity, novelty, surprise, complexity, incongruity, and conflict. Changes in response to repeated stimulation generally take the form of reduced responding or habituation. Exploratory behavior thus includes exploration, curiosity, and stimulation seeking and may be tied to concepts such as arousal and boredom. However, Berlyne also made one other important distinction. Exploratory behavior can be specific, in which the primary function is to provide "information about one particular object or event" or diversive, in which the "person ... seeks entertainment, relief from boredom, or new experiences ... from any of a wide array of sources" (Berlyne, 1960: 80). Much of the work from the period of intense interest in exploration and curiosity was brought together by Fowler (1965).

C. Hutt (1966) extended the distinction between specific and diversive exploration to play. She considered specific exploration as information extraction or learning whether, for example, an object is prey, predator, or nesting material. More recently, it has been suggested that diversive exploration be termed *exploration* and specific exploration *investigation*, as evidence accumulates for the dual nature of the underlying processes involved (Renner, 1998). Together exploratory and investigatory behavior reflect the presence of curiosity according to Renner (1998). Nonetheless, the literature continues to conflate the three terms: exploration, investigation, and curiosity. Diversive exploration typically follows specific exploration and is devoted to finding out what can be done with the object. This is what is traditionally called object play. Such diversive exploration or play can involve manipulating, pushing, hitting, and overturning. As Hutt points out, exploration consists of gathering information about the environment; play with an object is finding out what can be done with the object. I would add that much play is not just finding out what can be done with an object, but repeating similar acts that have similar results long after the animal clearly knows what can be "done" with the object. In fact, it is only after an animal discovers what the object can do, such as a cat with a suspended clump of feathers, that intense play may actually occur. Regardless, developmentally the two processes are linked (Welker, 1971) and thus may not be distinguishable early in ontogeny, including in human infancy.

R. N. Hughes (1997) noted that in recent years the sophistication of the early writings on exploration, responses to novelty, and related topics has been ignored as renewed interest in the topic has emerged. This seems particularly evident in some of the neuroscience literature. Hughes updated the analysis of exploration by emphasizing the difference between intrinsic and extrinsic exploration and focused on problems in evaluating the former. What seems clear is that early conceptions of an exploratory drive foundered on the issue of whether it "did little else than restate the facts that remain to be explained" (R. N. Hughes, 1997: 219). These facts included the observations that adequately cared for captive animals tended to approach and investigate moderate changes in stimuli, that such exploration declined over time, and that a stimulus change itself was sought out and may act as a reward or reinforcer in learning tasks. Such a stimulus change can be both spatial and temporal and involve sounds, changes in brightness levels, movement of familiar objects in space, etc., as well as the introduction of novel objects or provision of entirely new environments. In suggesting an agenda for future work, Hughes strongly advocated "free tests" in which animals are tested in their home environments or at least in familiar ones, rather than being put only in novel situations.

Some types of exploration, curiosity, and stimulation seeking could be both developmental and phyletic precursors to play, as defined later. Here, however, we need to decide if the two can or should be separated. Most of the behavioral definitions of play discussed up to now would not exclude exploration or curiosity. A useful definition of play should be able to exclude specific exploration. This is not to say that play cannot include aspects of exploration but, following C. Hutt (1966) and S. J. Hutt et al. (1989), not all curiosity and exploration should be considered play.

Although curiosity and exploratory behavior have long been associated with play, and while play of some kinds, most notably object play, may have its origin in curiosity and exploration, curiosity and exploration, like locomotion, can enter into almost any behavioral category. A definition of play should be able to exclude specific exploration because it is involved in virtually all behavior systems, including foraging, mating, and migration. Animals have to identify environments and the animate and inanimate objects in those environments. Doing so means that an animal engages in some exploratory forms of behavior. However, with objects of limited specific immediate biological value, the exploration does not shift to feeding, mating, nest building, or parenting, but goes in the direction of diversive exploration. In this book diversive exploration will not be used to refer to play since the use of the term *exploration* may not be appropriate. One could easily show that diversive exploration may be involved in nonplay behaviors such as a scavenger tearing apart a carcass, a bird incorporating artificial objects in a nest, or two fighting monkeys trying to maneuver into a good attack range. C. Hutt does note one important characteristic of playful diversive exploration: The animal is relaxed and has a positive affect. Table 3.1 lists some criteria for distinguishing play and exploration.

Exploratory behavior is often tied to arousal, novelty, and accompanying nervous system activity (Burghardt, 2001). Although play also involves arousal, this in itself does not define play. Similarly, generalizations that active foragers play with objects more than passive foragers, dietary generalists play more than dietary specialists, and predators play with objects more than herbivorous species (Fagen, 1981) may have their roots in the costs and benefits of exploratory behavior in the context of specific life histories. Animals may also differ in the reward value of varied and intense stimulation that often accompanies play, among other activities, such as serious violence. For example, in our species late adolescent males are often particularly focused on seeking intense stimulation (Zuckerman, 1984). Such processes may enhance interest in not only risky play (rough games, kayaking, auto racing) but also risky sex, fighting, drug use, and delinquency—behavior patterns society has had some difficulty controlling.

Exploratory behavior can also be expressed differently in male and female nonhuman animals. In rats, males and females used different cues (spatial and visual)

Table 3.1

Distinguishing characteristics of exploratory behavior (specific) and play behavior

Feature	Exploration or Curiosity	Play
Context	Novel object or setting	Familiarized object or setting
Timing	Before play	After exploration
Behavior	Stereotyped	Variable
Attention	Deliberate	Casual
Affect	Neutral or negative	Positive
Heart rate	Low variability	High variability
Effect of stimulant drugs	Increase attention	Reduce play and impulsivity

Sources: J. E. Johnson, Christie, & Yawkey (1999); Pellegrini (1993); Panksepp (1998b).

in locating objects such as glass bottles and cylinders when the rats were placed in an open field enclosure. They differed in the effects of repeated testing and females differed according to estrous state (Tropp & Markus, 2001), which suggests that exploration itself is more complex than might be thought. Animals that live in risky environments, such as small fish in water containing larger, predatory fish, may show less exploratory behavior (emergence from crevices) than when they live in predator-free areas (Sih, 1992).

Exploration and related topics have been the subject of much research since Berlyne and Hutt (Görlitz & Wohlwill, 1987; R. N. Hughes, 1997; Keller, Schneider, & Henderson, 1994; Renner & Seltzer, 1991), but the basic issues have not yet been totally resolved. Recent studies do show that rats raised in enriched environments have enhanced memory and learning and also show faster habituation to novel objects if they have been reared in more complex nonsocial environments (Zimmerman et al., 2001).

Power, in his recent review (2000), posits an intermediate category in responses to objects between "pure" exploration and true play that he terms functional exploration/practice play. This category, also referred to as mastery or sensorimotor play, is characterized as "exploring the functional capabilities of the object by examining the effects of various actions on object responses, as well as practicing and refining the skills involved in producing these responses" (Power, 2000: 107). Unfortunately, there is considerable inference here beyond objective description. Perhaps it is sufficient to simply note that exploration and curiosity may be components of play, but describing all play, especially extended and repetitive play, as nothing but exploration is not useful. Exploration and play may also have different neural substrates, which is suggested by differential responses to psychoactive drugs (Panksepp, 1998b; table 3.1).

Figure 3.2
Tongue play stereotypy in caged calves. (From Albright & Arave, 1997)

3.5.2 Stereotypical Behavior

Introducing the repetitive aspect of play highlights the second class of behavior that has some similarity to play as usually defined. This class includes the repetitive stereo-typies found in many captive animals (Hediger, 1950). Consider a parrot in a small cage repeatedly jumping from a perch to the metal wire side to the top and back to the perch. The animal never varies the performance, which my go on for hours. Bears pace back and forth in front of their moat. Birds pluck their feathers until most are gone. Caged calves engage in repetitive tongue-rolling movements up to hundreds of times an hour (Albright & Arave, 1997; figure 3.2). Wolves in small enclosures may develop aberrant pacing patterns, and parrots in captivity may develop stereotypies such as repeatedly flipping their wings in certain ways. Such obsessive, repetitive actions involve behavior that almost no one would ever consider play. These behaviors certainly do not appear useful, but they do incorporate modifications of species-typical behavior patterns and can satisfy all, not just some, of the four structural characteristics listed in the Martin and Caro definition of play. Behavioral stereotypies are one of the major categories of behavior that definitions of play have had difficulty excluding if they rely, as these do, only on structural features of play behavior.

"A stereotypy is a behaviour pattern that is repetitive, invariant and has no obvious goal or function" (G. J. Mason, 1991: 1015). This definition reflects common usage since the 1960s. In animals, such apparently abnormal stereotypies are limited to animals in captivity. In authoritative reviews, G. J. Mason (1991, 1993) points out that stereotypies comprise a heterogeneous category. There are problems in defining stereotypies that mirror those in defining play. In fact, depending on one's application of "unvarying," Mason's definition could apply to play. One feature of stereotypies, however, is that they develop during the animal's life. Another common feature is that they are induced by poor or inappropriate captive environments and hence suggest poor welfare, resulting in problems and abnormal behavior in farm animals, as in the example of "tongue play" in cattle kept in small enclosures (figure 3.2), which can occur at very high rates. Seasonal, social, and spatial factors may all be involved and influence the invariance in form, pacing, and physical location of stereotyped performances (Zlamal & Wieczorek, 2002).

Some stereotypical patterns are induced by drugs, leading to comparisons of stereotypies to some psychiatric conditions, such as obsessive-compulsive disorder, autism, and schizophrenia (C. Hutt & Hutt, 1965). G. J. Mason (1991) shows that the great diversity of stereotypies has led to difficulties in accepting any classification of them. The volume edited by Lawrence and Rushen (1993) is a comprehensive review of much research on stereotypies. The roles of motivation, stress, neural processes, learning, and other factors are addressed.

The view that stereotypies are not only without function but are always harmful precludes an unjaundiced evaluation of their costs and benefits. The costs may be self-injury of various kinds as well as high expenditures of energy. G. J. Mason (1993) and Fraser and Broom (1990) provide extensive references to some of these, such as, in horses, excessive tooth wear caused by crib biting and gastrointestinal problems that are due to wind sucking.

One of the earliest experimental studies that attempted to evaluate various theories for the development of stereotypies was the study by Keiper (1969) on various small domesticated and wild-caught birds such as canaries (*Serinus canarius*) and related finches. Both invariable route tracing and repetitive pecking of particular body parts (e.g., feet, feathers) or objects (e.g., a cage bar) were studied. The way the animals were reared in captivity seemed to have little effect on canary stereotypies. Route tracing was reduced in larger cages or in those with more features (such as a swinging perch). Keiper concluded that stereotypies resulting from physical restriction (route tracing) differ from those related to sensory or behavioral restrictions (spot pecking).

Huber-Eicher and Wechsler (1997) took the analysis of feather pecking in birds further in chickens (*Gallus gallus domesticus*). Is feather pecking due to restricted opportunities for dust-bathing or foraging by pecking at the ground? Providing chicks with sand (a dust-bathing medium) and/or straw (a foraging medium) tested this. Providing straw was the key to reducing feather pecking and animal injury and thus related feather pecking to the foraging system.

Although Keiper found that the rearing environment did not affect stereotypies in birds, a comparative survey of stereotypies in eight species of zoo primates (lemurs, Old and New World monkeys, apes) found that current environmental conditions were less important than past experiences and rearing conditions (Marriner & Drickamer, 1994). This was also clear in experiences we had at the Knoxville, Tennessee, zoo with polar bears (*Ursus maritimus*). These bears, on exhibit in the 1970s in a new and spacious enclosure, engaged in behavior in which the animal would pace a step or two in one direction, swing its head, step in the opposite direction two steps, and repeat the head jerk. This behavior became explicable when we found out that the bears had previously been in a circus and traveled and were exhibited in small circus boxcars with bars. Being crowded, the stereotypical movements developed in similar fashion in all the bears. Even after years in a larger enclosure, they spent long periods performing the behavior as if they were still constrained by bars.

Although stereotypies, like obsessive-compulsive behaviors in people, are considered aberrant, pathological, harmful, and indicators of barren, unsuitable environments or prior poor environments, they may provide benefits to the animal psychologically. Furthermore, stereotypies may develop from habits and motor routines that are themselves valuable, if not essential, in natural environments. Anyone who has a cat notices that various routines involving feeding, sleeping areas, petting rituals, and so on become established and that the animal seems "happier" when they are accommodated. A study of rock hyraxes (*Procavia capensis*—a small African herbivorous mammal) established that they develop a series of invariant behaviors performed on specific rocks in their environment. Such routines can be useful in rapidly negotiating their environment, especially when escaping predators. Such behavior may be accentuated in the stereotypies seen in captive animals in enclosures much smaller than their normal environments (Serruya & Eilam, 1996). Stereotypies may even be adaptive responses to abnormal or boring conditions and have a protective function. For example, the tongue play in cows depicted earlier is associated with less erosive ulceration in the calves that perform it at very high rates than those that do not (figure 3.3).

Stereotypies or "compulsions" may occur more frequently when the animal or person is under some stress or conflict. Preventing the animal or person from performing the obsessive act without removing the cause may actually harm the animal. Neural substrates for repetitive and compulsive motor activities are being identified in brain areas such as the basal ganglia (e.g., Graybiel, 1995) and further work may allow us to identify how such behaviors develop. The species-specific nature of many stereotypies has long been recognized (Hediger, 1950). There is now evidence that there are also genetic differences in susceptibility to the development of stereotypies,

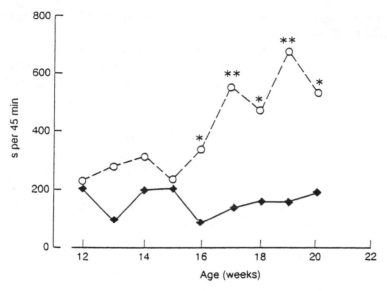

Figure 3.3
Data showing that extensive tongue play stereotypical behavior is associated with significantly less ulceration in calves by several months of age. Axis shows stereotypy frequency per 45-minute period. Open circles, little ulceration; closed circles, much ulceration. (From Albright & Arave, 1997)

since DBA/2 mice, but not C57BL/6 mice, developed stereotyped cage-climbing behavior in response to long-term restriction of food. Amphetamines also increased locomotor behavior in the food-restricted DBA mice, but not controls or the C57 mice. The authors suggested that these results show a neurological link between environmentally induced stereotypies and drug-induced behavioral sensitization (Cabib & Bonaventura, 1997).

A related phenomenon is wheel running in rodents and other animals (Sherwin, 1998). Literally thousands of studies have recorded the number of revolutions performed by a variety of wild and domesticated animals kept in small cages with a circular apparatus in which they can run continuously. Although the behavior of running is not abnormal in form, its occurrence in the laboratory often has the appearance of being compulsive in nature and has been interpreted as a measure of "general activity, exploration, migration, stereotypic activity, escape, play, level of deprivation (food, water, conspecifics, etc.), social rank, hormonal status, adrenal activity, body weight maintenance and parturition" (Sherwin, 1998: 11). After a comprehensive review, Sherwin (1998) concluded that the behavior is due to a variety of causes, but should be viewed primarily as an artifact of captivity and the nature of the running

Table 3.2
Twelve characteristics of play extracted from the literature

Attributes of Play
No obvious immediate function
Sequentially variable
Quick and energetically expensive
Exaggerated, incomplete, or awkward
Most prevalent in juveniles
Breakdown in role relationships
Special "play" signals
Mixing of behavior patterns from several contexts
Relative absence of threat and submission
Relative absence of final consummatory acts
Stimulation seeking
Pleasurable affect

Source: Burghardt (1984)

wheel apparatus, although it is also apparently self-reinforcing, is often the dominant activity in the animal's captive life, and is affected by many environmental and physiological conditions.

Finally, just as exploratory behavior may be a component of play or be on a continuum with it, so may play develop into stereotyped behavior with clearly dysfunctional properties. What initially started out as play or recreation may become a highly repetitive behavior that occurs in an almost unvarying compulsive mode. The informal enjoyable playing of cards or the occasional trip to the casino may lead to the drawn pale faces of near zombies dropping quarters in slot machines for hours at a time, or people playing the same computer game over and over. An effective definition of play must be able to distinguish, in a pragmatic fashion, play from initial exploration and play from its "hardening" in compulsive stereotypy.

3.6 The Use of Multiple Criteria in Defining Play

3.6.1 The Most Common Attributes of Play
Many writers on play, including some cited earlier, have tried to list a number of features shared by most, if not all, commonly accepted types of play (e.g., Thorpe, 1966). In my first major writing on play (Burghardt, 1984) I derived what appeared to be its most common attributes (table 3.2).

While this list of possible traits is a rather complete enumeration (Cohen, 1987), the problem here, as in the preceding definitions, is that guidance is not given as to which are the key identifying criteria. In addition, some criteria are specific to social play (play signals, role reversals). Although some of these criteria may be important in distinguishing among different kinds of play, they are often not easily uncovered without extensive study and thus are deficient in isolating good candidates for play of whatever type. What seems to be needed is a set of a few criteria that must all be met before a behavior can be labeled as play.

3.6.2 Play in Children

Play in children has been a major topic of study for over a century. Play has also been extremely important in many theories of development, education, therapy, socialization, and cognition. Perhaps this literature can provide some pointers toward a definition that can be useful in comparative studies. One complication is that the field seems to be going through some shifting between studying play as behavior that children perform, and play as a disposition or as a personality trait, usually termed playfulness (Rogers et al., 1998). Thus there is no consensus as to what should be measured and how or if play and playfulness are related in any clear fashion.

C. D. Clark and Miller (1998) concisely review the literature on play in children and articulated four criteria for play. These are listed below and include examples provided by the authors:

1. Nonliterality Transformation of meanings and actions, taking an "as if" stand toward reality.
Example: A child holds a hand to her ear and says "ring, ring" as if calling someone on the telephone.
2. Intrinsic motivation Activity done for its own sake, rather than being externally motivated.
Example: A child rides a tricycle purely for the fun of it, rather than to get somewhere.
3. Positive affect Enjoyment or pleasure.
Example: A child squeals with glee while descending a slide.
4. Process flexibility Flexible use of an object as means, rather than action directed by the object.
Example: A child freely tries many variations (of its own choosing) for using a Frisbee: throwing it, spinning it, using it as a hat, carrying marbles on it, throwing things at it as a target, and/or jumping on it.

In another recent treatment (J. E. Johnson, Christie, & Yawkey, 1999), a fifth criterion, free choice, is added. An activity freely chosen by a child and considered play, such as building with blocks, is viewed as work when instigated or assigned by a teacher.

These criteria cover a lot of ground and are quite abstract and general. However, all five do not appear to be necessary in all instances. For example, the process flexibility criterion refers to the use of an object and thus would seem to preclude locomotor and social play. Nonliterality is akin to the "pretense" aspect often discussed in the animal literature. However, any time a behavior does not seem serious, it may be too easy to apply concepts such as pretense, role playing, or intentionality. As an example of animal play, consider a cat chasing a rubber mouse. Since the cat does not eat the toy mouse, it "knows" the mouse is not real and thus is taking an "as if" stand toward reality. The behavior seems to be intrinsically motivated, although without the toy mouse it is unlikely that the cat would pounce, paw, and chase. That the cat is not in a feeding or aggressive state can often be ascertained; that the behavior is enjoyable or rewarding for its own sake may also be likely if critical anthropomorphism (Burghardt, 1997) is applied. The fourth criterion, process flexibility, is more problematic since we would have to know the range of behavior patterns shown toward real mice by cats. However, if the range of behavior shown toward the toy mouse is greater than that shown toward a live mouse in a serious predatory event, then perhaps we can apply the fourth criterion as well. If we are dealing with a far less well known species than a cat, then there may be additional problems in applying these criteria, especially if "positive affect" is made a central one. Nevertheless, these criteria are, overall, applicable to children and many animals and do not mandate a specific or general function, either immediate or delayed. Clark and Miller have developed a list of clear criteria. However, the terminology employed may not be suitable for much of the animal literature, especially as we move away from familiar mammals.

Additional criteria are sometimes added to the list of child play characteristics. These include active engagement in the behavior, emphasizing that the child is immersed in the behavior. Another one is that play is means oriented. This is another way of saying that the act itself is the end (autotelic). A third additional criterion is freedom from rules. This may help separate some kinds of children's games from others, but even in animals, much social play, including play fighting, has rules and regularities. When they are violated, true aggression can result (Bekoff, 1995).

A clear conception of play is also necessary for research and applied endeavors involving play in children. A number of play scales are used in research on children that are derived from explicit criteria. For example, the Test of Playfulness (ToP) scale is based on thirty-two observational items derived from four qualities felt to contribute to playfulness: intrinsic motivation, internal control, framing,[15] and suspending reality (Porter & Bundy, 2001). The thirty-two observational items all seem reasonable, but are more interpretation than description of specific activities. They include some fairly clear items such as initiating play, being engaged, showing joy and enthusiasm, and repeating activities, as well as others such as bending the rules, negotiating with others,

15. Framing is the setting off of play from serious activity and derives from Bateson's concept of metacommunication in play as described in the next chapter.

joking, and so forth. Psychometrically the test seems quite sound. Another recent observational instrument is the Playful Behaviors Observation Inventory (PBOI), which was used to measure the activities of toddlers in a classroom (Dodd, Rogers, & Wilson, 2001). Here a variety of measures derived from the first four criteria listed earlier were used and involved quantitative measures such as number of uses for an item, duration of focused attention, and number of repetitions.

Playfulness in people is largely assessed through questionnaires given to teachers, parents, friends, and peers (Porter & Bundy, 2001; Rogers et al., 1998) rather than the direct observation of play itself. A recent popular instrument is the Child Playfulness Scale (CPS) developed by Barnett (1998), which consists of twenty-three statements grouped into five categories: cognitive spontaneity, social spontaneity, physical spontaneity, manifest joy, and humor. In the psychoanalytic area, playfulness has been assessed using the Rorschach inkblot test (Handler, 1999). Patients were told to look for playful interpretations. Playful responses to the blots had to meet five criteria that also overlap the ones already discussed: unconventional, original, positive emotional tone, no hostility or aggression, reflect secure attachment. For some patients this was very difficult indeed; seeing a blot as representing two cats who died fighting among themselves was rated very nonplayful whereas seeing a blot as two little girls in pigtails on a seesaw was definitely playful. Having a good set of play criteria could enhance such research, as far from traditional play research as it appears.

Typically these child behavior play studies ignore or downplay the most commonly studied play behavior in mammals, play fighting, also called in children rough-and-tumble (R&T) play (Pellegrini & Smith, 1998). Indeed, even distinguishing R&T play from aggression has proven difficult, especially for adults (Pellegrini, 1989), although it is telling that children from different countries (Italy and England) had no difficulty in distinguishing serious from playful fighting in both their own and other cultural settings (Costabile et al., 1991).

In summary, the literature on children's play has addressed this complex phenomenon with diligence and often a conceptual and methodological sophistication rarely found in studies on animal play. However, the very richness of the phenomena and the option of using questionnaires and indirect measures, along with a rather firm belief that play is easily recognized, even if it cannot be defined, has made it difficult to translate the methodology to nonhuman animal studies. For example, joy is not an obvious attribute of most animals.

3.7 A Working Method for Identifying Play

We have seen that there are many, indeed innumerable, ways of characterizing and defining play. All single-criterion definitions such as "play is behavior done for its own sake," "play is not serious," "play is pleasurable behavior," or "play is preparation for the future" fail because they include much that clearly is not playful in any traditional sense even if the criteria could be objectively applied. When such definitions are supplemented with more detailed characteristics, only some of them apply in any given example; this is true for much of the child literature as well as that involving animals. Which, if any, characteristics need to be present are not specified. Definitions combining criteria suffer the same fate, especially if they contain words such as *may*, *often*, or *sometimes*. Definitions based solely on subjective or emotional criteria such as "fun" are often as difficult to apply as those based on a presumed but unidentified adaptive value (enhanced survival in adulthood). Moreover, even in humans, having fun is not isomorphic with expressions of glee or pleasure.

Thus we still face the dilemma of deciding in any given example or species whether we are dealing with a presumptive example of play. This is not just a pedantic question. In order to try to elucidate the genesis of play, we must use the comparative method. In order to apply the comparative method, we need to be able to know what we are comparing across species and populations. If we are studying the ontogeny of play and its fate and transformations in individuals, we also need to know whether we are comparing related activities or those that just look similar.

The definitions listed above, the many others enumerated in Fagen (1981), and the criteria list I used previously (Burghardt, 1984) are unable to do this for us. At best, they are lists of factors that may be involved in play, but they neither distinguish between the essential and the inessential nor indicate their relative importance. A usable operational method is required. The utility of operational definitions is not that they capture the entire nature of a phenomenon, but that they distinguish it from other phenomena in a manner sufficiently rigorous to allow scientific analysis to proceed. Such an approach should serve to separate the category we are interested in from most others with which it may be confused (fighting, predation, low-intensity intention movements, stereotypies). The more discriminating the better, but absolute discrimination, like a mind that forgets nothing, might be a goal not worth attaining.

This being said, what can we do to help in the day-to-day work of recognizing and analyzing play? The approach tried here is to produce a small set of criteria by combining commonly noted traits of play into smaller groups containing similar criteria.

In addition to the literature on child behavior, lists of criteria have been tried before. For Huizinga (1955) play was voluntary (related to freedom), distinct from ordinary life, disinterested (unconnected with any immediate satisfaction of biological wants or needs; not goal directed), and dependent on some order or rules. This is hard to apply to animal play. For example, Huizinga accepts as play any behavior of animals that is not purely physiological. Yet physiology enters into every and all action, and our understanding of biological needs has expanded markedly since he wrote.

Another early effort to characterize play in animals, as well as exploration, was that of Welker (1971). He articulated five general "criteria by which exploration and play have been defined and distinguished from other behavioral classes (such as reproductive, aggressive, fearful, maternal, ingestive, eliminative, etc.)" (Welker, 1971: 183). The five involved (1) stimulus goals and incentives, (2) terminal (consummatory) act sequences, (3) preterminal (appetitive) act sequences, (4) internal neurobiological states, and (5) adaptive features (functions). Although he discusses many of the features of exploration, and then play, as they relate to these criteria, he does not actually either define play or give the specific and essential features one should note in deciding whether an act is playful. In fact, he finally concludes that there are inherent difficulties with all these criteria and in effect punts.

Millar (1981) lists six criteria that are more easily evaluated. These are that play (1) is voluntary; (2) is paradoxical (out of context and dissociated from the normal goal); (3) is exaggerated; (4) may be accompanied by play signals; (5) entails random sequences of activities from different adult functional behavior systems; and (6) may be repeated, ritualized, or involve rules. Millar concludes, however, that only the first two are essential.

After considering all the proposed criteria and how they might be applied to the occurrence of play in animals never considered playful (e.g., turtles) (Burghardt, 1998a; Kramer & Burghardt, 1998), I have now decided that five key criteria are possible (Burghardt, 1999). It seems to me that applied in a careful manner, they can distinguish play from virtually all other phenomena with which it might be confused, including exploration and curiosity on one hand and stereotyped behavior on the other. The key here is that *all five* criteria have to be simultaneously satisfied for the label of play to be attached. Equally important is an additional proviso: When a criterion contains more than one attribute, *only one* needs to apply for the criterion to be met. Examples showing why none of these criteria can work alone are discussed as each one is introduced. I claim no originality for any of the criteria, but the packaging is new and that provides the added value.

3.7.1   The First Criterion

As shown previously, the most common attribute of play is some variant of the view that play behavior is not serious, is not of immediate use, and is not necessary for survival. However, showing that a behavior has some possible immediate function or current adaptive role cannot be used to eliminate the notion that the behavior is play. As arguments over adaptation have shown (Rose & Lauder, 1996), a behavior or structure can be of value even if it has not evolved for that purpose. For example, the vigorous exercise involved in much play may improve the oxygen-carrying capacity of the blood. Furthermore, every behavior that has no immediate function is certainly not play. If it were, then self-mutilation behavior and the stereotypical behavior of many captive animals would be considered play. On the other hand, play may indeed have some current function (arousal, physiological toning) and thus cannot be said to be

entirely nonfunctional even if no delayed benefits can be identified. Furthermore, play may often entail costs to the performing animal in terms of energy expenditure and increased predation risk. These suggest, for the frequent and complex behavioral performances often seen in play, that there should be benefits. These benefits can be current as well as deferred.

Another aspect of play, particularly play with objects, is that the behavior may be directed at normal stimuli (cats playing with mice), stimuli that might be construed as "normal" (a kitten with a ball of yarn or a rubber mouse), or stimuli that may have little or no reference to natural objects (monkeys playing with pegboards).

Although play has some nonfunctional or nonadaptive elements, these must be evaluated in a careful manner. After considering the various constraints listed here, the following criterion captures an essential property of play.

The first criterion for recognizing play is that the performance of the behavior is not fully functional in the form or context in which it is expressed; that is, it includes elements, or is directed toward stimuli, that do not contribute to current survival.

The critical phrase is "not fully functional," instead of purposeless, nonadaptive, or having a delayed benefit.

Now this clearly does not eliminate all instances of nonplay behavior. We know, for example, that many predatory chases of prey by lions are unsuccessful, as are defensive attacks by prey or rivals. Many courtship attempts, indeed most attempts in many species, are unsuccessful. We also can deceive animals with models, and nature does this with mimics. Thus, many performances of behavior do turn out to be ineffective, misdirected, and unsuccessful. We would not, for these reasons, call them play.

There are other more controversial and less easily dismissed examples of behavior patterns that do not seem to be play but that meet the first criterion. Animals deprived of appropriate mating or prey stimuli may substitute inappropriate or degraded stimuli. Indeed, the end result of this process, as put forth in the classical ethological model, is vacuum activity, behavior patterns such as feeding or flight performed in the absence of any external stimulus. (Burghardt, 1973; Tinbergen, 1951). On the other hand, low levels of motivation may lead to tentative incipient and apparently nonfunctional movements, called intention movements, that may be confused with play (Kruijt, 1964). Conflicting motivational states leading to redirected and displacement behavior may also be involved in play (Pellis et al., 1988). Such motivational factors greatly influenced early ethological theorizing on play (Lorenz, 1956; Meyer-Holzapfel, 1978). Early in ontogeny, behavior patterns often appear before they are needed. A useful term for these precocious responses is prefunctional behavior patterns (Hogan, 1988).

The problem with the "no immediate function" criterion so often found in play definitions is that there may in fact be a function, but we just do not recognize it. Many claimed instances of play have been tempered when more became known about

the natural history of the species. However, the same could be said about vestigial organs or claims about the lack of adaptiveness of any behavior or structure. Essentially the issue is one of probabilities. When we add other criteria to our definition, we solve this problem.

3.7.2 The Second Criterion

Play is often characterized as something that animals seem to engage in voluntarily. Play often appears to be spontaneous or intrinsically motivated, or the stimulation produced is rewarding or reinforcing. This suggests that no apparent external stimuli seem involved (this is particularly true in ungulate locomotor play). Sometimes this aspect is so reliable that claims are made that a drive or motivation to play is play's primary characteristic, leading to the view that play is an instinct (Groos, 1898) or autotelic. Applying this trait of play, however, also presumes that the first criterion is met.

While for some scientists "voluntary" and "spontaneous" are useful terms to apply to play, others prefer the oft-made claim that play is pleasurable or fun. The mere performance of play actions may be stimulating, rewarding, or in some other way reinforcing to the animal. Certainly, however, many behaviors that are not play have similar stimulus-seeking, self-reinforcing, and pleasurable properties. Eating is a prime example, and not just in people. Rats prefer food flavored with nonnutritive saccharin. Mating behavior and maternal care also seem to have similar intrinsic reinforcing properties. Combined with the first criterion, however, we can eliminate some of these phenomena where the performances of the behavior patterns are pleasurable or to some extent voluntary or spontaneous (e.g., feeding in animals when food is continuously available) as well as being highly functional.

Sometimes, as in social play, one animal will appear to pester another to play fight or wrestle. This is commonly seen in two dogs, where an older animal will tire first and opt out of the play encounter. I also saw this in the black bear cubs we raised (Burghardt & Burghardt, 1972); asymmetries appear in parent–offspring play in virtually all animals, including people (MacDonald, 1993). On the other hand, social play is often contagious; the jumping and leaping of one animal may stimulate another. This recruitment of animals to social games may have been the kind of behavior that led to repeated assertions that imitation is an important feature of play (e.g., Miklosi, 1999). In any event, play occurs when it appears to be, on the part of one participant at least, spontaneous and voluntary. Such behavior may be accompanied by signs that play is fun, pleasurable, and joyful. These latter aspects involve us in the difficult though not impossible task of assessing the subjective state of the animal. Such a determination will not be feasible in most species. Nonetheless, if the performance of the behavior or the stimulation received is hedonic, then play may be present.

The second criterion for recognizing play is that the behavior is spontaneous, voluntary, intentional, pleasurable, rewarding, reinforcing, or autotelic ("done for its own sake").

Only one of these often overlapping concepts needs to apply. Note that this criterion also accommodates any subjective concomitants of play (having fun, enjoyable), but does not make them essential for recognizing play.

Note the "or" in the definition. Scientists averse to anything tainted with anthropomorphism might not accept that a behavior is pleasurable for a rat, but may accept that performing it may be reinforcing. Physiologists may not want to use the concept of spontaneous because it may imply that the behavior is uncaused. Similarly, intention (or intentionality) may be key words for those who object to voluntary.[16]

3.7.3 The Third Criterion

Neither of the first two criteria tells us what play behavior will look like (its topographical and structural properties). If the behavior, even if it is spontaneous and not fully functional in obtaining a specific end, appears the same as the serious performance of the activity, we are unlikely to call it play. Thus to be play, the behavior must have some characteristic that sets it off structurally or temporally from the serious performance. This is especially important if the play behavior is highly species-typical and resembles the serious performance. Many such structural differences have been noted and some are incorporated into the definitions cited earlier that seem most comprehensive. These elements may include the observation that the motor patterns in play fighting, for example, while outwardly similar to serious fighting, may differ in the targets and frequency of various behaviors (Pellis & Pellis, 1987).

The behavior patterns in play may also be exaggerated in intensity or duration from their normal expression. The bow used by dogs in soliciting play from another animal or its master is an exaggerated form of social behavior (Bekoff, 1995). But the exaggeration aspect has rarely been quantified, and may often be lacking, as in black bear social play (Henry & Herrero, 1974).

Behavior patterns in play may also appear earlier in development than when the behavior is performed seriously. This may be especially true of fighting, chasing, wrestling, locomotor play, and courtship. It may also appear at one stage of life and not be present again later. Suckling behavior in young mammals is not just immature feeding behavior, but a system that is quite physiologically and evolutionarily separate from feeding on solid food. Similarly, it has been argued that much play fighting may differ in both causal mechanisms and function from adult serious fighting (Pellis, 1993). Nonetheless, adultlike behavior patterns that are performed precociously in young animals before their deployment in serious contexts are often considered play.

16. See Bekoff (1976) for an early prescient discussion of these issues.

Play behavior may also be in some respects awkward or unpolished. The charm of young animals often lies in this very awkwardness of performance. Play may also involve sequences of behavior that never appear in the same order when performed seriously. Such awkward or variable performances could be involved in refining or enhancing motor or perceptual skills. It may be difficult to quantify and measure awkwardness, but our subjective impressions can be clarified through careful analysis using diverse methods. For example, when the Laban Movement Analysis developed for human dance notation was used to analyze rats play fighting at different ages, it showed that as rats matured they became more forceful in their movements and had more control over their bodies. Specifically, they shifted to a more stable anchoring position when pinning their partner (Foroud & Pellis, 2002, 2003).

Another difference from the typical serious performance of a behavior may be that the end of the sequence may be dropped or inhibited. Thus cats playing with prey objects may not inflict killing bites. Play fights with conspecifics, parents, or littermates also may have inhibited biting or none. Animals that play with human caregivers are often seen to inhibit the roughness of their play with humans compared with conspecifics (Burghardt & Burghardt, 1972; Burghardt, 1992).

Undoubtedly, very few if any play examples will show all these structural characteristics. It would appear, however, that *at least one* of these structural or temporal characteristics needs to be present for behavior to be considered play.

The third criterion for recognizing play is that it differs from the "serious" performance of ethotypic behavior structurally or temporally in at least one respect: it is incomplete (generally through inhibited or dropped final elements), exaggerated, awkward, or precocious; or it involves behavior patterns with modified form, sequencing, or targeting.

Notice that this is a structural and temporal descriptive criterion that acknowledges, but does not require, that play may be found only during a limited period early in an animal's life.

Sometimes it is claimed that play must always be marked by distinctive communicative signals (see chapter 4), but this is not a requirement, although it could satisfy the third criterion. With criterion three, the claims that play is not only highly variable but also completely unstructured, free from rules, and creative can be addressed. If these claims were true, we would *never* recognize behavior as play. In fact, any and all behavior patterns can vary across individuals and among performances by even the same individual. Animals vary in the details of how they capture or ingest prey, approach a rival, court a mate, or build a nest. Evolution operates on individual differences. Thus it is not surprising that no "ideal" form holds sway except in the typological aspects of any behavioral categories we are forced to adopt. When is normal variation of behavioral performance an exaggeration? When is "awkward" merely in the eye of the beholder? Such considerations led to Barlow's redefining of instinctive movements (fixed action patterns) as "modal action patterns" (Barlow, 1968).

Although individual variation may be more common in play than in other behavioral contexts, this needs to be quantitatively assessed. The variances from normal "serious" ethotypic behaviors seen in various guises in play may offer the illusion that the play is free or creative when it is just the shift from the expected, coupled with our own fascination, that is at work. Also, since play may involve many kinds of different objects, many being artificial in captivity, variability is to be expected, just as a wolf stalks a bison differently than it hunts a rabbit.

3.7.4 The Fourth Criterion

There are many reports of rarely seen behavior that is often labeled play because it does not fit anywhere else. Crane (1975) reported a behavior in fiddler crabs that were deliberately attacking a rival's dome as play. How, in fact, do we deal with reports of abnormal but somewhat species-characteristic behavior seen only once or at a few scattered times? We need an additional criterion to eliminate the bizarre or non-replicated anecdotal report. For play to have evolved, it must have a fairly widespread currency in certain contexts, even if there is much individual variability.

The fourth criterion for recognizing play is that the behavior is performed repeatedly in a similar, but not rigidly stereotyped, form during at least a portion of the animal's ontogeny.

As with the third criterion, this criterion explicitly counters the apparent freedom, flexibility, and versatility of play that have been so often noted. It is clear from the literature that repetition of patterns of movement is found in all play and games in human and nonhuman animals. It is also useful in distinguishing exploratory responses to novel stimuli, which typically habituate quickly, from the play actions that may follow initial exploratory behavior. Repeated actions also facilitate the use of play in learning or improving skill and, as discussed later, an "urge" to repeat behavior (try and try again) may be essential for play to have functional and adaptive roles in behavioral development and psychological well-being.

Play, then, is something that is repeatedly performed, often in bouts, during a predictable period in the animal's life (which in some cases may be virtually life-long). Sometimes an animal seems not to tire of performing a behavior for long periods. Pellis (1993) makes the point that play is distinguished from nonplay or the merely "play-like" on the basis of the amount of time devoted to the putative play behavior as well as the length of individual play bouts (Byers, 1999a). The total time spent in play is a measure clearly related to the amount of repetition and has been used in the literature. However, a criterion of duration too often becomes enmeshed in arguments over the amount of time spent in play in relation to an animal's total activity budget (cf. P. Martin, 1984b; Miller & Byers, 1991). Duration measures do not deal with the number of times comparable patterns are performed; a single instance of play may take a long time. A long duration might mean that a behavior pattern was repeated many times, as in bouts, or that a series of different, but confusing, almost random behaviors were observed.

The qualification that the period of repetition may last for only a short time in the animal's ontogeny recognizes that play may wax and wane and be seen almost exclusively at certain periods in an animal's life. Play in adults is less ontogenetically constrained and may have more to do with contextual factors (having offspring, being bored) than juvenile play.

Related to the repetition aspect is the frequent observation that play seems to take on a life of its own, as in object or locomotor play, where an animal may repeat an action until it has somehow mastered it. This is the so-called "mastery play" of Piaget (1962) and underlies K. V. Thompson's (1996, 1998) view of play as self-assessment. The apparent awkwardness of many juvenile play behaviors compared with the adult form may serve as a cue to the animal to keep on playing until the behavior is mastered. Learning to walk in human infants may be an example (Thelen, 1995). This aspect of play is a crucial one that might provide a much-needed refinement of the practice theory.

The repetition of play behavior may be due to the self-reinforcing or related aspects of criterion two, although here we are only characterizing the behavior structurally. Repeatability is important in considering as play behavioral performances that do not obviously derive from serious instinctive patterns (with or without learned elements). Behavior patterns that may structurally satisfy some of the criteria, but which are performed rarely and unreliably within or across individuals are thus not considered firmly demonstrated play, whatever their other features.

Criterion four is also useful in distinguishing play from exploratory behavior, with which it is often linked. As discussed earlier, exploratory behavior is seen in novel environments and curiosity is directed at novel objects. Such behavior often wanes or habituates rapidly. Parents are often disappointed when a complex and expensive toy engages a child's interest for only a brief time. The toy was "explored" and found unsuitable for play.

The addition to the fourth criterion of not being highly stereotyped raises the question of when a repeated play behavior is a stereotypy. As noted earlier, play can become addictive and compulsive; when this happens, the behavior is often marked by repetitive rigidity. However, this must be assessed in the context of the normal behavioral repertoire of the species and the application of the other criteria.

Note that the first, third, and fourth criteria are descriptive. The second criterion is a combination of descriptive (spontaneous) and interpretive (reinforcing, fun) criteria. The subjective elements are to some extent derived from the descriptive. Observers may often rush to the interpretive aspect, however, even to the extent that some people claim that the sole essence of play is fun or pleasure. Nevertheless, once this move is made, then all kinds of problems arise. As pointed out in chapter 1, much that is called play involves serious rhetorics, such as power and fate. Applying the next criterion may solve part of this conundrum.

3.7.5 The Fifth Criterion

Behavior that is termed play is uncoerced, appears voluntary, and engages the animal's interest (criterion two). However, we did not specify how one could really know this. The last criterion not only helps in this regard, but also is in itself a critical point.

One of the prime characteristics of play is that the animal is not strongly motivated to perform other behaviors. The animal is not starving (or even very hungry), it is not at the moment preoccupied with mating, setting up territories, or otherwise competing for essential resources or escaping predators. It has long been recognized that animals that are well fed and free from environmental stresses play more than animals that are hungry, too hot or too cold, sick, or endangered by predators. This is a criterion of play shared by Spencer (1872), Groos (1898), and Hornaday (1922), and acknowledged by many describers of play in specific species (e.g., Pereira & Fairbanks, 1993).

Although this point seems similar to criterion one, it differs in that here the animal is not under the strong influence of any "primary" drive. Such an exclusionary approach may appear to be equivalent to the "proving the null hypothesis" approach decried by Beach (1955). On the contrary, play is often seen when the animal is not under the strong influence of other motivational systems. Thus a juvenile mammal will play more when it is warm, well fed, not in obvious danger from predators, and so on. This last criterion is one of the most important aspects of play; it occurs in a "relaxed field" (Bally, 1945; Lorenz, 1981). Such a relaxed field was used by C. Hutt (1966) to distinguish play from specific exploration. Play is related to lower stress (less cortisol) in squirrel monkeys (Biden & Champoux, 1999).

Recent work on using play in schools to stimulate creativity and problem solving has found that it is most effective when children are comfortable in their surroundings and with the adults (Tegano, Sawyers, & Moran, 1989). These workers independently arrived at the term *psychological safety* to label this phenomenon; it is remarkably similar to the "relaxed field" of Bally (1945), especially when we recognize that the more biological components of the relaxed field (good nutrition, good health, good weather) are assumed to be present in psychological safety as well. The hierarchical organization of behavior and behavioral priorities has been recognized for many years and was formalized by Tinbergen (1951) and included in many current models of behavior (Timberlake & Silva, 1995). Grooming behavior in animals typically follows feeding to satiation, and play may also be most likely in specific behavioral contexts.

The fifth criterion for recognizing play is that the behavior is initiated when an animal is adequately fed, healthy, and free from stress (e.g., predator threat, harsh microclimate, social instability), or intense competing systems (e.g., feeding, mating, predator avoidance). In other words, the animal is in a "relaxed field."

This criterion may underlie the finding that play is often much more common in well-maintained captive animals than in their wild counterparts (Burghardt, 1988b). Not every behavior seen when the animal is in the relaxed field will be play, and sometimes such a state, particularly in captivity, may be hard to ascertain completely. Stereotyped behaviors, such as pacing in captive animals, may occur because of overly small cages that do not adequately accommodate the behavioral needs of the animals, especially active ones, or cages that, while spacious, are barren and sterile (Burghardt, 1996). The occurrence of stereotyped behavior is not a response to a relaxed field.

Although the relaxed field criterion may seem straightforward in most cases, it cannot be applied, as is true of the others as well, without some thinking about possible problems or apparent exceptions. Much play and sport in our species is risky, if not dangerous, and part of the "fun" may be the adrenaline-induced arousal, excitement, and short-term stress engendered (I write this before embarking down class IV rapids on a Tennessee river). Note however, that such behavior seems to be engaged in voluntarily by people in resource-adequate (if not wealthy) environments. A factor underlying such play may be, in fact, a means of arousing "virtual emotions" in people living in environments where "real" versions are no longer common or necessary (Sutton-Smith, 2003a, b).[17] Much animal play may also have the consequence of arousing specific emotions or increasing general arousal. Thus some level of stimulation or internal motivation may be involved in instigating play. Sleepy, tired, overly sated animals, or those otherwise avoiding stimulation do not play unless they are aroused with highly salient play-inducing stimuli.

3.7.6   What the Play Criteria Do Not Do

The five criteria do not assume that play is due to a separate "play motivation" or is a part of other motivational systems, an issue discussed in chapter 5. It could be either or both or derived from a conflict between drives or moods. For example, some evidence supports the view that play occurs in conflict situations, such as the vacillation between approach and withdrawal that may occur in predatory object play in cats (figure 3.4), where it serves as a means of testing the potential danger of the prey (Pellis et al., 1988). The vigorous probing, leaping, and withdrawal responses in object play by cats could represent a means of avoiding possible injury and thus not be completely relaxed behavior. On the other hand, I have observed that if cats are either extremely hungry or very wary, predatory play either does not occur or is extremely attenuated. In satiated cats, play bouts with objects may be very prolonged.

17. Gregory Bateson (1972) mentioned that play was a simulation of emotion, but the idea was not developed.

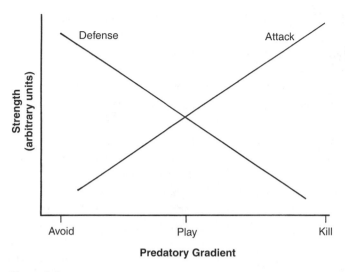

Figure 3.4
A model showing how predatory object play in cats may occur when both defensive (avoidance) and attack (approach) tendencies are simultaneously aroused. (From Pellis et al., 1988)

Play may serve immediate functions in social contexts, as in play fighting in male rats (L. K. Smith, Fantella, & Pellis, 1999) and courtship play in primates (Pellis & Iwaniuk, 1999a). A study of social status in rats paired with unfamiliar rats concluded that play fighting may "act as a quasi-aggressive means of testing the propensity to fight by potential competitors" (L. K. Smith, Fantella, & Pellis, 1999: 150). Play in some primates and other mammals can be a conditional courtship strategy. For example, males may engage in play wrestling as a means to overcome female reluctance to mate (Pellis & Iwaniuk, 1999a). The shift in use of behavior patterns from one context to another is known as ritualization, and to the extent that play behavior has become incorporated into various behavioral systems, it may be on the way to losing some of its playful characteristics and evolving into something else. This is only to be expected if play can sometimes serve as the source of behavioral innovation and be an important component of behavioral evolution (Burghardt, 2001; chapters 5 and 15).

3.7.7 Applying the Criteria

This long chapter is almost at an end, but it is essential to the tasks ahead. To summarize,

all five criteria must be met in at least one respect before the play label can be confidently attached to any specific instance of behavior.

Many tantalizing examples of play, especially in little-studied animals, can only be tentatively accepted as such because there is not sufficient information to make a judgment in all five categories (chapter 7). Animals under chronic stress or intense motivation (e.g., to escape, eat, fight, mate), or engaging in captivity-induced stereo-typed behavior, must not be erroneously viewed as playing.

A recent doctoral dissertation by Kathryn Lampard (2002) is the first empirical hypothesis-driven comparative study attempting to look at the effects of novel objects, novel sounds, and novel odors on exploratory, stereotypical, and play behavior. This almost 300-page work cannot be summarized here, but the study will be briefly de-scribed as it is a useful model for future work. Four species maintained at a zoo in quite naturalistic settings were looked at: plains zebras (*Equus burchelli*), oriental small-clawed otters (*Aonyx cinerea*), collared peccaries (*Tayassu tajacu*), and Barbary sheep (*Ammotragus lervia*). The species were chosen to represent different behavioral lifestyles. The sheep and zebras are herbivores, the peccary an omnivore, and the otter a carnivore. The sheep and zebras are prey species, the otter a predator, and the peccary both prey and predator. They also differ in their sensory emphases, with peccaries and otters having better olfactory capabilities than sheep and zebras while peccaries seem to have less hearing sensitivity than the others.

Although only a few members of each species were studied and then only in one setting, a systematic two-week presentation of the stimuli (movable and nonmovable objects, sounds, and odors) was carried out with baseline and postpresentation phases and some other variants. Behavioral measures recorded represented locomotor, social, and object play along with specific object exploratory (investigatory) behavior, stereo-typies, and behavior such as eating/foraging, courtship, grooming, aggression, and sleeping.

In all four species introduction of novel objects led to more exploration and play while stereotypies decreased. However, much more important were the findings from the series of twenty-one hypotheses that were tested, which showed interesting species differences that were often not predicted. For example, while it was predicted that all species would show increased levels of exploration to movable as compared to non-movable objects, this was only true of the otters and peccaries; the zebras showed little difference and the sheep responded more to the nonmovable objects. It was similarly predicted that object play behavior would be more common with the move-able than nonmovable objects. Although the peccaries and otters played more with the moveable objects, the zebras showed no play at all. Adult sheep did not play with either type of object but the juveniles played more with the nonmovable objects. On the other hand, the hypothesis that overall play behavior would increase with the introduction of novel objects was supported in all species, but only during the first week with zebras.

The distinction between specific exploration and play became clearer when comparing responses to the novel objects over the two weeks that they were present. Whereas the sheep explored and played with the objects both weeks, even more the second week, other species showed a different pattern. The otters showed a great amount of exploration the first week and none the second, but played a lot both weeks. The peccaries followed the same pattern with exploration as the otters, but differed in that they did not play at all with the object until the second week. What this study makes clear is that theories about the relationships among exploration (curiosity, investigation), stereotypy, and play cannot be settled by studying only one species or one category of stimuli.

The five play criteria do not characterize the forms of play, the distinctive characteristics of play, or the reasons for the occurrence of play in any given species. For example, some animals seem to use special postures, facial expressions, and even pheromones to signal a readiness to engage in social play. These are often termed metacommunication signals, and the best-known examples derive from play (chapter 4).

One value of these five criteria is that they effectively link the different kinds of play: locomotor, object, and social. Play manifests itself in many ways. Whether all play shares some common phyletic history or physiological underpinnings is not the question at issue now.

A main reason for developing criteria for recognizing play is the probability that play behavior evolved from nonplay behavior and may be still the most actively evolving system in many extant animals. This means that play can only be understood by linking it with "protoplay" or ancestral (plesiomorphic) processes that facilitated the further evolution of play. Thus later in this book there will be examples that meet the criteria for play laid down here that have never previously been considered play, playlike, or precursors of play. This is understandable given the examples of "true" play so often discussed. However, that does not mean that the phenomena are not in any way comparable, just that they have not been looked at through the same prism.

For the sake of convenience, I will refer to the "big five" criteria[18] for identifying play as:

1. Limited immediate function
2. Endogenous component
3. Structural or temporal difference
4. Repeated performance
5. Relaxed field

18. This is a deliberate play on the current popularity of the "big five" personality dimensions popular in personality and evolutionary psychology as well as human behavior genetics (e.g., Buss, 1999).

Keeping in mind the nuances underlying each word, a one-sentence definition could then read as follows: *Play is repeated, incompletely functional behavior differing from more serious versions structurally, contextually, or ontogenetically, and initiated voluntarily when the animal is in a relaxed or low-stress setting.*

As an example that satisfies the five criteria, the description of play fighting in rat pups by Panksepp, Siviy, and Normansell is exemplary. When two pups:

are placed together in a nonthreatening environment, they rapidly begin to exhibit vigorous fighting: animals chase and pounce on each other, sometimes unilaterally, sometimes mutually with rapid role reversals. They repeatedly poke and nip each other, often at the nape of the neck but also on the ventral surface when one animal is pinned. (Panksepp, Siviy, & Normansell, 1984: 466)

I chose this example, not only because it concisely satisfies all five criteria, but also because play fighting in rats is the type of play most well studied experimentally and physiologically.

Unfortunately, many descriptions of putative play are difficult to interpret because information that would enable us to apply the five criteria is absent. Thus a side benefit of these criteria is to indicate the kinds of information we need. Documentation and independent observation by several qualified investigators are also important in firmly establishing claims about play for some species. Eventually, as more is learned about the genetic, neural, and hormonal correlates of play, the criteria will be refined.

Armed with these criteria, it should be possible to cut through some of the confusion as to what play means in a phyletic perspective. Before embarking on our comparative journey, another detour awaits us. It is useful to review some additional attributes of play that are frequently observed in, but are not essential features of, play in the more playful species.

4 A Guide to the Diversity of Play

4.1 Introduction

Given that we can identify play when it occurs, the next task is to classify and describe various kinds of play. Classifying the diversity of play is necessary for developing integrative views about the origins of play and for evaluating research on the role of play in animal lives. Then we can answer such questions as why play is maintained in a species' behavioral repertoire and how differences may have evolved in various groups of animals.

How many kinds of play are there? Are the various categories of play just arbitrary points on a continuum? Do the various types of play differ in more than superficial ways? Just as a definition or set of defining criteria needs to accurately describe the phenomena involved if it is to be useful, so too do we need an extensive descriptive database on play if we are to answer these questions satisfactorily. As seen with horses, detailed information on all five ethological aims is largely absent. Nevertheless, although highly detailed "molecular" descriptions of play are needed for understanding the nuances of play and making refined comparisons among populations and species, enough information is available to describe the major types of play and some of their characteristics. As in any such classification, new examples may add to the mix or refine distinctions. Animal and human play researchers have somewhat different traditions of classifying play. Thus, these methods need describing as well. Finally, there have been several recent attempts to arrange play in a hierarchical fashion. These efforts may turn out to reflect an evolutionary progression, but much caution is needed.

The various descriptive classifications of play may be viewed as support for the qualitative distinctiveness of various play types. The evidence appears mixed. Ultimately we need to know much more about the internal causal and control mechanisms of play as well as developmental trajectories to validate various play categories as being more than fictions useful at one stage of study and best discarded at others.

4.2   Classifying Play

The most common taxonomy of animal play divides play into three types (Bekoff & Byers, 1981; Fagen, 1981): locomotor (or locomotor-rotational) play, object play, and social play. This classification scheme is used in many descriptive or ethogram studies of animal behavior and was introduced in chapter 1. Not only can each of these three types be divided into subcategories (this is especially true for social play), the distinction is not always clear and the categories get blurred. Are two dogs chasing a thrown stick engaging in locomotor, object, or social play?

In a recent survey of research on play and exploration in mammals, primarily monkeys, apes, and children, Power (2000) divided play into five major categories (locomotor, solitary object, social object/pretend, play fighting, and parent-child). As shown later, the children's play literature provides some alternative richness to play classification that is only recently beginning to be appreciated by animal play researchers.

4.2.1   Locomotor-Rotational Play

Locomotor, activity, or movement play are terms that have long been used for typically solitary activity in which a young animal performs intense or sustained locomotor movements (leaping, running, prancing), often without any apparent immediate reason or stimulus. The behavior often involves reversals of direction and exaggerated movements in three dimensions. Since head shaking and body twisting often accompany this behavior, S. C. Wilson and Kleiman (1974) coined the term *locomotor-rotational movements* (L-R), which has been increasingly adopted. Although it is often still called locomotor play as a shorthand term, I will occasionally use L-R play as well. The addition of "rotational" addresses the fact that some vigorous play does not involve the body moving from one place to another or, alternatively, that the behavior is more than normal locomotion. Thus, in humans, engaging in various movements that twist the torso can be included as L-R play if the five criteria are met.

Locomotor-rotational play is usually the first play behavior recorded, ontogenetically, in many species. This is especially true of nonpredatory precocial mammals such as the horses described in chapter 1. The gambols of foals released from barn stalls into a field, and the rush of schoolchildren onto the playground during recess are readily appreciated examples of locomotor play. Nevertheless, L-R play actually turns out to be not all that obvious when it is solitary and especially when animals other than mammals perform it. Anthropomorphic terms labeling L-R movements as "fun" and as an expression of "exuberance" and "joy" often accompany descriptions of this kind of play. Functionally, such play is often related to rehearsal or practice of flight and other antipredator escape maneuvers (Power, 2000). Nonetheless, referring to locomotor play as physical exercise play, as is often found in reviews, should be avoided since it includes a function (exercise) in the label.

4.2.2 Object Play

Object play is sometimes referred to as diversive exploratory play (Drickamer et al., 1996) following Berlyne and Hutt (chapter 3). It may also be called solitary object play (Power, 2000) or sensorimotor play (see later discussion).

Object play is typically recorded when animals mouth, paw, push, pull, grasp, lift, hit, carry, and otherwise manipulate objects that, unlike food or nesting material, seem to provide no immediate benefit. This is often called predatory play when seen in carnivorous species. Indeed, it is particularly common in many carnivores that incorporate predatory movements (stalking, grabbing, shaking) in their object play. Foraging movements generally play a major role in the object play repertoire. Even herbivorous horses (chapter 1) and cattle (Brownlee, 1954) show some object play and manipulation. One of the most fascinating kinds of object play occurs in whales and dolphins. Beluga whales (*Delphinapterus leucas*) blow bubbles that they then kick, bite, suck, or otherwise fragment (Delfour & Aulagnier, 1997). Bottlenose dolphins (*Tursiops truncatus*) blow bubble rings (like large smoke rings) and catch and join two together, swim through them, and manipulate them in various ways (McCowan et al., 2000).

A list of specific actions used by a number of mammals and human children in response to objects is given in the excellent tables and summaries provided by Power (2000). Object play may also involve elements of antipredator responses, conspecific fighting, nest building, courtship, and sexual behavior. Object play is often attached as a label whenever an animal interacts with an object beyond the mere "specific exploration" of Berlyne (1960).

A subset of object play that has been well studied in children is construction or building play. Here objects are moved, stacked, and otherwise manipulated to produce something new. Chimpanzees (*Pan troglodytes*) will often stack objects or insert one object into another, employing commercial toys in the same manner as young children. Many animals construct elaborate nests or seal their burrow entrances with stones arranged in intricate ways. Although such construction activities are rarely described as play in nonhuman animals, they may become more recognized as having a playful component as studies accumulate on the ontogeny of construction behavior in animals.

Although object play is often found in young animals, it is also frequently described in species that otherwise do not appear playful (see part II). The introduction of objects to "enrich" the environment of captive adult animals is a common procedure. Spontaneous manipulation of objects or access to "toys" can be used as reinforcers in learning experiments. The most important early demonstrations of this were by Harlow (1950) and P. H. Schiller (1957). In the former study, rhesus monkeys (*Macaca mulatta*) were given a set of manipulanda in which pins, hooks and eyes, and hasps had to be disengaged in a serial order. The monkeys would both learn to do this and persist for hours in repeatedly solving the problem without any apparent reward except "success." In the latter study, chimpanzees who had an opportunity to manipulate sticks and other objects were more able to quickly employ the sticks in solving problems, such as retrieving food, than chimpanzees without such "play" opportunities. Such studies suggest that tool use may be either enhanced or dependent upon object exploration and play.

Not only does Power (2000) separate solitary object play and social object play, he also subdivides the former into exploration, play, and tool use. The category of "functional exploration/practice play" has been advanced as an intermediate between object exploration and play (Power, 2000). The concept is potentially useful, but as in the term *exercise play*, it may be misleading to include in the label words that could prejudge the explanation for the behavior patterns seen (such as functional or practice). What is actually recorded is repetition with variation, a key criterion (four) for recognizing play in the first place.

The problems in identifying object play are several. One is in determining that the responses are not performed "for real" by animals that cannot distinguish the play object from the biologically meaningful stimulus: for example, a toy mouse from a real one. Is such behavior in a kitten comparable to the "pretend play" or pretense seen when children ride broomsticks, dress dolls, or use a finger as a gun? A second problem is that when young animals are observed responding to objects for the first time, the attempts may be tentative, incomplete, directed to "nonfunctional" stimuli, or otherwise just presage the onset of the normal movements through maturation. These are often labeled as prefunctional movements (Hogan, 1988) or maturational behavior intermediates (Fagen, 1981) and are found in early social responses as well (Kruijt, 1964). However, experience can also play a role. For example, European red squirrels (*Sciurus vulgaris*) need some experience opening nuts to do it proficiently. Manipulatory experience increases proficiency in young squirrels who (1) have never opened a nut or observed another squirrel doing so and (2) were given nuts in which the meat had been removed so food reinforcement was not responsible for any "learning" that occurred (Eibl-Eibesfeldt, 1970).

A third problem is that responses to objects by captive animals in deprived or sterile (boring) environments must be distinguished from abnormal stereotyped interactions. To complicate matters, the same object may be used in object play in some animals and be incorporated into stereotyped behavior in other individuals. For example, bears often respond playfully to balls, but at the National Zoological Park in Washington, D.C., one bear was reported to repeatedly kick a ball and bounce it off the cage wall in exactly the same manner over and over (Ben Beck, personal communication, 1997). For this bear, the ball seems to have been incorporated into a pathology resulting from environmental deprivation in its past or current life. Providing a different size or shape of ball might be a useful means of breaking the cycle of rigid (mindless) repetitiveness, which can also plague human behavior in boring environments.

4.2.3 Social Play

Social play is identified when play is directed at conspecifics, or other animals taking on the role, at least partially, of a conspecific. Classic examples of social play include chasing and play fighting "games" in canids (Bekoff, 1974) and juvenile rhesus monkeys (Symons, 1978). Social play can take many forms, but the most common are quasi-aggressive behavior patterns such as chasing, wrestling, pawing, and nipping. This is usually readily identified as play in animals (Pellis & Pellis, 1998a), but may not be always the case, as we have seen in chapter 3. Nonetheless, social play attracts attention, is interesting to watch, involves many often complex and even balletlike movements, and appears to presage the use of these behavior patterns in more serious adult behavior.

Play fighting is by far the most well-studied type of animal play (Aldis, 1975) and has received the most comparative attention theoretically (P. K. Smith, 1982). In a survey of the literature from 1984 to 1994, Pellis and Pellis (1998a) report that 82.5 percent of articles containing data on play were devoted totally or largely to play fighting. Thus in large measure, our total knowledge of play is skewed toward play fighting. If it is the case that play fighting is the most important, most common, or most easily studied type of play, then this emphasis is appropriate. In the case of our species, however, play fighting is not nearly so predominant as an area of study (Berk, 1996; Pellegrini & Smith, 1998; Power, 2000). This raises the possibility of a disjunction between the study of animal and human play that impoverishes our understanding of play in both human and nonhuman animals.

Play fighting is often separated into play chasing of conspecifics, generally age mates, and play wrestling. The latter also is referred to as rough-and-tumble (R&T) play and involves lunging, pouncing, biting, pushing, butting, grabbing, hitting, mounting, and pinning. The label play fighting also obscures the fact that it may involve elements of courtship rather than serious aggression (Pellis, 1993).

Although social play is generally considered dyadic and reciprocal (Fagen, 1981), social play can also be one-sided when it is playful for only one participant. In these situations, play may be erroneously attributed to both participants. Teasing and harassing behaviors are prime examples; from the teaser's point of view such play may be more akin to predatory play with live prey (cat and mouse) than reciprocal social play. Similarly, when one player tires of a social play bout and the other persists, serious fighting can erupt.

Although most social play involves conspecifics, other partners can participate. In the field, hyraxes often engage in social play with hyraxes of other species (Caro & Alawi, 1985) (see also section 8.2.10 in chapter 8). In captivity, play partners of other species are often employed in a mutual manner. This is often noted between human caregivers and pets (R. W. Mitchell & Thompson, 1991), and can even involve deception, as when a dog retrieves a ball, drops it in front of a person, and as the latter stoops to pick it up the dog grabs it and runs away (Mitchell & Thompson, 1986). Humans, of course, often do the same kind of enticing/removal of objects when playing with dogs and this seems to be legitimately termed a game. Social play also occurs between two nonhuman species as well. For example, Leyhausen (1948) described play between a dog and captive black bear (*Ursus americanus*) cub. Wolves (*Canis lupus*) initiated social play bouts with brown bears (*Ursus arctos*) in a large 2-hectare (5-acre) enclosure (Koene et al., 2000). More interactions occurred on days the wolves were fed, and wolves "lost" more than the bears. It is interesting that most wolf interactions were with the youngest of thirteen bears and also became frequent with two blind male bears. Rhesus monkeys reared by dogs also show mutual play (W. A. Mason, 1978).

It is important, however, to apply the five criteria to both partners in showing that the behavior is playful from the perspective of each participant. Thus, when a cat plays with a mouse, repeatedly catching and releasing it, this may be object play for the cat but not for the mouse. Similarly, a remarkable report of a wild female chimpanzee capturing, keeping, and playing with a hyrax (*Dendrohyrax dorsalis*) and keeping it almost as a pet is problematic as mutual social play (Hirata et al., 2001). Mutual social play can also be terminated by a partner and quickly turn into annoyance or even a fight. A good example of this is play fighting in black bears, which can escalate into a serious altercation (Burghardt & Burghardt, 1972; Henry & Herrero, 1974; Pruitt, 1974, 1976).

4.2.4   Interactions among L-R, Object, and Social Play

Many animals seem to engage in only one or the other of these play activities. For example, rats engage in social play as well as locomotor and object play, but laboratory mice are not thought to do so (Pellis et al., 1991; Poole & Fish, 1975). Such differences will be important in the comparative survey presented in part II. Many of the most playful species engage in all three kinds of play, however, and, as noted earlier, it may be difficult to distinguish and usefully classify them in many instances. Animals may use objects in social play; dogs and wolves will grab, push, and pull sticks and other objects in tug-of-war and chase games. Animals may leap, jump, swing, and swoop when with other animals. Chasing involves locomotion in a social context. If an animal darts and dodges with no one else around, could it still be engaging in a social game with an imaginary partner? These issues are not easily resolved. One solution is to view these three categories as a hierarchy so that locomotor play is always solitary, chasing an object is object play regardless of any locomotion involved, and a tug-of-war with an object is classified as social play. Thus, social play with objects is social play, locomotor play with moveable or detached objects is object play, whereas swinging from branches or sliding down a slope is locomotor play (but if children are using a slide is it now object play?). Object play involving vigorous locomotion by two or more animals is typically called social play. Although one could classify social play as play with or without locomotion and/or objects, this solution is awkward at best and is rarely seen in the literature. Furthermore, play of dogs with other dogs or with humans when objects were present showed distinct differences (Rooney, Bradshaw, & Robinson, 2000).

Another problem is that play may switch rapidly among the three play types as well as being associated temporally. Thus the black bears we raised (Burghardt & Burghardt, 1972) became very playful after their afternoon meal. A typical play sequence would involve individual locomotor play followed by one bear emptying the contents of a purse and manipulating the various small objects, thereby attracting the other cub. The animals might then switch to playful competition for the objects, leading to standup wrestling and chasing play, with the objects ignored. After several minutes of vigorous play fighting, the bears would return to the objects and manipulate them further in solitary activity. In other words, it is hard to motivationally separate the three kinds of play. It is clear that the simple threefold classification of L-R, object, and social play is conceptually deficient in fundamental analyses of play in the more playful species (carnivores, primates, ungulates) but is still useful for a preliminary classification.

4.3   Attributes of Social Play

There are several features of social play in mammals that are considered both indicators of social play and markers of more complex and advanced social play. Although a detailed review of the dynamics of highly complex play is not a part of this book, an introduction to some of the features of more complex social play will be useful in appreciating the scope of the phenomena considered to be animal play.

4.3.1   Role Reversal

The typical example of role reversal is when the "attacker" and "defender" engaged in a play fight change roles. There is reciprocity and turn taking in social play in many animals. One animal chases the other; when the gap closes, the chased individual may suddenly swing around and begin chasing the chaser up trees, around bushes and rocks, and so on. One animal may be on top in a play wrestling match and then appear on the bottom. Recall the squirrel monkeys in chapter 3 (Biben, 1986). Of course, such changes of status or role can also take place in the ebb and flow of a serious fight over territory, food, or a mate. However, the occurrence of reversals in the context of social play seems to mark an advance in complexity, and be a kind of turn taking seen in so much child play.

Play fights with reversals must have a certain duration beyond the merely sporadic interactions that may be considered incipient or marginal social play. Pellis (1993) provides a comparative survey of play fighting in rodents showing that the least play-ful species do not engage in play long enough for a reversal to take place within a bout. The duration of play bouts has been used as an important play metric (see chapter 9).

Another kind of reversal is possible, however. Roles may change, not within a play bout, but only across bouts. That is, one animal may chase another one day and be chased the next. Thus, even short play bouts may show no rigid status relationship. Why is this interesting? In many social species the dominance hierarchy in a group is established early in life or shortly after strange animals are introduced. In these cases, serious fighting may occur for only a short time. Examples would be when breeding season arrives and animals compete for territories or challenge the current dominant individual. In other situations, serious competition is usually demonstrated through deference and without overt fighting.

Both kinds of role reversals are often found in play among animals differing in size and status. These asymmetrical contests led to the discovery of another interesting feature of social play.

4.3.2 Self-Handicapping

In a serious fight, the dominant, stronger, or larger animal usually wins. Often there is only a brief altercation because the smaller or less dominant animal retreats, flees, or submits. In some way an animal seems to know, or quickly learns, that it will lose (L. K. Smith, Fantella, & Pellis, 1999). In a play fight in nonhuman animals or children, the stronger or more dominant animal might actually use less advantageous strategies, inhibit his or her behavior, or otherwise act to keep the "opponent" in the game. This is particularly true of much parent-offspring play in human beings and other mammals and can be readily seen when watching a large dog playing with a much smaller one. Here the objective of the play may be to keep the interaction going rather than quickly terminating it by the larger animal "defeating" the smaller, even if playfully. Children often use language to encourage self-handicapping. "You play too rough!" is a common plaint in childhood and verbally calling attention to it may lead the larger or stronger play partner to alter his or her tactics. Animals need to negotiate this poten-tially dangerous situation in the absence of humanlike language. A growl or nip may be sufficient to keep the interaction playful. Self-handicapping implies some type of mutual intentionality in aspects of animal social play (Allen & Bekoff, 1997; Bekoff & Allen, 1998), an issue the next series of phenomena brings to the fore.

4.3.3 Play Signals and Metacommunication

Play often involves behaviors borrowed from other contexts and these behavior pat-terns may be only slightly modified in play. Play fighting is the most common type of social play in animals. Fighting can be dangerous and animals can be hurt. Play fight-ing usually is accompanied by inhibitions of damaging bites, swipes with claws, and so forth. Such inhibitions or restraint in completing behavioral sequences are common in many types of play and are included in play criterion three. Nevertheless, an intriguing question now arises: How do both partners "know" that the fighting behavior is playful and not serious? Misreading a behavior as play could be risky for animals with formidable weapons. Can animals convey "intent?" Play fighting has been presented as a prime area for exploring the cognitive ethology of communicating behavioral meaning or intent (Allen & Bekoff, 1997).

How do animals know that fighting is not serious? Gregory Bateson (1956, 1972) applied to the play context the term *metacommunication*. This term refers to signals that qualify what subsequent behavior signals mean. For example, two dogs meet and perform an easily recognized posture called the bow (figure 4.1), which is associated with readiness to engage in social play (Bekoff, 1972, 1974). This is one of the most familiar and well-documented examples of a play signal. Thus a play bow can signal that what follows is play, in spite of how aggressive it appears. Symons (1978) argued that the signal means, more simply, "this is play." Bekoff (1995) showed that the play bow in canids can occur throughout a play bout and seems to have this function. Indeed,

Figure 4.1
The play bow in dogs, a metacommunication signal that what follows is play. (Photo by Marc Bekoff, reprinted from Bekoff, 1972)

coyotes (*Canis latrans*), which are less social and more aggressive to one another than wolves and dogs, punctuate their play with more play bows than the more social canids. These often prominent and distinctive features of play have led to much discussion and controversy. How and why are specific behavior patterns used in play that are not found in other types of behavior?

Social play could be identified unequivocally if a signal used in play is not found in any other context (e.g., Fagen, 1981). If such a social signal occurs, then the behavior can definitely be labeled play. Furthermore, if without such a play signal the behavior seen cannot be considered play, we would have a solution to the problem of defining social play, at least. The fact that play signals have not been found in many examples of social play in animals may only mean that we have not been able to identify them.

Play signals can be of several types and may perform different functions during play. A play signal, like the dog's play bow, might serve to solicit play from another animal, be it dog or human companion (Bekoff, 1974). The signal could also convey that "what follows is play and not for real; I am not about to hurt you." As mentioned, however, many such play signals are performed at times throughout a play bout; they "punctuate" it. Perhaps the meaning is "I am still playing." The anthropomorphic tenor of these interpretations is obvious, but such conceptualizations do lead to testable hypotheses, as shown later.

Play signals do not need to be limited to postures. Distinctive odors or play pheromones (S. C. Wilson & Kleiman, 1974) may accompany play in more olfactory-dominated mammals such as rodents, although little work on chemical play signals has taken place. A more easily documented class of play signals consists of vocalizations found in several species. Mongooses (*Helogale undulata rufula*) emit a whistle only heard during social play (Rasa, 1984). Play vocalizations also occur in squirrel monkeys (*Saimiri sciureus*) (Biben & Symmes, 1986). In this species the sounds do not act as play invitations or solicitations, as does the play bow in canids; however, social play bouts are usually accompanied by cackles and four types of play peeps. The vocalizations take place during play and the authors conclude that their main function is to indicate the signaler's interest in continuing to play (which may also be true of play bows in dogs during a bout). A waning motivation to play is shown by a decline in the rate of calling, which ceases suddenly when a play bout terminates. The play vocalizations are given more frequently by animals in the defensive or submissive position in the bout, not the one in the more dominant role. It is interesting that the sounds are much louder than needed for the play partners to hear them. Perhaps the vocalizations are meant to inform nearby adult conspecifics that the interactions are playful. Adult males will intervene in serious fights or in other dangerous situations. On the other hand, some social play is marked by the absence of vocalization. Social play and play fighting is silent in black bear cubs (Burghardt & Burghardt, 1972; Henry & Herrero, 1974; Pruitt, 1974, 1976).

The most complex putative play signals in mammals are "play faces," facial expressions that signal or accompany social play. Pellis and Pellis (1996) provide a thorough review of the play face in mammals. It is highly variable across species, even among primates in which the expression open-mouth play face is common. For example, in primates the play face can involve open, oval, or closed mouths; open, closed, or normal eyes; raised or lowered eyebrows; flattened or relaxed ears; relaxed, pulled back, or curled lips; exposed, partially exposed, or nonvisible teeth; or directed, relaxed, or eye contact-avoiding gazes (Pellis & Pellis, 1996). It is thus unclear whether similar behavior patterns are being described and recorded across species or if they serve comparable functions in play.

Communication plays an important role in social play, but the emphasis on play signals may have deterred study of the more nuanced and complex involvement of signaling in social play. Pellis and Pellis conclude "that not only are most so-called play signals not universal amongst species that engage in play fighting, but also that many such signals are not unique to play" (1996: 250). Both offensive and defensive agonistic signals are present in play fighting. In the canid play bow, careful observation shows that from the bow position the animal can quickly pounce upon or evade others (Bekoff, 1995; Pellis & Pellis, 1996). Such behavior that involves shifting weight onto the hindquarters is seen in other mammals as well. Thus, the play bow may also function as a highly versatile posture in the play bout itself, and not just act as a signal. There is much precedence for this since many postures in animals play a role in behavioral sequences and also act as signals (Tinbergen, 1951).

Not only are unique play signals not needed in much play fighting, but signals and movements used in serious fighting are present, as reported in Pellis and Pellis (1996). For example, in a prosimian primate, the ring-tailed lemurs (*Lemur catta*), adult males begin or inhibit fights by performing ritualized tail waving at the opponent. Before waving their tails, however, the males rub the end of the tail over scent glands on their wrists. In play fighting, juvenile males also perform the tail waving after rubbing the tail tips on immature, thus nonfunctional, glands. Most serious aggressive signals utilized in play fighting are not this elaborate, but may include slapping, swatting, and even the proverbial chest beating in gorillas.

The social play of black bear cubs, which we studied throughout their juvenile period, illustrates the role of postures and movements in the sometimes sedentary play of older cubs. One of several play invitations is a stylized biting movement (figure 4.2a), which may be followed by jaw wrestling (figure 4.2b) and head jockeying (figure 4.2c). Turning the head away can be a signal to terminate the bout (figure 4.2d). Based on hundreds of hours of notes and films gathered by Cheryl Pruitt (1974) and other graduate students, a simplified sequential model shows that even a short play sequence can involve many responses and decision points (figure 4.3).

Figure 4.2
Four aspects of play in two young female black bears. (*a*) Play-bite invitation. Note the muzzle twist by the recipient. (*b*) Jaw wrestling play. (*c*) Head jockeying play. (*d*) Head turning form of play termination. (From Burghardt, 1975; photos by Cheryl Pruitt)

c

d

Figure 4.2
(continued)

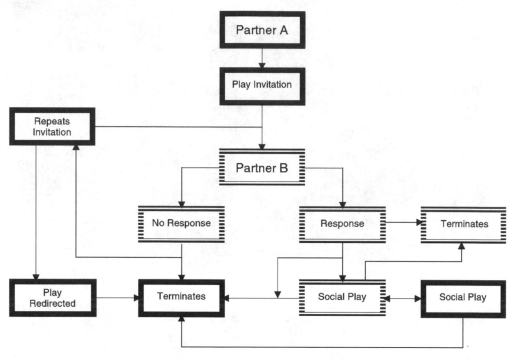

Figure 4.3
Diagram of the sequence of interactions in black bear social play. (Modified from Burghardt, 1975 and Pruitt, 1976)

In short, social play can contain complex features such as role reversal, turn taking, self-handicapping, and metacommunication. We are still far from having a solid comparative basis for speculating as to how these features arose. They may have had many independent origins.

4.4   Play in Children

Throughout the twentieth century, the study of play in children proceeded largely in isolation from studies on animals, although superficial comparisons were sometimes drawn and occasionally attempts were made to go further (Power, 2000; Smith, 1982). Nonetheless, play in children has been categorized in several influential ways, often employing terms and concepts rarely found in descriptions based on the standard tripartite scheme used for nonhuman animals. The schemes of Piaget (1962), Parten (1932), and Smilansky (1968) have been particularly influential. These schemes will be amalgamated here to provide an introduction to the categories typically employed in studies of human play (table 4.1). The terms have developed from several different

Table 4.1
Some types of play described in human infants and children

Type of Play	Additional Names
Sensorimotor	Functional or exploratory play
Construction	Building, piling, stacking
Parallel	Side-by-side, noninteractive
Pretend	Pretense, make-believe, symbolic play
Sociodramatic	Role playing, fantasy
Rough-and-tumble	R&T play, physical play
Language	Babbling, repartee, jokes, humor
Rule	Games with rules (either chance or skill, pairs or teams)
Ritual	Repetitive social routines, can include rule play

perspectives and often overlap. More detailed listings are available (J. E. Johnson, Christie, & Yawkey, 1999; Power, 2000). For each type of play, I will also mention at least one possible analogue in nonhuman animal play. Play interactions between parents and offspring are important as well, both building on and directing the scaffolding provided by the developmental stage of the infant and child (MacDonald, 1993).

A preliminary note: climbing, swinging, sliding, running, throwing, and other vigorous activities of locomotor and object play in children are often typed as "gross motor activities" and viewed as training for "gross motor skills" that, once acquired, are encouraged mainly through the pursuit of excellence in athletic sports and are too often neglected otherwise. (See the minimal discussion in the otherwise excellent and balanced treatments of Garvey, 1990, and Berk, 1996.) Play fighting, the most frequently studied form of play in nonhuman mammals, is rarely studied in children (Pellegrini & Smith, 1998) and merits only about two pages (0.5 percent) in an otherwise comprehensive authoritative text on child play (J. E. Johnson, Christie, & Yawkey, 1999). This is one of several areas in which the perspective offered in this book might challenge traditional views and practice in studies of human play.

4.4.1 Sensorimotor or Functional Play

This play category is usually applied to infants up to 2 years of age, encompassing the sensorimotor period in Piagetian theory (Berk, 1996; Piaget, 1962; Piaget & Inhelder, 1969). Although the behavior patterns described later (e.g., circular reactions) are generally accepted, the larger theory, which aims to explain cognitive development, is still debated vigorously. Essential to Piagetian analysis is the process by which infants *assimilate* information from their environment (including their own bodies) and *accommodate* their cognitive apparatus to it and thus proceed through the stages of cognitive development. The sensorimotor period is the first of four periods in Piagetian analysis.

The others are the preoperations period (2–6 years), concrete operations period (6–12 years), and formal operations period (12–18 years). Only the first two periods are currently used in studies of animal play and cognition.

There are six stages of sensorimotor play in domains such as physical knowledge, logical-mathematical knowledge, and social knowledge (S. T. Parker & McKinney, 1999). This play involves movements that may or may not involve objects. It is viewed as pleasurable activity. There are two subperiods, which in humans go from about birth to 12 months and from 13 to 24 months. Regardless of the acceptance of Piaget's theories of development, which have come in for much criticism in the past decade (Berk, 1996; Lancy, 1996), the observational base, although not the age-specific timing, seems secure (S. T. Parker & McKinney, 1999).

Newborn infants cannot locomote, so they are physically unable to engage in whole-body locomotor play. They can move their limbs and grasp objects reflexively. Insofar as performance of these reflexes is not reflected in any changes in their behavior, it is not play. This would include grasping, sucking, and orienting. *Circular reactions* are the means by which infants initially engage the world and by so acting, adapt their behavior to it. Circular reactions are labeled *primary*, *secondary*, and *tertiary*. *Primary circular reactions* are seen in the first 4 months of life and are marked by repeated performance of activities, such as opening and closing the hand or making anticipatory mouth movements before meals. The focus is on the infant's own body, not the external world. *Secondary circular reactions* are seen later, when the infant can reach for, clutch, and manipulate objects. He or she will repeatedly hit or nudge objects and become more skilled at doing so. This is the period when most people (nonparents) begin to think infants are fun and are having fun. The behavior also seems to acquire a more intentional or goal-directed quality. That is, the infant is not just responding to what is presented, but seems to seek out certain kinds of stimulation.

In *tertiary circular reactions*, the infant does not just repeat responses to gain the same outcomes (banging a spoon on a high chair), but will vary the behavior to see what will happen, such as banging the spoon on a glass. This may lead to a different enjoyable sound or, even more exciting (to the infant if not the caregiver), the glass may topple and spill. This is a type of experimentation in which the infant learns about objects, what they can do, and how variations in behavior can lead to new and interesting possibilities. All this learning is mediated through these playful activities. These circular reactions have their counterparts in much mammal play. In fact, many mammals, being more advanced at birth in their motor skills, seem to perform these kinds of behavior even more readily and earlier than human infants (S. T. Parker & McKinney, 1999).

The final substages in the sensorimotor period occur when the routines are established enough that the infant does not need to perform them to modify what he or she will do. For example, if a child is actively maneuvering a push toy through the house, and the toy gets hung up on the legs of the dining room table, observe what happens. If the child seems to randomly move the toy in different directions, pushing, pulling, and twisting it to get around the obstacle, we are seeing a tertiary reaction, or trial-and-error variation. If, however, the child immediately backs up the toy and changes direction so that the obstacle is easily bypassed, then it appears that the child has made some internal mental review of the consequences of different moves. Thus it can be argued that mental representations are present. If the child has never performed the behavior, but has observed someone vacuuming the house and going around obstacles, then it is possible that the child is showing deferred imitation. Although imitation and deferred imitation of facial expressions and movements have now been shown to occur very early in infant life (Berk, 1996), such demonstrations have themselves been criticized by Piagetians (S. T. Parker & McKinney, 1999). Although these various types of functional motor and object play are certainly present in infants, the breakdown into categories or substages may be merely convenient classifications. Also, it is probably the case that the circular reactions are involved in enlarging the range of responses infants make and the stimuli they react to, although Piaget considered them as causally instrumental in creating or forming abilities such as imitation or mental representations (Piaget, 1962).

These stages of sensorimotor play have been studied, along with other Piagetian developmental series, in several mammals and birds, though most diligently in primates (i.e., S. T. Parker, 1977; S. T. Parker & Gibson, 1990). The possible role of these stages in cognitive development is the reason for much of the current interest in play as a facilitator of mental development. Other Piagetian stages occur during the sensorimotor period as well; those underlying imitation and social development are especially relevant to play. Nonetheless, the fact that all primates studied go through a similar series of sensorimotor (0–2 years) and preoperations (2–6 years) stages, but stop at different levels (e.g., sensorimotor stage 5 in the object permanence series in rhesus monkeys) has brought renewed respectability to aspects of the recapitulation view of play (S. T. Parker & McKinney, 1999).

4.4.2 Construction Play
Construction or building play is generally viewed as piling, inserting, shaping, or in some other way creating an object with different characteristics than its component parts. Building blocks are the classic example with children. Today Legos and other commercial products are popular with European and American parents and children. Although chimpanzees will perform comparable behavior, such as stacking boxes (Kohler, 1925), much building behavior in animals that has more direct instinctive roots, such as nest building, may also show some commonalities with construction play and can also be considered play if the five criteria are met.

4.4.3 Pretend or Make-Believe Play

Pretending is a major component of children's play. Using a broomstick as a horse, talking to a stuffed bunny or doll as if it were real, and shooting toy soldiers with toy guns are standard types of make-believe play in children (Garvey, 1990; Berk, 1996). Pretend play has been associated with role playing and sociodramatic play (see later discussion), and many extensions of the Piagetian scheme have been developed, as recently summarized (S. T. Parker & McKinney, 1999). They all are considered to depend upon some form of mental representation. Examples include having a doll sleep, using different objects as a telephone, or pushing a box while making automobile sounds (S. T. Parker & McKinney, 1999; Piaget, 1962). With children, we can ascertain that they know the object is not "real"; with animals, this is more difficult, as noted earlier. Since pretend play comes after imitation in the Piagetian series, it is considered both symbolic and advanced; it is limited to apes and is not to be found in monkeys. Thus, a series of examples of pretend play in chimpanzees, orangutans (*Pongo pygmaeus*), and gorillas in captivity have been reported (S. T. Parker & McKinney, 1999). For example, apes use imaginary string toys, eat pretend food, feed a doll, hide pretend objects, and so on. Experimental studies have not found the extent and frequency of such behavior in apes very impressive compared with that in children, however. Isolated examples, such as this one recorded in the field by Matsuzawa (S. T. Parker & McKinney, 1999) are instructive. A mother chimp was carrying her sick infant from tree to tree and was followed by her 8-year-old daughter. The daughter found a large dead stick and carried it around, treating it as an infant by slapping it softly as if it was the back of an infant.

The limitation of pretend play to the Piagetian model may obscure similarities in nonprimates as documented in a review by R. W. Mitchell (2002). Does a dog retrieving a stick not "know" it is not prey? Does a kitten not "know" that the bunch of feathers on the end of a wand being waved in front of her is not prey. Consider this example of a red fox (*Vulpes vulpes*) from the field notes made by a leading researcher (Henry, 1986). Henry had been observing a 6-month-old fox that he went on to study for seven years. The fox caught and quickly ate one mouse, then caught another, played with it for several minutes and then cached it, as foxes often do with extra prey. Thus it is fair to assume the fox was not very hungry. However, the fox then caught a shrew, which, since they emit a bad smell, are not prized prey for foxes. The fox carried the shrew to an open area on a road and played vigorously with it, leaping and dancing, without injuring it, and then carried it back to the area where he had caught it and spit it out near a burrow opening, into which the shrew entered and was gone. Henry speculates that the fox returned the shrew with the idea it might provide food or serve as a play object some other time. Clearly this is reading much into the fox's behavior, but this example certainly makes us wonder about some exceptional animal performances. Still, the mice and shrew were both food and play objects, so making the distinction between feeding and play contexts can often be difficult.

Leyhausen (1979) reported observations on "angling play" in servals (*Leptailurus serval*), a small wild cat. These animals allow captured mice and rats to escape under a tree stump or hole and then try to retrieve them with a forepaw. If a suitable escape hole is not found

servals pick up the prey cautiously by the back fur, carry it to the vicinity of a crevice, and let it run; if the prey animal still does not slip into the hole, the servals often push it in with their forepaws in order to be able to "fish" it out again … this … is without doubt intentional. This becomes particularly clear when, instead of live prey animals, the servals are using small playthings such as pieces of bark for their game. Thus the animals must be able to bring together two objects which were not simultaneously in their field of vision at the start, and manipulate them appropriately before they can play their game. (Leyhausen, 1979: 139–140)

More generally, whenever animals treat an inanimate object as if it were a biologically meaningful one and independent information is available to show that the animal is able to make the distinction between it and the biologically appropriate one, then pretend play could be validly indicated, even if the cognitive underpinnings do not rely on imitation or are otherwise humanlike. Such play may in fact have far deeper and fewer learned components than is generally recognized.

In summary, some recent workers claim that pretend play is found only in some great apes and other primates (S. T. Parker & McKinney, 1999), although it is difficult to actually define this in such a way as to exclude play with objects in cats, foxes, and dogs that involves predatory behavior from the realm of pretend play. Sue Parker (personal communication, 2000) has agreed that pretend play in carnivores may have an independent origin from that seen in apes.

4.4.4 Simple Games

Dogs are well known for their interest in and enjoyment of object-retrieval games, in which they will bring back an object and then suddenly grab and run off with it when the human player reaches for it. This keep-away game is a complex social event with both players having a certain role to play and it involves a host of expectations, intentions, and rules (R. W. Mitchell & Thompson, 1991). Insofar as the object retrieved—be it a ball, Frisbee, or stick—is not a real prey item, this highly repetitive behavior is also based on pretense, but with a social component added.

Another type of play behavior that is related to pretend play is the peek-a-boo game indulged in between adults and babies, to the great entertainment of the latter. Six- to 8-month-old infants find it enjoyable to have a face hide and then reappear (Parrott & Gleitman, 1989). Smiling and other measures of emotional response to this game can be quantified, and it has been found that if the familiar face (the one that disappeared) reappears, the babies react with more smiling, laughing, and eyebrow raises than if an unexpected face appears. The same result occurs if the expected face suddenly appears in a new location (Parrott & Gleitman, 1989). Such results suggest that these young infants have "expectations" in simple games, but that certain rules need to be followed. It is interesting that with older children the unexpected in peek-a-boo leads to greater enjoyment, and the authors of this ingenious study argue that this response demands a higher level of cognitive processing that does not appear until after 1 year of age. They point out that the enjoyment of the reappearance of the familiar face is sufficient to provide "a sense of mastery over a cognitive challenge" (Parrott & Gleitman, 1989: 309). Other species may have similar kinds of challenges in their social play that should be investigated.

Eye-covering play has been recorded in many primates and a particularly careful study of it in orangutans and Japanese macaques (*Macaca fuscata*) has been carried out (Russon, Vasey, & Gauthier, 2002). Both species engaged in the behavior as they were involved in other kinds of play, usually solitary, although the monkeys engaged in the behavior less often and for shorter durations. Eye covering (with a hand) took place during walking, running, swinging, somersaulting, and when manipulating objects. Orangutans also did it during social play such as wrestling. The animals were not pretending to be blind, according to the authors, because they did not take dangerous risks (such as keeping their eyes closed in settings that might result in falls or collisions). Still, humans may do the same when closing their eyes. I have pretended I am in a dark room finding my way even when the lights are on, but I check myself or become cautious when I become less sure of my specific location in the surroundings. In fact, like humans, the other species sometimes peeked to avoid hitting something or checked themselves if they did. Still, the authors conclude that the animals engage in eye covering during play, not just for self-stimulation or autotelic reasons, but also to play with "discrepancies among multiple representations of a situation" and thus this activity involves both imagination and representational memory, which are elements of imaginative play (Russon, Vasey, & Gauthier, 2002: 253).

4.4.5   Parallel Play

When two or more children engage in various forms of locomotor or object, construction, or pretense play simultaneously in the same vicinity, but do not interact with one another, the term *parallel play* has been applied (Parten, 1932; Pellegrini & Boyd, 1993). The children are certainly aware of each other and may even influence or facilitate each other's behavior. This category of play may be seen in many social animals, but is rarely invoked since it seems to alternate with social behavior over short spans of time. It is easily scored, however, and is used in most observational research on young children's play (Pellegrini & Boyd, 1993; K. H. Ruben, Fein, & Vandenberg, 1983).

4.4.6 Rough-and-Tumble Play

Rough-and-tumble is the very active wrestling and chasing play found in early child-hood and most resembles the social play of mammals. During rough-and-tumble play, children play with age mates, older children, and adults. Older siblings and parents frequently get down on all fours and play vigorous contact games with children up to the preteen years. Unfortunately, this play is largely ignored in the child play literature (Pellegrini & Smith, 1998). This may be because it is often too rambunctious for researchers and does not seem to be so connected with the cognitive skills that "good" play is thought to instill. Girls, especially when young, enjoy and participate in this activity as often as boys. Children can distinguish serious from playful fighting, even cross-culturally (Costabile et al., 1991), although adults seem less adept. This mis-understanding and mischaracterization of rough-and-tumble play by teachers and daycare workers (S. J. Hutt et al., 1989), who are often sedentary females, leads to pro-hibitions against it in many contexts (J. E. Johnson, Christie, & Yawkey, 1999). As will be argued later, this may be one of the most developmentally critical kinds of play in nonhuman animals, and discouraging it in humans may have effects we do not yet appreciate.

Generally, play fighting has been considered the type of play that is most similar across humans and nonhumans, especially primates (Aldis, 1975; P. K. Smith, 1982). This type of human play usually has the strongest claim for an evolutionary origin in nonhuman animal behavior. This conclusion is supported by a careful review of the great similarity in many details of the behavioral patterns used by humans and animals in play fighting (Power, 2000).

4.4.7 Sociodramatic Play

Sometimes called role playing, this type of play occurs when children begin to engage in social games in which the players take parts, such as doctor and patient, cowboy and Indian, Luke and Darth Vader, and other characters, both fictional and real. Dolls and other figurines (toy soldiers, farm animals) can be employed here too, showing conti-nuity with more basic pretense play. Generally, think of sociodramatic play as pretense in a social context. Obviously culturally transmitted information is involved with most such human sociodramatic play. Baby goats playing "king of the hill" can, however, be viewed as engaged in similar role playing, as can any social play where role reversal occurs.

In the Parten (1932) scheme, play is divided into solitary independent play, parallel play, interactive associative play (unorganized), and cooperative or organized play. Parten also had categories of unoccupied and onlooker (the child watched others play). In the Smilansky (1968) scheme, the four divisions are functional (repeated motor actions), constructive, sociodramatic, and games with rules. These categories have been workhorse methods in child cognitive development and have often been combined. In these approaches, solitary and functional play behaviors are considered regressive beyond a very young age, while interactive, cooperative, and dramatic play behaviors are viewed as the most predictive of later cognitive ability (K. H. Ruben, Fein, & Vandenberg, 1983).

The hierarchical aspect of these schemes has been asserted without careful analysis, as has been the case in the typical tripartite scheme of animal play. A study by Pellegrini and Perlmutter (1987) combined the two schemes into one series involving solitary, parallel, and interactive play. However, within each category there were three subcategories: functional, constructive, and dramatic. This led to nine groupings plus those of unoccupied, onlooker, and R&T play. When this was done and eighty-six 4-year-old children were observed over 4 weeks, factor analysis showed that three factors explained almost half the variance. Most variance was explained by a dramatic-constructive factor that loaded positively on the dramatic measure in all three categories plus R&T and was highly negative on construction in the parallel and interactive but not solitary social categories. The second factor was called solitary and loaded positively on functional and onlooker behavior, and this was considered the socially and cognitively regressive aspect. The third factor was called functional-constructive and, while typically solitary, reflected active engagement with objects. The addition of R&T play was a nice touch in this study because the high loading on factor 1 suggests that R&T has a large pretense or dramatic component, although it is rarely studied from that perspective in either animals or children (Power, 2000).

4.4.8 Language Play

Young infants go through a babbling phase in which sounds are tried out, altered, practiced, and otherwise manipulated in a manner conceptually akin to movements and interactions with objects. Such verbal play may be solitary as well as social (Garvey, 1990). There are parallels of such play with vocalizations in animals, especially in birds, as will be elaborated later (chapter 11). Regardless of the role of play in language, human language is also an important feature in the more complex types of play and the cognitive accomplishments of humans compared with other animals. The emphasis on distinctly human language in human play is sometimes used to discount consideration of any important continuity between play in animals and humans (Power, 2000). The truth may be much more complex and interesting.

Gestural communication is common in many species, especially apes and humans. It is highly developed in those fluent in sign language for the hearing impaired. It is interesting that babies with normal hearing who are born to profoundly deaf, signing parents, and who have limited exposure to spoken language, perform gestural "babbling" with their hands that contains rhythmic features found in their parents' signing. This is never seen in the gestures of hearing babies raised with hearing parents (Petitto et al., 2001). This behavior seems to meet the play criteria.

A different twist to language play was a detailed study of language and emotional expression in babies from 9 months of age through the period they were learning to talk at around 2 years of age. When the children were playing with objects, the amount of language and emotional expression declined from the baseline (Bloom & Tinker, 2001). There was also a simplification of language, and the occurrence of language and emotional expression was inversely related so that more words meant less emotion and vice versa. The authors concluded that learning language is cognitively complex, even spontaneously, and thus when babies are cognitively challenged with play objects, for example, they have fewer cognitive resources for either language or emotion. Perhaps babbling before sleep is a time of release from competing activities and is important in vocal development.

4.4.9 Rule Play

Games with rules are considered fairly advanced play since the rules are viewed as part of a shared, learned, and culturally derived system. Still, as discussed with peek-a-boo and keep-away games, even here there are rules and expectations that seem to transcend both culture and language (see section 4.4.4). Regardless, Garvey states that "Games are play activities that have become institutionalized" (1990: 104). Games can be of many types, and classifications of games have been constructed that involve chance, turn taking, penalties for rule violations, and so forth (S. T. Parker, 1984). Suffice it to state here that much animal social play, including play fighting, seems to involve rules, yet rough-and-tumble play in children is rarely studied as rule play until it reaches the formal athletic contest stage. But, as argued earlier, by this time such activities may no longer really be play.

In animals with elaborate and prolonged play fighting bouts, there do seem to be rules (e.g., inhibitions) that must be honored for play to continue. However, if games with rules must be symbolic and language based, then perhaps it is true that "sociodramatic play and games with rules ... appear to be uniquely human and are apparent consequences of symbolic, communicative, and other cognitive abilities" (Power, 2000: 289). This conclusion, however, may be modified as more information on chimpanzees and other animals becomes available (S. T. Parker & McKinney, 1999) and the operational and objective means of comparing social play in animals and humans become more refined.

4.4.10 Ritual Play

Ritualized performances in dance, theater, religions, secret societies, governments, and even universities (e.g., commencement) are often viewed as being derived from play (Dissanayake, 1992; Huizinga, 1955). Some rituals, including sporting events, festivals, and carnivals, are themselves considered play (Sutton-Smith, 1997). Garvey (1990) defines rituals in children's play as potentially involving any "resource," including movements, language, objects, social conventions, and rule play distinguished by "controlled repetition." Thus, two children taking turns putting a curtain over their head and exclaiming "watch this!" followed by giggles are engaged in a ritual with object, movement, and language repetition. All of Garvey's examples are of a social nature and thus seem to exclude the stereotyped and obsessive-compulsive behavior found in individual behavior in both children and animals.

Garvey mentions several characteristics of ritual play that recall the five play criteria as well as other characteristics of social play. Certainly, repetitiveness (criterion four) is involved. Indeed, in "children, repetition is apparently enjoyable for its own sake, even in solitude, but in an intimate social situation it provides a basis and framework for continued interaction" (Garvey 1990: 120). Further, "its breeding ground is relatively quiet, undistracted togetherness" (Garvey 1990: 120). Together these reflect criteria two and five. Rituals may even employ signals and other cues. "Rituals are generally based on some other behavior that *could be performed* as nonplay, like peeking out of the door, exchanging greetings, asking and answering questions, and so on" (Garvey 1990: 121; emphasis in original). It does not take much effort to see the similarity to much social animal play.

Are the "high play" elaborate rituals of adult human societies derived from these satisfying rituals of youth? Perhaps Huizinga and Dissanayake and many others are on to an essential feature of human life, as the opening quotation from Huizinga in chapter 1 asserts. Garvey sees children's ritual play as "a formative principle in magical incantations and spells, religious chants, cheers for football teams, political rallies, riots, in fact many events where members of a group must be synchronized to express solidarity" (1990: 120).

4.5   Alternative Classifications of Animal Play

For a comparative survey of play, the standard tripartite division into L-R, object, and social play will be used to categorize the kinds of "simple" play analyzed in diverse species in part II of this book. Nevertheless, there are problems with this classification scheme, as noted earlier (section 4.2.4). Are there other ways to parse animal play without going into all the complexities found in human play? Two recent attempts are those by Fagen (1995) and Robert Mitchell (1990).

4.5.1   Fagen's Scheme

Fagen (1995) advocated a levels or grade hierarchy approach. In his scheme, depicted in table 4.2 with examples that he himself mentions, the traditional tripartite approach is completely abandoned and the classification deals mainly with different levels of social play. Level 1 consists of brief, isolated movements that are hard to interpret. These would often not satisfy the five criteria listed in chapter 3 and may, in young

Table 4.2
Robert Fagen's levels of animal play

Level	Characteristics	Examples
1	One-sided or noninteractive; isolated, brief single actions	Brief jerky movements, and single actions performed repeatedly. Common in rodents.
2	Social noncontact play and solo play	Locomotor-rotational behavior. Various movements may be combined. Little or no physical social contact, but some chasing. Common in hoofed animals, birds, some rodents.
3	Contact and noncontact social play	Active, "friendly" social play, including wrestling, sparring, and chasing. Contact and noncontact play may alternate. Solo locomotor and object play may involve signals used in social play. Chasing games using landscape features (hide-and-seek). Role reversals. Common in primates, carnivores, pinnipeds, ungulates, kangaroos, some birds, and some members from virtually all eutherian (placental) mammal orders.
4	Complex social play	Social games outside male-male and parent-offspring settings. Social games involving objects and landscape features. Found in social carnivores (e.g., wolves, lions), primates, elephants, cetaceans, birds in the parrot and corvid (raven) families.
5	Social play involving special intimacy or cognitive interaction	Tickling, construction play with objects, reciprocal mother-young play involving tutoring. Found only in chimps and other great apes.

Source: After Fagen (1995)

animals, be viewed as prefunctional movements (Hogan, 1988). The second clause in level 1, repeated single actions, may be more characteristic of stereotyped behavior. Swatting an object repeatedly with similar movements, but adjusted to the response of the object (as in a ball tethered to a cord) would not seem appropriate for level 1. Level 2 includes individual L-R play and rudimentary play chasing. Level 3 includes typical play fighting and solitary play involving social signals while level 4 involves more complex social games. It is unclear why female-female social play is put in level 4 and male-male social play is apparently restricted to level 3. The highest level, 5, is restricted to great apes and presumably, human beings. It involves tickling, mother-offspring play involving teaching, and construction play with objects. Grouping these disparate behaviors together seems arbitrary. While this taxonomy highlights apparent complexity across play types, it does not seem to have a rational basis other than apparent increases in complexity. No specific cognitive capacities or other factors are deployed in the framework. Fagen posited that animals capable of play at the higher levels will also show the lower levels of play.

Table 4.3
Robert Mitchell's levels of animal play

Level	Design Process	Name of Play	Examples of Play
1a	Perceptual-motor coordination	Autotelic	Locomotor-rotational; cat object play
1b		Schematic	Much play fighting, sexual play, escape play
2a	Learning	Learned autotelic	Badger somersaulting and ice sliding; bonobo funny faces and eye-closing game; bird dropping pebble for sound
2b		Teasing	Dog object keep-away; gorilla acting interested in infant to surprise mother
2c		Mimetic	Parrot vocalization; intentional play solicitation based on simulation
3	Intentional simulation	Pretend	Chimpanzee bathing doll; rhesus monkey imitating infant-carrying female
4	Intentional communication of simulation	Communicative pretend	Rhesus monkeys simulating play fighting; human sarcasm and parody

Source: After R. W. Mitchell (1990)

4.5.2 Mitchell's Scheme

Robert Mitchell (1990) attempted to deploy a specific process in developing a hierarchical system of play (table 4.3). He argued that adaptive and functional definitions of play do not work, a position adopted in this book as well (chapter 3), and neither do those based solely on the structure of behavior. For Mitchell, play involves actions not movements. Mitchell developed his ideas from two of the psychological theories presented by James Mark Baldwin (J. M. Baldwin, 1902a): the autotelic and semblance theories (see chapter 2), which Mitchell calls autotelic and simulation, respectively. These two views are combined with a focus on intentionality. "To say that an animal has a particular intention is to say that *the animal itself* is organizing its movements in a particular way to achieve, in a reasonable manner, a particular effect (R. W. Mitchell 1990: 200; emphasis in the original).

Intentionality is an important concept in current cognitive ethology (e.g., Allen & Bekoff, 1997), although one that seems difficult to define so that it can be unambiguously recognized in practice (R. W. Mitchell, personal communication, 1997). Note that "intent" in the technical philosophical sense used in cognitive ethology does not mean "conscious" or "purposive" in spite of having a goal or end; the animal may neither understand nor be able to control its actions. Mitchell claims that play is "intentionally directed towards ends, but is unlike other such activities in having (1) no end outside its own enactment, (2) a frivolous end or means, or (3) an end different from its apparent end" (1990: 201). For Mitchell, play is goal-directed behavior that involves some mimetic, pretense (simulation), or learned directed action. Play is a design feature, not random or a by-product of something else.

Mitchell's classification of play contains four levels and types of play (table 4.3). As in Fagen's scheme, the higher levels subsume the lower, with the lowest derived from "evolution and morphogenesis" (actually Mitchell's first level—nonplay). In fact, Mitchell is explicit that "Hierarchically more inclusive levels develop from the design processes of lower levels, and therefore *require* the processes of the lower levels" (R. W. Mitchell 1990: 208; emphasis in original). The first level of play is distinguished from evolution and morphogenesis by requiring a perceptual process.

In the same volume in which Mitchell's chapter appears, there is a much more pessimistic chapter by Rosenberg (1990), who argues that because play must be intentional, imitative, or pretense, it is impossible to have an evolutionary biology of play. Rosenberg's objections are important because they seem to capture the views of many people who approach play in an anthropomorphic commonsense "folk" approach. Most writers disagree (or more accurately, ignore) Rosenberg's objection to the possibility of an evolutionary approach to play by countering his arguments (e.g., Allen & Bekoff, 1997) or sidestepping them (as in chapter 2 and my five criteria for play). Mitchell's approach is to accept Rosenberg's focus on the critical role of intention in play, but to courageously confront head on his objection to an evolutionary approach.

4.5.3 Classification: A Means, Not an End

We divide, sort, label, categorize, and arrange almost all aspects of the natural and social world. We start as children, and pedantic scholars never seem to stop. We group plants, microbes, and animals using traits of all kinds. Indeed, all animals must classify objects as food, mates, offspring, enemies, shelter, and so forth, and make many subdivisions within each of these. No species would survive in the real world if it did not discriminate environmental, and even internal, stimuli, and in some way classify and prioritize them. Humans have grouped physical matter into various kinds—for example, elements, atomic and subatomic particles, and quarks. Without doing so we would have difficulty understanding the most basic phenomena (earth, fire, wind, and water) let alone seeing the repetitive patterns in the periodic table of elements or the essential links across the structure of all matter and energy. We have friends, enemies, acquaintances, and relatives of all degrees who are members of religious, ethnic, fraternal, national, professional, neighborhood, social class, and gender groups. These are also distinctions essential for survival and we start making them early in life.

Are classifications of play essential for understanding play? Probably. Do we have a classification as stable and accepted as the periodic table? Of course not. At this point, trying to deal with the elaborate variations of play before elucidating their commonalities and genesis has proven daunting. Fagen and Mitchell have taken on the task started modestly by Spencer, more systematically by Groos, and then largely neglected by those working with nonhuman animals. The careful evaluation of the course of play development in children and other animals may to some extent reflect the evolutionary origins and history of play. Although recapitulation theory as presented by Hall (see chapter 2) is out of favor, it is always in the background in the theories of Piaget, other influential child developmentalists, and in the hierarchical approaches of Fagen and Mitchell. These theories rely upon extensive descriptions and classifications of behavioral development that were unavailable to earlier writers. It is not a surprise that both Fagen and Mitchell studied play for many years before formulating the typologies presented here. But even more reliable and empirically based descriptions of play and related behavior patterns are needed to assess these and any other schemes that combine descriptive, comparative, and developmental data.

In chapter 1, Sutton-Smith's (1997) seven rhetorics of play were presented to illustrate the way that different styles of discourse and lack of a common set of terms can hinder agreement on what constitutes useful knowledge about play. Still, decisions have to be made as to the most promising areas to search for a unifying framework for play. My decision is to look at the biological foundations of play and adopt the working hypothesis that all play in all seven rhetorics should be viewed as a product of evolutionary history, in spite of how remote our evolutionary past might seem to be from political rallies, sporting events, and gambling casinos.

In the next chapter, some necessary tools will be gathered to begin the search for origins. Useful as observations on play and its development in our species (and even in most mammals) may be, the observations cannot be effectively applied without a broader consideration of the factors underlying play or associated with playfulness.

5   Nothing Is Simple: Studying the Hows and Whys of Play

5.1   Introduction

How did the many forms of play and playlike behavior originate? To answer this question, we cannot assume that all behaviors satisfying the play criteria have the same causal (neurobiological) mechanisms or that they are evolutionarily homologous and have common ancestral roots. The evidence presented in this chapter and throughout the rest of this book shows that the normal behavior, ecology, ontogenetic development, metabolism, neural organization, and phylogeny of a species influence the manner in which it expresses play. In fact, it is because play is, as part II shows, a heterogeneous category that arose repeatedly in the evolution of animals that we need clear criteria to help us sort out the processes and variables influencing playfulness and to point the way to experiments and critical phyletic comparisons. As the heterogeneous nature of play becomes recognized, it will become more acceptable to see play as a distinctive set of transitional behavior patterns linking a variety of behavioral phenomena with diverse qualitative and continuous attributes (Baerends, 1990).

Although many major concepts needed to understand play were extant near the beginning of the twentieth century (chapter 2), a half century later the most prominent comparative psychologist of the mid-twentieth century, reviewing animal play, concluded that "current views on the subject are considerably confused" (Beach, 1945: 523). Compartmentalization of play research (e.g., human versus nonhuman, neurological versus comparative, descriptive versus experimental, causal versus functional, field versus captive settings) is one reason for the slow progress in understanding play in mechanistic, developmental, or evolutionary terms.

Although there has been much relevant recent work on animal play (Bekoff & Byers, 1998; Burghardt, 1998b; Panksepp, 1998a; Pellis & Pellis, 1998a), a broader conceptual integration is needed. The preceding chapters have gathered some of the essential materials and tools needed to construct a framework for explaining the genesis of play.

In chapter 1 the need for an integrative approach built around the basic ethological aims was established. Chapter 2 reviewed early play theory, which, it turns out, contains the basic elements that can be used in a modern framework, although it took a century for theoretical clarification to occur. The necessary step of providing criteria for recognizing play was accomplished in chapter 3. A description of different kinds of play and play attributes was provided in chapter 4.

In this chapter basic biological factors helpful in the search for explanations of the origin and diversity of play are outlined. This is followed in chapter 6 by an attempt to join the causal mechanisms and developmental processes of play in individual animals within an evolutionary scheme. The goal is to explore how play originated in ancestral species and diversified in extant ones while gaining new functions that possibly facilitated behavioral, emotional, and cognitive complexity. In this chapter, which is updated from earlier analyses (Burghardt, 1984, 1988b, 2001), hypotheses and conclusions are emphasized. The model outlined in the next chapter is meant as a temporary tool to use in evaluating the diversity of behavior and species covered in part II. Empirical tests of the model's predictions, especially comparative ones, are thus not included in these two chapters.

I became professionally interested in play for two major reasons. The first was the difficulty researchers have had in demonstrating that play in any species has deferred benefits, in spite of appearing "purposeless." The second was that throughout my research career devoted to studying behavioral development in reptiles in both nature and captivity, I saw little that could be viewed as play in the traditional sense the concept was used (Burghardt, 1982, 1984). Yet reptiles are capable of considerable learning and complex sociality (Burghardt, 1977a,b). Why do they not play (Burghardt, 1982)? Most play theory in animals was focused on the most playful mammals, typically primates, ungulates, and carnivores (Bekoff & Byers, 1981; Fagen, 1981, 1993; Müller-Schwarze, 1978) along with laboratory rats (Hole & Einon, 1984). Thus the challenge was to try to understand why many mammals, but virtually no nonavian (ectothermic) reptiles, were considered playful (e.g., Fagen, 1981). Rather than the typical "top-down" approach to understanding the origins and radiations of playfulness, careful observations were needed of animals that seemed not to play (at least in obvious ways) or to play rarely, as well as of those animals that play a great deal. I have called this approach a "bottom-up" strategy versus the top-down view taken by most researchers on animal play (Burghardt, 1998a).

This chapter is not a review or detailed comparison of current theories of animal play, which are becoming increasingly sophisticated in trying to explain the role of play in animals that are highly playful (Bekoff & Byers, 1998; Caro & Alawi, 1985; Pellegrini & Smith, 1998; Pellis, 1993; Pellis & Iwaniuk, 1999a; Power, 2000; Spinka, Newberry, & Bekoff, 2001). Rather, it is an overview of issues related to searching for the origins of play constructed around the five ethological aims (chapter 1).

Table 5.1
General categories of proposed benefits of play

Benefit	Example
Motor development	Improve coordination in locomotion
Physiological development	Improve cardiovascular system and endurance
Perceptual-motor coordination	Improve integration of sensory modalities
Adult species-typical behavior	Improve prey capture or parenting abilities
Social-communicative skills	Improve ability to react appropriately to others
Social roles	Determine dominance-submission status or gender roles
Information	Learn what objects and other animals do
Neural development	Consolidate and integrate neural pathways
Cognitive abilities	Improve responses to environmental challenges
Creativity	Provide source of novel behavioral responses
Competence assessment	Allow parents to assess normative development

5.2   Searching for the Benefits of Play: Misplaced Priorities?

5.2.1   The Numerous Claimed Benefits of Play

For over a century claims have been made concerning the positive, perhaps crucial, role of play in the mental life and behavior of human and even nonhuman animals (Burghardt, 1999; Fagen, 1981). More than thirty functions have been proposed (J. D. Baldwin & Baldwin, 1977, 1981); table 5.1 lists the major (and overlapping) types of general benefits of play. These functions, derived from theory, have remained controversial and largely unsupported empirically (P. Martin & Caro, 1985; Power, 2000; P. K. Smith, 1988, 1996). Earlier writers concluded after reviewing all the factors influencing play in primates that multiple funtions had to exist (e.g., Poirier, Bellisari, & Haines, 1978; Poirier & Smith, 1974), but the search for *the* major function of play persists. Claims have been made that play perfects instinctive behavior and facilitates learning (including reading and mathematics in children) and imitation of novel behavior, imagination, socialization, behavioral flexibility, mental agility, and creativity (e.g., Fromberg & Bergen, 1998; Hartley, Frank, & Goldenson, 1952; Miklosi, 1999). Conversely, lack of play can lead to disruptive, hyperactive children who need to be drugged (Panksepp, 1998a,b) or suggests, if it does not predict, children who later may be prone to violent criminality (S. Brown, 1998). Evolutionary arguments based on selected comparative data often accompany these assertions (e.g., Fagen, 1984). In spite of the lack of experimental support (Power, 2000), such claims have certainly been viewed as plausible by many who have studied play. Even those most responsible for disproving experimental results on the value of play in children find it difficult to completely dismiss these putative benefits (e.g., P. K. Smith, 1996).

Play actually may have an important role in the behavioral, social, emotional, cognitive, physiological, and developmental realms in the lives of many animals, including people. However, this role is likely to be multifaceted, variable, and often involve complex, indirect, and subtle processes, as indicated by the finding that there is some plausible evidence supporting almost every claim in table 5.1. It is this protean complexity that makes play an often paradoxical and socially controversial topic, as chapter 1 asserted and which the last chapter will revisit.

Although most views of play focus on the benefits of play itself, there are other possibilities as to its function, such as David Chiszar's view of play as a signal to parents that their offspring are competent and developing normally (Chiszar, 1985).

5.2.2 How Do We Demonstrate That Play Is Adaptive?

Much has been written over the past 20 years or more on the importance and adaptive significance of play in animals (Caro, 1988; Fagen, 1981; Petersen, 1988; Power, 2000). The sources cited are scholarly and critical. Much in the popular press and child development literature is uncritical, however, and bald claims are frequent that play is central to all childhood learning and thus play needs to be facilitated at all levels. What play means in many such claims, however, is often unclear, except that it must be "fun." It is doubtful that we have a better understanding of fun than we do of play.

What is needed are means of evaluating evidence on the benefits (and costs) of play, not confident assertions. Five basic methods have been used in evolutionary and ethological studies to investigate adaptive function. Although this book is not devoted to evaluating the evidence for the adaptiveness of play in the most playful species, each method is briefly described and named for future reference (cf. Rose & Lauder, 1996).

The first step in the ethological study of any behavior is to describe both the behavior and the context in which it occurs, such as how, where, and when a hawk captures and eats a mouse. Such observations reveal that the talons and beak play important roles in such predation and this may be why they differ from the comparable parts of a chicken or a hummingbird. It is thus almost irresistible to conclude that the design of the feet and beak is adapted to the feeding requirements of the species. This *design feature approach* can also be applied to details of the predatory behavior itself.

Similarly, researchers have looked at certain kinds of play and concluded that the form of the playful acts, their timing in the life of the animal, and the later behavioral needs of the animal show that the play is designed to function in a certain way for clearly adaptive reasons. Exactly what these reasons are, however, is seldom clear, because for any given play, several features could be enhanced. Does vigorous play fighting enhance fighting skills in general, offensive fighting skills, defensive fighting skills, social role learning, or various measures of physiological competence (Pellis & Pellis, 1998b)? An especially strong version of the design feature approach is to view the animal's current behavior or structure as having been optimized for the function it is serving. When the adaptive function is itself unclear, such an approach is misleading as well as largely useless.

The second approach to "proving" that play must be adaptive is to focus on the costs of play, which must be countered by corresponding benefits or otherwise play would be eliminated by natural selection. Here calculations are made concerning the energy and time costs of play as well as the risks of death or injury that play often entails (Fairbanks, 1993; P. Martin, 1984b). Caro (1988) lists numerous "survival costs" of play, including self-injury, increased predation risks, separation from parents, retaliatory aggression, and reduction of food intake. This *cost-benefit approach* is weaker than the design feature method in that it merely asserts that play must be adaptive to persist in the face of the costs involved. It does not directly imply what the benefits actually are, just that they must exist. However, if the play is a by-product of, or linked in some way (genetically, physiologically, behaviorally) with another feature of an animal, play might have costs or benefits that are not due to the playing itself.

The third approach is to show a correlation or association between the type or amount of play and either survival (nonhuman animals) or later abilities (animals and children). For example, do cats that play more with objects have more predatory success than cats that play less or not at all? Do rats that engage in more social play have more reproductive success than animals that do not play as much? Do children that show more sociodramatic play have more complex language skills or cognitive development than those that engage in less sociodramatic play and more of the less complex "functional" play (chapter 4)? Less direct correlations would be between the amount or type of play and measures of neural development, metabolic rate, or other features that presumably benefit the organism. I will term this the *adaptive correlational approach*.

A second type of correlational approach ignores individual differences within a population or species and seeks relationships among different species (or populations) in the amount or type of play engaged in and features of the organism, such as brain size (or development of parts of the brain), cognitive ability, social organization, or some aspect of ecology. I will term this the *comparative correlational approach*. In both types of correlational studies, a positive relationship can only suggest, but cannot prove, a causal relationship among the variables compared. To carry out the comparative correlational approach most validly, it is important to use modern comparative methods that control for the phylogenetic relationships among the taxa being compared. For example, finding a significant relationship between object play and diet by comparing only large predatory cat species with herbivorous ungulates is spurious. This is because the individual species of cats and ungulates could be viewed as components of a single radiation of cats and a single radiation of ungulates, since all cats are predators and all ungulates are herbivorous (Martins, 1996). We need to compare many more groups to confirm that object play is associated with diet and not taxonomic group. Both adaptive and comparative correlational approaches are important because they can seriously question putative relationships about the value or role of play that abound in the literature, as well as suggest new ones (P. Martin & Caro, 1985; Pellis & Iwaniuk, 2000a; Power, 2000).

The fourth method of deciding what the adaptive value of play may be is to use mathematical modeling and simulations that draw on the power of modern computers and increasingly sophisticated methods of predicting outcomes based on the development of putative relationships among key variables and estimation of parameter values. This is being applied to everything from weather forecasting, the ecological consequences of global warming, neural networks and learning, and the effects of natural selection on almost every conceivable trait in plants and animals. The cachet of this *modeling approach* can be seen in almost any issue of the journal *Evolution*. Ultimately, formal mathematical modeling will be useful in understanding play, but the early models (Fagen, 1974, 1977, 1981) were premature (Burghardt, 1984). In any event, they often assumed the function of play rather than helping us to determine it. When and if various models for play can be contrasted and tested against empirical data, modeling will prove to be useful.

The most powerful method, the "gold standard" to many, of establishing causal relationships between play and other features of animals is the *experimental approach*, in which subjects are placed in different groups and given different experimental or control treatments. Does raising kittens without giving them opportunities for object play lead to less proficient killing of prey? Do rats deprived of opportunities for play fighting have less successful social lives than those who can play? Do experimental groups of animals that are reared in complex environments develop larger brains or better immune systems than those that are raised in simple environments? Do children given the opportunity for free play with objects later use them more creatively in problem solving than children who are never exposed to the objects or children who are allowed to use them only in specified ways? Certainly there are data that seem most convincing. Polecats (*Mustela putorious*) raised without opportunities for play fighting, which involves neck biting, were relatively incompetant at both mating and rat killing (Eibl-Eibesfeldt, 1970).

Unfortunately, there are great logistic difficulties in doing such research, and it is often hard to vary only the single aspect that one is interested in evaluating. This is particularly a problem in social play deprivation studies, which are difficult and controversial (cf. Caro, 1988; Müller-Schwarze, 1984; Power, 2000). Furthermore, given the great diversity of species, types of play, and possible independent and dependent measures, it is necessary to use plausible, but grounded and cautious, inferences based on methods other than direct experimentation to devise the experiments. Diversity among species and populations (including human cultural and ethnic groups, Avedon

& Sutton-Smith, 1971; Blurton-Jones, 1993) and even genetic differences within populations may lead to differences in the effects of variables or to contradictory experimental results. For example, social isolation can have different effects on play fighting in different inbred strains of laboratory rats, even those derived from the same outbred source (Siviy, Baliko, & Bowers, 1997; Siviy et al., 2003).

Furthermore, play may be only one path to an adaptive outcome: demonstrating that play, or variations in play, has limited effects in an experimental setting does not rule out the role that it may have in normal settings. For example, play may provide physical exercise benefits that could also be obtained by other activities (hunting, fighting over resources, stereotyped movements in confinement, etc.). Thus, even experimental studies may have limited value in determining the utility of play outside of very narrowly specified boundaries. In short, rather than being the gold standard or benchmark for a science of play, experiments are often rather limited and open to as many interpretive problems as the other methods. To understand play then, both comparative and experimental approaches need to be used to jointly test hypotheses generated from the cost-benefit and design feature approaches to the control, ontogeny, function, experience, and phylogeny of play.

5.2.3 Immediate versus Delayed Functions of Play

Characterizing play as behavior with no immediate function or contribution to survival and then inferring that the benefits of play are delayed has led to much theory, from Groos (1898) to the present (Power, 2000), on what these benefits are and how they are to be obtained. In spite of considerable research, the evidence for delayed benefits based on the adaptive correlational and experimental approaches is sparse (P. Martin & Caro, 1985; Power, 2000). Perhaps more interest should be taken in evaluating whether play has immediate current benefits, not long-term delayed benefits. There is good reason to suspect that this might be a more useful way to begin an approach to understanding the role of play in animals' lives.

In the past, the study of behavioral development in animals, including human children, was focused on development to an end point—the adult stage of life. Less focus was placed on the fact that animals go through different stages of life, with their own social and ecological demands. Their size, physiology, morphology, diet, and other traits change as they proceed through ontogeny. Many of the behaviors that they perform are better viewed as adaptations to the life stage they are in (such as use of the "egg tooth" to facilitate hatching in birds), rather than as behavior preparatory for the future. Many tadpoles have mouth parts and behavior specialized for eating plant matter, whereas their adult forms have jaws, tongues, and behavior specialized for capturing insects (McDiarmid & Altig, 1999). These tadpoles have features adapted to their juvenile ecology and there is little evidence that, beyond survival to metamorphosis, these feeding adaptations have any specific influence on adult feeding. In short, the details of juvenile feeding behavior are designed for current problems tadpoles face. Similarly, the behavioral processes involved in neonatal mammalian suckling behavior seem quite separate from those involved in eating solid food. So, even in mammals a form of behavioral metamorphosis can occur, and recognizing this phenomenon (including the role of play) may be crucially important in understanding behavior in mammals (P. Bateson, 1981; Coppinger & Smith, 1989).

Thus, the question now arises for all features of behavior seen in early development: Which behavior patterns serve juvenile functions and which are preparatory for later life? For example, secondary sexual characteristics and hormonal changes in females may be largely preparatory if the females cannot yet mate or have offspring. However, such changes could have immediate effects on the social life of young females and these may themselves have consequences later in life.

Instead of looking for long-term or delayed benefits of play, then, it is probably more useful, certainly initially, to focus on immediate benefits that play may provide (P. Martin & Caro, 1985). Of course doing so immediately discounts "purposeless," "nonfunctional," and other typical defining traits of play. Some of these immediate benefits include providing important physical exercise that develops endurance, control of body movements, or perceptual-motor integration. Other immediate benefits could include testing objects that represent food or danger, or establishing social roles and communication skills that contribute to current survival in the juvenile stage. Such immediate benefits might be even more evident in play in adult animals, a phenomenon too often neglected in animal play research (S. L. Hall, 1998; Pellis & Iwaniuk, 1999a). The emotional benefits of play in enhancing psychological and physiological well-being and resilience might be important as well (Sutton-Smith, 2003a). Ruling out the immediate benefits of play should, in typical scientific approaches, precede the more problematic study of delayed benefits. However, the typical definition of play as behavior with no immediate function has conspired against such research or even asking the proper questions.

5.2.4   The Processes of Play in the Origins of Play

In addition to evaluating whether the benefits of play are immediate or delayed, it needs to be asked whether play originally evolved, or currently serves, to aid in survival at all. The null hypothesis has been strangely absent in the study of play and is rarely even proposed. Play may not have any direct role, *as play*, in aiding either individual survival or reproductive fitness. As pointed out in chapter 1, play may have its ambiguous status in children as "good" or "bad" for valid reasons. One way to resolve this good-bad, benefits-costs opposition is to distinguish between primary processes, or the setting conditions through which "play" first evolved in ancient animals and their modern descendants, and derived secondary processes. These latter may currently provide, or in an earlier evolutionary time period did provide, physiological, behavioral, social, cognitive, or emotional advantages to those animals engaging in play. Thus, it would not be expected that playful-appearing acts that were due to primary processes would have either immediate or delayed benefits. They could be truly nonfunctional initially (and in some instances maybe still are), perhaps as the outcome of several processes described below. In trying to explain the possible origins of play, it is useful to divide play into three types that outline a broad evolutionary scenario.

Primary process play   This is play behavior (meeting the five criteria) that is an outcome of factors not related to any direct action of natural selection on the play behavior itself. Identifying primary process play is crucial to understanding the origins of play. Play of this type may have no role in subsequent behavior or may serve as a "preadaptation" or "exaption" providing variation that can be selected (Burghardt, 1984, 2001).

Secondary process play   This is play behavior that, once it occurred, evolved some role, although not necessarily an exclusive or even major one, in the maintenance or refinement and normal development of physiological and behavioral capacities (question M in Burghardt, 1977c). Just as certain experiences are important in the maintaining (preventing atrophy) of many other motor and sensory systems, such as suckling or visual perception, play may serve to maintain the precision of predatory, defensive, and social skills; neural processing; and physiological capacities.

Tertiary process play   This is play behavior that has gained a major, if not critical, role in modifying and enhancing behavioral abilities and fitness, including the development of innovation and creativity. There is not too much support for this seemingly commonsense interpretation (Fairbanks, 2000; P. Martin & Caro, 1985). The transition between secondary and tertiary processes, in particular, is probably on a continuum and graded, but the distinction seems important in resolving the issue of the evolution and current function of play (figure 5.1).

Primary process play is most likely to be found in animals that play rarely or simply. Secondary and tertiary process types of play have been selected to perform some adaptive functions, such as those outlined in table 5.1. These functions are both diverse and often difficult to evaluate; it is enough to state that if play serves even a small number of these adaptive functions, then this in addition argues for the multiple origins and heterogeneous nature of play phenomena across taxa. It also needs to be recognized that just because a behavior serves a function does not mean that it was directly selected to perform it. Which came first in the evolution of birds: feathers for insulation in incipient warm-blooded reptiles or feathers as lightweight devices for flying?

Primary processes for play are the proximate conditions, such as lowered thresholds for eliciting behavior as a result of stimulus deprivation, that underlie many "playlike" performances (see later discussion). Animals that have much tertiary play may also still

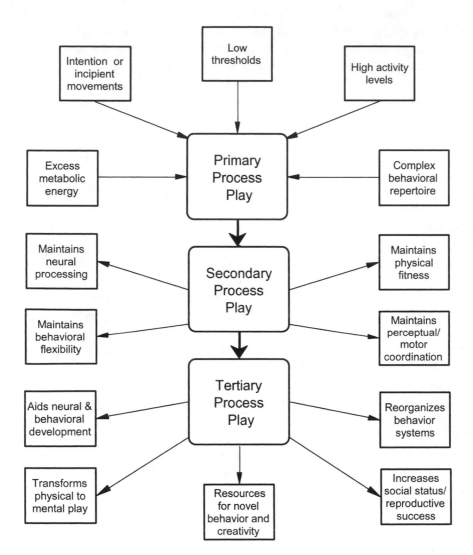

Figure 5.1
Attributes of primary, secondary, and tertiary play processes.

produce primary play because many of the factors are still present. In any event, primary processes provide an essential base upon which the highly diverse and complex structures of mammalian play can be built through the selective actions of secondary processes that provide important cognitive, emotional, and motivational functions useful in foraging, defensive, and social contexts (Burghardt, 1998a). For example, the exaggerated movements, role reversals, and testing of the individuals or objects being played with may allow an animal to learn about the reactions of other entities as well as aiding control of the animal's body. The distinction is similar to that underlying the process of behavioral ritualization, in which autonomic, thermoregulatory, defensive, or feeding responses are incorporated into social displays and can become essential for successful courtship, for example (Burghardt, 1973; Grier & Burk, 1992; Tinbergen, 1951).

The distinction between primary and secondary processes also allows recognition that both the surplus energy theory popularized by Spencer (1872) and the recapitulation theory of play popularized by G. Stanley Hall (1904) largely dealt with primary process in play. Neither explicitly addressed the derived (secondary and tertiary) processes of play that Groos (1898) and the modern proponents of play contend are the major reasons for play (chapter 2). Recall that the surplus energy theory held that play occurred when well-fed "higher" animals had an excess of energy and needed to release it through vigorous activity. The recapitulation view held that juvenile play, which resembled adult serious behavior, was a necessary biological developmental process that animals, including people, went through; it incorporated behavior patterns once necessary for survival in earlier times, but in and by itself it had no long-term effects. The instinct-practice theory held that play was important solely as a means of perfecting adult behavior in species with long periods of immaturity and extensive parental care.

The tendency of most early, and even some current, writers on play to confuse proximate mechanisms and adaptive value led to much needless controversy and especially a neglect of the former in evolutionary theorizing on play (Burghardt, 1984). *We now recognize that play can be viewed as both a product and cause of evolutionary change; that is, playful activities may be a source of enhanced behavioral and mental functioning as well as a by-product or remnant of prior evolutionary events.* It is probably a mistake to think that play originally evolved in order to provide such advantages, and this mistake may have hindered a more accurate and scientifically supported analysis of play.

If the distinction between primary, on the one hand, and secondary and tertiary processes, on the other, is appropriate, it becomes critical to ground the phenomena of play in a phylogenetic context. What are the processes leading to playfulness throughout vertebrate evolution? The answer to this question may be critical in the search for the putative consequences of play.

5.2.5 Studies on the Costs of Play

Although the controversial research on the possible functions of play is not reviewed in depth in this book, the costs of play have recently received renewed attention (Caro, 1995) and deserve mention. Play has costs in time and energy, although the extent of these costs has been debated (Bekoff & Byers, 1992; P. Martin, 1984b). Young mammals may spend 5–10 percent of their time in play and several percent of their metabolic energy (Fagen, 1981; P. Martin, 1984a). In a series of experiments with school children ages 7 and 10, Pelligrini, Horvat, and Huberty (1998) measured heart rate, movement speed, and behavior ratings to estimate caloric costs of physical play. They found outdoor play more costly than both indoor play and classroom behavior. Even though total play time was limited, the authors calculated that play consumed about 6 percent of the childrens' total energy budget. At some age periods, in some species, and in captive settings, the relative amount of play may be much higher than 10 percent; the amount of social behavior in adolescent chimpanzees that is devoted to social play may exceed 30 percent of their time (Paquette, 1994). Play thus uses metabolic resources and time that could be devoted to more "important" or "serious" activities. Pronghorn antelope fawns (*Antilocapra americana*) expend a steady amount of play until weaning at week 6, during which play decreases significantly and only recovers after the fawns shift to substantial independent browsing (Miller & Byers, 1991).

As noted earlier, play has costs in addition to time and energy, such as increased risk of predation and physical injury from performing vigorous activities. Harcourt (1991b) has shown that twenty-two of twenty-six fur seals (*Arctocephalus australis*) that he observed being killed by sea lions (*Otaria byronia*) were attacked while playing, although play only occurred during about 6 percent of their waking hours.

Wariness in exploring and foraging in environments populated with predators has been shown to increase survival (Sih, 1992). An interesting suggestion as to why animals spend so much energy in play is that by doing so they become exhausted and rest more, becoming less conspicuous to predators (Müller-Schwarze, 1984). No research seems to have tested this idea, but it is very similar to one of the theories for why animals sleep (Grier & Burk, 1992). However, becoming conspicuous through play to become subsequently inconspicuous does not, on the surface, seem very plausible.

A remarkable long-term field study of play in cheetahs (*Acinomyx jubatus*) was based on 2600 hours of observation of forty families during their cubs' first year of life (Caro, 1995). Locomotor play, object play, and contact (e.g., wrestling) and noncontact (e.g., chasing) social play were distinguished. This study shows both the strengths and weaknesses of the design-feature, cost-benefit, and correlational approaches. Caro found that the risks of injury, maternal separation, and predation were minimal in cub play. Mothers showed no increased "unease" when their cubs played. That energy expenditures during play may be a significant cost was shown by the positive relationship between time spent eating and playing. The possible benefits of play were modest. There were positive relationships between the amount of time spent in object play and contact social play and the number of contacts made with live prey released by the mother for her offspring to play with. Noncontact social play measures such as stalking, crouching, and chasing showed some subtle age-related changes.

Another recent field study of play in golden lion tamarins (*Leontopithecus rosalia*), a small South American primate, also was designed to test various hypotheses and resulting predictions about play using an approach similar to that in the cheetah study (de Oliveira et al., 2003). Juveniles 2–5 months old in nine social groups were observed. Some animals were reintroduced and given supplemental food. Play occupied 3.8 percent of the activity period and social play was more frequent than solitary object and L–R play. Highly energetic play occurred in short bouts, presumably to avoid overheating or excess energy depletion, but play did occur most during midday when it was hottest. Food-supplemented animals did not play more than wild non-supplemented animals, but this could have been due to less efficiency in foraging rather than having better nutritional resources available, so it does not contradict the squirrel monkey studies cited earlier. The predation risk hypothesis was supported since animals played more when in the center rather than the periphery of their group and they also chose less physically risky or exposed (to predator) locations for play. The authors also found that animals preferred to play with older partners rather than siblings (tamarins are often twins); they concluded that this supports the cognitive training for the unexpected model (Spinka, Newberry, & Bekoff, 2001) rather than the self-assessment model (K. V. Thompson, 1998). Injuries to young animals playing with older ones were nonexistent, suggesting that older play partners self-handicapped. Finally, some individuals and groups played extensively with juvenile and subadult common marmosets (*Callithrix* sp) found in the same habitat.

5.3 The Ontogeny of Play

5.3.1 Timing, Deprivation, and Critical Periods

Elements of play can appear remarkably early in an animal's life: as early as 2 hours after being born in wild beavers (*Castor canadensis*) in Canada (Patenaude, 1984). Ontogeny, then, is an important arena for addressing primary and secondary processes in the role of play. Play is typically found in juvenile animals, although in some, including human beings, it can endure throughout life. Most studies of ontogeny have looked at the course of play throughout the juvenile period: the type, context, frequency, duration, and targets of play. Among the many animals studied have been laboratory rats (Panksepp, 1980), olive baboons (*Papio anubis*; Chalmers, 1980), cats (P. Bateson & Young, 1981), canids (Biben, 1983), gazelles (Gomendio, 1988), and fur seals (Harcourt, 1991a). Different kinds of play or play movements may appear and

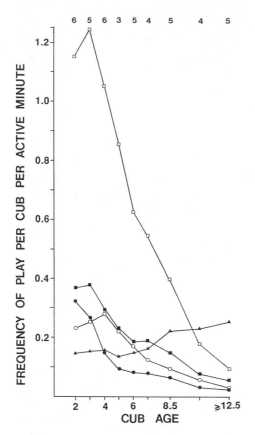

Figure 5.2
Occurrence of different play behavior patterns in young cheetah cubs in the wild at different weeks. □, contact social play; ■, noncontact social play; ●, locomotor play; ○, object play; ▲, exploratory (sniffing objects). (From Caro, 1995)

then wane at different time periods, suggesting that play behavior reflects different behavior systems in development. In slender-tailed meercats, *Suricata suricatta*, object play begins in week 4, wrestling with litter mates and play with adults in week 5, play soliciting signals such as head-rolling and stiff-legged walking during weeks 9–10, and vigorous play with juveniles and yearlings during weeks 11–14 (Doolan & Macdonald, 1999). In cheetahs, locomotor play peaks before social and object play (figure 5.2) and it has been argued that this is because of the need to perfect flight responses at a time of maximal vulnerability to predators (Caro, 1995). In spotted hyenas (*Crocuta crocuta*), the cubs are very aggressive in the natal den until they are moved, during weeks 2 and 3, to a communal den (Drea, Hawk, & Glickman, 1996). Social play emerges during week 2 but locomotor play begins at week 3 and object play at week 4. The authors conclude that the timing of the changes supports the socialization role of play in the clan. However, similar arguments for the role of play in integrating juvenile howling monkey (*Alouatta palliata*) clans (Carpenter, 1934) have been questioned as both sexes emigrate fairly soon from their natal groups (Zucker & Clarke, 1992).

Such studies of differences in timing of various play responses can, thus, provide clues for answering questions concerning the function, motivation, physiology, and evolution of play. However, mere observation that the type of play changes throughout life may lead to uncritically concluding that play has a formative role at certain times in the life of an animal, does its work, and fades away. For example, all mammals show a decline in play fighting after puberty. This is one of the main design feature arguments for the importance of play. Nonetheless, the fact that play appears at a certain point, such as play fighting in rats during the fourth and fifth weeks of life, does not mean that it (1) functions to perfect fighting behavior for use in adulthood or (2) necessarily has some other delayed function. It could have a function of giving a rat enduring experience with the defensive and offensive moves involved in fighting or even courtship (Pellis & Pellis, 1998b), but it may have neither of these roles (also see Paquette, 1994, on play and aggression in chimpanzees).

Studies that manipulate variables such as social contact, the presence of the mother, nutritional status, and presence and type of objects are subsequent steps in the analysis of ontogeny that have much promise, but they are still too infrequent. The reason such studies are needed is the possibility that play criterion one (incompletely functional) and the temporal or structural aspect of play criterion three (play as imperfectly organized behavior that appears before it is actually needed) have a simple explanation.

Good examples of careful developmental research on play are available for young domestic cats, one of the most extensively studied species. In an early study of social play in kittens from birth to 2 years of age, West (1974) isolated eight play behaviors first seen at different ages from 21 days (belly-up) to 42 days (face-off) with others such as pouncing, chasing, and leaping appearing at intermediate ages. The overall amount of play increased threefold from weeks 4–12 and then declined threefold by week 19. She claimed that the different play elements could have different functions and was one of the first to point out the potentially misleading use of the term *play fighting*. The development of all types of play in twenty-eight kittens was followed for the first 12 weeks of age (P. Bateson, 1981). Stalking, rearing, neck arching, neck flexing, wrestling, and object contact were six play elements followed during this period (mere contact between cats was also considered a play category, but I consider it ambiguous by itself). Of these six behaviors, rearing, arching, and neck flexing (performed in the presence of siblings) increased from weeks 4 to 7 and then declined rapidly. In contrast, stalking showed a marked increase at 7 weeks and stayed high thereafter. Wrestling continuously increased from weeks 7 to 12. Object contact play showed about a fivefold increase from 6 to 8 weeks and remained high thereafter. Patrick Bateson concluded that "Play is heterogeneous, and it seems likely that the factors controlling one system of play are not the same as those controlling another" (1981: 287). This is an important conclusion that argues against a unitary "play drive" or "play instinct." While there were positive correlations among all six play behaviors in the 4–7-week period, several were negative in weeks 8–12. This discontinuity suggests that after weaning, which begins at 6 weeks of age, a major behavioral reorganization is taking place and behavioral systems are becoming differentiated. Thus object play increases as exploration and independence from the mother occur. Some aspects of social play also have elements of predation (e.g., stalking).

Bateson and his colleagues were also able to shift the timing of the alteration in play behavior frequencies by enforcing early weaning at 4 weeks of age (P. Bateson & Young, 1981). Thus contextual factors might be important in the ontogenetic timing of various play behaviors.

Stamps (1995) has pointed out that locomotor play could be important in motor learning related to escape in familiar territories. If so, simple experiments involving transplanting animals to unfamiliar areas at different ages could test the function of play in general vs. age and context-specific escape ability.

The fact that vigorous behavior typical of play appears at a certain time could have more general long-term consequences unrelated to the specific behavior patterns seen in play. It is known that certain experiences in early life are essential for later behavioral expression and in fact may have to occur during certain sensitive or critical periods in life if they are to be effective. This is true of song learning in some birds, parent-offspring attachment and imprinting (Harlow, 1964; Hess, 1973), and in people, mastery of spoken foreign languages and the playing of many complex musical instruments. Could play have the role of facilitating the performance of certain essential behavior patterns at certain developmental periods?

A specific research question would be the following: If motor training or physical exercise is involved in the function of play, then why is play limited to a short period of time in most animals' lives? In a review of the functions of play, especially the exercise or "getting in shape" theories, Byers and Walker (1995) point out that none of sixteen different physiological exercise effects posited for play, such as increased oxygen-carrying capacity in the blood, increased blood volume, and increased endurance, have permanent effects. Once a long-distance runner shifts to the couch, he or she cannot keep the fitness accrued by prior exercise in the body's "bank," let alone accrue interest. By looking at the ages when play peaks in three domestic species (mice, rats, and cats), Byers and Walker found that these play peaks coincided closely with the ages at which permanent experience-dependent synaptic development occurred in the cerebellum and important muscle fibers were innervated (figure 5.3).

Although the Byers and Walker theory is based on a comparative correlational approach using a small sample size ($n = 3$ species) and the design feature approach,

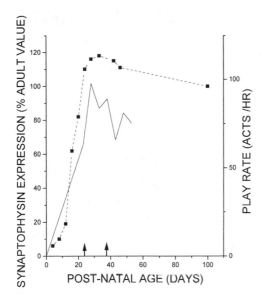

Figure 5.3
Timing of play (solid line) and cerebellar synapse development in rats. Arrows point to age range that muscle fiber differentiation occurs. (From Byers & Walker, 1995)

the idea that play is associated with a sensitive period for neural integration may be a key to understanding the timing of play (Byers, 1998). A study with male rats who were prevented from engaging in social play as pups found a decrease in the amount of social interaction as adults when the rats were not able to play during a period comparable to the period that Byers and Walker (1995) argued is critical for cerebellar synapse formation (van den Berg et al., 1999).

As indicated earlier, depriving animals of play and not interfering with other systems has proven very difficult. There is still no solid experimental evidence that play deprivation per se has long-lasting consequences for behavioral ontogeny (Caro, 1988; Power, 2000). However, a recent study in rats based on social isolation (Hol et al., 1999) found that social deprivation at week 4 but not week 5 reduced adult social interaction, suggesting a sensitive period. More refined tests are needed. Other critical changes may also be occurring. For example, bone growth and bone "remodeling" are known to be affected by events such as dietary experience, and it could be that prepubertal play functions in skeletal development.

The ontogenetic organization of play may have more specifically behavioral consequences. When 6-week-old experienced rats play, pinning is performed by the winners having their hind feet firmly anchored on the ground, whereas 30-day-old rats often pin by trying to balance their hind feet on the supine rat's body (Foroud & Pellis, 2002). Yet the obvious conclusion that such a skill must be learned does not hold as weaning rats (25 days old) anchor frequently as soon as they begin to play. So why the ontogenetic shift? The authors argue that by not anchoring the animals may be increasing the opportunity to gain experience in play tactics that may be developmentally beneficial, although they have no good idea as to what the benefits are (Foroud & Pellis, 2002). Nevertheless, this self-handicapping merits more detailed study.

The timing of primate play may also provide information on functional issues (Fairbanks, 2000). Fairbanks followed the development of several kinds of play in captive vervet monkeys (*Cercopithecus aethiops sabaeus*). She thus extends the Byers and Walker analysis and makes a strong case for extending it to all play and many functions.

Careful consideration of the developmental timing of primate play leads to the conclusion that each of the different play types influences later capacities via the process of neural selection, by increasing relevant experience during the time when the neural and cognitive mechanisms involved are undergoing ontogenetic modification. Thus, primate play contributes to the development of fighting skills, object handling abilities, and motor performance by selectively enhancing the basic neuromotor structures that will be later available to perform these tasks. (Fairbanks, 2000: 1578)

Unfortunately, this is still too much a just-so story, especially since these claims immediately follow a section in the chapter labeled "Play is not essential!" Certainly all these play types can "influence" later behavior, but the plausible must be made more convincing. In addition, adult play is ignored. As pointed out early in chapter 1, extravagant claims for play that have led to its lowly status in many scientific quarters and uncritical claims in the media also need to be considered (R. A. Thompson & Nelson, 2001).

If play is primarily a phenomenon of infancy and juvenile periods, then the amount and importance of play might be related to the length of such periods. Indeed, the famous statement from Groos that "animals do not play because they are young, but they have their youth because they must play" (1898: 76) leads to the claim that the longer the period of "youth," the more important play must be. Life history factors do play a role in differences in the amount and nature of play seen among animals, but Groos's statement is not supportable when the comparative information in part II is looked at even superficially. Nonetheless, the relative degree to which animals have their sensory, skeletal, and motor systems operational at birth or hatching (precocity) versus the amount of postnatal development needed for independence after birth or hatching (altriciality) is an important distinction that will prove useful later. Precocity and altriciality are themselves related to the amount of parental care needed by animals, which is why parental care is often considered an important factor that can help explain the amount of play seen.

The rapidity of postnatal development is also important. Some birds and mammals born in a very altricial state mature very quickly to independence, in a matter of weeks, while some animals born in a more mature state may stay with the parents a much longer time (S. T. Parker & McKinney, 1999). Thus the timing and duration of the parental care period may be more important than the degree of immaturity at birth. In some mammalian species the mother has only one or a few precocial neonates. These offspring are generally larger and entail more prenatal maternal investment per individual than species that have large numbers of smaller altricial young. The relationship of play to altriciality is not simple because phylogeny, physiology, body size, reproductive investment style, and other factors can preclude simple relationships. That is why the parental care system as a whole needs to be considered. Nonetheless, altriciality may be a useful marker in identifying animals in which play is prominent because species with altricial young often play more, or more complexly, than even close relatives that are more precocial (Burghardt, 1988b; Fagen, 1981; Ortega & Bekoff, 1987; Pellis & Iwaniuk, 2000b).

5.3.2   Is Learning to Walk a Model for Play?

An early type of secondary process in play may have been the maintenance or modification of basic species-typical motor activities by young animals. In altricial species, compared with precocial species, a more drawn-out process in the appearance of various behavior patterns would be expected, and there would be a greater window of time for incompletely functional performances to be influenced by playlike performances. However, even in human beings, the motor components of species-typical behavior (facial expressions, reaching, grasping, biting) may be only modestly influenced by experience, although their contextual deployment and perceptual-motor control may be influenced to a considerable degree.

A good test case in which the first type of secondary process (maintaining "instinctive behavior") in play may be relevant is learning to walk in human children. McGraw (1943) emphasized the importance of maturation; infants do not really learn to walk, they walk when the neuromuscular system is ready. Thelen (1995) has confirmed that human infants do indeed have many precocial locomotor skills, such as coordinated stepping movements at 1 month of age if they are held on a treadmill. Nevertheless, she argues, these congenitally highly complex behavior patterns still need much experience in order to develop fully, and walking and other behaviors should be viewed in a "multicausal" framework. Although hard evidence is limited concerning the basic features of locomotion in infants, it can be granted that practice is as important for perfecting locomotion in children as it seems to be for predatory behavior in some young snakes (Burghardt & Krause, 1999; Halloy & Burghardt, 1990).

Thelen argues that "new views of motor development emphasize strongly the roles of exploration and selection in finding solutions to new task demands. This means that infants must assemble adaptive patterns from modifying their current movement dynamics" (1995: 85). Although Thelen attempts to challenge the operation of genetic and neural inputs in behavioral development by emphasizing the role of the body's biomechanical features in producing "self-organizing" behavioral change (Metzger, 1997), a softer version in which the adaptive deployment and altering of much motor behavior may involve considerable ontogenetic input (growth and learning) has value. Aiding this process are motivational factors (as when an infant keeps trying to stand alone, crawl up stairs, or cross a room to get to a parent or toy), accompanied by the joy of success, which facilitates the learning of a novel means of accomplishing a behavioral outcome (see sections 5.4.1 and 5.4.2).

Central to Thelen's view is that action and perception are linked and "that each component in the developing system is both cause and product" and that "cognition is emergent from the same dynamic processes as those governing early cycles of perception and action" (Thelen, 1995: 94). Even "higher order mental activities, including categorization, concept formation, and language, must arise in a self-organized manner from the recurrent real time activities of the child just as reaching develops from cycles of matching hand to target" (Thelen, 1995: 94). She formulated a conceptual model for how sophisticated motor activities, often involved in play, are derived from the same kind of processes as those involved in the development of advanced mental abilities.

Applying the five criteria of play, including incomplete functionality, repetition, endogenous motivation, and structural or temporal factors, all speak to learning to walk and other behavioral tasks in altricial mammals as more than superficially playlike. The task now is to forge this link between the two kinds of secondary processes and go beyond the vague multicausal ("nonlinear") framework (B. Goodwin, 1994) that Thelen advocates. We need analytical research that separates and evaluates the various putative influences. For example, Meer, Weel, and Lee (1995) showed that spontaneous arm movements in newborn (10–24-day-old) infants are more frequent when the infants can see their arms. Furthermore, visual information is used to counteract external forces (weights, strings) on their limbs in maintaining a reference position. The authors speculate that such early developmental processes may be critical in the development of more purposeful reaching and grasping skills 3 months or so later. Playlike behavior may be important in many of these developmental transitions in human and nonhuman species.

Comparable experimental work with animals in which controlled and long-term manipulation of sensorimotor integration during social, locomotor, and object play is carried out could be an entrée to the analytical work that has been so lacking in play research. In later chapters, evidence that animals have a neural template like that found useful in understanding song learning in birds will be presented. Play may be a means to activate the behavioral work needed for certain necessary skills to be acquired and operate in behavioral systems, such as walking, which are rarely considered playful.

5.3.3 More on Play Sequences and Sequences in Ontogeny

Piagetian and neo-Piagetian developmental research in children and nonhuman primates (S. T. Parker & McKinney, 1999) focuses on research showing that the four periods of cognitive development (sensorimotor, preoperations, concrete operations, and formal operations; see chapter 4) build on one another sequentially, as do several stages within each period. Play, as characterized earlier, is an integral and important component in cognitive development (Piaget, 1962). For example, the sensorimotor intelligence series involves a sequence of stages that include circular and secondary circular reactions. The latter consist of repeated actions, such as repeatedly striking a mobile or shaking a rattle; similar actions are found in many species and usually considered playful. A famous example popularized by Piaget was the fact that infants from about 7 to 12 months of age who are shown a toy in one location persist in reaching toward that location even after the toy has been moved to a different location that the infants can see. This persistence is considered an error (the A-not-B error) that must be overcome, and Thelen has applied her field theory to this problem as well (Thelen et al., 2001). The controversial explanation she provides is an attempt to break down the dualism between cognitive and bodily movement processes. However, comparative evidence shows that many other animals show this phenomenon and it might very well be adaptive in situations where the object is not viewed as unique (Hailman, 2001).

Play behavior, as is true of many other behavior patterns, also has several sequential components that may have different causal bases. Even a circular reaction can be divided into sequences. For example, if an object such as a ball is introduced into a kitten's environment and play with it ensues, we observe the following: orientation to the object (initiation); running over to the object (approach); hitting it with a paw, perhaps several times in a row (engagement); and leaving the ball and switching to another activity (termination). Such sequences may occur repeatedly in bouts.

Recently Willingham (1998, 1999) has put forth a general model of motor skill learning that postulates a specific set of four processes involved in motor control of just the first part of the above sequence. Consider the process of reaching for and moving an object, such as when a cat reaches out to a dead mouse and pulls it to her mouth. This entails a "decision" to perform the act (strategic process), a translation of the spatial locations of cat, paw, and object into an "egocentric space" (perceptual-motor integration), a sequential ordering so that the paw is moved to the object (the "goal location") before being retrieved (sequencing), and finally the translation of these steps into appropriate muscle firing (dynamic process). In each of these four stages, learning of different kinds may be involved in enhanced behavioral performance. Play could be a means of ensuring that behavior patterns are both practiced and deployed in effective manners to either maintain skills removed from the operation of natural selection by

parental care or to enhance performance beyond that which could possibly be anticipated by innate wiring.

Even the most congenitally perfected behaviors (such as predation) may have to be
employed in widely varying environments and with widely disparate objects to increase the chances for survival, especially when environments change. Perhaps, however, object play in kittens is so exaggerated or otherwise so different from real
predation that such "unrealistic" practice interferes with predatory behavior. If so,
then object play has no secondary function related to predation and exists for other
reasons (e.g., compensation for stimulus deprivation, exercise of diverse body parts).
Evidence suggests, however, that predatory play in cats is linked to motivational systems that involve predation (S. L. Hall, 1998; Pellis et al., 1988).

An alternative conception, the possibility that play is just neurologically or motori-
cally immature behavior in the process of being prepared for its "serious" deployment,
must always be considered as a default hypothesis of primary play. Such a view would
explain the greater prominence of play in species with long developmental periods or
immense physical changes before adulthood (Burghardt, 1984; Ewer, 1968a). In other
words, play as behavior that has no current adaptive function or only a limited one
may be a consequence of developmental necessity. Play is seemingly nonfunctional
because it is, in fact, a largely nonadaptive consequence of other factors in the lives of
the organism. The most common examples of precocial behavior as play may be play
as a temporary maturational intermediate, an ontogenetic by-product of adult behavioral necessity. These examples, such as wing flapping, have also been termed prefunctional behavior (Hogan, 1988; Kruijt, 1964). Although some have argued that such
behavior is not true play (Fagen, 1981), others have argued that this is all that play
really is (G. C. Williams, 1991). George Williams (1991), for example, points out that,
just as with anatomical traits, much species-typical behavior (courtship, fighting, predation) in animals with parental care only becomes necessary after a juvenile period.
However, there may be a rapid onset of the need to include such behaviors in the animal's behavioral repertoire if it is to survive and reproduce. Since natural selection will
operate to ensure that the nervous system and other mechanisms underlying such behavior are available in functional form at this abrupt developmental transition (post-
weaning solo hunting, first courtship), and if the costs (and hence selection against) of
precocial performance of behavioral elements are low, such temporary maturational
intermediates are to be expected. Thus play is something that animals can afford to
perform if the costs are low and the benefits are great if the behavior is performed
adequately as soon as it is needed. The more complex the behavioral systems needed,
the less likely it is that they will be functionally integrated when first performed. This
is certainly one way to explain the occurrence of primary process play in development,
but to dismiss all play as prefunctional adult behavior is highly simplistic.

5.4   The Control of Play

5.4.1   Behavior Systems and the Question of Motivation

As mentioned at the end of the preceding section and in previous chapters, motivational issues have been at the heart of many controversies about play (Eibl-Eibesfeldt, 1970; Meyer-Holzapfel, 1978; Müller-Schwarze, 1978) and resemble those concerning exploration (Hughes, 1997). Early studies trying to demonstrate a relatively autonomous drive for play by depriving animals (deer and goats) of social play had mixed results (Chepko, 1971; Müller-Schwarze, 1968) and were challenged on methodological grounds (Fagen, 1976, 1981). These early studies were based on short-term deprivation, however, and avoided many of the social and environmental deficits that long-term social deprivation can create (Müller-Schwarze, 1984). In male rats, the ability of even short-term opportunities for social play to override the effects of isolation rearing (van den Berg et al., 1999) has been shown repeatedly (Ikemoto & Panksepp, 1992; Panksepp & Beatty, 1980). Rats are much more ready to play if they are separated from a partner for some time.

Motivation concerns itself with basic drives underlying physiological and reproductive behavior (e.g., feeding, drinking, mating, fighting, parental care) as well as extensions to social and cognitive behavior (e.g., altruism, achievement, status, addictions, social roles). All of these have been implicated in play. Nevertheless, despite a long history in psychology and ethology (Baerends, 1976; Mook, 1996), motivation has not been a central focus of recent work in animal behavior. Modern ethologists and behavioral ecologists have minimized the study of "drives." Behaviorist psychologists prefer to talk about "setting factors," such as environmental context or hours since last eating. Physiologists avoid the term and would rather measure body fluids (blood glucose, hormones). Neuroscientists image brain states and measure neurochemical concentrations to obtain their objective facts about psychological states. However, the fact remains that motivational analyses are still both common and needed (Mook, 1996).

A feature of play is its repeated nature and the persistence with which animals often pursue opportunities to play (Hole & Einon, 1984) and even learn tasks in order to gain a play partner. Repeated behavior patterns in moderately changing contexts might be particularly conducive to learning or improving complex skills and negotiating complex habitats. A descriptive behavioristic theory that has utility in relating play and other responses is the Matching Law (Herrnstein, 1997). At behavioral equilibrium, matching assumes that the ratio between any two behavioral responses (B) matches the ratio of the respective reinforcement (R) obtained such that $B_1/B_2 = R_1/R_2$. This also should hold for time allocation (t) such that $R_1/t_1 = R_2/t_2$. From this it should be possible to calculate the subjective (to the animal) value of different alternative behavior, since, to Herrnstein R_i is subjective value. It is interesting that behavioral ecologists have recently "discovered" the relevance of conditioning, matching, and other psychological models for understanding why animals persist in, for example, competing over space (Sih & Mateo, 2001). However, the motivational mechanisms underlying such persistence and their comparative, physiological, feedback and ecological correlates have barely been considered, which Herrnstein (1997) allows is necessary "before any actual behavior can be predicted" (Herrnstein, 1997: 76). Play could very well be a "safe" means of beginning such competition and learning behavioral and spatial tactics (e.g., Pellis & Pellis, 1998b).

A brief review of the traditional ethological model of behavior may be useful here. Animals are often predisposed to respond to rather specific stimulus cues from biologically important items in their environment (such as food, predators, potential mates, or offspring). These stimuli are often extractions from the complete set of stimuli an object possesses and, depending on the species, may be an odor, a sound, a color, a shape, a specific movement, or even a tactile stimulus, as well as a specific combination of stimuli. Such stimuli (often termed cues, sign stimuli, or releasers), when perceived, may elicit a response that is also instinctive (often termed fixed or modal action patterns, unlearned or instinctive movements, etc.), such as flight, attack, eating, courtship behavior, or care of young (e.g., retrieval of a pup upon hearing a high-pitched vocalization, movement toward the mating call of a male frog, capturing an insect). These stimulus-response units often occur in a series in which the animal first appears to "search" for the stimuli to which it can respond with the instinctive response. This initial phase is termed appetitive behavior (Craig, 1918) and is followed by the more stereotyped "consummatory acts" after the animal perceives the stimulus object (prey, mate) that "releases" the consummatory action sequences.

From Craig's pioneering work through the refinements of Lorenz, Tinbergen, and others to sophisticated newer models (Hogan, 2001; Timberlake & Silva, 1995), the appetitive phase is where the most learning and adaptability is found. In most learning experiments with nonhuman animals, quite complex responses are taught, from maze running to counting and deception (Bekoff, Allen, & Burghardt, 2002), while much less attention is devoted to teaching animals how to eat, mate, and flee. Learning for most people focuses largely on how to obtain important resources such as food, drink, shelter, and mates; how to chew and swallow food, how to sleep, or how to copulate receive far less attention. The performance of these behaviors is itself, in the ethological system, rewarding.

But why should animals strive to obtain stimuli that elicit adaptive behavior patterns even before they "know" that performing them is important to their survival or reproduction? A general drive might not accomplish this and so the ethologists postulated individual drives for different behavioral systems (reproductive, predatory), which

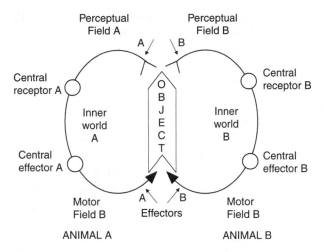

Figure 5.4

A double functional circle derived from the single actor circular system developed by Jacob von Uexküll. In social play the partner is both object and an experiencing actor/reactor. (From Burghardt, 1998c)

could in turn exist at rather fine-grained levels. Thus the reproductive drive could consist of a series of drives that involves establishing territories, courting mates, building nests, and giving parental care, each of which may have further stimulus-behavior connections and its own motivational system (action-specific energy) (Lorenz, 1981; Tinbergen, 1951). Positing a drive for every response is, however, overly reductive and minimizes the value of the concept of motivation itself, which is used as a shorthand for behavioral systems that contain a group of behaviors with common functional features (Mook, 1996).

Responses by an animal to an object or another animal can in turn alter the features of the object or produce responses by the object (e.g., a ball or rattle) or the mate, prey, baby, or predator and lead to a fairly complex series of interactions. Social play is precisely one of these types of interactions. Von Uexküll's (1921) concept of the unity of external and internal stimuli in a "functional circle" is a useful way to keep motivation from being viewed only as an internal mechanism (Burghardt, 1998c). Figure 5.4 shows a double functional circle illustrating the interactive nature of the functional circle when two animals interact (social play). Removing the right hand circle gives the original functional circle (object play, locomotor play) in which the cue bearer can be the physical environment as well as a specific object. The more complex the species' behavioral repertoire, the more complex the motivational system that would be present. In fact, William James, America's first great psychologist, asserted that humans have more instincts, not fewer, than any other species (James, 1890). It may be this complexity that makes possible the countless combinations of behavioral responses more frequently seen in animals with rich repertoires.

The "behavior system" approach (Baerends, 1976; Timberlake & Silva, 1995) is being employed today as a counterpart to the concept of modularity in evolutionary psychology (Buss, 1999). This approach is particularly useful in that it incorporates learning into the sequential organization of motivated behavior at certain points, a concept termed constrained variability (Timberlake, 2001). It derives, as we have seen, from the analysis of motivated behavior by Craig (1918) in which it is in the appetitive phase of behavior that most variation and openness to experience exists, whereas the behavioral organization of the end point of a sequence (drinking, killing, eating, copulating) is more impervious to modification. It is within this appetitive phase that most play occurs. In fact, the absence of the final consummatory acts has often been used as a major characteristic of play (chapter 3).

Clever recent experiments have shown that rats, even up to 4 weeks of age, do not show the appetitive responses for food or water until experienced with both food-deprivation or dehydration. Thus appetitive responses (drives) for basic biological substances may need to be learned (Hall, Arnold, & Myers, 2000; Changizi, McGehee, & Hall, 2002). If so, play may serve as a means to establish or enhance motivational systems and responses to stimuli in various behavior systems.

The main issues in motivation and play revolve around these four questions: Is play controlled by a separate or unitary motivational (or behavioral) system for playful behavior that is separate from the internal states underlying serious performance? Is play incomplete, unperfected, or simulated behavior that is derived from the same motivation as that underlying the serious version? Does play behavior involve a blending of both serious and play systems? Does play result from mixing two or more independent serious systems?

These questions are partly subsumed in the distinction between primary and secondary processes in play. It is possible that each alternative may underlie some forms of play and thus the diversity of play is best viewed as a continuum on which any separate motivational components of play are secondary processes, although they need not be. Thus, in learning to walk, at a certain age an infant seems very motivated to accomplish first crawling, then standing, then walking with support, then walking independently, then rapid walking and running. Piagetian and mastery-type processes can be involved. Here the motivational source is probably identical to that involved in locomotion itself. In play fighting, however, the motivational sources may be quite different from those underlying serious fighting. Motivational concerns are probably important in the evolution of play and underlie play as ritual as discussed earlier. Recall that the autotelic theory and the view that play is behavior done for its own sake are motivational constructs.

One way to study the question of the behavioral systems underlying play is to look for marker behaviors. Play signals (chapter 4) are often useful, but do not necessarily give unambiguous cues as to the behavior system being invoked. A rare exception is found in dwarf mongooses, which have a distinctive play vocalization that pulses 3–12 times per second throughout a play bout with an object (Rasa, 1984). The repetition rate is related to the intensity of play and associated behavior patterns. More typical is the finding that social play increases after feeding. For example, Pellis (1991) found that changes in object and social play occurred as a function of hunger in a group of captive oriental small-clawed otters (*Aonyx cinerea*). The typical object play sequence resembled the gathering, handling, fragmentation, and chewing of food. Typical social play involved attempts to gently bite a conspecific's cheek. As feeding time approached, the otters increased their object play and decreased their social play, even threatening each other over objects. Once the animals fed and were satiated, object play declined and amicable social play significantly increased. Such studies suggest that different kinds of play are linked to primary motivational systems rather than a separate play drive or instinct. Studies on the effect of hunger on play have led to a more complex picture of motivation and object play such that varying prey and toy size, type, and movement as well as satiation/hunger can lead to conflicting results (see Hall, 1998). Furthermore, different components of predation and other behavior systems may have separate thresholds and drives underlying the types of play performed and their sequential organization (Leyhausen, 1979). In this way the rarity of the final consummatory stages such as killing bites in play can be explained (Burghardt, 1984). Leyhausen's "drive surplus" view of play has been unduly neglected.

What we need are more detailed observations of play from the viewpoint of the various systems involved within what seems to be a single kind of play, such as play fighting. Play fighting in rodents has been most informative in this regard. Early work by Pellis and co-workers (Pellis, 1993; Pellis & Pellis, 1987) showed that the targets of play fighting were not those used in serious fighting, but those used in precopulatory encounters between males and females (see also Eibl-Eibesfeldt, 1970). Thus the view that play fighting represented a low level of aggression, but derived from the social aggression behavior system, was disproved at least in these species. In cats, both serious fighting and predation involved the same target (the nape of the neck) and thus other behavior patterns involving stalking, leaping, etc. were employed to decide whether the play represented predatory or conspecific fighting systems.

A recent study of the grasshopper mouse (*Onychomys leucogaster*), an unusual carnivorous rodent, showed that play fighting in this species involves the mixing of both predatory and nonpredatory (sociosexual) behavior systems (Pellis et al., 2000). Thus attacks to the nape of the neck are predatory and the other kinds of play behavior, such as nosing and allogrooming of the nape and nearby regions of the partner, are part of the precopulatory behavior system. Detailed observations of the sequential

organization of attack and defense in play fighting support this view. In another rodent, Richardson's ground squirrels (*Spermophilus richardsonii*), close analysis of play
fights found that most (86 percent) could be readily classified as either sexual or aggressive play fighting, and most of these were sexual in both sexes (Pasztor et al., 2001).
Furthermore, it was found that a play bout that began as sexual play fighting ended
that way; the same was true for agonistic play fighting. This suggests that play fighting
in other species also may only superficially appear to represent a unitary behavior system and questions the view that play is, by definition, a phenomenon of mixed motivations. Furthermore, in the ground squirrels, agonistic play fighting did not differ
between the sexes, whereas sociosexual play did differ; males initiated more attacks.

Play in the most highly playful species involves multiple behavior systems, but they
may remain largely separate causally. Mapping such diversity in the systems underlying play across taxa may be essential for tracing the evolution of play in its most highly
developed forms. The transfer of elements from one behavioral system to another
through ritualization (Grier & Burk, 1992; Tinbergen, 1951; Leyhausen, 1979) may also
have happened in play (Loizos, 1967). This complexity may be a major reason for the
lack of progress in understanding the evolution of play among playful families of
mammals prior to the careful comparative work instituted by Sergio Pellis, Marc Bekoff,
and others.

Can the motivational processes underlying social play be distinguished? Specifically,
when dogs play with human beings is the same system being expressed as when they
play with other dogs? Rooney, Bradshaw, and Robinson (2000) compared the details of
play with toys when the partner was another dog or a human. They found less interest
in the toy and more time spent in interacting with the partner in dog-human play.
They also studied more than 400 dogs being walked by their owners and found that
dogs who had the opportunity to play with other dogs played as much with their
owners as dogs being walked alone. Dogs in multi-dog households played somewhat
more with humans than dogs in single-dog households. The authors suggest that these
differences mean that play with each kind of partner is motivationally distinct and
cannot be used to predict levels of play with another type of partner. Clearly this is not
a definitive study, but it might point the way to more experimental testing of this and
related hypotheses. Still, the development of play from precursor behavior patterns
cannot be ignored, as shown by the work of Chalmers (1980) with baboon (*Papio
anubis*) infants (figure 5.5).

5.4.2 Emotion and Affect in Play

Whereas motivation is concerned with the "push" and the decision-making processes
underlying the choice among alternative behavior patterns available to an organism,
emotion and affect are viewed more as consequences of external stimulation or of the
behavioral performance itself. The joy, fun, thrill, or pleasure attributed to playful acts
is surely real in many cases and is an important and perhaps critical issue in the anal-

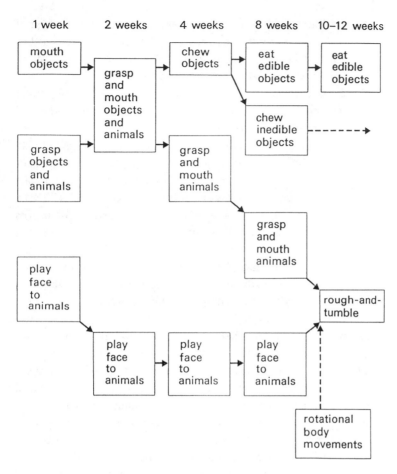

Figure 5.5

The emergence of complex play from precursor behavior patterns and the interaction among behavior systems in young baboons, *Papio anubis*. (From Chalmers, 1980)

ysis of play (Csikszentmihalyi, 1991; Spinka, Newberry, & Bekoff, 2001; Sutton-Smith, 2003a). For example, the positive (reinforcing) emotions associated with play have been interpreted as facilitating training to deal with more serious events when they occur (Spinka, Newberry, & Bekoff, 2001). Unfortunately these emotional attributes of play are not easily measured in diverse species, which is why affect, as well as motivation, were incorporated as alternatives in play criterion two. Certainly, any comprehensive theory of play will need to deal with affect and the way animals experience play, as the fifth ethological aim (private experience) posits. The performance of play, however, may not be conventionally "fun," as shown by the concentration and even fear involved in voluntary thrill-seeking behaviors in which humans often engage

(Sutton-Smith, 2003a, b); whether these are found in other species is less certain but it is probable because stress may accompany play fighting (L. K. Smith, Fantella, & Pellis, 1999). Although the emotional and experiential aspects of play are not emphasized in the comparative survey that follows, ultimately we will need to do so.

Not only are motivational and emotional issues difficult to study in play, they suffer from a more general problem. Mainline psychologists downplayed motivational and emotional aspects of play for much of the twentieth century as a focus on species-typical behavior (instincts) became unfashionable. This is shown in the review of play by E. D. Mitchell and Mason (1934), who were at pains to accept the then-ascendant "modern" anti-instinct perspective (Bernard, 1924) and stated that "Out of habits and attitudes arise motives and desires. These are the drives that lead to play" (E. D. Mitchell & Mason, 1934: 70). Thus emotions and drives are mere learned behaviors that have no special status. Modern research questions such dogma, but the effect it had still lingers.

Having fun seems to be the major characteristic of play to many. Humor is often associated with fun, and laughing; a repetitive and easily recognized vocalization is one good sign that children are playing. As in children, there is evidence that great apes laugh when they are tickled and played with gently (Provine, 2001). Using ultra-sonic detectors, we now know that rats too perform a laughterlike repetitive chitter response when tickled, and seek out opportunities to be tickled by a familiar person; they also perform the behavior in social contexts with other rats (Burgdorf & Panksepp, 2001; Panksepp, 1998a, 2000). Panksepp feels that such positive emotions aid social bonding and that the neurochemistry of such systems is a core mammalian attribute.

Is fun as a positive emotion an essential trait of play? It is not an essential part of play criterion two for a very good reason. Even if play is fun at times, this attribute is not only hard to measure in nonhuman animals in a noncircular manner, but it seems not to be true. Animals, including people, can be quite immersed in playful activities that arouse emotions other than benign fun or pleasure, such as intense fear, surprise, anger, and even grief as the play activity proceeds. Play may serve as a means of arousing emotions in settings where their serious deployment is muted through comfortable and socially constrained contexts. Sutton-Smith (2003a) has argued that much play in humans may be a means of triggering "virtual emotion" in safe contexts. In a sense, the psychoanalytic theory of Freud (Wälder, 1978) is a narrower version of Sutton-Smith's formulation. Regardless, play may be proximally controlled by a broad array of emotions, not just fun. If this view is valid, then the often rapid transition from play to serious behavior (fighting, sex) can be understood. Once the virtual emotion is aroused, the serious one is more readily triggered. Social play fighting, particularly in older juveniles, can escalate into serious fighting, as in black bear cubs (Burghardt & Burghardt, 1972).

Perhaps the discouragement of recreational dancing by many conservative religious groups, especially at church social events for adolescents, derives from a recognition that a transition from courtship play to consummated mating is a real danger and an unwelcome test of the efficacy of their moral teachings.

5.4.3 External Stimulation

Curiosity and exploration are directed to environmental stimuli, generally novel ones. Play, as discussed in chapter 3, can also be a response to stimuli in the environment, although novelty is not the key criterion. Play is clearly facilitated or even made possible by the presence of appropriate stimuli, be they objects or social play partners. Obviously locomotor play requires the appropriate environment—water for otters, trees for arboreal monkeys, fields for antelopes—as well as sufficient room. Object play is facilitated by items that provide appropriate interactive opportunities or "affordances" (J. J. Gibson, 1978) for the species involved. Much evidence supports the conclusion that animals often habituate to objects in their environment and increase their investigation and manipulation of novel objects when they are introduced (e.g., Renner & Seltzer, 1991). Social play partners of the appropriate age, size, and sex may be important, although social play between species is common, particularly in captivity.

Different species rely on different sensory systems, and this may influence the type and amount of play. Collared peccaries, as mentioned in chapter 3, rely heavily on olfaction, and in a field study playing was almost always accompanied by olfactory investigation and contact. This often took place in a 4 m diameter "playground" heavily scent marked (Byers, 1985). Play in the playground often involved many herd members in boisterous bouts four times longer in duration (about $6\frac{1}{2}$ min.) than play occurring elsewhere. Nocturnal primates rely on tactile, vocal, and chemical signals for communication more than on visual signals. If nocturnal and diurnal prosimian primates are compared, the former engage in much more play fighting than the latter, with New World monkeys and Old World monkeys continuing the trend toward use of visual cues in short-range communication, along with decreasing social play. It has been suggested that this is due to the use of play as a social evaluation and assessment method when visual cues are less available or less evolutionarily developed (Pellis & Iwaniuk, 2000a).

This finding is in line with much research suggesting that animals require certain types and amounts of stimulation for proper sensory, structural (muscle, skeletal), motor, and cognitive development. The environmental enrichment movement for captive animals is built on this premise (Burghardt et al., 1996), a premise so convincing that more and more legislation is being passed in the United States requiring that facilities provide not only adequate space for laboratory animals, but added structural features; varied diets provided in novel ways; and objects to manipulate, climb over, or push around. The concept of a range of necessary and optimal stimulation is central to this view. Clearly, apparatus, objects, and play partners are important in facilitating play. The notion that chemical, auditory, and tactile cues should be considered in enrichment schemes that are in line with a species' biology and life history needs to be formally addressed (Lampard, 2002). Too often enrichment is based on providing satisfying visual displays for humans rather than dealing with the needs of the species being maintained in captivity (Burghardt, 1996). Nonetheless, experiments that attempt to evaluate the role of specific sensory modalities, such as olfaction, in the development and performance of play can lead to confusing results, especially when neural circuits are manipulated (e.g., Loranca & Salas, 2001).

Excessive stimulation (crowding, too much noise), not just insufficient stimulation, can lead to increased stress and decreased play, as noted in play criterion five. But stress is best measured from the perspective of the animal and not just environmentally. For example, in one study, high-density housing of chimpanzee groups led to less agonistic behavior, less mutual grooming, and fewer submissive greetings, but more juvenile social play (adult social play was very low in both conditions) (Aureli & de Waal, 1997). In rats, social play was also increased in small cages (Siegel & Jensen, 1986) and small boring environments might be a reason for the common observation that well-cared-for animals play more in captivity than in the field (Burghardt, 1984). For juveniles, the increased availability of nearby play partners may have facilitated social play more than crowding inhibited it.

Although spare and sterile environments may inhibit play, animals are not passive reactors to environmental constraints. They can actively alter their level of stimulation, and this may be a crucial factor in the origins of play (Burghardt, 1984). Animals in stimulus-deprived (boring) environments may engage in various activities to relieve sensory and response deprivation and to increase arousal. Such boredom might be expected in the well-provisioned and protected environments (e.g., nests, burrows) provided by endothermic parents. This factor may be the critical one in the consistent finding that well cared-for captive animals play much more than their wild counterparts (Burghardt, 1988b). If juveniles are buffered from the demands of survival, and the species possesses a complex repertoire of evolved and active behavior patterns, then the animals have a behavioral resource to draw on when they are deprived of stimulation. Lowering of the stimulus threshold and reorganization of behavior sequences into less precise adultlike forms could result. Since the simplistic views of a unitary nonspecific arousal system are no longer accepted, having been replaced with a conception of functionally different neural systems mediated by monoaminergic and cholinergic neurotransmitters "contributing to different forms of behavioral activation" (Robbins & Everitt, 1995: 703), the plausibility of such processes has increased. For example, polecat (*Mustela putorius*) young, when reared alone, engaged in more than three times the social play than socially reared animals, and the author argues that the threshold for play sequences was lowered (Diener, 1985).

Related to this is the finding that many mammals that typically engage in social play may, if deprived of a play partner, respond to less-preferred partners or even play with inanimate objects as if they were a social play partner. If a preferred play partner is present, such object play responses are reduced (Power, 2000).

5.4.4 Genetic Differences in Playfulness

If play is subject to natural selection, then individual differences in playful behavior should be at least partially attributable to genetic differences, irrespective of sex or species. Laboratory rats from different strains play fight to different extents, and this play can be differentially affected by experience (Siviy, Baliko, & Bowers, 1997; Siviy et al., 2003). Individual differences in locomotor play in laboratory mice are heritable (C. Walker & Byers, 1991) and suggestive evidence exists for horses as well (Wolff & Hausberger, 1994). As noted earlier, temperament differences among individual animals from fish to snakes to humans are increasingly reported (D. S. Wilson et al., 1994). Such individual differences, as well as those in the level of neurotransmitters such as dopamine, are related to the occurrence of play and exploratory behavior in mammals (Burghardt, 2001; Depue & Collins, 1999; Siviy, 1998; Vanderschuren, Niesink, & Van Ree, 1997). Consistent with this theory, C57BL6 mice have more dopamine neurons than DBA2 mice and show more novelty-induced exploratory behavior than DBA2 mice (see also Cabib, Puglisi-Allegra, & Ventura, 2002; Depue & Collins, 1999). Rats would be the prime animals to test for exploratory and object play differences since different strains also vary in their dopamine concentrations (Depue & Collins, 1999). Recently, rats have been genetically selected for immature behavior (Brunelli & Hofer, 2001) and such a process, which may be prevalent in domestication, also shows the potential role of genetics and individual differences in playfulness. Rats have been bred for their laughter response when tickled, showing a marked change from baseline rates in four generations (Panksepp, Burgdorf, & Gordon, 2001).

Finally, if playlike behaviors can be selectively bred, then it is possible to begin looking at a host of associated changes in other behavior patterns—development, sociality, physiology, anatomy, and so forth. Silver foxes (*Vulpes vulpes*) bred just for social tameness showed many seemingly unrelated changes in morphology and behavior and became more playful, even doglike in their attachment to people (Trut, 1999). That this is not an isolated finding is suggested by studies such as those by Gariépy, Bauer, and Cairns (2001). These authors selected mice for high or low social aggressiveness. In a very detailed and careful study, they found that selection led to developmental changes in timing of behavior (heterochrony) so that low aggressive lines showed greater differences early in ontogeny (days 28 and 42) than as adults (day 280), especially early in the selection process. The authors point out that this is an example of neotenization of behavior, and it would be interesting to see how play behavior was altered, especially since domesticated laboratory mice are not very playful compared with rats (Pellis et al., 1991; Poole & Fish, 1975). Mink (*Mustela vison*) selected for approach (confident) reactions to people explored people more quickly and maintained much closer distances to them than did mink undergoing selection for avoidance (fear) of people (Malmkvist & Hansen, 2002). More interestingly, confident selected mink approached and played with novel objects more, explored tubes in a maze more, and would more readily approach and eat a new food.

Such studies may not always have clear results, but the differences can be illuminating as well. Girard et al. (2002) selectively bred mouse strains for high and low wheel-running activity and found, rather surprisingly, no effects on offspring size, litter size, growth, maternal behavior, or other life history measures. However, the mothers did not have access to running wheels during the time they were raising babies and the authors predict that when they have such an opportunity, reproductive performance in the high-running strain will suffer.

5.4.5 Neural Substrates of Play

Does play have its own neural underpinnings, a play module as it were, as suggested by Panksepp (1998a) and advocated for most behavioral systems by evolutionary psychologists (Buss, 1999)? Such play would most likely be tertiary play. Or is play a product of a special set of circumstances that could arise in almost any behavior system? Indirect evidence supporting the modularity view comes from studies indicating a specific motivation for play of certain types (Rasa, 1984). Contrary evidence comes from those who see play as derived from incipient behavior (intention movements; Lorenz, 1981), the emergence of prefunctional behaviors in ontogeny (Hogan, 1988, 2001; Kruijt, 1964), or conflicts between behavior systems (Pellis et al., 1988). These views would all reflect primary process play. We are far from an answer, but neural play circuitry would have evolved from the latter processes and thus we might expect both specific and more diffuse neural underpinnings for play of different types, different phases of the sequence, and in different species, as suggested in section 5.4.1.

The role of the brain in play has been reviewed repeatedly, although unfortunately most neuroscience research on play is based on play fighting in rats (Panksepp, 1998a; Panksepp, Siviy, & Normansell, 1984; Pellis & Pellis, 1998a; Siviy, 1998; Vanderschuren, Niesink, & Van Ree, 1997). Integrating this work with the literature on exploration and responses to novel objects led to the following conclusions (Burghardt, 2001), which are updated here with more recent studies.

The brain is central to behavioral performances as well as the cognitive, emotional, and motivational attributes of a behavior. The role of play in cognitive processes is often supported by pointing out that play is found most commonly in those birds and mammals that have large brains relative to their body size and are considered "intelligent" (Fagen, 1981). In fact, recent claims by primatologists make it sound as if we have all the answers and the skepticism underlying this book is misplaced: "The bigger the brain, the longer the life, the more the need for social living, the more complex the environment (including the social environment), the greater the importance of play"

(Poirier & Field, 2000: 262). The passage continues with all sorts of bald claims about the adaptive value of play, although the only reference for these claims is 30 years old (Poirier & Smith, 1974). Regardless, play and curiosity could be marks of intelligence as well as necessary for the development of a sophisticated mind. The view that play is most common in large-brained animals is rarely evaluated rigorously; what we find when we do such an assessment has not been very encouraging to date.

First, we need to determine if species with larger brains *are* more intelligent. This certainly is an attractive hypothesis: "The larger the brain, the more likely that the animal's behavior will appear highly intelligent. Large-brained species will have large motor repertoires and will construct complex, variable, goal directed motor sequences. They will recognize foods, mates, and other objects by means of object images constructed from varied perceptual features. Large-brained species will also exhibit greater ability to accommodate motor actions to environmental stimuli, and their behavior will appear more volitional" (K. R. Gibson, 1990: 109). Such putative relationships were at the heart of much comparative psychology; the problem was the lack of a general measure of learning ability that could be used across species with widely differing morphological, ecological, social, neural, and phylogenetic attributes. Thus a more limited emphasis on behavioral specializations of an ethological and ecological nature became popular (Burghardt, 1973). Nevertheless, the general pattern of increased brain size relative to body size among those mammals and birds considered most intelligent or adaptable in behavior is hard to ignore. Efforts to develop a comparative measure of intelligence that can cut across species are still under way; a recent attempt claimed to be promising for primates from prosimians to *Homo sapiens* is the transfer index, a measure of an animal's ability to learn from prior learning (Beran, Gobson, & Rumbaugh, 1999). The correlation with brain size is high enough (0.83) that the authors used it to predict the intelligence of extinct hominid species.

Even if we accept that animals with larger brains are, in some important senses, smarter or more cognitively adept than other species, does this relate to play? Claims are frequent that play seems more common in, if not limited to, species with large brains (Fagen, 1981). Whether this holds across diverse species in a taxonomic group will be explored in later chapters. However, play frequency and complexity can differ among even closely related species (Pellis et al., 1991; Poole & Fish, 1975) and among those with similar relative brain sizes. Thus one needs to look at the kinds of play shown and all the other factors enumerated earlier.

Additional complications arise. Domesticated species generally play more frequently than their wild counterparts (Burghardt, 1984), but they actually have considerably smaller brains, controlling for body size. Indeed, domestication seems to lead to a decline in brain size of about 30 percent (Kruska, 1987a,b; R. W. Williams, Cavada, & Reinoso-Suárez, 1993). A comparative analysis of relative brain size and play showed that while at the level of order or family, a relationship may hold (chapters 8 and 9,

Byers, 1999a), when studies controlled for phylogenetic effects or focused on closely related species differing in playfulness, the correlation largely disappears (Iwaniuk, Nelson, & Pelles, 2001). The ratio of neocortex size to play in primates does appear to be positively related to social play but not locomotor or object play (Lewis, 2000). Thus overall brain size may not be a crucial factor in variation in playfulness (Burghardt, 1999).

There are also some other problems with the putative relationship between play and cognition. Dogs raised in social isolation appear to be more social and curious than normally reared dogs, especially in novel situations; they are less neophobic. However, Melzack and Thompson (1956) showed that such dogs are rather stupid; even the most trivial items amuse them persistently. There is also considerable evidence that habituation—rapid boredom with stimuli—is a good measure of intelligence and can be used to test preverbal infants with considerable success (Colombo, 1993). If becoming bored is a sign that one has mastered what there is to know or do with an object, then choosing stimuli that are more complex might be a way to maintain play. This is exactly what Piagetian mastery play is directed toward. K. V. Thompson (1998) has advocated a similar process that she terms self-assessment; animals play to perform and "practice" a skill until it becomes mastered or too easy (habituated, boring).

However, curiosity killed the cat. Rodents, fish, and tadpoles that stray too far from secure retreats for food have been shown to be more at risk of predation (e.g., Sih, 1992), and evidence for predation as a cost of play was documented earlier. Thus prudent behavior has some advantages over the exuberant "joy of life" excitement many view as the essence of play. Clearly, some ecological contexts might have facilitated play in some contexts and opposed it in others.

It is also becoming increasingly apparent that external stimulation, including environmental enrichment, can enhance brain development in many domestic species (Kolb & Whishaw, 1998). In humans, the role of experience in brain development, including critical periods, is not very well known and there are fears that making large claims in this area in the public news media is both premature and could backfire (R. A. Thompson & Nelson, 2001). Nevertheless, Thompson and Nelson provide a summary graphic (figure 5.6). Play may be one of the ways that such enrichment has neural effects, although the diversity of types of play and the extent of play in mammalian species that have been studied preclude generalizations. What is interesting here is that the plasticity seen in the ontogeny of individual animals can be mimicked by rapid genetic changes in several thousand years of domestication (Ebinger, 1995) or even several generations (Trut, 1999). Perhaps, however, the role of the brain in play is not tied to the development of the "higher" brain centers, but true to its resemblance to instinctive behavior, is more accurately traced in its origins to the brain systems that underlie motivated and emotion-laden instinctive behavior: the striato-pallidal complex (basal ganglia) and the limbic system (Burghardt, 2001). These areas, along with

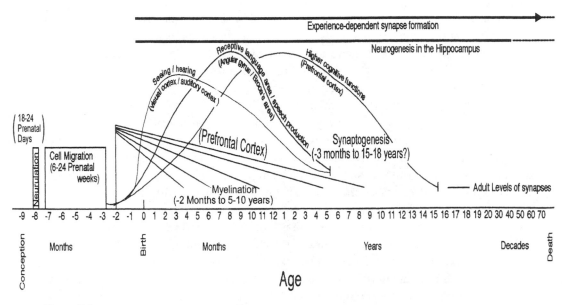

Figure 5.6

The course of human brain development showing the differential pacing of different brain regions and psychological processes. (From R. A. Thompson & Nelson, 2001)

the prefrontal cortex, link emotion, motivation, and reward conditioning (Cardinal et al., 2002). Some neuroscientists vigorously maintain that the mammalian brain evolved conservatively and while "Special [natural?] selection for specific functions does occur, . . . it is a minor factor compared to the large-scale covariance of the whole brain" (Finlay, Darlington, & Nicastro, 2001). However, convincing evidence for a more modular "mosaic" evolution of brain structures based on function exists (e.g., Barton & Harvey, 2000) and play may be a tool to investigate the "play module" idea.

The amygdala may be particularly important in social play. For example, lesions of it in male rats on days 7 or 21 led to decreases in social play one or two weeks post operation compared to sham and ventral hippocampus lesions (Daenen et al., 2002). However, social behavior deficits in adult rats were seen only in rats lesioned in the amygdala on day 7, suggesting a neurodevelopmental defect. This and other studies (Burghardt, 2001; Pellis & Iwaniuk, 2002) suggest that the amygdala and social play may be related. A phylogenetically controlled comparison of adult social play and brain size in primates found that amygdala size was correlated with sexual but not nonsexual play, whereas nonvisual neocortex was related to both play types (Pellis & Iwaniuk, 2002). Brain imaging studies will become much more feasible with small animals in the future and the possibilities are intriguing. For example, not only is laughing a stereotyped fixed action pattern response in people (Provine, 2001), the amygdala of the limbic system is itself activated when people hear laughter (Sander & Scheich, 2001) regardless of their mood or attentional state, suggesting that markers of play (as well as of distress such as crying) are neurologically and developmentally largely preprogramed responses in behavior systems.

The basal ganglia, prefrontal cortex, and dopamine systems are critically involved in the reward, anticipation, memory, social modulation, and goal orientation seen in the often fast-paced, contextually sensitive, and anticipatory responses (Pellis & Pellis, 1998a; Kolb, Pellis, & Robinson, in press) of locomotor, object, and social play. Dopamine is the main neurotransmitter involved in play and is heavily concentrated in the basal ganglia and its associated structures implicated in play. In fact, the substantia nigra and ventral tegmental area (involved in motor systems) have perhaps the highest concentrations of dopamine in the brain (Butler & Hodos, 1996). Dopamine is involved in reward, pleasure, arousal, and motor patterning systems of motivated behavior. Exploiting the sequential organization of play sequences (i.e., initiation, engagement, and termination) may be useful in clarifying the role of dopamine in play. This literature cannot be explored in depth here, but it is important to note that the studies of Siviy and others suggest that dopamine antagonists reduce play, but agonists do not always facilitate play. To resolve this inconsistency, Steve Siviy proposes that dopamine might be involved in the initiation of play through anticipated reward systems and summarizes suggestive experimental evidence. He speculates that:

Stimuli which predict a playful experience would result in increased activity in the dopaminergic mesolimbic pathway. This would result in an increased release of dopamine in mesolimbic terminal areas, such as the prefrontal cortex and nucleus accumbens, resulting in energization of the animal and behavior patterns that would increase the probability of a playful interaction. Because of the diffuse nature of noradrenergic, serotonergic and opioid pathways, these systems are likely to exert a more modulatory influence on how the play bout will unfold. Increased noradrenergic activity may enhance the ability of a rat to focus its attention on the task at hand (i.e., playing), while increased opioid activity may enhance the pleasure associated with playing. For all this to happen, serotonin levels must also be low. (Siviy, 1998: 232)

However, these systems are also involved in many nonplay activities, suggesting that the pathways involved may overlap, converge, or reinforce a variety of behavior systems. This supports the plausibility of the hypothesis that play originated in the initiation and execution of instinctive behavior sequences in which motor performance was itself rewarding. Repeating the behavior could enhance performance through practice in changing contexts and produce modifications of sequences based on experience. It turns out that the neural circuits underlying species-characteristic behavior may be very conservative and just a single gene may alter regulatory neuromodulation (Katz & Harris-Warrick, 1999). We also now know that 30 minutes of social play in rats can affect gene expression and lead to measurable changes in a variety of brain areas,

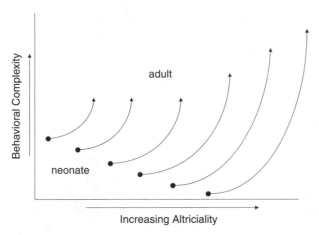

Figure 5.7

Behavioral complexity as an adult is often greater in animals born in a more altricial state and with a longer period of dependency on parents. Juvenile play then has a greater opportunity to become developmentally important.

including those in the striatum, tectum, somatosensory cortex, and hypothalamus (Gordon et al., 2002). Further work showed that such play experience leads to elevated levels of brain-derived neurotrophic factor (BDNF) in the amygdala and dorsolateral frontal cortex (Gordon & Panksepp, in press). BDNF is a key modulator of neuronal development and plasticity, and the authors suggest "that play may help program higher brain regions involved in emotional behaviors," a tertiary play process, even though decorticate rats can still play. Soon brain imaging during play may be possible. Child developmental psychologists are now attempting to study how to "turn on" genes that promote favorable outcomes (B. Brown, 1999). Although these initial discussions are based on the effects of stress, poor nutrition, and other markers of poor environments, a focus on the value of more active behavior such as play may not be far behind. Solid experimental work here will result in perhaps the most powerful tool available to assess the role of play in our lives.

Nevertheless, the difficulty in isolating specific long-term benefits of play may lie in the fact that play may provide only one of several ways to enhance behavioral, physiological, and cognitive performance, a facilitation that is not essential in every case (Burghardt, 1984; Fairbanks, 2000). In any event, neural systems underlie playful acts and may be affected by them. However, the origins of play do not solely lie within the brain itself. The brain is the mediator of animals' responses to their environment as well as a record of a long evolutionary history. If adult behavioral complexity, not just intelligence, is important in playful species, then slower rates of behavioral development, and opportunities for play, may both relate to behavioral complexity (figure 5.7) and be involved in the transition between primary and secondary play (see figure 5.1).

If play is closely linked in the brain to the many behavioral systems that underlie the repertoire of any species, then it is not surprising that play in any species resembles its normal behavioral repertoire, and that it often shares the motivational, perceptual, behavioral, and emotional pathways of these systems. The shift from play fighting to serious fighting can be thus understood in neural terms, although the detailed mechanisms are still not known.

The research discussed in this chapter and in part II supports the view that locomotor, object, and social play derive from different behavioral systems associated with the species-characteristic behavior of animals. The nature and the amount of play are not random, but are tied to a species' phylogeny, ecology, ontogeny, and normal behavior. Object play is typically predatory in carnivores and manipulatory in extractive foragers (such as cebus monkeys). Social play can be composed of chasing, stalking, wrestling, and other behavior patterns that may be derived from sexual, aggressive, or predatory behavioral systems. Many of the most playful species show all three major types of animal play, although the mix may differ. This level of complexity seriously hampers attempts to uncover the ancestral forms of play. It is because of such complexity in the internal dynamics of play that it is necessary to turn to other factors that may explain the origins and early evolution of play.

6   The Genesis of Play: An Integrative Approach

There are many factors influencing play, and chapter 5 considered those dealing with establishing the adaptive function of play; some costs of play; the development and genetics of play; and motivational, emotional, and neural substrates of play. All these topics could only be touched on, but it was important to present some findings relevant to understanding the true complexity of play, while not, I hope, signaling the impossibility of gaining some understanding of play as an evolutionary phenomenon. In this chapter, life history, social, and ecological factors underlying play will be covered, along with the difficult issues of energy and physiology that together help us predict in what species and contexts play should be found. It thus expands on conclusions reached in my first theoretical play foray.

The frequent observation that play occurs only when animals are in a "relaxed field," sated, warm, content, and so forth supports the view that play of various kinds originated in animals with (1) sufficient metabolic resources; (2) an efficient aerobic system; (3) a relatively familiar and often risk-free juvenile environment; (4) the ability to accumulate more energy than can be shunted to growth; (5) escape from the need to behaviourally thermoregulate to bring the body to the optimum for vigorous behavior; (6) innate precocial exploratory and arousal mechanisms; (7) specific motivational and behavioural systems; and (8) relatively high survival rate of offspring (Burghardt, 1984: 31).

6.1   Parsing the Problem of Energy and Play

The concepts of energy and excess (surplus) energy have been used in the analysis of play. However, the energy concept has been used to refer to quite different aspects of animals and their behavior, leading to considerable confusion. Four of these uses are outlined in table 6.1. For example, Spencer used energy in his surplus energy model to refer to stored nutritional reserves such as fat (use 2) that would be expressed in vigorous behavior (use 1), tapping into instinctive behavior patterns organized in neural motivational systems centers (use 3). The possible role of play in enhancing the arousal level of animals to an "optimal" state represents a fourth use. Throughout this book we

Table 6.1

Various connotations of the terms *energy* and *surplus* in reference to play

Meaning of Energy	Manifestation of Surplus
1. Vigorous (energetic) behavior	1. Elevated activity level (hyperactivity, fidgety, persistent, rambunctious)
2. Metabolic potential (i.e., from food)	2. Excess available metabolic reserves (e.g., fat)
3. Derived from specific behavior system(s) (e.g., motivation, drive, or instinct)	3. Extreme accumulated specific motivation, drive state, or action-specific energy (e.g., predatory, sexual)
4. Level of general behavioral arousal or responsiveness	4. High level of alertness

Source: Based on Burghardt (1984)

have seen application of all four energy concepts to play, and it is time to differentiate them.

The brain uses much of an animal's energy expenditure, up to 20 percent or more, even when it is only 2 percent of the body mass (S. T. Parker, 1990). Thus brain size and metabolic rate seem to be closely related (Burghardt, 1984). Endothermy (warm-bloodedness) is a trait that demands considerable energy and is also related to metabolic rate. I have discussed the details of this relationship elsewhere and noted that animals with very low metabolic rates and those relying on anaerobic metabolism (table 6.2), play less (Burghardt, 1984, 1988b). Very small mammals, such as shrews, have high metabolic rates and high thermoregulatory costs because of their large surface-to-mass ratio. These attributes may preclude having sufficient metabolic energy available to expend in playlike behavior that may not efficiently serve immediate survival needs. Very small (< 10 g) endotherms are rarely recorded as engaging in play. For example, many studies have experimentally determined the serious constraints on small hummingbird behavior (e.g., López-Calleja & Bozinovic, 2003). Likewise, nutritionally and energetically rich diets may foster play by providing both "excess" metabolic resources and the time for play. Time spent foraging may reduce or eliminate the time for play. Consider the parallel with laborers who work long, physically exhausting shifts for minimal pay. Such laborers are not the ones traveling the world searching for exciting adventurous play, such as trying to travel around the world by balloon, building a faster yacht, or climbing the highest mountains. Similar time constraints could explain why play in adult harbor seals (*Phoca vitulina*), generally solitary and locomotor, is more common outside the breeding season (Renouf, 1993).

Metabolic rates in animals are not easily measured. Basal metabolic rate (BMR), resting metabolic rate (RMR), and maximum metabolic rate (MMR) all have different measurement demands (see A. F. Bennett, 1982; Burghardt, 1984; Nagy, 1982, 2000) and different implications for the ability of animals to express the energetic behavior

Table 6.2
Metabolic terms related to behavioral performance in animals

1. *Basal metabolic rate* (BMR). Minimal metabolic rate when fasting under optimal environmental conditions. All metabolic rates may be measured indirectly (by oxygen consumption) or directly (by heat production).

2. *Standard metabolic rate* (SMR). Minimum metabolic rate at a given temperature in an ectotherm (no heat production).

3. *Resting metabolic rate* (RMR). The level of oxygen consumption or heat production when an animal is not engaged in any overt activity.

4. *Field metabolic rate* (FMR). Daily total energy costs of animals in the field engaged in all normal activities. Often measured by estimating CO_2 production using the doubly labeled "heavy" water method.

5. *Aerobic metabolism.* Release of metabolic energy by use of external (gaseous) oxygen, generally obtained through breathing, lungs, and associated systems.

6. *Aerobic scope.* The range of oxygen consumption rate between minimum and maximum aerobic oxygen utilization.

7. *Anaerobic metabolism.* Release of metabolic energy by the breakdown of stored glycogen to lactic acid. This occurs when insufficient molecular oxygen is available through ordinary respiration.

8. *Anaerobic scope.* Rate of lactic acid formation during the onset of vigorous activity (usually the first 30 seconds).

9. *Anaerobic capacity.* The amount of lactic acid formed during longer activity bouts, usually those preceding exhaustion.

10. *Maximum sustainable activity.* The amount of exertion (often measured in duration or rate of locomotion) an animal can carry out continuously without building up an oxygen deficit.

11. *Energy costs of activity.* Amount of energy (joules or calories) needed to perform a given behavior. Should be measured as a *rate* of energy output, as in metabolic rate (i.e., watts = joules/second) (P. Martin, 1984). The net cost of activity is the difference between the total energy expenditure rate during activity minus the RMR.

12. *Total metabolic scope.* The difference between BMR and maximum combined contributions of aerobic and anaerobic metabolism.

we are predisposed to label as play (table 6.2). Brain size in mammals appears to be more related to factors such as arborality and patchily distributed diets than metabolic rate (McNab & Eisenberg, 1989). Thus arboreal hunters have bigger brains than terrestrial counterparts. For example, a rather arboreal jaguar (*Panther onca*) has a relatively larger brain, but lower metabolic rate, than lions (*Panthera leo*) or tigers (*Panthera tigris*). Metabolic rate may thus be influenced by physiological demands that have little effect on brain size. Metabolic and brain size processes and measures will be invoked later in interpreting play diversity and play origins. For now it is sufficient to state that the complex relationships among brain size, metabolic rate, body size, endothermy, and thermoregulation argue against any simple relationships between play type or amount of play with any of these factors.

It is, however, germane to ask how energetically costly play is in the more playful mammals in which it has been measured. In cats, play seems to add about 4 percent to the energy budget (P. Martin, 1984b) and this has been used to argue that play is not very costly (and also perhaps not very important). This may not be a generalized conclusion because some species, such as pronghorn antelope, may expend so much energy in play that if the energy went into growth, it would produce 7 percent more growth at 12 weeks of age; play consumes about 20 percent more energy than that used at rest (Miller & Byers, 1991). Thus, allocation of time and energy in play is not a simple matter and warrants careful analysis (Bekoff & Byers, 1992). Such allocation has been a focus of optimization theory in recent animal behavior, including optimal foraging theory, where energy intake and time and energy expenditures, sometimes accompanied by risk, are central considerations.

One consequence of an energy constraint on behavior is that the energy costs of locomotion vary with the medium in which the animal operates. All things being equal, swimming consumes the least energy, flying is next in energetic cost, and terrestrial running or walking the most costly (McNab, 2002). These differences can be considerable. A 10 g mouse expends almost 30 times more energy walking than a 10 g bird does as it covers the same distance (McNab, 2002). Since swimming is less costly than terrestrial locomotion, play may be more common in aquatic animals, and in animals operating in both aquatic and terrestrial media, play should be more common and less energetically constrained in water. This is a robust prediction from an energetics perspective that has received support (Burghardt, 1988b). For example, marine mammals such as seals and dolphins are perhaps the most playful of all mammals (Fagen, 1981).

Although up to this point only stored metabolic energy and stored excess energy (fat) have been discussed, it is clear that metabolic energy is essential but not sufficient for play. For example, some species may have much stored energy and be fat, such as sloths, yet do not engage in vigorous behavior (use 1 in table 6.1) because of physiological constraints. One would not expect a fat tortoise to rapidly chase a sibling and wrestle with it. Vigorous behavior, which is often viewed as essential to play, may be an anthropocentric conceit based on the time scale of our own behavior. Thus gentle or slow-motion play might be ignored or viewed as not "real" play. This bias must be put aside when a comparative approach is taken. The nature of play and its "vigorous" execution must be viewed from the perspective of the performer, not the observer.

Play as a response to activity in specific neural centers or, more generally, the activation of specific behavioral systems, is another aspect of energy that has led to confusion (use 3 in table 6.1). The concept of energy accumulation as a driving force for the amount and intensity of behavior is an old idea easily transferred to the play context. Thus, as described earlier, Lorenz and other early ethologists advocated an action-specific energy (Lorenz, 1956, 1981) or action-specific potential (Thorpe, 1956) underlying the performance of species-specific behavior patterns (instincts). These were more molecular versions of the more general basic "drives" of the experimental psychologists (Mook, 1996). The application of such ideas to play goes back to other advocates of both instinctive energetics and surplus energy theory. The prolific and influential psychologist William McDougall (1924) described an energy model of instinct very similar to Lorenz's and also was an advocate of surplus energy. Spencer himself advocated a somewhat mentalistic neural center model in his surplus energy theory. In all these models, lowering of the stimulus threshold needed to elicit behavior, owing to deprivation (e.g., hunger) or lack of opportunity to engage in specific behavior patterns, was a key factor in both instinctive behavior and play (e.g., hunting).

Play as a consequence of a general arousal process (use 4) is invoked in models in which play is viewed as a way of self-stimulation or relieving boredom. Play may be a means of achieving optimal arousal for proper neural and physical development. For example, it has been argued that the exaggerated locomotor and rotational play in harbor seals promotes vestibular stimulation (Renouf & Lawson, 1986), which may be reinforcing or pleasurable. In the general arousal view, play is of interest primarily as an activation process that gets the animal "up and going" and is controlled more by internal endogenous factors (see play criterion two) than external stimuli, although the latter may induce or facilitate play, as when objects or partners are made available (Spinka, Newberry, & Bekoff, 2001). In young rats, postsuckling arousal leads to increasing behavioral activation so that at weaning the pups leave the nest (Gerrish & Alberts, 1997). These authors argue that play is activated at this time. There are considerable observations showing that play in young animals is more prevalent after feeding (e.g., Burghardt & Burghardt, 1972). Human infants, after feeding, initiate and maintain play with the mother, not vice versa (E. Blass, personal communication, 2002). Blass writes: "In order for the brain to develop, it requires punctate stimulation—what better time or way to get it than after a meal."

An old relationship in psychology may be relevant here: the Yerkes-Dodson law. In this relationship, task learning is viewed as influenced by arousal level (Mook, 1996). Easy tasks are most quickly learned and performed when the animal is highly aroused, whereas difficult tasks are most easily learned and performed when the animal is rather relaxed and not highly stressed or too "motivated." In other words, if you are starving when you are in a class on a difficult subject or taking a difficult test, you are not likely to do well, which is why there are recommendations to get a good night's sleep and have a nutritious breakfast before an important exam, meeting, or performance. For most tasks, however, research suggests that moderate arousal or anxiety may be most effective. The Yerkes-Dodson law has two implications for the study of play. First, it suggests that there is no single optimal set point of arousal, but that it is contingent on the behavior being performed and the state of the animal. Second, play might be a sensitive indicator of how an individual perceives a task or function. Thus the arousal level seen in play devoted to physical tasks such as simple locomotion may be quite different from that underlying more cognitively demanding play. Some graylag goslings (*Anser anser*) were more innovative than others in that they learned to trigger a food dispenser at 8–11 months of age while siblings in the social group never did learn and could only scrounge food dispensed by the "producers." These innovative geese were quicker at learning to uncover hidden food at 4–6 weeks of age and also had higher fecal corticosterone levels at 2 weeks of age (Pfeffer, Fritz, & Kotrschal, 2002). The authors note the research indicating that corticosterone is an arousal response to stress. The moderate levels seen in the goslings may be associated with enhancement of neural synapse reorganization and dentritic growth as well as priming memory formation and consolidation. Nevertheless, the response repertoire of the species, its metabolic and physiological capacities, and individual differences in arousal need to be considered in any comparisons.

In sum, the different and often subtle and indirect ways in which energy concepts are used in studying play need to be distinguished and the relationships among the uses recognized.

6.2   Ecology and Play

A variety of ecological factors seem to influence the type and amount of play seen in natural settings. These factors can be divided into two types: those involving the evolutionary adaptations of the species (e.g., typical diet and habitat) and those related to the changing circumstances in which the animal finds itself (e.g., food shortages). There is a wide range of evidence supporting the conclusions drawn here that will not be presented in detail. It is the implications of the conclusions that are important for the working model to be used in evaluating the comparative evidence. The "ecology" of the juvenile animal during development was considered previously. As is evident, however, brain size and metabolic rate covary with ecological relationships, and so determining causal pathways is not straightforward at all.

6.2.1   Some Species Attributes and Play
Body size within an animal lineage is often related to the complexity of behavior shown, although this is often related to brain size (K. R. Gibson, 1990). It is also possible that in larger endothermic animals, the metabolic costs of thermoregulation are reduced and thus more metabolic resources are available for behaviors that are less essential for immediate survival than in smaller species in a lineage (Burghardt, 1988b). Furthermore, larger species generally have longer life-spans, including longer juvenile periods in which behavior patterns and skills preparatory for adulthood can be developed, rehearsed, and consolidated, as well as longer adult periods during which continuing and changing social and ecological circumstances need to be accommodated (S. T. Parker & Gibson, 1990).

Within mammals, brain size, metabolic rate, and perhaps intelligence, are related to dietary niche. Carnivores, omnivores, and frugivores that forage widely for dispersed food resources have larger brains than more specialized species or those foraging on widely available food such as leaves (K. R. Gibson, 1990; McNab, 1980). In a modeling approach to the evolution of generalists, specialists, and plasticity, van Tienderen (1997) concluded that specialists only evolved when "selection within habitats was severe and optimal phenotypes for different habitats were widely different" (p. 1372). In contrast to such "hard selection," in all other contexts varied levels of generalists evolved. In other words, resources were more abundant and risks lower.

Active pursuit of prey or cooperative hunting is also associated with large brains and high metabolic rates (Jerison, 1973; McNab, 1980), as in dolphins and otters. These are often mammals in which play is quite common (Fagen, 1981; Iwaniuk, Nelson, & Pellis, 2001).

Among the animals reported to engage in considerable object play, extractive foragers (animals needing to search in leaf litter or under rocks for small animals, in flowers for nectar, in tree trunks for insects) are prominent (Fagen, 1981). Raccoons (*Procyon lotor*) and cebus monkeys are typical examples. Scavengers, such as condors (*Vultur gryphus*) and other vultures, are also highly playful, as I discovered at the Knoxville zoo (Burghardt, 1996). Why might this be? Such animals need a complex repertoire of motor actions, object recognition skills, learning abilities (for various food items and appropriate search and capture responses), and the capability to apply them in diverse settings. Quantitative studies on evaluating the complexity of various behavior patterns and the variability needed in their effective deployment should, by this perspective, be related to the amount of play seen. Methods used to assess the complexity of a seemingly trivial task, such as how gorillas eat thistles (Byrne, Corp, & Byrne, 2001), could be used to obtain empirical data to test this idea.

Furthermore, foraging typically takes up much of the daily routine of extractive foragers in the wild. In captivity, the need to engage in serious foraging is typically reduced because of the high-energy and easily obtained nutrition that is provided. Thus manipulating objects in a playful manner might be a consequence of time, energy, response availability, and exploratory motives.

6.2.2 Ecological Conditions and Play

In a class study of a captive group of nine baboons (*Papio hamadryas*) at the Knoxville zoo, play was recorded along with weather and temperature. Temperature varied little and did not affect play, but weather did (Lori Taylor, unpubl. ms, 1992). Play was more frequent on sunny than cloudy or rainy days for most of the nine play behaviors recorded. Considerable studies confirm that play of all types is readily curtailed in both the wild and captivity in times of food shortage, climatic adversity, social upheaval, and chronic stress (Burghardt, 1984; Caro, 1988; Sommer & Mendoza-Granados, 1995).

John Robinson carried out an extensive field study of seasonal variation in time budgets in capuchin monkeys (*Cebus olivaceus*) but did not publish data on play (Robinson, 1986). However, when he heard me speak about this phenomenon he looked up his data based on 14 months of intensive sampling of more than 15,000 intervals. Sure enough, during the 5 month (Dec. to Apr.) foraging stressed dry season, play was 18 times less frequent than during the following 5 wetter months (0.32 percent and 5.88 percent respectively) (John Robinson, personal communication, 2001). Exposing young rats to just several cat hairs (Panksepp, 1998a) suppressed play fighting dramatically (figure 6.1). Exposing pregnant rats to a cat greatly reduced pup survival and those that did survive grew more slowly, explored less, and had memory deficits (Lordi et al., 2000). Although play was not measured, it is likely that this would have been affected as well.

Play appears, then, to be a low-priority behavior that is readily curtailed when issues of more immediate survival are at stake. Recent work continues to support this conclusion, which is one of the most robust findings in the play literature. The effects of this phenomenon are shown in diverse ways, however. The amount of play seen in wild populations can be used as a measure of habitat quality in Hanuman langur monkeys (*Presbytis entellus*). A population with food and water shortages that is forced to eat low-quality leaves rather than energetically rich fruits played only about 15 percent as often as animals in a high-quality habitat, and the bouts of play were shorter (Sommer & Mendoza-Granados, 1995). Similar population differences in social play in rich and poor habitats have been reported in other species, such as squirrel monkeys (J. D. Baldwin & Baldwin, 1974). In this species, laboratory experiments in which food was reduced decreased play and replicated the field findings (J. D. Baldwin & Baldwin, 1976). Conversely, supplementing food to free-living Belding's ground squirrels increased social play in litters as compared to unprovisioned controls (Nunes et al., 1999). Comparable results were found with meerkats (Sharpe et al., 2002). Thus, measures of play might be useful in assessing the effects of captive environments as well.

Two experiments on the role of food restriction on social play in rats came to conclusions that might seem to contradict the role of food shortage in reducing play. In the first, rat pups were undernourished by removing them from the mother for 12 hours a day and placed in an incubator. This went on for the first 23 days of life, after which the pups were weaned and they, along with normally reared rats, were given unlimited rat chow (Loranca, Torrero, & Salas, 1999). Both male and female pups were significantly lighter than the controls, but from days 20 to 60 (puberty is at day 40) the undernourished rats played more! However, the authors noted that the incubator environment led to sensory deprivation, the mother-infant bond was altered, and overall, females played more than males, reversing typical findings. Thus interpretation is difficult. Another experiment was more transparent and was done on the same strain (Wistar) of rats (Almeida & de Araújo, 2001). During the lactation period, moms and

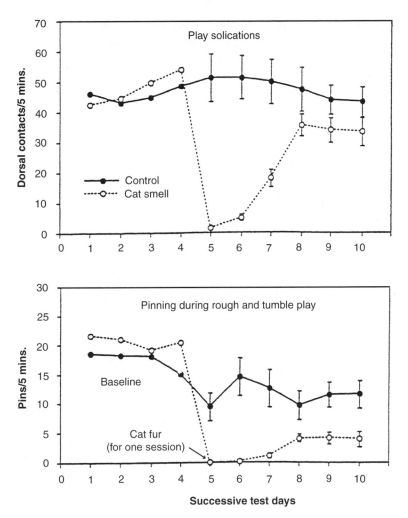

Figure 6.1
Exposure to cat hair on test day 5 abolished social play in rats for several days. (From Panksepp, 1998a)

pups were given either a diet with normal protein (16 percent) or low protein (6 percent), weaned at 21 days, and play observed during week 5. Half the low protein reared rats were switched to the normal diet and half stayed on the low protein diet. The results were clear. Rats continually malnourished played less than the controls and previously malnourished rats played more, replicating the previous study. The authors found the increased play in the now normally fed rats to be a compensation effect. They concluded by referring to studies showing "that chronic malnutrition causes less social involvement, less happy affect and greater timidity in free play in children during the first four years of age." (p. 50).

Marine mammals have high basal metabolic rates that are thought to be due to the high rate of heat loss in cold aquatic environments (S. D. Thompson et al., 1987). California sea lions (*Zalophus californianus*) show this feature particularly clearly, and young pups have very high metabolic rates along with a high growth rate (S. D. Thompson et al., 1987). Sea lion behavior, then, should be particularly sensitive to the availability of metabolic resources. A remarkable test of the relationship between nutritional resources available to pups and various measures of behavior in a wild population occurred when an ongoing study of maternal investment in sea lions was "interrupted" by an El Niño event in 1983 (Ono, Boness, & Oftedal, 1987). During an El Niño year, the major fish species eaten by sea lions decrease, and the adverse effect of this food shortage was reflected by the increased time mothers spent foraging and their higher metabolic costs during this period. This unusual "natural experiment" is described here in some detail.

Mother sea lions give birth to a single pup on land, where they nurse the pup periodically after extensive foraging trips. Pups are not active until after 3 weeks of age, at which time they associate in groups and begin to explore, swim, and play in tide pools and coves. Individual pups and mothers were marked and monitored, the pups being weighed shortly after birth and after about 2 months of age. Milk intake was measured using a deuterium-labeled "heavy water" method. Pup behavior was recorded and included such categories as resting, suckling, on-land social and object play, swimming, and aggression.

The study took place over several years, with the El Niño event in the middle. The authors expected that pups born during the El Niño year would maximize energy reserves by suckling more, resting more, and engaging in less high-energy behavior patterns. An exception was aggression, which they thought would be increased owing to stress and competition. Comparisons were made during the year preceding El Niño (PRE), during El Niño (EN), and for the 2 years following El Niño (POST1 and POST2). The PRE period was a good year for food resources, as was the preceding year. The POST1 period was a good year preceded by a poor food-resource year (EN). Differences between the PRE and POST years could then be attributed to the effect of El Niño in the year before the POST1 period.

The results were many, but in terms of play they were clear. Pup weight gain was significantly lower in the EN year compared with all other years, and infant mortality was also much higher in the EN year. The number of pups born was lower in both the EN and POST1 years. The POST1 effect was due to the poorer condition of females in the year following the EN. Pup behavior changes across the PRE, EN, and POST1 years were revealing. Active behavior significantly decreased between PRE (32 percent of observations) and EN (25 percent) and POST1 (22 percent). This category was further broken down into aquatic activity (including social play in water), aggression, and play on land. Neither aquatic activity nor aggression changed at all over the 3 years. Play on land, however, declined sharply and significantly between PRE (9.1 percent) and EN (5.2 percent). Furthermore, a significant further reduction occurred in the POST1 year (3.0 percent). The authors, in explaining their unexpected results concerning play, interpreted them as follows: The decline in terrestrial play was due to the effects of long-term food deprivation. The absence of a decline in swimming and aquatic play was due to the importance of learning swimming skills for later survival. The fact that play on land is energetically more costly than aquatic locomotion may be a more proximate reason why terrestrial play declined and fits the comparative findings more satisfactorily.

6.3   Social Factors and Play

6.3.1   Social Organization and Play

Except for some differences in male and female play fighting, the role of social organization beyond that of the family unit does not seem to be a major factor in the kind of play exhibited. Certainly locomotor and object play are not highly related, as would be expected. More social imitation in play might be expected in species where there are opportunities for observing conspecifics in nonamicable circumstances (Miklosi, 1999). Similarly, adult social play outside of courtship contexts should be more common in species that live in social groups, although many highly social animals, including primates, show little adult social play.

My skepticism about claims for play being more prevalent in highly social species is based on the fact that black bears we studied and orangutans both engage in intense play fighting as juveniles, although both are highly solitary species as adults (outside of the mother-infant bonds) and adult-adult play is rare. Thus the argument that play fighting in bears and orangutans is preparation for dealing with adult social life did not appear valid (Burghardt, 1982). In short, while the complexity of adult social organization may have some influence on the secondary features of play, it appears to have little to do with the occurrence of play itself.

Recently this paradox was at least partially resolved in a comparative analysis of adult-adult play in primates. Pellis and Iwaniuk (1999a, 2000a) found that such play in primates, both in sexual and nonsexual contexts, is more prevalent in primates with loose, even somewhat solitary, social organization in which unfamiliar animals interact, than in primates with more rigidly hierarchical or nuclear family types of social organization. Similarly, in a comparative analysis of sixteen macaque monkeys (*Macaca*), the type of social organization seemed related to the duration and nature of play fighting, with hierarchical species having briefer and more asymmetrical play fighting than the more loosely organized and more socially tolerant species (Thierry, Iwaniuk, & Pellis, 2000). Data were not available for many species; studies such as these suggest where additional data are needed.

6.3.2   Male and Female Play

Sex differences in play are common, especially in social play, and have been much reviewed (Power, 2000). In fact, being able to explain sex differences in play fighting (amount and type of play fighting and choice of partners) is considered one of the greatest accomplishments of modern animal play research (Caro, 1988; Pereira & Fairbanks, 1993; P. K. Smith, 1982). That is, males typically play fight more than females, do it more roughly, and prefer to play with other males. As discussed earlier (Biben, 1986), squirrel monkey males engage in directional (winner-loser) play fights more than females, who engage in nondirectional play fights. Hormones are involved in sex differences (Beatty, 1984), but the nature of the differences needs to be understood through a more contextual approach than merely a causal physiological one.

The extent of the differences in male and female play seem related to the importance of fighting among males in polygynous societies, with more male play fighting in polygynous species, or species in which males disperse and have to establish themselves in new groups. For example, it has been claimed that in gorillas, vervet monkeys (*Cercopithecus* sp.), and galagos (Galaginae) males fight more than females and also prefer male play partners that are equal or older in age, whereas females play fight less and preferentially choose younger play partners. On the other hand, ringtailed lemur females and males play fight equally. This difference was attributed to the fact that in the first three species male reproductive success is directly tied to fighting ability (Fairbanks & Pereira, 1993). Although the relationship seems to hold over a diversity of primates, only a few have been looked at and the pattern needs to be studied much more closely. For example, Richardson's ground squirrel is highly polygynous, with much male-male fighting during the breeding season; however, there is no difference between males and females in aggressive play fighting (Pasztor et al., 2001). The role of phylogeny and sociality in play fighting is thus complex and perhaps quite evolutionarily labile, as shown by a comparative analysis of muroid rodents (Pellis & Iwaniuk, 1999b).

One of the most intriguing studies of sex differences in play involves the spotted hyena, in which females are dominant to males, larger than males, and have external genitalia that look like the male scrotum and phallus. Females also have higher levels of circulating androgens (testosterone) relative to males than is typical in female mammals. What about play in this species? Juvenile hyenas have been observed for locomotor, object, and social play (Pedersen et al., 1990). Females were markedly more playful than males in several measures of locomotor and social play, but did not differ in object play. In no context did males play more than females. Although this reversal of the typical male-female difference may suggest that androgens play a causal role, gonadectomized hyenas did not differ from intact animals in playfulness. Circulating hormones were not measured, however.

Sex differences in morphology and behavior are undoubtedly related to hormones, hormone levels, and development, but the ways in which hormones function in different species need much more research, and the story seems to be getting less, not more, clear (Forger, 2001). For example, the development of attack and defensive moves in rat play fighting differs for males and females, with the former becoming rougher at puberty (Foroud & Pellis, 2003). For this to occur, males need neonatal androgens. However, while ovariectomy at either birth or weaning led to females adopting the male type of rough behavior, neonatal testosterone had no effect on females (Pellis, 2001). On this last point there are conflicting results (Hotchkiss et al., in press) both in rats and other species (e.g., sheep; Orgeur, 1995) in that androgenized (testosterone loaded) female fetuses become masculinized, including in play.

Hormones may be particularly important in restructuring neural circuits and behavior at puberty in rodents and other species (Romeo, Richardson, & Sisk, 2002), the time during which male social play often begins to differ from that of females. A recent, and disturbing, study highlights the value social play may have as a marker of proper development (Hotchkiss et al., in press). A commonly used fungicide, vinclozolin, is an environmental endocrine-disrupting chemical. To assess its possible role in mammalian sexual differentiation, neonatal rats were injected with vinclozolin and play and other behaviors recorded. Although general activities were not affected, at 7 weeks males showed female-style play. The incorporation of play into standardized behavioral measures (Rohlman et al., 2001), may prove useful in assessing the effects on children of neurotoxic environmental chemicals, which are becoming increasingly prevalent across the world.

Sex differences in object and locomotor play exist in some species, but are typically less marked. In young kittens, the increase in object play from weeks 8 to 12 is much greater in males than females (P. Bateson, 1981). If this object play is practice for effective predation, then such a difference cannot easily be explained, since both sexes need to be effective predators, females perhaps more so since they need to feed their litters. It is interesting that females from mixed-sex litters showed as much object play as their brothers. This could be due to prenatal hormonal influences ameliorating sex differences that may have no functional role in play at all. In fact, object play in cats has been shown to be unrelated to adult predatory efficiency (Caro, 1980). Individual and sex differences in play have not been looked at in terms of either learning ability, innovativeness, or production of novel behavior, although this seems a worthwhile issue. For example, in some species females and in others males, are the most innovative (Pfeffer, Fritz, & Kotrschal, 2002).

Human beings are somewhat of an exception in that gender differences in physical and locomotor play, object play, sociodramatic play, games and sports, where play occurs, and other aspects of play have been extensively documented (Pellegrini & Smith, 1998; Power, 2000). Although it was controversial in the past (e.g., Harper & Huie, 1978), the view that there are evolved male-female differences in human play that interact with social training and culture can no longer be doubted. The fact that male vervet monkeys (*Cercopithecus aethiops sabaeus*) prefer to play with "boy" toys (car and ball) and female monkeys with "girl" toys (doll and a pot) suggest that human object play may also been shaped by sexually differentiated selection pressures (Alexander & Hines, 2002). However, as with play fighting, sex differences in play are most likely derived secondary processes.

Insofar as male and female animals have different foraging, social, reproductive, habitat, and predatory avoidance behavior based on genetic predispositions, hormones, and neural connections, sex differences are to be expected (Burghardt, 1988b). The existence of differences between the sexes does not prove that some behaviors are designed for training or practice or that they originated for such purposes. The fact that play fighting may have diverse roles in behavioral development speaks to the evolutionary ease with which it can gain or lose functions (Pellis & Iwaniuk, 1999b). The increase in risky play and risk-taking behavior in human adolescents, especially males, may have a hormonal basis in postpuberty changes (Spear, 2000). A note of caution on hormonally mediated sex differences needs to be added. In mammals with multiple offspring in litters, males and females may be influenced by hormones produced by their intrauterine siblings or, more specifically, by the position of a fetus to neighboring fetuses. Many effects have been noted, particularly masculinized behavior (Ryan & Vandenbergh, 2002). Such effects are also found in human multiple births and effects on sex typical play may prove of considerable interest.

6.3.3 Play as a Signal

Play is often studied only from its consequences for the player, but perhaps play is also a signal to others (Chiszar, 1985). Play may have been selected for in social species and in those with parental care as a sign that offspring and other conspecifics are healthy, adequately nourished, and ready to learn or even obtain their independence in various behavioral realms as they move toward weaning or other forms of adult independence. In addition, playful animals may be socially more friendly with one another.

Another twist is found in squirrel monkeys, which play in peer groups somewhat removed from adults. Although the monkeys are rather unattentive to predators while engaged in their vigorous games, they also emit loud play vocalizations during this time, vocalizations that do not seem to have any role in the play itself (Biben & Symmes, 1986). The function of this signal appears to be to alert adults, who are now more vigilant themselves while the play bouts occur (Biben, Symmes & Bernard, 1989). Many mothers know that when the rambunctious sounds of play cease, it is time to check what mischief or danger might be afoot.

The actual form of the play may be less important since it has been co-opted for another use. Ghiselin may have an important point when he writes: "many of our educational practices may be seriously misguided as a result of folk psychology. Little boys playing soldier are not practicing to slaughter their fellow men, but furthering peaceful life in their own society. The way to make a killer out of a child is to put him into a genuinely competitive situation—such as Little League baseball" (1974: 261).

The next extension of this idea is to sexual selection. Males and females both want friendly, helpful mates, and a sense of humor is often high on the list of desired traits (Buss, 1999). If such qualifications also include a playful attitude toward life, then play can be a force in sexual selection (Chick, 2001). This possibility moves play into the realm of artificial selection. If true, it may also lend plausibility to H. G. Wells's view about the future of human evolution (chapter 1)! Nonetheless, play as used as either a propensity, an attitude toward life, or as an approach to life is a fascinating proposition and could explain the enigma of adult play. Play is indeed used in courtship in some primates (Pellis & Iwaniuk, 1999a), in other species as claimed by Groos (1898), and may underlie precocial play in other animals as well.

6.4   An Instructive Comparison: Mammals and Ectothermic Reptiles

Why has play been historically most described in and attributed to mammals? Several processes have been suggested earlier favoring play in animals and these may be the very factors most likely to be found in combination in mammals. They are listed in table 6.3 as a contrast between "typical" mammals and their closest sister taxa, nonavian reptiles. These factors have been incorporated in an evolutionary-developmental perspective called the surplus resource theory, or SRT. Developed earlier in Burghardt (1984, 1988), some of the core ideas have been extended and elaborated by Coppinger and Smith (1989) and Nigel Barber (1991). Surplus resource theory incorporates physiology (e.g., activity metabolism, thermoregulation), life history (e.g., parental care, altriciality, food niche, ontogenetic shifts), behavioral repertoire (complex movements, behavioral diversity, social organization), and psychological factors (stimulus deprivation, habituation, exploration). It is focused on the origins of primary process

Table 6.3

Contrasts between typical mammals and ectothermic reptiles relevant to the occurrence of play

Mammals	Reptiles
Metabolic and physiological contrasts	*Metabolic and physiological contrasts*
High basal and resting metabolic rates	Low basal and resting metabolic rates
Rich vascular system and highly oxygenated blood	Fewer capillaries and less efficient blood-transport system; blood capable of carrying far less oxygen
Capable of sustained, vigorous activity (aerobic metabolism)	Vigorous behavior sporadic and short lived; reliance on anaerobic metabolism for sustained vigorous activity
Endothermy provides high resting metabolism, allowing rapid onset of vigorous play. Costs of overcoming inertia increase with weight	Ectothermy allows a low-energy (conservation) life-style; the behaviors needed to raise body temperature to aerobic optimum are often incompatible with play
Young, growing animals typically have higher basal metabolic rates than adults	Young, growing animals do not have basal metabolic rates different from those of adults
Rapid recuperation after sustained activity; short period of vulnerability to predators	Recuperation from sustained activity (to normal lactic acid levels) measured in hours; extended period of vulnerability to predators
Exercise increases cardiovascular and endurance functions	Little evidence of physiological benefits of exercise; exercise may even be harmful
Developmental contrasts	*Developmental contrasts*
Young often enter world with incompletely functional sensory and motor systems	Young enter world with highly functional sensory and motor systems
Neonates have food, heat, shelter, and protection provided by parent	Neonates must provide most, if not all, their own resources
Neonates have many motor and perceptual systems restricted to juvenile period (e.g., sucking)	Most neonatal behaviors show clear continuities with adult motor and perceptual systems
Neonatal/juvenile period available to develop or perfect functional social, feeding, locomotor, or antipredator skills	Most behaviors necessary for adult survival are highly functional at birth; however, skill improvement can occur
Young typically interact with, and individually recognize, siblings, parents, or other colony members	Young often have little opportunity for social interaction and learning involving siblings, parents, or other colony members
Relatively determinate juvenile growth allows for excess metabolic energy in "good times"	Relatively indeterminate juvenile growth leads to most energy intake being channeled into growth
Neonates capable of sustained activity	Even well-fed neonates have less endurance than adults
"Relaxed field" common in juveniles	"Relaxed field" rare in juveniles

Table 6.3

(continued)

Mammals	Reptiles
Behavioral and ecological contrasts	*Behavioral and ecological contrasts*
Play occurs most frequently when juveniles are well fed, often after feeding	Postingestion behavior in reptiles is characterized by lethargy, distended stomachs, and basking or holing up out of harm's way, often due to greatly elevated metabolic rates needed for digestion
Relatively few offspring, especially in the more "playful" families	Relatively more offspring, with higher mortality, over equivalent adult life-spans
Almost universal highly developed parental care with social bonding between parents and offspring and among siblings	Typically only rudimentary parental care or none, with little development of social bonds with offspring
Large brains with extensive neocortex needing more energy and allowing more variable and flexible behavior	Smaller brains with less neocortex needing less energy, but constraining behavioral complexity and flexibility
Limbs and faces allowing more complex manipulatory and communicative responses	Limbs (or none at all) and faces with more limited motor and expressive capacities
Often extensive integration within and across perceptual and motor systems	Often limited integration within and across various perceptual and motor systems

play as well as the conditions in which derived process play will flourish. The most important of these are classified and depicted in figure 6.2.

6.4.1 Energetic Differences

The first suite of traits affecting play involves energetic differences between ectothermic reptiles and mammals. Reptiles typically are metabolically constrained from performing vigorous, energetically expensive behaviors, especially those of any substantial duration (A. F. Bennett, 1982; McNab, 2002). This constraint is due to their low resting and maximal metabolic rates, limited aerobic capacity, and long recovery times after anaerobic expenditures. Reptiles have about 10 percent of the metabolic rate of a comparably sized mammal (although most reptiles are much smaller than mammals). Both metabolic rates and typical body sizes are further reduced in amphibians. It is difficult to deduce the vigor and endurance of animals at the dawn of tetrapod vertebrate evolution since atmospheric oxygen may have reached 35 percent in the Late Paleozoic (Graham et al., 1995), and possibly fostered radiation of many groups, giganticism, and novel behavioral phenotypes. Small body size leads to greater heat loss and expenditures of time and energy to maintain body temperature by moving back and forth from cool to warm locations to behaviorally thermoregulate (ectotherms) or to obtain calories to maintain body temperature (endotherms). It is relevant

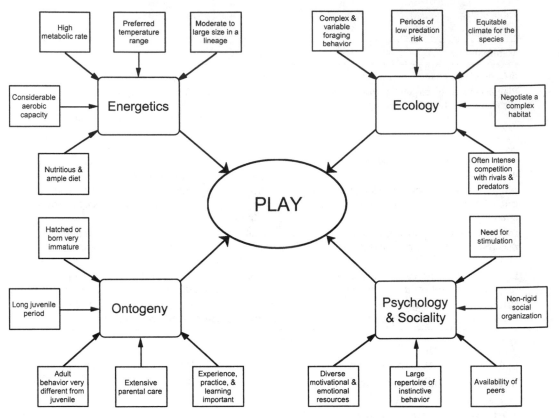

Figure 6.2
The surplus resource theory model of play indicating the major factors underlying playfulness.

to note that the traditional theory that endothermy evolved via increasing metabolic rate has been questioned through experiments that increased the metabolic rate of *Varanus* lizards to the mammalian level with no substantial increase in metabolically produced heat or thermogenesis (Bennett, Hicks, & Cullum, 2000). Taken together, in ectotherms these factors inhibit the performance of, and selection for, costly, vigorous, playlike behavior that has limited utility or none.

Very small mammals also appear to play less than larger species in a lineage (Burghardt, 1988b). Countering this trend is the fact that play occurs more often, at least in mammals, in juveniles that have not yet reached adult size. In these cases the animals, such as rodent pups, have grown fur and become better able to thermoregulate, and secondary derived processes may underlie playful behavior.

Phylogenetic factors and other traits such as type of parental care and quality of diet complicate the role of metabolism in play. Among primates, folivorous species (animals that eat leaves) with diets containing few calories play less than frugivorous (animals that eat sugar-laden fruit) or omnivorous species that eat diets containing more energy (Fagen, 1981). They also typically have lower metabolic rates and such relationships with diet hold across many species (McNab, 1980; Burghardt, 1988b).

Studies also suggest that the endurance of young reptiles, such as snakes, is less than that of adults and this may be related to lowered blood oxygen-carrying capacity (Pough, 1977, 1978). Furthermore, studies on a diverse set of lizards and a turtle show that growing neonatal ectothermic reptiles do not have higher basal metabolic rates than adults, whereas the energy costs of growth are considerable in mammals and birds and thus these young animals have higher metabolic rates than adults (Nagy, 2000). These differences also make the costs of vigorous behavior such as play much higher for ectothermic reptiles. On the other hand, feeding induces greatly increased metabolic costs in reptiles (Secor & Phillips, 1997; Wang, Busk, & Overgaard, 2001), often tenfold over resting BMR, that mitigate the propensity to vigorously play after feeding found in many mammals. Furthermore, the necessity for reptiles to use anaerobic metabolism for vigorous activity greatly increases post-exercise metabolic costs and recovery (Hancock, Adolph, & Gleeson, 2001), which probably increases the risk of predation. In fact, reptiles rarely ever perform at maximal capacity and do so "only in situations that have a critical impact on fitness" (Hertz, Huey, & Garland, 1988: 927). Still, they incur the high behavioral costs of thermoregulation in order to "be prepared" for emergencies and thus, as the authors suggest, are "more like Boy Scouts than Olympians" (Hertz, Huey, & Garland, 1988: 934).

6.4.2 Life History Factors

The second suite of characteristics involves developmental factors, almost all of which revolve around the limited parental care and attendant precocity of juvenile nonavian reptiles. With the exception of all crocodilians, most neonatal reptiles are not cared for by their parents (Shine, 1988). Consequently, immediately upon birth or hatching, they must devote their activities to obtaining food, finding shelter, avoiding predation, and growing rapidly. This limits the safe time or opportunity for practicing or perfecting behaviors (motor abilities, perceptual-motor coordination, and social skills) to be used in an uncertain future. Most young reptiles are very small, and selection will have shaped abilities that enhance juvenile survival, such as remaining quiet and inconspicuous. Such behaviors are, of course, incompatible with vigorous play. There is also no source of high-fat, high-protein nourishment available at little cost, as in juvenile birds and mammals.

Although nonavian reptiles are highly precocial and superficially resemble and behave like miniature adults, they nonetheless may learn many things as they go about their serious activities. Reptiles also grow as rapidly as food resources allow; unlike mammals and birds, there is no necessary age-defined period of youth. Young reptiles, unlike young mammals, typically do not get fat; again, they just grow as fast as food resources permit. This characteristic of reptiles is termed indeterminate growth. Reptiles convert a higher percentage of assimilated energy to biomass and thus can grow on a smaller ration than a mammal.

Given plentiful food, however, endotherms can add weight at a higher rate than an ectotherm amniote; this might be a major benefit of endotherm parental care. N. Barber (1991) has advanced a "brown fat" hypothesis in which vigorous play is a means for well-provisioned young mammals to avoid obesity through increased heat production (thermogenesis), a view very akin to Spencer's surplus energy theory. Although there is no supportive play data, thermogenesis could be a primary play process. Thermogenesis can be induced by high-fat diets (Bachman et al., 2002) as a means of obesity resistance. More controversial evidence also implicates fidgeting and related activities as a major factor in thermogenic resistance to obesity in humans (Levine, Eberhardt, & Jensen, 1999). In any event, obesity is not a problem for wild reptiles, although many captive reptiles of the larger species are often fed excessively rich or abundant food, leading to overweight, lethargic adult animals. How could a mechanism to reduce fat through play evolve when, for example, simply reducing caloric intake would seem to be simpler? We know that there is a complex Lipostatic (fat-sensing) system that aids in regulating fat storage in mammals, though rather loosely in humans (Mercer & Speakman, 2001). "Some mammals appear able to cope with excess energy by burning it off" (p. 102). Why not just eat less? Well, consider fruit-eating animals that must take in lots of food (and energy) to meet their protein requirements. "Rather than store the excess as fat they burn it off by flying" (p. 102). Thus mammals, as compared to reptiles, have many more mechanisms to produce surplus activity that could lead to play. Interestingly leptin, a hormone regulating body mass and energy output in mammals, has been shown to increase preferred body temperature, activity, and metabolic rate in fence lizards (*Sceloporus undulatus*); at the same time they ate less but did not differ in weight gain from controls (Niewiarowski, Balk, & Londraville, 2000).

The last life history characteristic I will mention is that reptiles typically have large litter and clutch sizes, with both smaller neonates and higher juvenile mortality than endotherms. Thus, any delayed benefits of play would be less important than current risks.

Since reptiles have a low-energy life-style and a limited capacity for extensive, vigorous movement, they also may not suffer the adverse consequences of not moving or being otherwise unstimulated for extended periods. Parental care may have led to animals being kept in protected, but often boring (nonstimulating) burrows and nests. Performing activities or responding to siblings may have been a means to increase arousal and consequent neural and muscular activity during the active development of the neural and morphological systems that are more precocially developed in reptiles. Ancestral mammals would have used various instinctive behavioral repertoires available to them, not because they needed to be practiced, but because they were the legacies of a more precocial ancestry and were a means to increase arousal and sensorimotor stimulation.

6.4.3 Behavioral and Ecological Factors

Certain kinds of complex ecological and social interactions and operations upon the environment seem to characterize the more playful species. For example, object play is found most often in active predators, scavengers, extractive foragers, and generalist feeders that rely on manipulation by limbs and mouth. Reptiles do not have the rich repertoire of possible movements of limbs and face seen in many mammals. The lack of parental care may have prevented the evolution of social bonding and affiliation in reptiles to the extent that it is seen in birds and mammals (MacLean, 1985), and thus social play is less likely than object and locomotor play. It is interesting that it is in those reptiles with more variable diets and active foraging techniques, such as soft-shelled turtles (Burghardt, 1998a; Burghardt, Ward, & Rosscoe, 1996), that more exploration, curiosity, and sometimes play are found. The same probably holds in fish (part II).

6.4.4 Surplus Resources and Play

The various kinds of differences (metabolic, developmental, neural, behavioral, and ecological) help explain why some groups of animals play and others do not. As a guide to identifying behavior in nonavian reptiles that could be candidates for traditional-appearing play, I have used the above and related physiological, psychological, and life history contrasts to predict that mammalian or avianlike play in reptiles should be rare and occur only in specific contexts in which those factors facilitating play in mammals and birds are also present. This exercise also provided suggestions of mammalian groups in which we would expect to find the most complex play and the most time spent in play (Burghardt, 1988b). A series of predictions was supported that suggest that many of the factors listed earlier are associated with the occurrence of play and may in fact have facilitated its evolutionary origin. For example, as indicated earlier, since less energy is needed for locomotion in water than on land, aquatic mammals should be particularly playful—and they are. The first play we confirmed in reptiles was in aquatic turtles (Burghardt, Ward, & Rosscoe, 1996; M. Kramer & Burghardt, 1998), supporting predictions made a decade earlier (Burghardt, 1988b).

Thus metabolic, behavioral, and ontogenetic (e.g., available time) resources are involved in incipient play and may have been the basis for the first inklings of playlike behavior, only some of which, through natural selection, were elaborated into complex and functional play.

6.5   The Surplus Resource Theory of Play

6.5.1   Four Important Processes Underlying Play

The preceding sections have shown that a simple or unitary functional, neural, developmental, or ecological explanation of play is improbable. The fact that social play is most prevalent in some animals, object play in others, and locomotor play in still other species, along with varying degrees of overlap, underscores the complexity in behavior that meets the five play criteria. The many subdivisions of these general play types and the elaborations found, especially in apes and humans, also are consequences of evolutionary processes and biological properties that vary among animals, even within placental mammals. This makes it likely that the initial advantages of incipient playlike behavior did not involve any particular functions, such as perfecting later behavior, increasing endurance, or facilitating behavioral flexibility.

Four main factors appear to underlie play in animals and some of these may be necessary, although not sufficient, for play to occur: (1) There is sufficient metabolic energy (both energy stores and the capacity for sustained vigorous activity). (2) The animals are buffered from serious stress and food shortages, which is especially important in species with a prolonged development until reproductive age (e.g., young animals are well cared for by parents). (3) There is a need for stimulation to elicit species-typical behavioral systems or to reach an optimal level of arousal for physiological functioning (e.g., there is susceptibility to boredom). (4) There is a life-style that involves complex sequences of behavior in varying conditions, including diverse and unpredictable environmental and/or social resources (e.g., generalist species should play more with objects than those with more rigid, specialized behavioral repertoires).

Play in all species, then, including human beings, will be most prevalent when there are excess resources along with appropriate evolved motivational, physiological, and ecological systems. Play can evolve independently whenever physiological (including neural), life history, metabolic, ecological, and psychological conditions, in conjunction with a species' behavioral repertoire, reach a threshold level. Play then appears, and its fate depends on its consequences in the lives of animals. As seen in later chapters, specific types of play are beginning to be mapped on evolutionary trees to trace their path, just as other traits of animals have been tracked through time.

6.5.2   Parental Care, Relaxed Selection, and Play

The evolutionary processes that led to the extensive parental care found in mammals and birds are, like the evolution of endothermy, little understood. Although ectothermic reptiles, specifically lizards and snakes, have evolved some parental behavior toward eggs and offspring multiple times (Shine, 1988), it was not till the advent of endothermy that parental care reached the high levels of complexity seen in birds and mammals. Ted Case (1978) argued that while postnatal care occurred before endothermy evolved, endothermy was necessary for its radiation. Furthermore, care of precocial young preceded the evolution of small, helpless altricial young and may have originated from larger reptilian ancestors, which were longer lived and better able to defend their offspring. Also, as we have seen, larger endotherms are less energetically constrained and thus could devote more "excess" energy to offspring care. In addition, as Case (1978) points out, they are more energetically able to have relatively large precocial young. The scenario that Case (1978) advocates is the following: early mammals were shrew or mouse sized. Being energetically constrained, they could only produce small eggs relative to body size as do reptiles, but unlike reptiles, they could only afford to produce undeveloped altricial young that needed extensive postnatal care. The main constraint here was the larger, more complex nervous system in endotherms. Although dated in many ways, Case's scenario raises questions that the study of play may help answer.

However it occurred, it is in the transition to extensive parental care that the need to distinguish between primary and secondary processes in play becomes critical. More specifically, I propose that the advent of parental care led to the deterioration of some aspects of neonatal response systems through less precise functional motor patterns, the lowering of the stimulus thresholds necessary to elicit such responses, and the broadening of the range of effective stimuli inducing such ethotypic behavior. In addition, the increased aerobic metabolic capacities resulting from endothermy modified or even reorganized developmental processes so that incipient play and other experiential avenues were not only available to some species, but may well have had to be exploited by them for continued survival to replace lost, suppressed, or maturationally delayed response systems.

In this way, new response patterns could arise that would themselves be retained by natural selection if they had an advantage over animals with different modes of response. For example, if natural selection is continually honing predatory skills so that less successful juvenile predators starve or are otherwise less fit than more skilled predators, once selection is removed, the mechanisms for capturing prey should show a reverse process and become less precise. Individual developmental processes involving both maturation and experience may become necessary and animals able to be developmentally flexible should have an advantage over those that are not.

A prediction would be that domesticated cats removed for generations from preying on live animals would be less competent hunters as juveniles than nondomesticated small cats. Among gartersnakes (*Thamnophis*), we have shown that species specializing in aquatic prey capture fish more efficiently than those that are prey generalists or earthworm specialists. Experience, however, can make up for some of the deficits in terrestrial prey specialists (Burghardt & Krause, 1999; Halloy & Burghardt, 1990). In fact, experience-altered prey preferences are themselves heritable in snakes (Burghardt, Layne, & Konigsberg, 2000), so natural selection could act upon such plasticity rather than the behavior and preferences themselves. Indeed, the importance of practice and repetition in all sorts of behaviors, including the most "hard-wired" or "innate" behavior in animals from flies and frogs to birds and mammals, is becoming increasingly documented in developmental psychobiology (DeVoogd & Lauay, 2001; Fentress & Gadbois, 2001; Hirsch et al., 2001; Oppenheim, 2001). The effectiveness of such practice and experience will often prove to be heritable and thus open to selection. Since natural selection operates less intensely on neonatal behavior after the evolution of parental care, play may evolve some role in refining behavioral performance and capability and become itself a heritable trait. This removal of the operation of selection on the original role of a behavior also provides an opportunity for it to operate on different aspects of behavioral phenotypes.

The longer the developmental period before effective adult action, the less need there is for rapid maturation of behavioral systems and the more drawn out the process can be. A secondary process of play derived from the primary processes outlined earlier would be supported if research showed that vigorous rough-and-tumble play of young rats and dogs enhances adult performance, promotes socialization, or increases behavioral flexibility. However, it is precisely because the more primary processes of play have been ignored that predictions made from secondary processes have fared poorly. An example of an important primary process derived from SRT would be the role of metabolic rate or parental care in production of "surplus" behavioral "mutants" that could in turn be selected ontogenetically and phylogenetically. An apparent secondary process derived from a detailed consideration of primary processes is based on the claim by Byers and Walker (1995) that there is a correlation between the onset of vigorous motor play and the age at which permanent long-term changes occur in the muscular and cerebellar systems of several species of domesticated animals. If play is essential or even useful in establishing these permanent physiological systems, then a secondary process has been established. If the play behavior is a mere accompaniment to this developmental process, with no causal role, then it is but another primary process.

6.5.3   Play as a Joint Outcome of Genetics, Experience, and Selection

Today we know that phenotypic expression of behavior patterns is a complex epigenetic outcome of interactions and feedback occurring at many levels from allele to protein synthesis (gene expression) to behavioral performance and social experience. Selection can operate on all these levels and more, at least indirectly. Therefore, play may have a subtle yet profound role in behavioral ontogeny and phylogeny that we are only beginning to appreciate.

The study of the role of play in development should initially focus on the primary processes leading to behavior satisfying the five criteria for play. Increased endurance, functional endothermy, parental care, major developmental changes during early ontogeny, and lack of sufficient external stimulation facilitated incipient playlike behavior. As the trends favoring this incipient play expanded, play acquired secondary functions, including those underlying greater behavioral, social, and cognitive complexity through the evolution of secondary processes. Animals that are initially more precocial in their behavior systems will have less opportunity for primary playlike processes to occur because of their great need to engage in highly functional behavior early in life. The contrast between the "efficient" mouse and the less efficient neurodevelopmental course of the more slowly maturing laboratory rat (Whishaw et al., 2001) may be reflected in the fact that laboratory rats are among the most playful rodents, and mice are among the least. Such developmental processes underlying the probability of low-cost inefficiencies could reflect the model that G. C. Williams (1991) suggested.

Could play be a "random process generator" or a means of creating "adaptive variability" (Sutton-Smith, 1999)? Fagen (1974) compared the variability seen in play with that found in genetic systems. Play shows similarities to chromosomal inheritance in that play sequences may display recombination, fragmentation, translocation, and duplication. Such variation, if inherited, can provide raw material for natural selection to operate. Perhaps play also produces behavioral mutants. Recent molecular genetics methods that produce overexpressed alleles, add genes, or eliminate loci (gene knockouts) allow further genetic metaphors. Such genetic-like events may be involved in the ancestral stages of primary process play as well the production of novel behavioral phenotypes that, if adaptive, can become secondary or tertiary play. Such processes may involve surplus resources producing dispersal phenotypes that not only expand their ecological niche but also produce novel adaptations for surviving in new habitats (Geist, 1978).

However, much play is far from random, is species-typical, and seems to operate within tight boundaries. Pellis (1993) has shown how play fighting can differ among closely related species with little or no overlap. This suggests that play in these species may have become secondary process play and genetically fixed, whereas primary process play may be the source of more nonadaptive mutants. There is virtually no support for any of this speculation. Thus the challenge is not just to state that play creates novel behavioral phenotypes but to uncover the actual processes underlying such behavioral variation.

Neural and physiological changes resulting from experienced-based learning and plasticity may have opened up new possibilities for cognitive and emotional complexity in many mammals and some birds as compared to nonavian reptiles. For example, play among littermates in Belding's ground squirrels (*Spermophilus beldingi*) (figure 6.3) may help establish or consolidate kin recognition cues that later facilitate recruitment to aid in defense against predators in social mobbing species (Holmes, 2001). In this species littermates live in underground burrows until they are weaned and emerge on day 27, at which time social play is a prominent activity involving both littermates and

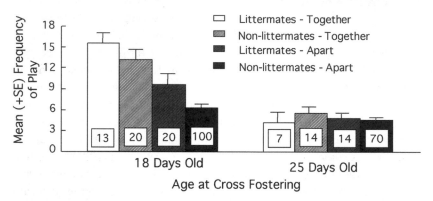

Figure 6.3
Play partner preferences in Belding's ground squirrels are influenced by kinship and familiarity. Animals were cross-fostered at 2 or 9 days before typical emergence from natal burrows. Mean play frequencies among pairs during the first 20 days above ground. Number of pairs of juveniles in boxes inside bars. (From Holmes, 2001)

other juveniles. Both genetic (kinship) and age-specific early experience (familiarity) influence the amount of play seen after pups emerge from nest burrows. How might these more advanced secondary processes have operated? Were they in fact tertiary processes? Could they have jump started a cognitive revolution? Such extensions are not the issue here since the focus is on the initial origins of play, but the consequences of such behavior may, as this question suggests, have important ramifications for studies of behavior, evolution, and neuroscience.

Even if play is more frequent and diverse in animals with larger telencephalons (or parts thereof), we still have to decide whether this is a circumstance supporting enhanced mental abilities, maintaining instinctive responses that are now far more plastic than ancestral states, or is a currently epiphenomenal or atavistic phenomenon, as suggested by the original surplus energy and recapitulation play theories.

According to SRT, play originated through nonadaptive indirect means (primary process), but could also have incorporated secondary processes that allowed behavioral and psychological abilities to shape new behavior and capacities, perhaps through positive feedback. A hallmark of mammalian behavioral evolution is the rapid diversification of behavior, the genome and the size of the telencephalon in a relatively short time span (geologically speaking) compared with many ectothermic vertebrates and invertebrates, whose core behavior patterns and abilities may have changed little over millennia in spite of often rapid microevolutionary adaptation. The persistence of core perceptual and behavioral systems as legacies from the past needs to be incorporated into our thinking more than it has been (Coss, 1991, 1999; Coss & Goldthwaite, 1995; Panksepp, 1998a).

But are mammals not vastly different from other vertebrates? Consider that physical and behavioral adaptations involving milk production and its delivery and ingestion are restricted to modern mammals. Facial expressions and vocal repertoire are also much more complex in all mammals than in the extant reptilian sister groups (squamates, tuatara, and turtles). The fine motor control of many parts of the body (limbs, digits, tail, snout, mouth, ears) almost simultaneously is probably more developed in many mammals (and some birds) than in ectothermic reptiles and amphibians. True, but the mechanisms underlying these differences may be more superficial than we typically think (Burghardt, 1988b). For example, play gets animals doing things, and doing things may cause rapid changes in dendritic spines (Coss & Perkel, 1985) as well as activating chemical changes and brain areas (Gordon et al., 2002). Animals capable of being more active and active in diverse ways are going to have many more opportunities for these brain changes to take place and lead to even more behavioral change in a positive feedback manner (see Petersen, 1988, for a provocative but little-known non-neural feedback model of play and Baldwin, 1896, for a recently resuscitated "organic selection" model).

6.5.4 Domestication as a Model of the Evolutionary Consequences of Parental Care

A parallel model for testing the evolutionary scenario of surplus resource theory is the course of domestication. Many of the processes postulated here as having occurred in juvenile mammals with the onset of parental care and the consequent buffering from the demands of life are also found in domesticated species. The match is remarkable. Price (1984) documented these processes completely independently of the theory outlined here. Domesticated species, such as dogs, are much more playful than their wild counterparts, even taking into account captive conditions. Many behavioral skills found in wild populations (wolves) show deterioration in domesticated forms (dogs). Domesticated dogs have larger litters and considerably smaller brains (Coppinger & Coppinger, 1998). In fact, it has been argued that most changes in the physical structure of domesticated dogs compared with their wolf ancestors are due to changes in rate of development, specifically the retention of juvenile traits or neoteny (paedomorphism). There is now evidence that those dog breeds most physically different from wolves also have the smallest and most juvenile visual signaling repertoire (D. Goodwin, Bradshaw, & Wickens, 1997). But studies of dogs in one category, working sheep dogs, provide a glimpse of the actual processes involved in relation to play (Coppinger et al., 1987). One type of sheep dog herds and moves sheep from place to place while the other type guards and protects sheep. These two types are behaviorally quite distinct and were bred separately in similar habitats for many generations. Adults of both breeds were observed. The herding dogs never exhibited social play approach behavior toward sheep but guard dogs did so frequently. Conversely, the herding dogs, but not guard dogs, approached sheep with the stalking behavior seen in early stages of predation. Furthermore guard dogs would not even hunt, let alone kill and eat, either live or anesthetized chickens, while wolves and herd dogs would. Thus guard dogs, through domestication, have lost the predatory sequence. The authors argue that during domestication the guard dogs were selected for a prepredatory developmental stage and treat sheep more as social playmates while herding dogs "retained at least a segment of the full ancestral predatory sequence" (Coppinger et al., 1987: 105).

The pattern of increasing playfulness as brain size decreases may be quite common. Kruska (1987a,b) has shown that in many mammals, domestic populations have brain sizes 5 percent smaller than wild populations after only a few generations. This is shown in both a rodent (bank vole, *Clethrionomys glareolus*) and carnivore (polecat). Ferrets were domesticated from wild polecats 2500 years ago and now have brain sizes 30 percent smaller than wild animals. The effects of domestication on brains result in a relatively greater decrease in neocortex and those brain areas involved in planning and problem solving as well as inhibiting impulsive, emotional, and instinctive behavior. Relaxed selection in farm or hatchery-reared animals can be rapid and dramatic and affect not only overall brain size but specific brain areas involved in various types of behavior (see Marchetti & Nevitt, 2003).

In chapter 5 behavioral genetic studies of domestic species showing changes that are due to selection in play and exploration were discussed. A careful study of play behavior in wild animals undergoing domestication might be a most useful method to see how buffering animals from the harsher aspects of existence may change the amount, type, and frequency of play as well as cognitive capacities. Similarly, studies of feral animals undergoing the reverse process would also be useful. In any event, it is important to be critically anthropomorphic, because it is all too easy to conclude that the more affectionate or compliant dog is smarter than the more elusive, unpredictable, high-strung wolf or devious coyote. In fact, hand-reared wolves are more insightful and better at problem solving and observational learning than dogs (Frank et al., 1989). Frank (1980) argues that wolves also have more stimulus boundness in the sense that selection has honed components of a behavioral system "responsive to only a narrow bandwidth of cues and releases highly stereotyped behaviors" (Frank, 1980: 394).

Perhaps only less smart animals were actively selected for domestication by human beings and thus they were selected to have smaller brains. This appears unlikely, as in the most careful study of the process of domestication by Belyaev and Russian colleagues (Trut, 1999). Merely selecting silver foxes (*Vulpes vulpes*) for tameness alone led, after 10–35 generations, to animals that showed marked changes in coat color, ear and tail morphology, more rapid sensory development (e.g., eyes opened earlier), and delayed onset of fear and the plasma corticosteroid surge. The foxes thus had a longer period for bonding with humans and other animals and showed much more interest and "friendliness" to people (which seems to include playful interactions) than the initial stock population. Although I could not find any data on brain size, cranial height and width were both reduced in the selected foxes (Trut, 1999) and brain measurements are planned (Trut, personal communication, 2001).

A nice statement of how domestication may have facilitated play and altered behavioral orgaization is provided by Coppinger et al. (1987: 104) in regard to the guarding sheep dogs where "play-bites and play-chases were apparently separable motor units of their behavior system that may be combined at any opportunity with other motor units to produce non-functional, non-systematic sequences of mixed social behaviors that strung together are commonly referred to as 'play' behavior."

Similarly, the initial forms of play in vertebrates are most likely derived from instinctive behavior patterns whose form and motivation are controlled by the basal ganglia and limbic system of the telencephalon and structures in the diencephalon. The rapid rate of evolutionary changes in endothermic animals, especially mammals, in brain size and behavioral complexity are remarkable and still little understood. One consequence may have been increased amounts of primary process play during periods of rapid speciation and diversification of mammalian lineages beginning about 65 million years ago. Surplus resource theory suggests that primary processes involved in play may have been a major engine in this rapid cascade of evolutionary change that led to increased behavioral diversity and later to cognitive complexity in endothermic animals (chapter 15). This may have occurred by natural selection for behavioral play variants that were then incorporated into serious endeavors and functions, so that the once playful behavior was eventually transformed and fixed so that it shifted to being outside the realm of play defined according to the criteria developed earlier.

The thesis here, then, is that after a period of evolutionary reorganization in behavioral ontogeny accentuated by the lengthening of parental care (Burghardt, 1988b), play came to facilitate rapid behavioral and mental development by providing altered phenotypes for natural selection to prune and shape. The motivational and emotional concomitants of play are probably, as neurological findings suggest, more conservative than the behavioral expressions, and so motivational and emotional concomitants of play will need to be studied along with play behavior. Ethologists, behavioral ecologists, and physiologists will need to consider the experience of play, ethology's fifth aim. To speak metaphorically, play is on a leash, yearning to be free.

In chapter 1 it was established that play is paradoxical, not to say ambiguous (Sutton-Smith, 1997), in many ways. We are on the path to understanding it, but the trail is still tangled with vines and hidden in mist. This chapter has ranged widely in the search for processes that may underlie playful behavior in order to at least help orient the directions that explorers of play might take using more rigorous methods. The view of play and its origins outlined here suggests that playlike behavior evolved episodically throughout animal evolution under suitable ecological and physiological conditions. Play, in this approach, is both evolutionary detritus and an evolutionary pump. Using the five criteria for play and the general features of surplus resource theory as a compass, it is now appropriate to explore and evaluate evidence on the diversity and radiation of animals and their many types of playful behavior.

II The Phylogeny of Play

7 The Path Through the Major Evolutionary Landscapes

7.1 The Complexities of Evidence and Phylogeny

In the following chapters, I review evidence about the occurrence of play in various groups of animals. In order to test the relationships outlined in chapter 6, it is critical to know what behavior patterns of which animals meet the play criteria. The amount of space devoted to a particular taxonomic group in part II of this volume is not related to how much we actually know about play in that group of animals. Since this book is oriented toward the genesis and origins of play behavior, the species that are most relevant for our examination lie mainly at the boundary between playing and non-playing animals.

Unfortunately, most play research has focused on what seem to be unequivocal and clear examples of play, prominent in the lives of their subjects; much of this has been well reviewed recently (Power, 2000). Part I has presented the case for a different approach, a bottom-up strategy that is necessary for understanding the processes leading to playful acts in the first place, not just their elaboration and usefulness after they are already present. Part I also ended with an articulation of surplus resource theory. The major value of SRT is in its possible helpfulness in predicting and explaining where we might find play or playlike behavior in the diverse animals of the world. Figure 7.1 shows the major lineage of vertebrate groups. There is still considerable controversy centered on the relationship among some major groups, such as turtles and mono-tremes (Zardoya & Meyer, 2003), but the current consensus view is depicted.

Most evidence for play and studies of play come from a small number of animals, primarily placental (eutherian) mammals, which constitute about 4300 of the one to two million animal species estimated to currently live on earth (Nowak, 1999). The vast majority of the examples in part I are from this group, but since this book is about the origins of play, it is important to have data from a wide range of taxonomic groups to test various views on the evolution of play. For example, Groos discussed possible play in many animals, although eutherian mammals dominated (Groos, 1898). However, by the time of Fagen's authoritative review (1981), mammals were discussed in

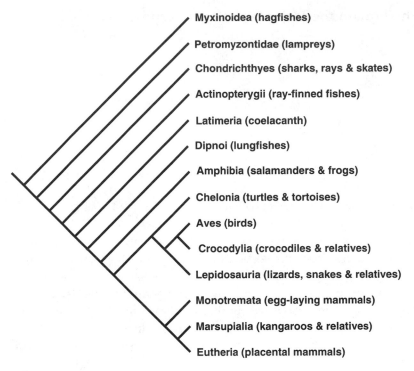

Myxinoidea (hagfishes)

Petromyzontidae (lampreys)

Chondrichthyes (sharks, rays & skates)

Actinopterygii (ray-finned fishes)

Latimeria (coelacanth)

Dipnoi (lungfishes)

Amphibia (salamanders & frogs)

Chelonia (turtles & tortoises)

Aves (birds)

Crocodylia (crocodiles & relatives)

Lepidosauria (lizards, snakes & relatives)

Monotremata (egg-laying mammals)

Marsupialia (kangaroos & relatives)

Eutheria (placental mammals)

Figure 7.1
Phylogeny of major vertebrate groups living today.

about 124 pages (105 if *Homo sapiens* is not included), birds in 17 pages, and all other animals in less than 1 page. In the most recent review, mammals dominate even more (Power, 2000). Here the priorities are reversed, with relatively little attention given to placental mammals and most time and space devoted to the animals that take up only 1 page in Fagen's seminal review. A study of play and playlike behavior in more diverse groups of animals may change the picture greatly.

In looking for the origins of play, we need to ask a number of questions. For example, is play and playlike behavior distributed throughout many animal groups other than endothermic animals (birds and placental mammals)? If so, is it comparable in organization complexity and function? What are the implications?

7.2   The Continuing Legacy of Anecdotal Evidence and Anthropomorphism

A serious problem in searching for the origins of play is the often abysmal nature of the evidence available. Although the five criteria for play are useful in isolating play from nonplay in the more playful mammals discussed previously, such as rats, dogs, and monkeys, their application to other groups of animals is not without difficulties. Many physical attributes of humans are found in other animals (e.g., legs, eyes, brain, and heart), so the issue is how far we can go in attributing cognitive, motivational, and emotional traits to other species based on our own experiences. Although the five play criteria aid in removing the intuitive anthropomorphic labeling of behavior as play, reliance on these criteria also means that such intuitive labeling is not available for us when we study animals that are rarely considered playful. There are good reasons why a radical extension of Fagen's single-page treatment of nonendothermic animals has not been seriously attempted to date. At the very moment when we need to use all available information in categorizing behavior as playful, it seems we cannot rely on such standard criteria as "having fun" or "purposelessness." And if this is not enough, our need to seriously consider informal, sparse, or nonexperimental data and observations compounds the difficulty. In short, we are faced with examples largely based on anecdotes. It was the twin reliance on anecdotes and uncritical anthropomorphism that doomed the comparative psychology of a hundred years ago (Burghardt, 1973, 1985b; Whitman, 1899). After being skeptical of anecdotes myself (Burghardt, 1973, 1988a; Burghardt, Ward, & Rosccoe, 1996), I nevertheless find myself needing to use them. How can this be justified? How can I live with myself as a scientist?

There are four ways to answer these questions. The first is to point out that anecdotal evidence is now back in fashion. Qualitative research methods have become very popular and defended as sources of data that are lost in quantitative and pooled subject research. Verbatim reports of transcripts of conversations are widely used in psychological research. More to the point, collections of anecdotes on nonhuman animals have been gathered and analyzed quantitatively. For example, Whiten and Byrne (1988) showed that by gathering information from professional scientists who informally observed rare or hard to recognize deception behavior in primates, it is possible to document species differences and phylogenetic trends. Animal emotions have also been explored by professional scientists in comparable fashion (Bekoff, 2000). Thus the strictures on anecdotal information may have been legitimately loosened.

A second response is to point to the wave of recent work on animal minds, consciousness, and cognitive ethology that requires different inferential methods than those of traditional behaviorism to probe and identify cognitive processes in animals (Allen & Saidel, 1998; Griffin, 1976; Ristau, 1991). The recent culmination of these discussions can perhaps best be appreciated in a comprehensive edited volume on anthropomorphism and anecdotes (R. W. Mitchell, Thompson, & Miles, 1997).

A third response is to argue that anecdotes can be useful in drawing attention to phenomena that warrant more careful consideration and study. By themselves anecdotes are always suspect, but if there is fire along with smoke, further research will uncover it. This is the position I have taken in the past (Burghardt, 1973).

A fourth response is more nuanced. Sometimes anecdotes are all we have available at a certain stage in ethological study, yet they are still useful for drawing conclusions, however qualified. This is especially true in comparative studies in which little information is available for many species. Just as there are differences between uncritical and critical uses of anthropomorphism (Burghardt, 1985a), so in addition, one can distinguish between critical and uncritical uses of anecdotes (Burghardt, 1973). It is the latter that I want to discuss more fully before going on to our comparative survey, because often qualitative descriptive accounts are the only data available.

7.3   Two Useful and Forgotten Perspectives

One of the most treasured books in my library is *The Animal Mind* (Washburn, 1908). I paid $2 for it in a used bookshop in Milwaukee, Wisconsin, during my college days, and have revisited the book periodically ever since. The author was Margaret Floy Washburn, one of the first eminent female psychologists. In addition to serving as president of the American Psychological Association in 1921, she was also the first woman psychologist to receive a Ph.D. and the first to be elected to the National Academy of Sciences. Her book went through four editions, the last in 1936.

This information on credentials is useful because Washburn had the misfortune to start writing on animal behavior at the time of the ascendancy of "mindless" behaviorism, as exemplified by J. B. Watson. A generation of psychologists thought that virtually all behavioral phenomena were best explored through application of a few basic processes and concepts. The careful and scholarly attempts by Washburn and many others to closely evaluate evidence for diverse mental phenomena were forgotten, along with the issues that they were trying to understand. In her day, much of the evidence she had to work with was often anecdotal and much of it could be easily discredited. Soon nonexperimental data were to be excluded from the science of animal behavior.

Washburn was herself concerned with the limitations and misuse of anecdotal data. Her brief description, with examples, of the difficulties involved in trying "to separate the grain from the chaff" (Washburn, 1908: 8), has never been equaled. Since the evidence presented in the following chapters sometimes raises these issues, I quote her at some length:

Method of Anecdote. It consists essentially in taking the report of another person regarding the action of an animal, observed most commonly by accident, and attracting attention because of its unusual character. In certain cases the observer while engaged in some other pursuit happens to notice the singular behavior of an animal, and at his leisure writes out an account of it. In others, the animal is a pet, in whose high intellectual powers its master takes pride. It is safe to say that this method of collecting information always labors under at least one, and frequently under several, of the following disadvantages: —

1. The observer is not scientifically trained to distinguish what he sees from what he infers.
2. He is not intimately acquainted with the habits of the species to which the animal belongs.

3. He is not acquainted with the past experience of the individual animal concerned.

4. He has a personal affection for the animal concerned, and a desire to show its superior intelligence.

5. He has the desire, common to all humanity, to tell a good story.

(Washburn, 1908:4–5)

Washburn gives examples of each of these problems. Although her focus was on evaluating evidence of animal cognitive accomplishments, an attempt to evaluate possible examples of play leads to quite similar problems. In the later chapters in part II, evidence tainted to varying degrees by the above five problems is presented because it is all we have to go on. Some of these examples came from noted scientists that I specifically asked "Have you ever seen any behavior in 'X' that appeared to be play, or would be considered play by you if you had observed it in a dog, cat, monkey, etc.?" I have used some of their answers. I consider these examples rather reliable because disadvantage 1 is avoided. Since these experts were commenting on animals they knew well, I consider disadvantage 2 avoided as well. Generally, especially with captive animals, disadvantage 3 is avoided and is not as severe a problem with examples of play as it is with animal intelligence. Disadvantage 4 is problematic, especially if the example is based on a pet or a species to which the author is committed. References to Marc Bekoff's dog, Jethro, are sprinkled throughout Bekoff's writings and interviews on animal play and cognition. However, scientists like Bekoff use such animals as exemplars of an already known phenomenon, rather than as the documented source of a new phenomenon. On the other hand, this is not always the case. Kenneth Shapiro provides a careful analysis of the world as experienced by a single pet male dog, Sabaka (Shapiro, 1997). Many of the classic descriptions of animal play are based on detailed study of one or very few animals (Fagen, 1981). Disadvantage 5 is always present as a potential problem. What Washburn is referring to is the tendency to anthropomorphize the animal's behavior. Yet this impulse, to tell a good story, is one that confronts all scientific work. Both the rash of exposed fraudulent research and the careers of most successful science popularizers testify to the persuasive power of the good story. All the best scientific work derives from the search for a good story. In many cases, however, self-deception and faulty memory may be at work; the dedicated fisherman might really believe, after some time and several retellings, that his 25-cm fish was a near 100-cm record breaker!

Small sample size is not an inherent limitation to solid scientific contributions. Phenomena based on careful study of one or two individuals can be more illuminating of essential details than a more superficial, but controlled study of a large sample. Both operant analysis and neurophysiology have made important discoveries from a study of only a few animals. The necessity to replicate findings independently applies regardless of sample size.

I have tried to keep faith with my skeptical colleagues by noting here, and in context, the problems with some of the putative examples of nontraditional animal play. In my discussion, replicated examples will count more than a single instance, and comments by trained scientists concerning animals whose behavior patterns they are familiar with are viewed as more valid than older reports or those by nonprofessionals. Examples elicited from experts, often somewhat reluctantly or with a tinge of embarrassment, are less infected by the affectations and narrative viruses of the self-promoters in the popular press. Examples from the early literature will generally be credited only if more recent accounts by modern trained scientists can also be adduced. Some of the early literature, however, may be the more valuable because it was less tainted by the skeptical responses of modern scientists, who may be overly willing to close off topics for study, especially on "lower animals," based on scientific political correctness (Griffin, 1976).

Refusing to even consider whether "lower animals" possess certain abilities is, however, the acme of unrecognized anthropomorphism (anthromorphism by omission, Rivas & Burghardt, 2002). Thus to close this section, I want to refer to one of the least-known papers by my doctoral advisor, the late Eckhard H. Hess (1964). Hess devoted his career largely to the study of filial imprinting in birds: the process of how chicks and ducklings bond with their mothers. He was careful never to draw comparisons between the processes involved in birds and the attachment processes of human mothers and infants. He was thus somewhat disturbed by work such as Harlow's maternal deprivation studies in rhesus monkeys (Harlow, 1964), which were touted as experimentally equivalent to what went on with human beings, a comparison much encouraged by Harlow himself (1971). Hess pointed out that other primates, including those phylogenetically closer to us than rhesus macaques, had rather different bonding processes than those found in this one species of macaque. Hess then used the phyletic distribution of play to make a most pertinent point.

I once showed to [a psychology seminar group discussing play and curiosity] a typical psychologist's phylogenetic scale, which, of course, would be a horror to any biologist, with man on top and the invertebrates on the bottom.... I asked, "If you were studying play behavior or curiosity behavior and you had a series of organisms, starting with man and going down to the monkey, cat, rat, crow, chicken, fish, and cockroach, where would you draw the line as to whether you can still legitimately study a behavior process like curiosity or animal play, or play?"

It appears that almost everyone has his own cutoff point. Some will draw the line at the cat because they can identify the kitten's actions with a ball of yarn as play. They are not so sure about a rat, and certainly not a bird or fish or cockroach. Others are likely to have had some experience watching a crow, perhaps because they raised one on a farm, and know the kinds of behavior that the crow engages in, so perhaps are willing to go down that far. Others assume immediately, not intellectually but deep down inside, that there is a distinct separateness between man and any animal, that somehow man is absolutely and not just quantitatively but qualitatively different from any other organism.

I think, if we objectively describe such behaviors as curiosity or play, or the kind of affectionate systems that Dr. Harlow discussed, and discuss them in objective terms, we have to accept that these behaviors can occur at various levels as long as you can find the behavior and fit it into the paradigm that you have set up in the situation in question. (Hess, 1964: 176)

Hess wrote these paragraphs for a major conference on the future of behavioral science research, in which his talk followed Harlow's presentation. I was then a graduate student in his laboratory and at the time was not particularly interested in play or curiosity in animals in more than a casual sense; yet his point resonated and was retained somewhere in my brain. The issues raised in the following chapters now make his comments extremely relevant and I am even more appreciative of having known this iconoclastic and controversial figure.

The chapters in part II with the thinnest and most controversial evidence are the longest because the data need to be presented and examined in sufficient detail so that readers can draw their own conclusions about whether play is shown. Simple gut reactions of either yea or nay are not the stuff of science, although unfortunately they affect the reactions of many scientists. How do we evaluate and interpret evidence? Where does each of us draw the line? Can we justify our conclusions with objective evidence and rational arguments separated from the intuitive anthropomorphic biases we all have? Armed with the five Washburn cautions and the five play criteria, the next chapters proceed through some tangled evolutionary landscapes. I will try to be both critical in my use of anecdotes and critically anthropomorphic. Thinking about play is far more than a game.

8 Play in the Placental Mammals

8.1 Is Play Ubiquitous among Placental Mammals?

Play is generally considered the province of the placental (eutherian) mammals (Bekoff & Byers, 1981; Fagen, 1981). These mammals include the great majority, over 80 percent, of all mammals. A thorough treatment of play in placental mammals would be longer than the treatment of all other groups of animals combined. This chapter presents examples of play in some of the less familiar mammalian groups and then gives some recent findings on the evolution of play diversity within selected groups of placental mammals: canids, rodents, ungulates, and primates. Extensive treatments of play in many groups of mammals are found in Fagen (1981), Power (2000), and Bekoff and Byers (1998), and in thousands of primary sources.

As discussed earlier, the challenge faced in this book is to explore with an objective approach and broad sweep the entire realm of phenomena that can be considered playful. If play is not the sole province of placental mammals, its appearance must depend on variables other than those associated with the biology and phylogeny of these mammals. However, if play is an ancient placental mammalian trait rather than a derived trait, then it should be found in all orders of mammals and be homologous. Some authors have claimed that this is the case (e.g., Fagen, 1981; Spinka, Newberry, & Bekoff, 2001). The truth, however, is more complex.

The living placental mammals are divided into nineteen orders (Nowak, 1999) that vary in number of families, genera, and species (table 8.1). More than two-thirds of all mammals are either rodents or bats. All major groups of mammals differentiated by the late Cretaceous, before the extinction of the dinosaurs, more than 65 mya (Lillegraven et al., 1987) and the earliest placental mammals may have lived more than 100 mya (million years ago). The phylogenetic relationship among mammalian orders is still controversial or unresolved, and a consensus tree is presented here with the major categories of play (locomotor, object, social) mapped onto the tree (figure 8.1). Although carnivores, primates, rodents, and hoofed animals dominate the literature on

Table 8.1
Prevalence of play in the orders of living placental mammals

Order	Number of Families/Genera/Species	Locomotor Play	Object Play	Social Play	Play Rating	Selected Common Names
Xenartha	4/13/29	Yes?	Yes?	Yes	1.5	Armadillos, anteaters, sloths
Pholidota	1/1/7			Yes	1.5	Pangolins
Lagomorpha	2/13/81	Yes	Yes?	Yes	1.5	Pikas, rabbits, hares
Rodentia	29/468/2052	Yes	Yes	Yes	2.0	Mice, rats, squirrels, gerbils, beaver, porcupines, pacas
Macroscelidea	1/4/15	Yes			1.0	Elephant shrews
Insectivora	7/68/440		Yes	Yes?	1.0	Tenrecs, hedgehogs, shrews, moles
Carnivora	8/97/246	Yes	Yes	Yes	3.0	Cats, dogs, bears, raccoons, hyenas, mongooses, weasels
Pinnipedia	3/18/34	Yes	Yes	Yes	3.0	Sea lions, seals, walrus
Scandentia	1/5/16	Yes	Yes	Yes	2.5	Tree shrews
Primates	13/66/279	Yes	Yes	Yes	3.0	Lemurs, galagos, marmosets, monkeys, apes, humans
Dermoptera	1/1/2			Yes	1.0	Flying lemurs
Chiroptera	18/192/977		Yes?	Yes?	1.5	Bats (fruit and vampire)
Tubulidentata	1/1/1			Yes	1.0	Aardvark
Artiodactyla	10/86/221	Yes	Yes	Yes	2.0	Hogs, hippos, camels, deer, giraffes, antelope, cattle, sheep
Cetacea	13/41/78	Yes	Yes	Yes	3.0	Dolphins, whales, porpoises
Perissodactyla	3/6/17	Yes	Yes	Yes	2.5	Horses, zebras, tapirs, rhinos, hoofed ungulates
Hyracoidea	1/3/7			Yes	2.5	Hyraxes
Proboscidea	1/2/2	Yes	Yes	Yes	3.0	Elephants
Sirenia	2/2/4	Yes	Yes	Yes	1.5	Manatees, dugongs
Total species	4508					

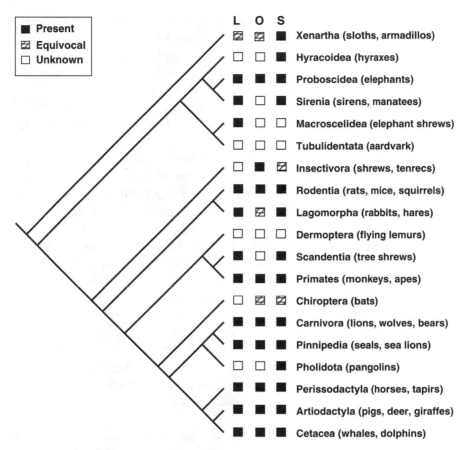

Figure 8.1
Phylogeny of eutherian mammal orders and occurrence of different kinds of play. L, locomotor play; O, object play; S, social play.

play in eutherian mammals, the emphasis here is on animals in which play is subtle, doubtful, or nonexistent.

The distribution of mammalian play given in table 8.1 shows that most groups exhibit play in all three major categories. In terms of distribution across orders, social play is most common, followed by locomotor and then object play. If only two play types occur, they are usually locomotor and social play. This reinforces the view that object play may have a different set of facilitating factors than the other two forms. Social play is typically rather active and involves locomotion, so the link between these two is not surprising.

Another consideration in evaluating table 8.1 is that some of the orders in which evidence for play is absent or questionable are also orders containing either only a few species or species whose behavior has been little studied (Eisenberg, 1981; Fagen, 1981; Nowak, 1999). The prominent exception is the bats. Even within the bats, however, detailed behavioral ethograms and behavioral development have not been major areas of research. Furthermore, many species, even in orders in which play seems prevalent, have not been studied, so the phylogenetic distribution of play reflects, to some extent, a sampling bias. Some orders have been studied much more than others, irrespective of number of species. For example, the order that contains the two species of elephants has been much studied, and play is common in both species. On the other hand, insectivores are rather little studied, although there are several families and quite a few species. At this point, the focus is on whether play occurs in an order, what types of play occur, the relative prevalence of types of play, and how these findings relate to the factors outlined in chapter 6 as important in the occurrence of play.

Although the distribution shown in figure 8.1 suggests that play was an ancestral character found in the earliest placental mammals, the wide variation in the ubiquity and complexity of play within these orders suggests that play evolved and was later lost or greatly modified repeatedly during the evolution of placental mammals. Our comparative database is still too limited to draw final conclusions within orders, but the overall outline of the course of play diversity in mammals suggests that there are major differences in the types and extent of play in different orders of placental mammals. A brief look at some of the more problematic orders precedes a more careful look at play variation within selected orders containing highly playful species. Unless noted in the text, the information in sections 8.2 and 8.3 is based on Nowak (1999).

The topic of the formal comparison of play in mammalian orders was addressed recently by Iwaniuk and co-workers (Iwaniuk, Nelson, & Pellis, 2001). They largely limited themselves to using Fagen (1981) as a primary resource and rated play complexity on a scale of 1.0 (very limited play or none) to 3.0 (much complex play), as did Byers (1999a). Table 8.1 shows the ratings modified from Iwaniuk et al. for placental mammals. The benchmark for play complexity was the occurrence of long sequences incorporating many behavioral elements, as found in primates and carnivores. In social play, play wrestling (physical contact) was rated as more highly developed than play chasing. Given the paucity of the comparative database, the prevalence of play was not included in their scale. Nonetheless, play is common in virtually all primates and carnivores, and eventually a more quantitative approach will be necessary. Here I have discounted groups in which fairly complete study of some species shows that play is rare, even if it is found in fairly complex form in one or two species. However, such cases are key targets for analyzing the conditions under which play emerged from a phylogenetic backdrop of limited play or none, assuming that the nonplaying majority represent the ancestral condition.

8.2 Do These Mammalian Groups Play?

8.2.1 Xenartha

The xenartha (formerly called edentates in the order Edentata) are eutherian mammals with perhaps the most conservative traits, along with specializations such as few teeth or none. They have low metabolic rates, often well below typical eutherian levels. They include the families containing sloths, anteaters, and armadillos. Since there are ten times as many fossil as living genera, they are a relic group dating to before the Cretaceous. Sociality seems very undeveloped by mammalian standards and solitary living is the rule (Eisenberg, 1981). Aggressiveness to conspecifics is generally low. They are typically long lived and develop slowly. All current families evolved in South America.

There are brief reports on social play in two-toed sloths (*Choloepus didactylus* and *C. hoffmanni*) and social, locomotor, and object play in giant anteaters (*Myrmecophaga tridactyla*) (Fagen, 1981; Kawata & Elsen, 1994). These species represent the largest living sloths and anteaters, respectively, and are the most active members of their groups. There are no reports of play in armadillos, although the twenty species and eight genera provide a good diversity in habits and size (up to 60 kg). Armadillos are generalist predators on many small vertebrates and invertebrates. One species is reported to throw itself on snakes and dispatch them by slicing them with its sharp plates. The species most common in the United States, the long-nosed armadillo (*Dasypus novemcinctus*), can show considerable aggression toward conspecifics and this can include chasing and stand-up "boxing" fights. It is not known whether play fighting is seen in juveniles (McDonough, 1994). Armadillos are typically weaned at several weeks of age, and all species, including the largest, reach sexual maturity within a year. Xenartha are rated 2.0 in play complexity (Iwaniuk, Nelson, & Pellis, 2001), but this seems to be based largely on the giant anteater. My estimate would be closer to 1.5.

8.2.2 Pholidota

The pangolins are scaly-appearing mammals that have converged with the Xenartha anteaters in also specializing on ants. They have a similar small elongated head and snout and also lack teeth. They are strictly Old World, being limited to Asia and Africa. At one time they were considered to be closely related to or even part of the Xenartha, but now their relationship with other mammals is uncertain. There are only one or two young at a time and the mother-infant bond seems well developed. There is some evidence for mother-offspring and subadult social play fighting (Fagen, 1981). Iwaniuk and colleagues (2001) did not separate these taxa from the Xenartha; I would also rank them as 1.5 on their play scale.

8.2.3 Insectivora

These relatively small animals, which include the shrews, hedgehogs, and tenrecs, have relatively small brains and play is rarely mentioned, even in descriptions of well-studied species such as the tenrec (*Solenedon paradoxus*). Other reports are problematic anecdotes with perhaps the exception of several reports on hedgehogs (*Erinsceus europaeus*). These latter have been reported to exhibit inhibited play bites, play invitations, and perhaps some object play (Fagen, 1981), although the descriptions are not detailed or convincing using the five criteria (i.e., Dimelow, 1963). This species is now a popular pet and yet play is not mentioned in the pet trade manuals that I have consulted and thus may not be very common. The following unpublished description of object play in an adult dwarf hedgehog (*Hemiechinus albiventris*) provided by Andrew Iwaniuk seems to meet the five play criteria:

The hedgehog, while in a large open area (kitchen floor) was provided with the cardboard cylinder from a roll of toilet paper. She approached the cylinder and after investigating it, she wedged her head into one end. The cylinder fitted snuggly around her head and remained in place while the hedgehog walked forward waving her head around, mostly in the vertical domain. When she bumped into a wall, the cylinder fell off. She re-oriented so that she was face-on with an open end and once again wedged her head into the cylinder. This sequence of actions was repeated many times. Interspersed with these sequences of forward movement, she walked backwards and waved her head more forcefully. If the cylinder fell off, she re-oriented and again wedged her head into the open end. On this particular evening these repeated interactions with the cylinder went on for over 15 minutes. During the interactions with the cylinder the hedgehog seemed relaxed and did not emit either fear-typical or agonism-typical vocalizations. Also noteworthy was that the hedgehog engaged in such interactions with a cardboard cylinder on many separate occasions. That is, this behaviour was repeated many times on the same day and on many different days. Overall, the behaviour seemed playful, as it was voluntary, repeated and seemed enjoyable. (Iwaniuk, personal communication, 2002)

Play is ranked 1.0 in this group (Iwaniuk, Nelson, & Pellis, 2001). Still, that might be low.

8.2.4 Macroscelidea

Elephant shrews were once considered part of the insectivores, but are now considered a completely separate order that is perhaps phylogenetically close to the lagomorphs (rabbits and hares). A few highly precocious young are born and development is rapid, with the young attaining sexual maturity in 6 weeks or less. These animals are considered to be highly nervous and alert. Thus the interpretation of short dashes and leaps reported in unpublished observations on unidentified species (quoted by Fagen, 1981) as locomotor play is suspect. They are not separated from insectivores by Iwaniuk, Nelson, and Pellis (2001) and I rank them as 1.0.

8.2.5   Scandentia

Tree shrews are small squirrel-like animals once considered an early offshoot of primates and thus were the focus of considerable research, especially in neuroscience. This faded when their status as a "primitive" primate diminished (Nowak, 1999). They have been variously considered an advanced insectivore, allied to the elephant shrews, or most commonly today, in a separate order closely related to the primates, bats, and flying lemurs. Their brain size is about midway between that of insectivores and primates (Iwaniuk, Nelson, & Pellis, 2001). One unusual feature of the development of baby tree shrews is that the mother visits them and provides milk only once every 48 hours. Adults are essentially solitary. Individual locomotor (running, rolling) and social (chasing, mounting, boxing) play have been reported, along with role reversals, but not play wrestling (Fagen, 1981). Adult play has not been reported. Play has been described in the most-studied species, but the absence of object play and play wrestling led Iwaniuk and colleagues (2001) to rank them as 2.0.

8.2.6   Lagomorpha

Rabbits and hares, even adults, show some social play (Fagen, 1981), although this has not been systematically studied. Fagen did not report object play, but a student studying enrichment in a research colony of laboratory rabbits at the University of Tennessee documented object use in adult rabbits that appeared playlike. Play complexity was rated 1.5 by Iwaniuk and colleagues (2001). It could be that since lagomorphs, unlike rodents, rely on cryptic, motionless (freezing) behavior for avoiding predation, the more active behavior leading to play is selected against in juveniles as well as in adults in this group.

8.2.7   Tubulidentata

The single species in this order, the aardvark or ant-bear, is another species that has converged on a largely ant and termite-eating life-style, with great tooth reduction. They are often considered part of the Afrotiera, the first major radiation of mammals that took place in Africa, and may be among the most ancient living placental mammals. The young are relatively large and precocial at birth. Their behavior is largely unstudied and play has not been reported. I would rate them 1.0 based on current information.

8.2.8   Dermoptera

The Dermoptera are another small order, found only in Southeast Asia, that includes two species of flying lemurs, neither of which have been reported to play. Then again, little is known behaviorally about these largely nocturnal animals variously considered closely related to insectivores, bats, and primates. They are largely folivorous, although they may also eat flowers and fruits. I would give them a 1.0 based on the lack of current information.

8.2.9   Chiroptera

Bats are numerous, second only to rodents in number of species (almost 1000). Yet play has been described in only a few of these highly successful but very specialized mammals. Bats are divided into two suborders: the small insectivorous Microchiroptera and the generally larger fruit-eating Megachiroptera. The latter do not echolocate.

Vampire bats have highly developed social behavior that may involve reciprocal altruism; some social play has been reported in them and in fruit bats (Fagen, 1981). The milling about of neonates in crèches containing tens of thousands of young Mexican free-tailed bats in caves could involve play (Fagen, 1981), but more basic descriptive information on the behavior of the young is needed. A mother bat has only one offspring at a time but all babies are born at the same time and are crowded together on cave walls and ceilings. All the mothers leave at dusk to hunt insects and return hours later to nurse their babies; they seem quite able to find their own offspring even as they move about (McCracken, 1984). Studies of the babies in the absence of mothers are needed to see if the play criteria are met in this situation.

Object play has not been specifically described in bats, although food enrichment devices have been employed. A film of several species of fruit bats given to me by the Lubee Foundation (which carries out studies on captive fruit bats and supports much valuable research on all bats, as well as conservation and education efforts on their behalf) provided suggestive evidence for object play. The bats displayed some intriguing puzzle-solving behavior as well as manipulation of nonfood objects that could be classified as play using the five criteria. The importance of providing novel objects to maintain interest was demonstrated. Play in Chiroptera was rated as 1.0 by Iwaniuk and colleagues (2001). I would tentatively raise the ranking to 1.5, based on vampire and fruit bat behavior.

8.2.10   Hyracoidea

The vegetarian hyraxes live in Africa and Southwest Asia. Vocal communication is well developed. Some species of hyraxes live in large social groups and it is in those species that play has been most well documented. Social play in the gray hyrax (*Heterohyrax brucei*) has been especially well described (Caro & Alawi, 1985). This is one of the orders for which Fagen (1981) could report no evidence of play but for which good evidence now exists. Play complexity is rated a high 2.5 by Iwaniuk and colleagues (2001). However, this may be premature given that solitary locomotor and object play have yet to be documented.

8.2.11   Sirenia

This small group of relatively slow-moving, herbivorous aquatic mammals has been described as engaging in locomotor and gentle social play, although Fagen (1981) is skeptical because some of the behavior described as play could actually be social grooming. Locomotor play consisting of twisting and tumbling seems to be better verified. The Sirenia are often considered to be closely related to the elephants (Proboscidae), which are highly playful. This again points out that the complexity and amount of play can differ greatly across related orders. They were not rated by Iwaniuk and colleagues (2001); I would rate them as 1.5.

8.2.12   Conclusions

These eleven orders illustrate the difficulties in any claims for the ubiquity of play, and certainly common, sustained, or complex play, in many groups of mammals. Except for the tree shrews and hyraxes, play seems quite uncommon in these orders. This is especially true of object play. Seven of the orders show no object play, and the evidence for the other four (Xenartha, Insectivora, Lagomorpha, and Chiroptera) is sparse or anecdotal. What can we conclude? All these orders, with the possible exception of many bats, are born in an advanced state of precocity or rapidly develop to behavioral independence.

Relative brain size is often measured by the encephalization quotient (EQ), which is the ratio of the brain size expected for an animal of a given size to the value actually measured. The mean EQ for the six orders included in Iwaniuk et al. (2001) is 0.876. Lagomorphs and insectivores had the smallest mean EQ (0.592 and 0.681, respectively). Without the tree shrews, which have a large EQ (1.369) and the only one over 1.000, the mean is 0.778. Omnivores, carnivores, frugivores, and other dietary modes are represented in these orders. Scavengers and extractive foragers except for anteaters are rare or absent and these two apparent feeding modes are found in some of the species showing the most complex and common object play. Those groups with complex social lives, such as hyraxes, show considerable social play, but so do the tree shrews, which live solitary lives and have minimal contact with offspring. These orders need to be studied much more completely using the play criteria developed in chapter 3 and then classified according to the hierarchical schemes in chapter 4. However, the overall picture of playfulness in these orders will probably not change much, although it is much more likely that nocturnal species or those that raise young in burrows will harbor more surprises.

8.3   The Most Playful Orders of Placental Mammals

The remaining eight placental orders contain a large percentage of very playful species according to virtually all experts on mammals (Bekoff & Byers, 1981; Eisenberg, 1981; Ewer, 1968a; Fagen, 1981; Iwaniuk, Nelson, & Pellis, 2001; Spinka, Newberry, & Bekoff, 2001). Power (2000) has collated the details of play in about sixty representative species of these mammals (from six orders) in many useful tables. Many examples of play in part I were based on these species, particularly Rodentia (rodents),

Carnivora (cats and canids), Pinnipedia (seals and sea lions), Primates, Artiodactyla (deer, antelope, bovines, pigs), and Perissodactyla (horses). Proboscidea (elephants) and Cetacea (whales, dolphins) are well known for play as well. For example, there is evidence that killer whales (*Orcinus orca*) may teach their offspring techniques of beaching and escaping (entering and leaving shallows to capture seals) through play, and animals with this training appear to become better hunters at an earlier age (Rendell & Whitehead, 2001). Imitation of both motor and vocal behavior may also occur in cetaceans, and all this evidence is used to support true cultural transmission in this group (Rendell & Whitehead, 2001). Since imitation can also occur through play (Miklosi, 1999), play could be a major factor in the generation of novel behavior (tertiary process play) as well as in the refinement of essential basic behaviors such as prey capture (secondary process play).

Virtually all these groups contain animals with large brains and high metabolic rates, although there can be significant variation and, as discussed earlier, large brains and high metabolic rates may be dissociated. Relative brain size is generally larger in these orders than in the less playful ones, but comparative analysis shows that the relationship is weak (chapter 5; Iwaniuk, Nelson, & Pellis, 2001) and may represent a threshold that allows, but does not ensure, high levels of play (Burghardt, 1984; Iwaniuk, Nelson, & Pellis, 2001). Nevertheless, a comparison of brain size data across orders is suggestive and it is easy to see how brain size and play have been considered causally related through rough correlational analysis (chapter 5). Using the review already cited (Iwaniuk, Nelson, & Pellis, 2001), the mean EQ of these eight playful orders is 1.400. Since these authors combined the Pinnipedia with the Carnivora, the mean for orders might have been even higher. Of these more playful orders, the Artiodactyla had the smallest EQ with 0.775, and the Primates had the highest (2.151), followed closely by the Cetacea (2.071). These numbers are significantly different, although, as discussed in chapter 5, such a comparison is highly suspect.

If, however, we add the hyraxes and tree shrews to these eight orders and compare all groups scoring 2.0 or above in play complexity with those scoring 1.0 or 1.5 (Iwaniuk, Nelson, & Pellis, 2001), the mean decreases to 1.210 for the more playful orders and to 0.745 for the less playful orders. Using the play complexity criteria, Cetacea, Primates, Proboscidea, and Carnivora (and Pinnipedia) are the only orders scoring 3.0, and the mean EQ of these four orders is 1.768. It might be tempting, then, to see a causal relationship between brain size and play. Many other factors enter in, however, such as body size, feeding habits, metabolic rate, and degree of parental care, which is lengthy in most species in these orders except for some of the smaller carnivores, such as weasels.

In the better-studied orders of playful animals, it is possible to look more closely at the differences and similarities among species in the nature and extent of play behavior. This can give us insight into the ways in which play has evolved as animals have adapted to different ecological and social niches. In all eight playful orders, all three types of play are commonly seen, and social play in many members of these orders involves the more complex attributes of wrestling, role reversal, play signals, and self-handicapping.

8.3.1 Play in Nonhuman Primates

Play has been recorded in every species of primate from all twelve families (excluding humans) for which even marginal descriptive data are available. Primates range in size from tiny mouse lemurs to gorillas and live in almost all habitats except arctic and very cold temperate areas. They can be dietary generalists or specialists, arboreal (most) or terrestrial, and have social organizations that vary from adult solitary living (orangutans), to monogamy (gibbons), to cohesive and rigid dominance hierarchies with single or multimale harems (some baboons), or looser "fission-fusion" structures (chimpanzees). Diets can range from omnivory to a focus on fruits, leaves, tree sap, invertebrates, and vertebrates, including other primates.

Play in juvenile primates is very common, although locomotor and object play may be somewhat less ubiquitous than social play. Even the former, however, is more common and more complex than that seen in almost all other groups of mammals. Tool use, which is often linked to play in primates (Power, 2000), is most common in this order as well.

Unfortunately, although there is much information on play in primates, including comparative studies (Kawata, 1980; S. T. Parker & Gibson, 1990; Pereira & Fairbanks, 1993; Power, 2000; E. O. Smith, 1978; P. K. Smith, 1982; Symons, 1978), it has not been until recently that we could begin to identify major phylogenetic patterns and relate them to diet, sociality, brain size, or other factors in any detail. There does seem to be, within primates, significant relationships of social play with the size of cerebellum, amygdala, neocortex, and striatam (Lewis, 2003; Lewis & Barton, 2004) (see figure 8.2).

Complex social play in adult primates may be one area where the growing impact of comparative evolutionary analysis may be useful in understanding variation across species (Pellis & Iwaniuk, 1999a). A recent analysis of patterns of social play among adult primates based on the published literature reached some important conclusions (Pellis & Iwaniuk, 2000a). The questions asked in this analysis derive from the fact that play is used in both sexual and nonsexual contexts. Usable play data were available for seventy-one primate species from all thirteen families, and a consensus phylogeny based on both molecular and morphological data was employed (Purvis, 1995), along with the method of independent contrasts (Felsenstein, 1985). Unlike juvenile social play, adult social play is absent in some primates and very common in others. Thus the data used for each type of social play (sexual or nonsexual) were a simple ranking on a three-part scale.

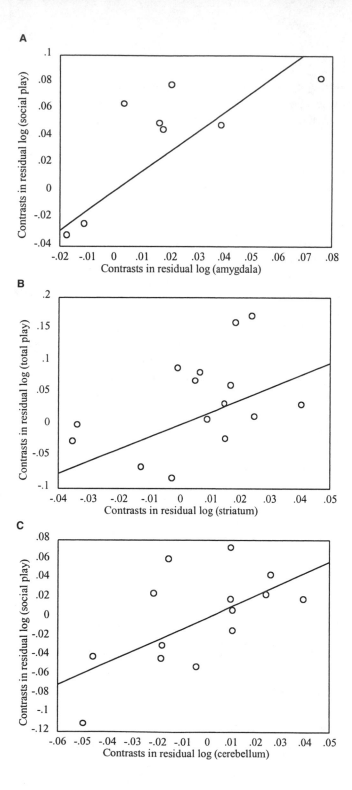

Play in sexual contexts explained a significant amount of the variation in play in nonsexual contexts. More interesting was the finding that reduced social familiarity among adults accounted for even more (30–40 percent) of the variation in play in nonsexual adult-adult play. Overall, play among adults was more frequent in primates living in social settings that had reduced contact between the sexes and other group members. Both sexual and nonsexual play was mapped onto a phylogeny of primates (figure 8.3). Rare to moderate levels of play in nonsexual contexts was the most likely ancestral state, with play becoming more or less prominent in various taxa. The functional interpretation of these phylogenetic patterns in terms of social organization and nocturnal habits has been discussed earlier (chapter 6). What is evident from the phylogenetic tree is that even at the coarse level at which play was rated in this most universally playful order of mammals, play has repeatedly changed and evolved. Thus "deep" phylogeny, or preprimate evolutionary history, has little effect on the nature of play across species in primates. This suggests that complex social play has important functional consequences and responds to social demands. These most likely relate to social affiliation and assessment (Pellis & Iwaniuk, 2000a). However, the measure of play used was very simple, which suggests that a more refined comparative analysis would show even more variation among closely related taxa. In any event, the multiple origins of complex play are certainly supported by this analysis.

8.3.2 Play in Rodents

Unlike primates, rodents are classified as only moderately playful as a group (Fagen, 1981), although some species, such as gray squirrels, are very playful, live in three-dimensional habitats as do many primates, and have large brains in relation to body size (Horwich, 1972). Prairie dogs (*Cynomys ludovicianus*) are ground squirrels that live in large colonies and are very social. They have an extremely complex communication system that seems to encode information that includes the type, direction, and distance of human and other intruders (Slobodchikoff, 2002). They are also extremely social and playful within the group (coterie). Fathers are especially playful with offspring, and the young have elaborate means of enticing play (Masson, 1999). Beavers (*Castor* sps), large semiaquatic rodents that live long and have complex social lives, also play frequently, including "dancing," and several authors mention the inhibitions on biting and other consummatory aggressive responses that may facilitate social play (Wilsson, 1971; Ryden, 1997). Holmes has shown that play is the most common social behavior among groups of young Belding's ground squirrels and results from a complex interaction of kinship relatedness and familiarity (Holmes, 2001; figure 6.3).

◀ **Figure 8.2**

The relationship between play and the size of three noncortical brain components across a sample of representative diverse primates. (*a*) Social play and the amygdala, (*b*) total play and the striatum, and (*c*) social play and the cerebellum. (From Lewis, 2003)

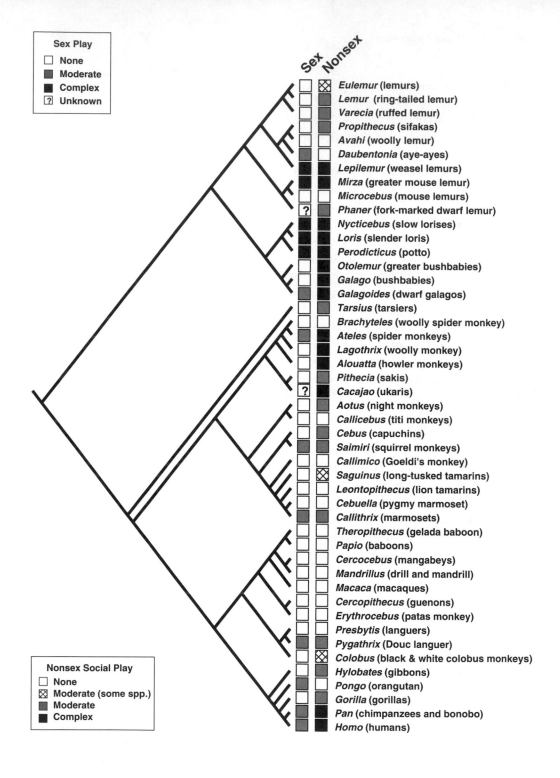

Rodents are promising subjects for a phylogenetic analysis of play because variation in play is so much greater in rodents than in primates, even within the same family (Pellis et al., 1991; Poole & Fish, 1975). The Muridae comprise the largest family by far of the 29 rodent families. About two thirds of the more than 2000 rodent species are members of this single and most successful (in terms of species and distribution) of all mammalian families. There are some interesting little-known phenomena in these animals that are poorly understood but that provide opportunities for comparative study. For example, there is a radiation of mice (*Pseudemys*) in Australia that manipulate pebbles and other objects into rather elaborate mounds that may have some defensive, thermoregulatory, or visual marking function, although the development and details of the behavior seem to be little known (Cermak, 1996).

Although laboratory rats are the species most studied for social play, the comparative data on play are far less systematic and comprehensive in rodents than in primates. Thus a phylogenetic study of social play fighting in rodents was limited to thirteen species, although these ranged over eleven genera and five subfamilies of muroid rodents (Pellis & Iwaniuk, 1999b). For comparison, it should be noted that there are sixteen recognized subfamilies (Nowak, 1999). Even in this limited sample, however, the range of social play is great (Pellis, 1993). Pellis and Iwaniuk carried out a comparative analysis of social play in these thirteen species similar to that performed with primates. Instead of adult-adult play, they used juvenile play fighting but a similar rating scale. Remarkably, they found that phylogeny explained little of the diversity that they found (figure 8.4). However, differences in sociality also explained little of the variation. The presumptive ancestral state was low to moderate play, which then increased or declined in various lineages. Clearly much more work needs to be done, but these results strongly suggest that more complex social play has roots in recent, rather than ancient, evolutionary history. Furthermore, using the kinds of functional analyses listed in chapter 5, such differences among play styles almost certainly are due to either important functional roles or are by-products of other behavioral differences having functional, and ultimately adaptive, roles.

8.3.3 Play in Canids

All members of the canid line of carnivore evolution (wolves, foxes, bears, raccoons, weasels) are playful in all respects. Many of these carnivores, especially bears and weasels, are born in a highly altricial state (hairless, eyes closed, no mobility). Some, such as the highly intelligent bears, also have very large brains. These findings are exceptions to claims that the more altricial species are cognitively inferior to precocial ones

◄ Figure 8.3

Phylogeny of sexual and nonsexual social play in adult primates. Cross-hatching depicts genera in which only some species show nonsexual adult social play. (From Pellis & Iwaniuk, 2000a)

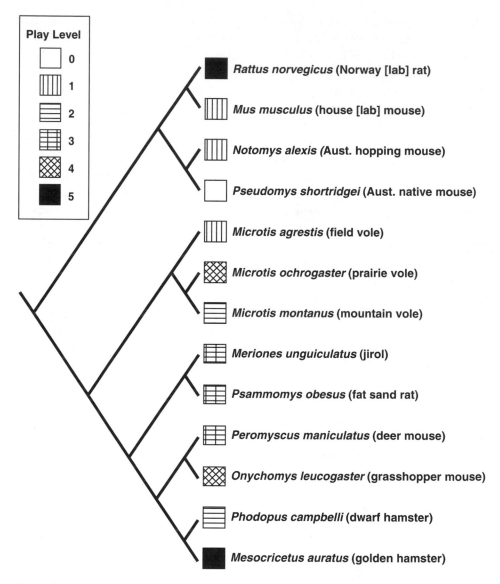

Figure 8.4
Phylogeny of social play in juvenile muroid rodents. Note that the most complex play is found
only in the two species most distantly related to each other. (From Pellis & Iwaniuk, 1999b)

(S. T. Parker & McKinney, 1999; Portmann, 1990). Furthermore, bears are not very social but still have elaborate play behavior (Burghardt, 1982). One spectacled bear (*Tremarctos ornatus*) (Kawata, 1990) outdid by far any American black bear that I ever studied in his use of objects in escapes as well as his dexterity in twirling broomsticks in one hand, picking up a small metal feed pan and carrying it to a water trough, where he "floated and pushed the pan as a child would do" (Kawata, 1990: 13), and other spontaneous and untaught behaviors (although imitation cannot be completely ruled out).

Although play has been documented in many species of carnivores of all families (Fagen, 1981), comparative work has been most intensive on a portion of the sixteen genera and thirty-six species of the family Canidae (wolves, dogs, foxes, jackals), and a few of these comparisons are mentioned here to show the nature of differences among these often familiar animals and how such differences have been interpreted.

Canids show enormous diversity in levels of adult sociality and social organization. Even within the single genus *Canis*, there is great variation, from the social hunting packs of the gray wolf (*Canis lupus*) to the family units typical of jackals and coyotes (*Canis latrans*). The controversial red wolf (*Canis rufus*) is considered intermediate, if not a hybrid, between the gray wolf and coyote (Wagener, 1998). Social play differs in wolves and coyotes in several respects, although there are no sex differences (Bekoff, 1974, 1978a, 1995; Fox et al., 1976). Play in the red wolf is somewhat intermediate. For example, the red wolf shows the extensive parent-offspring play and exaggerated double leaping of gray wolves, along with the absence of vocalizations during play fighting. Like coyotes, however, young red wolves do not engage in sexual play and show infrequent submissive behavior; social play first appears after serious agonistic behavior has developed. Thus data on play may be useful in resolving questions concerning the relationships of closely related animals and is consistent with, but does not prove, the hybrid origin hypothesis of the red wolf.

The play behavior of three other canids, all from South America, has also been compared (Biben, 1983): the maned wolf (*Chrysocyon brachyurus*), the crab-eating fox (*Cerdocyon thous*), and the bush dog (*Speothos venaticus*). All three are the sole members of their genus and have different kinds of social organization. The maned wolf is generally solitary and monogamous during the mating season; the crab-eating fox forms long-lasting monogamous bonds, and mated pairs travel together but hunt individually. The bush dog is highly social, monogamous, lives in packs up to ten, and hunts cooperatively. All can live in wet savannahs, but the maned wolf favors grasslands while the other two species are more woodland adapted.

All three species displayed virtually the same behavior patterns in play, such as chasing, pawing, rolling over, biting, gaping, and muzzle wrestling. It is interesting that the highly social bush dogs did not engage in grappling (bipedal wrestling) or play bows (as seen in dogs, wolves, and coyotes), but they did vocalize much more during play than the other two species. Bush dog play was also less variable. In all three species, there were no sex differences in social play, nor are the species sexually dimorphic in size. Although the ontogeny of play was roughly similar, social interactions were more frequent and peaked later in life in bush dogs than in the other two species.

Biben suggests that the bush dog retains more juvenile morphological and behavioral features than more ancestral species. For example, the adult bush dog has the short muzzle, large head, and short legs typical of young canid pups. On the other hand, the bush dog had "a less rich and varied repertoire during interactions and had showed a higher frequency of behaviours considered aggressive (e.g., biting, growling)" (Biben, 1983: 824). In bush dogs, the typical limits on play fighting that keep it from escalating to serious fighting were absent. Submissive behavior patterns were more common. This difference might be related to the role of social organization in patterns of social play as reported earlier for primates. Species with a looser social structure showed the richer and more complex play. In spite of the maned wolf and crab-eating fox having different levels of sociality, there were few differences between them. Biben concludes that standard predictions that more social species should have more complex play, be less aggressive, and have a dominance hierarchy are not supported.

Biben also studied object play in both the crab-eating fox and the bush dog (Biben, 1982, 1983). Pups of both species brought objects into the den beginning at about 5–7 weeks. Bush dogs chose larger objects and they hunted larger prey relative to their body size than the foxes. Foxes, but not bush dogs, maintained a hoard of "toys." Much object play was social, involving tug-of-wars and chasing in foxes, but the bush dogs, although biting on objects together and carrying them around, did not engage in tug-of war (figure 8.5). Unlike social play, object play differences among the two species seem more readily understood. Bush dogs hunt cooperatively while foxes do

Figure 8.5
Group object play in bush dogs. (From Biben, 1982)

not. Apparently, although they group hunt and kill prey, bush dog methods are quite unsophisticated; they surround prey and bite at it repeatedly. Foxes, on the other hand, use a variety of attack modes to capture prey and thus may need more complex and acquired skills. Thus the smaller repertoire of bush dog object play may be related to their later less complex predatory behavior.

The less competitive nature of bush dog object play also is congruent with the social and food-sharing characteristics of the species. In bush dogs, 77 percent of social object play bouts were amicable compared with only 13 percent for crab-eating foxes (Biben, 1982). The type of predatory object play witnessed in the foxes was similar to that seen in other individual hunting carnivores, such as domestic cats and dogs. It is interesting that "hunting play," defined as stabbing with one or both forepaws at an apparently imaginary prey item in the grass, was common in the maned wolf, rare in the fox, and absent in the bush dog.

These comparative studies on canid species support Fagen's (1981) prediction that there will be few play differences between the sexes in carnivores because of their similar roles in hunting, territorial defense, and parental care. This was also predicted in a more general form from SRT (Burghardt, 1988b). There is recent evidence relating the level of play in selected carnivores to neocortex size, excluding domestic dogs (Lewis, 2003)

8.3.4 Play in Deer

Young ungulates are quite playful, and comparative reviews document the basic patterns in many species (Byers, 1984; Fagen, 1981). Although no phylogenetic studies are available, considerable data exist on play in field or naturalistic settings in Artiodactyla, as well as on the domesticated species. Unlike many species of mammals, which are often small, nocturnal, or live in dense habitats in which observation is difficult, many ungulates are easily observed in the field and there are several fine field studies of social and locomotor play in these species, especially those found in North America (e.g., Byers, 1997; Miller & Byers, 1998; Power, 2000). Here just one comparative study is presented.

A comparison of the behavior of three species of North American Cervidae is available (Müller-Schwarze, 1984). Caribou (*Rangifer tardanus*) live in arctic and subarctic terrain, where they may seasonally migrate hundreds of kilometers. Caribou have a quite open social system; they can aggregate in the hundreds. Mothers stay with their fawns for about a year and leave before calving occurs. However, both family units (mothers and offspring) and male pairs may travel together for years. The other two species studied were the white-tailed deer (*Odocoileus virginianus*) and mule (or black-tailed) deer (*Odocoileus hemionus*). Mule deer stay with their mothers for only 3 months before weaning and are "hiders." That is, they stay motionless under cover for long periods while the mother forages. Social groups are smaller and more stable than in caribou, and intergroup and even fawn-fawn, aggression is frequent. Whitetail deer have a somewhat more open social system than do mule deer, although the basic social unit consists of the female, fawns, and yearlings from the previous year.

Play behavior in all three species contains similar elements, primarily motor patterns involved in escape behavior, with some also derived from fighting and mounting but not courtship or threat (Müller-Schwarze, 1984). Indeed, after listing all the motor patterns involved in threat and courtship, Müller-Schwarze stated that "None of these motor patterns occur in play, although they are precisely the ones whose practising, especially in various pattern combinations, would confer benefits to the individual" (1984: 156).

There were differences among the three species, however. The usually single caribou offspring is "remarkably precocious. It is able to follow its mother after 1 hour of life and can outrun a human when 1 day old" (Nowak, 1999: 1130). Play behavior begins on the second day of age and the amount and complexity of play increase over the next 9 days. Although over 90 percent of play is running, "leaping, butting, striking, mounting, and pawing" (Müller-Schwarze, 1984: 153) also occur. Play occupied a little over 1 percent of total activity time on average, but was more frequent on better quality range.

The kinds of play and their ontogeny in white-tailed and mule deer were very similar and only data for the latter are given. In mule deer play began later than in caribou, at 6 days of age, and peaked at 2.5 months, after which it declined, but could still occur in intense bouts. Play not only included social running (following, chasing, intercepting) but also "head jerks, leaping, running, butting, striking, mounting, pushing, neck-craning, neck-twisting, head-shaking, and reclining" (Müller-Schwarze, 1984: 154–155). Besides this additional complexity and the longer period of juvenile life during which play occurred, play was much more frequent than in caribou, taking up 8.9 percent of total activity time in 2–4-month-old fawns. The greater amount of agonistic behavior in mule and white-tailed deer play was interpreted by the author as being related to their greater aggressive and competitive behavior as adults. Although these results are consistent with both the developmental and ecological predictions from SRT, more detailed comparative work with more species is needed for rigorous comparative analyses.

8.3.5 Conclusions

Although a thorough phylogenetic review of play in the most playful orders of mammals is lacking, this section has shown that there is sufficient variation within orders and families to test hypotheses about the relationship of play to variation in a number of life history, social, physiological, and ecological factors. As emphasized in chapter 5, a particular relationship may not be either causal or functional, but its study is certainly necessary in order to test the generality of conclusions about play derived from intensive experimental research on a single species such as laboratory rats or rhesus monkeys. Social play, in particular, may be rather evolutionarily labile in its complexity, frequency, and association with the factors listed above. Although play is more or less highly developed, especially in the rodents and ungulates, the basic primary and even secondary sources of play were undoubtedly present in the ancestors of all these groups. Play has flowered in many ways.

The limits of comparative analysis across orders or even species must also be recognized. Different populations of the same species must be studied carefully and population differences assessed. Indeed, current and recent selection pressures as well as the role of current ecological factors must be considered in studies of behavioral evolution (Foster & Endler, 1999). The amount of food available and group size are both positively related to the amount of play found in squirrel monkeys (J. D. Baldwin & Baldwin, 1974).

Another example of the importance of ecology is apparent in work on behavioral development and play in populations of bighorn sheep (*Ovis canadensis*) inhabiting desert and mountain environments (Berger, 1979). In these sheep many components of sexual, threat, contact, and locomotor-rotational behavior are incorporated into play shortly after birth. Berger studied three populations of sheep—a Canadian mountain population, a desert population in California, and a mountain population in Oregon derived from animals transplanted from the Canadian population about 20 years previously. Although the behavioral repertoires of all populations were similar, the desert animals played less, matured faster, and lived in smaller social groups. Both lambs and adults had lower behavioral diversities in the desert. However, the desert population appeared better nourished than the mountain population. So, why did they play less when well-nourished squirrel monkeys played more? Berger suggested that food in the desert, although more plentiful, is more dispersed and this would lead to smaller group sizes. His data showed that social play was more frequent in groups of three or more lambs, and that desert animals were more often isolated from their peers, with less opportunity for social facilitation of play. In addition, animals in desert areas achieved independence more quickly than those found in the other two habitats. Furthermore, there were more hazards in the physical environment in the desert. Thus these ecological, physical, and social factors could underlie the difference between desert and mountain populations in playfulness.

Although genetic differences might partially underlie the differences, as shown in the transplant population along with other data (Berger, 1979), later maturity in the mountain population, larger social groups of peers, and a physical environment more conducive to play were all involved in the greater play in mountain animals. Bighorn sheep living in a very arid desert environment such as that of Death Valley, California, might be a good test of the relationships among resources, group size, and play. Berger (1979) predicted that social play would be very infrequent. These studies, by demonstrating the lability of play even within species, teach us that intensive and costly detailed studies of wild populations are needed, not just species-level descriptions and measures such as brain size, typical habitat, and diet.

8.4 More Questions than Answers

If play is not ubiquitous in all placental mammals, it is certainly widespread. Furthermore, it has been found in almost every order to at least some, albeit minimal, degree. Play is not as complex or common in some groups as in others. For example, play seems rare or absent in almost all insectivores and uncommon in bats, lagomorphs, and elephant shrews. Taking play as a single measure, simple associations of play with brain size, metabolic rate, body size, intelligence, ecology, sociality, altriciality, and other factors are modest at best. It is only when several of these factors are taken together or play is broken down into subtypes that relationships appear, as in rodents and primates. At this point, the data necessary to do multiple regression and other integrative analyses are not available.

In any event, although play appears less complex, energetic, and frequent in mammals from older or more archaic groups (e.g., Insectivora, Macroscelidea), it does occur in some species, and an effort to study these groups in closer detail is definitely needed because so many species appear to show no play at all. A formal application of objective criteria is seldom discernable in the literature, in spite of the heroic and insightful analysis of this literature by Fagen (1981). Since then, little new comparative data have accrued for most of the orders reviewed in section 8.2. Nonetheless, the ubiquity of play in mammals (Bekoff & Byers, 1981; Fagen, 1981) means that play in some form occurred in the earliest mammals, and it is to other groups that we must look to critically assess the place of placental mammalian biology in the origin of play. Do other vertebrates have play behavior and is it comparable in diversity and complexity?

9 The Alternate Radiation: Play in Marsupials

9.1 Introduction

Most of our comparative knowledge of play is necessarily based on the familiar mammals of the world: cats, dogs, monkeys, rats, and horses. These are the animals studied by most scientists exploring the mysterious world of animal play. In an earlier chapter, I used a comparison of ectothermic reptiles with typical (eutherian or placental) mammals as a way of developing some understanding of what may be involved in the occurrence of playfulness. Differences from reptiles were related to the evolution of mammalian characteristics such as endothermy, parental care, high metabolic rates, and large brains. Within mammals, preliminary attempts are being made to systematically catalog variations in playfulness and relate such variation to differences in these same characteristics within and across mammalian groups (Iwaniuk, Nelson, & Pellis, 2001). Going further, I used the mammal–reptile contrast to outline an evolutionary scenario to help understand some of the diversity within placental mammals (chapter 6). However, the relationships are only correlational and have not yet been rigorously analyzed; alternative explanations abound. For example, any comparisons among the various radiations of eutherian mammals (primates, canids, rodents) could really be viewed as only one radiation (placental mammals). Controversy about the independence of taxa in comparative testing of hypotheses (Felsenstein, 1985) has made conclusions suspect if all animals compared share the same trait. Rather than argue about the quality, independence, and appropriateness of making comparisons among eutherian mammals in order to understand the processes underlying play, it would be useful to have another comparison group that is independent from the eutherians. Since play is found in almost every placental mammalian order, it is plausible to postulate that play occurred in the earliest mammals and was lost in some lineages. Thus play did not originate in eutherian mammals and only secondary, not primary, factors can be identified.

We are left with two hypotheses. One is that the variation among mammalian groups in "reptilian" traits and the positive correlation with playfulness is more than just a singular relationship existing only in one group, placental mammals. The second hypothesis is that play arose once in mammalian evolution. It would be a useful test of these ideas to have another mammalian radiation with comparable traits to study. Fortunately, we do.

As the world of play description and theory that emerged at the end of the nineteenth century was being formulated and debated, an independently evolved, and evolving, mammalian radiation was being uncovered. These are the marsupials, the now-familiar kangaroos, wallabies, koalas, and opossums, along with dozens of other species about which we still know little. It is only with the rapid development of world-class science in Australia that the details of a wide range of marsupials are becoming known. An excellent, well-illustrated volume by Walton and Richardson (1989) summarizes this work.

The Marsupialia split off from the eutherian line at least 100 mya, in the Cretaceous (see figure 7.1; Clemons, 1989). Based on amino acid substitutions, these dates may be pushed back a bit farther (Clemons, Richardson, & Baverstock, 1989).

Marsupials are members of the Metatheria. It is often thought that with the exception of the domesticated dingo and the monotremes, the marsupials are the sole native mammals of Australia. This is not true. Australia has an extensive representation of bats and rodents, including many endemic species. Bats have been in Australia for upward of 50 million years, while rodents have been there no more than 4 million years (Strahan, 1995). In contrast, humans probably introduced the dingo less than 10,000 years ago. Many marsupials are also found on other nearby South Pacific islands, especially New Guinea, which has a number of endemic species. One order, the Didelphimorphia (opossums), has an extensive radiation in South America, with one species, the Virginia opossum (*Didelphis virginiana*) being very common in North America. It is so successful that its range is still expanding northward. There are many other families of marsupials, with thirteen being found in Australia alone (Walton & Richardson, 1989). The taxonomy of the entire Metatheria is in flux, and the phylogenetic relationships of many families are in dispute (Nowak, 1999). I follow Nowak (1999) in recognizing seven orders of marsupials. Table 9.1 provides a nested taxonomy down to the level of the family.

Do the types of play seen in marsupials vary along the same dimensions as in comparable eutherian groups? To claim that the Metatheria are a useful control group for testing hypotheses derived from placental mammals, one needs to show comparable ecological and behavioral diversity in the two groups. That there is. Marsupials can be carnivores, granivores, frugivores, omnivores, and folivores. There are species that specialize in eating termites or just nectar and pollen. Although no marsupials are truly aquatic, there are arboreal leapers and gliders as well as burrowing molelike forms. Other marsupials hop, climb, and swim.

Marsupials do not reach the great body mass of many eutherians or reptiles, but they do range from a mouselike form (Dasyuridae) weighing less than 5 g as an adult to large kangaroos weighing 85 kg, a range of 1 to 17,000! Although it has not been well studied, antipredator behavior in marsupials is similar to much of that in placental mammals (Coulson, 1996). However, predation on macropods (kangaroos and wallabies) may be less than that on ecologically similar placentals (Croft, 1989). Marsupials and placental mammals often converge in physical appearance and behavior, as shown by the similarities between Australasian possums and Madagascan lemurs (Winter, 1996). The macropods are herbivorous mammals generally viewed as the ecological equivalents to the ungulates (Croft & Ganslosser, 1996). The total number of marsupial species is rather small, about 300. More than 25 percent of these are South American opossums, the oldest and most conservative living marsupials. Didelphids were presumably already present in South America when the continents separated and have speciated extensively since then.

Although the invasion of Australia by placental mammals (rabbits, foxes, cats, deer, and goats among others) and the resulting impact on native marsupials is well known, several members of the kangaroo family (macropods) have themselves become established outside of Australia and the southeast Pacific islands.

9.2   Play in the Metatheria

Until recent years, the research on play in marsupials was limited. Fagen (1981) only reviewed work in two families of marsupials, and this was in less than three pages. His tables (1981: 221–222) include reports on four of the twenty-one currently recognized families (in three of the seven currently recognized orders). Nonetheless, Fagen clearly recognized the importance of marsupials for a comparative study of the evolution of play by looking at convergent processes, although this was funneled through his reliance on brain size: "Whether marsupial play is less elaborate, less frequent, or less stable than the play of corresponding mammals (as the brain-size hypothesis might predict) is not known" (Fagen, 1981: 81).

The situation is better today. Play has been documented in more marsupial species, families, and orders. Detailed studies of several species are also now available. The current situation for research on marsupial play is summarized by Lissowsky (1996), who reviewed play in marsupials, and Watson (1998), who reviewed play in the Macropodoidea, the superfamily that includes the Macropodidae (kangaroos and wallabies) and Potoridae (rat kangaroos). Both authors cite recent and unpublished observations and theses. The marsupial species accounts in Strahan (1995) also added taxa to the list of animals studied (e.g., the Myrmecobiidae; see also Friend & Burrows, 1983). Among other references consulted, Grzimek (1972) contains considerable anecdotal

Table 9.1
Nested taxonomy and play occurrence in the Metatheria (marsupials)

Order/Suborder/ Superfamily/Family	Genera/ Number of Species	Loco- motor Play	Object Play	Social Play	Byers play index	Iwaniuk, Nelson, & Pellis play index	EI	Selected Common Names
South American Radiation								
Order Didelphimorphia								
Marmosidae	8/53	?		Yes		2/3	116	Pouchless mouse opossums
Caluromyidae	2/4							Woolly opossums
Gironiidae	1/1							Bushy-tailed opossums
Didelphidae	4/8							Pouched opossums
Order Microbiotheria	1/1							High-altitude Monito del Monte
Order Paucituberculata	2/7							Shrew opossums
Australasian Radiation								
Order Notoryctemorphia	1/1							Marsupial mole
Order Dasyuromorphia								
Dasyuridae	17/62	Yes	Yes	Yes	1–3	1–3	100	"Mice," "cats," "Tasmanian devil
Thylacinidae	1/1						148	Tasmanian wolf
Myrmecobiidae	1/1	Yes		Yes	3	3		Numbat or banded anteater
Order Peramelemorphia								
Peramelidae	4/11	Yes		?	1	1–2	99	Dry-country bandicoots, bilbies
Peroryctidae	4/11						128	Rainforest bandicoots
Order Diprotodontia								
Suborder Vombatiformes								
Phascolarctidae	1/1			Yes	2	2		Koala
Vombatidae	2/3	Yes		Yes	3	3		Wombats

Table 9.1
(continued)

Order/Suborder/ Superfamily/Family	Genera/ Number of Species	Loco-motor Play	Object Play	Social Play	Byers play index	Iwaniuk, Nelson, & Pellis play index	EI	Selected Common Names
Suborder Phalangerida								
Petauroidea								
Petauridae	3/10	Yes		Yes	?	1–3	156	Gliders, striped possums
Pseudocheiridae	6/16	Yes			1/2	1–2		Ringtailed, greater gliding possums
Tarsipedoidea								
Tarsipedidae	1/1	Yes		Yes	2	2		Honey possum
Acrobatidae	2/2				1	1		Feather-tailed possums
Macropodoidea								
Macropodidae	12/61	Yes	Yes	Yes	3	2–3	142	Kangaroos, wallabies
Potoroidae	5/10	Yes		Yes	3	2–3	166	Rat kangaroos
Phalangeroidea								
Phalangeridae	6/22	Yes			2	2	130	Phalangers, possums, cuscuses
Burramyoidea								
Burramyidae	2/5				1	1	98	Pygmy possums
Total species	~295							

information. Two recent papers based on comparative analyses of degree of play and brain development in marsupials offer additional information (Byers, 1999a; Iwaniuk, Nelson, & Pellis, 2001).

For comparative purposes, the marsupials can be divided into several groups. Here I emphasize those for which some data on play are available (table 9.1). This arrangement is derived from Walton and Richardson (1989) and chapters therein, especially Clemons (1989), and from Nowak (1999).

Lissowsky (1996) begins her review of marsupial play by stating that her "aim is to demonstrate that play behaviour occurs in very similar ways in both subclasses, and that marsupial play is neither less frequent nor less diverse than play in placentals" (1996: 187). This claim may be overstated, but given the lack of behavioral research on marsupials, it still may be a question of insufficient study. Watson (1998) also points out that the view of marsupials as inferior (see later discussion) may have biased observers against interpreting some of their behavior as play. He makes a good case that such misinterpretation has in fact taken place.

9.2.1 Locomotor Play

Locomotor play is found in all families for which any play has been recorded. Southern hairy-nosed wombats (*Lasiorhinus latifrons*) are heavy bodied and highly social. They are arid country grazers living in large underground warrens and have long life-spans, living up to 17 years in captivity (R. T. Wells, 1989). They engage in leaping and bipedal jumping play, as well as extensive social play with a keeper (Fagen, 1981; Lissowsky, 1996). The carnivorous dasyurids show running play as well. All the larger dasyurids engage in locomotor and other forms of play, while the smaller species show virtually none (Croft, 1982). One of the smallest dasyurids, the fat-tailed dunnart (*Sminthopsis crassicaudata*), showed no clear play, but at 11 weeks of age the young engage in a period of short, quick runs with no apparent external stimulus, a phenomenon termed incipient locomotor play (Ewer, 1968b). Bandicoots (*Isoodon obesulus*) perform a variety of nonagonistic behaviors that were considered play by Fagen (1981): leaping, burrowing, climbing, and chasing. Lissowsky (1996) lists this species as engaging in play chasing, but omits it from the list of species that engage in locomotor play. Winter (1996) reports that the arboreal phalanger (*Trichosaurus vulpecula*) plays at climbing. Rat kangaroo (*Potorous tridactylus*) juveniles move extremely fast during play (Lissowsky, 1996). All these phenomena are also common in placental mammal play.

The greatest amount of locomotor play is shown by the macropods, where it seems largely, but not always, related to simulations of predator avoidance behavior (Watson, 1998). Locomotor play seems to decline rapidly with age in macropods. Sex differences exist in some species in the frequency and duration of locomotor play. For example, juvenile male red kangaroos (*Macropus rufus*) played more than juvenile females, but eastern gray kangaroo (*Macropus fulginosus*) females played more than males (Lissowsky, 1996; Watson, 1998).

9.2.2 Object Play

Object manipulation of all kinds seems rather undeveloped in marsupials, and play with objects has been reported only for the dasyurids (Croft, 1982) and macropods. Among the dasyurids, object play in the large carnivorous Tasmanian devil (*Sarcophilus harrisii*) is most documented. A captive individual seized various toys in its mouth and vigorously shook them (Ewer, 1968a). Another captive devil incorporated objects such as water troughs and hollow logs into social and locomotor play (Fagen, 1981). Lissowsky (1996), commenting on a species of broad-footed marsupial mice (*Antechinus stuartii*) suggests that tail-pulling by siblings is a form of predatory object play. These animals also play with twigs, leaves, and small harmless insects by catching, releasing, nipping, patting, or tossing them.

Macropods are almost exclusively herbivorous, but still show object play (Lissowsky, 1996; Watson, 1998). Watson describes this in some detail; unfortunately, all reports are anecdotal. Some macropods use their dexterous forelimbs and mouth to bite, grab, and manipulate items such as sticks, bark, grass, leaves, food, paper, feathers, and novel objects left in their enclosures. They may also wrestle with bushes and throw sticks against their chest. Red kangaroo males engage in more object play than females (Lissowsky, 1996). However, only juvenile macropods have ever been reported responding to objects with play. It is interesting that the much smaller omnivorous rat kangaroos (potorids), the other family in the Macropoidea and the sister group of the macropods, have never been recorded to engage in object play. In other marsupial families, species that manipulate food and other objects do not appear to do so in accord with the definition of play used here.

9.2.3 Social Play

Social play in marsupials is sufficiently well known in some species that it can be grouped into various kinds of play (also see chapter 4).

Parallel Play   In this type of play, two individuals engage in the same play behavior, but do not directly interact. This is usually locomotor or object play. Lissowsky (1996) lists three species of macropods and one potoroid (rat kangaroo) as engaging in parallel play.

Contact Play   Lissowsky (1996) has described this type of play as being the earliest play behavior seen in *Dasyurus maculatus*. It occurs in preweaning individuals where the young of both sexes climb on the back of the mother; the behavior does not seem to be related to predatory, defensive, or courtship behavior (Settle, 1978), although given the theories from Groos (1898) to Pellis (1993), the latter should not be dismissed without further study. One macropod has been reported to engage in "pouch play" in which the young lies on its back and tries to catch hold of the mother's forelimb or fur.

Play Chasing This behavior, which occurs in marsupial herbivores, seems similar to that seen in eutherian herbivores. It may involve subadults or adults and juveniles (Lissowsky, 1996). In addition to the three families she mentions (dry-forest bandicoots, dasyurids, and macropods), it also has been reported in the sole members of the Tarsipedidae, the honey possum (Russell, 1986), and the Myrmecobiidae, the numbat (Byers, 1999a; Friend & Burrows, 1983).

Play Fighting This is the most common form of social play in marsupials, as it is in placentals. Although widely studied in marsupials, especially in macropods, we still know less about it than in placental mammals (Lissowsky, 1996; Watson, 1998).

Until recently, play of any type had not been recorded in the American marsupial radiation (didelphids), but this has now been rectified in a description of play fighting in the gray short-tailed opossum (*Monodelphis domestica*) (Fadem & Corbett, 1997). In this species, both climbing over the back of another animal and bipedal boxing with the front paws is recorded in juveniles of both sexes. Play wrestling occurs in the honey possum (Russell, 1986). Young animals chase each other, followed by wrestling and huddling together "amicably."

Play fighting has been reported in several of the largest carnivorous marsupials, but not the smaller species (Croft, 1982; Iwaniuk, Nelson, & Pellis, 2001; Lissowsky, 1996; Morton, Dickman, & Fletcher, 1989). For example, the largest Australian dasyurid, the tiger quoll (*Dasyurus maculatus*), begins wrestling play as soon as its eyes open at 61–63 days of age, while aggression is not seen until a week or more later. By 90 days of age, social play is well developed and the young chase, stalk, and wrestle with each other. These opportunistic carnivores eat insects and mammals supplied by the parents, but do not kill and eat their own prey until later and are not weaned until 120 days of age or older (Settle, 1978). Play fighting is also well developed in the southern hairy-nosed wombat (Fagen, 1981). It is recorded in virtually all macropods (Lissowsky, 1996; Watson, 1998) and there are several reports for many species. Some of these studies rival the most detailed studies of primate and carnivore play in placental mammals. Play fighting in macropods is thus the aspect of marsupial play that I will present in depth.

There are several thorough ethograms of play fighting in macropods (figure 9.1). Probably the most thorough published studies are the series of papers by Watson and colleagues (Watson, 1993; Watson & Croft, 1993, 1996) on red-necked wallabies (*Macropus rufogriseus banksianus*). Based on observations of captives in naturalistic settings, these workers set forth a meticulous ethogram; traced the ontogeny of play fighting, sex differences, and partner preferences; and made inferences as to whether there is support for the theory that play fighting serves as motor training or whether it enhances socialization.

Figure 9.1
Play fighting as stylized boxing in kangaroos, *Macropus giganteus*. (From Russell, Lee, & Wilson, 1989)

Red-necked wallabies are sexually dimorphic, with males larger than females. Sexual competition seemed more important to males than females. Furthermore, males, but not females, disperse from their natal area upon reaching sexual maturity.

Play fighting in red-necked wallabies involved twenty-one actions that can be placed in five categories (Watson & Croft, 1993): play initiation (approach and orient toward), fighting (skip, grab, spar, paw, push/hit, attack, kick, and defend or break contact), affiliative/sexual (sniff, touch, hold, allogroom, mount), acts during pauses (feed, autogroom, shake, head arch), and acts associated with terminating bouts (orient away, leave). Play fights could be high or low intensity. They were repetitive and had a definite, but not rigid, structure. Play fighting was noted to be "relaxed," and potentially dangerous acts such as kicks were inhibited. Skipping was seen only during play and thus is viewed as a good candidate for a play signal. Other acts were exaggerated or differed from their typical context, such as autogrooming and shaking. Play fights were also characterized by the absence of the following acts seen during serious fighting in macropods: stiff-legged walking, grass-pulling displays, and agonistic vocalizations

Figure 9.2
Play fight sparring in mother and young kangaroos. (From Russell, Lee, and Wilson, 1989)

(Watson, 1993). Furthermore, no resource was identifiable as the object of competition (e.g., food, water, resting sites, sexual partner). All these characteristics of play fighting in red-necked wallabies show that the behavior easily meets the five play criteria.

Males play fought almost thirty times more than females, although the three females that did fight had bout durations as long as those of males. Play fighting began as early as 7 months after birth, which was soon after the young began to leave the pouch and 2 months before permanent emergence (figure 9.2). Following weaning at about 16 months of age, the duration of play fights decreased, but the frequency increased. It declined sharply at 20–22 months of age, which is the onset of sexual maturity in males.

Watson and Croft (1993) subdivided the development of play fighting in male wallabies into three stages in which different patterns of play fighting predominated. The first involved high-intensity fights that increased with age from prepouch emergence to weaning. The second lasted from weaning to sexual maturity. As this stage progressed, play fights were shorter and play initiations and solicitations were increasingly rebuffed. Peak instability took place at sexual maturity. During this time, true agonistic behavior increased and partner relationships became unstable. The third stage was found among older adult males and was characterized by low-intensity play fights.

More than 90 percent of the play groups were dyadic. Male wallabies preferred play partners of the same sex and comparable age and dominance status. Females initiated play bouts with younger males as well as with their male offspring. No play between females was ever recorded. Play partnerships developed among males, but these were only weakly related to affiliative behaviors outside the play context (Watson, 1993). A further study established that wallabies adjusted their play tactics to the age of their partner. Older partners seemed to self-handicap when they played with younger and smaller wallabies. They did this by standing flat-footed, pawing rather than sparring, and not using the strength and power they were capable of deploying. Younger animals were more likely to spar and take on a high stance posture (Watson & Croft, 1996). Shaking apparently functions as an appeasement or metacommunication ("it is only play") signal.

The presence of some of the more advanced features of play fighting, especially self-handicapping and play signals, has been established in several species of marsupials. No exclusive and necessary play signals have been documented for any marsupial, however (Watson, 1998), and are rare in placental mammals as well (Pellis & Pellis, 1996); self-handicapping seems more common (Watson, 1998). Role reversals are frequent in red-necked wallabies (Watson & Croft, 1996) and red kangaroos (Croft & Snaith, 1991), and probably occur in other macropods as well (Watson, personal communication, 1997).

Watson and Croft (1993) and Watson (1998) make a strong case that many reports of adult ritualized fights in macropods are misclassified play fights. The basic argument is that the agonistic elements described above (as in red-necked wallabies) are absent and no resource is ever identified as the reason for serious competition. If this view is sustained, then macropods show more frequent adult play than that found in many placental mammals.

Sex Play Sexual behaviors such as sniffing, tail pawing, mounting, thrusting, and other precocial sexual activity may occur in juveniles. Adult females may also take on the male role (Watson, 1998). Such behavior may occur alone or in the context of play fighting, much as we have seen in rodents; this is even true of a didelphid (Fadem & Corbett, 1997).

Interspecific Social Play This form of play has been recorded in several species, primarily in hand-reared animals in response to their caregivers (Watson, 1998, personal communication, 1997) and in wombats as mentioned earlier.

A similarity with eutherian mammals is the greater frequency of play in well cared-for captive marsupials compared with animals in the field (Watson, personal communication, 1997). Red-necked wallabies are rather solitary and when they were observed in the field during a severe drought, no play of any type was seen, although it has been reported in the field (Watson, personal communication, 1997).

9.3   Phylogeny of Play in Marsupials

Fagen (1981) noted (in his table 3.2) that play was recorded in four families, the carnivorous Dasyuridae (five species), the bandicoot family (Peramelidae), wombats (Vombatidae), and kangaroos and wallabies (Macropodidae). From the more recent literature
we can add examples from one of the three American orders of marsupials (opossums)
as well as the Potoroidae (rat kangaroos), Phalangeridae (possums), Myrmecobiidae
(numbat), and in fact members of eleven of fifteen families in the Australasian radiation. New marsupials are still being discovered or even rediscovered. Three of the four
families in which play has not been observed consist of only one to five species, most
little studied. These include small marsupials such as pygmy possums and the marsupial mole. The Virginia opossum has been studied for years without any references to
play that I could locate (cf. Fagen, 1981; Lissowsky, 1996). This is of interest because
the Virginia opossum is a foraging generalist and perhaps the most successful marsupial in competition with placental mammals. Play must not be currently important
to its success. Although play may not be at all prominent in opossums, Glickman
and Sroges (1966) noted that in their brief curiosity tests, Virginia opossums did grab
and manipulate small objects. This was not a study of play, however, and the five play
criteria are not met.

In table 9.1, I list the types of play that have been found by family. Note that by far
the most diverse play is found in the Dasyuridae and the macropods. These are, except
for the little-studied neotropical mouse opossums, the most speciose (i.e., rich in species) extant families. Furthermore, the most diverse play has been recorded for these
species, especially the macropods (Lissowsky, 1996; Watson, 1998). As we have seen,
play in macropods is rather common and highly developed, while in the dasyurids, it is
limited to the larger species. Dasyurids can be very small, whereas macropods are all at
least several hundred grams as adults. The one large family in which play has not been
reported until recently is the superfamily Petauroidea, the gliders. Based on ecology (it
is an extractive forager) and brain size, it might be expected to play, and this has now
been confirmed (Iwaniuk, Nelson, & Pellis, 2001; Russell, Lee, & Wilson, 1989).

The conclusion that locomotor play is the earliest-appearing type of play (Byers,
1984) is supported by the findings in marsupials. Ten families show this behavior. Five
of them show play chasing, which seems easily derived from locomotor play when a
conspecific, especially a sibling, is present. Play fighting and play signals are reported
for three families (wombats, dasyurids, and macropods), but sexual play and object
play are reported only in the latter two. However, in macropods, play fighting is even
more common than locomotor play in animals that have permanently left the pouch.
In red-necked wallabies, play by pouch young is more often locomotor. Adult females
never play fight and rarely perform locomotor play; young adult males do both
(Watson, personal communication, 1997).

A problem in comparing marsupials with placental mammals now needs to be pointed out. Until recently, all 300 or so marsupials were placed in a single order, the Marsupialia, while living placental mammals are currently organized into 16 (Novacek, 1992) or 19 (Nowak, 1999) orders. There are also about fifteen times as many placental species as marsupial species. Thus comparing orders of eutherians with the approximately same number of families of marsupials could be considered an apples-and-oranges error. Maybe not. The higher taxonomic levels are always somewhat problematic, and what constitutes genera, families, orders, and the many intermediate groups often seems arbitrary across groups of animals. The number of species involved and our anthropomorphic determination of what makes for useful categories are important considerations. The diversity among marsupials certainly is apparently beyond that seen in any single eutherian order, both in amount and type of play. With the recognition that marsupials are best viewed as consisting of at least seven orders, the diversity between placental and marsupial orders is not inordinately extreme. That there are fewer orders and species in the marsupials could be related to the more limited geographic areas where most of their modern evolution has taken place (i.e., Australia).

Play, often very complex, has been found in most of the eutherian orders. Play is sometimes rare or simple in very small mammals, mammals with very low metabolic rates, and mammals feeding on low-nutrient diets. Marsupials do have lower metabolic rates than placentals and have a smaller average body size. These limitations, especially body size, do not apply to many marsupials, yet marsupial play, outside of macropods, seems rather simple and undeveloped in all but a few species, in spite of the enthusiasm of Lissowsky (1996). The macropods include the largest marsupials and they are rather long lived. Even compared with comparable placental species, however, macropods are not as energetically and continually playful as are many large herbivorous eutherian mammals, such as deer and horses. However, as described for reptiles in chapter 11, play does not have to be the frenetic, vigorous activity seen in many placental mammals to be true play.

Thus in spite of macropod social play being both common and complex, it may seem that play is not nearly as common in marsupials as in eutherian mammals, at least at the family level. Object play and manipulation seem particularly undeveloped. With the possible exception of social play in some macropods, there do not appear to be any marsupial player equivalents of otters, bears, or monkeys, all of whom have stages in their life in which play is very prevalent. Perhaps this is a bit unfair. Many placental mammalian families have not been reported to play, but the three groups mentioned (aquatic carnivores, terrestrial carnivores, and primates) have larger brains and higher metabolic rates than other groups.

The South American opossums have been little studied as a group. The finding of quite well-developed social play fighting in the gray short-tailed opossum led to the authors claiming that since didelphids are one of the oldest marsupial orders, play is very ancient (Fadem & Corbett, 1997). Indeed, this mouse opossum, which has been shown to play, is so primitive it has no pouch. Other South American marsupials, so little known, need to be studied. One likely candidate for playing, based on SRT, is the little-known yapok or water opossum (*Chironectes minimus*) found throughout much of Central and South America, although it is seemingly rare (Nowak, 1999). An adult weighs up to a kilogram or more. The yapok is an excellent swimmer, has webbed feet, and is carnivorous on small aquatic animals that it locates with its forefeet. The sole member of the Microbiotheria, the Monito del Monte (South American high-altitude opossum), should be studied as well, since it is considered the most primitive of living marsupials, even retaining some monotreme traits not found in any other marsupials (Nowak, 1999).

9.4   Why Do Marsupials Differ from Placental Mammals?

When first discovered, marsupials were considered clearly inferior in brain development, intelligence, and behavioral complexity compared with eutherians (Grzimek, 1972). Nonetheless, the brains of marsupials are in many respects similar to those of eutherian mammals (Butler & Hodos, 1996; Rowe, 1996). They vary in amount of cortex (encephalization) and cortical convolutions, as do eutherian mammals. There are some differences in the connections between the two hemispheres, with the marsupials being more similar to monotremes. Despite the similarities, it has been shown that the relative brain mass of marsupials, controlling for body mass, is generally less than in comparable placental mammals (Eisenberg, 1981; Jerison, 1973). For example, the didelphids (opossums) seem to have the lowest brain development and the macropods (kangaroos and relatives) the highest within the marsupials (Dawson et al., 1989). The didelphids are considered among the oldest groups of living marsupials, and an opossum the size of a cat has a brain less than 20 percent the size of the cat's (Hoffman, 1982). On the other hand, the tammar wallaby (*Macropus eugenii*) has a larger brain for its body size than diverse placental mammals such as a laboratory mouse, rat, guinea pig, or pig, and the brain is nearly equivalent in size to that of sheep (Renfree et al., 1982). Still, as a group marsupials are less brain laden than placental mammals. If play is related to brain size, then marsupials should play, but less frequently and with less complexity, as Fagen (1981) suggested. But brain size is also related to metabolic rate and this is generally lower in marsupials. Furthermore, adult altricial mammals have smaller brains for their body size than adult precocial mammals (Harvey & Bennett, 1983), and marsupials are the ultimate altricial species if birth, rather than emergence from the pouch, is considered. Is brain size, metabolic rate, or neither related to play variation in marsupials?

The eutherian-marsupial behavior comparison has been revisited with more data and insight than have been hitherto available (Croft & Ganslosser, 1996). Based on more recent data, marsupials are about at the relative brain size level of advanced insectivores and some prosimians, but have relatively smaller and less complex brains than all monkeys and apes (Rowe, 1996).

The brain size data are worth exploring further. Since larger species have relatively smaller brains in terms of body mass than smaller species, an allometric relationship has been established between body size and brain size that allows species of different sizes to be compared (Jerison, 1973). As indicated in chapter 8, this ratio is called the EQ (encephalization quotient). Rowe (1996) adjusted the EQ to 100 for values based on dasyurids (and called it the encephalization index or EI). Using this index, opossums in the genus *Didelphis* (including the Virginia opossum) have a value of 75, the lowest yet found in a marsupial (but see Iwaniuk, Nelson, & Pellis, 2001, for lower values in some other marsupials using a different measure). The EI values reported by family are listed in table 9.1. Note that the families reported to play have generally larger values. Since these values vary so much within families, a better approach would be to compare playful and nonplayful species within each family as well as the mean level of play, using some play metric, and mean brain size by family or even genus.

Table 9.1 lists the play values, by family, for Australasian groups as used in brain size and play analyses by Byers (1999a) and Iwaniuk, Nelson, and Pellis (2001). Comparing these values with placentals, it appears that the basal insectivore EI is 60 and that for the entire order about 100; prosimians average 256 and monkeys and apes 543. The highest EI for a marsupial seems to be an arboreal possum in the Petauridae (*Dactylopsila trivirgata*). The one individual measured had a value of 224, but has not been reported to play (Iwaniuk, Nelson, & Pellis, 2001). This species has forelimb digits specialized for foraging and extracting ants from crevices in tree bark (Nowak, 1999; Rowe, 1996). This "outlier" species is not represented in the table. The mean of 156 is for the genus *Petaurus* itself. I have talked to people who have had sugar gliders (*Petaurus breviceps*), another member of this family, as pets and they have mentioned play with objects. Thus these animals are included in the table with a question mark.

Studies on the cortical representations in the brains of placentals, monotremes, and marsupials cannot tell us which features, or which species, reflect the ancestral mammalian form (Rowe, 1996). Even the similarities that exist "may reflect parallel evolution rather than the retention of attributes characteristic of an ancestral form of cerebral cortex" (Rowe, 1996: 33). In spite of their having somewhat smaller brains than eutherians, the amount of neocortex in marsupials, contrary to earlier reports, is about the same. Learning abilities in the marsupials studied have not been found to be inferior to those of ecologically similar placental mammals when their ecological and behavioral adaptations are considered, although their intellectual inferiority is often assumed. This may not be entirely appropriate. For example, the dasyurid *Sminthopsis crassicaudata* weighs only about 10 g as an adult, which is much smaller than a house mouse, and has a very small brain with little neocortex for its body size (Bonney &

Wynne, 2002; Jerison, 1973). Yet it is the first marsupial to be shown to have the "win stay, lose shift" learning strategy found in many eutherian mammals (Bonney & Wynne, 2002).

Marsupials are born in a more altricial state than eutherian mammals. Consider the tammar wallaby, which at birth weighs about 0.5 g, whereas the adult weight is around 5 kg, a difference of 10,000 (Rowe, 1996)! Full brain development is not reached until more than 6 months after birth (Renfree et al., 1982). During the first 180 days after birth, the brain increases from 4.5 to 60 percent of the adult weight. At emergence from the pouch at 250 days, the brain is about 70 percent of the adult weight. This provides a great opportunity to not only follow neural and sensory development but to observe the details of behavioral ontogeny. However, just as placental mammals are born at different stages of development, as in the altricial–precocial dichotomy, so are marsupials born with different levels of cortical development (Rowe, 1996). Some marsupials are born with less developed brains than others (Rowe, 1996), but all are much more altricial than any placental mammal.

If we consider emergence from the pouch comparable to placental birth, then the precocial–altricial range is more similar to that seen in eutherian mammals. It also has been argued that a better equivalent to placental mammal birth is when the young become endothermic and insulated with fur (Russell, 1982). Macropods are more likely to have extensive parental care after leaving the pouch and may have brains that are less fully developed (Renfree et al., 1982) than other marsupials from other families or species. Thus postpouch parental care may indicate less behavioral precocity and be reflected in more play. This extreme initial altriciality, with most neural development taking place in the womb in placentals, but after birth in marsupials and monotremes, also suggests that the latter are the animals of choice to test the suggested relationship and continuity between prenatal spontaneous movements and play (Bekoff, Byers, & Bekoff, 1980).

Metabolic rates in marsupials are significantly lower than those of placental mammals (McNab, 1988). They also do not vary as much as in placental mammals. Marsupials may have evolved in tropical forest environments and many macropods (e.g., tree kangaroos) and the potorids still live in these environments in Australia, as do all three South American orders of marsupials. However, tree kangaroos appear to have secondarily invaded arboreal habitats and adapted the macropod locomotor style to living in trees. Low metabolic rates may have facilitated the success of so many diurnal marsupials in the hot, arid areas of Australia as the continent dried out beginning in the Miocene; high metabolic rates could have mitigated their success. Lizards, for example, are more successful (in biomass) in deserts than many mammals and birds because they can endure food shortages and wait for highly seasonal food resources. The lower metabolic rate in marsupials suggests a constrained life in the ectotherm direction, and thus may dampen the expression of play in spite of other favorable factors.

In the first formal study of brain size in Australian marsupials and play, Byers (1999a) found a significant relationship at the family level, correcting for body size, with all four of his most playful families (numbat, potorids, macropods, and wombats) above the regression line. According to Byers, only these families, and some dasyurids, have juvenile play. On the other hand, there was no relationship with metabolic rate, leading to the comment that we find here "mind over metabolism" (Byers, 1999b: 40) and the claim that young playful marsupials "are directing their own brain assembly" (Byers, 1999b: 45). The latter statement reflects Byers's view that play may be important in developing the brain at certain critical stages in life (Burghardt, 2001; Byers & Walker, 1995). In addition, according to SRT, play should be related to energetic, ecological, and behavioral factors. The koala has a restricted behavioral repertoire, a low metabolic rate, a sedentary way of life (it is inactive 20 hours a day), a specialized plant diet, a slow rate of locomotion (although it is capable of quick bursts of speed), and a smooth-surfaced brain that is much smaller than its brain cavity (Byers, 1999a; Strahan, 1995). The wombats, closest relatives to the koala, are at the opposite of the koala in almost every dimension. Wombats are playful, koalas far less so.

It should be pointed out that Byers (1999a) used only a measure of play frequency on a three-point scale: (1) no play, (2) play bouts of less than 5 seconds occurring less than once every 45 minutes over fewer than 3 days after leaving the pouch, or (3) play occurring for bouts of at least 20 seconds on most days after leaving the pouch. I assume that there were no species in between categories 2 and 3.

A more recent study (Iwaniuk, Nelson, & Pellis, 2001) pointed out some problems in Byers's analysis and added more species. Byers averaged play across families using his three-point scale (see table 9.1); one or two playful species in a larger family could skew the results. In addition, the relatedness of the families was not considered, resulting in comparisons that were confounded by the degree of relationship among the families. For example, almost all the playful species except for the dasyurids are in one order, the Diprotodontia.

Iwaniuk and colleagues (2001) used the same play scale as Byers did, but included more species. They used an accepted phylogeny for the relationships among the forty-five species for which they had data. Overall brain size (EQ) was significantly correlated with both play frequency (replicating Byers, 1999a) and play wrestling (play fighting); the results were attenuated by using the method of independent contrasts. Although positive correlations between overall brain size (EQ) and neocortical size were found for both play frequency and play wrestling, only the relationship between play frequency and neocortex size ($r = 0.59$) approached statistical significance at the family level, and only that of play frequency and overall brain size ($r = 0.26$) approached significance using the full data set. In a study of eighteen diverse marsupials, forelimb dexterity (wrist, paw, digits) was also significantly related to cortex size, not total brain size (Iwaniuk, Nelson, & Whishaw, 2000). Relating forelimb dexterity and play holding brain/cortex size constant would help test more of the foraging mode hypotheses in chapter 6 and could be carried out across all terrestrial vertebrates (Iwaniuk & Whishaw, 2000).

In placental mammals, play, especially social play, is somewhat related to social organization. Among marsupials, even the large macropods show far less diversity and complexity in social systems than eutherians. Beyond mother-infant bonds, there is no complex social network and there are no instances of hierarchical control of mating opportunities as extreme as that found in wolves and chimps (Hendrichs, 1996). On the other hand, the kinds of choices made by females are similar for marsupials and placental mammals (Walker, 1996). Also, as in many lizards, birds, and eutherian mammals, male size-based dominance hierarchies that enhance access to females have been documented in many kangaroos (Croft, 1989).

When contrasting two distinct stocks of animals in order to "detect the influence of phylogenetic constraints we need to show consistent differences (a patterning of differences) between two phylogenetically distinct arrays when faced with similar sets of niche opportunities" (Jarman & Kruuk, 1996: 80). To evaluate sociality, these authors classified female spatial-social organization into six categories of style as shown in table 9.2.

All but two of the thirteen families of marsupials Jarman and Kruuk evaluated had 100 percent of all species studied in category D. The exceptions were six of sixty-three macropod species, categorized as E, and all of the Petauridae, whose species fall into categories A, B, or C, many of which carry out group defense. The latter group consists of small arboreal nectar and sap specialists comparable to small marmosets and galagos. Since they show convergence with these placentals in niche and social system, marsupials can evolve more complex social systems, although most have not.

The authors argue that style D is the original and ancient mammalian style of adult female sociality and that all other styles can be derived from it. "There seems to be no general adaptive reasons for the metatherian failure to evolve sociality or defence of

Table 9.2

Styles of spatial-social organization in adult female mammals

Range Defense	Sociality	Style
Defended by female	Forages solitarily	A
Defended by group	Forages solitarily	B
Defended by group	Forages socially	C
Undefended range	Forages solitarily	D
Undefended range	Forages in ephemeral groups	E
Undefended range	Forages in persistent groups	F

Source: Jarman & Kruuk (1996)

range. On the evidence, the Metatheria either have not met the same evolutionary challenges as some Eutheria, or they are relatively behaviorally plesiomorphic, perhaps the victims of phylogenetic constraints" (Jarman & Kruuk, 1996: 96). Thus social organization, at least the female style looked at here, is not of value in understanding the distribution of play among marsupials. That territorial defense can occur in marsupials is shown by Bennett's tree kangaroo (*Dendrolagus bennettianus*) in Australia (Strahan, 1995). Males of this species defend discrete territories and are intolerant of each other. Their polygynous system is similar to that in many eutherian mammals as well as many lizards. When the radiation of tree kangaroos in New Guinea is studied, we may find much more complex social organization. Two other members of the genus *Dendrolagus* that have been studied have high play frequency scores and play fighting (Iwaniuk, Nelson, & Pellis, 2001).

No dasyurids, which include the carnivorous marsupials, show social foraging or social range defense. This is in contrast with eutherian carnivores and insectivores. In terms of predatory behavior, the typical view is that marsupial carnivores are less flexible in response to prey than are eutherians (Pellis & Officer, 1987). In a comparative study of both the attack strategy predators used prior to prey contact and how they performed head shaking after grasping prey, Pellis and Officer (1987) compared four carnivorous dasyurid marsupials from three genera with the well-studied domestic cat. Responses to prey such as mice, rats, chickens, guinea pigs, and invertebrates were filmed. There were differences among the marsupials with one species, *Dasyuroides brynei*, having the only frontal attack tactic. Head shaking was found in all species, but might be modified by habitat constraints (e.g., arboreality). Having only a highly domesticated placental mammal for comparison, they judiciously drew no conclusions about the relative plasticity of marsupial and eutherian predators. In a later study (Ben-David, Pellis, & Pellis, 1991), the predatory tactics of the marbled polecat (*Vormela peregusna syriaca*) were described in which the location of bites was related to the size of prey and whether the prey were fleeing or defending themselves. This variability was interpreted as related to the opportunistic and nonspecialized nature of the prey this species eats. However, the authors pointed out that many placental mammalian predators are also quite stereotyped in their predatory tactics. These include species that are considered highly playful, such as mongooses (Rasa, 1984). More detailed comparisons of predatory tactical diversity among placental and marsupial lineages would be most useful in establishing the relative degree of flexibility shown both across taxa and within individuals and whether such flexibility is at all related to amount or type of play. Object play, so common in predatory placentals, is present, but does not seem highly developed even in the carnivorous marsupials. It is too soon to relate generalized predatory behavior to amount of object play, although predators clearly engage in object play in ways that resemble aspects of real predation.

Does the lessened social complexity in marsupials explain the lessened variability in their behavior? Hendrichs (1996) closely compared marsupial and placental mammal sociality. Although there is indeed overlap with some eutherian species, he also recognized that marsupials nonetheless differ from eutherians in body size (smaller), metabolic rate (lower), hemispheric connections (fewer), sociality (less complex), and cognitive competence (less), among other differences. He evaluated sociality in light of four factors: social, physiological, mental, and behavioral. In all domains marsupials, even macropods, seem to function on an overall lower level than their eutherian counterparts. Hendrichs concluded that cognitive and behavioral competence requires physiological complexity, but not social complexity. On the other hand, complex social organization requires physiological (varying stress and coping reactions) and behavioral (varying social and reproductive roles) differentiation, but not necessarily high mental competence. He thus concluded that the lower average mental competence of marsupials is not due to lack of more complex sociality, but may be the result of less pronounced physiological and behavioral differentiations. Nevertheless, the "less pronounced physiological and behavioural differentiations possibly do not favour the quick and precise—and therefore costly—activations and regulations necessary for efficiency in complex mammalian systems" (Hendrichs, 1996: 131). This conclusion bears a close, and apparently independent, resemblance to the arguments I previously made in comparing mammals and nonavian reptiles in general (Burghardt, 1988b). On the other hand, the exceptions are often the most illuminating. A comparison of different groups of marsupials and eutherian mammals of similar size, diet, and microhabitat would allow more precise understanding of the exact methods being employed, including the role of any playfulness.

In summation, many of the more complex patterns of social play seen in placental mammals (play fighting, play signals, role reversal, self-handicapping) can be found in at least some marsupials. However, is it also safe to conclude that play is not as ubiquitous in the families with smaller marsupials as it is in those with larger-bodied species? Could the fact that play is more common in larger-bodied and more speciose families of marsupials be related to their relative success? We cannot yet answer this question.

Nevertheless, we can give tentative answers to the two questions posed at the beginning of this chapter. The absence of play in the families of marsupials with relatively small brains, such as the didelphids, the oldest known lineage of marsupials with the exception of the one extant member of the Microbiotheriidae (the South American high-altitude opossum, about which little is known), suggests that brain size is involved. It also suggests that the earliest marsupials did not play, at least complexly, and thus play is not homologous in metatherian and eutherian mammals. As for the other issue, whether the ectotherm–endotherm contrasts used with eutherian mammals can be also used with marsupials, the answer is a tentative yes. Degree of altriciality, body size, metabolic rate, captivity effects, all seem to vary in marsupials according to SRT, but the data are still very sparse. The macropods are a critical group for this evaluation, but most of the smaller and more cryptic kangaroos, wallabies, and their relatives have not yet been studied. Since macropods are so often compared with ungulates as their placental ecological equivalents, more formal analysis should be carried out here as well, using comparable methods and data gathering so quantitative, not just qualitative, comparisons can be made.

10 Does the Platypus Play?

10.1 An Informative Relic Group

When the marsupials split off from the lineage that became the eutherian mammals about 100 mya, dinosaurs dominated the terrestrial landscape. Many millions of years earlier the mammal-like reptiles evolved and perhaps about 200 mya the monotremes first appeared (figure 7.1). Today the remnants of this ancient group live only in Australia and New Guinea, although fossils have been found in South America. These mammals have retained the most primitive, that is reptilian, characteristics, and their exact relationships to other mammals are still controversial (Musser, 2003). Although I portrayed the monotremes as splitting off the lineage leading to marsupials and eutherians (figure 10.1), this is not the only hypothesis available. Unfortunately, fossil evidence for the relationships among Mesozoic mammals is quite sparse.

Four scenarios have been advanced over the past century for the relationship of monotremes with other mammals (M. Griffiths, 1978). The most radical view is that monotremes independently evolved from therapsid ("mammal-like" reptiles) and the similarity with marsupials is convergent. Another view is that monotremes are derived from early marsupials, sharing derived characters such as the dentition of the milk teeth. A third view, based on brain case morphology, is that the monotremes are allied with extinct mammalian nontherian orders such as the Multituberculata and the Triconodonta, and with these and other groups belong in a separate subclass of mammals called the Prototheria. Other specialists would link monotremes just with the Multituberculata and place the placental mammals and marsupials in the Theria subclass. The current consensus seems to be to consider all living mammals a monophyletic group evolved from a cynodont mammal-like reptile with monotremes most closely related to the long-extinct mammalian groups, the multituberculates and triconodonts (Colbert, Morales, & Minkoff, 2001). Since there are problems with all these views, it is most conservative to divide living mammals into three subclasses for the monotremes, marsupials, and placentals. Molecular evidence may shuffle the relationships still more (Grützner et al., 2003; Zardoya & Meyer, 2004). Regardless, if play is found in monotremes, the potential for evolving play would go back at least to the earliest mammals.

Unfortunately, only two families of monotremes exist today: the duckbilled platypus (one species) and spiny anteaters (two genera, two species). These fascinating animals have been increasingly studied in recent decades. Excellent concise overviews of anatomy, life history, reproduction, and physiology are available (Eisenberg, 1981; Grant, 1989; M. Griffiths, 1978, 1989; Nowak, 1999) along with a fascinating book on the history of the scientific controversies surrounding them (Moyal, 2001). A brief review is given here in addition to addressing the question of play in this group of mammals that might be critical in understanding the genesis of mammalian play.

The echidnas (spiny anteaters) live in New Guinea (*Zaglossus*, long-nosed echidna), where they are large (5–10 kg); and in Australia, Tasmania, and nearby islands (*Tachyglossus*, short-nosed echidna), where they are small (3–6 kg). *Tachyglossus* is highly specialized for feeding on ants and termites. *Zaglossus* feeds on earthworms and small arthropods, but is otherwise little studied, and most of our knowledge of echidnas is based on *Tachyglossus* (M. Griffiths, 1978). Both species have long tongues, no teeth, and powerful bodies covered with hedgehoglike spines. They can dig burrows with ease.

The platypus (*Ornithorhynchus anatinus*), an aquatic specialist, lives in eastern non-arid Australia and along rivers into South Australia. Its streamlined body is considerably smaller than that of echidnas (0.5–2.0 kg), but shows more sexual dimorphism; adult male mass is almost twice that of females (Grant, 1989). A fine, but dated, review of the sensory and behavioral biology of the species is available (Burrell, 1927) in addition to a later review (M. Griffiths, 1978). Platypuses, with their ducklike bill, primarily feed on soft aquatic invertebrates and crustaceans. They seem to eat prodigious amounts for their body size: a 2-pound (0.9-kg) female was recorded eating 1 3/4 pounds (0.8 kg) of washed live food in 1 day (Fleay, 1944)!

Both groups of monotremes are highly specialized animals. While retaining more reptilian characteristics than other mammals, they certainly are not living fossils in the narrow sense. Although monotremes do have some ancestral traits, they also have many derived specialized traits. However, for the echidna, "the overall skeletal characteristics do suggest a living species that might represent the ancestral mammalian condition" (Jerison, 1973: 7), while Musser (2003) argues that platypuses are the much older family. The monotreme reproductive mode of laying eggs, the structure of their sperm, their possession of internal testes, and the structure of their pectoral girdles all show strong reptilian affinities. The name Monotremata derives from the fact that like all reptiles, a single orifice, the cloaca, is used for passing urine, digestive wastes, and gametes. Marsupials also share this trait.

Monotremes maintain lower body temperatures than most other mammals, about 30–32°C. Monotremes, especially the echidna, do not regulate their body temperature as precisely as most eutherian mammals and thus they have been termed heterothermic (M. Griffiths, 1989). However, some placental mammals, such as sloths, also show less than precise thermoregulatory abilities. The neonates of many placental species that have altricial young lacking insulation (hair and fur) also have a limited ability to thermoregulate. It is possible that the heterothermic tendencies of sloths may have been secondarily developed as an evolutionary response to a slow-paced life-style relying on a low-energy diet (leaves). The situation with the platypus is similar. The platypus is able to maintain a stable body temperature of 32°C until an ambient temperature of 30°C is reached. However, in cool weather the extremities may only be 1 or 2°C above ambient air or water temperature (Grant, 1989). Since the ability of ancestral monotremes to thermoregulate is not known, the extant, highly derived forms may also be showing a secondary response.

All monotremes are relatively long lived (close to 20 years) and reproduce slowly, having clutches of only one or two offspring yearly. Being long lived, it might pay to benefit from experience. In fact, a feature of monotremes that is not primitive is that they possess very large and differentiated brains compared with some basal groups of placental mammals (insectivores such as the hedgehog) and marsupials (didelphids such as the opossum) (Jerison, 1973). The purpose of these brains has been the subject of a debate that is still unresolved.

Little is known about the natural behavior of monotremes, but play does not appear prominent. Fagen (1981), summarizing the types and distribution of mammalian play, does not report observations on the spiny anteaters. Echidnas have a very large and convoluted brain (Butler & Hodos, 1996) and can learn some tasks as quickly as laboratory rats (M. Griffiths, 1989). The behavior patterns recorded for the echidna may preclude typical play. Their antipredator strategy is to roll up into a spine-protected ball, thus obviating the need for the active defensive maneuvers often seen in play. Similarly, the forelegs of the animals are modified so much for digging that the use of the forepaws in manipulation or grooming is limited (Eisenberg, 1981). Sometimes these two traits operate in concert, as when the echidna digs an escape burrow while its spines protect its exposed dorsum. Echidnas have highly specialized food habits.

Clearly, we need to know more, but all the above features, combined with their low-energy diet, which demands a high rate of intake, suggest that play would not be conspicuous in these animals. Brattstrom (1973), a scientist specializing in reptiles and their behavior, described the social and maintenance behavior of *Tachyglossus* in detail, listing more than sixty postures, feeding and defensive behaviors, locomotion, bodily maintenance, and investigative responses such as sniffing. He reported nothing resembling play and concluded that the echidnas' behavior was quite simple and less complex than that found in many lizards. They are primarily solitary as adults.

In the platypus, the brain is smooth (it has an unconvoluted cortex, like that of a laboratory rat) but relatively large. Although no formal learning studies appear to have been performed on the platypus, there are considerably more behavioral observations available than in the echidnas. The animals occupy a semiaquatic niche in Australia that is not occupied by any marsupials. They are quite active at times and when not in the water remain in burrow retreats. Platypuses seem to possess a richer array of foraging and defensive behavior patterns than do echidnas, although I am not aware of any comparative ethograms. Foraging on a wide array of aquatic animals, they also have almost twice as high a metabolic rate as echidnas and an even larger brain, almost at the eutherian mammalian average for their body size (Eisenberg, 1981).

10.2   Play in Monotremes

Play has not been noted in echidnas, and all evidence for play in the platypus is anecdotal (Fagen, 1981); given the importance of this group, I will review what we know.

The classic description is from Bennett (1835), who had a captive pair in his room in Sydney. "One evening both the animals came out about dusk, went as usual and ate food from the saucer, and then commenced playing one with the other like two puppies, attacking with their mandibles and raising the fore paws against each other. In the struggle one would get thrust down, and at the moment when the spectator would expect it to rise again and renew the combat, it would commence scratching itself, its antagonist looking on and waiting for the sport to be renewed" (1835: 256).

Later he writes: "Sometimes I have been able to enter into play with them, by scratching and tickling them with my finger; they seemed to enjoy it exceedingly, opening their mandibles, biting playfully at the finger, and moving about like puppies indulged with similar treatment" (Bennett, 1835: 256). After providing them with a pan of shallow water "with a turf of grass in a corner, they enjoyed it exceedingly. They would sport together, attacking one another with their mandibles, and roll over in the water in the midst of their gambols; and would afterwards retire, when tired, to the turf, where they would lie combing themselves. It was most ludicrous to observe these uncouth-looking little beasts running about, overturning and seizing one another with their mandibles, and then in the midst of their fun and frolic coolly inclining to one side and scratching themselves in the gentlest manner imaginable" (Bennett, 1835: 256–257).

Although this certainly sounds like social play, Burrell (1927) was skeptical and, aware of the enormous appetite of these animals, thought that the responses Bennett observed were the death agonies of starving animals. Moreover, many of Bennett's observations were of animals on land, on which they are apparently quite awkward (Burrell, 1927). However, supporting Bennett's observations, apparently independently, were those of Fleay (1944), who was the first to breed the platypus in captivity. After about 5 months of age, the single young female behaved somewhat similarly to the animals that Bennett observed a century earlier. "Feeding vigorously whenever the occasion presented itself, rolling on her back and playfully scratching herself, clinging

Table 10.1
Application of the play criteria to the anecdotal reports of play in the platypus

Play Criteria	Social Play	Sensorimotor Play
Incompletely functional	Yes	Yes
Endogenous component	Yes	Yes
Structural or temporal difference	?	?
Repeated performance	Yes	Yes?
Relaxed field	Yes	Yes

with all four feet to any hand that approaches her, or playing "chasie" by holding on to her mother's tail with her beak, or even pursuing her own tail like a pup, Corrie at the end of March, 1944, had become the most frolicsome, fat, and engaging little duckbill one could imagine" (Fleay, 1944: 43).

More recent captive observations and observations in the field are rare concerning play in the platypus, although an authoritative review of monotreme biology accepted Bennett's conclusions and noted the accuracy of his many other observations on platypuses (M. Griffiths, 1978). Moreover, a few years later a leading monotreme biologist (Grant, 1983) did note the following, which suggests locomotor play: "During the crisp early mornings and evenings of this season [Autumn], the newly emerged juveniles can be seen 'playing' in the water with much more splashing than is normally seen when adults are going about the daily business of obtaining their food. For the young this playfulness is shortlived and is soon replaced by normal feeding behaviour and the behaviour that ensures their future survival" (1983: 55).

How do these sparse observations stack up against the five criteria (table 10.1)? The main problem is that the observations are limited and anecdotal. The similarity with puppies claimed by both Bennett and Fleay could be due to their own familiarity with dog play and their desire to convey some idea of the behavior seen to readers who presumably are also familiar with dogs.

Surplus resource theory would predict that under benign conditions play might indeed be seen in these aquatic animals. Platypuses eat aquatic invertebrates in the wild and will eat earthworms, grubs, and small shrimp in captivity. However, their need for food is enormous, up to or equal to their body weight each day. Although one might expect a generalist feeding on hidden prey to show some foraging-related play, it may be virtually impossible for these animals to reach satiation in the wild. Could their physiology be such that although they attained endothermy, they did it at the expense of not having any spare time, especially in the wild? Could Spencer, without even knowing about them, have had the platypus in mind as an "inferior animal"? Too little is known about their social system to be more precise than that. We do know that platypuses have the aquatic specializations, brain size, and ecological niche that might

Figure 10.1
Phylogeny of the major mammalian groups and occurrence of play.

be conducive to the occurrence of play. Young animals do have a period during development when they are protected and provided for by the mother. Burrow observations would be most informative. However, growth rates are quite rapid, and available energy may be channeled to growth, as in most reptiles.

An apparent paradox here is that many marsupials seem to have relatively smaller brains than monotremes, and yet many are socially playful. Again, we see that the relationship of play to brain size is murky indeed. According to SRT, it would be predicted that the platypus would be more playful and more diverse in its play than the echidna. Eisenberg (1981) has related brain size (encephalization quotient) in many mammals to the kind of antipredator strategy used (passive or active) and locomotion dimensionality (two or three dimensions). In both cases, relatively larger brains should be found in the latter categories. The platypus has a more active escape strategy than the echidna and operates in a three-dimensional environment; it also has a larger, if less convoluted, brain. Since arguments have been made that the most basic play may be locomotor and be related to antipredator tactics (Byers, 1984), then to this extent the observation of more play in the platypus makes sense.

Recently a new wrinkle has developed. Both the platypus and at least one species of echidna have been shown to be electroreceptive (Moller, 1995; Proske & Gregory, 2003). This means that they can perceive weak electric fields, as can many fish and some amphibians. They may use this information to locate food. However, their detection threshold is much higher than in fish (Moller, 1995). Monotreme electroreception is passive, however, while many fishes possess an active electrosensitivity system. In active mode, fish produce weak electrical signals that can be used to detect prey and other environmental features in a way similar to that of bats employing ultrasonic sounds that reflect from objects and convey information on distance, size, and movement. Those fish species with the most advanced electrosensory abilities have brains far larger than is typical for fish, by a factor of 100 or more. Electrophysiological investigations have shown that the large brain of some fish is related to their electrosensitivity (Moller, 1995). Early neurophysiology investigations of the echidna brain showed that much of the large association cortex was "silent." Could the larger brain of the monotremes be related to possession of this sensory modality?

10.3   Evolution and Mammalian Play

A chapter has been devoted to these enigmatic animals, in spite of the weak evidence for play, because they may be central to the issue of origins. If we accept that some play or very playlike behavior may occur in the platypus, then play might be plesiomorphic in mammals, and found in their common ancestor. Conversely, the appearance of play in eutherians, marsupials, and monotremes might be due to a suite of traits involving energetics, ecology, life history, and brain development that favor behavior meeting the five play criteria (figure 10.1).

As even earlier radiations of animals are covered in the following chapters, even more time will be expended on questionable data concerning the occurrence and form of play in nonmammalian taxa. Given the occurrence of play in all subclasses of mammals, however, such exploration is essential in the quest for its origins.

11 Play Is for the Birds Too

Play is one of the most mysterious activities of animals.
—Ficken (1977: 573)

Play in keas is less a set of ritualized behaviors than an attitude to the world at large.
—Diamond & Bond (1999: 76)

11.1 Introduction

Birds are known for their diverse ways of obtaining food, for navigating long distances, for performing spectacular courtship displays, and for possessing many other complex behavioral abilities. They have captured the attention of scientists for centuries. The traditional class Reptilia is an assemblage of diverse groups (primarily turtles, lizards, snakes, and crocodiles), placed together primarily because of historical reasons. Birds, like dinosaurs, are today considered reptiles. Whether birds evolved from dinosaurs or archosaurs more closely related to crocodilians is still somewhat controversial, although most authorities today accept the dinosaur origin (Colbert, Morales, & Minkoff, 2001). Regardless, the history of birds goes back at least to the Lower Cretaceous (Sanz et al., 1997). When Marc Bekoff and I, in our edited book on behavioral development and evolution, called our section on birds, "Feathered Reptiles," we were not being facetious (Burghardt & Bekoff, 1978). Birds may have feathers and other reptiles do not, but birds still have scales on their legs. Behavioral similarities with crocodilians, the closest living relatives of birds, are extensive and compelling (Coombs, 1989). Recent discoveries in reptile behavior have only strengthened the connection, as will be emphasized in the next chapter. Nevertheless, birds are considered a natural monophyletic group. They are feathered, endothermic, vigorously active, have high metabolic rates, and engage in diligent, highly developed parental care.

Many species of birds have large brains, relatively larger than many mammals (Jerison, 1973), although the "bird brain" slur is still common. To many laypersons and scientists, birds are considered cognitively inferior to mammals. Much evidence, not reviewed here, counters this impression (see T. X. Barber, 1994; Skutch, 1996 for enthusiastic accounts). In fact, song learning in birds has been used as a model system for studying human language for many years (Marler & Peters, 1982; Pepperberg, 1991, 2002; West & King, 1985). Peter Marler, reviewing the evidence on bird cognition, concludes that "there are more similarities than differences between birds and primates" (Marler, 1996: 22), a conclusion reinforced by recent findings (Emery & Clayton, 2004). It might be more accurate to say that this is true of some taxonomic groups of birds just as primates are a special subset of all mammals. Nonetheless, the parallels between birds and mammals in tool use, cooperative hunting, learning of motor patterns, and complex social cognition are quite striking. Similarly, the richness of play in some birds rivals that seen in the most playful mammals.

A distinctive characteristic of both birds and mammals is the virtual universality of parental care (Clutton-Brock, 1991). Following the discussion in chapter 3, parental behavior is viewed as all "things parents do to offspring that may have either positive (what we now call "care") or negative effects on offspring or alternative parent's fitness" (Gowaty, 1996: 519). Play may have been involved in the origin or elaboration of parental behavior. Gowaty (1996) has described the seemingly superfluous, but not energetically costly, activities that many birds engage in with offspring while they are parenting as "fiddling." She has argued that such parental "fiddling" may be an important factor in the origin, evolution, and maintenance of parental care in birds. Gowaty's application of fiddling to parental care may seem somewhat different from the common usage of the term. Still, she sees fiddling as a means of producing novel behaviors that can be selected and shaped into adaptive repertoires by natural selection. This represents the incorporation of primary process play behavior patterns into nonplay behavior systems (parental behavior). Birds with high activity levels may be particularly prone to the "surplus" behavior patterns that may underlie the prominence of play in endothermic animals (Burghardt, 1988b, 1999, 2001).

In the nineteenth century birds were often considered playful; Groos (1898) cited many avian examples. However, he frequently confused courtship with play. As ornithology developed early in the twentieth century and provided much of the basis for the revival of the concept of instinct and the rise of ethology, much of the uncritical early work on avian behavior was either dismissed or more parsimoniously interpreted. Consequently, professional bird ethologists, ornithologists, and animal play researchers slighted play in birds. There certainly were descriptions of play in birds. Naturalists filled the ornithological literature with anecdotal accounts of play by birds (Ficken, 1977). Although many are fragmentary and uncritical anecdotes, several are still compelling today.

When my mother purchased a pet budgerigar for me many decades ago, the standard procedure even then was to outfit the bird's cage with bells, mirrors, ladders, and various odd-shaped food treats that could be manipulated in various ways. Pet stores sold entire lines of toys—and the birds used them. It is hard to find a modern pet store that is not overflowing with toys for birds. "Environmental enrichment" for birds in zoos is beginning to become more common (Burghardt et al., 1996) as a means of improving the captive lives of birds, although it lags behind comparable efforts with mammals (King, 1993). There is even a newsletter for Grey parrot owners called *The Grey Play Roundtable*.

Why then was play in birds ignored when animal play was again taken seriously beginning in the 1970s? Was a lingering popular bias against "mere bird brains" at work, supported by the growing popularity and intellectual prestige of primatology? If, as many thought, play was a mark of cognitive dexterity and creativity, was it not obvious that the focus should be on the most humanlike animals? Since birds were not considered smart compared with mammals, it followed that any "play" could only be superficially similar to that seen in mammals.

The bias against the cognitive accomplishments of birds was criticized by many scientists beginning two decades ago (T. X. Barber, 1994; Beck, 1982; Griffin, 2001; Pepperberg, 1991), although the bias remains strong, if less stridently expressed, today. Nevertheless, if birds, a well-studied and well-loved group of animals, are not considered to really play, in spite of the rich evidence provided by a number of species, then the occurrence of play in other groups should be even less favorably considered. In retrospect, the revalidating of playfulness in birds was a major step in creating a climate in which play in other disdained groups could be explored.

Although it might be argued that the classical ethological emphasis on instinctive behavior in birds militated against the study of play in this group, this emphasis certainly did not stop many ethologists from such study. Konrad Lorenz (1956) often wrote about the playfulness of his beloved jackdaws (*Coloeus monedula*) and other birds. Wallace Craig (1918) mentioned doves "toying" with nest material. Still, examples of play in birds are often hard to distinguish from incompletely performed behavior and may be easily missed or misinterpreted, a problem to which we will return. In birds, the distinction between juvenile and adult play is particularly salient.

An avian ethologist, Millicent Ficken, wrote a review of play in birds (Ficken, 1977) that was followed and extended by Fagen (1981) with further updates by Ortega and Bekoff (1987) and Skutch (1996). I will rely on their coverage, although I have consulted original descriptions of cited examples and have included additional and more recent examples. Earlier useful reviews of play in birds are those by Armstrong (1965) and Thorpe (1956).

Fagen points out that while birds have been extraordinarily important in ethology, especially those species that are easy to observe, "Play research is not one of the many feathers in avian biology's cap" (1981: 202). He decries the anecdotal, scattered, and uncritical treatment of avian play. Nonetheless, play in birds has been described for locomotor, object, and social categories. Rather than thoroughly review the various kinds of play in birds, much of it anecdotal, I will emphasize several recent and detailed studies that go beyond mere documentation and broad description. Then I will add the evolutionary picture to see how play maps onto bird phylogeny.

Play has been described most frequently and in most detail in birds of two major groups, the parrots (parrots, parakeets, macaws, keas) in the order Psittaciformes, and in two converging families, the Corvidae (ravens, crows, magpies, jays) and Cracticidae (Australian magpies) in a distantly related order (Passeriformes). All three major types of play have been recorded in these families as well as in woodpeckers and their relatives (Piciformes) and raptors and their relatives (Ciconiiformes).

11.2 Some Examples of Avian Play

11.2.1 Locomotor Play

Locomotor play has been described most often in adult and fledged juvenile birds. The soaring of raptors and vultures on fine windy days has often been described as play, since it seems to be nonfunctional, and appears as if it would be fun or enjoyable if we were doing it. These features by themselves are not very convincing evidence that play is involved. The first feature ignores the fact that soaring may involve foraging (why are few if any insectivorous, seed, or fruit-eating birds described as soaring?). The second is uncritically anthropomorphic without more evidence (Burghardt, 1997).

Pandolfi (1996) describes communal soaring by Montagu harriers (*Circus pygargus*) with members of the same or other species as play using clearly specified criteria. Adult soaring is done without any interaction among birds, but young birds may repeatedly dive at each other nonaggressively, so-called "nuisance play" (Pandolfi, 1996). Young peregrine falcons (*Falco peregrinus*) also engage in "mock fights" (A. Parker, 1975). Perhaps communal soaring functions as flight training for young birds and the diving flights serve as physical training (Fagen, 1981; Pandolfi, 1996). Skutch (1996) also describes soaring in herring gulls (*Larus argentatus*) as play. Often this flying is done in groups, so it is not strictly solitary locomotor play, if it is play at all. Much of this locomotor activity is embedded in chases and may be more akin to social play chasing as described in mammals. Nevertheless, even if the activity is truly solitary locomotor behavior, if the five criteria are met, then this behavior can be considered playful even if it has some current function.

Most other examples of locomotor play are both more fragmentary and less convincing than that of the soaring birds. Juvenile song sparrows (Nice, 1941) and woodpeckers engage in "wild, erratic flights" (Kilham, 1974: 37). Kilham observed these in the field for seven species of woodpeckers. Kilham also raised tame and hand-reared birds of several species in captivity where such erratic flights were also seen. Other examples of this erratic flight behavior are cited in Ficken (1977) and Fagen (1981). Such behavior could be an ontogenetic precursor of more skilled adult flight; whether it is actual training for improved flying ability is not known. Kilham (1974) notes that this behavior often occurs after a social or interspecific encounter and calls it dodging. Both Ficken and Kilham note that Lorenz labeled such flight behavior as emotion-dissociated fleeing movements and considered them escape behavior without an evident stimulus. This fit in with Lorenz's ideas of vacuum activities, behaviors that are performed when so much action-specific energy for a given response accumulates that it overflows even when no sign (triggering) stimulus is present. However, while Ficken (1977) claims that if this is true then such locomotor behavior is not play, Fagen (1981) points out the similarity of this kind of behavior to mammalian locomotor-rotational play, where external stimuli are also often not evident in the gambols of colts and calves. Here we see the implicit role of motivational criteria. Must play be under a different motivational system than the appropriate ethotypic behavior in order to be called play? As we have seen, the difficulty of assessing motivation, even when observing people, has led to my rejection of such a criterion. Play can be under complex internal controls that can even shift among closely related species (Pellis & Pellis, 1998b).

In any event, recent observers have also reported on flying play in young common ravens (*Corvas corax*). This activity may involve elaborate aerial play acrobatics by large numbers of young birds (Heinrich & Smolker, 1998; Skutch, 1996). These authors also report that ravens engage in other possible forms of locomotor play, including sliding down inclines, pushing and plowing through snow, and hanging upside down from branches. Watching ravens slide down snow banks on their backs, while holding objects, must be a delightful experience!

As an example of the anecdotal nature of much of the bird play literature, I will mention the frequently cited observation of Stoner (1947) on hummingbird locomotor play, the sole example of "play" in these generally diminutive and energetic birds. This report, all of twelve lines, mentions observations of an Anna's hummingbird (*Calypte anna*) that approached water streaming out of a hose, attempted to land on it as it would on a tree limb, and, floating down the stream a bit, repeatedly returned to ride again. The report's final phrase "apparently enjoying her fun as much as I enjoyed watching her" (Stoner, 1947: 36), captures the anthropomorphic quality of much of this literature. According to SRT, small hummingbirds, with their high energetic requirements and rapid heat loss, should play little, if at all (Burghardt, 1984). Complicating the picture, however, is the fact that hummingbirds, such as Anna's, go into torpor (lowered body temperature) at night and, unlike shrews and equally small mammals, are able to spend 90 percent of their time perching or roosting and expend only 50 percent of the energy expended daily by a same-sized shrew (*Sorex* sps.), (McNab, 2002). Some small mammals also have daily torpor. Anna's hummingbirds are also relatively large for hummingbirds and this could be the rare response of a well-fed, relaxed, animal. The behavior could also be derived from object curiosity, because many birds have a strong attraction to bright, shiny objects (Rheingold & Hess, 1957;

Wilcoxon, Dragoin, & Kral, 1971). Furthermore, this behavior is rather reminiscent of one of the earliest published examples of ectothermic reptile play, which will be discussed in the next chapter.

11.2.2 Object Play

The role of approach and avoidance of novel objects (neophilia and neophobia) is particularly important in object play. As we have discussed earlier, curiosity, exploration, and play are often linked and may be hard to distinguish early in development. Recall that exploration is a response to novelty itself; animals manipulate objects to test them and gain information. Play occurs only when the animal repeatedly engages and interacts with the object in order to "see what I can do with it." Exploration of a given stimulus habituates quickly; even if the stimulus is removed and reintroduced later, it evokes little further response. This distinction between play and curiosity is particularly important in evaluating object play in birds.

Play with objects has been described as occurring most commonly in young birds. It is most often described for birds of prey (hawks, eagles, owls) and other predaceous (but not insectivorous) birds such as pelicans, hornbills, and cormorants as well as scavengers. The behavior may involve manipulating or releasing (dropping) and recapturing dead prey or sticks, stones, or leaves. The behavior patterns involved may also include swooping, tossing, flinging, jumping on the object, biting, shaking, and tearing (Fagen, 1981). Ravens also will drop and catch objects in flight (Heinrich & Smolker, 1998).

Herring gulls not only drop clams onto rocks to break them open, they also drop other objects and will catch them in midair. While many have viewed this as play, such as Beck, who carried out an extensive set of experiments (1982), a number of questions remain as to whether this is play (Gamble & Cristol, 2002). In a nice set of observations, Gamble and Cristol (2002) tested the play hypothesis against two others. Perhaps the birds caught the clam before it hit the ground to test whether other birds in the area were lurking around to steal it (the kleptoparasitism hypothesis). On the other hand, perhaps catching the clam allowed the bird to reposition it in its beak for a more effective drop (the repositioning hypothesis). The authors developed a number of measures that would distinguish between the three and found the play hypothesis the most valid. Among other results they found that the birds drop-caught nonfood items more than food items, drop-caught over soft ground more than hard substrates, clams that were drop-caught were less likely to be eventually eaten, and drop-catching was more common on warm days when the gulls were not cold stressed. Also, they did more drop-catching on days with higher winds. Although the authors argued that this supports the play hypothesis since flight costs are lower in the wind, it could also be that in play the birds were testing their limits or challenging themselves, as the mastery and self-assessment theories suggest. Observations did not support the other two hypotheses. This is a fine example of testing play using systematically collected field data with clearly developed measures.

Nevertheless, as Ficken wrote 25 years earlier: "It is difficult to see any substantial difference between a hawk repeatedly releasing and catching an object in midair and a kitten pouncing on a ball of yarn. Such activities in mammals are usually considered play and no valid reasons exist for not applying the same term to similar activities of birds" (1977: 576). We have already discussed work that forces us to reevaluate the motivational systems underlying predatory play in cats (Pellis et al., 1988), but this reevaluation does not rule out that this is play. Does the same logic apply to the following example?

For decades my students and I have studied the early weeks of life in domesticated chicks in animal behavior laboratory classes. One of the most conspicuous behavior patterns in newly hatched chicks is pecking. Even when they still have a full yolk sac and are not interested in ingesting food, the chicks will peck at all manner of objects, especially small or shiny ones. Certain colors and shiny objects are particularly attractive, including moving objects. Students are usually charmed, then annoyed, when the chick runs over to the notebook in which they are writing their notes and persists in pecking at the pencil tip, eraser, or marks on the paper. If there are small seeds; miniscule pieces of paper or metal foil; scattered mash; or small insect larvae, pupae, or beetles on the table, the chick may repeatedly grab an item, run off, drop it, push it around as it repeatedly pecks at it, and otherwise engage in activity with it. The chick is easily distracted, though, and it will often run over to another spot, especially if the student taps a finger (mimicing a hen's pecking at real food, which may function to direct a chick's behavior to new, or newly found, food resources). The persistence of this behavior, especially in chicks during the first days of posthatching life, is remarkable.

The fact that many of the stimuli the chicks respond to are those associated with species-typical food or water (Hess, 1973; Rheingold & Hess, 1957) does not belie the argument that these initial responses meet the five play criteria. Many of the stimuli responded to might be what ethologists have called supernormal stimuli in that, by accentuating a feature of a natural biologically important stimulus, artificial stimuli might elicit more intense responses, or greater preference, than the natural one. The junk food industry in the United States exploits this feature in our behavior toward foods by focusing on the visual, tactile, "chewing," taste, and odor properties of processed food stimuli that are much more salient to us than the real foods they replace. "Toying" with food has already been discussed as play in our species and this, along with the chicks' pecking of a wide range of objects with little or no nutritive potential, could be a comparable phenomenon. Pecking in birds may play an important role in learning about potential food resources even in the absence of serious hunger. Studies show that there is an early sensitive period for modifying pecking (Hess, 1973) and seed preferences (Burghardt, 1969) in chicks in the first week of life.

Pecking behavior in birds is perhaps the most well-studied response in all of animal behavior, not just avian behavior. Operant psychologists find it an ideal measure in studying animal learning; pigeon pecking has thus replaced rat lever pressing in many laboratories studying the general properties of operant behavior. The fact that pigeons, like people, are highly dependent upon vision is a major reason for use of these birds. Pigeons quickly learn to peck stimuli in a test apparatus. It may be the easy conditioning of this highly motivated, generalized means of exploring and testing the environment that has sustained the experimental analysis of behavior for decades. Yet, if a playful response is at the heart of this success, it has never been recognized.

Young peregrine falcons have been reported to playfully break off pieces of ivy stems and pass them to each other repeatedly, before departing to engage in "aerial mock battles" (A. Parker, 1975). Aerial food passing in raptors, however, is a dramatic behavior that anyone lucky enough to observe will not soon forget. This should be distinguished from food stealing in which a bird harasses a food-carrying bird into releasing prey from its talons. In Montague's harriers, aerial food passing, in which one bird releases prey so a partner can catch it in midair, rarely happens between young birds. However, mothers engage in aerial food passing to their fledgling young, and this has been interpreted as a form of parental training through play (Pandolfi, 1996). It is interesting that among adults only males pass food to females, whereas females never pass food to males, even to their mates. It would be interesting to find out if mothers pass food preferentially to males or females. Many passes to young birds are unsuccessful, so such practice may be necessary to perfect the skill. On the other hand, similar to predatory play in kittens, such experience may not be important at all and maturational factors may explain the increase in performance.

Kilham (1974) reported that red-bellied woodpeckers (*Centurus carolinus*) frequently manipulated and stored objects such as toothpicks, bent nails, and small wads of paper, trying to insert them into holes. This kind of manipulation was not seen in the six other woodpecker species studied except for one performance by a yellow-bellied sapsucker (*Sphyrapicus varius*). Eibl-Eibesfeldt (1970) noted similar behavior in the unrelated Galapagos Islands woodpecker finch (*Cactospiza pallida*). Heinrich and Smolker (1998) also describe play caching in common ravens.

Watson (1992) observed and videotaped sequences of object play in a laughing kookaburra (*Dacelo novaeguineae*), a long-lived, highly social kingfisher, near Sydney, Australia. He saw a bird, probably an adult female, repeatedly grabbing a 2–3-cm stone in its bill and then striking it sideways on a branch, making a distinctive sound that first drew Watson's attention to the bird's behavior. It did this with two separate stones. Watson classified the behavior as play for several reasons: It was repeated; it resembled behavior used by kookaburras to kill prey important in their diet, such as rodents, lizards, and snakes; there was no attempt to swallow the stones; and the behavior was performed in a context that ruled out aggressive or territorial display. Watson suggested that the bird was practicing prey-killing behavior. It was able to practice movements important in dispatching potentially dangerous prey. Regardless of the reason, these and other observations indicate that predatory object play is not limited to the juvenile stage.

Australian magpies (*Gymnorhina tibicen*) in the cracticid family show an elaborate head and foot coordination in prey handling and object play (Pellis, 1983). This ability improves rapidly beginning 4 weeks after fledging. In this behavior, the bird fragments an object such as a twig into smaller pieces by head shakes and by rubbing the object on the ground while holding it in its bill. The foot grasps objects that do not fragment while the bird pulls upward and bill shakes. Pellis used the Eshkol-Wachman Movement Notation to describe the behavior at different ages after fledging. The bird begins to use its leg in this behavior by flicking its leg upward to the bill holding the object at the same time as the head is lowered. Although such leg flicks were seen 1 week after fledging, they did not become successful until 4 weeks after fledging, when the success rate jumped to 52 percent. Success was 75 percent at 6 weeks and 93 percent at 8 weeks. At 8 weeks, however, the birds may fall and if this occurs, they immediately drop the object. After this period, however, the birds improve their coordination further so that they retain the object when falling. In the final stage, they seem to actually amplify the fall, continuing to manipulate the object while lying on the ground. Indeed, by 8 weeks after fledging, the birds do most of their object play while lying on their sides or backs. Finally, the birds sometimes will even begin to roll onto their sides as soon as they grasp the object.

This object play may also be a social activity, with birds playfully competing over an object. Pellis interpreted this behavior as practice of complex skills in a playful context, and cites comparable findings in other birds as well as baboons. Pellis (personal communication, 1997) has also observed American black-billed magpies (*Pica pica*) and has not seen any interaction with objects going beyond "rudimentary forms of exploratory play."

It is in the superfamily Corvoidea (crows, shrikes, vireos, etc.) (Sibley & Ahlquist, 1990) that object play has been most well described and experimentally studied; within this group the Corvidae, especially the subfamily Corvinae (crows, ravens, jays, and magpies) have starred. These birds have, like parrots, large brains and are opportunistic generalist feeders. These adaptations seem to underlie much of the high level of object interaction found in this group. Ficken (1977) and Fagen (1981) discuss much of the early literature that documents the attraction to and use of objects in these animals. However, this is also a group where the distinction between foraging-related curiosity and object play is often problematic. It must also be emphasized that only a few species in even these large taxa may actually play in such elaborate ways. Such variation may be particularly valuable in testing the functions of play using design features, correlational studies, or, preferably, experimentation.

Heinrich and Smolker (1998) carried out a set of detailed studies of object play in common ravens. These studies raise several important issues and test the border between play and food-related curiosity. In one study (Heinrich, 1995b) looked at responses to novel objects in four hand-reared fledging ravens and twenty-two adult or semiadult wild-caught ravens tested in a large, naturalistic aviary. With the young hand-reared ravens, he found that they contacted 980 natural objects in 95 categories present in this rich environment in ten 30-minute sessions. Over the next 28 sessions, Heinrich introduced 44 different objects, including edible and inedible organic matter (e.g., blackberries and mushrooms), edible and inedible animals (caddisfly larvae and butterfly wings), conspicuous inorganic items, and other objects that these birds might find in the wild. The birds were strongly attracted to novel objects of all kinds, edible and inedible, conspicuous and cryptic, but virtually always ignored the natural inedible objects that were present in this environment. Heinrich found, using relative pecking rates, that there were no initial differences in responses to the new items, regardless of edibility or conspicuousness; the key was that they were novel.

These results at first suggest that the animals were not responding to the objects with food-related responses. However, the birds very quickly stopped responding to the inedible objects, which suggests that these responses were indeed related to foraging. Although the birds missed no edible items, even highly cryptic caddisfly larvae, by the second session inedible objects were virtually always ignored. In short, young ravens avidly and thoroughly tested every available object in their environment for its edibility. Comparable results were found in additional experiments. It would seem that by the five criteria for play, the lack of repeated and varied manipulation of the objects makes these responses short of playful.

Furthermore, the responses were age related. At 1 year of age the birds began being much more hesitant in contacting novel items, often either ignoring them or approaching them while emitting alarm calls. At 1.5 years the two males showed some hesitant approaches, but the two females ignored all novel, inedible objects. Experiments with older wild-caught birds showed that they responded to novel organic inedible objects (e.g., hazelnuts and apples), but ignored conspicuous artificial objects that would have immediately attracted juvenile ravens. If these same animals were food deprived, however, the birds examined all of the edible objects and eleven of thirteen artificial objects.

Heinrich (1995b) interpreted these data as showing that ravens, a generalist species found in many habitats, have to respond to many different objects and thus demonstrate high levels of neophilia (love of novelty, attraction) when young. This neophilia decreases and is even replaced by neophobia (dread of novelty, avoidance) as the birds age, but can be increased with food deprivation, even in adults. He supported the contention (R. Greenberg, 1992) that birds with narrow habitat breadths show neophobia to novel objects and those with wide habitat breadths show neophilia. For a generalist species, rapidly testing large numbers of objects, accompanied by an ability to rapidly learn about those that are potential food, possibly dangerous, or useless, would be an asset. When the young are with their parents, they have an "intense curiosity and at first contact virtually everything that they encounter" (Heinrich, 1995b: 703). Heinrich concluded "I first thought that the ravens' exploratory behavior of pecking at inedible objects and often tearing them apart had no utilitarian goal. The present study, however, suggests that this seemingly useless behavior has a direct payoff, allowing ravens to learn the background milieu of their environment, and to quickly locate any new sources of food, sometimes even hidden food such as cryptic and encased insect larvae" (1995b: 703). However, this extraordinary curiosity is replaced in subadults by a growing neophobia to types of objects not encountered earlier in life.

Thus in object play we see a relationship to feeding ecology that might prove useful in assessing such kinds of play in many groups of animals. Ravens may just be remarkably adept. Nevertheless, the question lingers: If rats, which are generalist feeders, test all kinds of items, why is this testing not called play? Could it be because they test with nose and taste buds and tiny bites rather than the dramatic pecking, tossing, and energetic actions of birds? Alternatively, by our criteria, if an animal explores and then quickly ignores an object, it may show rapid learning and other cognitive abilities, but it is not playing.

The relationship between exploration and neophobia may be even more complex and involve two separate motivational systems (Mettke-Hoffman, Winkler, & Leisler, 2002). In a comparative study of tendencies to explore and neophobia in seventy-six species of parrots, Mettke-Hoffman and colleagues (2002) tested exploration (a novel object, a wooden ring hanging in an enclosure distant from food or water) and neophobia (a novel cotton mop or a familiar empty food dish placed near food and water) by recording both latency to and duration of contact. They found that not only were the two responses dissociated (birds high on one measure were not high on the other) but also that there were some ecological associations. For example, species living in complex habitats such as forest edges had the shortest duration of exploration, as did those feeding on patchily distributed foods such as buds. Birds feeding on seeds and flowers had long exploration latencies. Those eating nuts or originating from islands explored for long durations, while those typically feeding primarily on seeds explored for a very short time. Birds eating insects (which can be distasteful and poisonous) showed the greatest neophobia and those eating leaves the least.

Insofar as these kinds of ecological relationships affect responses to novel objects that appear to have no similarity to natural foods and differ within one order of birds, the role of ecology in the genesis of play is supported. This study involved many species, but only a few of each kind were tested in different home settings. Also, a different object was used in the two settings. In spite of such problems, studies such as these have the comparative breadth needed for phylogenetic work. Future studies should also consider brain size since the occurrence of feeding innovations in bird species has been related to forebrain size (Lefebvre et al., 1997, 1998). Whether this relationship co-varies with exploration or object play is still unknown, although both brain size and foraging innovations predicted the invasion success of sixty-nine introduced bird species around the world (Sol, Timmermans, & Lefebvre, 2002).

Returning to ravens, there is no question that they not only test novel objects and quickly learn about them but are also extremely capable of learning how to obtain desired food objects. Many workers have shown that these birds are able do remarkable things virtually unheard of in other birds, let alone mammals, and have demonstrated "insight" rivalling that demonstrated in the great apes (Heinrich, 1995a; Emery & Clayton, 2004). Heinrich added to this reputation with a remarkable experimental demonstration of the raven's ability to learn to obtain food attached to a string hanging down from its perch. To do this a bird had to pull up a short section of string with its bill, and holding the retrieved section with one foot, release the string from the bill and grab another section of string, holding this while the foot changed position to hold onto the newly retrieved section of string and so on for five times until the food reward was obtained. The birds were not taught this behavior, but seemed to come up with the solution through a mental representation of the necessary sequence of actions needed. Heinrich also tried this experiment with wild birds. While most showed neophobia and would not approach the meat on a string, a few did so and showed the same ability.

Is this ability related to play? Could the great interest in visually assessing and then manipulating objects provide an intellectual store from which the bird can draw? It is important to note that Heinrich attempted to exclude less cognitively advanced explanations of the behavior, such as random responding, genetic programming, sequential learning through trial-and-error, and imitation, concluding that "insight" is the best explanation (Heinrich, 1995a). Budgerigars learned to choose correctly which string to retrieve when only one was attached to the bait, but a jackdaw and Indian starling (*Acridotheres tristis*), although quickly learning to pull a string with food attached, were not successful in choosing the correct uncued string because the birds played with the strings; in other words, "pulling of strings was rewarding in itself" (Dücker & Rensch, 1977: 169). It would be interesting to see if ravens could also solve the perceptual task posed by the multiple string problems. Here we see how play may interfere with, as well as enhance, learning new tasks.

Juvenile common ravens also play cache (hide) small objects as well as food. Caching attracts raiders who try to steal the items. The cost of losing an object should be low as compared to losing a food item. Tom Bugnyar (personal communication, 2003) observed a group of six ravens for 10 weeks after fledging and found that they cached objects while interacting with other juveniles but cached food secretly. Ravens that cached objects more frequently were more successful in preventing others from raiding their cached food and more successful in raiding other's food caches than ravens doing little object caching. Bugnyar suggests that low-cost play object caching enhances social skills needed for successful raiding.

Members of the order Psittaciformes (parrots, macaws, cockatoos, lories) are well known for their repeated pecking, grabbing, and manipulation of objects in captivity, as recognized by anyone keeping a parakeet or parrot as a cage bird. Surprisingly, Ficken (1977) does not mention object play in this group at all. In fact, observations of parrots in the wild are limited and their play in captivity has attracted little scholarly interest. However, the great interest in objects shown by an African grey parrot (*Psittacus erithacus*) was almost certainly a major factor in his remarkable ability to learn and communicate the properties of objects (Pepperberg, 1991).

Keas (*Nestor notabilis*) are large parrots limited to the South Island of New Zealand; they may be the most playful avian species in the world, even among a family with such cognitive stars as gray parrots. Keas are noted for their remarkable attraction to, and ability to destroy, various human artifacts, such as windshield wipers and vinyl trim on automobiles, campers' tents and backpacks, as well as rain gutters on houses. They have been known to steal television antennas from houses, let the air out of automobile tires, and remove covers from garbage cans (Diamond & Bond, 1999). The authors of the first comprehensive study of play in wild keas (Diamond & Bond, 1999) report observing a kea roll up a doormat and push it down a flight of stairs. Keas are readily observed in the field because of their peskiness and the often quite open terrain where they live. They can also be more easily observed individually than most parrots, who are restricted to forests or live in large colonies.

Keas have powerful bills and dexterous grasping feet that allow utilization of many food resources, including many plants, snails, grubs, grasshoppers, rodents, rabbits, deer, and sheep (Diamond & Bond, 1999). Although some of the mammals listed may be scavenged, keas also learned to attack live introduced domestic sheep; pecking through the skin, they ate the animals' flesh. Beginning in the late nineteenth century, this led to persecution of keas by sheep ranchers and the institution of government-sponsored bounty programs (Diamond & Bond, 1999).

The ability to shift to such novel food resources was early on attributed to the keas' remarkable "intelligence, curiosity, and mischievousness" (Diamond & Bond, 1999: 39). It also links play to its often destructive and cruel aspects that we recognize in our own species. In fact, Diamond and Bond (1999) called the destruction of objects, such as the chair in figure 11.1, demolition and emphasized its relation to object play as well as its distinctness from foraging motivation by hungry animals. Persistence and repetitiveness are clearly major components in the keas' response to objects. Although experimental studies are needed, it is clear that many of their responses to objects are not done solely to test them for edibility. Their behavior meets all five criteria for play.[19]

19. Recent reports in eastern North America document that vultures, particularly black vultures, engage in similar livestock and object destruction as human populations move into their habitat (Dao, 2003).

Figure 11.1
Demolition play with an abandoned chair by keas. (From Diamond & Bond, 1999)

What does seem to be involved in the objects played with or destroyed are the kinds of things that can be done with the object, or the "affordances" of the stimuli (Gibson, 1978). An object with a hole the bird can pry into elicits more attention than the same object without the hole. Soft objects seem to be particularly favored, but the birds will interact with almost anything. A bird was recorded playing with an anchored stick for 20 minutes during which he chewed it, jumped on it, hit it with his wings, rolled under it, and otherwise treated the object as if it was an opponent or play fight partner (Diamond & Bond, 1999). The finding that solitary object play is more frequent in mammalian species without a play partner has been often noted (Power, 2000).

As the incorporation of historically introduced mammals in the kea diet shows, keas can exploit many novel food resources and thus are generalist feeders. However, they are threatened in their native areas because, although they can exploit many novel potential food sources, they also are tied to the high alpine beech forests, which are declining. Nevertheless, keas may survive even as many native New Zealand birds become extinct. Since keas live in an unpredictable environment where food is often limited and more specialized competitors are common, Diamond and Bond (1999) argue that object play and social facilitation are the processes by which keas learn the flexible deployment of their behavioral repertoire, which they will need to survive as sophisticated adults (see also Huber, Rechberger, & Taborsky, 2001).

This point is strengthened by observations of the kaka (*Nestor meridionalis*), the sister species of the kea, which lives on all three New Zealand islands. Morphologically similar to the kea but with a stronger bill, it is a lowland forest bird that chisels out grubs from trees and eats fruit. It has never been recorded eating any vertebrate. Solitary object play involving sticks and branches is present, but it is less common, less complex, and of much shorter duration than in keas. The most likely basis for the origin of the species difference in object play involves different selection pressures on foraging demands over evolutionary time, even if the object play in keas is divorced from feeding motivation.

After these examples from parrots and ravens and Australian magpies, the brief and cursory manipulation of objects by other birds might seem rather uninspired. The important point is that the evolution of traits has to begin with moves in the right direction. With keas and ravens, the ultimate opportunistic foraging generalists, this ability has been highly developed. These examples again clearly prove that viewing play as having no immediate benefit is an assumption that is most harmful to an analysis of play. Responses to novelty may not only help the individual bird identify the immediate use or danger of objects in the environment, but may also be transformed into the most amazing avian abilities.

11.2.3   Social Play

Social play is the type of play most unlikely to be confused with exploration or captive-induced stereotypy. On the other hand, it can be confused with courtship and true fighting. In nestling birds, competition for food can be intense, leading to starvation, fighting, and even siblicide by nestmates. Thus, the fifth criterion (a relaxed field) is critical in identifying social play.

In birds, as in mammals, social play can be divided into fighting and chasing. The latter seems more common in birds, but this may be due to our tendency to see them in flight at a distance rather than close up and wrestling. Nonagonistic social play is also often reported. Ficken (1977) and Fagen (1981) provide critical evaluation of the earlier examples. Kilham (1974) described various kinds of social play in several species of woodpeckers. Flickers perform a bill-waving dance in adult courtship. Kilham saw hand-reared juveniles performing this behavior within 3 weeks of the time they would have fledged. He also saw young hand-reared red-bellied woodpeckers tapping on objects in an apparent courtship mode directed to Kilham himself and a woodpecker of another species. This precocious courtship as play has been increasingly reported in animals (Pellis, 1993) and may explain why courtship and play are often confused in birds (Groos, 1898). On the other hand, playlike responses can be involved in adult courtship, so it is important to consider the details and context of behavior, not just the label, in identifying play.

Kilham also described dodging games in which woodpeckers, both in the field and in captivity, would dodge and shift around tree trunks using a smaller harmless species as a pretend enemy. During this behavior, their wings would be extended backward. Species to which the behavior was directed included black-capped chickadees (*Parus atricapillus*), redpolls (*Acanthus flammea*), pine grosbeaks (*Pinicolae nucleator*), and white-breasted nuthatches (*Sitta carolinensis*). This dodging could be considered inter-specific play, although there is no indication that the other species joined in the behavior.

Unfortunately, there are few quantitative descriptions of social play in birds. One exception is social play among Australian magpies (Pellis, 1981, 1983). In this species, social play interactions seem to last for rather long periods (up to 10 seconds or more), compared with the often short interactions usually described in birds. Pellis ob-served three family groups of magpies every 2 weeks for 16 weeks after fledging. Play chases (32 percent) and play fights (62 percent) were the most common interaction, with a few instances of attempts to take another bird's play object and some precocious courtship behavior as well. Play fights were often followed by play chases and preceded by contests over objects. Most play fights were vigorous and involved pecking, attacking, defending, and counterattacking in a manner reminiscent of the play fighting of rats. Juveniles instigated fights most often with other juveniles; although adult-juvenile fights were also common, adults, usually the male, instigated the vast majority of them. In evenly matched pairs, attack, defense, and counterattack roles changed rap-idly. Certain postures were more likely to lead to launching of play attacks. About 20 percent of play fights involved more than two birds if other possible partners were present.

Pellis (1983) also noted some possible play signals. These were never observed out-side of the play context, although they were not always present. These play signals included a soft guttural sound of long duration, a "bouncy" walking gait, and an open-bill display. Self-handicapping was also sometimes observed. Play bouts lasted as long as a few minutes. In earlier reports (see Fagen, 1981), these features of play are also described in several other species including keas and various parrots. Here birds may hang from their feet and "wrestle" and engage in other behaviors comparable to the wrestling play described earlier in squirrel monkeys.

A quantitative study of the frequency of different kinds of play in Montague harriers was based on 272 play events in field observations of 23 pairs of birds and their off-spring in Italy (Pandolfi, 1996; table 11.1). Aerial play fights differed from flight play as described earlier by including sudden bursts of acceleration and then gliding. Many also included flight rolls and talon presentations. Aerial play fights could involve con-specifics or members of several other species, including the black-billed magpie, Eur-asian kestrel (*Falco tinnunculus*), common buzzard (*Buteo buteo*), and hooded crow (*Corvus corone*). However, play with other species did not involve talon presentation

Table 11.1

Frequency and duration of different forms of play in Montague's harrier based on 272 instances in 23 family groups

Behavior	Percent of Total Instances	Time of Day Generally Seen	Duration (minutes)
Flight play (reciprocal chasing and diving)	35	0630–0730	2–20
Aerial play fights (intraspecific)	35	1300–1400	2–10
Aerial play fights (interspecific)	16	0800–0930	2–25
Communal soaring	12	—	3–5
Aerial food passing	3	—	—

Source: After Pandolfi (1996)

and thus was distinguishable from the much smaller number of aggressive interactions among conspecifics.

The distinction between intraspecific aerial play fights and flight play is not that clear from the descriptions and might only represent differences in intensity. The vast majority of play fights involved nonsiblings. On the surface, this difference from what is typically found in clutchmates suggests serious competition, but may be a consequence of the small number of young in successful nests (on average less than three) and asynchronous hatching and fledgling of the birds. There was a high rate of adult play in these 272 play events (24 percent) and males were twice as likely to participate as females. More such studies are needed. Diurnal birds are more easily observed than most mammals in the field.

Although not quantitative, the descriptions of social play in ravens (Heinrich & Smolker, 1998) are additional evidence that ravens compete with keas as the play champions among birds. Ravens engage in social acrobatic aerial games where pairs of birds roll, tumble, and soar together. They play "keep-away" with objects in a fashion comparable to that seen in dogs and other canines. They engage in play chases and play fights. While hanging upside down, birds may pass sticks and other objects back and forth.

Parrots are known not only for their object play but also for engaging in much social play. Most of this research is based on studies of captives; those of Skeate (1984; 1985) on white-fronted Amazon parrots (*Amazona albifrons*) are a good example. Social play is found in juveniles only, lasts up to 11 minutes, and consists of a mixture of courtship (bill nibbling, mutual preening, and pseudocopulation) and agonistic (foot lifting, attack sidling, bill gaping) behaviors. Virtually all social play is considered play fighting and several behaviors are only seen in play, such as gentle play biting and foot clawing. A play signal, termed play solicitation, occurred in which one bird sidled up to the other with head and body lowered. Here we see a pattern also established in mammals; social play is mostly play fighting, but courtship components are involved.

A thorough quantitative and descriptive field study of social play has been carried out in keas that rivals any such fieldwork performed on any species of mammal, including primates (Diamond & Bond, 1999). Social play in keas is extremely vigorous and elaborate and can occur with one to five partners. Building on earlier descriptions of kea social play, the authors find two major kinds of social play involving seven classes of behavior (locking bills, biting, pushing with feet, hanging by the bill or upside down using the feet, jumping and wing flapping, rolling over on the back while often squealing and waving the feet, and tossing an object with the bill). The two major types of play are tussle play and toss play. Tussle play (figure 11.2) is basically rough-and-tumble play or play wrestling involving all the seven behaviors listed except for hanging and tossing. Aggressive movements, feints, and other behaviors occur rapidly and look almost choreographed. The similarity with the analysis of defensive and offensive moves in play fighting in rodents by Pellis and Pellis (1998b) is quite remarkable. Careful field observation of the rates of occurrence and partners used in such play found that fledging animals of both sexes do it most; juvenile females and sub-

Figure 11.2
Tussle play in keas. (From Diamond & Bond, 1999)

adult males do it the least; adult females and subadult females tussle play with fledgling and juvenile males; and adult males only tussle play with adult females. The exact nature and reason for these sociometric age and sex class differences warrants detailed study. This play seems to be strongly related to agonistic behavior according to the authors, although the adult male-female play suggests to me that courtship might also be involved.

The second type of play is toss play in which tossing and exchange of objects is involved and rolling over and biting are absent. This form of play has been interpreted as related to courtship and maintenance of the pair bond (Diamond & Bond, 1999), although subadult and adult females engage in it most often and males rarely do any of the tossing if they do participate. Objects are also included in much kea social play and, as mentioned earlier, may substitute for a play partner. Several birds grab a single object in social play interactions that are similar to those in the bush dogs depicted earlier (figure 11.3).

Developmentally it appears that fledgling play is hard to distinguish from aggression, while in juveniles its motivational distinctiveness becomes apparent. Tussle play is performed more frequently by males than by females in the juvenile and subadult stages, a pattern seen throughout the mammals as well. However, a number of play signals were identified that became more prominent with time.

Although unpredictable food resources may underlie the intense object play in keas, why do these birds also show levels of intensity and complexity in social play that surpass those in the more docile and socially amiable kaka (Diamond & Bond, 1999)? The

Figure 11.3
Social object play in keas. (From Diamond & Bond, 1999)

authors point out that limited nest sites and climate uncertainty make reproduction a rare event for keas, and strict dominance and status concerns rule such opportunities. Males play important roles in raising the young and seem to need to be 4 or 5 years old before they can rear young. Thus there is a prolonged adolescence as compared with kakas as well as most other birds, and play complexity in birds is related to age at first reproduction (Diamond & Bond, 2003). Winter survival of juveniles is not at all certain, and Diamond and Bond (1999) argue that adults are lenient to offspring, both their own and others, and give way to them in feeding aggregations; adults offer a relatively relaxed childhood in which to gain skills through play needed for survival. In the kea, I predict, will be found a definite function for both object and social play, which has been so hard to demonstrate (P. Martin & Caro, 1985). The conclusion to be reached is that social play in some birds attains a level of complexity comparable to that found in the most playful groups of mammals.

11.2.4   Construction Play

Is there anything akin to construction play in birds? Male bowerbirds build elaborate structures, often artistically decorated, used to attract females for courtship and copulation. These structures incorporate sticks, pebbles, and other colorful objects. An individually marked population of satin bowerbirds (*Ptilonorhynchus violaceus*) has been studied for many years by Gerald Borgia and colleagues. In this species males do not achieve full colorful adult plumage, build bowers, and mate until they are 7 years old, although they produce viable sperm much earlier and females can breed at an early age as well. Females assess the bower, the courtship behavior, and the vocalizations of males as they check them out. Typically, younger males, in drab female-style plumage, spend much of the mating season observing mature males as they construct bowers from sticks, decorate the entrances with colorful pebbles and other objects, and paint the insides with saliva combined with plant materials (Coleman & Borgia, unpublished). Blue is the favorite decorating color and the one preferred by females. The young males may enter and work on a bower if the resident male is absent. Resident males may also court the young males, treating them like females; such male-male courtship is common.

In their fifth and sixth years young males go through transitional molts approaching the adult male blue coloration and at this time, they are often attacked, not courted, by resident males. They thus move off and build temporary bowers elsewhere where they also practice courtship behavior and vocal displays. These bowers are not high quality as measured by objective criteria (Collis & Borgia, 1993; Coleman & Borgia, unpublished). Are these practice bowers, displays, and vocalizations forms of play and, if so, do they have an adaptive function? Certainly, it is not for mating that season. Although the details are complex, the males that had more practice building bowers and engaging in male-male courtship with resident males were more attractive as mates than males who engaged in fewer such activities over the 4–5 years prior to onset of adult plumage. Male-male courtship seems important for young males to learn how not to startle and scare off females, even though the basic courtship behavior appears innate. But is experience and practice really responsible for the greater success of more experienced males?

A series of experiments with young birds implanted with testosterone sheds some light on the function of precocious bower building (Collis & Borgia, 1993). Young birds were captured and implanted with testosterone or used as controls and their behavior followed closely during the following mating season. Implanted males molted into adult plumage, some as much as 5 years earlier than expected. When these implanted birds visited bowers of resident males they, unlike control birds, often stole decorations or destroyed bowers. They were less tolerated by resident males, understandably, and some went on to make their own "real" bowers and set up for courtship without the years of previous experience watching and building. However, these bowers were of low quality with fewer decorations and not attractive to females. The authors concluded that bower building excellence depends on information (and skill?) obtained through both practice building bowers and observing bower building by adults during the long juvenile period. They advocated the "facilitated-learning hypothesis" and suggested that delayed plumage maturation in this species evolved to provide young males the opportunity to obtain various skills needed for successful courtship. Perhaps this is the best example supporting Groos's (1898) dictum that youth in animals evolved in order that they could play and practice skills needed as adults.

11.2.5 Vocal Play

Most birds, especially the well-studied Galliformes (chickens and turkeys), Anseriformes (ducks and geese), and Columbiformes (doves and pigeons) have a vocal repertoire that is not very developmentally labile (plastic), especially in terms of the need for postnatal practice. All baby chicks and many other precocial birds, when well fed and content, twitter in a soft call termed the contentment or contact call. This could be considered a form of play according to our five criteria. It has some immediate function, but certainly seems on a continuum with spontaneous locomotor play. In addition, if play is a means of parental assessment of the condition of offspring, could this not also be true of vocalizations as well as locomotor activities?

Consider again the baby domestic chicks given to my students for observation and study. Some chicks are given small injections of testosterone using a procedure modeled after a classic experiment by Noble and Zitrin (1942). Students are always amazed when newly hatched, androgenized chicks, male or female, begin to crow after a few days. They do so for no apparent reason except that the hormone has precociously sensitized target tissues controlling the expression of crowing. Is this spontaneously produced vocalization with its accompanying species-typical posture being performed as a kind of play? If so, have we in a way stimulated a precocial form of reproductive behavior that may occur naturally in the development of many species, including mammals? These ideas can be viewed as either intriguing or as evidence that the play label or the play criteria are problematic. I think that what they do is further the claim that play is derived from a multitude of processes in diverse ways and that we have to consider conceptual links that challenge conventional intuitive labels. Strutting, a form of precocial courtship in young turkeys (*Meleagris gallopavo* L.), is found in both sexes without hormone injections (Schleidt, 1970).

Recall that precocial sexual behavior is found in the play performances of many neonatal animals, including cattle, horses, and rodents, and it may be directed to inanimate objects. Since the crowing vocalizations are performed by solitary animals and do not seem to be responded to by others, a label of social play may appear unwarranted. It has already been established that one partner may be playing while another is not, and there is no way to rule out the solitary performance of social behavior as play, especially if the performance of the behavior improves with practice.

Vocal play has typically only been applied to the most vocally complex birds, especially the passerines (songbirds). Many of these species possess, next to human beings, the most experience-dependent and developmentally complex vocal system. The canary that sings for no apparent reason, the similarities of juvenile bird song with the babbling of human infants, and other parallels are used to argue that subsong in birds may be a form of play (Fagen, 1981; Ficken, 1977). The low-intensity "rehearsal" of songs in many birds seems to serve no immediate purpose, and Thorpe (1956) has argued that this could be play. Studies have classified and quantified the ways in which birds, including cowbirds (West & King, 1985) and sparrows (Marler & Peters, 1982), vary aspects of their vocalizations in rehearsals before they take on their adult forms. In the satin bowerbirds described in the preceeding section, solitary male practice may help in producing the more complex songs, often involving mimicry of other species, that females prefer; such improvements continue after males assume adult plumage, even up to 12 years of age (Coleman & Borgia, unpublished).

The vocalizations used by many songbirds to attract mates and establish territories can be quite complex and even provide clues to individuality and population (dialects). These complex songs develop gradually. Zebra finches (*Taeniopygia guttata*) are one of the most-studied birds in terms of song development (F. Johnson, Soderstrom, & Whitney, 2002). In zebra finches, subsong begins about 28 days after hatching; it consists of a series of relatively soft and variable sounds and variable intervals. About 40–50 days after hatching, the plastic song phase begins in which the notes used in adult song become recognizably clear, but the arrangement of notes is still variable. Beginning at about 80 days of age, the birds enter the crystallization stage, where the sequence of notes becomes more and more stereotyped. After subsong, it may be a developmental intermediate and eventually lead to the "crystallized" song of adults (F. Johnson,

Soderstrom, & Whitney, 2002). Birds emit both directed and undirected songs; this is true of adult male zebra finches. Could undirected song have a playful aspect?

The parallel of bird subsong and plastic song phases with the babbling of infants has often been noted. In infants, such behavior is considered a form of play. When performed by adults, neither bird song nor human speech is typically considered playful except when employed in "play." For example, Spencer (1872) included conversational repartee as a kind of play. When adults babble we rarely consider it play. (Well, perhaps we do when someone is so enthusiastic or taken up with him or herself that they go on and on, seemingly for the pleasure of hearing themselves talk, not for the edification or entertainment of the listener.) Babbling in babies can be solitary and is often recorded by researchers at night as the baby drops off to sleep. It has been viewed as a type of rehearsal in which the infant recreates, rehearses, and masters the sounds heard during the day while in a relaxed and contented state (Kucza, 1983).

One of the major concepts that came from the songbird learning literature is the template, the idea that birds are born with a brain-determined mold that channels learning in a certain direction and that birds are thus "wired" to learn some kinds of songs rather than others. An interesting parallel with the self-assessment and mastery views of play is found here. Zebra finches were recorded giving subsong, plastic song, and crystallization-stage song (F. Johnson, Soderstrom, & Whitney, 2002). It was found that spontaneously produced sounds were performed most during the plastic and crystallization phases and decreased as the stereotyped adult-style song was attained. These authors also found that the more the birds produced plastic song, the fewer "errors" were found in adult song. Adult zebra finches when socially housed develop significantly more new neurons in the three brain areas involved in vocal communication than birds housed singly or in pairs (Lipkind et al., 2002). Whether the richer auditory environment, increased vocalizations by the birds, or other activity mediated the increase is not known, although females do not sing and thus vocalizing could not be a factor for them. All this is very comparable to findings with more traditional play. In fact, selective learning and social shaping of babbling in birds has recently been applied to human speech in infants, and the resulting data provide strong support for a parallel in function between vocal precursors of songbirds and infants (Goldstein et al., 2003).

The term *babbling* in human language development is misleading. What researchers of human language development focus on is termed monologue speech, which can itself be divided into private speech, as in the solitary bedtime behavior referred to earlier, and social-context speech, in which the presence of others may facilitate performance, but no communicative function is apparent. Social speech, on the other hand, is directed at others and has a communicative function (Pepperberg, Brese, & Harris, 1991). Monologue speech in infants has been hypothesized to function as a form of play in which a communication code can be practiced without the costs of failure; novel forms can be tried out and there is freedom to choose topics and contexts. Other forms of language learning are much more constrained, and failure can inhibit both practice and learning (see Pepperberg, Brese, & Harris, 1991 for references and discussion). The true function of monologue speech has, however, been difficult to demonstrate for a variety of methodological reasons that are compounded by great individual differences in this type of speech.

Although crows and ravens are not known for beautiful sounds, if we go beyond our anthropomorphic and superficial aesthetics, we may learn more from them than from the song sparrow and nightingale. A remarkable example of vocal play has been described in common ravens (Heinrich & Smolker, 1998) that is perhaps even better than that of the song sparrow and typical songbirds usually studied.

Young ravens, even before fledging engage in long monologues, unlike anything heard in adults. During this behavior, ravens produce a variety of sound types (low gurgling sounds, barely audible chortles, squeaks, quacks, loud yelling, trills and sounds that resemble water running over pebbles in a swift stream), some of which resemble calls typical of adults. These monologues are often accompanied by continually changing gestures and feather postures, as if the birds were play-acting numerous roles in apparently random sequence. For example, loud trills and rasping quorks are accompanied by "macho displays"—ear and throat feathers erect and flashing nictitating membranes. In adults, these displays are mating and assertive displays directed at mates or rivals. In young birds (during the first few months out of the nest), these monologues occur out of context, often either when the bird is alone or not directed at any other individual and not eliciting any obvious reaction from others. They do not appear serious since the bird may intermittently perch, stretch, yawn, pick at twigs, etc., and then abruptly change to a different "tune." (Heinrich & Smolker, 1998: 40)

Clearly, ravens should be formally studied in an experimental context to better understand what is taking place during these monologues. However, the most rigorous and quantified research on vocal play in birds comes from the studies of parrots, especially the work on Alex, an African Grey parrot, by Pepperberg, Brese, and Harris (1991). Alex was studied in a manner closely modeled after work on children. For example, the training that Alex underwent in learning to communicate using English words in appropriate contexts involved correction and denial of rewards. Would Alex rehearse words and phrases in private or solitary vocalizations in a context in which no criticisms would apply?

The training method used by Pepperberg involved a close relationship with the bird and a model-rival approach in which a second human "trainee" was a rival for Alex's attention. Diurnal taping of Alex's monologues just before nightfall, when the bird was alone, allowed assessment of the effects of the words and concepts being trained on the form of "private speech." In 1986 the concept and word "none" were being trained, and in thirty-five evening sessions more than 10,000 sounds were recorded, of which 51.5 percent were English word labels or recognizably related. The other sounds were parrot calls and whistles, cage noises, ringing phones, door closings, etc., but most were, remarkably, humanlike vocalizations. The word *none* or its variants increased from none at all to a small percentage, but the overall number of English vocalizations of any kind increased. In 1988 a more detailed experiment involving acquisition of *nail*, *sack*, *bread*, and *green bean* led to results that were more dramatic. More than 24,000 vocalizations were recorded and 71 percent were English or related sounds. During baseline recordings before training Alex never made sounds similar to the words to be trained, but during training they were made during monologue periods and showed increasing accuracy over time, as if the practice was having an effect. Furthermore, the parrot practiced all vocalizations privately before he was able to reliably use the label in training. Still, the total amount of vocal play using the targeted words was relatively small ($<$ 6 percent).

In comparing Alex's monologues and acquisition of human speech by children, Pepperberg and colleagues (1991) pointed out that children also only practice more difficult words; Alex emitted a series of variations that led to the targeted version rather rapidly. This is also seen in children. A similarity between children and Alex in the need to assimilate and accommodate the new idioms (Piagetian terms are discussed in chapter 4) was also noted. Pepperberg et al. also pointed out that since Alex was already quite sophisticated in his use of English before these studies were carried out, having been trained for 10 years, he may have been entering the subsequent stages seen in children where monologues become more like solitary dialogues than social context speech. In addition, it seems as if Alex differed from children in practicing words not yet in his repertoire, whereas children use words they have already learned but arrange them in different ways. As the authors noted, many questions cannot be answered from this study of one animal already advanced in training. However, the parallels with human speech are compelling and open the door for a less anthropocentric look at other birds as well, who learn, not an arbitrary, human-derived language, but one evolved to serve their own needs in nature.

11.3 Miscellaneous Related Phenomena

To many of the classical ethologists, the hallmark of play was its motivational independence from the serious performance of the activity observed. Thus, low-intensity or incipient versions of a behavior (such as flight, nest building, courtship) that did not have a clear function (called intention movements) or animals so highly motivated that they performed a behavior (e.g., predation) in the complete absence of an appropriate stimulus (vacuum activities) should not be confused with play (Eibl-Eibesfeldt, 1970; Lorenz, 1956). If, however, a duck performs predator escape actions when it is swimming, but without the "panic" seen during real escape, then there is motivational independence and the behavior can be considered an elementary form of play (Lorenz,

1956). The difficulty of assessing motivation and emotion in many species makes application of this criterion difficult as a sole measure of play, but it may help identify the basal kinds of playlike activities (primary processes) that could serve as the evolutionary foundation of ritualized displays. As birds develop, the adult repertoire (such as fighting in chickens) may appear first as isolated or incompletely performed acts that are only gradually integrated into the adult version. The latter might be less variable than the incomplete sequences seen during ontogeny and often have playlike characteristics (Kruijt, 1964). A foremost student of behavioral development in precocial birds calls such early versions of adult behaviors prefunctional behavior (Hogan, 1988). These behaviors are typically studied in the more primitive precocial bird families (table 11.2).

Rather different is the peculiar habit in many birds, primarily passerines, of anointing themselves with ants or ant substances, as well as other materials such as fruits (e.g., lime fragments), beetles, millipedes, mustard, vinegar, tobacco, tree gum, and many other things (Dumbacher & Pruett-Jones, 1996; Parks, Weldon, & Hoffman, 2003; Whitaker, 1957). The birds may apply the ants with the bill, or passively posture or dust bathe in a clump of ants or an anthill. Anting, or, more generally, self-anointing, can be active or passive. The behavior may often be of long duration: 20, 45, even 90 minutes. Passively anting birds may often show a deliberate and elaborate behavior as well as posturing in attempts to facilitate the invasion of ants on their bodies. Anting always involves ants that eject repugnant substances; stinging or biting is not a factor. Ants, millipedes, and beetles produce a variety of defensive chemicals, including formic acid, aldehydes, esters, ketones, and carboxylic acids among others (Dumbacher & Pruett-Jones, 1996). Whitaker reports that anting occurs in 148 species of birds, all but 16 being passerines, although whether nonpasserines engage in true anting has been disputed (Simmons, 1966). Simmons (1966) lists 108 species of passerine birds in more than 20 families, so the behavior is clearly phylogenetically widespread in the passerines. Whether this behavior has any relationship to play has been disputed, although it does not seem likely. The difficulty has been in experimentally confirming any function for the behavior.

Whitaker (1957) evaluates the many proposed functions, which include removing substances preparatory to ingesting the ants, using their secretions to repel ectoparasites, using ant-derived acids for medicinal effects (self-medication), using ant substances to help condition the feathers, and using the ant acids to intercept light and produce vitamin D, among others. No experimental tests have supported any of the proposed functions of anting, although work has been limited (Dumbacher & Pruett-Jones, 1996). The person who did the most early descriptive and experimental work on this problem, Holger Poulsen, studied fifty-six anting species and concluded that the behavior was merely unintentional activity associated with feeding in most cases and in any event has more than one function (Poulsen in Whitaker, 1957).

The behavior may indeed have originated as an incidental response and later acquired other functions. One of these could have been applying substances that make the bird's feathers distasteful or repellant and hence likely to be released when grabbed, although early work did not consider this sequestration hypothesis. What are intriguing are the reports and evidence presented by Whitaker (1957) that suggest that the behavior has also acquired a distinctly positive tone. She reports an extensive series of observations and experiments on a captive hand-reared orchard oriole (*Icterus spurius*). The details are quite remarkable; the bird had no ectoparasites yet was selective in gathering wads of ants that it would apply to its feathers. Some were eaten. Dead or frozen ants were also tested. Those that had lost their odor and flavor were eaten but not used for anting.

Whitaker noted that many birds respond to smoke in a way similar to their response to ants. She also established that the chemical substances of the ants the birds used for anting had irritating "thermogenic" properties and that this was true of most of the substitute materials, including smoke. Furthermore, the ants were frequently deposited around the cloaca and thin skin surrounding the vent, which are highly sensitive areas. She suggests that stimulation caused by the ant secretions provides "sensual pleasure, possibly including sexual stimulation, from the thermogenic effect of the ants" (Whitaker, 1957: 250). Whether this could be considered a form of play derived from some functional precursor is not known.

It is of interest that anting, like play, is found primarily in passerine birds. All the other orders of birds in which anting or antinglike behavior have been recorded also have been reported to play (table 11.2) including gallinaceous fowl, owls, parrots, and woodpeckers. More than 11 percent of the anting passerines are members of the Corvidae. Before anting can be accepted as play, however, the third criterion, that the behavior differs in some way from the "real" performance of the behavior, needs to be determined. It would be remarkable indeed if such a phylogenetically widespread and complex behavior did not originate from some functionally important response.

The self-stimulation hypothesis of anting and its relationship to play was evaluated some years ago in a major volume on animal play (Simmons, 1966). The main argument against self-stimulation put forth by Simmons is that such a costly behavior must have adaptive value. However, highly adaptive behaviors such as eating and mating can be pleasurable when performed functionally, and can also be engaged in for their pleasurable component only (e.g., gourmet cooking, masturbation), in which case the play criteria are met. On the other hand, anting seems to have an important learned component in that birds have to learn, not only which ants have the appropriate chemicals, but also how to recognize and best apply the chemicals (Simmons, 1966). To Simmons, only use of proper stimuli in a proper manner is true anting, and "most instances of aberrant anting with substitutes have been recorded in captive birds, especially hand-reared ones" (1966: 155). Furthermore, "the use of ant-substitutes has a

Table 11.2
Taxonomic distribution of the major play types in birds

Order	Number of Families/ Genera/ Species	Altricial (A) Precocial (P) sA = semialtricial	Locomotor Play	Object Play	Social Play	Selected Common Names
EOAVES						
Struthioniformes	4/5/10	P				Ostrich, emus, rheas, cassowaries, kiwis
Tinamiformes	1/9/47	P				Tinamous
NEOAVES						
Craciformes	2/17/69	P				Guans, megapodes
Galliformes	3/58/214	P	Yes	?	?	Chickens, grouse, pheasants, quail, guinea fowl
Anseriformes	4/48/161	P	Yes			Geese, ducks, screamers, swans
Turniciformes	1/2/17	P				Button quails
Piciformes	5/51/355	A	Yes	Yes	Yes	Woodpeckers, honeyguides, barbets, toucans
Galbuliformes	2/15/51	A				Jacamars, puffbirds
Bucerotiformes	2/9/56	A		Yes	Yes	Hornbills
Upupiformes	3/3/10	A				Hoopoes, scimitarbills
Trogoniformes	1/6/39	A				Trogons
Coraciformes	3/34/152	A		Yes		Rollers, motmots, kingfishers, kookaburras, bee-eaters
Coliiformes	1/2/6	A				Mousebirds
Cuculiformes	6/30/143	A			Yes	Cuckoos, anis, coucals, hoatzen, roadrunners
Psittaciformes	1/80/358	A	Yes	Yes	Yes	Parrots, parakeets, macaws
Apodiformes	2/19/103	A	Yes	Yes		Swifts

Play Is for the Birds Too

Order						Common names
Trochiliformes	1/109/319	A	Yes			Hummingbirds, hermits
Musophagiformes	1/5/23	sA			Yes	Turacos, plantain-eaters
Strigiformes	9/45/291	A		Yes	Yes	Owls, nightjars, nighthawks, oilbirds, frogmouths
Columbiformes	3/42/317	A		Yes		Pigeons, doves
Gruiformes	9/53/196	P/sA		Yes		Bustards, cranes, trumpeters, rails, gallinules, coots
Ciconiiformes	29/254/1027	A/P	Yes	Yes	Yes	Snipe, gulls, hawks, vultures, pelicans, storks, penguins
Passeriformes	45/1161/5719	A	Yes	Yes	Yes	Wrens, antbirds, ovenbirds, crows, magpies, sparrows
Total species	~9672					

Source: After Sibley and Monroe (1990), Nice (1962)

logical, causal explanation that does not require any additional speculation about self-stimulation." Indeed, reports of the excitement, ecstasy, and pleasure accompanying anting in birds is dismissed by Simmons as "a subjective interpretation of very high intensity anting" (Simmons, 1966: 156). Simmons's paper, which is useful in many respects, in effect argues that since anting is almost certainly part of a "feather maintenance system," neither self-stimulation (criterion two) nor the play label is useful in understanding it. Still, anointing behavior is certainly playlike in some respects in its control features, and its possible restriction to certain groups of birds raises intriguing questions. Recent work has shown that some primates apply plant and millipede chemicals to themselves, and these chemicals are known to deter other insects (Weldon et al., 2003; Zito, Evans, & Weldon, 2003). It has been demonstrated that passerine birds such as the Corsican blue tit (*Parus caeruleus*) place aromatic plants in their nests at night, plants that repel blood-sucking insects such as mosquitos (Lafuma, Lambrechts, & Raymond, 2001).

11.4 Evolution of Play in Birds

No one can read about the exploits of keas and ravens and not accept that some birds play in highly complex ways. When a series of conditions prevails, play occurs opportunistically in many species. Birds have the sound-producing apparatus, activity levels and metabolism, parental care system, and brain development to exploit and develop the actions produced from primary process play into functionally important responses.

The fact remains, however, that putative play in birds is often confused with highly functional behavior that we do not recognize or appreciate. Thus many presumed examples of avian play have been dismissed as artifacts of captivity, "maturational behavioral intermediates" (Fagen, 1981: 204), or vacuum activities. Fagen, following Ficken (1977), concludes that "most avian play seems somewhat ambiguous by mammalian standards, either because it has not fully emerged from maturational intermediate status or because existing accounts relied on inadequate criteria and failed to provide necessary information" (1981: 218). He also argues that birds, unlike mammals, "are primarily visual and aerial, object play is common and vigorous, whereas aerial maneuvers of various sorts confuse the uninitiated" (Fagen, 1981: 218). Why being visual should enhance object play, which involves tactile, and often chemical and kinesthetic, reception, is not obvious. No review that I have seen supports the notion that more visual or diurnal mammals have more object play than less visual or nocturnal ones when phylogeny, diet, social organization, and other factors are controlled.

These arguments, rather than suggesting that avian play is particularly ambiguous, may actually suggest that much mammalian play is also ambiguous, but that we do not recognize it as such for essentially anthropomorphic reasons. Indeed, Heinrich and

Smolker (1998) point out that the common definitions of play still leave observers with no objective and applicable criteria for what is and what is not play. Thus, they opt for identifying as play behavior that strikes them as playful and with which most other observers would intuitively agree. However, this only works with the most mammalo-centric kinds of play. Play in ravens seem to meet the Heinrich and Smolker criterion. Much play does not, and that is why we need to apply a list of uniform criteria as consistently as possible.

Even with this list, however, because there is not enough information, many of the examples in the literature cannot be confidently assessed using the five criteria. The idea that only pseudoplay manifests maturational behavioral intermediates is of limited value. Although the quality of evidence is often marginal and anecdotal, enough has been gathered by seasoned ethologists who are familiar with natural behavior to show that instances of playlike behavior are often common and are related to phylo-genetic, ecological, physiological, and other factors.

How does play map onto a phylogeny of birds? The birds retaining the most primitive characteristics (table 11.2) are the Eoaves, including the ostrich, emus, rheas, and cassowaries. Parental care in these birds is even less developed in the megopodes (Cra-ciformes). Play has not been recorded in these animals. It is interesting that the related archosaurs, the crocodilians, have many similar parental behaviors and even more postnatal parental care than some of these birds (Coombs, 1989). Perhaps some non-avian reptiles will prove more playful than some birds.

Ortega and Bekoff (1987) provided a good start for a formal analysis by categorizing the three kinds of play (locomotor, object, and social) across all the orders of birds. They found evidence for play in thirteen of twenty-seven orders. They then related the presence of play to whether the orders contained species with primarily altricial or precocial young. This distinction between precocial and altricial is not always clear-cut and an eight-stage continuum has been proposed (Nice, 1962). One of the playful orders could not be so classified and thus was dropped, leaving twelve of twenty-six playful orders. Only two of the ten precocial orders (Anseriformes—ducks, geese, and swans, and Galliformes—chickens, turkeys, etc.) showed evidence of play and in both cases this was primarily limited to locomotor play (although I have made a speculative case for both limited foraging object play and vocal play in chickens). In contrast, ten of the sixteen orders with altricial young show play, and, except for penguins, this play includes object and social play. The association of play with degree of maturity at birth is statistically significant.

The study by Ortega and Bekoff (1987) thus supports a prediction from SRT (and other theories) that altricial animals should play more. Furthermore, the discussion of these authors is important in a number of other respects. They pointed out that social play is found in seven altricial orders. They speculated that this may be due to the prolonged time spent "socializing with adults and nest mates" (Ortega & Bekoff, 1987:

339). Similarly, they pointed out that this factor may be less important than the fact that precocial young spend more time feeding.

The evolution of the earliest birds is still little known, but fossil finds are providing some information (Sanz et al., 1997). Were the earliest birds precocial or altricial? Both monotremes and marsupials are highly altricial compared with eutherian mammals. Although crocodilians are precocial in that all their senses and locomotor apparatus are functional at hatching, there still is a period of parental care, a period that may last much longer than the parental care period of most altricial birds. It is this period that may be a more important determinant of possible play than the relative change from helplessness to competence, which can be measured in days and weeks in most altricial birds. Since the Eoaves secondarily lost powerful wings and the power of flight, they may not be the best model for seeking the ancestral conditions for the occurrence of play.

Since Ortega and Bekoff (1987) published their analysis, some major and controversial realigning and reconstituting of avian families have occurred (Sibley & Monroe, 1990). I have updated their list in table 11.2. A current phylogeny of orders and play types is presented in figure 11.4. Some resolution is lost because some orders with altricial young have been folded into one another, such as penguins and birds of prey. Each of these orders often contains many families. I have included in the table the number of genera and species. Note that almost 60 percent of all birds are in a single order, the Passeriformes. Most of the most playful species are in this group. But of the almost 10,000 species of birds, play has been described in only about 1 percent. Thus the idea that play is rare in birds may indeed seem to be justified, especially since, as pointed out earlier, even closely related species may differ greatly in the degree of playfulness observed. A more detailed phylogeny of play in birds would allow a more careful analysis of the details of trends in its evolution and the determination of whether play is homologous or independently derived within the orders, some of them very large, in which play does occur. However, this project is beyond the scope of this book. If play has arisen and developed complex forms independently in eutherians and marsupials, and in various avian orders as well, then multiple origins of play have indeed occurred. It is the convergence among the play types (e.g., more object play in generalists and scavengers, more male than female play fighting, play signals restricted to highly socially playful species) that needs explanation.

Although they are critical of the crude quality of the comparative evidence for avian play, Ficken (1977), Fagen (1981), and Ortega and Bekoff (1987) all stress that the evidence for play in many birds is not only compelling but rivals that seen in the most playful mammals. The more recent evidence presented here on ravens and keas supports this conclusion. Thus note where we are now in the evolutionary search for the genesis of play. First, we showed that the picture found in eutherian mammal play was mirrored in marsupials, an independent radiation, but one that still shares the basic

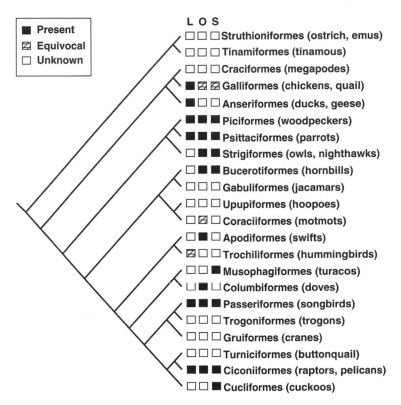

Figure 11.4
Phylogeny of avian orders and occurrence of different kinds of play. L, locomotor play; O, object play; S, social play.

mammalian biology. Now we see that avian play also seems to follow the same schema of an independently evolved playfulness manifested in all three categories (locomotor, object, and social) and having similar associations with feeding ecology, brain size, activity level, etc.

When we compare avian play with marsupial play, we find different similarities. Most groups of marsupials have not been shown to perform any play and play is found primarily in the most derived radiation (kangaroos and wallabies) and in the larger predatory species (dasyurids). Even the most playful marsupials, however, show far less elaborate play, especially with objects, than that seen in many birds. Birds rival eutherian mammals in relative brain size, and the Passeriformes and parrot orders have brains much larger relatively than those of most mammals.

Byers (1998) argued that the most basal form of play is locomotor-rotational play. The fact that Ortega and Bekoff (1987) found that locomotor play was seen in fewer avian orders than object play, and about equally as often as social play, may seem to counter this hypothesis. This may not be an appropriate conclusion for the following reasons: (1) locomotor play is found in families that are precocial and show no other form of play and (2) locomotor play is probably the form most open to uncritical anthropomorphic attribution. For example, Fagen's (1981) survey of play in birds contains hardly any locomotor play that is not included in a social game. Yet, locomotor play is rather widely attributed to mammals. Recall the gambols of fillies and colts and mountain sheep hopping over rocks. It seems that locomotor-rotational play must be of a spectacular bent before it attracts our attention sufficiently to be labeled play. Thus seeing "play" in birds in flight may be more difficult for us than identifying leaping and prancing as play.

In conclusion, we can accept without doubt the observation that birds with complex repertoires of behavior and big brains perform many playful acts. The fact that many families of birds show behavior that satisfies the criteria for at least rudimentary (primitive or primary) play demonstrates again that play arises when several favorable factors coalesce, and that large brains are not necessary. When sufficient comparative data are available, birds will provide a third, and very distantly related group, to compare with eutherian and metatherian mammals in mapping the distribution of play onto phylogenetic, ecological, life history, physiological, and central nervous system variation. What about other reptiles that are closer to a shared ancestry with mammals?

12   The Cool Reptiles

The virtual absence of play behavior in the lower vertebrates attests to the minor role of learning in their life compared to mammals.
—Case (1978: 867)

12.1   Introduction

Did ancient ectothermic reptiles, the ancestral group giving rise to both birds and mammals, play? Do the living representatives of ectothermic reptiles play? A close look at reptiles will further test the proposition that play becomes a recognizable category of behavior as a consequence of a series of adaptations and historical legacies that may arise repeatedly during evolution. If some reptiles play, then no group of animals should be summarily dismissed as not being capable of showing some playful behavior without good reason. "Good reason" involves careful observation, critical anthropomorphism, and objective, unbiased application of the five criteria. As this and subsequent chapters get under way, this admonition becomes more important at the same time that the more typical intuitive criteria for recognizing play become less readily applied.

For zoo visitors, observing a motionless snake or alligator in a cage is the typical experience. Indeed, historically all ectothermic reptiles have been viewed as sluggish, stupid, and behaviorally simple (Burghardt, 1977a). Although considerable evidence to the contrary has been available for more than a century, it has often been resisted in the scientific community as well as by the public. In fact, herpetologists themselves are frequently reluctant to either appreciate or study the flexibility often found in the remarkable and complex behavior of reptiles (Bowers & Burghardt, 1992; Burghardt, 1977b). The most recent editions of excellent major herpetology textbooks, unlike comparable texts on mammals and birds, contain no index entries on play (expected), but also none on learning, cognition, emotion, exploration, curiosity, conditioning, experience, intelligence, plasticity, or similar concepts (Pough et al., 2001; Zug, Vitt, &

Caldwell, 2001). The opening quotation by Ted Case seems to still reflect the received wisdom about reptilian mentality.

As indicated earlier, birds are reptiles, as that group is broadly conceived today, because a modern taxonomic grouping should include all the animals with a common ancestor and their descendants, called a clade. That is, a taxonomic group should be monophyletic and by this view, dinosaurs and birds are clearly reptiles (figure 7.1). If some descendants, such as birds, are excluded, the group is paraphyletic, merely a "grade," and this is unacceptable in modern systematic biology (Greene, 2002). A modern phylogeny of reptiles shows that the groups making up the traditional reptiles are rather distinct from one another. It is possible that existing reptile groups evolved independently from different nonreptilian (amphibian) lineages. If this happened, then reptiles are polyphyletic, and since reptiles without birds refers only to a grade of organization, the very term *reptile* loses even more standing as a useful scientific term.

Many orders of reptiles are now extinct. Even living nonavian reptiles differ in many more ways than they are similar. Only the fact that they are covered in shells, scales, or bare skin rather than feathers or fur seems to unite them. Nonavian reptiles can be divided into four extant major groups (orders): the Chelonia (about 300 species of turtles and tortoises), the Sphenodontida (2 species of tuatara), the Squamata (4500 lizards, 3000 snakes, and 160 amphisbaenians or worm lizards), and the Crocodylia (23 species of crocodiles, alligators, and gavials). Of these four groups, the squamates are by far the most diverse and successful today.

A modern arrangement of the Amniota, the traditional mammals, reptiles, and birds, would view reptiles as the sister taxon to mammals (Greene, 1997). Within modern reptiles, the Chelonia are the sister group to the Sauria, which include all other reptiles and birds. The Sauria are divided into two major groups, Lepidosauria (Sphenodontida and Squamata) and Archosauria (Crocodylia and Aves [birds]).[20] In previous chapters, play has been reviewed in all the Mammalia and the Aves. This may be confusing from a phyletic perspective, but if we view our trip as going from the more recent mammalian lineage (eutherian mammals) to the oldest (monotremes), then it can

20. The Chelonia have traditionally been considered "anapsid" reptiles, based on skull characteristics, and thus a lineage separate from all other reptiles and birds, which are considered "diaspid" (Gauthier et al., 1989). Recent studies have shown that this supposed critical character is not valid and that turtles are diaspids, as are other reptiles and birds (Rieppel & deBraga, 1996; Rieppel & Reisz, 1999). This removes the polyphyletic issue. However, it is now controversial whether the Chelonia are sister taxa to the archosaurs rather than to the Sauria as a whole (Pough et al., 2001) and turtles may be closer to crocodilians than the latter are to birds (S. Hughes, Zelus, & Mouchiroud, 1999). Here I consider turtles as the sister group to the Sauria.

be seen that a similar "descent" is being done within the Reptilia, beginning with birds.

Chapter 11 showed that many birds play and several have a degree of playfulness rivaled by only a few mammals. The playfulness of these avian play champions seems to be associated with large brains, prolonged postnatal development, a complex behavioral repertoire and fine motor control, high metabolic rate and endothermy, generalized foraging abilities, and even, in some species, complex sociality. Parental care is highly developed and protects the young from a hostile environment. Overall, play is less ubiquitous and complex than in placental mammals, but many more of the latter have slow development and larger body sizes. When we come to ectothermic reptiles, even the mainstream scientists who study them apparently have little confidence in, or at least curiosity about, their capacity for noninstinctive behavior.

Until recently, the lack of unequivocal documented evidence of playlike behavior in nonavian reptiles supported the view that play was not found at this grade of organization. In his exhaustive survey of the literature on animal play, Fagen (1981) could locate only two purported examples of reptile play; both were anecdotal reports of object play in single individuals. These will be discussed here along with more recent reports showing that play is not as rare as might be thought. Several life history, ontogenetic, physiological, and psychological factors mitigate against, but do not preclude, the occurrence of typical mammalian playfulness in nonavian, ectothermic reptiles (chapter 6; Burghardt, 1984, 1988b).

12.2 Crocodilians

The social system, interaction patterns, and parental care of present-day crocodilians are as advanced as those of many conservative eutherians and metatherians and probably reflect a nearly comparable level of neural organization.
—Eisenberg (1981: 74)

Alligators, crocodiles, and gavials represent the three families of living crocodilians. Their order, Crocodylia, is grouped with extinct dinosaurs, thecodonts, and pterosaurs and all birds in the subclass Archosauria. They are the living animals most closely related to living birds. About twenty-five species have survived virtually unchanged morphologically since the time of the dinosaurs (upper Cretaceous). Dinosaurs, crocodilians, and birds can be viewed as a monophyletic group. Although it is controversial, most paleontologists currently accept the evolution of birds from small bipedal dinosaurs (Colbert, Morales, & Minkoff, 2001; Pough, Janis, & Heiser, 2002). The alternative view that birds evolved from an archosaur more similar to a crocodilian is still supported by some scientists.

12.2.1 A Little Detour—Did Dinosaurs Play?

In recent years attempts to revise our view of dinosaurs have permeated the scientific and popular press (Bakker, 1986; Desmond, 1976; Horner & Gorman, 1988). Dinosaurs, it is claimed, were warm-blooded (endothermic), very active, highly social, had extensive parental care, and some were probably rather intelligent as well. According to a recent authoritative film series on dinosaurs, they also played. All these attributes are said to be vastly different from the common view of sluggish, dull, and behaviorally simple living reptiles. Without getting into the details here, this view of living nonavian reptiles is highly suspect. The many statements by paleontologists who would rather ally dinosaurs behaviorally with birds than with other reptiles, such as crocodiles, are often misleading and based on an unfamiliarity with the behavior of living ectothermic reptiles (Burghardt, 1977b). Nevertheless, if play occurs in reptiles other than birds, it most likely would have been found at least in some dinosaurs as well.

Dinosaur behavior is most parsimoniously interpreted in light of current archosaurian behavior as found in crocodilians. Analysis of dinosaur bones suggests that they had growth rates intermediate between those of bird-mammals and other reptiles (Chinsamy & Dodson, 1995). There is also evidence that the earliest birds were not as warm-blooded as living birds. Birds typically mature faster than many mammals, so growth rate may not be that central to the issues of metabolism, brains, and behavior. Studies on lung mechanics also suggest that the metabolic rate of dinosaurs was significantly lower than that found in living birds and mammals (J. A. Ruben & Battalia, 1979; J. A. Ruben et al., 1997). On the other hand, there is also evidence that some monitor lizards and turtles, discussed later, can sustain high oxygen exchange rates that are comparable to those of mammals, and that only minor modifications in several parameters, such as blood oxygen-carrying capacity, could raise ectothermic reptiles to endothermic metabolic levels (Hicks & Farmer, 1998).

12.2.2 Crocodilians, Dinosaurs, and Birds Compared

Crocodilians are all large; even the smallest outweigh most members of the other major groups of reptiles, such as turtles, lizards, and snakes. As archosaurs, they share a more recent common ancestor with birds than with squamates or turtles. In fact, crocodilians are more similar to birds in many physiological and life history characteristics than they are to other traditional reptile groups such as turtles. For example, crocodilians have a four-chambered heart that allows them to keep venous and arterial blood more separate than is the case in other nonavian reptiles; presumably it allows greater sustained activity (aerobic scope; see chapter 6). This type of heart may have been a factor in the subsequent evolution of endothermy. In fact mammals and birds have even more complete separation.[21] In addition, crocodilians provide postnatal parental care that may extend for many months, if not years (Gans, 1996; Shine, 1988). They also have a complex vocal communication system that includes contact and distress calls as found in many birds (Herzog & Burghardt, 1977).

As with birds, all crocodilians lay eggs. Female crocodilians also dig or build nests and frequently tend and defend both their nests and hatchlings. Nest tending and parental care have not yet been reliably documented in any turtle (Shine, 1988), all species of which also lay eggs. In a detailed comparison of the nesting and parental care behavior of crocodilians, dinosaurs, ratites (ancient large flightless birds), and megapodes (primitive turkeylike birds that lay eggs in mounds and show no parental care), it was shown that crocodilians have most of the behavioral attributes attributed to dinosaurs (Coombs, 1989). Thus both early avian and dinosaur behavior "are arguably retentions of ancient behavior patterns from archosaurs" (Coombs, 1989: 21). More direct fossil evidence of dinosaur nesting behavior suggests that parental care is a shared ancestral trait in all three groups, while brooding, which is also present in some squamate reptiles but not in crocodilians, may have been independently rederived in dinosaurs and birds (J. M. Clark, Norell, & Chiappe, 1999). Regardless, in terms of physiology and parental care, crocodilians have features that are often associated with play (Fagen, 1981). If play occurs in crocodilians, then it most likely could have been a feature of some dinosaurs as well.

All crocodilians are semiaquatic and spend most of their time in water. They can run quickly on land by raising up on their legs and galloping (Zug, 1974), even becoming bipedal. Crocodilians are carnivores and eat a high-protein diet. All these features might predispose them to show some play (chapter 6). In actuality, the data are sparse. But since even the advanced parental care shown by crocodilians was not accepted by most herpetologists until after the 1970s,[22] it is premature to rule out the extent and nature of play crocodilians might demonstrate.

21. Scanning of a presumed dinosaur heart suggested the presence of a bird-type heart (Fisher et al., 2000) in at least one dinosaur, although not one from the lineage thought to have given rise to birds. The authors of this report suggest that such animals had intermediate to high metabolic rates. Metabolic studies of oxygen consumption and exercise in alligators show that they are as much constrained in performance of sustained activity as are typical lizards (Emshwiller & Gleeson, 1997). Rather brief nonsustainable (anerobic) activity leads to large postactivity oxygen consumption and extensive recuperation costs. In this way they are typical nonavian reptiles.

22. For example, in spite of observations by fine observers, parental care in ectothermic reptiles was rejected by both the then-dean of crocodilian behavior (Neill, 1971) and other knowledgeable reviewers (e.g., Case, 1978), although on varying empirical and theoretical grounds.

12.2.3 Curiosity and Play in Crocodilians

Crocodilians do seem to engage in exploratory and investigative behavior (Glickman & Sroges, 1966). This classic paper assessed visual and manipulatory responses in many birds, mammals, and reptiles. None of the twenty diverse reptiles (several each of snakes, lizards, and turtles) were nearly as responsive as the single crocodilian tested, a male Orinoco crocodile (*Crocodylus intermedius*). He responded to all of the introduced objects (wooden blocks and dowels, a steel chain, rubber tubing, paper) by attacking and biting them, sometimes even pushing them about with his snout. As with mammals, habituation was rapid over the 6-minute trial. However, objects were not repeatedly presented, a procedure that might have been used to assess a play interpretation by seeing if the animal would return to the object and manipulate it after it found it posed no risk. Remote viewing without visible humans would also have been an asset here. Furthermore, the introduced objects might have been confused with food, for many captive reptiles develop a pronounced and startlingly quick "feeding reflex," as it is called by zoo curatorial staff. The objects were presented on land, which might have led to fewer interactions than if they had been presented in the water, where crocodiles typically live except when basking.

The sole published report on crocodilian play is tantalizing, but is restricted to one field observation session on one individual. An American alligator (*Alligator mississippiensis*) was repeatedly attracted to, and snapped at, water dripping from a spout (Lazell & Spitzer, 1977). The published account omits some important details (J. D. Lazell, personal communication, 1996). The observations were made on a young, wild alligator on St. Catherine's Island, Georgia, where the species had been unmolested for many years. Artesian well water was supplied to a small pond by a pipe that extended 2 m over the surface of a full pond. Periodically a pump would run and a torrent of water would exit the pipe and loudly fall about a meter to the pond's surface. The authors were present when the pump shut off and a 1-m-long alligator swam toward the point where the trickling water from the pipe hit the surface. The animal slowly circled and observed the dripping water. Finally, facing the pipe head on, it paused, moved slowly toward it in a straight line, and then suddenly swerved away at a 45° angle; it swam away about 3 m and then repeated the action. After doing this three to four times, it approached the drip and let the water hit its snout. Then the gator suddenly snapped at the drip, swam away, returned, snapped again, and repeated this "many times" for a period of 45 minutes.

The authors reject the interpretation that the animal was showing displaced aggression toward the observers since there was no such response by any of the alligators in the pond before the pump was turned off. ("All appeared unafraid and frankly curious.") Consistent with criterion five, the day was warm and sunny. It is reasonable to accept this anecdotal report on putative play behavior as tentatively valid, since trained herpetologists observed it and the play criteria seem to be satisfied. There are also recent data on the sensory aspect of this behavior (Soares, 2002). Alligators, like all crocodilians, have extremely sensitive dome pressure receptors on their faces, that respond to pressure changes such as those caused by water dropping on a surface. Blindfolded alligators can locate prey and other objects using this sense organ. It could be that the animal was responding to the sensory stimulation and performing a predatorylike act; again, this is similar to the visually mediated object play in cats and birds.

Although this is the only published account, reptile behavior experts have provided additional accounts of captive young alligators engaging in locomotor-type play, such as repeatedly sliding down slopes into water (Paul Weldon and Harry Greene, personal communication), but these have not yet been confirmed with film or video. Captive juvenile dwarf caimans (*Paleosuchus palpebrosus*) have been reported to stand on their hind legs in a shower in an inexplicable manner not seen in other species (Heinbuch & Weigman, 2000). Andrew Odum of the Toledo Zoo has observed a male Cuban crocodile (*Crocodylus rhombifer*) attacking and pushing around a large ball and approaching it while blowing bubbles used in courtship. Altogether, from the observations to date it would appear that crocodilians do not provide strong evidence for play behavior. However, the nature of their housing in captivity may preclude play, and young animals have not been studied sufficiently in either captivity or the field. Animals in warm, nutritionally adequate, and ecologically appropriate settings need to be studied.

12.3   Squamate Reptiles

Squamate reptiles include the lizards, snakes, and worm lizards. The latter are little-known fossorial reptiles with a mix of snake and lizard traits (Gans, 1975), and few behavioral reports, none suggesting play, have been published. Therefore this group is not discussed further. Lizards, on the other hand, have been well studied in the field and captivity. Although many are small and suffer from the constraints limiting play discussed earlier, many are large and many species show some parental care, especially the skinks (Shine, 1988; Somma, 2003). In fact, one extensively studied Australian skink, the sleepy lizard (*Tiliqua rugosa*) has virtually lifelong social monogamy, small litters, and mother-offspring recognition (Bull, 1994; Main & Bull, 1996). There are nocturnal, crepuscular, and diurnal species. They can live in trees, shrubs, rocks, underground, in the desert, and near and in water.

Many lizards show highly developed exploratory behavior and curiosity directed toward objects. One dramatic example is the lizard *Anolis agassizi*, found only on Malpelo, a rock island in the Pacific owned by Colombia (Rand, Gorman, & Rand, 1975). Anolis lizards are typically small insectivorous animals. An exception, the Malpelo anole, a rather large species feeding on a wide variety of small animals found in its harsh and barren habitat, approached the scientists studying them and even jumped on them. They were attracted to, and investigated, all kinds of objects, particularly orange and yellow ones. They readily ate novel food items such as colored candies. Such behavior seems similar to the response to objects described for ravens in chapter 11 and is not play.

My colleagues and I have watched neonate, juvenile, and adult green iguanas (*Iguana iguana*) for hundreds of hours in the field and have never seen any behavior that seemed playful, although they would approach and tongue flick at novel objects. Observation of these large, herbivorous lizards supported the original tenets of SRT that would find play rare in reptiles. However, there are now substantial data available on play in one group of remarkable lizards.

12.3.1 Monitor Lizards

The largest living lizards are the monitor lizards in the genus *Varanus* and the largest of these is the Komodo dragon (*Varanus komodoensis*), a species known to science for less than a century. Play by a captive Komodo monitor lizard was described in a short article full of interesting observations on a variety of birds and mammals (Hill, 1946), although Komodo play was briefly mentioned in an even earlier report (Proctor, 1928). Hill's entire description (which originally was accompanied by a photo) is as follows:

Even some reptiles, it seems, have a rudimentary sense of play. At the Reptile House to-day you can meet a Komodo "dragon" in whose den the keeper often deliberately leaves his shovel after the morning clean-up. This the dragon loves to push about over the stones, and the more noise he can make with it, the more it seems to please him. He is indeed the only Zoo reptile, so far as I have been able to discover, ever to be intentionally provided with a "toy." (Hill, 1946: 26)

For a long time this anecdotal brief paper has stood as the first and best example of reptile play (Fagen, 1981). That it was not an aberrant observation or animal is shown, however, by recent observations on a Komodo monitor at the National Zoological Park in Washington, D.C. that we have studied for several years. This animal, a female named Kracken, was the first dragon bred in captivity in the Western Hemisphere. In the initial observations on Kracken it was noted that she would repeatedly and noisily push a bucket around. She also removed notebooks and other items from her familiar keeper's pocket and walked around with them in her mouth, but did not chew or destroy them. Since then, extensive playful interactions with all kinds of objects, including blankets, shoes, small rubber statues, boxes, rings, and Frisbees, have been studied and videotaped (figure 12.1). Extensive social interactions and tug-of-war games with keepers involving handkerchiefs, beverage cans, and other objects were common and have also been filmed (Burghardt et al., 2002).

We carried out a series of trials with different objects with or without the familiar keeper present, all of which were videotaped. The most frequently used objects were a sturdy plastic ring and shoes (clean or used sneakers). The animal would perform a

Figure 12.1
Response of a Komodo dragon to a ring. (Photo by Trooper Walsh)

wide variety of actions, including nudging, grabbing, shaking, putting her head inside the shoe, and so on (figure 12.2). Her behavior, particularly with the shoe, was similar to a dog's and became even more similar when the tape was run at twice the normal speed. We tested the alternative hypothesis that she was just performing feeding behavior under a feeding motivational system by presenting the plastic ring coated with rat blood, her common food being rats. First she shifted to actually trying to swallow the ring and performed side-swiping movements with it in her jaws, behavior that is used to reposition prey for better swallowing (figure 12.3). These actions were never seen with the nonbloody objects except for the first trial with linseed oil. Second, when her keeper, whom she typically tried to engage in interaction with her and the objects, was present, she became more nervous, possessive, and even threatening toward him in the presence of blood-coated objects. This was shown by the typical lateral display and tail lashing. Since these animals often feed at carcasses and are very protective of their food, even toward mates and offspring, it seems clear that she was readily able to distinguish the toy from real prey. The overwhelming importance of chemical cues in her behavior was also demonstrated. The Komodo dragon is the only

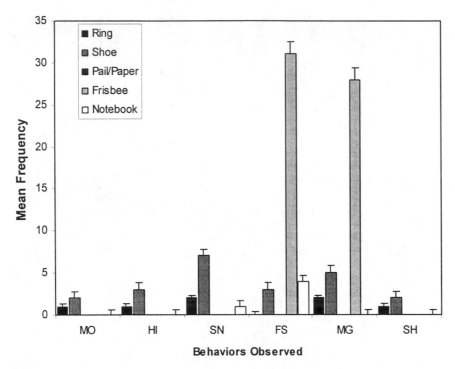

Figure 12.2
Quantitative data on the frequency of different acts performed with various artificial objects by a Komodo dragon over several 30-minute sessions. MO, move object; HI, head inserted into object; SN, snout nudges object; FS, foreclaw scrape ("pawing"); MG, mouth grabs the object; SH, shakes the object while held in the mouth.

monitor that makes a habit of often eating large prey, tearing it apart, eating communally (but often competitively), and having many other quite remarkably complex behavior patterns (Burghardt et al., 2002).

Play might be rather common in these lizards. Monitor lizards have high metabolic rates compared with most reptiles and are considered quite intelligent (A. F. Bennett, 1982; Christian & Weavers, 1994). Although monitor lizards apparently show no parental care after their eggs hatch, Fagen (1981) was correct in predicting that this group of lizards would be a prime candidate for play in reptiles.

Play was not mentioned by Walter Auffenberg in his seminal monograph on the behavioral ecology of the Komodo monitor (Auffenberg, 1981); curiosity and exploration were also not explicitly mentioned. However, the behavior of one particular male, 34W, might have been misinterpreted. This animal was considered "crazy" and dangerous since it seemed to have so little fear of humans. The entire description is worth quoting.

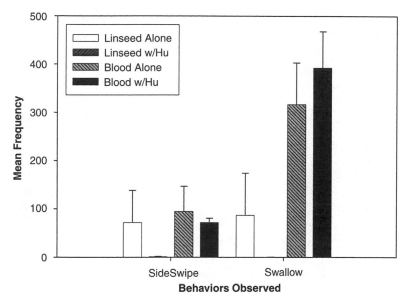

Figure 12.3

Data comparing responses to blood-coated and nonblood-coated rings by a Komodo dragon with the keeper present. Sideswiping and swallowing only found when object coated in blood except for one trial with linseed oil. (From Burghardt et al., 2002)

In fact, it often entered our camp and once almost stepped into our shelter, though we were clearly visible inside. It often came to our Poreng camp shortly after our arrival, perhaps because it was drawn by the scent of our campfire (a pattern frequently noticed by villagers as well). On one trip to Poreng it drove our expedition members out of their tent, stuck its head into a knapsack, removed a shirt, and tore it to shreds. Other pieces of clothing and things we handled were similarly manipulated or carried off. There was no question in our minds, or in the minds of villagers, that if given the opportunity this animal might attack, whether provoked or not. (1981: 123)

This animal might well have attacked if it thought that a person was appropriate prey or posed a threat. Any interaction with large, dangerous animals, including bears, elephants, gorillas, and tigers, poses such a risk to people, a risk that usually does not color our interpretations of similar behavior by a smaller or less potentially dangerous animal. Consider the same behavior described in a similar manner for a grizzly bear and a cat. What is evident from this description is the similarity to the behavior with objects shown by Kracken. That such behavior is related to foraging is not surprising; 34W was a dragon that was not intimidated by people, but perhaps was wary enough to show open-mouth and bowed-tail defensive postures. His boldness may have led to showing a level of interaction with objects, in the presence of people, that is not seen in the typical more flighty monitor lizard. This example suggests that remote video-taping of dragons in the field, perhaps provided with objects with and without added odors, as in the National zoo study, would be worthwhile.

There are other species of monitor lizards, varying in adult size from less than 100 g to the more than 50 kg of some Komodo adults. The size range is such that hatchling Komodo lizards are larger than adults of some other species (Auffenberg, 1981; Christian et al., 1996). Although monitors are found in Asia and Africa and the South Pacific, the most diverse radiation is in Australia. Many monitors are highly active predators with high metabolic rates and considerable aerobic scope (chapter 6). For example, during the dry season, one Australian species, *Varanus panoptes*, moved about an average of 3.5 hours a day, with some individuals on the move for more than 6 hours a day (Christian et al., 1995). This contrasts with the much lower metabolic energy consumption of sit-and-wait lizards from other families, which may be active only 2 percent of the time when they are outside their burrows (Anderson & Karasov, 1981). Furthermore, monitors seem to have overcome one of the problems lizards have, compared with mammals, in obtaining enough oxygen for continuous activity—the absence of a diaphragm. Monitors have a large throat pouch that can expand and force air into their lungs and provide more oxygen for aerobic activity. Not all monitors are highly active predators, however, and their metabolic rates are not always higher than expected for a typical (e.g., iguanid) lizard of their size (Christian et al., 1996; Christian & Weavers, 1994). Finally, some monitor lizards have a constraint on excess activity only found in their close relatives, snakes. Eating a large meal causes greatly increased metabolic rates, up to ten times normal, and this without moving at all (Secor & Phillips, 1997).

A study of sixteen hatchling black-throated monitors (*Varanus albigularis*) in collaboration with the Dallas zoo demonstrated the intense and persistent investigatory and manipulation tendencies of monitors (Manrod, 2003). Half of the animals were reared in complex environments with live prey and other nontraditional features and half were reared in typical captive environments with only dead prey. The enriched animals were given Plexiglas containers containing live prey that they could obtain by opening a door; all eight learned the task on the first trial and did so twice as quickly on the second trial.

Although much of the activity of the lizard at the National zoo concerned object play, note that the lizard also frequently involved its keeper in tugs-of-war and even keep-away games. Social play in conspecifics is not known; however, precocial sexual behavior has been reported in the savanna monitor (*Varanus exanthematicus*) (Bayless, 1994) and has been observed in our laboratory as well.

Mosasaurs were large Cretaceous aquatic, diving, predatory lizards closely related to the monitor lizards. In appearance and perhaps habits they were similar to the toothed whales (Cetacea) and seals (L. D. Martin & Rothschild, 1989). They were capable of deep dives and had a morphology adapted to agile and quick swimming. They apparently laid their eggs on land. They ate their prey whole, as do most monitors today with the exception of the Komodo dragon. The Komodo dragon is capable of swimming between islands, and other monitors, such as the water (*V. salvator*) and Nile (*V. niloticus*) monitors, enter the water frequently and even forage there. It is thus not out of the question to suspect that mosasaurs, along with their even more aquatic dolphin-like relatives, the ichthyosaurs and Loch Ness monster-appearing plesiosaurs, engaged in some playlike behavior. Be that as it may, the conclusions about monitors summarize their status among reptiles. Varanids are to lizards what nonhuman primates are to other mammals. They have broken through the constraints of their respective ancestral lineages and reached new pinnacles of complexity in physiology, foraging, sociality, and cognition. In fact, varanid lizards vary in size as much as do bushbabies and gorillas—these majestic lizards can attack prey chimps can only dream about, and they have conquered life underground and in water where primates fear to tread.

12.3.2 Other Lizards

Although the Komodo dragon presents the best example of object play in squamate reptiles, additional anecdotal claims of play in lizards are sometimes found in the pet literature (e.g., green iguanas, *Iguana iguana*; Hatfield, 1996), although careful behavioral descriptions are typically lacking. Play has been proposed as a possible explanation for what seems to be nonfunctional and enigmatic behavior, such as nonsocial head-bobbing displays in hatchling fence lizards (*Sceloporus undulatus*) (Roggenbuck & Jenssen, 1986), and "wrestling" in neonate African chameleons (Burghardt, 1982). Since systematic description and experimental analysis are not available for these examples, the existence of social play in lizards other than monitors remains in doubt. However, both head-bobbing displays and wrestling in juvenile, sexually immature animals are reminiscent of the play fighting so common in young mammals and some birds.

Fence lizards, shortly after hatching, will perform simplified head-bobbing displays to no apparent conspecific and for no apparent reason. The displays are normally employed in courtship and territorial establishment and defense, neither of which is found in these young animals. Similarly, Australian frillnecked lizards (*Chlamydosaurus kingii*) at 1 day of age directed frill erection and "handwaving" displays toward other hatchlings and people. Dominance among hatchlings was not related to either sex or androgen level; however, androgen levels were far more similar between the sexes in hatchlings than they were later in adults (Christian et al., 1999). Hormones also play a role in the ontogeny of head-bobbing displays in neonatal green iguanas (Phillips, Alberts, & Pratt, 1993), and some head-bobbing displays seem unique to juveniles. Perhaps these are motivationally transient behavior patterns, as suggested for many birds (Fagen, 1981; Ficken, 1977). Whether they are essential precursors to later behavior has not yet been established, but the similarity to play fighting in mammals should not be ignored. On the other hand, these behavior patterns are all communication displays. Could such "gestural" behavior be a motoric equivalent of the vocal play so often described in birds and human beings, albeit with a much less diverse communicative repertoire? Repetition could help in filling out a template or providing practice. Here, as so often in this book, identifying something as play does not answer a question, but merely raises problems for analysis. Viewing such phenomena as trivial epiphenomena discourages closer analysis.

Although physically large species of lizards might be predicted to show play behavior if appropriate nutritional, energetic, ecological, and life history factors are present, these, like the planets in our solar system, might rarely be in alignment in reptiles. For example, one might expect that Galapagos marine iguanas (*Amblyrhynchus cristatus*) would be seen playing in water since they forage in the ocean in the tropics. However, the water they forage in is very cold, despite the Galapagos Islands being on the equator. In addition, iguanas in general are adapted to a low-protein, low-fat diet and thus the conditions facilitating play are minimal.

12.3.3   Snakes

In the snake, all the organs are sheathed: no hands, no feet, no fins, no wings. In bird and beast, the organs are released, and begin to play. In man, they are all unbound, and full of joyful action. With this unswaddling he receives the absolute illumination we call Reason, and thereby true liberty.
—Emerson (1870: 22–23)

The origin of snakes from lizards is widely accepted, but the exact scenario is still controversial. The consensus view is that snakes arose from a burrowing lizard, related to the monitors, perhaps in the late Jurassic about 140 mya (Tchernov et al., 2000). The most primitive living snakes are the blind snakes (Scolecophidia) (Greene, 1997). They are still quite numerous, with more than 300 species, but are little studied because of their generally small sizes and secretive habits. There is fossil evidence that the basal Alethinophidia (e.g., pipe snakes, sunbeam snakes) and basal Macrostomata (e.g., boas, pythons) arose by the late Cretaceous. The advanced snakes (Colubroidea), comprising more than 80 percent of all living species (colubrids, cobras, sea snakes, vipers, and pit vipers), may not have appeared until long after the extinction of the dinosaurs, perhaps in the Oligocene or Miocene 25–35 mya, with the major radiation in the Pliocene (Holman, 2000). Most living snakes, then, are recent animals that are demonstrably younger than the major recent bird and mammal lineages, including the great apes. Indeed, the rapid evolution of diverse species of birds and mammals may have opened up food niches for these specialized reptilian carnivores.[23]

23. All snakes eat other animals (or their eggs) whole, with the primary exception of some Asian homalopsine water snakes that sometimes remove the legs from crabs and swallow only the bodies (Greene, 1997) or swallow only the legs (Jayne, Voris, & Ng, 2002).

The evidence for play in snakes is sparser than in lizards. Clearly, snakes do not have the means to manipulate their environment nearly as effectively as limbed animals and must rely on chemosensory, tactile, and visual information that is often received more passively. Tongue-flicking movements are the most elaborate and finely controlled of snake behaviors and seem to serve primarily as a means to gather chemosensory information and also sometimes to convey a visual signal (Gove & Burghardt, 1983). Whether there is any playful aspect to the ubiquitous tongue flicking by most active snakes is something that may be difficult to determine. On the other hand, Aristotle did claim that snakes have a forked tongue so that they could get double pleasure from their food. If we extend this to stimulation in general, then perhaps some tongue flicking could be less than completely functional and thus fit the five criteria.

Given their basic body plan, snakes have radiated into an amazing diversity of forms, habitats, and behavioral repertoires (Greene, 1997). Some snakes are highly arboreal and others highly aquatic. The behavior patterns of most snakes have seldom been observed in the wild. The behavior of young snakes in nature is rarely observed at all. Those species that have been studied have not been reported to show any behavior that might be termed play, but then it is difficult to know what might be called play in these animals. A captive gopher snake (*Pituophis catenifer*) would often repeatedly climb through a 5-cm loop of light fixture cord at the top of his cage for periods of 15 minutes or more (Dan Mulcahy, personal communication, 1998). Snakes are not known to push toys with their snouts, but what about burrowing snakes? Do those deprived of substrate show any kind of substitute movements? What about young snakes raised in restricted environments? No one has really looked at the behavior of the more active, prey generalist snakes from a playful perspective. As pointed out in chapter 6, the behavioral endurance of neonate snakes is less than that of adults. Thus play appears to be physiologically constrained in snakes.

We might expect that tropical sea snakes, those rarely leaving the water at all, might be most likely to play because their locomotion is less costly. I have seen, as have others, the sea snake (*Pelamis platurus*) wind its body in knots and contort itself repeatedly. One interpretation is that this is parasite removal behavior, but there is little evidence for this, and other sea snakes do not knot, even those that have barnacle infestations (H. Voris, personal communication, 1997). I have seen knotting in captive snakes (Naos Marine Laboratory, Smithsonian Tropical Research Institute, Panama) that showed no sign of external parasites. Knotting has been found to be associated with shedding in this pelagic species, where there are few objects to rub against to stimulate the periodic shedding of the entire skin that all snakes must undergo throughout their lives (H. Voris, personal communication, 1997). Knotting may be frequent in some species of snakes living in "low-friction" environments (Lillywhite, 1989), but is not necessary. Muscular contractions also stretch the skin and facilitate removal. Could knotting also be play if it is found in well-fed "bored" snakes between sheddings? No one seems to have suggested this possibility. As we will see in the next chapter, a similar issue has been raised in a long-standing controversy concerning fish behavior and parasite removal.

Recently, David Cundall, a herpetologist and functional morphologist, has suggested that the drinking behavior of snakes has some playful aspects (unpublished manuscript, 2001). Using very precise kinematic methods with sixteen diverse species, he found that snakes did not drink efficiently and engaged in periodic "high irregularity" in drinking that appeared nonfunctional in that water was expelled. He concluded that the behavior was best interpreted as play. Since drinking is both complex (it involves sucking and jaw movements) and risky (owing to exposure to predators) for snakes, selection should maximize efficiency. There was some evidence showing reduced efficiency as snakes became satiated. Drinking, however, is a rather low-energy behavior and Cundall argued against mechanistic explanations based on physiology. He could not rule out the possibility that the behavior is influenced by the captive environment, since risk of predation and limited access to water are not typical concerns of snakes in captivity; field studies of the sort he carried out in the laboratory are not yet technically possible. As Cundall suggested, the behavior in his snakes seemed to be similar to the sucking behavior people use with straws; children often engage in repeatedly sucking in and blowing out liquids, making bubbles, etc. Snakes, as do mammals, will drink before they need to for physiological reasons. Given the limited scope physiologically and morphologically for behavior in snakes, the parallels are intriguing. As Cundall stated, "Despite distant phylogenetic relationship, . . . some aspects of drinking behaviour in snakes bear uncanny similarity to drinking in humans (unpublished manuscript, p. 22).

Although I have received anecdotal reports of snakes engaged in playful activity, such as the bull snake example provided by a herpetologist, discussed earlier, they are rare. In all my years of watching snakes, I have not seen playlike responses, certainly not in the mammalian manner, and remain agnostic on tongue flicking as play.

Snakes might be less prone to play than lizards for several reasons. The absence of limbs greatly limits the complexity of their behavioral patterns and the ability to engage in novel behavior. Recall that distal forelimb size was related to some aspects of brain size. Physiologically, their locomotion is often more costly than that in legged reptiles. They also have smaller brains than comparably sized lizards (about half the size, E. Font, personal communication, 2000), although we have seen that the role of brain size in play is not at all clear (chapter 5). Postnatal parental care is absent in virtually all species, although increasing evidence for neonatal pit vipers and other snakes staying with their mothers for several days after birth or hatching is accumulating from field studies (e.g., Greene, 1997). Snakes, being solitary predators and having to locate, subdue, and ingest prey animals from the beginning of their life, need to have much of their hunting expertise present instinctively. If mammalianlike object or locomotor play is to be found in a snake, I suspect it would be in a species with a high metabolic rate that lives in a warm, structurally complex or aquatic environment, or one that forages on a variety of small prey that are difficult to capture and ingest. Snakes such as mambas, cobras, and racers may have the greater endurance and active predatory behavior that would predispose them to playlike behavior. Nonetheless, even snakes with small regular meals have post-feeding metabolic costs much higher than other reptiles except for some monitors (Secor & Phillips, 1997).

Social play in snakes should be even less common since snakes are generally nonterritorial animals that show little direct fighting or vigorous competition with one another, even in the context of mating. One exception is the male-male wrestling combat of adult rattlesnakes (see Greene, 1997). Observations of socially housed young snakes of species showing such combat might uncover some playlike neonatal interactions. Social aggregations of snakes outside of mating, including juveniles, are common in many species (Burghardt, 1983; Greene, 1997).

Certainly, squamate reptiles in general, in spite of being very successful, show only scattered evidence of play in the mammalian way. Lizards, and especially snakes, typically have rather small brains compared with birds and mammals (Jerison, 1973). But we are also finding out that many lizards and even some snakes have limited, but perhaps critically important, postnatal parental care. Some lizards, particularly some of the larger skinks and insular lizards from several families, have monogamous bonds, small clutches or litters, and maternal care (e.g., Case, 1982). Thus careful study of these animals might lead to more definitive examples of behavior that fit the five play criteria.

12.4   Turtles

All turtles living today are divided into the aquatic side-necked turtles (Pleurodira) and the more diverse and widespread hidden-necked turtles (Cryptodira). Only Pleurodira are found in Australia, but many are also found in South America. The Pleurodira are considered the more ancient lineage (but see Meylan, 1996) and are relatively little studied. All currently available examples of turtle play concern cryptodires.

12.4.1   Object Play

The first well-documented instance of play in turtles was object play in a Nile soft-shelled turtle (*Trionyx triunguis*) (Burghardt, Ward, & Rosscoe, 1996). This turtle is a large aquatic species with a carapace length up to 95 cm and a mass of 90 kg. The little that is known about the species' natural history, fossil record (at least 5 million years), and taxonomic position is reviewed in Burghardt, Ward, and Rosscoe (1996). It is pertinent to note that turtles were found in the Triassic at least 200 mya (Rougier, Fuente, & Arcucci, 1995) and members of the soft-shelled lineage go back to the early Cretaceous or even the Jurassic; that is, more than 144 mya (Meylan, 1987).

The initial subject was a long-term captive male (called Pigface) at the National (Washington, DC) zoo and the details have been presented at length elsewhere (Burghardt, 1998a; Burghardt, Ward, & Rosscoe, 1996). Pigface was provided with a series of objects in a successful attempt to reduce self-injury from stereotyped clawing and biting. The solitary adult turtle was provided with sticks, balls, hoops of hose, and other objects. In addition to frequently approaching, following, and visually inspecting them, he would nose, bite, grasp, chew, push, pull, or shake them with his mouth. He would also use his forelimbs to hold down objects or to pull them closer. The behavior patterns used varied with the object; for example, basketballs were pushed with the snout and lunged at with open jaws (figure 12.4). When the hoop was present and floating vertically, the turtle nosed, bit, chewed, shook, push, pulled, and sometimes swam through it. An activity budget showed that the turtle interacted with the objects a great deal of the time as well as being highly active in general. Active over two-thirds of the time when filmed over several days, the turtle interacted with the objects 31 percent of the time. If objects were continually present, the turtle lost interest; thus the proportion of time spent with the different objects was even higher if calculated only for periods that the individual objects were available. The value of toy rotation is thus shown in a turtle.

A common criterion for play is that it is fun or pleasurable to the participant. This common play attribute is included in criterion two. Although emotion in reptiles, except perhaps anger or rage, is rarely studied, evidence is accumulating through careful experiments that turtles and lizards have emotional responses that physiologically and behaviorally are comparable to those in mammals (Balaskó & Cabanac, 1998; M. Cabanac, 1999; M. Cabanac & Bernieri, 2000). It seems particularly hard to document pleasure in nonhuman species and especially in a species where it is difficult to easily, if anthropomorphically, interpret gestures and facial expressions (but see Bekoff, 2002). Did Pigface show any signs of pleasure? When his tank was being refilled with water, which streamed from a hose at the bottom, Pigface would orient toward the hose so that the stream of water flowed over his head. He appeared unsatisfied until he had adjusted the direction of the hose so it was "just right." When everything was set, he would remain there motionless for some time. This was rather striking given his usual high rate of activity. When the water was turned off, the turtle rapidly became restless and moved off. Could this be akin to our pleasure with a jacuzzi or the wind in our face on a spring afternoon? This is a species often found in rivers where there are currents, and his enclosure had no current otherwise.

Regardless, by any traditional criteria the turtle "played" with the various objects in his tank and, furthermore, this behavior made up a considerable portion of his activity

Figure 12.4
Response of a Nile soft-shelled turtle to a basketball. (Photo by Paul Weldon, from Burghardt et al., 1996)

budget. This impression is magnified if the video tape is replayed at two or four times regular speed. Furthermore, the behavior of this turtle was not exceptional. Although the species is extremely rare in captivity and field observations are scarce, we carried out subsequent analyses of videotaped trials with various objects by two members of this species at the Toronto zoo. The reptile curator there (Robert Johnson) had written me that that their two males responded in a manner similar to that of Pigface when objects were supplied. Together we planned a systematic videotaped series of tests with four objects. Behavior with objects similar to that exhibited by Pigface was recorded when the turtles were singly housed in small tanks (but spacious for most zoo exhibits). When the turtles were in a new, large pond in a naturalistic primate exhibit, the level of interaction decreased, as would be expected from SRT. Some of the data have been published and show a somewhat lower level of play in a large tank than in a small one (Krause, Burghardt, & Lentini, 1999). Interestingly, rats play more when in small rather than large enclosures (Siegel & Jensen, 1986); thus close confinement may be another factor in the greater play found in captive vs wild animals. The absence of substrate in the tanks may also have encouraged the play behavior. When we provided sand to our juvenile Nile soft-shell, she gave up manipulating intake and outlet tubes and colorful toys and spent most of her time buried. Thus tactile stimulation may have taken priority.

What factors facilitated play behavior in these soft-shelled turtles? Several possibilities derive from those previously identified as factors in endothermic animal play (Burghardt, 1988b). These include its life in an energy-efficient medium for locomotion (water), ample provision for nutritional and thermal needs in captivity, the spartan captive environment, and the prior evidence of stress (boredom?), as indicated by the earlier history of self-mutilation behavior for Pigface.

Other recent evidence for turtle object play has surfaced. Mann and Mellgren (1998) reported that young loggerhead (*Caretta caretta*) and green (*Chelonia mydas*) turtles approached and contacted small objects in a manner that could be considered object play as well as curiosity. These authors discussed whether the behavior with the objects was play or autogrooming, since the turtles contacted the objects with their carapace and flippers by using rubbing motions. The authors systematically added and removed objects. The results showed that initially the turtles were neophobic, but as time went on, they began to seek out and then to interact with the objects more and more frequently. Thus these observations tracing the initial reaction to objects and its later development made clear the distinction between investigation and play (see chapter 3). That the behavior is not just an artifact of captivity is supported by professional scuba divers who observed adult green turtles approaching and behaving similarly toward objects in the ocean, and who also interpreted the behavior as both playlike and pleasurable (R. L. Mellgren, personal communication). More recently Mellgren (personal communication, 2002) recounted additional experiments with green turtles that approached objects after a neophobic period. This researcher found that with these animals, objects and structures (such as a ledge made from rocks) that were rough seemed to stimulate rubbing behavior, while round, smooth objects were ignored. Tactile stimulation may thus underlie the object interactions that they saw. Green turtles, unlike loggerheads, usually have clean carapaces. To find out whether this is play according to the five criteria, it is essential to see if the behavior is done only for direct cleaning purposes.

Barbara Savitsky (personal communication, 1998, 2001) has provided observations on a juvenile captive loggerhead turtle that would approach, bite, and chase a floating red ball (but not a gray ball) for up to 20 minutes at a time. This animal would also grab onto the tail fluke of a nurse shark kept in its tank. It would hang on for several seconds and go for a ride while the shark tried to escape the turtle. This was seen repeatedly. Subsequently Stephanie Day (personal communication, 2002), carried out some systematic videotaped trials of this now larger (9 kg) female about 5 years old. A number of objects were provided, but the response to a semibuoyant ring was, to me, especially dramatic. The animal would grab and carry around the ring, release it, and grab it again as it rose in the water column, perhaps stimulated by the movement. The soft tubing received no bite marks, indicating no ingestion attempts. Consistent with SRT, play with this and other objects was most frequent after feeding.

12.4.2 Locomotor Play

The behavior of Pigface with the hoop and his frequent swimming, floating, and other locomotion may be considered locomotor play akin to soaring in birds and leaping and brachiating in mammals. However, locomotor-rotational play seems to be invoked as a label only when dramatic or exaggerated movements are observed, an often problematic task in little-known species. More anecdotally, Levoen (personal communication, 1997) observed a captive wood turtle (*Clemmys insculpta*) that repeatedly climbed and slid down a board into water.[24] More generally, many aquatic turtles "spontaneously" swim in an aquatic three-dimensional space. Certainly, Pigface spent much time swimming, although he should have known he was not going anywhere. Is this locomotor behavior comparable to the soaring of hawks, the brachiation of gibbons, and the gamboling of colts? Alternatively, is such locomotion akin to the stereotyped behavior

---

24. Wood turtles have a reputation for being particularly clever among turtles and were the subject of perhaps the first formal learning study in a turtle, a maze study by Robert Yerkes in 1901. Wood turtles even tap on the ground to produce vibrations that cause earthworms to come to the surface and be easily captured. Wood turtles (and perhaps other species) also seem to seek out anthills; ants may prey on the leeches that are often found attached to their shells (McCurdy & Herman, 1997). In this form of anting, a turtle will sit on an anthill and allow ants to run over its body for up to 20 minutes, then amble off. They neither fed on, nor appeared irritated by, the ants.

so common in active species in captivity? Such questions cannot be answered at this point. However, adult green sea turtles nesting in the field have been shown to have high aerobic scope during land-based vigorous activity. Unlike most reptiles, much of the metabolic tenfold increase was not accompanied by high levels of lactate accumulation (Jackson & Prange, 1979). The authors compared the phasic (intermittent) alternation of vigorous activity and rests with interval (wind sprints) training by human athletes.

12.4.3 Social Play

Although Pigface was raised apart from other turtles, he did develop a relationship with his keeper. The rubber hose used to refill the tank in the morning session was lowered from the top of the tank with the outlet resting on the substrate. The turtle nosed, bit, clawed, and push or pulled the hose. If the keeper pulled the hose when it was in the turtle's mouth, almost pulling him out of the water, the turtle would respond by trying to swim backward, pulling the hose back into the tank. This was reminiscent of a tug-of-war game. According to the keeper, this took place regularly over a period of years (Roger Rosscoe, personal communication, 1995). This behavior is also similar to that seen in the Komodo dragon.

Monique Halloy (personal communication, 1996), a professional researcher on reptile behavior, recounted observations that suggest teasing behavior on the part of an American emydid turtle.

I kept an aquatic turtle (I think it was from the genus *Chrysemys*) for a few months in a small pool in the garden. One day I noticed the dog barking at the pool, stopping, running around, barking again. I went out and kept watch. The turtle was coming to the surface, approaching the dog just enough to "taunt" her (or so it seemed) and when the dog barked, plunged back under water and reappeared just a little further away. The dog then moved to that area, desperate to grab the turtle. Again the turtle approached just out of reach of the dog and slipped back under water. I saw this several times and on different days. I wanted to get this on film but my camera was broken ... so it's just a little story.

What about social play between turtles? An intriguing example involves juvenile courtshiplike behavior reported in some aquatic species of North American emydid turtles (subtribe Nectemydina) well before they attain sexual maturity and develop morphological secondary sexual characteristics. The genera reported include *Chrysemys*, *Graptemys*, *Pseudemys*, and *Trachemys*. The following discussion is derived from a detailed report on the playlike nature of precocious courtship that includes a literature review and original observations (M. Kramer & Burghardt, 1998); it is supplemented by the comparative courtship review by Fritz (1999). In these turtles, both sexes of juveniles have been noted to engage in the titillation display otherwise seen only in courtship, and then only in males. In order to appreciate this behavior and why it might be a form of play, a possibility not entertained by previous writers, it is useful to look more closely at normal courtship in these animals.

In most emydid turtles, the mature females are considerably larger than the males. Adult males have an enlarged tail and very elongated foreclaws. Both characteristics are related to courtship and copulation, and are not used in agonistic competition between males or in any other context as far as is known. Consider the description of courtship by Florida redbelly turtles, *Pseudemys nelsoni* (M. Kramer & Fritz, 1989). Adult courtship begins with the male's approach and investigation of the female. This proceeds to active following, interspersed with the courtship display termed titillation. During titillation the male swims above and parallel to the female, facing the same direction, and periodically and repeatedly thrusts his front limbs forward, rotating them so that the palms face out, and rapidly vibrates the digits of his front feet. The display is clearly oriented toward the head (eyes) of the female. The male's long front claws appear to emphasize the display. Titillation may continue for many minutes and be repeated in bouts for hours. At some point, the male may attempt to mount and, if the female permits it, to copulate. If unsuccessful, the male may continue to display or leave the female. Courtship in other species of *Pseudemys* appears to be similar. It is interesting that in painted turtles (*Chrysemys picta*) and sliders (*Trachemys scripta*), males face the female during titillation (Ernst, 1971; C. G. Jackson, 1972) instead of swimming above her. Indeed, this is true of turtles in all other genera where males titillate during courtship (e.g., *Graptemys*; Vogt, 1978). In any event, adult females always lack the elongated foreclaws and are rarely observed titillating.

Titillation is not restricted to mating. In these slowly maturing animals, juvenile turtles, even those only a few days or months old, show this behavior. Titillation behavior is even occasionally shown toward inanimate objects, generally in a transient manner when turtles are very young. Precocious sexual behavior can be frequent, however; one juvenile approaches another and displays (titillates) one or more times in a series of bouts (M. Kramer & Burghardt, 1998). The vibration rate of the front claws of juvenile turtles seems comparable across species and similar to adult male courtship rates. Unlike adults, however, both male and female juveniles approached and titillated other turtles. Titillation bouts were often longer in duration than those in an adult male observed in the same setting. These preliminary observations suggest that juvenile titillation displays may be exaggerated compared with adult displays. Certainly they were not just tentative or brief intention movements or mere intimations of adult courtship. The behavior was repeated and if they were in mixed colonies, the turtles preferentially displayed toward conspecifics rather than congeners. Furthermore, the turtles had partners with whom they preferred to display (M. Kramer & Burghardt, 1998). All this is similar to many social play traits found in mammals.

Titillation displays often terminated when the displaying animal abandoned the recipient. The response to the displays varied. The recipient often appeared to ignore the displaying individual, retracted or rubbed its head, or used a front leg to push the displaying animal away. Less often the recipient appeared to be more disturbed by the display and turned or moved away from the displaying individual. Mounts rarely followed displays but, when seen, females even mounted males (M. Kramer & Burghardt, 1998). The behavior was vigorous and involved considerable maneuvering of the displaying turtle to maintain its position with respect to the often moving recipient. Precocious courtship appeared to be the most energetic behavior performed by these animals.

Although it is clearly similar to adult courtship, precocious courtship behavior of juvenile turtles differs from adult courtship in several ways. The initiation phase (M. Kramer & Fritz, 1989) is cursory or absent, although displaying individuals often sniffed the cloacal or head region briefly prior to, but rarely during, a display. And although the display was performed by very young turtles, the stimuli eliciting displays seemed to become more specific as the turtles matured, and species differences in performance of the behavior were evident.

A most fascinating aspect of the differences between immature and adult turtles, besides the sex difference, is in how the turtles oriented while performing the titillation displays. In juvenile *Pseudemys nelsoni* and probably other species (Rives, 1978), titillation displays occur from two positions: (1) head-to-head, in which the displaying animal faces the recipient and (2) swimming above, in which the displaying animal swims above the recipient and faces in the same direction (figure 12.5). As already noted, the first position is characteristic of adult courtship in all genera except *Pseudemys*; the second position is characteristic of all *Pseudemys* species in which adult courtship has been observed and it has been seen in no other species (Fritz, 1999). Most filmed juvenile *P. nelsoni* displays were head-to-head, not the orientation used in adult courtship in this species. More comparative work is needed on the occurrence in juveniles of precocious courtship postures that are not found in adult conspecific courtship. Are such occurrences due to the retention and ritualization of plesiomorphic behavior patterns?

Courtship in adult and juvenile turtles could be an important source of evolutionary information about the phylogeny and ritualization of courtship displays. Perhaps precocious courtship retains ancestral traits that are lost in the more stereotyped serious adult behavior. What we do know is that the chicken turtle (*Dierochelys reticulata*), considered the closest relative of the nectemydid turtles, lacks both the elongated male foreclaws and titillation behavior during courtship (Fritz, 1999). The genus *Malaclemys* lacks the elongated male foreclaws, but rudimentary titillation is seen in adults (although it has not yet been observed in juveniles). All members of the other four genera (*Chrysemys, Graptemys, Pseudemys,* and *Trachemys*) have elongated male foreclaws and all show titillation in courtship except for the probable secondary loss in some species of *Graptemys* and *Trachemys*. Only *Pseudemys* species show adult titillation from the dorsal position, yet juveniles show titillation from both positions. Does juvenile courtship represent a recapitulation of ancestral serious (highly functional) adult be-

Figure 12.5
Two courtship postures found in American emydid turtles and seen in juveniles. (From Kramer & Burghardt, 1998)

havior? A phylogeny of precocial courtship and associated features (figure 12.6) shows that the behavior is quite, but not totally, consistent across the taxa. Some South American *Trachemys* lack both the long male foreclaws and the titillation display in courtship. These turtles have elongated snouts and blow bubbles at the females to excite them instead. The phylogeny of these genera are still under study (Stephens & Wiens, 2003).

Titillation is not the only behavior used by adult males. Chasing and biting also occur. A recent study looked at the role of age of male in the courtship behavior directed toward females (Thomas, 2002). Older males of *Trachemys scripta* turn black and so two black, two "normal male," and two female groups were observed in captive trials with field fresh animals. Older, large melanistic males chased and bit females at rates far above nonmelanistic males, while the latter did more titillation. Could younger males, those much smaller than females, rely on persuasion while large, older males dispense with the nice guy routine? Foreclaw growth ceases when males turn black and although they titillate, they do so often outside the mating season and also frequently direct it toward males, not females.

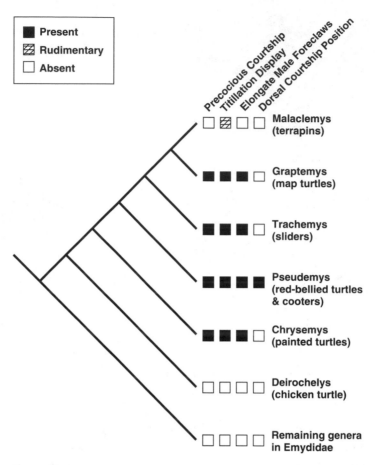

Figure 12.6
Phylogeny of precocial courtship and associated behavior and structures in American emydid turtles.

The evolution of the sexual elements in juvenile courtship may be comparable to the proposed model of the evolution of play fighting in rodents that was discussed earlier (Pellis, 1993). Recall that precocious sexual behavior patterns already present in immature rodents (e.g., voles), were interpreted by Pellis as the bases from which sexual play and play fighting were derived. According to this scenario, in the later evolutionary stages such juvenile social play became a necessary developmental precursor to successful sexual behavior as an adult and could be valuable in other social contexts as well. Rats have well-developed social play that seems to be clearly a secondary process, whereas in mice and voles social play is more rudimentary and may reflect maturationally transient behaviors. Perhaps turtles show a similar evolutionary trend.

An alternative interpretation of precocious courtship was put forth by Rives (1978), who suggested that titillation in juvenile *Chrysemys picta* and *Trachemys scripta* was aversive to the recipients and could serve to establish and maintain social dominance. Our observations on *P. nelsoni* juveniles with a long history of prior social interactions with one another did not show any relationship to dominance order or size. However, recipients of displays in all these species often responded neutrally or even negatively to the displayer. The displayer, but not the recipient, seemed motivated to engage in the precocious courtship behavior and found it in some way rewarding, if not exactly pleasurable. Although this behavior is social play, it is possible that like bullying, only the instigator finds it playful, and thus precocious courtship may represent an early stage in the evolution of social play in which conspecifics do not reciprocate in such a way that mutually playful interactions ensue. However, the fact that mutual titillation was seen by Rives (1978) in other genera indicates that the social nature of this activity needs to be evaluated more closely.

Unfortunately, there are virtually no observations in the field of the underwater behavior of juvenile aquatic emydid turtles and so the possibility that precocious displays are artifacts of captivity cannot be eliminated. However, precocious courtship has been observed in recently wild-caught turtles as well as in captive hatched and reared animals of several species. Furthermore, adult courtship in the field resembles that in captivity.

Unlike the object and locomotor play described earlier, precocious courtship behavior seems clearly limited to early ontogeny. If the behavior is playful, does it have a function or is it merely the nonfunctional outcome of primary play SRT processes? Elsewhere various functions such as maturation, practice, and motor training are discussed in some detail (M. Kramer & Burghardt, 1998). Precocious mounting behavior, though not courtship, has been seen in many mammals, and is routinely considered play. In many species juvenile mounting of adult females, not necessarily the mother, is frequently performed by juveniles of both sexes (Vaňková & Bartoš, 2002). In farmed red deer (*Cervus elaphus*) juveniles, such mounting is considered as a means to obtain the attention of mothers to obtain another feeding, as a response to "tense situations" by females, or as a way of "sexual training" when done by males. These do not appear too likely in the turtles, but suppose that the function is related to acquisition of permanent motor-neural-physiological functions during a critical period (Byers & Walker, 1995). Could precocious courtship in turtles serve some similar function? Perhaps precocious courtship behavior is a means of consolidating, not specific behavioral routines (the titillation display is in adult form when first performed), but the neural (cerebellar) and muscular substrates necessary for complex negotiation in a three-dimensional world. If so, then this explanation might account for display behavior in juvenile females. Of course, one can posit other functions that explain female performance. Perhaps juvenile females are role playing; performing male-typical routines may help them in courtship and mate choice when they are adults. This seems rather improbable, perhaps, but at this stage of our ignorance, all possibilities should be considered.

Although the motor performance of the titillation display is adultlike when it is first observed, the orientation and movements associated with behavior may need to be practiced. Unlike adults, juveniles always titillated animals on the substrate rather than those actively swimming. This suggests that juveniles may need to perfect the behavior while actively negotiating and maintaining contact with a swimming animal. It may be similar to the childhood game of circling one hand on one's chest while using the other hand to pat the top of one's head with an up-and-down motion. Either motion is easily performed singly; doing both simultaneously needs practice. There is evidence that the stimulus control for precocial courtship shifts with age. The youngest animals display to many small objects while older juveniles and adults display mostly to con-specifics. The high frequency of this behavior among juvenile *P. nelsoni* allows each individual to have many interactions with others, providing substantial opportunities for learning to occur. This explanation, however, fails to account for display behavior in juvenile females, nor does it explain partner preferences.

12.5 Evolution of Play in Nonavian Reptiles

Although rare, behavior with the characteristics of play, especially object play, is found in squamate reptiles (especially lizards) and turtles (figure 12.7). Much of this may be primary process play, but I have tried to suggest how it may have taken on some functional secondary process roles. Surprisingly, however, the evidence for play in crocodilians is now the weakest. This is surprising because they have the most advanced parental care, they all live in water, and they have the most advanced heart

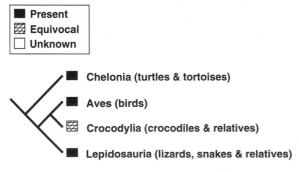

Figure 12.7
Phylogeny of major reptile groups and occurrence of play.

and circulatory system found in nonavian reptiles. Furthermore, their learning abilities are quite advanced (Burghardt, 1977a). Juvenile behavior in naturalistic surroundings (maternal pods) has not been well studied, however. It may also be that predation pressure on juveniles is so great it discourages less than essential noncryptic behavior, such as play. However, this last argument does not explain why neonate turtles and lizards, which are smaller and have no parental protection at all, may show some play.

Finding play in some turtles may not be surprising since, with the exception of parental care and high metabolic rates, they share other traits with the more playful species in the mammalian radiation, including generalist food habits and manipulatory abilities. Aquatic turtles live in an energy-efficient medium and have less need to adjust to rapid temperature fluctuations than terrestrial ectotherms. Thus, turtles live in an environment where some of the metabolic advantages of endothermy are less critical for life-style differentiation. Some aquatic turtles have evolved physiological adaptations that provide greater aerobic metabolic rates and thermoregulation than found elsewhere in nonavian reptiles (Gatten, 1974; E. N. Smith, Robertson, & Adams, 1981; Stone, Dobie, & Henry, 1992). One of the precocious titillating turtles, *Chrysemys picta* is not only an alert and active species, but it has perfected anaerobic metabolism so that it can essentially live without any atmospheric oxygen for long periods (D.C. Jackson, 2000). This might be a factor in allowing more active "voluntary" spurts of activity than aerobic processes could support. Finally, turtles are both long lived and take many years to reach sexual maturity, which would give many of the proposed long-range benefits of play (see Fagen, 1981) sufficient time to accrue. Once they reach a sufficient size, the hard shell of turtles provides considerable protection from enemies. However, many of these features are also found in crocodilians, where bony plates and large size provide protection.

The features that are similar among the five play criteria and the more detailed examples of reptile play described here are summarized in table 12.1. It is noteworthy that such reptile play as exists is often found in adult rather than very young animals. In addition to the ontogenetic endurance effects discussed earlier, we now know that adult reptile brains can show considerable addition of neurons late in life (Font et al., 2001).

If turtles are diapsids and diapsids are the sister group to the synapsids, which led to the therapsids and modern mammals (Gauthier et al., 1989), the last shared ancestor is ancient indeed. The Chelonia may go back to the late Triassic, more than 200 mya (Rougier, Fuente, & Arcucci, 1995) and the Mammalia to at least 200 mya. The common ancestor of turtles and mammals probably lived in the Permian era, more than 300 mya. Therefore, we have pushed the possible first occurrence of play back a long time. However, unlike the tetrapod limb, play is not a plesiomorphic trait. It is more conservative to view play in isolated taxa as independently derived when a series of ecological, life history, and physiological factors converged. But such isolated

Table 12.1
Application of the play criteria to the reports of play in ectothermic reptiles

Species	Play Type	Incompletely Functional	Endogenous Component	Structural Modification	Repeated	Relaxed Field
Alligator	Sensorimotor	Yes	Yes	?	Yes	Yes
Komodo dragon	Object, social with keeper	Yes	Yes	Yes	Yes	Yes
Chameleon	Social	Yes?	Yes	?	Yes	?
Fence lizard	Social	Yes	Yes	Yes?	?	Yes
Snakes	Sensorimotor	Yes	Yes	Yes?	Yes	Yes?
Nile soft-shelled turtle	Object	Yes	Yes	Yes	Yes	Yes
Loggerhead and green turtles	Object	Yes	Yes	?	Yes	Yes
Emydid turtles	Social	Yes	Yes	Yes	Yes	Yes

Note: Data for alligators and chameleons are nonreplicated and thus weak until better documented.

situations are nonetheless important, for they can allow us to compare and contrast the underlying mechanisms, developmental precursors, and functional consequences of such playfulness. What observations on nonavian reptiles suggest is that the primary processes shaping play run deeper in evolutionary time than has been typically appreciated, and that the difficulty of demonstrating clear adaptive functions for play may reside in the atavistic nature of some types of play in some animals.

Evidence supporting continuity in play among ectothermic reptiles, birds, and mammals would be enhanced if similar neural structures (e.g., basal ganglia, limbic system) were involved across these groups. This we do not know, although the possible role of the cerebellum in play in mammals (Byers & Walker, 1995) and in the three-dimensional world of aquatic turtles could be a place to look (Burghardt, 1998a). Furthermore, the basal ganglia are involved in learning in lizards (Punzo, 1985) and it is the basal ganglia that have been implicated in mammalian play fighting (Siviy, 1998). Hippocampal analogues have also been found in spatial learning in lizards (E. Font, personal communication, 2000).

Another source of continuity in play is exercise and its role. Although studies have shown that sustained exercise does not enhance the endurance of lizards (chapter 5), more recent work suggests that in some instances intermittent locomotion does increase endurance. For example, when frog-eyed geckos (*Teratoscincus przewalskii*) were given a bout of 15 seconds of treadmill exercise followed by a 30-second pause, their endurance, as measured by the distance they were capable of traveling, increased 1.7-fold compared with that of lizards that were exercised continuously (Weinstein & Full, 1999). Such observations, if replicated in other species of vertebrates, may help explain the relatively short nature of most playful interactions, which have often been considered too erratic and fleeting to provide the benefits associated with cardiovascular fitness and endurance. Nonetheless, the costs of vigorous activity in producing lactate through anaerobic metabolism are great indeed in reptiles. For example, a desert iguana has a maximum aerobic locomotion speed of less than a foot (0.27 m) per second, whereas in escaping from predators it can run ten times as fast, but rarely for more than 15 seconds (Hancock, Adolph, & Gleeson, 2001). Thus vigorous play in the mammalian way, even in monitor lizards, should not be expected, but that does not mean the behavior cannot be play.

Finally, their nonexpressive faces and the absence of any indicators of pain, joy, suffering, and other emotions in reptiles has led to their stoic reputation. However, the manifestations of pleasure noted earlier are not the only indicators that can be used. A series of papers has argued that emotion, and thus incipient consciousness, in reptiles as in birds and mammals, is indicated by increased heart rates when animals are handled or undergoing mild stress, and such reactions have been found in lizards and snakes (A. Cabanac & Cabanac, 2000; M. Cabanac, 1999; M. Cabanac & Bernieri, 2000).

With this chapter, our search has entered the darker paths of the evolution of play. Even those who might accept the premise that perhaps some ectothermic reptiles show some glimmerings of play as typically viewed may feel a rising skepticism as evolutionary history is pushed farther and farther back. However, if we strive to apply the criteria for play objectively and temper our anthropomorphic, hot-blooded arrogance, there may be answers, one way or the other, as we push on along these paths through the evolutionary landscape.

13   The Origins of Vertebrate Play: Fish That Leap, Juggle, and Tease

Before we have the complete solution of the whys and wherefores of herding and flocking and schooling, there must be a great deal of uncomfortable climbing and diving, hiding in unpleasant places, getting wet and hot and cramped and weary. And then, after we have tried to be sandpipers and ants, silversides and mackerel, we may attain to the honor of such knowledge as our prejudiced, but humbled minds will permit.

—Beebe (1932: 252)

Even fish seem to play, or engage in what is called *playlike behavior*, since biologists are rather doubtful whether fish can really play.

—Goodwin (1994: 193)

13.1   Amphibians and Discontinuity

In chapter 12, it was established that reptiles, under certain circumstances, show behavior that meets the play criteria useful in recognizing mammalian and avian play. Amphibians are the first terrestrial vertebrates (tetrapods) and the ancestral group for nonavian reptiles, birds, and mammals (see figure 7.1). With amphibians, however, we seem to hit a dead end. None of the early writers on animal play, even the most speculative nineteenth century writers, provided any amphibian (frog, toad, salamander, caecilian) examples. In the first major book on amphibian biology, including life history and behavior, G. K. Noble (1926) did not mention play. Fagen (1981) did not present any examples of amphibian play, anecdotal or otherwise, and recent reviews do not provide any (Crump, 1996). Environmental enrichment involving perches, caves, and ramps has been reported to enhance the welfare of captive bullfrogs (*Rana catesbeiana*), although play was not reported (Bang & Mack, 1998).

Most amphibians have an aquatic larval mode and undergo metamorphosis, although some frogs develop directly into miniature-appearing adults. Many species spend most of their life away from water. However, the development of amphibians is constrained. Swimming behavior of larvae seems little affected when eggs are reared without external stimulation, so practice seems unimportant for locomotor performance (Oppenheim, 2001). Early commentators make much of the "stereotyped and specifically determined behavior" of amphibians (N. R. F. Maier & Schneirla, 1935: 217). For example, their feeding system involving prey capture, although highly diversified, largely exists within a narrow scope. The head is mainly a housing for the large jaws, tongue, and eyes; the brain itself is small (Jerison, 1973). Perhaps more significantly, their metabolic rate is much lower than that of even reptiles, and their average body size is also much smaller (Pough, 1980, 1983), although treadmill training has increased the aerobic capacity and anaerobic endurance (35 percent) in the leopard frog (*Rana pipiens*; Cummings, 1979) in contrast to the typical finding for ectothermic reptiles (chapter 6). Still, in the aquatic stage many tadpoles (anurans) are gregarious, setting the stage for social play. Salamander larvae, however, are typically predatory and even cannibalistic.

Parental care is found in some species of salamanders and frogs. The relatively small number of young in dart poison frogs (dendrobatids), which are cared for by the father or mother in small puddles of water (often in bromeliad leaves high up in trees), suggest they may be a good group to consider for possible play. Their aposematic (warning) coloring limits predation risk as well, allowing behavior that might otherwise attract predators. They also can be active in foraging for long periods and have a fairly high metabolic rate and aerobic capacity (Pough et al., 1992). This is especially true of the blue and green dart poison frog (*Dendrobates azureus* and *D. auratus*). I have videotaped both species engaged in vigorous chasing and jumping upon and wrestling with each other in same and mixed sex pairs. Although this behavior is considered variously as territorial defense or courtship related (Wells, 1977; Hurme et al., 2003), the similarity to play seems to have been ignored. This behavior is frequent after feeding and in benign enriched conditions (pers. obs.). Hurme et al. (2003: 298) described "harmless agonistic behavior such as short bouts of wrestling," but stopped short of the "P" word! Blue dart poison frogs at the Baltimore zoo have also been reported to push around dice when placed in their enclosure (Eli Bryant-Cavazos, personal communication, January 2004) and I have seen them jump on a small leaf or a vine in the excitement of an extended bout of social interaction.

Salamanders have a basic body plan comparable to lizards (in Tennessee and elsewhere in the Southeast, salamanders are sold in bait shops as "spring lizards"). Salamanders, especially, have a simplified brain compared with other vertebrates, including most fish (Roth et al., 1993). In fact, a cladistic analysis of twenty-three sensory and nervous system characters showed that nineteen of them are best viewed as simplified in salamanders (Roth et al., 1993). This simplification from more complex nervous systems has been interpreted as being due to paedomorphosis (neoteny), the retention of juvenile traits into adulthood. Paedomorphosis turns out to have been important in the evolution of all three amphibian lineages. Not only does this finding disprove the kind of linear progressive evolution still rampant in biological theory when it comes to "mental" qualities, it also provides an opportunity to gauge more clearly how the process works. For example, the cerebellum is greatly reduced in amphibians and may even be entirely absent in some groups. This contrasts with the closest living relatives of the tetrapods, the lungfish and *Latimeria*, which have well-developed cerebellums (Roth et al., 1993). Since of all the major brain regions, the cerebellum is the last one to develop ontogenetically, perhaps the evolutionary process in amphibians is reverse recapitulation, in which an ancestral condition is restored in the adult.

What does this have to do with play? Perhaps not much, since play has never been reported in salamanders. However, it turns out that the group of salamanders that is most successful in number of species is the Plethodontidae. Plethodontids are lungless salamanders and are extremely common in some areas of temperate North America. The red-backed salamander (*Plethodon cinereus*) is perhaps the most well-studied salamander and the one for which many complex behavioral traits have been found, including parental guarding of the terrestrially laid eggs, territoriality, mate and individual recognition, monogamy, and the ability to assess mate quality and competitors by chemical cues deposited in feces (e.g., Gillette, Jaeger, & Peterson, 2000; Lang & Jaeger, 2000). Males even punish female mates that have been experimentally manipulated to appear to have been unfaithful to them (Jaeger, Gillette, & Cooper, 2002). The bolitoglossines subfamily contains about 50 percent of all salamanders and has radiated extensively in the New World tropics. These species "lack larvae and have direct development, they have diverse locomotor specializations, including acrobatic ability for life in three-dimensional environments (e.g., walls of caves, trees, bromeliads, etc.), and have highly developed and extremely specialized feeding and visual systems" (Roth et al., 1993: 162). Their prey capture methods are quite flexible because they have long tongues and the ability to capture prey from a variety of positions and angles. Bolitoglossine salamanders also have the most simplified brain among *all* vertebrates (Roth et al., 1993). Even frogs have ten to twenty times more neurons in their visual system, and these are more differentiated than in salamanders. How can this be? Citing many other authors for support, Roth et al. argue that "ontogenetic repatterning establishes new sources of variation by uncoupling processes that previously were organized in particular ontogenetic sequences. Such uncoupling may offer an escape from specialization" (1993: 163). It is interesting that this paedomorphic process in salamanders is accompanied by an enormous increase in genome size, with the bolitoglossine salamanders averaging, as a group, close to the maximum genome size found in any salamander except completely neotenic species. Could playlike behavior have been important in the reorganization of the neural and developmental processes in these salamanders? Could play still be found if these salamanders are carefully observed? It is worth investigating if the vertebrates with the simplest brains show primary process play.

The first example of possible amphibian play was drawn to my attention by Kevin Zippel, curator of the National Amphibian Conservation Center in Royal Oak, Michigan (personal communication, August 2001).

I wanted to tell you that I might have found your first example of play in amphibians. We have a large school of *Theloderma corticale* tadpoles that repeatedly swim into a rising air column from an airstone and ride it to the surface. At first I thought they were just getting caught up in the current and dragged passively (or against their will), but they seem to return to the same spot and do it repeatedly. There are plenty of other places to go in this 300 gallon aquarium, if they wanted to get away. It might also have something to do with respiration—how could you ever know for sure?

Further information from Zippel indicated that the group size is twenty-five to thirty and that only some individuals repeatedly swim into the bubbles, while others avoid the current. This would argue against the interpretation that the tadpoles were simply obtaining oxygen for respiration from the bubbles; in any event, play behavior can have some immediate function by criterion one. I have been able to videotape this behavior and tested the respiration hypothesis by bubbling helium, an inert gas, instead of air and found that it still occurs. This species, the Vietnamese mossy treefrog, is a rare and little-known animal with some unusual characteristics. The species seems restricted to cave and rocky habitats along mountain streams in Northern Vietnam. Thus, in spite of its name, it is largely aquatic as an adult. Only recently bred in captivity, these "playing" tadpoles are rarely available for study. Unlike the tadpoles most people are familiar with, which eat algae and other plants, Tonkin treefrog tadpoles are omnivorous from birth. Full metamorphosis can take up to a year; they may leave the water and become terrestrial for a short period and then return to the water and only then become sexually mature. I have observed similar repeated locomotion horizontal airstreams in salamander (axolotl) larvae (*Ambystoma mexicanum*).

Even if the examples given here do not stand up under scrutiny, and play according to the five criteria is indeed absent from amphibians, does this mean that the search for the origins of play has ended? It has been argued that amphibians, unlike reptiles, lack emotions (Cabanac & Cabanac, 2000; Cabanac, 1999) as they do not show, for example, handling stress changes in heart rate. Frogs, at least, may show post-feeding metabolic increases to handle intermitant feeding (Secor, 2001) and this could interfere with nonessential activity as much as in snakes. Perhaps the story is as follows: Play can occur under certain favorable circumstances in amniote vertebrates, including a few nonavian reptiles and numerous species of birds. The line leading to mammals, however, provided the most scope and potential for the elaboration of play and its near ubiquity. Such a plausible story would, if true, simplify our search for the origins of play. Before accepting such a conclusion, it is important to fairly evaluate any evidence that suggests that the processes leading to play extend back even more than the 300 million years since mammals and reptiles had a common ancestor.

13.2 Fish: The Most Successful Vertebrates

One of the important predictions of surplus resource theory is that play should be more likely to arise in aquatic environments since locomotion in water costs less energetically than terrestrial locomotion. This led to the prediction that aquatic mammals, taken together, should be very playful, which is indeed the case.[25] It would also be expected that play would be most likely in aquatic turtles and other nonavian reptiles, which was also supported. But what about fish? What about the earliest aquatic vertebrates? Placoderms, the primeval armored jawless fish, are not available, but many other ancient vertebrates have extant descendants and we have thousands of species to consider (see figure 7.1).

My original informal inquiries about play to fish ethologists and fish biologists in general were not promising (Burghardt, 1984). The very notion of fish play was, at best, an amusing thought entertained for 5 minutes while relaxing in a bar after a hard day at a scientific conference. Fagen did list two references on fish in a table titled: "PLAY" (?) IN OTHER SPECIES, REAL OR OTHERWISE (1981: 247). The fish references, not discussed, were tucked away between a short list of questionable references to play in insects and literary descriptions of play in mythical dragons![26] This was the only one of a long series of tables in Fagen's book in which play appeared in quotes or was followed by a question mark. Fish were also not mentioned in the contemporary comprehensive review by Bekoff and Byers (1981), who explicitly stated that fish do not play. Since the book in which this statement appeared was coedited by a leading ethologist specializing in fish behavior, it is understandable that most writers on play would assume that an absolute discontinuity existed in the occurrence of play between mammals (and perhaps birds) and all other vertebrates. Certainly, the leading figures in animal play research felt this was the case not too long ago.

It was with great surprise, then, after finding that play could be observed in turtles, that I discovered a substantial literature on play in fish. As a result, this chapter developed into the longest in this book in spite of being mostly descriptive, anecdotal, and too often inconclusive, but ultimately quite informative as to how behavior is classified and described. Carefully considering whether and how fish play serves as a lens through which to examine the nature of play. Looking closely at putative play in fish serves two functions. First, it addresses the issue at the heart of this book, the genesis of

25. The exception in mammals may be manatees and other Sirenidae, but this may be due to their reliance on a low-energy vegetarian diet because almost all other aquatic and semiaquatic mammals are carnivorous.

26. In an earlier paper, Fagen (1976) listed a few other sources for possible fish play that did not make it into his seminal review. Most fell into the category of low-intensity "intention" movements at the onset of nesting, courting, and so on.

play. Second, it highlights the problematic aspects of characterizing play, applying play criteria, evaluating evidence, and, most of all, the hidden anthropocentric notions at the heart of virtually all play theory.

As the examples are presented, keep in mind the minimal criteria developed earlier for identifying behavior as a candidate for play: (1) The performance of the behavior seen does not appear completely functional, that is, it includes elements or is directed toward stimuli that do not contribute to immediate survival. (2) The behavior appears to be spontaneous, voluntary, pleasurable, or in some way "done for its own sake." (3) The behavior may resemble "serious" performance of ethotypic behavior, but differs in being incomplete, exaggerated, awkward, precocious, or involves altered sequencing of modal action patterns. (4) The behavior is repeated during at least one developmental period in life. (5) The behavior is most reliably initiated when the animal is not seriously stressed or under intense competing motivations (the "relaxed field").

All five criteria must be met in at least one respect before the play label can be attached. Many tantalizing examples can be only tentatively accepted because insufficient information is available to make a judgment in all five categories. Further study is thus needed; if this review results in experimental work testing the interpretations offered here, our understanding of the evolution of vertebrate behavior will be enhanced, whatever the conclusions. Certainly animals under chronic stress or intense motivation (e.g., to escape, eat, fight, mate), or engaged in captivity-induced stereotyped behavior must not be erroneously viewed as playing. In addition, when dealing with fish, it is extremely difficult to attribute pleasure or enjoyment to their activities. This appears to be the main reason my ichthyological colleagues are skeptical about play in fish. It may be that they are not aware of the problematic nature of many examples of play in mammals and birds.

When I contacted many leading fish behavior researchers about play in fish, most had really never considered play as occurring in fish, or thought it would be just too difficult to identify. And yet, when pressed, many of those I consulted and who initially rejected the notion of fish play—usually because the behavior could be attributed to immediate functional categories such as feeding, escaping, and competing—often allowed, as did Susan Foster, an expert on freshwater stickleback behavior, that "I can't see why some could not have a play element" (Foster, personal communication, 1997). It is such an open mind that is all that is needed right now. Indeed, minds are opening in regard to fish cognitive abilities. Leading fish ethologists have recently pulled together data indicating that fish can have complex social lives, cooperate, imitate, deceive, use tools, develop cognitive maps, and otherwise do "primate" things (Bshary, Wickler, & Fricke, 2002). Furthermore, sprint and endurance exercise training does increase the metabolic and performance levels of some fish (Johnston & Moon, 1980; Pearson, Spriet, & Stevens, 1990). So why *not* play in fish?

13.3 Some Early Observations

E. P. Thompson (1851) suggested that the "wallowing" of "carp" in shallow water, during which they vigorously expose their backs above water, may be play. From the shore and dock at my home on the backwaters of Ft. Loudon Lake in eastern Tennessee, I too have observed this behavior in huge carp. The glistening gold and silver of their flashing bodies in the late afternoon summer sun is truly an impressive sight. Considerable effort may be expended in this behavior. Thompson stated that it occurs early on misty mornings; I have seen it more frequently at dusk, but then I am not often up and about by the dock early in the morning. Jarmer (1928) reported that the many kinds of play he described took place in early morning or at dusk. No one else seems to have viewed this performance as play, however. Could it be a social or courtship display?[27] A foraging or grooming behavior? A response to low oxygen levels in the water? An exuberant (fun) performance of high spirits? The latter would most certainly be rejected without strong evidence in fish, although it would perhaps be readily accepted in describing the gambols of deer and horses.

Romanes (1883), the first great synthesizer of comparative psychology and mental evolution, constructed a comparative scale of psychological evolution. Fish and amphibians were at level 21, the level at which jealousy, anger, and play first appear. Romanes also claimed that fish showed fear; curiosity; and strong social, sexual, and parental bonds, although these latter did not originate in fish, since all occurred earlier in phylogeny in invertebrates as well. Yet Romanes's sole sentence on fish play concerned the "emotions conducive to play; for nothing can well be more expressive of sportive glee than many of their movements" (1892: 247). Although amphibians were listed as having play, which is necessary for Romanes' ladderlike view of mental evolution, he actually never gave any examples of play in amphibians.

Groos (1898), in his seminal review of play in animals was more skeptical than Romanes, but mentioned schooling, "flying" (by flying fish whose coordinated leaps from the water so delight ocean travelers), and courtship as possible play. Since play was for Groos "at first an instinct, producing activity without serious motive" (1898: 101–102), the apparently limited mental endowment of fish was not a hindrance to attributing play to these animals. He quoted many well-known nineteenth-century authorities, including Brehm and Humboldt, on the "exuberance of spirits" (1898: 101) that fish often exhibit. Groos also held that "curiosity is a play closely connected with some of the primary instincts, such as flight and feeding" (1898: 219) and quoted

---

27. James Murphy (personal communication, August 2001) has seen such leaping by hundreds of carp in the Blackwater Wildlife Refuge in southern Maryland. The water was heavily oxygenated. He interprets the leaping as courtship. In my observations, the fish were generally solitary, at least in terms of the jumping.

Romanes on the acknowledged curiosity of fish toward fishing lures and even unnatural objects, such as spear points. However, recognition of play in fish before 1900 was problematic indeed, especially because the knowledge of natural behavior of fish was so limited.

Our knowledge of fish play is not, fortunately, limited to these brief, anthropomorphic anecdotes by amateurs in the area of fish natural history. Beginning about the time Groos wrote, a more substantial literature was being developed by ichthyologists. Some of this was buried in anecdotes recounted in popular books, perhaps indicating its lack of allure as a field of study for serious scientific workers. Uncovering this neglected literature has given me some playful pleasure. I want to provide sufficient discussion of this literature and its history so that readers can decide for themselves if at least some fish play in a way that is compatible with the way we have been using the term. I think that there is no question that some do, and this conclusion surprised me.

There are two early sets of literature that we need to evaluate. These have been summarized well (Gudger, 1944; Meyer-Holzapfel, 1960). These two reviews refer to mostly nonoverlapping sets of reports on fish (in English and German, respectively) from the late 1800s through the middle of the twentieth century. These reports are not only fascinating but are also common enough in the writings of experienced fish observers that they must be taken seriously. Gudger was at the American Museum of Natural History in New York City and Meyer-Holzapfel was, as noted earlier, one of the first mammalian ethologists and an important ethological theorist on motivation, play, and communication. I have examined the cited sources and others in evaluating the claims for fish play. I have not found any new explicit accounts of fish play published in the past 40 years, although my own observations, ongoing studies with colleagues (Michael Kuba, James Murphy, Trooper Walsh), reinterpretation of published reports, and unpublished observations by correspondents support many of the conclusions reached in the following discussion and will be briefly noted.

Although I group putative fish play examples into the traditional categories, many of the examples combine locomotor, material (object), and social elements.

13.4 Curiosity and Exploration

Anyone who has gone fishing, particularly still fishing for centrarchid fish such as bluegills, has no doubt that fish are curious. They approach, investigate, and nibble novel prey or artificial lures. Many experiments on schooling, mate selection, and predator recognition in fish document investigatory and assessment behavior in other contexts as well. The startling, and controversial, studies on individual recognition, "tit-for-tat," sexual selection, and other strategies involving complex cognitive decision-making in fish suggest that the flexibility and plasticity of fish behavior may have been greatly underestimated (Dugatkin & Sih, 1995; S. W. Griffiths & Magurran, 1997; Milinski, Külling, & Kettler, 1990; Murphy & Pitcher, 1991). For example, fish inspect model predators, live predators, nonpredatory fish, and inanimate objects (Murphy & Pitcher, 1991). A diverse array of fishes has been shown to behave more dominantly toward intruders when living in enriched rather than structurally simple environments (Nijman & Heuts, 2000), suggesting that investments in learning and exploration are valuable resources.

Curiosity and exploration toward objects are necessary precursors to object play involving repeated contact and manipulation. Kirchshofer, studying mouth-breeding cichlids (*Astatotilapia* [= *Haplochromis*] *desfontainesi*), found that whereas adult fish often fled from novel situations, the young did not (Kirchshofer, 1953). For example, when she threw a small stone, leaf, or edible object into a small school of young fish, they might at first disperse, but then would come back and approach, observe, and nibble on the object. Testing for edibility is a factor underlying the intense interest that ravens have in shiny objects, and this is true of many other animals as well, including monkeys and young children. Certainly, it is a characteristic exploited by the use of shiny fishing lures. In bait and fly fishing the lures move quickly and often erratically. Fish strike at them rapidly without stopping to investigate and test them.

Such curiosity and exploration may be very old in vertebrates. Mohr (1952) observed the responses of sturgeon (*Acipenser ruthenus*) to the shiny, unbaited hooks used in commercial fishing in Eastern Europe. Neither the stimulus nor the reactions toward it seem in any way similar to those for natural prey, which the sturgeon normally obtain by digging in the substrate using their upturned snout. In fact, while investigating the hooks as they flashed in the current, the sturgeons were hooked by the tail! More details of this behavior would definitely be necessary before one could conclude that the reactions to the shiny objects do not resemble any ethotypic behavior.

Curiosity may not be limited to stimuli with obvious connections to food, predators, or conspecifics. In cold mountain streams I have had my legs surrounded by small fish, generally minnows, that would repeatedly dart in and nibble at my legs for almost any length of time if I kept still. Certainly, my leg was far too large to be confused with food and the behavior, while cautious, did not indicate that I was viewed as a predator. Perhaps my skin had salt or some other chemical stimuli that the fish needed. The light skin color, leg hairs, or novel chemicals may all have contributed to this response. Even so, the fish would approach, identify, and contact my skin repeatedly.

Many persons snorkeling or swimming in lakes or rivers have had similar experiences when wearing wetsuits of various colors. The diversity of species showing such behavior is large. The social aspects of this behavior are also interesting because many fish respond in schools. Small groups of 30-cm-long riverine garfish repeatedly swam near, hovered around, and then left an ichthyologist who was swimming in the San Marcos River in Texas (R. Coleman, personal communication, 1997). Thus such responses to objects too large to be food show that exploratory behavior in fishes may be induced by a wide range of novel stimuli, including those that may be dangerous (Murphy & Pitcher, 1991). Such behavior may derive from the predator inspection behavior shown by many species of fish and be interpreted as a cognitive process to which game theory can be applied (Dugatkin & Sih, 1995). Exploration and curiosity, established in part I as necessary precursors of play, thus appear in fishes. What about play itself?

13.5 Locomotor Play

Ichthyologists do not typically consider the leaping of flying fish schools as play in more than a metaphoric sense. The role of such leaping in helping these relatively small fish escape from predators seems obvious. But do they only leap when threatened by a predator? Do they respond as a group when only one of them senses the threat? Do they jump periodically, even in the complete absence of a predator? How do weather and time of day affect occurrence of the behavior, irrespective of the presence of predators?

One behavior has attracted the attention of fish experts and natural historians: the leaping (leapfrogging) of fish over objects floating in the water, such as plants, leaves, sticks, and other animals. Perhaps this might be more appropriately considered object play, although since the object is not manipulated, locomotor play seems the more congenial classification. I will cover the major groups in which the behavior has been reported in roughly the order of discovery. Many of the groups in which the behavior has been most frequently reported are closely related to one another and to the flying fishes as well. Although the discussion is long, the issues raised here, the kinds of evidence available, the alternative explanations advanced, and the rhetoric employed get to the core issues in evaluating play in fishes and other animals.

13.5.1 Family Belonidae (Needlefishes)

Charles Holder, a zoologist, avid sportsman, and biographer of Charles Darwin, seems to be the first to have described leapfrogging behavior (Holder, 1892, 1899, 1903) in fish around the Dry Tortugas off Florida. His first report was contained in a popular book and provides the best illustration of the behavior I have found (figure 13.1). As he later described it in *Scientific American*: "Once while lying quietly on the wall of an inclosed aquarium on the Florida reef, I saw a number of garfishes ... leaping over the back of a small hawksbill turtle which was floating on the surface of the enclosure, fast asleep and innocent of the purpose to which it was being put. The animal's back was probably eight inches across, and the fishes cleared it several times with ease" (Holder, 1903: 151). In Holder's 1899 book he vividly described the "astonished and indignant" reaction of the turtle when a fish seemed to miscalculate the distance, fell on the turtle's back, and woke it up. Holder went on to write: "I also observed small sardines

Figure 13.1
A belonid fish leaping over a turtle. (From Holder, 1892)

leap over a floating twig. These instances illustrate the fact that fishes have games, and jump in the sense of children over some obstacle; in a word, perform acts that are entirely unexplainable under any other motive" (1903: 151). Holder's anthropomorphism and too easy comparisons with human beings should not prevent us from focusing our attention on the behavior being performed. He noted that such jumping was not related to escape from predators.

Holder set the stage for many such reports by even more eminent biologists. His observations of needlefishes were probably made in the 1860s (Gudger, 1944). Subsequent reports have identified three species of belonid fish as leapers in the Dry Tortugas (Gudger, 1944). These are *Strongylura ardeola, S. natatus*(sp?), and *S. raphidoma*. The ichthyologist W. H. Longley, director of the Tortugas Marine Laboratory, recorded the behavior many decades later (before World War I), as described in a monograph based on his posthumously published notes (Longley & Hildebrand, 1941). Hildebrand, who collated the work, in the section on *S. raphidoma* remarked that "Dr. Longley made the following interesting note" (1941: 29) and quotes verbatim a description of this species jumping over a bit of floating paper, as many as three times in succession. The fishes also jumped over a floating feather, and, rather callously, over a floating dead conspecific!

Apparently unaware of Longley's notes, the eminent ichthyologist C. M. Breder also noted this behavior in needlefishes during his extensive work at the same laboratory. He described it in two papers (Breder, 1929, 1932a). He saw fish of all three species

Table 13.1

Data on leaping over sticks in needlefish

Length of Stick (inches)	Length of Fish (inches)	No. of Fish Leaping	No. of Leaps
4	12	2	1 each
12	14	1	1 (tried 3 times before success)
8	12	4	1 each
8	12	1	9 times back and forth
6-inch piece of *Cymodocea* (seagrass)	12	1	3 times back and forth

Source: Breder (1932a)

leaping back and forth, up to a dozen times, over a single piece of floating straw. Since he noted that throwing out splints or straw would "invariably cause at least one to leap over it" (Breder, 1932a: 8), he then carried out a small experiment in which he threw out sticks of various lengths (all about 3 mm square). I have reprinted his table as the first example of quantitative data on playlike behavior in fish that I have located (table 13.1).

Breder also described the responses of the fish to the objects. Being a schooling species, they will not venture too far from a group of conspecifics to follow a stick. His careful description of the behavior itself is worth quoting.

First the fish will swim up slowly to the stick so as to be nearly at right angles to it (in a horizontal plane) and gently protrude the beak through the surface of the water, sliding the tip over the stick. Usually, if the stick is too small and gives way too easily, or too large and gives way too little, the fish will withdraw. If it is of the proper buoyancy and sinks ever so little under the weight of the beak, a violent tail action follows and the fish clears the water, but in such a manner that usually part of the body rubs against the stick in passing and the fish falls to the other side, from which it may turn and leap back again (1932a: 9).

Although Breder stated that still and motion-picture records of the behavior were obtained, they were apparently never published or made available.

Why does a fish engage in this behavior? Breder noted that the fish may be parasitized by leeches and argulids (carp-lice, parasitic crustaceans) and that "It is thought that the function of this well-marked habit is that of scratching to remove ectoparasites, for it was noted that usually some part of the fish was rubbed against the straw in passing. Second leaps were most often noted when this did not succeed" (Breder, 1929: 280). Furthermore, the species that leaped most (*S. ardeola*) was claimed to harbor the most ectoparasites, although no data were presented. Swanson (1949) reported what he termed hurdling behavior in needlefish off Lemon Bay on the Gulf of Mexico, a little south of Sarasota, Florida. He saw fish approach and slide over a floating mango leaf. Swanson took issue with the behavior being parasite removal since the leaf was far too soft and yielding. He also thought that the deliberate approach to the object suggested that "exuberance" was also not the explanation. Instead, Swanson suggested that many fish actually seem to enjoy the physical sensation of being rubbed "much as a cat rubs her back on furniture" (1949: 219). Thus the behavior is more scratching than parasite removal. Swanson also suggested that bottom-dwelling and pelagic fish have other, less conspicuous, means of obtaining comparable sensations.

13.5.2   Family Hemiramphidae (Halfbeaks)

The halfbeaks are a group similar to the needlefishes, except that only the lower jaw is elongate. They are considered closely related to the needlefishes and the flying fishes as well. Concerning the halfbeaks (*Hemiramphus brasiliensis* and *Hyporhamphus unifasciatus*), Gudger (1944) quoted observations made by Louis Mowbray, then director of the Bermuda Aquarium, showing that this species actually "somersaults." Mowbray recorded the former species approaching, inspecting, and placing "the tip of his long lower jaw under the object and at the same time give a flip which almost invariably lands him tail first on the other side of the object and on his side generally.... This may be repeated five or six times within twenty seconds. Once I saw three fish of this species performing at one time on a single box of wood about 15 inches long" (1944: 460). This species is about 30 cm in length. He saw the second species perform in a similar manner, but it is smaller, only about 13 cm long. Neither fish ever landed head first.

13.5.3   Family Clupeidae (Herring and Shad)

Breder (1932b) noted that Atlantic herring (*Clupea harengus*), a schooling species (observed off Rhode Island) that is about 8 cm long, leapt over plant fragments "in a manner similar to that described for various Belonidae at the Dry Tortugas" (1932b: 31). He noted also that "more frequently specimens were noted to "scratch" themselves on entirely submerged fragments." In this paper, Breder clearly felt that the scratching (parasite removal) hypothesis had been proven, although no evidence is discussed, let alone presented.

As mentioned earlier, Holder (1903) stated he saw small sardines leap over a floating twig. The species was not given and, as Gudger (1944) stated, "sardine" is often used colloquially for any small fish.

13.5.4   Family Atherinidae (Silverside Minnows)

Atherina harringtonensis   William Beebe (1932) described the behavior of large schools of this species in Bermuda. They are generalist feeders on animal prey, geographically widespread, and successful. Vision is the dominant sense. Beebe found that tossing a sliver of wood or wooden match among them on a calm, cloudy day did not disturb them, but within a few minutes they "drift up to the bit of wood and begin to leap over it. First one, then another goes over the hurdle, from this side or that, sometimes balking at the start and swimming away, more often flinching sideways, a leap clear of the surface, but very unlike the high forward course when fleeing for life from an impi [group] of mackerel" (1932: 248–249). Beebe followed this evocative description with the surmise that the leaping behavior with the match "may accomplish some real purpose, either practice or achievement, to which we have no clue, but as far as appearances go, it is sheer exuberance, relaxation, a momentary forgetting of the myriad dangers which menace even these favored fishes of the king from above, below and around, day and night, from birth to death" (1932: 249). He was careful to allow that play is much harder to recognize than fear and that "what to us appears complete relaxation may be far otherwise" (1932: 248). Gudger (1944) quoted two personal communications from scientists who confirmed Beebe's descriptions.

Gudger (1944) also quoted observations provided by Mowbray. He described this species of minnow "flipping" across grass and sticks in harbors. However, he also saw the fish perform somersaults across the objects. An individual would approach the object slowly, push its lower jaw against it, and quickly flip the tail so it would fly tail-over-head, land on its side, and repeat the behavior up to nine times. He could not see if there was any parasite removal during the act, but believed it was a combination of play and parasite removal.

Atherina area   Another schooling species was observed in Port-au-Prince Bay, Haiti, leaping over sticks and straw on quiet days. The behavior was only performed by one or two fish at a time, although the "performance was repeated, as if the little fish found it enjoyable" (personal communication from Tee-Van to Gudger in Gudger, 1944: 457).

Menidia notata   Gudger (1944) also presented two observations by staff of the American Museum of Natural History. One, an avid fisherman, reported the years of delight he has had watching these little fish jumping over the loop of fishing line at the cork float regardless of whether the line was slightly above or below the surface. It is interesting that most of the time the fish hit the line and did not clear it, often landing sideways or tail first. He also saw the fish leap over a floating matchstick. The second observer called the behavior spearing and saw fish jump over objects varying in size from stalks of grass to driftwood as thick as broom handles. The behavior was highly predictable and the fish would not only follow each other but also turn around and jump again.

Atherinops affinis cedroscensis (Kelp Topsmelt)   Another distinguished ichthyologist, Carl Hubbs of the Scripps Institution of Oceanography, described leapfrogging in this species (Hubbs, 1948). The animals were at the end of the Scripps Institution pier near La Jolla, California. For 15 minutes a group of fish repeatedly leapt over a floating stick about 5 by 22 cm. Up to ten fish jumped in close succession, sometimes two at the same time, and the behavior seemed "contagious." Hubbs noted that sometimes the fish scraped their bellies on the board, but also jumped clear.

Membras vagrans (Rough Silverside)   A member of this small species was recorded interacting with a white nylon line (3/16-inch diameter) during current measurements in Bay Adam, Louisiana (Gunter, 1953). If the line was slightly under the water surface, the fish was attracted to it, and swam back and forth across it, often in figure eights, for a few minutes at a time. The fish never swam under the line. The behavior was slow and deliberate, not exuberant. However, a second response was more vigorous. The fish swam at the line at a rapid speed and butted it full force. Typically the fish flipped tail-over-head across the line in a repeated performance.

In addition to these examples, all from older papers, I received a note from a former student, Dan Cunningham (personal communication, September 1997), who had read an early draft of this chapter and was wading in the surf at Wrightsville Beach, North Carolina. He noticed some splashing around a reed or piece of grass floating in the water and approached to within 1 m. The fish he observed, though unidentified, was about 5 cm long and had a shape similar to the fathead minnows (*Pimephales*) he had worked with extensively in my laboratory, so it could have been in the Atherinidae.

This "minnow" leapt over the reed no less than 5 times and followed this display with a curious "vaulting" behavior.... The fish proceeded to swim at a high rate (no means of measurement) of speed head first into the reed. Upon contacting the reed, the fish would propel itself 20 to 30 cm (best estimate, easily 5 times its length) into the air and flop (literally) down onto the surface of the water, landing on its side (laterally contacting the surface and creating quite a splash). This behavior re-occurred approximately 10 times. I moved closer to get a better look, but the fish interrupted another run at the reed by turning abruptly and proceeding to swim immediately to deeper water.

After the fish moved away, I waited for about 5 minutes near the reed. The fish did not return, and upon realizing the connection between what I had read weeks before, I became almost giddy with excitement and ran up on the beach to discuss it. Unfortunately, there were no ethologists in the nearby vicinity, and I was left to replay the incident in my mind for a few minutes. Although I had two more days of watching floating objects in the surf, I saw no other evidence of these behaviors.

13.5.5   Family Mugilidae (Mullet)

Jumping in mullet has been frequently reported and discussed over the years (see Hoese, 1985); in fact the striped mullet (*Mugil cephalus*) is sometimes called jumping mullet. George Barlow (personal communication, June 1997) observed mullet (*M. cephalus*) jumping in captivity and off the coast of Hawaii. In the former setting, a porpoise pool, the water was clear and he could easily see what the fish were doing in the water.

Here is what I saw from underwater. The jumper is in a "relaxed" state, not doing much of anything. Suddenly it darts to the surface and on into the air. Often the fish lands on its side. Why would it do that? Play? I doubt it. In nature mullet travel in schools, pause, and spread out to feed, reassembling to move on. The water is typically turbid. Thus visual signals are not of much use. I hypothesize jumping is an acoustic signal, transmitting low frequency sounds that travel far and can be heard by fish. The function? Maintain some degree of coherence among the group of mullet.

This is certainly an ingenious idea that should be tested. Note that here no stick was jumped over. Barlow noticed no "exuberance" in the performance, and states that in nature these fish feed constantly and thus would not have leisure time, in spite of the apparently relaxed setting in which the behavior appears. Although Barlow's idea is plausible, an alternative interpretation has been proposed.

Hoese (1985) observed jumping behavior repeatedly and rejected the play interpretation as well as those involving parasite removal. He focused on the theory that such jumping aids in respiration. This hypothesis is a tempting one, since striped mullet live in warm, shallow, brackish water that often is poorly oxygenated. Also, other species of mullet engage in "air pumping," during which they hold their heads high out of the water and expose a large cavity containing pseudobranchia and gill filaments (Hoese, 1985). Hoese conducted field studies at seven locations in Texas and Louisiana over entire 24-hour periods in 3–5-minute intervals. Every jump was recorded either through seeing or (especially at night) hearing it. Jumps associated with flight from predators were distinguished from typical jumps both in how the body was held in the jump and because many fish jump simultaneously in such escape behavior. In dense populations, escape jumping rates as high as 200 per minute were recorded. Along with the jumping data, information on levels of dissolved oxygen in the water was recorded.

The results showed that most jumping took place above 20°C and when oxygen saturation was low. Also, most jumping took place in late afternoon and rarely between midnight and late morning. Hoese argued that mullet are bottom feeders on anoxic or hypoxic sediment; jumping can refresh the animals through gas exchanges in the upper pharyngeal chamber. When oxygen levels in the upper water column are adequate, the fish do not need to jump and more likely just roll or produce a whirl on the surface. Hoese noted that his "internal diving bell hypothesis" may be objected to because no previous work proves that fish leap for air. Furthermore, the energy expenditure involved may be greater than the benefits received. Hoese answered the latter criticism by suggesting that by jumping the fish may move toward a new and richer feeding site.[28] He also suggested that jumping and air pumping allow higher metabolic scope

28. This seems somewhat dubious since Hoese also emphasized the dense aggregations in which the fish forage and that jumping fish are not always feeding.

in mullet as the temperature rises, and cited a study documenting an absence of such an increase when fish were prevented from jumping.

The example of carp rolling in shallow water on sunny, late summer afternoons may now be explained. Goldfish, our small domesticated carp, can also use oxygen that has been trapped in their upper pharyngeal chamber (Burggren, 1982). Most of us have seen dying fish or those in stagnant aquaria gulping air at the surface.

Although the jumping of mullet and wallowing of carp may have a physiological interpretation, this does not explain why fish jump over objects in open, oxygen-rich waters as described in the previous section. Furthermore, the high levels of jumping in mullet and carp may not be totally explained by oxygen deficits. In fact, Barlow's observations were of fish in well-filtered water, with no indication that the fish had an oxygen deficit. The jumping could be stimulating, pleasurable, or even social, as suggested by Barlow. It may not be easy to adopt Beebe's advice offered at the beginning of this chapter. More experiments are needed.

13.5.6 Other Species

Aquatic mammals such as whales and porpoises leap. Holder (1903) pointed out that when whales leap, especially gray whales, they use the tail to remain almost perpendicular to the surface. He also mentioned a whale that leaped into the air and over a boat, clearing it by 20 feet! Behavior such as this, he claimed, is considered a game by every sailor. Fagen (1981) accepted the observation that cetaceans play, especially with objects and conspecifics. He also mentions that locomotor behavior of cetaceans such as breaching, spinning, and surf riding have been attributed to play, but that the difficulty of making observations and the lack of clear knowledge of social and locomotor behavior makes interpretation premature. Although Fagen did not go on to discuss comparable behavior in fishes, Holder did. He mentions sharks that jump high out of the water, such as an oil-shark (now soupfin shark, *Galeorhinus zygopterus*) observed in deep water near Catalina Island off the southern California coast. Apparently unaware of Holder's report, a colleague of Carl Hubbs at Scripps reported seeing a great blue shark (*Prionace glauca*), over 2 m long, repeatedly jumping on and sliding over a corrugated cardboard box until the box was broken (Hubbs, 1948). Arthur Myrberg (personal communication, June 1997) noted that spinner sharks (*Carcharhinus brevipinnus*) often spin three full times in the air when they jump, and this may occur during feeding as well as when they are hooked. Blacktip sharks (*Carcharhinus limbatus*) and Mako sharks (*Isurus oxyrinchus*) also jump when they are hooked and apparently when feeding. However, most of the reports are anecdotes from fishermen and, according to Myrberg, are repeated in the literature although they are based on very few observations.

Holder (1903) also reports that in shallow water mullet and pompano leap vigorously, as do tarpon (*Megalops atlanticus*), the related "tenpounders" or ladyfish (*Elops saurus*), and tuna. Jarmer (1928) reproduces a figure of a large 2-m-long tarpon jumping more than a body length out of the water.

13.5.7 Interpreting Leaping and Leapfrogging by Fish

Schubert (1973), in discussing the great leaps of tarpon, asks why they jump. He answers that the behavior may be "an attempt to escape predators and other irritants; but the jumping itself may also be just for fun" (1973: 154). Although fish often perform such jumping without any apparent function, Holder and Schubert both point out that attacked or hooked fish jump as a means of escape. Tuna also actually leap out of the water as they follow fleeing schools of flying fish, and can even catch their prey in midair. Holder also brings in aesthetics: "Its leap is the personification of grace; rising to a distance of eight to ten feet, it turns and plunges downward like an arrow, having preserved the perfect lines of the curve" (1903: 152). Jarmer (1928) rules out oxygen deficits and predator avoidance as proximate causes since fish engage in such jumping in well-aerated water and in predator-free captive environments.

Except for Breder's brief experiment, surprisingly and unfortunately there have been no systematic, experimental, or quantitative observational studies of leapfrogging in fish and few studies of leaping in fish, Hoese (1985) being a notable exception. Why has the possible play aspect of such behavior been ignored when comparable behavior in mammals is readily called locomotor-rotational play? Frank Beach wrote the influential, but critical, paper on play we discussed in an earlier chapter (Beach, 1945). He promoted the Breder ectoparasite removal theory so authoritatively that it seemed to explain fish jumping so adequately that play in fish became a dead issue. Indeed, I think it was a convenient conclusion given that the next generation of ichthyologists was reared in a behavioristic era that made attributions of emotion, complex cognition, or appearing in any way anthropomorphic taboo in the study of fish behavior. Interestingly Beach (1945) was careful to state that there were *no* data supporting the ectoparasite theory. Yet that was not the message that prevailed. For example, an influential review stated that Beach "refers to a species of fish who have the habit of leaping over sticks and other objects floating in the water. This looks like an enjoyable game. Actually it scratches parasites off the fishes' back" (Millar, 1968: 32–33).

Why did Beach's skepticism prevail? Was it just the trend toward behaviorism? Or was Beach, who was then also at the American Museum of Natural History, replying to his colleague Gudger's (1944) paper? Beach could very well have been inspired by Gudger to write his critique of play. His paper on play was one of only a few the prolific Beach ever published in a zoological journal, rather than in psychological or physiological publications. Beach never again wrote anything substantive on play, but his speculative disproving of fish play has endured.

Based on Gunter (1953), we can summarize the observations on fish leaping over objects by noting that the responses fall into several classes. These are (1) straight jumping with complete clearance, (2) jumping without complete clearance, (3) making a standing jump or sliding over the object after placing the head on or just over the object, (4) turning a flip or somersault with the head initially placed against or under the object, (5) repeatedly swimming over a slightly submerged object, and (6) swimming at the object full force and utilizing that energy to propel the body over the object tail first.

13.5.8 Leaping in Fish: The Interpretive Options

If we dismiss the oxygen-deficit theory as only applying to fish in warm, shallow, oxygen-poor environments, what are the options for explaining leaping and jumping?

1. Jumping is nonfunctional play representing exuberance. Here the motor activities are primary.

pro It is usually recorded during calm days in the absence of stress, predators, or hunger. The behavior is spontaneous and often repeated.

con Jumping may be most easily detected on calm days. The true antecedents of the behavior can never be established without careful experimental and descriptive work.

2. Jumping is a functional, probably instinctive, mechanism for removing ectoparasites.

pro Fish may scrape themselves in ways that could remove ectoparasites. They sometimes appear to seek out objects with certain characteristics and investigate, even evaluate them, before jumping. The behavior may be derived from object chafing in nonjumping fishes as described later in this chapter.

con Often no physical contact is made with the object. Many jumping fish rarely if ever have ectoparasites, and no direct evidence has ever been presented that even one ectoparasite has been removed in this way. The objects selected do not seem optimal for dislodging parasites.

3. Jumping is a means of obtaining physical (and physiological) stimulation—from rubbing and scratching to the experience of tumbling and somersaulting in the air.

pro This can explain physical contact without parasite removal. Barlow has noted that "fish in aquaria commonly chafe, sometimes showing signs of urgent need, but with no visible parasites" (Barlow, personal communication, 2001). Furthermore, rubbing can be a positive reinforcer for fish in some circumstances (Losey & Margules, 1974).

con As I write this, my back is itching and I occasionally stop and scratch. I do not consider this play. But the stimulating effect of jumping and diving into water, the love I still have for roller coasters, whitewater canoeing, and driving fast are forms of commonly appreciated stimulus-seeking play in our own species. We do not have physiological measures for the possible effects of such stimulation in fish.

4. Jumping is a means of communication among schoolmates.

pro Barlow suggested this and it may operate in this way among dolphins and whales. It explains the noise that much jumping creates.

con Jumping occurs in some species when they are apparently not schooling and it cannot explain the use of sticks.

5. Jumping originates in curiosity and exploration.

pro Gunter suggested this and it certainly is a necessary first step, as we have seen in the discussion of the relationship of curiosity and play. Insofar as the response is leap-frogging over an object, object play may be a possibility.

con If jumping is not directed at an object, what is being explored?

At this point the best conclusion may be that the leaping of these fish is most likely related to all five of the above explanations, which incorporate several of the five ethological aims. What is needed are careful experimental and quantitative studies exploring these phenomena from the perspective of all the five aims of ethology: causation, function, evolution, ontogeny, and private experience. The motivational processes underlying such behavior particularly need to be addressed. For example, a good first start would be to design an experiment testing the jumping propensity of fish with and without parasites in naturalistic captive settings. We can also compare the behavior seen here with jumping and leaping in terrestrial mammals, much of which writers such as Fagen (1981) unequivocally attribute to play. Do we deny the label to fish because of uncritical anthropomorphism? Or is the uncritical attribution labeling such behavior in mammals as play?

I have discussed leaping as locomotor play, although objects are frequently involved. If all jumping over objects is linked with parasite removal, our understanding of the behavior will change but will not necessarily eliminate it as a form of play. Surplus resource theory and other modern play theories accept that play behavior may have some current function. We also need to remember that leaping out of the water is the mark of most locomotor play attributions. Vigorous locomotor behavior under water, in the animals' natural element, is rarely described as locomotor play. Yet aerial play, swinging in trees, and leaping on the ground are all considered play in the natural environments of birds and mammals. Is this another instance of inadvertent anthropomorphism?

If we apply the five major criteria for identifying play, the jumping and leaping of fish is certainly a major candidate for play as identified in other taxa. The observations on fish support a play label since this behavior (1) is not always immediately functional or necessary for survival, (2) often appears spontaneously or voluntarily, as when small objects are thrown in the water, (3) appears to consist of modifications of more serious performances and seems exaggerated, etc., (4) is often repeated, and (5) is most common on still or calm water when the fish do not appear either threatened by predators or preoccupied with food, mates, or other serious matters.

A final note: Wolfgang Klausewitz at the Senckenberg Nature Museum and Research Institute in Frankfurt, Germany reports on the remarkable training of groups of two species of cyprinid fish, the redeye (*Scardinius erythrophthalmus*) and the rudd (*Leuciscus cephalus*) by one Herrn May (Klausewitz, 1966). Mr. May fed these fish in Lake Maggiore and trained them to accept food from his hand. He then trained them to come and rest in his hand at the surface of the water, even without feeding them. Then he began to suddenly raise his hand and throw a fish (up to 2 kg or more in weight) up to 2 m away where they hit the water. Rather than swim away, the fish returned again and again for the experience of being thrown. Indeed, the fish often competed vigorously to be the next one in line to fly! Such proximate factors seem to send us back to the questions in the first paragraph of section 13.3.

13.6   Object Play

Jarmer (1928) claimed that tuna, tarpons, and sharks often hunt as a form of play, even when the prey is not needed for nourishment. This claim is difficult to evaluate for several reasons, including the difficulty of observing predation in the wild in these wide-ranging animals and our lack of knowledge about their normal ethology and nutritional needs in the wild. However, anyone who keeps aquarium fish (e.g., cichlids, goldfish) has noted how, when they are offered commercial or even live food, many fish may suck in a piece of food or prey, spit it out rather forcefully to some distance, recapture it, and do this several times before either swallowing or rejecting the object. This occurs with both familiar and novel food items. Jarmer (1928) is the first writer I have come across who considered this mouthing of food as possibly playful. We may initially reject that interpretation; isn't the fish just testing the item, attempting to kill it, or trying to break it apart (as when fish are offered small blocks of frozen prey)? Perhaps. But when thought about a bit more deeply, this behavior raises some questions. Don't infants and children often put objects, not always food, in their mouths and take them in and out (spaghetti seems to be a great favorite when solid food is just starting to be eaten)? Perhaps a more appropriate analogy with the fish would be a cat playing with a rodent or a clearly inedible substitute; repeatedly seizing, capturing, manipulating, releasing, and recapturing it. Doesn't the cat often injure the mouse or mutilate the toy during its play? In fish, does such play with prey occur more frequently when the fish are less hungry or even sated, as is typical in cats? Jarmer said yes. The fish ethologist Arthur Myrberg (personal communication, June 1997) noted that if he "saw an isolated fish repeatedly take up and spit out a clearly inedible object, such as a stone or similar object, I might well consider that the poor guy was bored and would have little angst in noting that the behavior appeared to be play. I have just never seen such."

13.6.1 Sturgeons

Earlier I described field observations of sturgeons being attracted to shiny hooks. Ladiges (1954) described how active the same species, the sterlet (*Acipenser ruthenus*), is in an aquarium, and how one fish pushed and pulled objects such as thermometers and filter hoses. The latter equipment became detached and had to be very firmly reattached. The fish also attempted to remove the plates covering its tank. This species primarily lives on worms, crustaceans, and mollusks that it grubs up from the bottom with its snout. Perhaps the behavior toward the objects is derived from foraging movements, as Meyer-Holzapfel (1960) suggested. But the sturgeon, just like Pigface (the Nile soft-shelled turtle described in chapter 12), did not eat, nor attempt to eat, the objects. Here boredom (environmental deprivation) and lowering of the stimulus threshold may have played a role, as it did with Pigface. But, as with Pigface, field observations by fishermen suggest that such behavior with objects can occur in the wild as well.

13.6.2 Mormyridae (Weakly Electric Fish)

The earliest detailed and convincing descriptions of object play in fish come from the superfamily Mormyridae. These are weakly electric fish found in Africa that are quite basal on the teleost line. Two independent reports on object play were published almost simultaneously more than 40 years ago (Meder, 1958; Meyer-Holzapfel, 1960), although Ladiges (1954) also noted that mormyrids were particularly playful, perhaps based on his knowledge of the observations cited below.

Meder (1958) was a medical doctor who, as an avocation, studied mormyrid fishes and kept them in well-planted aquaria, breeding them successfully. But when he obtained an elephantnose fish (*Gnathonemus petersii*), it performed so many fascinating actions that he set it up in an aquarium right in front of his desk so he could observe it better. The fish would strip water plants of their leaves and hide them behind rocks to make a home. It would also select a particular leaf and pull and push it around, to the exclusion of other possible "toys." It manipulated large snails the same way and then one day, to Meder's astonishment, balanced one on its snout like a sea lion. When the snail fell off, the fish would repeatedly rebalance it. Meder then added small nylon balls to the tank and found that the fish treated them in a similar fashion. That is, if several were put in the tank, they would be gathered up and moved to the home behind the stone. He also found that the balls soon began accumulating in the filter, which was up in a corner of the aquarium 14 cm from the bottom. It seems that the fish, in its balancing, would somehow release a ball so it went into the filter and the balls would accumulate there. If Meder removed them, the fish would quickly redeposit them there. If Meder did not remove them, the fish would retrieve them itself and repeat the game. Finally, a frustrated Meder suspended a ball on a string about 5 cm from the bottom of the tank. Now the fish could bat, balance, and retrieve the ball from the filter housing without it getting lost or stuck. This was like the tether ball that we had in our yard for our twin girls, which delighted them for several years when they were young. The nocturnal fish would frequently use the tethered ball at night; Meder could hear it batting the ball back and forth, even if he was not watching.

This remarkable fish moved the good doctor to reflect on how we interpret the *Umwelt* (environment) of other animals. He realized that many readers of his paper, especially in the fish fraternity, would consider his writing anthropomorphic. But he asked (Meder, 1958: 170, my translation) "How otherwise should we experience the Umwelt of other animals than as human beings. It appears important only to seek other ways of doing so." Meder was stimulated by his observations of this "simple" fish to reflect on philosophical issues concerning humanity, technology, and other topics.

Meder described one remarkable animal, sex unknown. However, he published photographs, and his findings were cited in an authoritative treatment of the Mormyridae (Gery, 1973). Independently, the respected classically trained ethologist, Monica Meyer-Holzapfel, wrote the aforementioned review of play in fish in the context of her own observations, and those of aquarium colleagues, on mormyrid play (Meyer-Holzapfel, 1960). Her own observations were on a single elephantsnout or tapir trunk fish (*Mormyrus kannume*), held in the city zoo of Bern, Switzerland, for 7 years. She supplemented her findings with observations provided by correspondents at aquaria in Denmark and Germany. Apparently these fish were at the time not very often kept in captivity, a situation reminiscent of our experience with the Nile soft-shell. Her observations were based on two other specimens of *M. kannume* and a related *Petrocephalus* specimen. As with Meder (1958), all specimens of these species were very active.

The Bern fish first showed unusual behavior by manipulating the filter pipe with its snout until the pipe finally came loose and fell off; it repeated the actions when the pipe was replaced. Now, like the sturgeon, this species digs in mud to find food and so this might appear to be nothing but a redirected feeding response. However, the behavior was most common after the animal was sated, which is similar to conditions already established with mammals and now considered a prime characteristic of play. Not only did the fish manipulate the pipe, it swam around it vigorously and even turned somersaults in the water. The *Petrocephalus* also would circle around plants in a lively, playful manner in contexts independent of feeding.

To solve the problem with the filter pipe, which was rapidly being destroyed, the caretaker gave the fish a three-pronged twig. This was a successful diversion, for from then on the fish spent hours with it. The fish would pick the twig up from the bottom and balance it on its long snout. If it fell off, the fish would often circle under the twig and retrieve it with its snout before it had even hit the bottom. But only the three-pronged stick was chosen, apparently because it was easiest to hold on its snout. He would not play in this way with heavy sticks or small celluloid (a precursor to plastic) toy animals such as frogs. Since playing with the stick was not restricted by season or year, courtship or other reproductive behaviors were considered unlikely explanations. Meyer-Holzapfel reported that two other individuals of this same species also manipulated twigs and snails and stones in a similar manner.

In trying to interpret these observations, Meyer-Holzapfel considered a number of ideas that are worth reviewing:

1. The juggling behavior was merely an aberrant behavior of one abnormal animal. This was ruled out since a few animals, independently observed, showed comparable behavior.

2. The behavior was merely redirected feeding behavior. This was eliminated not only because the object manipulation was independent of hunger, but because the *M. kannume* responded differently when hungry. Its behavior toward its normal food, tubifex worms and earthworms, was to slurp the prey out of the gravel.

3. The object manipulation was scratching behavior. Meyer-Holzapfel ruled out this possibility in two ways. First, the behavior of the animal toward the twig was not at all performed in such a manner as to rub, scratch, or remove parasites. Second, when the fish did have a yeast infection, it did not play with the twig at all. The fish did, however, then and only then rub itself sideways over the bottom of the tank in a scouring action.

4. The behavior with objects was a form of nest building. Meder's observations on the behavior of his fish with leaves might support this. Apparently some members of the family do build large floating nests and others glue their eggs to grass roots. Nothing was known to Meyer-Holzapfel about the reproductive behavior, or even sex, of the *M. kannume*. Indeed, courtship behavior is still little known in mormyrids (B. Kramer, 1990). But she ruled out this interpretation on the basis that the fish did not show any interest in grass except for ripping it out of the bottom of tanks (foraging?, clearing a nesting area?).

5. The behavior was a redirected form of courtship or aggressive behavior. The lack of information on sexual identification of all these fish as well as their normal ethology is a serious problem. But the former (courtship) is made less likely by the ubiquity of the behavior all year long. The latter (aggression) is rendered unlikely by the lack of similarity to aggressive or attack behavior directed toward conspecifics or other species in captivity.

6. The behavior with the object was a form of positive, but nonsexual, social interaction. This is countered by the Bern zoo's experience, because initially the zoo had two fish and for 2 years they were kept together. They never played with each other, but were so aggressive toward one another that the zoo finally shipped one fish off to another institution. Later, other species of fish were kept with the remaining *M. kannume*, along with the twig, but the play was only directed toward the twig. However, at the Danish aquarium, a different scenario unfolded. The aquarium obtained two new small *Mormyrus* in 1949 and put them in the tank with the 10-year veteran. The old

fish immediately gave up playing with the sticks and seemed to bond with one of the new fish. These two then both ganged up on the third fish to the point that the latter had to be removed. The old fish used the new fish as a playmate and performed the same motions with the new partner that it had with the stick; that is, they alternately chased each other over short distances while shoving upward with their snouts and pushing against the tail of the other fish. Finally, when the old fish died, the remaining fish started playing with pebbles and even treated the other fish in the tank, especially a catfish, as if they were conspecifics. These observations suggested to the Danish aquarium director and to Meyer-Holzapfel that the twig served as a substitute play partner.

It will be recalled that in mammals object play has often been shown to increase when social partners are not available (Power, 2000). The varying reactions to other fish could be a consequence of their individual characteristics and behavior. But still, Meyer-Holzapfel pointed out, this behavior with a play partner could be an exception because the species seems generally so intolerant of conspecifics. While this social intolerance has been noted in many mormyrid fish, the Schilthuis elephantnose (*Gnathonemus schilthuisae*) has been recorded as, gregarious, peaceful with other species, and showing "a marked playfulness" (Baensch and Riehl, 1993: 1142) although no more details are provided.

Clearly we need more work on the ethology of mormyrid fish in both field and captivity. But there is no question that this behavior is highly reminiscent of object play in mammals and birds.

Intrigued by this behavior, I obtained two *Gnathonemus petersii* and kept them individually in 80-liter aquaria for some months. The first time I added to the tanks small, plastic, hollow, perforated balls used in bird cages, both fish immediately approached and pushed it around with their highly mobile "trunk." They would dart out to them repeatedly and then retire to their retreat and come back out (they were somewhat shy in light). They would push the balls around their retreat and bounce them up into the water column (figure 13.2). We have several hours of filmed data that show this object play quite convincingly.

However, we now know some things that Meder and Meyer-Holzapfel did not. Mormyrids gain much information from their environment through emitting and detecting electrical signals (Bell, 1989; B. Kramer, 1990; Moller, 1995). They can detect objects—including their electrical properties, size, and distance—with considerable accuracy and even appear to develop cognitive "representations" (Bell et al., 1997; Cain, Gerin, & Moller, 1994). The details of various probing behaviors with novel objects have been reported in the scientific experimental literature in mormyrid fishes (Toerring & Belbenoit, 1979), but the behaviors are never referred to as play and in fact correspondence with several active electric fish researchers resulted in somewhat amused, if not bemused, responses. An exception is a note from Curtis Bell (September

Figure 13.2
An elephantnose fish (*Gnathonemus petersii*) with a ball toy.

1997), who wrote "A propos of play and *Gnathonemus*" that a student had "noticed a *Gnathonemus* balancing a small snail shell on its chin appendage and bringing it up to the surface of the water where it dropped off (was dropped off?) and fell to the bottom and picked it up again. Apparently this was repeated 3 or 4 times."

What is not, in doubt, however, is that these fish are considered quite intelligent and personable by those who study them. The electrical organ discharge (EOD) rate is altered (a startle response) when novel visual, electrical, chemical, or tactile stimuli are presented, and this knowledge has been used in many discrimination studies such as assessing spectral sensitivity (Ciali, Gordon, & Moller, 1997). Habituation of EODs to novel objects in *G. petersii* demonstrated rapid learning in discriminating different-sized objects (De Fazio, 1979). More recent studies also document habituation and compare the electrical discharge response with the orienting response of mammals to sounds or visual stimuli (Post & von der Emde, 1999). Gerhard von der Emde, who studies learning in this species, wrote me (personal communication, September 1997) that they not only learn more quickly than other fish, but that he has also seen many other kinds of learning, including operant and classical conditioning, with these electric fish. The unique brain of these animals will be discussed later in this chapter.

13.6.3 Cichlidae (Cichlids)

Cichlids are one of most successful and speciose of all the families of fishes, especially in freshwater environments (Barlow, 2000). They have radiated into many niches, so that hundreds of different species may live in a single large tropical lake. They are known for diverse social behavior, including advanced parental care, intelligence, and complex foraging tactics. As noted in chapter 6, species that have diverse diets, such as prey generalists, active foragers, and those using variable or complex tactics should play more with objects than fish with narrow diets, ambush foragers, and those using a very limited number of tactics in obtaining food. Fish with dexterous jaws, such as some cichlids and wrasses, appear to also be good candidates for the feeding innovations that might encourage behavioral flexibility.

Natural Objects   Ronald Coleman, a fish ethologist, recounted (personal communication, June 1997) the following incident concerning a pair of pike cichlids (*Crenicichla lepidota*), who were fed live goldfish.

The female was a bit of a pig and never wanted to pass up on a goldfish if she could possibly avoid it. I dropped in the first goldfish and she snagged it right away. She was only 6 inches long so a feeder goldfish was a big chunk to swallow. It was going down her throat so I put in another one, thinking the male could get this one because she was busy. Wrong! She snagged it instantly but caught it amidships and it was going down middle first with the head and tail still pointing out her mouth. In goes the third goldfish, destined for the male.... BUZZ. Wrong again! Even though she had one in her throat, one in her mouth, partially sticking out, she was still able to get the end of her lips around the third and hold it in place while she worked the other two down using her pharyngeal jaws. It was an awesome demonstration of the flexibility of the cichlid mouth.

Myrberg (personal communication, 1997) described an incident involving the convict cichlid (*Archocentrus* [= *Cichlasoma*] *nigrofaciatum*), a species in which both parents take their wriggling young a few days old into their mouths and carry them about. When Myrberg mixed such young with those from another species, the parents repeatedly took in and spit out the young until they started swallowing the alien animals and ended up with a mass of only their own young beneath them. This is clearly an area where experimental research on captive fish should be easy to carry out. In any event, this example shows that the fish are very discriminating, and thus arguments that fish who seem to play with objects in their jaws are unable to distinguish food from nonfood are no more credible than those that claim cats cannot tell a rubber ball from a real mouse.

Kirchshofer (1953), in observations on a mouth-breeding cichlid (*Astatotilapia desfontainesi*), found that the adults often moved quickly across stones and water plants as if they were dealing with some irritable skin stimulus (chafing). Young of this species (and also Sumatran barbs, *Barbus sumatranus*) also performed this behavior repeatedly, but rapidly alternated it with behavior patterns associated with different motivational systems. The young fish were quickly joined by others; Kirchshofer explicitly mentioned that this social aspect fits Bally's (1945) criteria for a social game.

Of course the imitation or social facilitation nature of play has a long history. Thus developmental studies may be needed to more completely study the rubbing of objects as play. Could it, as Meyer-Holzapfel (1960) and Beach (1945) point out, be merely a grooming instinct and thus not be play? Myrberg (personal communication, June 1997) has noted many species that chafe on tubes, substrates, and aquarium walls, but rarely on rough objects. He has also seen this in the wild when predatory trumpet fish (*Aulostomus maculatus*) are exposed to underwater speakers transmitting the sounds made by favorite prey fish. Myrberg concludes that such chafing and grooming are most parsimoniously interpreted as the thwarting of an instinctive response (here access to the food) if the animal does not have a skin disease (ich), and not as play. As argued earlier here and in preceding chapters, play can involve instinctive elements and even be functional in the short as well as the long term.

A comparative review documenting chafing in hundreds of species from thirty fish families (Wyman & Walters-Wyman, 1985) concludes that it is an ancient behavior. The authors state that while "The most frequently reported function of chafing is as a maintenance activity ... To our knowledge the significance of chafing as a maintenance activity or its proximate causation has not been rigorously demonstrated" (1985: 287). They thus performed some experiments in a cichlid, the orange chromide (*Etroplus maculatus*), and a poecilid (*Xiphophorus helleri*), in which they loosened a few scales or inserted a small piece of charcoal under a scale. Both these manipulations increased the chafing rate. Individuals of the former species with a fungal growth on the tail or fins increased chafing dramatically over that of controls. However, the behavior was also quite common in the absence of any irritation (occurring two to three times per hour). They also showed that the behavior was performed at a rather constant rate throughout ontogeny and although it occurred in bouts, seemed to occur more rapidly when it was used as a maintenance behavior (more adaptive?); it also appeared to be more rapidly performed in the field. If the behavior is an ancient and instinctive one, as suggested (Wyman & Walters-Wyman, 1985), then it may have been retained and performed even when somewhat removed from its original function and thus appear playlike. A test that would support interpreting this behavior as play would be to find out if it is more common in its nonfunctional state when the fish are healthy and well fed. There is also a social aspect that will be discussed later.

Artificial Objects Meyer-Holzapfel (1960) argued that behavior with objects that differ markedly from the natural objects used in instinctive behavior provides more convincing evidence for true play, because the interaction is less likely to be confused with eating, parasite removal, or other functional patterns. Certainly the Nile soft-shelled turtles' interactions with basketballs and hula hoops have been important in convincing skeptics that turtles play in a way that would not have been produced by interactions with sticks and prey. Barlow (personal communication, December 2001) reported that he has had large, isolated, aggressive male cichlids attack filter plumbing and aquarium heaters. He attributed this to threshold lowering in animals deprived of normal outlets who were perhaps stimulated by noise in the former and flashing thermostat lights in the latter. The following examples seem to make the redirected aggression hypothesis less feasible in all cases.

James B. Murphy, a noted zoo curator and herpetologist, has kept and observed cichlid fishes in his home for decades. He observed (personal communication, September 1997) that a captive-bred male African cichlid (*Tropheus moorii*), an algae-scraping species, when fed algae flakes would scrape algae from the sides of the tank and from rocks. He also noted that the fish would repeatedly push the top of a floating thermometer (with a weighted bottom) into the side of the aquarium, where it would produce a loud sound audible in the next room. Sometimes it would do this up to a dozen times in a burst of activity. This would occur at any time of day until the lights went out at night. No algae were on the thermometer. Later the fish began to attack its heterospecific tank mates (two birchirs and a catfish) and was traded. In addition, an isolated adult female of a related species (*Tropheus duboisi*) performed a similar behavior with the same kind of thermometer (figure 13.3). Although the first example could be interpreted as an isolated incident of redirected aggression rather than as thwarted feeding behavior, the second example suggests that the behavior is more common and

Figure 13.3
A *Tropheus duboisi* cichlid fish striking a bottom-weighted thermometer, which would often occur
many times a day in bouts. (Photo by Ann Hawthorne)

its motivational roots not clear. More recently Murphy has filmed two *T. duboisi* performing the same behavior with the thermometer and we have obtained sufficient
quantitative data to indicate the behavior is not redirected aggression. Although the
fish would often knock over the thermometer after tying to attack another fish in an
adjacent tank, it would engage in the behavior with the thermometer at about the
same rate even if her view of the other fish was blocked. The behavior is not at all
similar to feeding since this is an algae-eating species.

Finally, Murphy reported the following (personal communication, April 2001):

One of my Tanganyikan cichlids, an adult male *Petrochromis trewavasae* roughly 6 TL. has shown
behavior which might be loosely interpreted as "play." I put a red glass frog, suspended from a
floating plastic ball with monofilament, in the tank (15 gal. show tank). The fish bangs the frog
around, especially when it is trying to get at the adult *Tropheus duboisi* in the adjoining tank. Both
species are highly aggressive, in fact they had to be removed from my large tank as they were

tearing up tank mates. I don't want to make too much of this, however, as I have no idea what's happening, nor does it happen that often. What can be said is that I've never seen any other non-cichlid do this stuff with objects and I've kept fishes for over 40 years.

13.6.4   Opistognathidae (Jawfish)

One of the most dexterous and fascinating behaviors to watch in any fish is the use of rocks, shells, and other small objects by jawfish to seal or close off their burrows. These often colorful, active fish repeatedly carry objects up from inside the burrow or retrieve objects from outside the burrow to construct a wall to block the entrance, presumably to keep out predators at night. I often show my classes a film made by Wolfgang Wickler to illustrate how the rapid and frequent decisions a fish (most likely *Gnathy-pops aurifrons*) must make about the appropriate placement of such objects would readily be labeled cognitively complex behavior in a mammal or bird. As seen in adults, the behavior could always be considered functional and instinctive, even if it is frequent in captivity, where no predators are present. There does not appear to be enough knowledge of the ontogeny of this behavior to determine if it has any playlike aspects in early ontogeny, although digging is seen as early as 15 days of life, only 6 days after fins are formed (Debelius & Baensch, 1994). Still, the behavior is not only complex, it involves using available objects of various sizes, shapes, and densities, and thus some secondary process play might be expected.

13.6.5   Other Teleost Fishes

Grey triggerfish (*Balistes carolinensis*) at the Salzburg (Austria) Aquarium approach, grab, and carry around objects such as wooden brushes and sponges. Inge Illich, the curator, also described how, when she cleaned the tank, the fish would approach and manipulate the gold bracelets on her wrist (personal communication to Michael Kuba, November, 2003). Kuba has videotaped similar behavior with small balls at the Vienna Aquarium in a joint research study we have under way. Perhaps the most remarkable example is of fish who make their own toys. The curator of fish and invertebrates at the Aquarium of Long Beach reports that surgeonfish (*Paracanthurus hepatus* and *Acanthurus thompsoni*) will go to the surface of their tank, gulp air, swim to the bottom of the tank, release the air, and chase the bubbles up to the surface (Sandy Trautwein, personal communication, June 2003).

13.6.6   Chondrichthyes (Sharks and Rays)

Unlike aquatic mammals such as dolphins and seals, predatory sharks are not usually considered playful with objects. Yet sharks have brains that are among the largest of those in all fish (Jerison, 1973); they have complex behavior, often are viviparous, and may be endothermic. A radical revision of our view of sharks is under way, including that of the fabled great white shark (*Carcharodon carcharias*) (Klimley, 1994; Pardini et al., 2001). Great white sharks, like killer whales, are large, long-lived predators on seals and other prey. Unfortunately, little is known about their life history and behavior, including how many young they have, their social and mating systems, how foraging behavior develops, and how they navigate long distances. But what we do know is intriguing indeed.

Many presumed predatory shark attacks on humans may be at least initially just the investigatory responses found in many animals to novel stimuli—and people swimming in colorful, if not garish, bathing suits, wetsuits, and even life preservers are bound to attract the attention of wide-ranging foragers that can ingest large quantities of food. Certainly, like all large predators, be they bears, tigers, anacondas, or Komodo dragons, sharks might target humans as the occasional prey. And the occasional group feeding frenzy cannot be ruled out, especially when we consider what mobs of our own species can do. That being said, the great white shark is now known to be "a skilled and stealthy predator that eats with both ritual and purpose, and it may find human prey unpalatable" (Klimley, 1994: 122). The latter is because humans do not have enough fat. However, in some areas where it lives, high-fat prey may not be available, so more data are needed (Boustany et al., 2002; Eric Ritter, personal communication, 2002).

Great white sharks are long lived (females may not be sexually mature until they are 12 years of age or older), have offspring only every 2–3 years, have sexed-based dispersal (stay-at-home females), and along with several other sharks and other fish, are functionally endothermic, being able to maintain their body temperature many degrees above that of the water. In fact, "in some respects these sharks behave more like whales and dolphins than other fish" (Pardini et al., 2001: 139). So, do they play?

Although great white sharks are known to investigate and strike novel objects, such as surfboards (Klimley, 1994), I was unprepared for a video of sharks and some footage of great white shark object play that was sent to me by a behavioral ecologist specializing in shark behavior (Erich Ritter, personal communication, 1998). The film showed two things. First, if a large barrel-sized chunk of frozen fish was suspended in the ocean where sharks are common, several species of sharks swam to the food and systematically tore off chunks to eat them (Ritter, 2001). Up to the beginning of 2002, more than 35,000 tourists and photographers have swum among the sharks unmolested during these "chumsicle" events. Thus nondiscriminate feeding frenzies may be rare or occur only under certain conditions. However, the sharks in the filmed scenes were not great whites. Even photographers need to be cautious. This film was commercially released and shown worldwide.

Ritter found that great white sharks went into a play mode when the ship's crew tied a sturdy bag with some fish inside it to a floating ball and threw it overboard. Several sharks were repeatedly attracted to the bag, initially by scent, but then nosed and grabbed it. Often they shook it vigorously while the crew would pull on the line hold-

Figure 13.4
Object play in a great white shark. (Photos by Erich Ritter)

ing the bag, as if they were playing tug-of-war with a dog and a scarf (figure 13.4). The behavior often appeared violent, but the shark had postures, such as turning on its back, that were never seen in any predatory context. According to Ritter, this behavior is only seen with "relaxed" sharks and never in a socially aggressive context. Ritter wrote: "Whenever a white shark 'plays' he/she is looking at you and does not turn its eyes backward for protection." Since the sharks were individually recognizable by size, gill markings, etc., Ritter was able to document that individual sharks repeatedly returned to engage in the behavior with the bag after minutes or even hours. Moving as well as floating objects kept their attention. Later, Ritter (personal communication, 2002) added:

When a white shark lifts its head out of the water it is "unprotected" meaning that [it] can't use hearing or vision as an "early warning system" and only the lateral line will give some "warning" from other white sharks. But that system can only be used in closer distance to the shark (about 1–2 body lengths away). And so as a precaution these sharks (the ones who "play" with us) squeeze their gill slits together (to tighten them for protection). Gill biting is the most common "attack spot" for other white sharks. So it is interesting to realize that when they "play" with us, they are "aware" that they could get harmed by other whites but still interact with us.

I have shown brief excerpts of this tape at several talks, and it seems to be the most impressive display of extreme object play in any fish to date.

That the behavior is not just thwarted predation is also shown by the observation that the sharks pushed the float or ball around, even in preference to the frozen fish or when the fish were not present. Cardboard was one of their favorite floats. Ritter has found similarities between how the sharks mouth, bite, and grab the bag and the wound patterns suffered by surfers.

Ritter also has observed that a 2000-kg shark will attack penguins on a beach and release them, even though they are securely within the shark's jaws. Could this be sham or practice hunting or motivationally similar to a cat capturing and releasing rodent prey? Such targeting has been noted by others (Fallows & le Sueur, 2001). The latter authors note that in 9 years of study at Seal Island, False Bay, South Africa, the premier location for seals and great white sharks, only one penguin has been seen being eaten, although sharks have even been seen beaching on top of them. Ritter thinks that multiple bites without tissue loss are an indication of target practice. He also claims that young great whites may do the same with seals because the tooth shape of young sharks precludes their eating them; they eat the seals only after their tooth shape changes. He states (personal communication, 2002) that "they 'tune in' on this prey source [seals] and often 'nail them without harm' in order to get used to them when their jaw structure (teeth) gets finally ready."

Recent observations and videotapes made by Michael Kuba at the Vienna Aquarium document extensive interaction by white-blotched river stingrays (*Potamotrygon leopoldi*) with small round balls similar to those used by elephantnose fish (figure 13.2). Two individuals even competed with each other for access to it.

Clearly such observations are only a beginning, but the more we learn more about the world of fishes, the more remarkable the phenomena we might observe. In this case, given what we know, the five criteria seem to be met.

13.7   Social Play

On a hot day in March, visiting Death Valley in California, I hiked up a boardwalk into a small draw to see Salt Creek, one of the few spring-fed streams that run above ground for short distances in this austere but beautiful, parched landscape with scorching heat, the hottest valley on earth. I was on my way to see one of the species of the famous, and threatened, pupfish (*Crypinodon salinus*). Suddenly the water beside me was alive with small fish 3–4 cm long, chasing and whirling and whizzing back and forth. Seeing these amazing little survivors was a high point in my biological career. The fish were almost constantly interacting with each other in the shallow clear water.

According to Phil Pister of the Desert Fishes Council (E. P. Pister, personal communication, 1997), Carl Hubbs, the scientist most identified with the early study of these fish, gave them the name pupfish because they seemed to play like puppies. We have already seen that Hubbs wrote a short paper on fish play. But were these pupfish playing? Sadly, probably not, at least by the five criteria used here. The fish have a short life-span, grow fast, and must vigorously compete with others for mates and territories (Barlow, 1961). The constant activity of the pupfish is more likely a consequence of having to continually maintain small territories and compete for food and mates in a stressful environment than of playing. Supporting this view is the paucity of data indicating play in the many relatives of the several pupfish species living in more benign settings.

This negative conclusion should not deter us, but it should give pause as we turn to a most fascinating behavior sequence that suggests that fish may play a kind of game.

13.7.1   Fish Games: Food for Thought

We have seen that dogs play catching and retrieving games with people and that they and many other species engage in tug-of-war-like games. What about fish? The great white shark object play was in part a tug-of-war with the deckhands. But do fish play catch? Turning once again to Jarmer (1928), we find his affirmative answer. As in the case of goldfish, many fish will take up and spit out food items repeatedly. This was compared to predatory play as seen in many mammals. Now if two fish are doing this to different prey or food objects, as I have seen in our family fish tank, we could have an instance of parallel play and social facilitation. The next step in this putative sequence is a step most scientists will be reluctant to take. For Jarmer's most remarkable observation was of two predatory fish ("pike"), engulfing and then ejecting the same prey animal back and forth at one another. Each fish in turn took the hapless fish in its mouth and then forcibly ejected it (a throw?). Eventually, after being passed back and forth repeatedly, the chewed-up and mangled prey item, now dead, sank to the bottom and a new more lively prey animal attracted their attention and the "game" started again. The fish were fairly sated when this occurred. How often the game was observed, in what species, and whether it was partly an aberration facilitated by having many fish in a crowded tank, and other questions cannot be answered. Barbara Farrell, my former lab manager, has seen similar behavior in gouramis. Mouth-brooding chocolate gourami (*Beta anabatoides*) pairs spit just-spawned eggs back and forth (Kühme, 1961). Most fish ethologists would definitely not be comfortable calling this behavior playing catch.

In interpreting this behavior when it involves food, it must first be recognized that prey kleptoparasitism occurs in many species. In such kleptoparasitism, a food item in one animal's mouth seems much more attractive to a conspecific than a comparable unmolested prey item. In this case, an already captured prey fish may be a more easily gained meal than going after a vigorous, uninjured animal. I have seen snakes ignore an easily obtained earthworm and attempt to grasp one being swallowed by another snake, and it is not at all uncommon to see prolonged tugs-of-war over who will get the prey item. Injury, death, or at the least considerable wasted time and energy may be the reward for such kleptoparasitic behavior in snakes. Furthermore, when I have seen such behavior in snakes, the possessor of the prey attempts to quickly move off with it or very rapidly finish swallowing it. In the case of the pike exchanging prey back and forth, Jarmer reported no rushed attempts at ingestion. However, Jarmer did not report important details, such as how often the catching game was played. Although the text implied that the game was seen at times in several species, if it was rare and unrepeated, this example fails criterion four. It could be merely chance that two fish were attracted to the same item and were acting purely as two individuals oblivious to the other, testing and rejecting the item or perhaps killing or softening it. Perhaps, however, the behavior really was a short-term diversion developed by two rather bored fish in captivity.

Jarmer (1928) notes that the locomotor movements of fish are constrained by their physical limitations. "Unfortunately, no other movements other than swimming or jumping movements can occur. But the initiation of these motions by mutual encouragement consisting of bumps, mock fight, and simulated rage gives them typical note and distinguishes them sharply from actions meant in other ways" (Jarmer, 1928: 77, trans. C. J. Mellor). The movements here can be chases, rapid dives, or sideways or vertical jumps out of the water. Jarmer even claims that his observations in several species suggest that these teasing chases are not only a form of social play, but that isolated fish perform similar behavior toward nonexistent imaginary playmates (*"den imaginären Gespielen"*).

Recently, observations by James Murphy (unpublished observations, 2001) support the notion of teasing play in fish. A cichlid, *Tropheus duboisi*, in a large communal tank would repeatedly approach a larger (but slower) male *Labeotropheus* sp. and perform a lateral display that would elicit a brief chase by the latter. This went on repeatedly for days. I have several hours of video tape of this behavior and, if we set aside our anthropocentric views (Rivas & Burghardt, 2002), this behavior, seen in a dog or monkey, would unhesitantly be labeled teasing play. A detailed analysis of this behavior by the *T. duboisi* is planned.

13.7.2 Development of Social Behavior and Play in Fishes

Most putative play in fish is limited to adults. Jarmer (1928) dogmatically claims that young fish do not play, and uses this as an argument against a developmental role for play in fish comparable to that posited for mammals. His knowledge of neonatal fish was probably not great. The lack of observations on baby fish is understandable. Fish are often born at a minute size compared with adults, are often nearly invisible and hard to observe, and the larval period or that involving parental care may last only days or a few weeks. Still, the widespread hobby of breeding and rearing tropical and other small fish in captivity would seem to provide ample opportunity for observations.

Behavioral ontogeny has been generally neglected in many fishes, but several research groups have studied this in detail in the laboratory (J. A. Brown, Wiseman, & Kean, 1997; Noakes, 1978) and even the field (McNicol, Scherer, & Murkin, 1985) to aid the fisheries industry. The adaptive significance of both species differences and the timing of the appearance of a behavior have also been addressed. Although much of this is correlational (J. A. Brown, 1985), experimental studies are also becoming available (Schütz & Barlow, 1997). The observation of playlike behavior in young fish is a necessary first step in determining any functional role in the future lives of fish.

It might be argued that the great mortality in juvenile fish and their need to put all their activity into obtaining food for growth and avoiding predators precludes the kind of limited functional behaviors considered playful. This is perhaps true in many cases, but with more than 30,000 species of fish, many diverse phenomena may have arisen. Furthermore, Pederson (1997) demonstrated that metabolism and growth rate are not correlated at the youngest stages; there may be "apparent cost-free growth" in some young fish; and classical energetics may not apply. Thus, the conditions of SRT may have scope to operate as instigators of primary process play. There also is evidence in young Atlantic salmon that social dominance is predicted by the standard metabolic rate. Differences in SMR appear before aggressive encounters, and relative size, mass, or age at first feeding are not predictive when SMR is controlled (Metcalfe, Taylor, & Thorpe, 1995). This raises the possibility that primary process play may occur in salmon as a consequence of individual differences in SMR, with individuals having higher metabolic rates being more prone to engage in behavior at higher rates, including extraneous variants that could appear playful.

Kirchshofer (1953) performed a careful observational field and aquarium study of the reproductive and parental behavior of a population of the mouth-breeding cichlid fish, *Astatotilapia desfontainesi*. In this species the brood is carried about in the mother's mouth for 14–16 days. Fighting movements, apparently not completely adultlike, were seen at 3 weeks of age, before the author thought fighting was functional. Such observations could be comparable to the social play fighting seen in many young mammals. However, perhaps the behavior is at least partially functional. Myrberg (1965) described the ontogeny of behavior in *Pelmatochromis* (= *Chromidotilapia*) *guentheri*. He found siblings both fighting and defending tiny pieces of substrate by the time they were 26 days old. Myrberg (personal communication, June 1997) pointed out that since such behavior is functional, it was not play. Barlow (personal communication,

December 2001) reported that in a nonschooling cichlid, *Julidochromis marlieri*, fry "start serious fights within the first few days after emerging from the nest; this appears to be a behavioral mechanism promoting early dispersal." Nonetheless, juvenile behavior, such as butting, wrestling, and chasing in mammals, is typically considered play, even if it may have some hypothesized current function in the social hierarchy or learning of social roles.

Chafing behavior as presumptive maintenance behavior has already been discussed (Wyman & Walters-Wyman, 1985), but this behavior may also be related to social behavior in cichlids in interesting ways. For example, in another cichlid species (*Pterophyllum scalare*), adult mated pairs will groom (clean) each other (Bergman, 1968). One fish presents itself at right angles to the other, and the latter performs the grooming. Various fin and head postures are involved. Although only seen in adults in complete form, it was found that in young fish, low-intensity lateral aggressive displays may change over into grooming (by the nondisplayer), and Bergman suggested that this might be play.

Another possible candidate for behavior with playlike characteristics is "glancing" behavior in young cichlids. For example, in orange chromides (*Etroplus maculatus*), an extensive experimental study was preceded by the following:

We had observed that the young orange chromides, beginning the first day of free swimming, proceed to either parent and make contact as though chafing on the parent or eating something from it. It was also clear that while this behavior remains relatively the same during the period of parental care, its proficiency of execution, frequency of occurrence and orientation change as the young grow older. We wanted to know what the young, and possibly the parents, are deriving from this behavior. For we found it hard to believe that such behavior is without adaptive significance (Ward & Barlow, 1967: 2).

The authors point out that early descriptions of such behavior showed it to be variable and often incomplete, occurring in many species. In adult orange chromides, however, the behavior is also seen not only in presumptive ectoparasite removal, where it seems unusual for a fish in that both participants seem to cooperate, even groom each other (Barlow, personal communication, 1997), but is also seen in adult courtship. Ward and Barlow point out that it is rare to find a juvenile behavior so clearly employed in adult courtship in a "lower vertebrate." They do document that the behavior is targeted to specific body regions of the parents and, after 3 days of age, the young are ingesting mucus from the parents during glancing that may have nutritional value. However, until after day 7, prior feeding has no effect on the rates of glancing behavior. This suggests that early in ontogeny the behavior is performed for intrinsic or self-rewarding (autotelic) reasons, even if it has some current function.

Such contacting and mucus ingestion is seen in about thirty species of cichlids, though typically only in the young. In the orange chromide, such contact with the parent may aid survival of the young. Furthermore, another study showed that if parents were removed, the young did more of the chafelike glancing behavior on the substrate, suggesting to the authors that this was a substitute for a parental stimulus (Wyman & Walters-Wyman, 1985). Such redirected social responses to objects have been noted in mammalian play (Power, 2000).

Contact behavior by young also occurs in the Midas cichlid (*Cichlasoma citrinellum*), which was first described intensively by Noakes and Barlow (1973); subsequently an active non-nutrient compound from the mucus was identified (Schütz & Barlow, 1997). In the early behavioral development of this species, incomplete versions are seen (similar to birds, see chapter 11). One of the few noncichlid species of fish to show juvenile glancing behavior, and which similarly involves some ingestion, is a damselfish, *Acanthochromis polyacanthus* (Kavanagh, 1998). Thus there is still much that we do not yet know about such behavior. Nonetheless, it is a behavior that may serve a number of functions, including parental bonding, tactile communication, parasite removal, and growth and nutrition, about which little is definitely known and which may have a variety of consequences in some species, and perhaps very limited ones in others.

There may be more going on in Midas cichlids because they are found in two sympatric color types, or morphs. Studies of social interaction among juveniles have found that the specific color morph that individuals are reared with does not seem related to later mate choice, as might be predicted from an early experience or imprinting model (Barlow & Francis, 1988; Barlow & Siri, 1987). A fine descriptive study showed that in captivity fry grew at different rates and small ones could be eaten by larger siblings; such cannibalism did not begin until fish were more than 40 days of age and it peaked when they were more than 60 days old. By days 7–8 they began to eat mucus from a parent's body; aggressive interactions were not seen until about 14 days of age and then they developed gradually and sequentially (Valerio & Barlow, 1986). Could the early development of agonistic behavior be playlike? "Chase was first recorded at an age of 23 days, and it was performed in a seemingly pointless manner. For example, the chaser often stopped chasing without gaining any apparent benefit. Many times the chaser was unable to reach the escaping fish" (Valerio & Barlow, 1986: 24). This behavior fell to low levels well before the cannibalism phase began, as did "social" biting, which began on day 21. In large fry, chasing rebounded to high levels (about 80/hour) around day 76, well after the peak cannibalism phase. The final behavior to be mentioned is the lateral display, a defensive maneuver that first appeared on day 30 and was most common in small fry. It is interesting that this behavior dropped off remarkably during the peak cannibalism phase (days 58–72), and peaked again on day 79. The authors noted that the lateral display actually was rather different in its later manifestation and was initially scored as a different action pattern.

Could this early development of agonistic behavior, prior to serious fighting or cannibalism, be comparable to the fighting and chasing games of animals such as rats? In the latter, it has already been established that the behavior appears before the serious contests begin, that both offensive and defensive maneuvers are involved, and that targeting and response to bites are different than in serious fighting.

Brown bullheads (*Ameiurus nebulosus*) are highly social fish with advanced parental care that can involve both parents (Blumer, 1985). Sexual maturity is not reached until about 3 years of age, and the behavior of most catfish can be quite complex (Etnier & Starnes, 1996). The avian ethologist Anne Clark (personal communication, August 1993) reported students who observed in the field young bullheads 3–5 cm long engaging in social interactions that seemed playful. Groups of two or three young would break off from the main natal group, chase each other around a rock, and then return. Clark saw in this behavior a similarity to the budgerigars she mainly studies, where some birds would break off as a group and "flutter fly" (an energetic, exaggerated flight) around some object.

Observations of neonatal fish in the many species with advanced parental care would be worthwhile. The Cichlidae are probably studied by more ethologists than any other group of fish. This huge family of small and medium-sized fish has radiated throughout the tropics; a single lake can contain 200 species. They also possess a remarkable diversity in modes of parental care. Surplus resource theory predicts that play is likely to occur in situations where adequate nutrition and parental buffering of predator risks are both present.

A final example of play in fish is of a behavior tantalizingly similar to the precocial courtship observations in reptiles and mammals. However, although derived from reproductive behavior or courtship behavior, it was observed in an apparently nonsocial context. In a study of coho salmon (*Oncorhynchus kisutch*), fish that reach sexual maturity at about 3 years of age, Jennifer Nielsen (1990) recorded this brief observation: "Floaters were observed performing belly displays without provocation. In this behavior the fish rolled to the side, displayed a full belly and moved their tail up and down at the substrate, much like an adult female's movement when digging a redd" (1990: 55) (a redd is a nest in which the female lays her eggs). After I discussed this with Nielsen, she elaborated on the precocial aspects: "The precocial sex thing was something that haunted me as well" (Nielsen, personal communication, 1997). She dissected seven animals showing this distinctive female behavior and found two males among the seven. Furthermore, she found that other "juvenile salmon watchers" had also seen this behavior, which is common only in stream habitats with fine sand that can be easily dislodged and moved. Some of the fish swam into the small amount of floating particulates they stirred up by their activity and were observed to bite. To counter the argument that the nestinglike behavior was primarily a means of dislodging small food particles, she did both stomach content analyses of the fish and micro-drift net capture of the debris to see if anything edible was present. There was nothing. As in the turtles, this behavior, found in only one sex as adults, was found in both sexes as juveniles, making the direct practice interpretation unlikely.

If we apply our five criteria to social behavior, we find that they hold to varying degrees as well, but that the data are uncomfortably limited. Given the often large changes in size and ecology during the ontogeny of fish, it would be valuable to evaluate the role of playful rehearsals in their developmental history. That active fish may play some kinds of primitive games with each other, from playing catch with prey to chasing games, especially in nonstimulating captive environments, is not hard to appreciate, but it is hard to confirm.

Table 13.2 summarizes the types of play found among some of the fish discussed here. Although diverse play and playlike behavior seems to occur in fish, whether the mechanisms underlying this play and the functions it performs are comparable to those of tetrapods cannot be answered. Nevertheless, applying the criteria we developed for "truly playing" animals has brought us to this point, and there may be no going back.

13.8   Physiology, Brains, and the Play of Fish

In addition to expecting to see some relationship between play and parental care (e.g., provisioning and protecting neonates), we might also expect that certain physiological conditions might also predispose some fish to engage in playful behavior. Endothermy, as we have established earlier, is one such predisposing factor in tetrapods. Would effectively endothermic fish such as tuna thus be expected to show some playful behavior under appropriate conditions? Metabolic rate, activity level, and temperament vary across species of fish just as much as they do within mammals, birds, and nonavian reptiles. These factors should also be associated with amount, type, and complexity of playfulness. The energy obtained from the diet and the amount of time needed to obtain sufficient energy in rich environments also affect the metabolic expenditures and the probability that play will occur under favorable conditions. Fish that eat a variety of foods, especially other animals, and that deploy variable and complex tactics, might also be expected to show more variability in behavior and be predisposed to play. Well cared-for fish in predator-free but rather stimulus-poor environments might also be more likely to evince play behavior.

13.8.1   Brain Size and Fish Behavior
The three physical components of the von Uexküllian functional circle are the receptors, effectors, and nervous system. We earlier established that having diverse and complex ways of interacting with the environment will predispose animals to playful movements. These include tactile and kinesthetic cues obtained through body movement and manipulation. Larger brains within a class or order do seem to be associated

Table 13.2

Application of the play criteria to several suggestive examples in diverse species of fish

Species	Play Type	Incompletely Functional	Voluntary	Structural or Temporal Modification	Repeated	Relaxed Field
Needlefish	Locomotor	Yes	Yes	?	Yes	Yes
Mullet	Locomotor	?	?	?	Yes	?
Sturgeon	Object	Yes	Yes	?	Yes	Yes?
Mormyrids	Object	Yes	Yes	Yes	Yes	Yes
Cichlid	Object	Yes	Yes	Yes	Yes	Yes
Shark	Object	Yes	Yes	Yes	Yes	Yes
Cichlid	Play fighting	Yes	Yes	Yes	?	?
Cichlid	Social teasing	Yes	Yes	Yes	Yes	Yes
Coho salmon	Precocial nesting	Yes	Yes	Yes	Yes?	Yes?

with greater playfulness across nondomesticated species, at least according to crude analyses (Eisenberg, 1981; Fagen, 1981; Iwaniuk, Nelson, & Pellis, 2001), but specific brain regions are more informative (Lewis, 2004).

There is an extensive database on comparative brain size in various groups of teleost fishes. The Bauchot laboratory in Paris, France has been particularly interested in relating overall brain size and the relative development of different brain regions to phylogeny, diet, habitat, importance of the various senses, morphology (body plan or bauplan), and other factors. Fish overall have generally small brains compared with endothermic vertebrates, but this is not universal. Levels of encephalization can differ greatly among fishes as well as vertebrates (M. L. Bauchot et al., 1989; Ridet & Bauchot, 1990a). Although taxonomic position plays a role, other factors seem to be more important.

Body shape influences encephalization, with elongate animals having lower brain-to-body mass ratios and stout fish having larger values. The following characteristics have been positively associated with brain size: active predation, fusiform body shape, active defense or escape behavior, diurnal habits, territoriality (which entails a need to know details of spatial habitat), and complex sociality (the need to know about conspecifics and congeners) (Ridet & Bauchot, 1990a). In the goby fishes (Gobioidei), mud-dwelling species have very small brains, with torrent-dwelling and amphibious gobies having mean relative brain sizes almost five times larger (M. L. Bauchot et al., 1989). The relative size of the cerebellum is related to the body size and activity level of a fish, with more active species having a larger cerebellum (Ridet & Bauchot, 1990b). Relative reliance on chemical and visual stimuli is also reflected in degree of development of the brain systems related to chemical and visual signal processing (R. Bauchot, Ridet, & Bauchot, 1989; Kassem, Ridet, & Bauchot, 1989). There is ample opportunity to test hypotheses about the role of playlike behavior and related neural systems as more data are collected.

13.8.2 Is There Anything Peculiar about Mormyrids?

How does brain size relate to the remarkable behavior of some mormyrids? For if otters are the mammalian play champion (Fagen, 1981), parrots and corvids the avian champs, and Komodo dragons the squamate reptile champ, mormyrids may be the fish play champions. Since the behavior and electric discharge rate profiles of mormyrids in captivity are readily altered, Moller (1995) has provided a rationale for a "mormyrid captivity model" as an ideal system to study synaptic, physiological, and other forms of plasticity in fishes.

It could be a rich field. There are more than 200 species of mormyrids. Some body plans are shown in B. Kramer (1990) and Moller (1995), and a recent molecular phylogeny is available (Sullivan, Lavoué, & Hopkins, 2000).

The chin appendage (trunk) of many mormyrids is capable of some mobility and flexibility. Mammals with long, flexible snouts can perform many fine manipulations. While elephants are the most prominent example, bears, pigs, and primates also can use the mouth, jaws, tongue, and snout to push, pull, grasp, and separate objects. The mormyrid chin extension may have evolved in the service of foraging for food on littered substrates and crevices. This ability opens up entirely new perceptual—especially tactile—worlds to explore. Some sturgeons have a snout that seems to function similarly.

There are some other fish that should be investigated. Within the electric eels, there is a small family of mildly electric fish (Apteronotidae) that has species, particularly *Sternarchorhynchus*, with trunklike "snouts" that are virtually identical with those of some mormyrids, and that have similar feeding and social habits as well. The role of feeding ecology in the development of fine motor control, dexterity, and object manipulation has been studied in extractive foragers among primates, such as the cebus monkeys (Fragaszy & Adams-Curtis, 1997), and it is possible that a similar evolutionary trend has taken place in fish.

Most interesting here, however, is the central nervous system of mormyrids. Franz (1912) was one of the first to draw attention to some remarkable features of the brain in these animals. Their brains (figure 13.5) are remarkable (Butler & Hodos, 1996) in that the cerebellum of these fish is the largest, relatively speaking, in the vertebrates and is much larger than their forebrain. The cerebellum actually grows up and around the rest of the brain and is many times larger than any other brain structure. In fact, the brain of an adult *Gnathonemus petersii* is 4.4 percent of its body mass (Bullock,

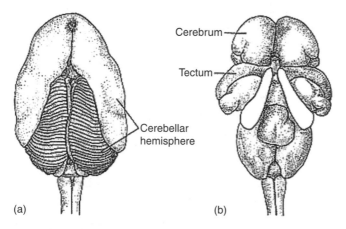

Figure 13.5
Dorsal view of the brain of a Mormyrid fish both with (*a*) and without (*b*) the cerebellum. (From Butler & Hodos, 1996)

1977), which is higher than in an adult human (in which 3 percent is large for even a rather small 100-pound or 45-kg person). Although Franz knew little if anything about the behavior of these animals, and certainly nothing about play, he hypothesized that the function of the immense cerebellum is to connect and integrate associations among many stimuli.

Recent studies have supported the role of the cerebellum in learning, target-directed behavior, and other cognitive processes (chapter 5; Burghardt, 2001; Bell, Cordo, & Harnad, 1996). The dexterity and flexibility demonstrated in the object-directed behavior of these fish apparently needs the support of a complex nervous system. So larger brains do seem to be supportive of the more complex types of play behavior even in fish, although they may not be needed for primary process play. The fact that play behavior is found in adult mormyrids seems to contradict the theory of Byers and Walker (1995) about a cerebellar sensitive period. With much more being known about the regeneration of nerve cells in adult vertebrate brains (citations in Burghardt, 2001), it is perhaps not surprising that regeneration of new cells is also common in fish brains; in electric fishes, such as mormyrids, 75 percent of this regeneration occurs in the cerebellum (Zupanc, 1999).

13.9   Evolution of Play in Fish

Fish were the first group of vertebrates, and fossil forms go back to the Ordovician period in the Paleozoic era (Janvier, 1996). The diversity of fishes is great indeed and includes groups much more different from each other than some fishes are from land vertebrates. Many of the earliest forms, such as placoderms, are extinct. As the phylogeny in figure 13.6 shows, the examples of playlike behavior described here are widely dispersed over the radiation of fishes. Play appears too uncommon to be plesiomorphic as playlike behavior, but, as established for other groups, might be a phenomenon that appears when the conditions are right.

The earliest tetrapod (terrestrial vertebrate) fossils can be dated from the Devonian, about 370 mya. Thus if play is found in any of the fishes, the lines of common ancestry are at least that old. In any event, play in living representatives of ancient lineages shows that it is not due to subsequent evolutionary events. The radiation of living fishes most closely related to terrestrial vertebrates consists of the fleshy or lobe-finned fish, the Sarcopterygii, represented today by the Actinistia (coelacanths) and Dipnoi (lungfishes). The former is represented today by the deepsea fish *Latimeria*, and the latter by a few species of freshwater animals that live in shallow-water habitats subject to drying. It is interesting that fossil coelacanths were also freshwater species. Behavioral knowledge of both these small relic groups is limited, but no play has been described (Hans Fricke, personal communication, 2002), although some underwater films by Fricke near Madagascar show some enigmatic behavior by *Latimeria*, including

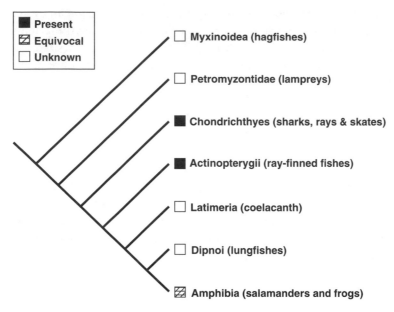

Figure 13.6
Phylogeny and play in major fish groups.

standing on their heads. The fossil record of both groups can be traced back to the Devonian. The lungfish are generally considered the group closest to the tetrapods. The Sarcopterygii broke off from the lines leading to the Actinopterygii (ray-finned fish) in the Silurian, more than 400 mya.

It is the ray-finned fish that provide most of the play evidence presented in this chapter. Their origins are even deeper in the Silurian. Figure 13.7 provides a simplified phylogeny of the living members of this group. The earliest radiation was the Cladistia (represented by two freshwater genera, including *Polypterus*, the bichir). These animals have retained some generalized characteristics shared with sharks. No playlike behavior has been recorded in the Cladistia. The next radiation was the Chondrostei, represented today by the Acipenseridae (sturgeons) and Polyodontidae (paddlefishes). These are large fish found in Eurasia and North America. Sturgeon, but not paddlefishes, have been reported as being curious about objects and engaging in some object manipulation. The foraging behavior of sturgeon, with their upturned snouts used for rooting in substrates, was probably the crucial adaptation of the group that led to the significant, but still rather elementary, manipulation of objects. What the sturgeon example does show is that the play behavior of the more advanced teleost fishes is not based in its origin on derived features in these animals.

In the line going to the more advanced fishes, the Ginglymodi, represented by the garfish (*Lepisosteus*), were the next to diverge, followed by the Halecomorphi, repre-

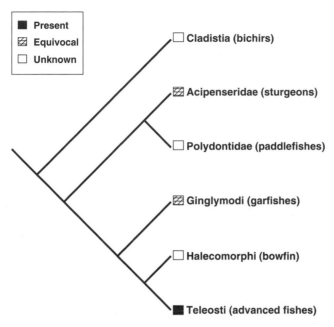

Figure 13.7
Phylogeny of play in major ray-finned fish groups. (After Helfman et al., 1997)

sented by the bowfin (*Amia*), the sister group to the true bony fishes or Teleostei. Clear play has not yet been recorded in the garfish or bowfin, but appears to have arisen several times in the teleosts. In figure 13.8 the major families of teleosts are shown in a current phylogeny (Janvier, 1996; Helfman et al., 1997). The examples of presumptive play are not randomly distributed. The Mormyridae split off very early in the teleost radiation. Tarpon are in the group of families that split off next. The next groups include the herring, pike, carp, and catfish, in all of which there is evidence of some playlike behavior in at least one species. There is then a break in the occurrence of play until the closely related silversides, flying fish, and needlefishes appear. It is most interesting that the many independent observations of fish leaping over objects are limited to these last two groups. The leaping behavior could well have been the ancestral condition that led to the remarkable performances of flying fish. Cichlids are in the huge perch group, and any social play in the young may be highly derived.

Recapitulation has been mentioned in chapter 2 as an old and largely discarded aspect of play, now receiving renewed attention in comparative cognition research. If it is to have substantial biological support as an evolutionary process, examples should be available in diverse groups. Recently the ontogeny of the fascinating needlefishes, halfbeaks, and flying fish has been studied through the recapitulation lens, and some

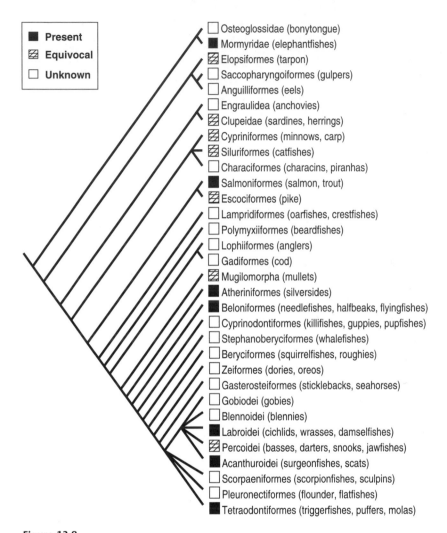

Figure 13.8
Phylogeny of major teleost fish groups with evidence for play.

major taxonomic revisions may be in the offing (Lovejoy, 2000). Young needlefish have a juvenile stage in development in which they have only the elongated lower jaw and thus resemble the halfbeaks. Traditionally, halfbeaks have been considered to be derived from ancestral relatives of the needlefish and selected to retain the juvenile character (paedomorphic). However, modern molecular and other data are most parsimoniously interpreted as having the needlefish derived from the halfbeaks, not the reverse (Lovejoy, 2000). If so, the conclusion is compelling that needlefish recapitulated the halfbeak adult stage and then subsequently added the elongated upper jaw as a terminal addition (peramorphosis). If so, the development of behavior should be studied in these animals as well. The more important conclusion is that this example supports the possibility that primary process play may often be an instinctive way station on the road to adulthood.

The common ancestor of all ray-finned fish and tetrapods lived at least 420 mya. How far back can we go? Janvier (1996) considers the hagfish (Hyperotreti) to be the oldest Craniata and the lampreys (Hyperoartia) the earliest vertebrate lineage. The two groups are often combined as jawless fish (Agnatha), but they differ in many respects in spite of being jawless. Their origins are in the Cambrian, more than 510 mya. No evidence of any kind of play, even the most anthropomorphic or anecdotal, has been reported in these groups to date. The common ancestor of the jawless (Agnatha) and jawed vertebrates (Gnathostoma) must date back to the Ordovician, more than 440 mya. The jawed cartilaginous fish (Elasmobranchii—sharks, skates, and rays) are the earliest group to then diverge (sharks are ancestral to both skates and rays).

Modern-appearing sharks were already around in the Carboniferous, 300 mya. Some locomotor and object interaction behavior that may be play has been recorded in sharks and stingrays. Nonetheless, many sharks and rays are truly viviparous, have small litter sizes, slow growth rates, large brains, endothermy, and a high protein or fat diet. This suggests that playlike behavior may be more common than might initially appear plausible. These ancient and highly successful animals, too often considered soulless killing machines, may have many secrets to tell us. Although some sharks are sedentary, many sharks, lacking a swim bladder, move almost constantly in the water. This constant activity might provide more opportunities for exploration, investigation, and play than in more energy-constrained or sedentary fishes.

Within the vertebrate lineage we can go back no farther, but then there is not much farther to go. It has indeed been a remarkable journey. For there is evidence, as problematic as it may be, for the existence of types of behavior in fish that some consider the hallmark, indeed the source, of much that we consider distinctly mammalian, or even human. There is something edifying, as well as humbling, in identifying behavioral similarities between us and huge sharks, snuffling sturgeons, flashing silversides, and the acrobatic elephantnose fish.

14 Play at the Margins: Invertebrates

14.1 Introduction

While play certainly does seem most prominent in eutherian mammals, it also occurs in marsupials, birds, some ectothermic reptiles, and fish. The prized discontinuity between mammals and birds on the one hand and "lower" vertebrates on the other, which initially drew me to the question of the evolution of play, is crumbling. This is particularly true of locomotor and object play, which can be linked together as sensorimotor play. Is there, however, a discontinuity in all types of play between vertebrates and the invertebrates, which encompass more than 99 percent of all living animals? Animals such as paramecia, rotifers, sea urchins, clams, squid, earthworms, scorpions, spiders, butterflies, and honeybees have a diversity in levels of activity, neural complexity, sociality, parental care, behavioral sophistication, and learning ability far greater than that found in vertebrates, from fish to chimpanzees. The communicative and learning abilities of honeybees, for example, are much documented (Gould, 2002; E. O. Wilson, 1975).

The story of invertebrate play is shadowy and unclear; the lack of clear definitions of play has haunted this part of our trek on the trail of play more than anywhere else. Although the data are admittedly quite thin, this might not be so 30 years from now. The reason for this is that development is now the main problem in biology. The genetic code has been broken and its nature explored. Today the issues of contention revolve around how structures and behavior develop from the genetic code. The remarkable accomplishment of cloning a complete organism from a differentiated cell taken from an adult, not just from fertilized eggs, shows the power inherent in the genome. But the fact that genetics does not specify more than 40–80 percent of the variance seen in even identical human twins shows that the developmental pathway is not completely predetermined. If play, in a broad sense, is important in development as well as being a source of behavioral novelty and adaptive responses in many vertebrates, then it may also be important in some invertebrates, although it may be hard to recognize if anthropomorphic conceptions of "fun" are applied to species as alien as the invertebrates often seem to be to us.

The biological and behavioral diversity among all the phyla of invertebrates is over-whelming and adds to the difficulty of defining and recognizing play. Furthermore, students in university programs in the biological sciences rarely take more than one course, at most, in invertebrate zoology, while they have many hours of instruction that focuses on vertebrates. In psychology, there is virtually no exposure to inverte-brates. Of course, in neurophysiology courses students will meet up with sea slug (*Aplysia*) and squid axons. In genetics courses they will study fruit flies (*Drosophila*) and minuscule nematode worms. In ecology courses they will study the role of earthworms, soil microbes, insect pollinators, and many other invertebrates in complicated food webs. In animal behavior courses they will hear about communication and social evo-lution in Hymenoptera (bees, ants, and wasps).

In ethology, invertebrates, especially insects, are used as model systems for the study of all kinds of problems, including those involving ontogeny and metamorphosis. As the shift to the study of development proceeds in invertebrates, will playfulness be among the topics studied? The identification of play behavior in invertebrates is not an end in itself, but reveals the kinds of flexibility and plasticity in behavior and devel-opmental trajectories that are found in invertebrate phyla.

The common ancestors of the external-shelled arthropodlike invertebrates go back much farther in time than the vertebrates. The now-extinct trilobites, as well as crus-taceans and chelicerates (today's crabs and spiders), were present 520 mya in the Mid-dle Cambrian (Osorio, Bacon, & Whitington, 1997). Insects themselves appeared in the Devonian, about 375 mya. Evidence is accumulating that the basic plan of the nervous system of animals as diverse as crayfish and insects is homologous and highly similar in both anatomy and physiology (Osorio, Bacon, & Whitington, 1997). As in verte-brates, complexity in invertebrate behavior may be mapped onto a basal plan that ori-ginated once in evolutionary time and proved successful. This basic plan then became elaborated and diversified as ecological, physiological, developmental, and behavioral needs and conditions changed. As in the case of vertebrates, playlike behavior in in-vertebrates should be expected to reach the threshold of a "separate" category only when other life history, physiological, ecological, and behavioral conditions converge. How this development plays out in invertebrates may be quite different in details, however.

Today play is rarely mentioned in conjunction with invertebrates, be they barnacles, earthworms, spiders, or bees (Aldis, 1975; Bekoff & Byers, 1981, 1998; Fagen, 1981). But it was not always so. One of the first books on comparative psychology quotes an au-thority who saw a crab "play with little round stones, and empty shells, as do cats with a cork, or small ball" (E. P. Thompson, 1851: 62). Groos quickly passes by "the lower orders, though some of their actions, especially the swarming of insects, is very sug-gestive of play" (1898: 100). He does quote Schiller (see chapter 2) and W. H. Hudson (1892). The latter was a fine naturalist, especially concerning birds, but he was limited by the general lack of information on much insect behavior. Hudson devoted a chapter to fireflies. It was not known then that they flash to attract mates; the most current theory in Hudson's time was that the flashing acted as a warning signal. Although they are soft-bodied and slow flying, fireflies are distasteful to many insectivorous predators. Hudson accepted as a partial explanation the possibility that the flashing might scare off potential nocturnal predators. However, he brooded over why fireflies only flash during part of the night and why they do not flash when they are at rest and still vulnerable to nocturnal predators. Hudson also pointed out that one species of firefly he knew about was diurnal and the flash would offer no protection to them; then he states:

We are thus forced to the conclusion that, while the common house fly and many other diurnal insects spend a considerable portion of the daylight in purely sportive exercises, the firefly, possessing in its light a protection from nocturnal enemies, puts off its pastimes until the evening.... I have spoken of the firefly's pastimes advisedly, for I have really never been able to detect it doing anything in the evening beyond flitting aimlessly about, like house flies in a room, hovering and revolving in company by the hour, apparently in amusement. (Hudson, 1892: 170)

This quotation is a prime example of why play as a category has such a difficult time being accepted in nonmammalian species. Fireflies, of course, are far from aimless in their flights, and, as indicated, the role of the flashing in mate communication was not then recognized. Sufficient natural history information is always needed to confidently recognize play. Our knowledge of many invertebrates then and even now is insufficient to measure the extent of playlike behavior. Furthermore, the parsimony principle requires solid evidence before such a higher-order trait as play can be attributed to "mere bugs." Should our ignorance of the great majority of invertebrates discredit all examples of play in invertebrates? If play, as characterized here, is not necessarily a highly complex and cognitive process, but appears when a suite of traits comes together, then perhaps it does occur in them.

When one is in doubt on many topics in behavior, evolution, and psychology studied in the nineteenth century, it is often rewarding to consult Charles Darwin. He wrote that "Even insects play together, as has been described by that excellent observer, P. Huber, who saw ants chasing and pretending to bite each other, like so many puppies" (Darwin, 1877: 65). Darwin thus found it credible that ants play fight. It has usually proven brash to disregard Darwin's claims without compelling reasons. Is this an instance where Charles Darwin, himself an avid observer of ant behavior, was wrong?

14.2   Play in Insects

14.2.1   Play Fighting in Ants
E. O. Wilson, immersed in the study of ants since childhood, parlayed and transformed what he learned about them into a major revolution in the way we look at invertebrate, vertebrate, and even human behavior (E. O. Wilson, 1975). Although he has

frequently been criticized for extrapolating his sociobiological ideas on the genetics and evolution of behavior from ants to people, Wilson does not do the reverse of extending playfulness from mammals to invertebrates such as ants. The genes that code for eyes in insects and vertebrates appear to be homologous (Carroll, Grenier, & Weatherbee, 2001). Could not the phenomena of play also prove to be homologous?

As usual, Darwin picked the best available authority for his claim that ants play. The classic example of play in an insect still discussed (but not endorsed) today is the Huber reference Darwin cited (Huber, 1810). Huber was not a dilettante who just recorded an observation here or there, but was an eminent Swiss scientist who was a pioneer in ant biology and behavior. What did Huber actually describe? He saw ants (*Formica* sp.) approach each other waving their antennae and then engage in wrestling. This involved rising up on their hind legs, seizing each other's mandible or grabbing onto other body parts, releasing them, trying again, and overturning their partner or falling themselves. Although there did not seem to be any injuries, the defeated ant would escape and hide. Is this social play fighting (Aldis, 1975)?

Huber's observations, although well publicized, "won little credence with the reading public" according to some critics (Groos, 1898). In fact, Aguste Forel (1929), another seminal ant researcher (and psychologist), stated that initially he was very skeptical of Huber's observations, until he also observed the behavior that Huber described. Indeed, he eventually concluded that "It is a well-established fact, therefore, that on fine, calm days when they are feeling no hunger or any other cause for anxiety, certain ants entertain themselves with sham fights, without doing each other any harm; but these games come to an end directly they are scared. This is one of their most amusing habits" (Forel, 1929, vol. 1: 469). The well-regarded observer of ants, the cleric Wasman (1905), claimed to have made similar observations on ants in the same genus (*Formica*) as those studied by Huber. For Wasman, these observations suggested behavior patterns that "are instinctive no less than the romps and scuffles of young cubs, or the frolics of lambkins. They are due, I suppose, to the natural impulse of exercising the muscles, which is pleasurable to animals as well as to human beings" (1905: 67). Wasman thus brings in the notion that the ants' behavior is instinctive (and thus does not need social learning or practice?) as well as the ideas of muscle exercise, pleasure, and, less directly, surplus energy.

Groos, although presenting the observations of Huber and Forel, was "not altogether prepared to make" (1898: 140) the admission that ants engaged in true play. This conclusion stemmed largely from his view that play fighting was preparation for courtship and he knew that courtship practice could not be involved in sterile castes of female ants. "The mock fights of ants must then be entirely for practice preparatory to their unusually quarrelsome and predatory way of living. Notwithstanding, I must hold to the belief that mock fighting in general is preparatory for the courtship contest" (Groos, 1898: 140–141). Groos then went on to a discussion of dogs, cats, wolves, bears, raccoons, ungulates, primates, and birds that more clearly supported his views.

In the early twentieth century, Stumper (1921) recorded similar play combat in *Formicoxenus nitidulus* in the summer on apparently pleasant, but not hot, days. The ants would pull each other about, and again the behavior did not seem harmful or serious. He attributed the behavior to surplus energy, supported the Schiller–Spencer theory, and was scornful of Groos's adaptationist theory (*"théorie finalisté"*).

In their magisterial opus on ants, the world's reigning ant experts cited some of these reports of play fighting, but dismissed the play interpretation (Hölldobler & Wilson, 1990). They viewed the interactions between ants recorded by Huber and others as struggles between two colonies, although they acknowledged that this behavior seldom resulted in death or injury to the participants. They also claimed that even Stumper later recanted his interpretation. Thus at the end of a short section titled simply "Ants Do Not Play," they state that "we know of no behavior in ants or any other social insect that can be construed as play or social practice behavior approaching the mammalian type" (Hölldobler & Wilson, 1990: 370). However, this statement is not as unequivocal as it first appears. Why would one expect mammalian-type play in ants? This appears uncritically mammalomorphic. Also note that play was equated with "social practice." In contrast, Darwin used the criteria of "pretense" in his description of ant play. Note that, as in examples of possible fish play in chapter 13, the postulation of a plausible current function for any putative play behavior, even without any evidence, leads to it being dropped as an example of play.

The conclusion of Hölldobler & Wilson (1990) that serious fights were being observed in ants may very well be correct, although their conclusion is not yet definitive. But Hölldobler & Wilson (1990) totally ignored observations of a different type of "play" made by Henry Bates (1864), the eminent naturalist who discovered the form of mimicry between palatable and unpalatable insects now known as Batesian mimicry. In his observations of the army ant (*Eiciton drepanophora*), he noted that a column of ants would frequently stop in a sunny nook in the forest and "seemed to have been all smitten with a sudden fit of laziness." The ants would approach and clean each other's legs and antennae; others would just stroll about or clean themselves.

The actions of these ants looked like simple indulgence in idle amusement. Have these little creatures, then, an excess of energy beyond what is required for labours absolutely necessary to the welfare of the species, and do they expend it in mere sportiveness, like young lambs or kittens or in idle whims like rational beings? It is probable that these hours of relaxation and cleaning may be indispensable to the effective performance of their harder labours, but whilst looking at them, the conclusion that the ants were engaged merely in play was irresistible. (Bates, 1864: 423)

We see here again, as in generally accepted "true play," the conflict between current function (cleaning), delayed benefit (effective performance), and "mere play."

The quotations from Bates raise many issues about play still current 140 years after he wrote. Current studies on the daily round of ant colony activities above ground classify them into five categories. Three of these have been used for about 20 years (e.g., Gordon, 1986; Sanders & Gordon, 2002): foraging, nest maintenance, and midden work. Patrolling, however, has been changed to the less functional "meandering" and convening at the nest entrance to "loitering." When colonies were given supplemental food to harvest, meandering and loitering decreased (Sanders & Gordon, 2002). Given the behavioral categories the authors use and the traditional dichotomy of work and leisure, neither Bates's observations nor boredom in ants should be peremptorily rejected. The dogma remains. Play is something not necessary, merely a product of excess nutrition and energy. If a behavior seems important, then it is probably not play. Play, unlike important activities, is pleasurable and associated with laziness.

Romanes (1892) discussed many additional examples of play in ants, but was quite uncritical, as was too often the case in Darwin's protége. Since Romanes's discussion of ant play was followed by a discussion of the funeral habits and burial ceremonies of ants, his credibility was sorely stretched. In addition to reliable observations from John Lubbock, the polymath scientist, who was Darwin's friend and neighbor, he included brief anecdotes by "the pen of an observer not well known" (Romanes, 1892: 91).

One of the few mentions of ant play in modern play theory is the treatment by Bekoff and Allen (1998). They introduce their discussion of intentionality and play (see chapter 3) by quoting Darwin on Huber and then discuss Huber's (1810) claim that only our bias in viewing insects as machines prevents us from attributing emotions to them. But Bekoff and Allen use the ant story merely to note that play is "a great challenge." Wouldn't pretenses and emotion be difficult to identify in ants even if they existed? So these authors quickly forget about ants and turn their discussion to play in mammals and some birds, where intentional communication is a more promising topic for exploration. Ironically, their chapter ends with a criticism of primatologists who, in their view, are too quick to reject other mammals, such as dogs, as having sufficient cognitive capacity to be intentional, let alone self-aware.

Another problem with attributing play to ants is that it has only been applied to adults, whereas play is often most associated with young or immature animals, at least in birds and mammals. Indeed, the major theories about play in mammals concern the value of play in development and preparation for the serious work of adulthood. Perhaps little in insect life is associated with this developmental role. To assess this with currently available evidence, other groups of insects need to be discussed.

14.2.2 Training Flights in Honeybees

The other major groups of social insects in the Hymenoptera are the bees and wasps. Honeybees (*Apis mellifera*) have been studied more than any other species. In the old literature I could find nothing on play in bees or wasps, but more recent detailed observations by behaviorally sophisticated bee researchers offer some tantalizing hints.

Allen Moore (personal communication, 1998) has seen newly emerged workers, about 3–5 days postemergence, climb to the top of the hive, jump off, flap their wings, float to the ground, and then climb back up and do it again. Other descriptions of "play" flights in bees have also been published, as have descriptions of scouting flights as playful (e.g., Lindauer, 1961). These play flights appear regularly until the bee takes up foraging at about 20 days of age. Although serious discussion of possible play in honeybees will not help one's reputation as a serious scientist,[29] honeybees are not that far-fetched a species to study for playlike locomotor processes. Honeybees engage in various hive-bound and nonflying activities until they begin foraging. In fact, they go through a sequence of roles in which they work as cell cleaners, nurse bees, comb builders, receivers and storers of nectar and pollen, guard bees, and finally foragers. When they adopt the foraging role, the level of muscular effort and spatial orientation skills needed increases manyfold. J. M. Harrison (1986; personal communication, 1998) showed that bees increase their flight capability at the onset of foraging. This increase involves a change in both maximal aerobic capacity and glycogen stores. Whether the increase is due to a training effect or a maturational increase in juvenile hormone is not known. Body mass also decreases at this time. The caste sequence (temporal polyethism) in bees can, however, vary greatly, and foraging can begin at 5 to more than 40 days of age, depending on season or population (Harrison, 1986) or if the number of bees in various castes is altered (e.g., by removing forager bees). Bees engaged in hive duties then accelerate their shift, over a short number of days, to forager status (Seeley, 2001).

14.2.3 Development of Social Fighting in Cockroaches

Termites are the other great radiation of social insects. No one appears to have described anything akin to play in them. Christine Nalepa, an authority on the evolution of sociality in termites (Nalepa, 1994) also informed me that she has never seen or read anything that might be construed as play behavior in termites (Nalepa, personal communication, 1997). In their behavioral, taxonomic, and life history traits, cockroaches represent the best ancestral group for deriving termite eusociality. Could playlike behavior been a source of key behavioral innovations in their sociality?

---

29. I found this out when I gave my first public lecture summarizing the results of my full comparative survey of the literature to a joint neuroscience and psychology audience at the University of Lethbridge in Alberta, Canada, in March 2002. Some audience members were even willing to entertain the idea of play in sharks, but thought I had really lost it when I suggested play in honeybees. My assertion that the entire comparative survey exercise is meant to encourage thinking about the nature of play, and that these observations by excellent scientists deserve a hearing, did not convince them. Yet I believe that bees are in fact one of the best invertebrates to examine for play.

Cockroaches have been around for 300 million years, since the Pennsylvannian or Carboniferous eras. They have not only been very successful in many habitats, but can reach huge densities in environments occupied by humans. Many studies have shown the complexity of their behavior and also their rather advanced cognitive abilities. In foraging studies, individuals have experimentally been shown to remember what food was found in what location and also to use learned visual cues to locate food sources (Durier & Rivault, 2001).

Cockroach development and early instar ("larval") behavior appear to be key traits in the evolutionary origin of termites from a cockroachlike ancestor (Nalepa, 1994). Nalepa (personal communication, 1997) studied wood-feeding cockroaches, *Cryptocercus punctulatus*, a group of roaches closely related to the presumed ancestors of termites. She reported that "two half grown nymphs will square off, scuffle a few moments, and then move on." Australian wood cockroaches (*Shawella couloniana*) are non-territorial and lack dominance hierarchies; they also lack a volatile sex pheromone (Gorton, Colliander, & Bell, 1983). Gorton and co-workers (1983) studied behavioral sequences in paired males and paired females. The scientists assumed that all acts were agonistic, including approaching one another, touching another animal with antennae, and all other actions not seen in paired-sex encounters. They ranked these acts by intensity. What they found was that female-female pairs were overall much more aggressive than male pairs, engaging in high-intensity behavior patterns with serious consequences, such as kicking and biting. Males, on the other hand, were more likely to engage in low- or moderate-intensity behavior patterns, such as touching another male with the antennae, establishing a truce (breaking off the encounter but staying close to each other), jerking (rapid body vibration), and climbing onto the back of the other animal. They interpreted the sex difference as derived from the longer life-span and direct intrasexual competition among females. It would be interesting to see what nymphs do in this species.

Olomon, Breed, & Bell (1976) reported on the ontogeny of fighting in American cockroaches (*Periplaneta americana*). Pairs of females or pairs of males were observed as either adults or early to late instar nymphs. Olomon and colleagues found that nymphs showed lower levels of aggression than adults, and that there was no sex difference until adulthood, when the males were more aggressive than the females. One interpretation that they advanced was that "the ontogenetic development of agonistic behavior may simply be preparation of motor patterns used by adults, analogous to play behavior observed in mammals" (1976: 248). No further testing of this idea seems to have been carried out, but it is telling that the play alternative was advanced almost as a default null hypothesis. It is also interesting that both sexes showed levels of fighting similar to that of nymphs, although the typical male sex bias was found in adulthood.

Another study focused on the development of aggressiveness after the final molt in young adult male *Nauphoeta cinera* cockroaches (Manning & Johnstone, 1970). Males were reared either paired with another newly molted male or in isolation. They were tested daily with a legless male mounted on a handle and his antennae were brushed against the test animal to simulate "fencing" the preliminary response to a normal aggressive sequence, which includes an aggressive curved abdomen posture, charging, butting, and grappling, wrestling-like behavior. All paired males showed the aggressive posture to the stimulus male by the fourth day, but after 12 days half of the isolated animals had not responded at all. Another experiment showed that the daily probe tests themselves had no effect on the developmental rate of isolated males. Remember that in rats, isolated males play fight more than social-reared animals. Of course, the probe male was not a natural partner. Longer contact with the probe, up to three 4-minute probes a day, delayed the onset of aggressive posture even more and many animals appeared stressed and died. On the other hand, young males raised together "show considerable bouts of antennal fencing when paired but this does not lead into the more intense stages of aggressive sequence outlined above" (p. 15). The males did spend much time in quiet contact and perhaps such "non-aggressive contact plays a part in the normal development of aggressiveness" (p. 15).

Given, as recounted in chapter 7, the difficulty that some of Hess's students had in accepting that play occurs in cockroaches (Hess, 1964), it is ironic that these insects may actually show social play, in addition to their well-developed investigatory abilities and parental care. Among the insects, cockroaches are one of the most ancient groups, having changed little since before the dinosaurs. Could features associated with play be responsible for some of their ability to adapt to changing environments for so many millennia?

14.2.4 Peculiar Behavior in a Predaceous Aquatic Insect

What about other nonsocial insects? During the 4 hours after a molt, nymphs of predatory water stick insects (*Ranata linearis*) "perform many particular foreleg claw and femur movements which have never been observed at other times" (Cloarec, 1982: 549). The presence of prey during this period increases the number of movements, but the insects do not capture the prey or direct any behavior at them at all, although general activity is increased. Experiments showed that nymphs need to be stimulated by prey into increasing their foreleg movements during a 4-hour period following a molt if they are to have proficient and accurate prey-striking ability later. This increased proficiency occurs even when the animals are reared with prey in the dark. Light plays a considerably smaller role. This seems to be a case of apparently immediately nonfunctional movements having a long-term effect on the development of an important species-characteristic behavior during a highly restricted ontogenetic period. Cloarec (1982) rightly recognizes that this is a most unusual phenomenon to be found in an insect; she does not, as might be expected, point out the similarity to play or its putative functions.

14.3   Play in Arachnids

It might not be surprising that no reports of play in spiders, most of whom are sedentary ambush foragers, have been reported, even in Groos (1898). Yet, spider play may not be that unexpected, given that these creatures are all carnivores and capture other live animals that are often larger than themselves. There are even spiders that capture fish, frogs, and birds. The variety of insects caught in webs must be diverse and necessitates different techniques for identifying, subduing, and ingesting (or rejecting) them. Constructing webs and wrapping prey are both complex skills. Certainly much of this behavior is unlearned, but experience during development may play a role and this has rarely been looked at. Indeed, cognitive capacities in spiders have been almost totally ignored. One exception, and the only one I will discuss, is the work of Wilcox and colleagues, who have demonstrated some complex strategies and learning abilities in spider behavior, in which some playlike elements may reside.

Portia is a small genus of jumping spiders (fifteen species) that eat other spiders. These spiders have two large central eyes that provide resolution unique in animals this small (R. R. Jackson & Wilcox, 1998) as well as other eyes on the side of the head that detect motion. They can distinguish among spiders, egg sacs, live insects, wrapped insects, and other stimuli, including the sex of conspecifics. In approaching potential prey spiders on their webs, a portia uses wind disturbances to the web as a smoke screen to get in closer to the spider and kill it (Wilcox, Jackson, & Gentile, 1996). These spiders also resemble detritus and thus camouflaged, capture unwary spiders by perching at the edge of a web.

More remarkable is their ability to invade another spider's web by sending vibratory signals through the web that mimic the signals created by insects captured in the web. These signals lure the resident of the web toward the stimulus, and the spider is then captured. The portia may have a preprogrammed tactic in which specific signals are used for hunting particular species of spiders. But sometimes a portia does not know the signal used by the species of spider it has targeted and so it begins to send out a range of signals. When it finds one that begins to attract the spider, the portia begins to repeat the successful signal and drops the others from the repertoire. It also learns to use different signals for different "caught insects" (R. R. Jackson & Wilcox, 1993b). Thus the portia is using a type of aggressive mimicry, a form of deception (pretense) in which an animal appears to be something other than it is in order to capture prey. It is the way in which this spider generates the almost limitless array of signals that is impressive. It can move several appendages in different ways almost independently and pluck, slap, and otherwise manipulate the web to produce signals; it can also flick its abdomen in concert with the appendages.

Another ability of the spider is to use visual cues to determine the appropriate detour path. Some prey spiders are just too wary to be captured in the normal way, and so the portia has to climb above the web and drop down on a line of silk, capturing the unaware spider from above. Experiments show that the spider makes this assessment ("planning ahead") and will even move a considerable distance away from the target web in order to reach the best position for jumping (R. R. Jackson & Wilcox, 1993a). The development of behavior has not been systematically examined in these spiders, and no mention of play is found in the reports. All the behavior engaged in is in dead earnest, including courtship, in which females attempt to kill unfavored males before mating, or favored males after mating. In closing a comprehensive review on the behavior of these remarkable animals, Wilcox and Jackson write:

When we began research on *Portia*, few thoughts would have seemed more foreign to us than that one day we would seriously be discussing cognition in a spider. Yet over and over again, *Portia* has defied the popular image of spiders as simple animals with rigid behavior. One of the challenges of this work has now become to clarify where the limits lie in *Portia*'s cognitive ability, but the greater challenge is to understand how it is that an animal with so little in the way of brain can nevertheless do so much. (1998: 428)

Outside of the varying of the vibratory signals, it is hard to see any role for play here, but the evolution of these remarkable abilities had to have its origin in some causal mechanisms producing novel behavior. It could also be that in the early life of these animals they go through a stage in which one sees some of these behaviors in a play-like guise, even if, like the stick insect, they do not shape the specific behavior patterns expressed by adults. But do consider this: While adult females try to balance treating adult males as both mate and meal, late juvenile females, who do not mate, nevertheless attract males and will capture and eat them. Could this play a role in successfully incorporating mating into a dining experience?

14.4   Play in Crustaceans

14.4.1   Play in Crabs

The example of object play in crabs cited by E. P. Thompson (1851) has not been replicated to my knowledge, although a noted fiddler crab biologist has seen some playlike elements toward objects by these animals (Crane, 1975; J. Crane Griffin, personal communication, 1998). In a section of her opus on fiddler crabs, Jocelyn Crane has a section on unusual behavior in the chapter on social behavior (Crane, 1975: 506–507). She quotes an early fiddler crab researcher's description of male behavior, which I have excerpted here from the original source.

Some of the activities of the fiddlers were like those displayed by higher animals while at play. The crabs frequently darted about apparently without a serious purpose, and were sometimes downright mischievious. On one occasion a male was half-heartedly pursuing a female. She went to her burrow, secured a plug nearby, and shut herself in. The male then came directly to the burrow, seized the plug, and cast it to one side.... Another time, two males (an *Uca marionisnitida* and *U. forcipata*) of medium size were seen running about for perhaps half an hour over an area about 12 m in diameter. They kept close together and acted like two mischievous sailors ashore. The tide was coming in rapidly, and in their rambles the pair came to a place where a large slow-moving *U. forcipata* was carrying a plug to close his burrow. They waited until the plug had been pulled down over its owner, then the *U. forcipata* went to the hole and removed it; and as the outraged owner emerged, the plug remover and his mate scuttled off toward the former's burrow some 4.5 meters away.... To all appearances activities such as these were carried out in a spirit of sport. (Pearse, 1912: 2)

Crane (1975) notes that such destructive behavior is characteristic of aggressive wandering males. While noting the anthropomorphic nature of the comments, she also records several examples of males going over to animals with newly made shelters or hoods for their burrows and tearing them down and even seizing and wrestling with the owner. She also recounts an additional example of an adult male tearing down the hood of another animal. As she adds in a letter: "Perhaps, as Pearse suggested, this rare variable behavior, with the large aggressive component, is one of Play's antecedents. If so, fiddlers surely play rough" (J. Crane Griffin, personal communication, 1998). These examples from experts on fiddler crabs in the wild (Philippines, Panama, Sri Lanka) are certainly interesting. However, the rarity of descriptions of these behavior patterns in species that have been observed for thousands of hours in the field argues against play being part of fiddlers' typical behavioral repertoire, as social play turns out to be in rodents and monkeys. It is also easy to be uncritically anthropomophic about animals so different from us. Still, these crabs are active and successful, and playlike activity might have had a role in the remarkable ritualization of their communicative displays.

14.4.2 Object Play in Mantis Shrimp

The crab examples are, admittedly, not overly convincing. This next example may be more so. Stomatopods (mantis shrimp), another crustacean, have as adults a very active and complex predatory repertoire in which they pound open shelled mollusks with their hammerlike claws. They do this with a wide range of natural and artificial stimuli. An authority on stomatopod behavior, Roy Caldwell (personal communication, November 1997), has unpublished studies showing that stomatopods can easily learn to discriminate stimuli and improve their feeding efficiency when given novel prey with a new type of snail shell morphology. They become more proficient at learning where to strike shells, as well as glass cubes, to most easily break them. Although Caldwell initially wrote that he had not seen anything he would call play, he pointed out that the shrimps do test things. Later he elaborated (Caldwell, personal communication, December 1997). Stomatopods may test objects by rotating them with their mouth parts, striking at them weakly, and even holding objects and apparently peering at them (stomatopods have remarkable eyestalks). Caldwell also reported that stomatopods will "play" with floating corks by trying to pull them down. He wrote "I get the impression that while they are originally trying to obtain food, that the 'resistance' that the cork puts up continues attack and investigatory behavior." He also noted that stomatopods "will occasionally 'rearrange' their entire tank, moving rocks around, etc. Again, I view this as construction of dens, but sometimes they almost seem bored and just start manipulating things." Clearly, these are remarkably complex invertebrates that readily discriminate individual conspecifics, feed on diverse and difficult prey, and spatially navigate a complex undersea environment (e.g., Caldwell, 1985). A close observation of their behavioral development might uncover even more playlike behavior.

14.4.3   Object Manipulation in Lobsters

A final example of crustacean behavior involves research on one of the largest crustaceans, the American lobster (*Homarus americanus*). Here a role for natural playlike processes shows up in an interesting context: the development of asymmetries in claws (Govind, 1989).

One of the most noticeable features of lobsters, crawfish, and crabs is that one claw is usually much larger than the other. In fiddler crabs the large claw is used in communication through species-specific waving patterns and the small one for grooming and feeding (Crane, 1975). Lobsters also have bilateral asymmetry in which one claw, called a crusher, is wide but short, and the other, called a cutter, is narrow and long. The latter has many sharp "teeth" and can snap closed in 20 ms, faster than the human reflex. The crusher has more massive muscles and closes more slowly, but with enough force to crack open clam and oyster shells. The two claws have different types of muscles, with the cutter having the "fast" type.

Lobsters are not born asymmetrical; the claws do not begin to differentiate until the fourth larval stage, when both gain a cutterlike appearance. It is not until the sixth stage, well into the juvenile period, that one claw begins the transition to the crusher morphology and muscle physiology. The crusher can develop on either the right or left side and equal numbers of either type are typically found. All this might seem remote from the topic of this book except that in a series of elegant experiments, it has been demonstrated that experiences during the juvenile period play a critical role in whether any claw becomes a crusher and which claw becomes a crusher (Govind, 1989).

Govind's (1989) paper is a fine example of scientific detective work that suggests that the role of playlike processes may be functionally much more common in invertebrates than our conception of them allows. First, if juvenile lobsters were reared on oyster shell substrates that they could manipulate (but did not ingest), they developed the typical asymmetry, with equal numbers of right- and left-handed lobsters. If they were reared in tanks with nothing to manipulate, the lobsters developed two cutter claws and no crushers at all. Second, the asymmetry derived from manipulating oyster shells was not due to anything specific to oyster shells (oyster being natural prey), because raising lobsters on manipulable plastic shirt buttons instead of pieces of shell had the same effect. Third, painting shell-like spots on the bottom and sides of the rearing tanks had no effect; all the lobsters reared in such conditions had two cutter claws. In all these experiments, lobsters were reared in social isolation because they are very aggressive toward one another. Fourth, two lobsters reared together with no substrate (buttons or oysters) fought with their claws and one usually lost a claw. The lobster keeping both claws developed both a crusher and a cutter. Fifth, providing a mirror instead of a conspecific had no effect since the animals rarely interacted with the image and thus visual cues alone were eliminated as important determinants of the development of asymmetry. Sixth, two crusher claws were never produced in the laboratory.

The researchers then tested additional hypotheses experimentally and got some perplexing results. When isolated lobsters were reared with oyster shells, but one claw was unable to manipulate the shells, or sensory input to it was reduced, no effect was found on which claw became the crusher. Thus it was not simple use of the claws that led to the asymmetry. Perhaps it was muscle activity itself. A series of fairly complex experiments were performed supporting the following interpretation: "In nature, as in the laboratory, initial use or contact of one claw with a substrate sets in motion an increasingly greater activity on that side. The greater neural input of that side determines, in the central nervous system, its fate as a crusher and at the same time inhibits the opposite side from ever becoming a crusher.... While the critical period for development of lobster claws is genetically fixed, the actual trigger is experience. It is possible that the development of lobster claws is an example of an innate program that is followed unless modified by experience" (Govind, 1989: 473).

Govind (1989) argues that the lobster could be a good model for studying the development of asymmetries, such as lateralization in the human brain. The way in which experience works in these invertebrate systems may provide more reliable and clear models for determining the role of experiential processes in behavioral development than many of those based on vertebrates. Lobsters are large, long-lived, and active predators, and the use of the claws in actual feeding may also involve predatory play-like behavior. In addition, the role of chance in determining a major morphological structural rearrangement in lobsters may give support to those who see play as either random or chaotic behavior, or more likely, it may challenge their conceptions of how such randomness or deterministic chaotic processes operate.

14.5   Play in Cephalopods

Cephalopods are behaviorally complex, large-brained invertebrates living a completely aquatic existence (Hanlon & Messenger, 1996). Although they are mollusks and related to clams and oysters, cephalopods, except for the nautilus, are in the subclass Coleoidea. Consisting of squid, octopods, and cuttlefish, this group includes the largest invertebrate known, the enigmatic giant squid. Cephalopods are active predators living in most regions and depths of the oceans. They have been viewed as invertebrates converging on fish in many aspects of their morphology, behavior, ecology, and physiology (Hanlon & Messenger, 1996), although they are relatively less successful (700 species versus more than 30,000). Unlike fish, however, cephalopods have short life-spans, rarely living more than 2 years. It is interesting that the major cephalopod radiation began in the Mesozoic era in the Jurassic period, as is true of teleost fish (Hanlon & Messenger, 1996). Still, the two lineages are today separated by more than a billion years.

Just as brain size differs among fish, it also differs among cephalopods. Still, in cephalopods brain size as a function of body size has a larger ratio than any other invertebrate group; it is generally in the fish and reptile range or above, but not quite into the bird or mammal range. Squid and cuttlefish have somehat larger brains than octopods, based on a small sample (Hanlon & Messenger, 1996). The rest of this section is devoted, however, to research on several octopus species.

Individual octopuses in captivity vary in temperament and even have individual personalities (Mather & Anderson, 1993). They build shelters and even use tools (Mather, 1982, 1994). One would expect that if any invertebrate would play it might be an octopus, since they are active predators, can perform many complex movements with their eight limbs, and live in an environment (salt water) where the costs of locomotion can be low. Many learning studies have been carried out on cephalopods (review in Mather, 1995), and these animals can readily learn many discriminations using visual and tactile stimuli. It is even claimed that octopuses can learn observationally from experiences of other conspecifics (Fiorito & Scotto, 1992). Although cephalopod behavior has been extensively studied in captivity, in the past play was not reported for any species of cephalopod (Hanlon & Messenger, 1996; M. J. Wells, 1978). However, their lack of both an external or internal skeleton makes it difficult to describe regularities in even normal behavior (Mather, 1998).

The comments by Caldwell in section 14.5.2 that describe stomatopods playing with corks and rearranging their cage décor also apply to octopuses (Wood & Wood, 1999). However, recent systematic study strongly suggests that octopuses can engage in object play. Mather and Anderson (1999) presented eight individually housed octopuses (*Octopus doefleini*) with sealed, partially filled, small plastic bottles that floated at the surface of their aquarium. Each tank had an 8 liter/minute inflow of water in one corner. The "toys" were painted white or black with smooth or gritty paint. These modifications were incorporated because octopuses have excellent (noncolor) vision, and tactile cues are very important. The toys were presented in a systematically rotated design, two per day for 5 days. The initial exploratory responses were differentiated from later repeated manipulatory responses that were called play using four criteria. These were that the responses had to (1) be different from the initial actions toward the objects, (2) involve some manipulation of the objects, (3) occur for at least 5 minutes, and (4) incorporate repeated instances of similar behavior.

Most of the animals responded initially by capturing and exploring the objects with an arm. Later behavior was considered playful. This included repeatedly aiming jets of water at the toy (squirting). The octopuses used their funnel to move objects. Two octopuses developed a "bouncing ball" routine. They would direct their jets at a toy and push it back to the inflow, where it was pushed back to the center, at which time the octopus again jetted it back to the inflow. One octopus observed a bottle bobbing around near the inflow for 4 minutes before starting the game and another one watched for 1 minute. These were the only two octopuses that fulfilled all four play criteria used by Mather and Anderson.

In a study with the more active and agile *Octopus vulgaris*, Michael Kuba and colleagues at the Konrad Lorenz Institute in Vienna presented animals with either live prey, a bottle on a string, or a red and white Lego block at three different food deprivation levels (Kuba et al., 2003). The Lego block was the preferred "toy" and was manipulated and carried around by some animals. If the animals were food deprived, contacts were mostly predatory but if the animals had recently been fed, the interactions were both exploratory and playful as based on the five play criteria (figure 14.2). Extensive further analyses are available (Kuba, 2004).

Other examples are available. *Octopus briareus* would repeatedly grab a hydrometer floating in her tank, pull it down, release it, and watch it shoot up to the surface (Wood & Wood, 1999). She would also hold onto the side of the tank and cover the air inlet with her body, fill her web with air, and float to the surface repeatedly. As the authors stated: "If these behaviors occurred in a vertebrate they surely would be called 'play'" (p. 2).

Finally we appear to have an example of object play in an invertebrate that seems similar to that found in vertebrates. Octopuses, with their complex brain and sensory and behavioral repertoire, seem to have reached the point where, in the fine captive settings we can now provide, they can exhibit some evidence of play (figure 14.1). There is also some evidence that other mollusks "play." Several people have mentioned to me aquatic snails in aquaria that fill their shells with air, float to the top, release the bubbles, sink, and repeat the activity.

14.6 Is Any of This Really Play?

It is time to judge the invertebrate behavior discussed here by the five criteria for identifying behavior patterns as candidates for play. As before, all five must be met in at least one respect before the play label can be attached. First I readily admit that most

Figure 14.1
Play in an invertebrate—an octopus interacting with a Lego block. (Photo by Michael Kuba)

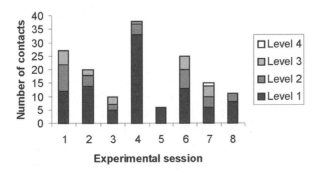

Figure 14.2
Representative example of behavior levels shown by an octopus given eight sessions with an object, either a bottle or plastic block, 30 minutes after being fed. Level 3 and 4 interactions represent repeated interactions meeting the five play criteria. (From Kuba et al., 2003).

of the reports are anecdotal, sometimes ancient, and, with the exception of the octopus, not yet available on film or video tape for independent appraisal. No experiments have been performed to elucidate the ways in which the criteria are met. That being said, let us look at the criteria (table 14.1) as they apply to the major examples discussed in this chapter.

1. Limited immediate adaptive significance   This was evident to all the observers in all examples. But if a proximate function can be shown, then the criterion is not met; a plausible adaptive function should also give pause. This is the point made by Hölldobler & Wilson (1990). The ants were involved in intercolony aggression. One might ask how this interpretation was missed by other astute observers. Perhaps uncritical anthropomorphism was characteristic of the nineteenth century and we know better now. Curiously, however, Groos, Bückner, and other nineteenth-century writers claimed that the ant play theory was not widely accepted, even then. Since the intergroup competition theory was not yet advanced, one wonders on what basis others rejected the play interpretation 100 years ago. It was not due to criterion one. Perhaps it was the inability to apply the anthropomorphic criteria that many of us may be employing when we confidently assert that many mammals do play.

2. Has an endogenous (pleasurable, autotelic) component   This seems to be the case for all examples except for the play fighting category. The grooming seen by Bates (1864) on warm, relaxed days could be the maintenance behavior that is often inhibited by more pressing matters. This in and of itself would not seem to prove playfulness.

3. Structurally or temporally different from ethotypic source behavior   This may have been the case in the crab with stones, octopods, and the play fighting in cockroaches and ants.

4. Repeatability   Except for the octopods, we have no clear information on how often the behavior occurred, e.g., in bouts or singly.

5. Occurs in a relaxed field   This apparently holds in most cases, but information is limited.

14.7   Nowhere to Go But . . .

This chapter provides a tantalizing glimpse of play in invertebrates, a group separated from vertebrates by perhaps as much as 1.2 billion years (Wray, Levinton, & Shapiro, 1996). Applied to an evolutionary tree, the distribution of putative play in invertebrates is spotty and disjunct, although it is more common in those groups considered the most complex in morphology and behavior (figure 14.3). Unless homeobox genes are identified showing that play genes are carried by species that do not play, the view that play is homologous is not tenable. Spinka, Newberry, and Bekoff (2001) argue that unless play is viewed as evolutionarily homologous, it is useless to study it as a general phenomenon. If this is true, then a discussion of the diverse phenomena described

Table 14.1
Application of the play criteria to reports of play in invertebrates

Species	Play Type	Incompletely Functional	Voluntary	Structural or Temporal Modification	Repeated	Relaxed Field
Ants	Play fighting	?	?	?	Yes	Yes?
Ants	Social, amiable	?	Yes	?	?	Yes
Honeybees	Locomotor	Yes	Yes	Yes	Yes	Yes?
Cockroaches	Play fighting	Yes	Yes	Yes	Yes	?
Water stick insects	Sensorimotor	Yes?	Yes	Yes	Yes	Yes?
Fiddler crabs	Object	?	Yes	?	Yes	?
Stomatopods	Object	Yes	Yes	?	Yes	Yes?
Lobsters	Sensorimotor	?	Yes	Yes?	Yes	Yes?
Octopods	Object	Yes	Yes	Yes	Yes	Yes

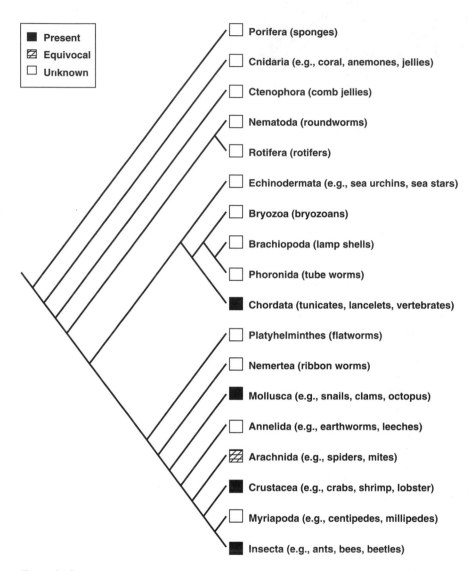

Figure 14.3
Phylogeny of major animal groups, noting evidence of play.

here, which most certainly have different causal, developmental, functional, and phylogenetic roots, has no purpose. But differences are as important as similarities, and they are informative.

The occurrence of play in invertebrates that firmly meets all five criteria is not yet established with confidence in species other than the octopuses. It should be possible to gather data, including video tapes, on a series of invertebrate species and settings in both the field and captivity to reach a definitive conclusion by applying the five criteria rigorously with sufficient natural history information. While the "ants do not play" assertion of Hölldobler and Wilson (1990) cannot be definitively disproved, neither should it be uncritically accepted at this time.

The study of octopus object play by experienced students of cephalopod behavior is so far the most convincing evidence we have for play in invertebrates. If these findings are valid, then the roots of the biological ability to evolve and perform playful acts go back over a billion years! In one solid example, we have doubled the ancestry of playful species.

This chapter concludes our meanderings along the evolutionary paths of diverse animals. Play is a genuinely heterogeneous phenomenon in almost every way, including its repeated evolution. This has to humble those of us in the twenty-first century who confidently disparage the romantic enthusiasms of the nineteenth century.

15   The Legacy and Future of Play

15.1   Conclusions from the Journey

This evolutionary trek has shown that diverse phenomena in an extensive series of animals can be considered play. Regardless of the quality of the information available for any given example outside mammals, the comparative data demand attention. Anyone interested in understanding play in specific taxa—such as human beings, monkeys, rats, dogs, or ravens—needs to be aware that common assumptions about play are often misleading and claims for the role of play are often suspect. In this final chapter some ideas lingering in the phylogenetic shadows are partially exposed.

Play is often viewed as a mystery, perhaps because it is full of paradoxes that do not allow the straightforward analyses scientists prefer. We still do not know how much play reflects atavistic remnants of instinctive behavior, how play is guided by specific internal (emotional and motivational) and environmental factors, and what kinds of playlike behavior are based on specific processes in the brain. We do not know how much play, or what kind of play, is useful, even essential, for proper development and maintenance of behavioral and psychological integrity. This volume makes no pretense at having resolved these issues; rather the aim has been to draw attention to them and the importance of an evolutionary, comparative perspective. An additional aim has been to provide integrative proposals that seem plausible at this stage of our knowledge, a process continued even more provocatively in this final chapter. Most important, this book will have served its purpose if it has convincingly demonstrated that a thorough comparative survey is an essential first step in understanding the genesis of play and its place in the evolutionary process as well as in the lives of individual animals and species.

Despite the caveats, we do know quite a bit about play, and I have drawn numerous general conclusions about play and its many variants in this book. I will list some of them here before touching on some final phenomena and paradoxes that need to be addressed in any view of play that claims to be both general and comprehensive. The following conclusions, while they are based on different levels of analysis, reflect the five ethological aims discussed in chapters 1 and 5. These conclusions might, should, and most certainly will be disputed and tested in the future; they are presented here in broad strokes before the more speculative turns in future research paths are briefly noted.

1. Play behavior is recognized by five criteria. Playful activities can be characterized as being (1) incompletely functional in the context expressed; (2) voluntary, pleasurable, or self rewarding; (3) different structurally or temporally from related serious behavior systems; (4) expressed repeatedly during at least some part of an animal's life span; and (5) initiated in relatively benign situations.

2. Play is a heterogeneous category and different types of play have their own phylogenetic and developmental trajectories.

3. The comparative evidence shows that play is not limited to some or even all placental mammals, but is found in a wide range of animals, including marsupials, birds, turtles, lizards, fish, and invertebrates.

4. Animals that play often share common traits, including active life styles, moderate to high metabolic rates, generalist ecological needs requiring behavioral flexibility or plasticity, and adequate to abundant food resources. Object play is most often found in species with carnivorous, omnivorous, or scavenging foraging modes. Locomotor play is prominent in species that navigate in three-dimensional (e.g., trees, water) or complex environments and rely on escape to avoid predation. Social play is not easily summarized, but play fighting, chasing, and wrestling are the major types recorded and occur in almost every major group of animals in which play is found.

5. Play may be arranged along a continuum so that much play may have no important evolved adaptive function (primary process play), while other types of play may have secondarily evolved important roles in maintaining or developing and enhancing behavioral performance and cognitive and emotional well-being. Demonstrating such roles, however, has been fraught with difficulties.

6. The genesis of play lies in primary process play with few, if any, immediate adaptive consequences. Such playlike behavior may then be favored by natural selection and eventually become adaptive, even essential, and incorporated into the behavioral repertoire. Play may also represent the precocious maturation of behavior before it is required for survival. Rich and complex play repertoires were facilitated by the evolution of parental care. Much play may be derived from juvenile instinctive behavior that is no longer honed by natural selection operating on its original precocial form and thus is open to neural and behavioral reorganization.

7. Play originally arose from proximate processes such as instinctive behavior and associated neural organization, and the performance of playful acts may be rewarding (autotelic) regardless of their adaptiveness or function. Thus play may be derived from, as well as incorporated into, many different behavior systems. The emotional aspects of play found so compelling are typically found in social animals or those from a highly social ancestry.

8. The evidence for the functional role of play is limited and consequently play has not entered the mainstream of behavioral research in biology, psychology, or the social sciences. The proponents of play in people too often operate on faith in the power of play, supported by anecdotal and correlational studies, rather than empirical evidence of its efficacy, except in very narrow contexts. The limited data supporting the efficacy of play may have actually held back wider acceptance of play as an important scientific phenomenon. However, play may be an important component in our understanding of human behavior. It may help explain aggression, war, morality, sex (including gender differences, courtship, sex roles), drug use and risky thrill-seeking behavior, educational endeavors, cultural achievements, creativity in virtually all realms, economic development, social class differences, and even the rise and fall of civilizations.

9. The brain mechanisms underlying play are diverse. The neural substrates of play in vertebrates have their origin in structures in the basal ganglia of the forebrain, the cerebellum, and may involve projections to the limbic system (affect) and cortex, especially the premotor and prefrontal areas (context assessment and performance skill). Midbrain structures (e.g., thalamus and hypothalamus) are sources of the sensory and motivational processes that underlie behavioral performance in play. Neurotransmitters (such as dopamine and opioids) and hormones also have influences on play that are still poorly understood, but undoubtedly important.

10. Our understanding of play will only be enhanced when its study is embedded in the normal lives of animals and looked at from a phylogenetic perspective. Experimental and neuroscience studies of play in a few model species can identify some mechanisms and developmental processes, but they will never be able to solve the conundrums of play in isolation from evolutionary processes.

11. Play is a crucial test for the power of science to understand "mysteries," and its effective study requires integrative and interdisciplinary work by the best scientific minds as well as intensely focused research by specialists.

It is now time to revisit and extend some of these conclusions, and point to future directions.

15.2 Play and the Evolutionary Process

The survey of play in diverse animals and the resulting phylogenetic trees show that it is a diverse phenomenon that evolved independently and was even secondarily reduced or lost in many groups of animals (figure 15.1). A phylogeny of the major animal groups shows that the craniate vertebrate (backboned) animals and invertebrates have long and separate lineages with many branches. Although major changes in our current understanding of the evolutionary relationships among animal groups may still occur (Zardoya & Meyer, 2004), it is unlikely that they will dramatically alter the broad comparative conclusions drawn here. Only in animals with several life history,

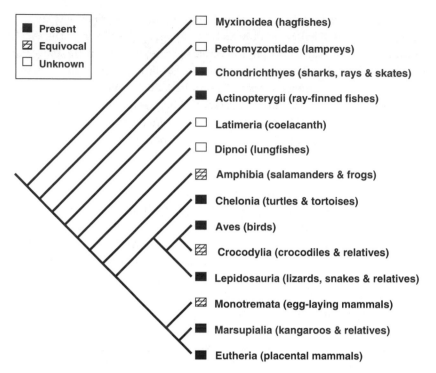

Figure 15.1
Phylogeny of all major vertebrate animal groups, noting evidence of play.

ecological, and physiological attributes did play appear, become prominent, and evolve complex forms. Important adaptive roles for play are thus derived and perhaps evolved in tandem with putative "plasticity genes" (Pigliucci, 2001). The independent evolution of wings in birds and insects, eyes in vertebrates and invertebrates, and other convergent or homoplastic processes served as the model for the evolution of such heterogeneity. However, the story may become even more complex.

The field of molecular genetics has begun to pay attention to the interaction of specific genes with developmental and life history processes in the expression of many traits of animals. Underlying the grand biological diversity in the world is a surprisingly conservative genetic toolkit (Carroll, Grenier, & Weatherbee, 2001). Traits that were thought to have arisen completely independently in animals separated by hundreds of millions of years, such as eyes in flies and mice, are controlled by similar genes; introducing the corresponding mouse gene into a fly induces compound eye tissue, not mouse-type eye tissue. Thus although play arose many times in evolution, it may have been the result of common environmental contexts that activated a suite of retained homeotic hox genes which, although they may have other functions, could be repeatedly co-opted in the service of playlike traits. With a conserved and widely shared genome available, play, as surplus resource theory posits, could then readily appear whenever physiological (including neural), life history, energetic, ecological, and psychological conditions, in conjunction with a species' behavioral repertoire, reached a threshold level to activate genetic processes. An important task for the future is to tease apart these conditions, including the genes, and rigorously evaluate their contribution to both the origins and elaboration of play, as is currently being advocated in the study of attention deficit hyperactivity disorder (ADHD) (Stokstad, 2003). This should be done in conjunction with studies of gene activity, particularly of the neural structures underlying the behavior patterns involved in play.

What is needed first, however, is to isolate those factors that seem to have facilitated the appearance of primary process, or incipient play, and test them across the different radiations in which play has appeared. The aim is to specify with some predictability the taxa in which play appears by presenting models that integrate much of the comparative material related to the origins of play and generate predictions. This is one important role of SRT and any other conceptual framework. Unfortunately, a simple quantitative model such as those prominent in current behavioral ecology (Dugatkin, 2001) will not be generally applicable. However, the growing amount of quantitative data on play in some groups should make such models useful and actually predictive, something not possible in the past.

15.3 Play: Beyond Fun and Games

Pre-nineteenth-century views of play and recreation, including those of Burton (1883) and the Puritans (Mergen, 1982), emphasized its dangerous aspects and evils, including gambling, sex, and idleness. Play can have certain downsides, such as animals engaging in activities that put themselves at risk or expending energy that they might be better off preserving or shunting to other activities. The costs of play, as discussed in chapter 5, are often used to support its benefits. Generally, however, the costs of play are rarely mentioned in books and tracts promoting play in humans, but these should not be neglected.

15.3.1 Play Can Be Cruel
Charles Darwin, in a letter to Asa Gray in 1860 (Darwin, 1888: 105), commented on cats playing with mice; he mentioned the apparent cruelty (to the mice) of such play and compared this to the apparent cruelty of wasp larvae feeding on the living bodies of caterpillars. Together these were actions that Darwin could not envision that a "beneficent and omnipotent God would have designedly created." In short, play was a phenomenon that fueled, or at least supported, his rejection of divine creation. In chapter 2 a story was recounted of a magpie playfully stoning a toad.

As established earlier, play with objects is behavior in which an animal investigates not just their nature (food, danger, nest material) but what he or she can *do* with them. Novelty, complexity, and unpredictability are factors in the amount and type of interactions seen in object play and may be related to any learning that takes place. This has often been discussed in infant play (Berk, 1996; Frost, Wortham, & Reifel, 2001; Garvey, 1990; Johnson, Christie, & Yawkey, 1999). Much animal play with objects is destructive of the object; animals can play rough and toys for pets and exotic zoo animals are thus made of much more indestructible materials than comparable objects for children.

Object play in many species is often derived from feeding or predatory play, as noted in the above examples. Infants and toddlers often engage in mouthing, chewing, pulling apart, and generally manipulating objects in a way that could be dangerous to them but is rarely viewed as cruel. What appears to be cruel to us is how the prey is treated in predatory play and the apparent fascination of the player in inflicting such cruelty. Adults typically recoil at children who play cruelly with animals, from pulling off wings of flies to hitting kittens or throwing stones at dogs. However, "cruelty" to inanimate objects does not lead to such disapproval at the ethical level unless valued objects such as artworks are the target. Concern about cruelty to animals stems from notions about destruction of a living creature. Few people are probably concerned about the real pain suffered by flies, but are concerned about the disregard for life such behavior indicates, a disregard that could be expressed later in socially destructive ways.

What motivates many animal welfare and animal rights proponents is that current practices create conflicting messages about how we treat animals (Burghardt & Herzog, 1980). Why is putting a live worm, cricket, or bait fish on a barbed hook acceptable, but not dewinging a fly? Why is dropping a large lobster into boiling water acceptable to many seafood lovers, but microwaving a live animal abhorrent? Why should laws in the United States mandate that laboratory research dogs have room to exercise and monkeys have psychological enrichment at the same time other current U.S. laws permit pigs and chickens to be maintained on factory farms in spaces so small that often they cannot even turn around or stand up to their full height? Is it the accepted human use that allows these differences? Regardless, cruel animal play can degenerate to dowsing cats with kerosene and igniting them for "fun." Such occurrences of cruel play, as well as deficits in appropriate social play with other children, have been found to be very high in retrospective biographies of criminals in jail for abuse, murder, and other violent crimes (S. Brown, 1998).

Cruel play with objects or other species may link diversive exploration (sensu Berlyne, 1960) and social exploratory play, in which animals test their social environment and presumably learn about it. What looks like playful quasi-aggression (teasing) may follow patterns similar to those of object play and thus tie the two phenomena together. These ideas were tested in chimpanzees at the Arnhem Zoo in the Netherlands (Adang, 1985). Here young chimps harassed other chimps by hitting them or throwing sand and sticks at them. Both young male and young female chimps directed these hostile "play" reactions to adult females and the adults responded in varying and unpredictable ways. If a target female responded aggressively, the youngsters prolonged the bout, in contrast to situations in which the female ignored the behavior. Adang considered this phenomenon "uncertainty reduction."

When young males directed such behavior to adult males, however, the latter often responded with considerable "bluff" rage and the youngsters responded with more submission and withdrawal. It is interesting that adult male responses were more predictable and bouts were shorter; indeed, 70 percent of the time, adult males ignored the youngsters' provocations. Adang considered this phenomenon "investigating authority." Thus what appears to be harassment of an adult may be a derived play process. In this case, the harassment was of a dominant or adult animal, and not the cruelty often playfully perpetrated on smaller, younger, or lower-ranked conspecifics that in our own species we call bullying. In a subsequent paper Adang (1986) studied the development of this "teasing" in chimpanzees and called for comparative studies in human children.

Human play can be cruel to the victim, even if that is not the perpetrators' intent. Richard Wagner's opus *The Ring of the Nibelungen* is one of the major mythological creative works of western civilization. It tells the story of the Norse gods using myths from the pre-Christian era. These are integrated into a major musical drama, a series of four operas[30] totaling 15 hours in performance. The plot centers on the Rhine gold, a treasure horde kept in a crevice in a rock in the middle of the Rhine River and guarded by the Rhine maidens.

The opera opens with the two of the Rhine maidens, Woglinde and Wellgunde, "teasing and playing, they chase each other" (Wagner in libretto book, p. 27). A third maiden, Flosshilde, warns her sisters that their job is to watch over the Rhine gold, not to play. But eventually she too joins in the game: "They dart about like fish from reef to reef, joking and laughing." Into this gay scene Albrecht, an ugly dwarf, intrudes from the netherworld. He observes their play with pleasure and then infatuation. When he is spotted by the Rhine maidens, they are initially spooked and circle the rock containing the treasure in order to protect it. But, seeing his infatuation, they conclude he is harmless and decide to play a chase game with him. They are nimble and he is awkward. Albrecht repeatedly lunges at them and always misses, falling or toppling as the sisters escape with "squeals of laughter" and become ever crueler. Albrecht becomes increasingly frustrated, then filled with rage when he realizes that the sisters are making a fool of him. Just at that point the rays of the rising sun penetrate the waters and illuminate the gold, and "a magical gold light suffuses the water."

---

30. *Das Rheingold, Die Walküre, Siegfried, Die Götterdämmerung* (Twilight of the Gods).

The maidens, rejoicing at the sight of the glimmering gold, carelessly reveal the treasure's secret: whoever possesses the gold and fashions it into a ring will have unlimited power. In exchange for the power, however, the capability of knowing love must be relinquished forever. For Albrecht, aware of his ugliness and steaming mad at the maidens, this is no big sacrifice. He steals the gold at an opportune moment and escapes with it to the deep netherworld. Thus is set in motion the complex series of events that lead to the destruction of the gods themselves in the final opera in the series, *The Twilight of the Gods*.

Here play has an awful consequence. Play is not something to be played with! Obviously this work of art is just a story and a myth at that. But what makes all good literature endure is that it captures some essential truths that resonate yet today and confirm Darwin's concerns with which this section opened.

When predators kill many more prey than can be eaten or stored, elements of play may be involved. Thus foxes and other predators may engage in "surplus killing" of chickens in a henhouse, something most people view as both cruel and wasteful (Short, Kinnear, & Robley, 2002). Why? There may be both external and internal processes at work. All the confined prey present an overload of stimulation that can trigger the end, consummatory, stages of the predatory behavior system independent of the hunger level and nutritional needs of the predator. Yet, unlike typical predatory object play, the rich stimulation triggers drive surplus motivational reserves (Leyhausen, 1979) that override the typical killing inhibitions characteristic of most play. This may be especially true if animals have been deprived of performing the final stages of species-typical behavior systems. Nonetheless, such slaughter may be playful from the perspective of the predator in the absence of strong learned inhibitions. Rats reared in social isolation become much more aggressive, and socially incompetent, in social interactions. Bullying on playgrounds may be a social counterpart to surplus killing in that certain types of children are often selected out for targets of aggression. The temptation to exert power in what often seems to be a perversion of playfulness on the part of the perpetrator has been divorced from social inhibitions for some children. But bullies do not always outgrow their predilections and circumstances may create them.

Mistreatment of prisoners by guards may be comparable phenomena. From biblical times to the present, many soliders have exploited opportunities to kill, torture, rape, and humiliate captive or defenseless populations. Classifying them as enemies, criminals, liars, or subhuman serves to remove any inhibitions against performing otherwise outrageous acts by significant numbers of any human population, especially when such activities are implicitly, if not explicitly, condoned by leaders. Modern technology can now document the mirth, glee, and short-term satisfactions accompanying this reprehensible behavior. Such activities afflict the armed forces of even those countries that confidently assert their morality, benevolent intentions, and rightness with God and are especially unfortunate when both sides pursue such activities. Not only soldiers and guards engage in this behavior, which can extend to the general population. Too many people can end up taunting, harassing, hurting, or even killing members of targeted racial, sexual, religious, economic, or other minorities in their midst. The endgame in H. G. Well's *The Time Machine* may have begun with such play. Clearly, the most playful species is also the most deadly! We need to recognize this ubiquitous relationship if we are ever to control cruel behavior and truly understand play.

15.3.2   Play Can Be Risky and Dangerous

In the example from Wagner, play was not only cruel, it turned out to be disastrous for the Rhine maidens and the gods. Engaged in play, the maidens were distracted from their serious task of guarding the treasure. Play can also distract animals from recognizing incipient predatory threats and lead to risks of physical injury in vigorous social, object, and locomotor play. In the United States, at least, the risk of injury has led to changes in playground equipment to eliminate virtually all risk to children (no one wants to be sued), such that much of what growing up entailed in the past has been lost in modern societies. The great urge to engage in physically challenging behavior that intrinsically entails some risks comes to the fore in teenagers with inventions of high-risk activities, most notably the X-games.

The apparent universal occurrence of risk-taking in children's play throughout the world suggests that challenge and risk-taking are important developmental processes facilitated by play (Jambor, 1998). Indeed "the play environment becomes a testing ground for the development of decision-making skills, understanding social implications of decisions, and weighing those decisions based on risk factors. Within this sociophysical environment children need to take risks to explore their skills in the social context of their peers to find out what they can and cannot do" (Jambor, 1998: 319). This view is remarkably similar to K. V. Thompson's self-assessment theory of animal play (K. V. Thompson, 1998) and the concept of mastery play seen in Piagetian and psychoanalytic schemes, although embedded in a more social framework. To Jambor, locomotor, object, and social play are directed at enhanced functioning in our most important social world. Jambor's views appear to embed play in a functional context true to human nature, but they still need rigorous evaluation.

Nonetheless, the role of risk-taking in life has a face validity to it, as does the realization that the risks need to be appropriate for the physical and social development of the animal. Indeed, Jambor claims that children often strive to play at appropriate developmental levels, but that adults are often unable to provide the necessary facilities because some children may use them in ways that frighten adults and cause injuries. In a litigious society this has led to restrictions on providing the playground and adventure-fulfilling facilities necessary for young people. In a perverse way, it encourages even more risky endeavors by children because boring equipment is often used creatively in novel and dangerous ways.[31] These concerns apply to nonhuman animal play as well, and especially to the nature of environment enrichment opportunities provided for captive animals.

Risk-taking is also related to sensation-seeking (Zuckerman, 1984) and is particularly a concern with adolescents (Weisfeld, 1999), where hormonal changes may be a factor (Spear, 2000). A number of studies have documented that older, but not yet adult, nonhuman animals engage in risky behavior. For example, 2- to 3-year-old vervet monkeys were more likely to approach humans in the field and also approach strange males, enter a new area, or approach novel objects than were younger monkeys or adults (Fairbanks, 1993). Similarly, adolescent mice were more likely to enter closed arms of a maze (entering a strange hole in the field?) than adult mice (Macrí et al., 2002). Thus what Jambor claims for younger children is especially true of adolescents in whom controlling "negative" risk-taking behavior involving drugs, sex, shoplifting, fast driving, theft, vandalism, violence, gangs, and the like is viewed as a problem that, if not solved, will doom civilization. If risk-taking, as a form of sensation-seeking in adolescence, is part of normal development (more so, but not always, among males; adolescent sex is historically much riskier for the future of girls and their families than for boys and their families; e.g., Weisfeld, 1999; Nell, 2002), then eliminating risk itself may be quite counterproductive. A study of 12- to 16-year-old Norwegian adolescents who were assessed for both negative and "positive" (kayaking, rock climbing, downhill skiing) risk-taking behavior showed that a standardized measure of sensation-seeking was related to both forms (Zuckerman, 1984). In fact, negative risk-taking behavior in this and other studies seems to be largely an outgrowth of a lack of opportunity or encouragement to engage in positive risk-taking in adolescence for those individuals with a strong need for intense stimulation. If play, including risky play, is a factor in sexual selection, however, as discussed earlier (Chick, 2001; see also Nell, 2002), then the interest in females for risk-taking males needs to be studied.

Could interest in loud and—to adults—raucous music, violent or sexual video games, and steamy or antiestablishment literature also represent such sensation-seeking? Maybe so, but the risks may contain some benefits. For example, unlike most perceptual learning tasks, habitual playing of action video games actually provides a general improvement in visual attention (Green & Bavelier, 2003). A recent study showed that chess players have a high sensation-seeking profile (Joireman, Fick, & Anderson, 2002). Chess is definitely a low physical risk sport and this also points to another way to address the risk-taking issues. Chess playing and tournaments have

31. Jambor provides guidance for providing appropriate play opportunities at different ages and appreciates individual differences (see also Harper & Huie, 1978 for male and female differences in space and equipment use).

been used in some poor urban and rural areas where teenagers are at great risk for negative risk-taking behavior.

There are other kinds of risky social play in people that may be enjoyed by all parties and which may be deeply entrenched in cultures. One example is "recreational aggression," which has been recently analyzed by David Ingle (2004). This kind of aggression, which occurs almost exclusively among males, is often violent and even dangerous to the participants, but it does seem to be sought out, as in soccer club hooliganism in England and elsewhere that results in quite serious but rarely fatal fights between clubs. Other fights begin in recreational settings, often involving alcohol, and the precipitating factor often involves a female. Ingle has compared the propensity of different cultures for this kind of "sport" by analyzing folksongs and drinking songs, as well as different occupational groups such as nineteenth-century cowboys and lumberjacks in the United States. By drawing on primate behavior and other biological data, he makes a strong case for the generality of alcohol as integral to recreational aggression wherever it appears.

This type of "play" is to be distinguished from survival games using paint guns or war reenactors playing "soldier" in sanctioned settings with strict codes of conduct. A "play" approach to hooliganism or fan violence is clearly not popular among social scientists. A recent review discussed almost every other interpretation but decried the lack of understanding and called for interdisciplinary approaches (Ward, 2002). Apparently evolutionary and biopsychological approaches don't count.

15.3.3 Play May Be Addictive

Recall that dopamine receptors in the basal ganglia, especially the ventral tegmental area (VTA) are involved in reward systems. Recent work has shown dopamine release in these brain areas occur within a tenth of a second before conditioned rats press a lever for cocaine (Phillips et al., 2003). Increasingly, research is showing that play can become addictive. Gambling becomes addictive when external rewards (e.g., money) become tied to the performance of a game (even with a machine) and thus the repetitive component of play becomes integrated into another reward system.[32] Modern technology can produce play activities that become just too rewarding just as it can produce designer drugs and fast foods that can lead to substance abuse and obesity. But reward systems and their subversion may be very old. The previous section showed that aggression and fighting is itself rewarding and can spill over from athletic contests to serious rows.

32. Professional gamblers may share some of the addictive traits of gambling, but they can also be viewed as highly rational experts supporting themselves through high-risk endeavors in a manner that is more acceptable when it is found in capitalist entrepreneurs or stock market investors (e.g., McManus, 2000).

Recent studies show that different kinds of novelty seeking are related to different dopamine receptor genes and that these underlie individual differences in risk-taking and susceptibility to alcohol and other "self-medication," and may also be related to personality differences (Cloninger, 1987; Burghardt, 2001; Berman et al., 2002; Hansenne et al., 2002). Rats learn to prefer environments in which they have had access to novel objects in a manner similar to appetitive learning involving sex and drugs of abuse. Different dopamine receptors underlie the aquisition versus the expression of the conditioned preferences (Bevins et al., 2002).

In a book that is otherwise extremely positive on play, the statement appears that "Adult computer game addicts say that the games give them the same feeling they get when on amphetamines—feeling euphoric, craving more and more games, feeling unable to stop, neglecting family and friends, lying about game playing, experiencing stress disorders and sleep disturbances, feeling empty and depressed, and having school and job problems" (Frost, Worham, & Reifel, 2001: 103). Video games with highly aggressive content may have other consequences we do not yet appreciate.

Although psychologists have long recognized that behavioral addictions share many similarities with drug addiction, mainstream biomedicine has not been keen on accepting the view that gambling, obsessive-compulsive disorders (OCD), and compulsive shopping, eating, and even internet surfing have mechanisms in common with drug addiction. However, newer research on brain reward circuits, especially in the basal ganglia and dopamine opiate receptors, shows that many such behavior patterns tap into common pathways (Holden, 2001; Osborn, 1999; Panksepp, 1998a). Even "positive" addictions such as running and other athletic activities may involve mechanisms similar to those underlying the "highs," withdrawal symptoms, anxieties, and guilt associated with "negative addictions." Wheel running in rats is a well-studied phenomenon discussed earlier; recent studies suggest that rats can be bred for compulsive running and that similar biochemical reactions are involved in both running and cocaine consumption in these animals (Holden, 2001). Furthermore, just as the basal ganglia are involved in reward learning, conditioned behavior easily supports such behavior; drugs and some behaviors "co-opt memory and motivational systems, not just pleasure pathways" (Helmuth, 2001: 983).

It is thus no accident, perhaps, that stereotyped repetitive behaviors in animals and people—gambling, hyperactivity, excessive athleticism that compromises health, and other seemingly voluntary activities—may often be confused with play. It may be that play is on a continuum with such activities, perhaps owing to its reliance on comparable brain mechanisms coupled with altered neurotransmitter concentrations. If some kinds of play and related behavior can become addictive, we can claim that they are then not play. Perhaps they are "good" addictions. However, gambling is not a good addiction, and neither is nymphomania, bulimia, and other compulsions that are aberrations of natural and necessary behavioral systems.

The origins of play go far back in time; play, in its various guises, largely makes life worth living. Yet play is largely ignored as a serious research topic while we devote the lion's share of resources to support the play of the world's leaders, who, safe in their war rooms, find war, and planning for war, to be the ultimate form of play. Perhaps we cannot face the truth of Huizinga—civilization is built on violent play, and the goal of politicians is to play risky games. Gambling is an addiction derived from play and chemicals in the brain. So too, the drumbeat of war arouses adrenaline and action.

Is this play? For the actors, perhaps, but it must be disheartening for those who view play as a means of freeing behavior from the rigidities of ancient instincts to see it put in the service of nation-state competition.

15.4   Beyond Play Behavior

Play is motor poetry.
—G. S. Hall (1904: 231)

15.4.1   The Leap to Mental Play

In chapter 4 various kinds of play were mentioned (pretense, fantasy, and dramatic play) that, especially in human beings, seem to involve mental (neural) activities that are the real play, the behavioral manifestation being less important. Perhaps here behavioral play is an indication of mental play. A case can also be made for deriving imagination and mental play from behavioral play, and a detailed treatment has been outlined elsewhere (Burghardt, 2001).

Play involves activity with the self, objects, other species of animals, and especially conspecifics. Prominent features of vigorous play activities include feints, exaggerated movements, and other actions critical to predicting and anticipating the actions of objects or other organisms (Spinka, Newberry, & Bekoff, 2001). Visual-motor integration may be heavily involved, although, of course, other sensory systems may be operating as well. Can these aspects of play be linked in any way to planning, mental rehearsal, imagination, and creativity?

A body of work is accumulating on the relation among motoric acts, mental imagery, and the brain. Circuits in the basal ganglia are involved in both motor learning and cognitive behavior, suggesting that the links between motor performance and cognitive processes are either very ancient or are slight modifications from ancestral vertebrate systems (Katz & Harris-Warrick, 1999). Striatal projection neurons depend on afferent and loop circuits in both the neocortex (especially premotor, parietal, and prefrontal cortex) and the thalamus. We also know now that new neurons can be added to adult brains (Gross, 2000), and thus continuity from childhood play may have a physiological basis.

Particularly intriguing are a series of papers from a research group in Parma, Italy, that suggest a mechanism whereby a more direct cognitive link may be made. Initially this research group showed that neurons in area F5 of the premotor cortex (near the arcuate sulcus) fired when monkeys (*Macaca nemestrina*) performed a goal-directed action, such as reaching for and grasping a piece of food. However, some of these same neurons also fired when the monkeys simply observed the experimenter doing the same thing (Gallese, Fadiga, Fogassi, & Rizzolatti, 1996). The authors termed these "mirror neurons" because they mirrored what the animal itself could perform. They found several types of these neurons. Some were specific to single actions by the monkey or the observed experimenter, such as grasping, holding, manipulating, and placing. Other mirror neurons were specific to two or three actions combined, such as grasping and placing, placing and holding, or grasping, placing, and holding. It is interesting to note that this area of the premotor cortex has been considered homologous with Broca's area in the human brain. The authors argued that such mirror neuronal systems in humans could be involved in the recognition of both actions and sounds. Further experiments showed that the mirror neurons did not fire when the observed experimenter reached for food that was not present or if he was in darkness and could not be seen. Suggestive evidence has been gained from humans also (Fadiga, Fogassi, Pavesi, & Rizzolatti, 1995). Mirror neurons might underlie imitation, and some evidence suggests that play in animals facilitates imitation of novel behavior (Miklosi, 1999).

These and other studies suggest that mental imagery, physical movements, and perception can be linked in areas of the brain even down to involvement of the same neuron (Jeannerod, 1994). Thus "imagery is a bridge between perception and motor control" (Kosslyn & Sussman, 1995: 1040). This may be a common phenomenon. With accumulating evidence on the great dendritic (synaptic) changes that can rapidly occur in the brain, practice and repetition of similar, but not identical, behavior during play may serve a role in the shifting mental states involved in anticipating, predicting, and controlling one's own behavior in relation to external stimuli. More recent work on monkeys identified areas in the premotor cortex and prefrontal cortex that integrate information on serial sensory information, motor sequences, goals, and rewards (Matsumoto et al., 2003; Ohbayashi et al., 2003; Richmond et al., 2003). Thus, as cortex develops, mechanisms evolve to channel and "use" the sensory and motor activities generated by play via instinctive behavior generated in more ancient regions of the brain.

The studies cited here model how we could move from play as a motoric, active response to stimuli, to active play involving pretense and make believe and eventually to behavior largely divorced from physical actions such as imagination, fantasy, new ideas, and complex social assessments (Carruthers, 2002). These phenomena may all be more closely linked than our theories suggest, perhaps because of the enduring mind-body dualism that disparages mere animate movement (Sheets-Johnstone, 1999). Certainly we all need to draw, sound out, or act out ideas to "test them." Gesturing appears useful in facilitating verbal expression of ideas (Goldin-Meadow, Nusbaum, Kelly, & Wagner, 2001), and gesturing has been argued to be the basis for human language as well (Corballis, 2002). Talking to oneself is commonplace; doing it soundlessly may be the essence of "thinking," which is often the rehearsal of different actions and possible outcomes. Is there any evidence that merely thinking can affect motor behavior?

Motor imagery is the process of imagining behavioral actions. When people are asked to imagine movements, the neurophysiological responses in various brain regions resemble those made when such movements are actually executed (Kosslyn & Sussman, 1995; Yágüez, Canavan, Lange, & Hömberg, 1999). This also happened with mental rotation tasks in people and in monkeys when they prepared to move an arm in a specific way (Kosslyn & Sussman, 1995). When people were asked to imagine writing a letter and then actually wrote the letter, the same areas in the cerebellum, the prefrontal cortex, and the supplementary motor cortex were activated (Kosslyn & Sussman, 1995).

Is it possible that there is a functional link between mental imagery and physical performance in that the former enhances the latter? Intriguing support is provided by the controversial experiments of D. Smith, Collis & Holmes (2003), who demonstrated that merely imagining exercise had beneficial effects on subsequent physical ability. Two groups of subjects engaged in mental (imaginary) or actual physical performance of strength training of a finger, along with a no-performance control group. All three groups were tested afterward for changes in the strength of their finger. The control group had no change and the physical practice group showed an improvement of 33 percent. What is remarkable is that the group that did mental practice only showed a significant strength improvement of 16 percent. We know that exercise, including that gained through play, might have at least short-term benefits physiologically. This study actually posited a physical benefit from just thinking about a specific action.[33] Children trained on a virtual maze on a computer did better on a real maze, even if the virtual maze was misleading (Foreman et al., 2000). The ability to focus attention and not be distracted by external stimuli as athletes rehearsed an action appeared to separate skilled from average performers in activities from golf and diving to target shooting (e.g., Bird, 1987; Crews & Lander, 1992).

If merely imagining activity is functional and thus evolutionarily adaptive, the next step is to mentally rehearse different actions. What might lead to such rehearsal?

33. Brain imaging (fMRI) during imagined and overt finger movement showed that while cortical and cerebellar activity was present during real movement, the latter was absent during imagined movements, although motor cortex was activated (Nair et al., 2003). In a similar fMRI study of real versus imagined rehearsals by pianists, comparable results were obtained (Meister et al., 2004).

Some demand or problem facing an individual could certainly lead to the adaptive strategy of choosing among alternative actions before making a behavioral commitment. Linking these mental rehearsals with possible outcomes is a hallmark of creativity, innovation, and social adeptness (Greenberg, 2004). Those organisms producing more of these mental options should then have, through natural selection, an advantage in producing more of the innovations that succeed. Play can thus be involved in creativity and behavioral innovation, not just in the choice of different behavioral options, but through selection for animals that can create such options via internal processes.

Note that a criterion for play is that it be initiated when the animal is not under serious stress. Yet we know that in our own species, at least, play can itself become stressful as the social competition or difficulty of the game becomes frustrating. Thus we can view play plus stress as fostering creativity by rewarding novel ways of solving some challenge (Greenberg, 2004). Recall the studies showing that some arousal (stress?) is important for optimal learning and performance (chapter 6). In fact, play used as an escape may become not only repetitive, but obsessively so. Such behavior not only ceases to be play, but is definitely not destined to be creative. Play performed under appropriate levels of arousal and complexity may facilitate a mental rehearsal mode that could be a means of fostering creativity. On the other hand, because of the diverse origins of play, much play may be repetitive and not novel for the species.

If these ideas have some merit, we would expect to be able to trace the operation of brain mechanisms in a comparative fashion. Although this has not yet been done, initial studies in human adults and children seem promising (Frith & Frith, 1999). Functional magnetic resonance imaging and positron emission tomography have both indicated that the medial prefrontal cortex and superior temporal sulcus are involved in the interpretation of the mental states (intentionality) of characters by someone listening to stories or watching cartoons. These authors, in trying to explain the origin of such mental imagination, suggest that they arise from the following four "preexisting abilities that are relevant to mentalizing," all of which have a demonstrated neural basis (Frith & Frith, 1999: 1693). These are the ability to (1) distinguish animate from inanimate entities, (2) follow the gaze of another individual, (3) represent goal-directed actions, and (4) distinguish actions of self from those of others.

There might indeed be similar neural involvement in motor representations and the highest cognitive abilities attributed to imagination, role playing, fantasy, and other types of mental play. Moreover, dopamine may be the link among them all. As indicated earlier, brain size is not necessarily related to play (Iwaniuk, Nelson, & Pellis, 2001), although certain noncortical sections of the brain may be (chapter 5). Rather, play may have secondarily provided expanded opportunities for behavioral flexibility, plasticity, and cognitive decision making through the operation of natural selection on behavior, and thus the nervous system, instigated by the evolution of parental care, endothermy, and increased metabolic rates.

We can now add a twelfth conclusion to the eleven that opened this chapter: Behavioral (physical, motoric, sensory) play may be an important developmental precursor to mental play involving rehearsal, prediction, planning, imagination, problem solving and creativity in realms such as social adeptness, language and communication, cognitive (decision-making) abilities, and emotional (empathic and "mind-reading") processes.

Thus physical play with self, partners, and objects leads to learning about how to effectively respond to unpredictable, unexpected, or complex features of the world (Spinka et al., 2001). It is an essential evolved and developmental process in mental rehearsal, where one can try out scenarios internally before choosing which, if any, would be most productive if physically carried out. We often value this type of abstract exercise more than physical performance, which may be why persons skilled in crafts have lost status (and especially income) in many modern societies compared with those who are mentally agile and abstractly accomplished. However, such "abstract" workers may be dependent on skills gained in actually working with material objects in the world. As already mentioned, language, which we value as the most human of all our capabilities may, ironically, be derived from gesturing and signing. Such gesturing, in turn, may have emerged from the variability attendant in social play. Again, G. S. Hall may have been ahead of his time when he asserted that play is poetry in motion. Play has been linked with freedom, gracefulness, and creativity[34] as well as with risks, obsessions, cruelty, and wastes of time. It may be all of these, which is why play has always provoked controversy.

15.4.2   Sleep and Dreams: The Ultimate Relaxed Field?

Panksepp (1998a) has noted the similarity of play with dreams, even postulating common neural pathways. This would be the extreme of mental play without overt behavioral manifestations or even conscious awareness. It is interesting that young birds may rehearse, refine, and learn aspects of their songs while they sleep. Apparently during sleep, neurons in two brain areas important to song learning responded to the songs, while neurons in only one of the areas did so in birds that were awake (Dave & Margoliash, 2000; Dave, Yu, & Margoliash, 1998).

Recently, the neurobiology of sleep and dreaming has received much attention. An entire issue of *Behavioral and Brain Sciences* (Vol. 23, No. 6, 2000, pp. 793–1121) was devoted to five target articles and more than seventy-five commentaries on them by other scientists. Dreams turn out to be controlled by many of the same brain areas that control instinctive, cognitive, and emotional responses in animals and people (Hobson, Pace-Schott, & Stickgold, 2000). The idea that dreams are simulations of threat behavior was advanced (Revonsuo, 2000) and much other enticing speculation and

---

34. This has been romantically expressed by more recent authors as well (Fagen, 1995; Kortmulder, 1998).

debate was put forth. Are dreams the play of a largely disembodied brain? If so, is computer play (not play with computers) on the horizon as the evolutionary journey continues?

15.4.3 Play, Work, and Flow

Play, leisure, recreation, flow, all are enmeshed in space and time. We need the psychological, as well as physical, space in which to play and the time and resources to effectively engage in it. To many scholars over the years, play is the child's "work" and play is also the most effective method by which children learn (Frost et al., 2001; Hall, 1904; Preyer, 1893). Educators can exploit play to teach physical, cognitive, academic, and social skills as well as creativity (Hartley, Frank, & Goldenson, 1952; Slentz & Krogh, 2001).

But play made into work, in the sense of compulsory dreary activity, is not then play. As discussed in chapter 2, the play/work dichotomy may be a modern conceit. One's "work" can become playful, a game, and even a compulsion and addiction. Necessary or serious activities can become playful when they become ends in themselves. A sign of this may be when there is such deep immersion in an activity that an awareness of the passage of time, as well as the irrelevant external world, is blunted or absent altogether. Such immersion is the hallmark of what is now popularly termed flow (Csikszentmihalyi, 1991). Play certainly has many of the characteristics attributed to flow, which, like play, has been linked to creativity (Csikszentmihalyi, 1996).

15.4.4 Play, Morality, and Ethics

Play is not just play. As seen from chapter 1 and this chapter, play raises issues of moral concern. After all, don't many games and ballroom dancing lead to gambling, drugs, and fornication? This argument is widely entrenched among some groups, as are rules against kids playing cops and robbers, with or without toy weapons, on playgrounds. When is play so wasteful of time, money, and effort that it is a societal evil? The opposition to lotteries and casinos is often on the moral ground that gambling is inherently evil.

When does some play foster violent and other anti-social behavior? Indeed, is behavior that is pleasurable inherently less worthy than behavior that is serious, dour, and onerous? Tragedy has always been valued more than comedy in "high art." Is it just coincidence that Aristotle's work on tragedy survived, but his treatise on comedy did not?[35]

---

35. The ambivalence raised by this "lost" book by Aristotle is the source of the plot in the wonderful novel *The Name of the Rose* by Humberto Eco. The novel was made into a motion picture starring Sean Connery. In the book a series of murders was instigated to prevent people from reading a book on comedy.

Play may, however, have positive ethical value. Through play people and other animals may learn about rules, sharing and reciprocity, interacting with others, and the values of ends other than winning. The issue of whether animals have moral systems is a long-standing one (see references in Burghardt & Herzog, 1989). The idea that social play and games inculcate fairness has been around for some time (e.g., Carr, 1902; Sutton-Smith & Abrams, 1978). That play may be an essential precursor to the evolution of social morality has been explored recently in a provocative article (Bekoff, 2001) and subsequently modeled mathematically (Dugatkin & Bekoff, 2003). As noted before, play is a protean concept.

15.5   Play, Leisure, Culture, and the Rise and Fall of Civilizations

If surplus resource theory approximates a generally valid and widespread behavioral process, the implications are profound. Some of these reach deep into social values and have political implications that I had not envisioned and that initially I resisted. The full explication and working out of the following speculations needs to be deferred. Readers who have made it this far through a rather daunting book may welcome this attempt to make the journey into the primeval ooze of ancient evolution serve some higher human purpose. Geist (1978) provides extensive complementary ideas.

Differences in the availability of time, energy, and resources are critical to understanding the variability seen in play across individuals and species. Such differences have been shown to underlie the variability in play seen in different wild populations of monkeys or differences throughout the year or even across years, as in El Niño–year differences seen in seals. The general increase in play in captive animals also is related to greater access to time, energy, and resources when they are made available. Play in children occurs more often when children are healthy and have adequate time and resources, along with appropriate supervision.

Can play underlie differences in the cultural attainments and relative successes of civilizations and, if so, are these also mediated by the availability of time, energy, and resources? At one level this seems obvious. Middle class and wealthy children, young adults, and adults often spend much more time in leisure pursuits and in self-selected and intrinsically motivated behavior than those of lesser means.

Similar to Spencer (chapter 2), the ancient Greeks viewed leisure as "the higher employment of the mind once the necessities of life have been dealt with" (Minogue, 2001). High western culture is often viewed in this way (Peiper, 1999). While many who inherit or earn wealth may waste time and money in vain, decadent, and luxurious pastimes (Veblen, 1899/1994), some, such as Charles Darwin, use their educational and material advantages and leisure time to move beyond the current state in art, technology, and science to create new possibilities and innovations in art, music, architecture, and science. The obituary of Edward T. Hall (Young, 2001) made clear how his immense creativity in physical science and archeology—he invented many now essential geological methods, including those used in dating ancient artifacts—was fueled by his family's wealth and educational opportunities.

Recent archeological scholarship studying the earliest civilizations is increasingly finding that climatic changes involving flooding, cooling, and warming, but especially droughts, have been the leading cause of the collapse of civilizations. Such changes seem to be behind Old World societal collapses such as the Natufian in southwest Asia about 6400 BCE, the Late Uruk in Mesopotamia around 3000 BCE, and Egyptian and Early Bronze III civilizations in Palestine, Crete, and Greece around 2200 BCE. Similar stories can be told about societal collapses in the New World involving civilizations such as the Moche in Peru around 600 AD, the Tiwanaku in the Andes around 1000 AD, the Mayan around 900 AD, and the Anasazi in the North American Southwest around 1300 AD (Weiss & Bradley, 2001). Many of these societies were hierarchical and had a wealthy class—supported by slaves gained through warfare—that could build the temples, and raise the arts, learning, technology, and sports to levels unattainable in more traditional and egalitarian societies. Yet when their resource bounty failed, so did the creative capacity of their world.

Thus societies with a class of players may be the most successful. Military prowess and new weaponry for hunting and war may also be derived from play, and the expression "war games" is not an oxymoron. In the United States today, research on military technology sucks up much of the federal government's research dollars. Anyone who can not appreciate the "play" aspect of Star Wars anti-missile programs based on highly impractical "science" can never hope to counter the political games behind them. Regardless, environmental events, including those caused by the societies themselves, swept aside societies that could not control them, a lesson worth remembering.

The economic system may also have been an important factor in the rise of playful societies. How much of the creative explosion of the Renaissance was due to the role of patrons and the development of a mercantile middle class? How important in the flourishing of the arts and sciences was the ability of people to escape the lot of serfs and peasants subservient to feudal lords and kings who appropriated all surplus production and impoverished the people with onerous taxes? And did capitalism capitalize on playful behavior in its rewarding of the innovative entrepreneur?

In all societies many in the middle and upper classes squander their resources or use them for status competition. Veblen's critique of the leisure class is still a scathing indictment (1899/1994). Still, all modern societies have one, even those borne on the crest of the most equalitarian of dogmas, the Marxist and communist countries.

But such waste by societies may be essential for progress. I will use a reproductive analogy to clarify the argument. Males produce many millions of sperm, although only one is needed for fertilization of an egg. The majority of sperm produced by male animals are thus wasted (as, to a lesser extent, are most eggs produced by females). Why are so many sperm produced? There are many reasons (Judson, 2002). One possibility is that producing lots of sperm increases the chances that one will actually be successful, as many hurdles prevent even good sperm from reaching the egg. Another may be sperm competition, both among sperm produced by a male and also among sperm populations produced by different males when the female mates with more than one male. It has been pointed out that polyandrous females can increase the chance of producing the most fit offspring by encouraging what seems, at first blush, to be wasteful competition. Selection can operate in many ways.

When such selection is removed, as in many fish hatcheries producing trout and salmon where eggs and sperm are indiscriminately mixed, the number of deformed and behaviorally incompetent offspring increases manyfold and brains degenerate (Marchetti & Nevitt, 2003). Thus excess production ensures quality and may be essential not only for sustaining a population but improving it. Neither we nor nature can predict what traits or individuals will be most adaptive. The answer is to produce a surplus. The same argument has been made in scientific research as in natural selection (Hull, 1990, 2000). Most experiments and scientific studies are not breakthroughs and lead nowhere. But some do, and although we can make some predictions as to what kinds of research by what kinds of scientists may be most promising, the scientific landscape is littered with erroneous concepts and assertions supported by the establishment that are now disproved. As Hull argues and demonstrates in looking at the recent history of three competing approaches in evolutionary biology, science itself is most successful when it uses the same processes Darwin discovered in biology. When scientists oppose shifting major research resources to narrowly focused targeted fields with immediately applicable findings, they are unwittingly recognizing that surplus resources need to go to testing good ideas that do not fit current wisdom.

The argument here is that surplus resources are essential for progress in both biological and cultural evolution. But there is a price to be paid. Some individuals will suffer and lose out both reproductively and economically. Does this mean that the "social Darwinism" supposedly used to justify the actions of wealthy robber barons and oligarchs in the nineteenth century (Bannister, 1988) is what we need? Absolutely not. A society needs to have surplus resources above and beyond what is essential for a decent life for all citizens. Too much of a difference is bad for both the elite and the general population (Wilkinson, 2000). Nevertheless, my exploration of surplus resource theory in animals convinces me that we need to see as socially adaptive the ubiquitous phenomenon that many progressives find offensive: many of the leisure (e.g., inherited) wealthy are societal parasites who contribute little other than (hopefully) paying taxes and purchasing goods. However, some support cultural, educational, philanthropic, and, increasingly, conservation activities that democratically run governments may only reach consensus on and decide to fund when it is too late. And a few, a very few, may take their talents and material resources and, stimulated by ancient basal forebrain systems, playfully accomplish wonderful things and enrich their societies manyfold.

15.6   Play and the Meaning of Life

The value of a humorous, playful approach to life is often touted as an ideal. Is this true even if cruel jokes or bitter sarcasm are excluded? Laughter is often considered an aspect of humor, easily measured (Provine, 2001). But laughter punctuates many mundane aspects of life, and serves to diffuse social tension as well as be a marker of joy and playfulness (Provine, 2001). The health or medical benefits of laughter and humor have received no solid experimental support (Provine, 2001; Martin, 2002). But true happiness, so elusive in a world awash in material abundance (Csikszentmihalyi, 1999) may have deeper roots in play.

The Hebrew Bible is not considered a humorous or playful book (but see Friedman, 2000). Nonetheless, in chapter 1 I used a passage from the Old Testament to show that the patriarchs viewed the relationship of the human body and soul to those of animals in a far more modern and complex way than in the earlier creation stories in Genesis. The verse immediately following the ones quoted in chapter 1 gives this book closure.

I see there is no contentment for a human being except happiness in achievement; such is the lot of a human being. No one can tell us what will happen after we are gone (Ecclesiastes 3: 22, NJB).

A productive life, then, is the goal, and play, behavioral and mental, is the sum of those activities that, while seemingly directed toward survival, are intrinsically satisfying in the process, in the means, and in the satisfaction of accomplishment. Attesting to this surmise is a wonderful book on the joys of hard labor in reviving the old New England craft of building a stone wall (Jerome, 1996). The same effort devoted to personal accomplishment and fun has quite different effects than when performed as forced labor. The similarity to the distinction between appetitive behavior and consummatory acts in analysis of instinctive behavior in animals is not coincidental (Craig, 1918). It was the classical ethologists who argued that the proximate goal of much animal behavior was the performance of the behaviors themselves, not their functional or evolutionary consequences (Lorenz, 1969, 1981). Modern learning theory is building on these insights (Timberlake & Silva, 1995). Nevertheless, a recent paper on the "evolution of happiness" ignores them, as well as play itself (Buss, 2000). So focused are most "evolutionary psychologists" on competition and questionnaire-based studies limited to people that they seem to lose sight of the ancient roots of our behavior in our vertebrate brain (MacLean, 1985; Panksepp & Panksepp, 2000). Indeed, I think a recent popular book on adapting our physical play and exercise regimes to our evolutionary past provides a more useful path to health and happiness (Forencich, 2002).

The Old Testament view of "happiness in achievement" is supported by much recent work on "positive" psychology and the psychology of happiness and a fulfilled life. However, just as flow is not a new concept, neither is our connection with other animals. New views on the well-being of captive animals in zoos and farms focus not only on the need to provide animals with adequate food, housing, and health care but also with the means to perform their biologically derived instinctive behavior patterns (Burghardt, 1996).

An explicit recognition of the affinity of the goals and rewards of activity for humans compared with other species was remarkably captured by an eighth- or ninth-century Celtic poet and monastic scholar who insightfully noted intriguing similarities between his endeavors and those of his companion cat, Pangur Bán. Picture the monk at his desk in a somewhat dark and dingy rodent-infested room in a massive stone monastery.

I and Pangur Bán my cat
'Tis a like task we are at:
Hunting mice is his delight,
Hunting words I sit all night.

Better far than praise of men
'Tis to sit with book and pen;
Pangur bears me no ill-will,
He too plies his simple skill.

'Tis a merry task to see
At our tasks how glad are we,
When at home we sit and find
Entertainment to our mind.

Oftentimes a mouse will stray
In the hero Pangur's way;
Oftentimes my keen thought set
Takes a meaning in my net.

'Gainst the wall he sets his eye
Full and fierce and sharp and sly;
'Gainst the wall of knowledge I
All my little wisdom try.

When a mouse darts from its den,
O how glad is Pangur then!
O what gladness do I prove
When I solve the doubts I love!

So in peace our tasks we ply,
Pangur Bán, my cat, and I;
In our arts we find our bliss,
I have mine and he has his.

Practice every day has made
Pangur perfect in his trade;
I get wisdom day and night
Turning darkness into light.

(Translated by Robin Flower. From *The Irish Tradition*, The Lilliput Press, Dublin, 1995)

Play can be desultory or intense and focused. The latter type seems to be most productive, be it hunting prey or hunting insight, but the former type may be more primary and serendipitous. Although the Celtic author used the language of sport and game, it might be said that the cat was not playing; it is going after prey for real, for a meal. And our cloistered monk is after a soulful meal as well. Entering into and immersing one's self in an activity may be the essence of play to us. Surplus resource theory offers an important avenue for deriving such a feature of play from the primal instincts, as Huizinga suggested.

15.7   The End of the Journey

15.7.1   Back to the Ancient Scripts

Time is a child moving counters in a game; the royal power is a child's.
—Heraclitus (~500 BCE)[36]

Plato recognized the value of play in his ideal society as recorded in The Republic:

The free man should learn no study under bondage … study forced on the mind will not abide there … train your children in their studies not by compulsion but by games, and you will be better able to see the natural abilities of each. (Plato, 1957: 288)

Thus play, to Plato, was not only the best way to learn but was useful to teachers and others to enhance individualized instruction by assessing natural talents and interests. The Kindergarten movement for preschool children was similarly based on the work of Friedrich Froebel and his development of play materials, songs, and games through which children gain perceptual, cognitive, social, and emotional knowledge, preparing

36. Heraclitus of Ephesus was a presocratic philosopher who is thought to be the first to develop an integrated philosophical system, although only fragments exist. This is Fragment 79 according to the Bywater Greek text (Bywater & Patrick, 1969). The fragment is translated in many different ways and I think the one used here, by William Harris (unpublished), an emeritus professor at Middlebury College, is particularly apt. Other variants include the translations by Patrick in 1889 (Time is a child playing at draughts, a child's kingdom), Crowe in 1996 (Lifetime is a child at play, moving pieces in a game. Kingship belongs to the child), and Borst in 1991 (Existence is a child playing at a board game; a child holds the sceptre). Note that this short fragment encompasses several of Sutton-Smith's rhetorics of play described in chapter 1.

them for the world they will soon inhabit (Blow, 1894). But both Plato and Froebel knew that life is not all fun and games. Wisdom is found in distinguishing how play can best be used in education. The current goal of educating lifelong and creative learners, beginning in early life (e.g., Singer & Lythcott, 2002; Rike, 1993), is an implicit recognition of the value of transforming learning, work, and, I might add, physical activity, into intrinsic and challenging processes rather than compulsory ends. How to accomplish this in later years in life is one of the true challenges a successful culture might want to seriously address.

15.7.2 Paradoxes Revisited: Play as Evolutionary Detritus or Evolutionary Pump

In the end, the paradoxes of play remain. Is the essence of play a positive force in evolution as well as the main source of a happy, fulfilled life? Or is the essence of play found in its negative, destructive aspects such as gambling, teasing, law breaking, war gaming, and recreational aggression? Many comedians and humor researchers find most or all humor to be hostile toward some target, and many comedians prove the point, using a hostile brand of humor against themselves or the audience, but more often against some other character (Herzog & Anderson, 2000). Or is play a waste of time or sin of idleness, a relic, if not degenerate, behavior that at most we patiently wait for children, but usually not other animals, to outgrow?

Perhaps these are not the correct questions. Play is and can be all of these: neither inherently useful nor useless, neither good nor evil. Play is—play endures—play may be something that creates a spark, lighting a candle where there was darkness. Play may prevent achievement or corrupt lives, because the lower cortical areas in which its origins lie interfere with adaptive behavior. Play may also be something like food, drink, sex, and competition, which are only good in moderation: extremism may not be a virtue in play, although the most valuable or creative play may be extreme.

Play is above all a process. Play involves old neural systems yet becomes transformed and ritualized. We cannot ignore an activity that occupies so much of our lives and directs our goals. We need to wrestle with it; play with it; immerse ourselves in understanding it. The ultimate paradox may be that play can only be understood through itself.

Revisiting the Serpent's Tail. The Mehen game played in Egypt during the Predynastic and Old Kingdom Periods (earlier than 3100 through 2150 BCE), one of the oldest documented "board" games known. This game is based on moving tokens in the form of lions up the spine of the serpent god Mehen, who protects the sun god Ra from outside evil during his passage through the netherworld. The gods themselves are both born through the serpent and need to play the game themselves for their deification and resurrection (exiting the board through the snake's head). Thus it appears that the god Mehen is *both* serpent and gameboard! Here play is both structure and process, originating and ending in mysterious and serious events. In this example the "tail" is a duck or goose head (through which the nascent god enters), but it could also be another snake head, deepening the mystery that is play (see Piccione, 1990). Shown is an alabaster Old Kingdom gameboard, 38 cm in diameter (no. 16950) in the Oriental Institute Museum. (Courtesy of the Oriental Institute Museum of the University of Chicago)

References

Adang, O. M. J. (1985). Exploratory aggression in chimpanzees. *Behaviour, 95*, 138–163.

Adang, O. M. J. (1986). Exploring the social environment: A developmental study of teasing in chimpanzees. *Ethology, 73*, 136–160.

Albright, J. L., & Arave, C. W. (1997). *The behaviour of cattle.* New York: C. A. B. International.

Alcock, J. (2001). *Animal behavior: An evolutionary approach.* 7th ed. Sunderland, Mass.: Sinauer.

Alcock, J., & Sherman, P. (1994). The utility of the proximate–ultimate dichotomy in ethology. *Ethology, 96*, 58–62.

Aldis, O. (1975). *Playfighting.* New York: Academic Press.

Alexander, G. M., & Hines, M. (2002). Sex differences in response to children's toys in nonhuman primates (*Cercopithecus aethiops sabaeus*). *Evolution and Human Behavior, 23*, 467–479.

Allen, C., & Bekoff, M. (1997). *Species of mind.* Cambridge, Mass.: MIT Press.

Allen, C., & Saidel, E. (1998). The evolution of reference. In D. Cummins & C. Allen (eds.), *The Evolution of Mind* (pp. 183–203). New York: Oxford University Press.

Almeida, S. S., & De Araújo, M. (2001). Postnatal protein malnutrition affects play behavior and other social interactions in juvenile rats. *Physiology & Behavior, 74*, 45–51.

Altmann, J. (1974). Observational study of behaviour: Sampling methods. *Behaviour, 49*, 227–267.

Alverdes, F. (1927). *Social life in the animal world* (K. C. Creasy, trans.). London: Kegan, Paul, Trench, Trubner.

Anderson, R. A., & Karasov, W. H. (1981). Contrasts in energy intake and expenditure in sit-and-wait and widely foraging lizards. *Oecologia, 49*, 67–72.

Armstrong, E. A. (1965). *Bird display and behavior.* 2nd ed. New York: Dover.

Auffenberg, W. (1981). *The behavioral ecology of the Komodo monitor.* Gainesville: University of Florida Press.

Aureli, F., & de Waal, F. B. M. (1997). Inhibition of social behavior in chimpanzees under high-density conditions. *American Journal of Primatology, 41*, 213–228.

Avedon, E. M., & Sutton-Smith, B. (1971). *The study of games.* New York: John Wiley & Sons.

Bachman, E. S., Dhillon, H., Zhang, C.-Y., Cinti, S., Bianco, A. C., Kobilka, B. K., & Lowell, B. B. (2002). βAR signaling required for diet-induced thermogenesis and obesity resistance. *Science, 297,* 843–845.

Baensch, H. A., & Riehl, R. (1993). *Aquarium atlas* (Vol. 2). Melle, Germany: Hans A. Baensch GmbH.

Baerends, G. P. (1976). On drive, conflict and instinct, and the functional organization of behavior. In M. A. Corner & D. F. Swaab (eds.), *Progress in Brain Research* (Vol. 45, *Perspectives in Brain Research,* pp. 427–447). Amsterdam: Elsevier/North-Holland Biomedical Press.

Baerends, G. P. (1990). On spontaneity in behaviour, the modal (fixed) action pattern and play. *Netherlands Journal of Zoology, 40,* 565–584.

Bakker, R. T. (1986). *The dinosaur heresies.* New York: William Morrow.

Balaskó, M., & Cabanac, M. (1998). Behavior of juvenile lizards (*Iguana iguana*) in a conflict between temperature regulation and palatable food. *Brain, Behavior and Evolution, 52,* 257–262.

Baldwin, J. D., & Baldwin, J. I. (1974). Exploration and social play in squirrel monkeys (*Saimiri*). *American Zoologist, 14,* 303–315.

Baldwin, J. D., & Baldwin, J. I. (1976). Effects of ecology on social play: A laboratory simulation. *Ethology, 40,* 1–14.

Baldwin, J. D., & Baldwin, J. I. (1977). The role of learning phenomena in the ontogeny of exploration and play. In S. Chevalier-Skolnikoff & F. E. Poirier (eds.), *Primate Biosocial Development: Biological, Social, and Ecological Determinants* (pp. 343–406). New York: Garland.

Baldwin, J. D., & Baldwin, J. I. (1981). *Beyond sociobiology.* New York: Elsevier.

Baldwin, J. M. (1896). A new factor in evolution. *American Naturalist, 30,* 441–451, 536–553.

Baldwin, J. M. (1902a). Play. In J. M. Baldwin (ed.), *Dictionary of philosophy and psychology* (Vol. 2, pp. 303–304). New York: Macmillan.

Baldwin, J. M. (ed.). (1902b). *Dictionary of philosophy and psychology.* New York: Macmillan.

Bally, G. (1945). *Vom Ursprung und den Grenzen derm Freiheit. Eine Deutung des Spiels bei Tier und Mensch.* Basel, Switzerland: Benno Schwabe.

Bang, D., & Mack, V. (1998). Enriching the environment of the laboratory bullfrog (*Rana catesbeiana*). *Lab Animal, 27*(6), 41–42.

Bannister, R. C. (1988). *Social darwinism: Science and myth in Anglo-American social thought.* Philadelphia: Temple University Press.

Barber, N. (1991). Play and energy regulation in mammals. *Quarterly Review of Biology, 66,* 129–147.

Barber, T. X. (1994). *The human nature of birds.* New York: Penguin.

Barkow, J. H., Cosmides, L., & Tooby, J. (eds.). (1992). *The adapted mind: Evolutionary psychology and the generation of culture.* New York: Oxford University Press.

Barlow, G. W. (1961). Social behavior of the desert pupfish, *Cyprinodon macularius*, in the field and in the aquarium. *American Midland Naturalist, 65*, 339–358.

Barlow, G. W. (1968). Ethological units of behavior. In D. Ingle (ed.), *The Central Nervous System and Fish Behavior* (pp. 217–232). Chicago: University of Chicago Press.

Barlow, G. W. (2000). *The cichlid fishes: Nature's grand experiment in evolution.* Cambridge, Mass.: Perseus.

Barlow, G. W., & Francis, R. C. (1988). Unmasking affiliative behavior among juvenile Midas cichlids (*Cichlasoma citrinellum*). *Journal of Comparative Psychology, 102*, 118–123.

Barlow, G. W., & Siri, P. (1987). Consorting among juvenile Midas cichlids (*Cichlasoma citrinellum*) in relation to own and to parents' color. *Journal of Comparative Psychology, 101*, 312–316.

Barnett, L. A. (1998). The adaptive powers of being playful. In M. C. Duncan, G. Chick, & A. Aycock (eds.), *Diversions and Divergences in the Fields of Play* (Vol. 1, pp. 97–119). Greenwich, Conn.: Ablex.

Barton, R. A., & Harvey, P. H. (2000). Mosaic evolution of brain structures in mammals. *Nature, 405*, 1055–1058.

Bates, H. W. (1864). *The naturalist on the river Amazon.* 2nd ed. London: Murray.

Bateson, G. G. (1956). The message "this is play." In B. Schaffner (ed.), *Group Processes* (pp. 145–242). New York: Josiah Macy, Jr. Foundation.

Bateson, G. (1972). A theory of play and fantasy. In G. Bateson (ed.), *Steps to an Ecology of Mind* (pp. 177–193). New York: Ballantine Books.

Bateson, P. (1981). Discontinuities in development and changes in the organization of play in cats. In K. Immelmann, G. W. Barlow, L. Petrinovich, & M. Main (eds.), *Behavioral Development: The Bielefeld Interdisciplinary Project* (pp. 281–295). Cambridge: Cambridge University Press.

Bateson, P., & Young, M. (1981). Separation from the mother and the development of play in cats. *Animal Behaviour, 29*, 173–180.

Bauchot, M. L., Ridet, J. M., Diagne, M., & Bauchot, R. (1989). Encephalization in Gobioidei (Teleostei). *Japanese Journal of Ichthyology, 31*, 63–74.

Bauchot, R., Ridet, J. M., & Bauchot, M. L. (1989). The brain organization of butterflyfishes. *Envionmental Biology of Fishes, 25*, 205–209.

Bax, M. (1977). Man the player. In B. Tizard & D. Harvey (eds.), *Biology of Play* (pp. 1–5). London: William Heinemann Medical Books.

Bayless, M. K. (1994). Zur Fortpflanzungsbiologie des Steppenwarans (*Varanus exanthematicus*). *Salamandra, 30*, 109–118.

Beach, F. A. (1945). Current concepts of play in animals. *American Naturalist, 79*, 523–541.

Beach, F. A. (1955). The descent of instinct. *Psychological Review, 62*, 401–410.

Beatty, W. W. (1984). Hormonal organization of sex differences in play fighting and spatial behavior. *Progress in Brain Research, 61*, 315–330.

Beck, B. B. (1982). Chimpocentrism: Bias in cognitive ethology. *Journal of Human Evolution*, *11*, 3–17.

Beebe, W. (1932). *Nonsuch: Land of water*. New York: Brewer, Warren, and Putnam.

Bekoff, M. (1972). The development of social interaction, play, and metacommunication in mammals; An ethological perspective. *Quarterly Review of Biology*, *47*, 412–434.

Bekoff, M. (1974). Social play and play-soliciting by infant canids. *American Zoologist*, *14*, 323–340.

Bekoff, M. (1976). Animal play: Problems and perspectives. *Perspectives in Ethology*, *2*, 165–188.

Bekoff, M. (1978a). Behavioral development in coyotes and eastern coyotes. In M. Bekoff (ed.), *Coyotes: Biology, Behavior and Management* (pp. 97–126). New York: Academic Press.

Bekoff, M. (1978b). Social play: Structure, function, and the evolution of a social cooperative behavior. In G. M. Burghardt & M. Bekoff (eds.), *The Development of Behavior: Comparative and Evolutionary Aspects* (pp. 367–383). New York: Garland.

Bekoff, M. (1995). Play signals as punctuation: The structure of social play in canids. *Behaviour*, *132*, 419–429.

Bekoff, M. (2001). Social play behaviour: Cooperation, fairness, trust, and the evolution of morality. *Journal of Consciousness Studies*, *8*, 81–90.

Bekoff, M. (ed.). (2002). *The smile of a dolphin: Remarkable accounts of animal emotions*. New York: Discovery Books.

Bekoff, M., & Allen, C. (1998). Intentional communication and social play: How and why animals negotiate and agree to play. In M. Bekoff & J. A. Byers (eds.), *Animal Play: Evolutionary, Comparative, and Ecological Perspectives* (pp. 97–114). Cambridge: Cambridge University Press.

Bekoff, M., & Byers, J. A. (1981). A critical reanalysis of the ontogeny and phylogeny of mammalian social and locomotor play: An ethological hornet's nest. In K. Immelmann, G. W. Barlow, L. Petrinovich, & M. Main (eds.), *Behavioral Development: The Bielefeld Interdisciplinary Project* (pp. 296–337). Cambridge: Cambridge University Press.

Bekoff, M., & Byers, J. A. (1992). Time, energy and play. *Animal Behaviour*, *44*, 981–982.

Bekoff, M., & Byers, J. A. (eds.). (1998). *Animal play: Evolutionary, comparative, and ecological perspectives*. Cambridge: Cambridge University Press.

Bekoff, M., Allen, C., & Burghardt, G. M. (eds.). (2002). *The cognitive animal: Empirical and theoretical perspectives on animal cognition*. Cambridge, Mass.: MIT Press.

Bekoff, M., Byers, J. A., & Bekoff, A. (1980). Prenatal motility and postnatal play: Functional continuity? *Developmental Psychobiology*, *13*, 225–228.

Bell, C. C. (1989). Sensory coding and corollary discharge effects in mormyrid electric fish. *Journal of Experimental Biology*, *146*, 229–253.

Bell, C., Bodznick, D., Montgomery, J., & Bastian, J. (1997). The generation and subtraction of sensory expectations within cerebellum-like structures. *Brain, Behavior and Evolution*, *50* (Suppl. 1), 17–31.

Bell, C., Cordo, P., & Harnad, S. (1996). Controversies in neuroscience IV: Motor learning and synaptric plasticity in the cerebellum. *Behavioral and Brain Sciences, 19*, 339–527.

Ben-David, M., Pellis, S. M., & Pellis, V. C. (1991). Feeding habits and predatory behaviour in the marbled polecat (*Vormela peregusna syriaca*): I. Killing methods in relation to prey size and prey behaviour. *Behaviour, 118*, 127–143.

Bennett, A. F. (1982). The energetics of reptilian activity. In C. Gans & F. H. Pough (eds.), *Biology of the Reptilia* (Vol. 13, pp. 155–199). London: Academic Press.

Bennett, A. F., Hicks, J. W., & Cullum, A. J. (2000). An experimental test of the thermoregulatory hypothesis for the evolution of endothermy. *Evolution, 54*, 1768–1773.

Bennett, G. (1835). Notes on the natural history and habits of the *Ornithorhynchus paradoxus*, Blum. *Transactions of the Zoological Society of London, 1*, 229–258.

Beran, M. J., Gobson, K. R., & Rumbaugh, D. M. (1999). Predicting hominid intelligence from brain size. In M. C. Corballis & S. E. G. Lea (eds.), *The Descent of Mind: Psychological Perspectives on Hominid Evolution* (pp. 88–97). New York: Oxford University Press.

Berger, J. (1979). Social ontogeny and behavioural diversity: Consequences for bighorn sheep, *Ovis canadensis* inhabiting desert and mountain environments. *Journal of Zoology, London, 188*, 251–266.

Bergman, H. H. (1968). Eine deskriptive Verhaltensanalyse des Segelflossers (*Pterophyllum scalare* Cuv. & Val., Cichlidae, Pisces). *Zeitschrift für Tierpsychologie, 25*, 559–587.

Berk, L. E. (1996). *Infants, children, and adolescents*. 2nd ed. Boston: Allyn and Bacon.

Berlyne, D. E. (1960). *Conflict, arousal, and curiosity*. New York: McGraw-Hill.

Berman, S., Ozkaragoz, T., Young, R. M., & Noble, E. P. (2002). D2 dopamine receptor gene polymorphism discriminates two kinds of novelty seeking. *Personality and Individual Differences, 33*, 867–882.

Bernard, L. L. (1924). *Instinct: A study in social psychology*. London: Allen and Unwin.

Bevins, R. A., Besheer, J., Palmatier, M. I., Jenson, H. C., Pickett, M. S., & Eurek, S. (2002). Novel-object place conditioning: Behavioral and dopaminergic processes in expression of novelty reward. *Behavioral Brain Research 129*, 41–50.

Biben, M. (1982). Object play and social treatment of prey in bush dogs and crab-eating foxes. *Behaviour, 79*, 201–211.

Biben, M. (1983). Comparative ontogeny of social behavior in three South American canids: The maned wolf, crab-eating fox, and bush dog: Implications for sociality. *Animal Behaviour, 31*, 814–826.

Biben, M. (1986). Individual- and sex-related strategies of wrestling play in captive squirrel monkeys. *Ethology, 71*, 229–241.

Biben, M., & Champoux, M. (1999). Play and stress: cortisol as a negative correlate of play in Saimiri. In S. Reifel (ed.), *Play and culture studies* (Vol. 2, pp. 191–208). Stamford, Conn.: Ablex.

Biben, M., & Symmes, D. (1986). Play vocalizations of squirrel monkeys (*Saimiri sciureus*). *Folia Primatologica*, *46*, 173–182.

Biben, M., Symmes, D., & Bernhards, D. (1989). Vigilance during play in squirrel monkeys. *American Journal of Primatology*, *17*, 41–49.

Bierens de Haan, J. A. (1947). *Animal psychology*. London: Hutchinson University Library.

Bird, E. I. (1987). Psychophysiological processes during rifle shooting. *International Journal of Sports Psychology*, *18*, 9–18.

Bloom, L., & Tinker, E. (2001). The intentionality model and language acquisition. *Monographs of the Society for Research in Child Development*, *66*(4, serial No. 267), viii+104.

Blow, S. E. (1894). *Symbolic education. A Commentary on Froebel's "Mother Play."* New York: Appleton.

Blumer, L. S. (1985). The significance of biparental care in the brown bullhead, *Ictalurus nebulosus*. *Envionmental Biology of Fishes*, *12*, 231–236.

Blurton-Jones, N. (1993). The lives of hunter-gatherer children: Effects of parental behavior and parental reproductive strategy. In M. E. Pereira & L. A. Fairbanks (eds.), *Juvenile Primates: Life History, Development, and Behavior* (pp. 309–326). New York: Oxford University Press.

Bonney, K. R., & Wynne, C. D. L. (2002). Visual discrimination learning and strategy behavior in the fat-tailed dunnart (*Sminthopsis crassicaudata*). *Journal of Comparative Psychology*, *116*, 55–62.

Borst, A. (1991). *Medieval worlds: Barbarians, heretics and artists*. Chicago: University of Chicago Press.

Boustany, A. M., Davis, S. F., Pyle, P., Anderson, S. D., Le Boeuf, B. J., & Block, B. A. (2002). Expanded niche for white sharks. *Nature*, *415*, 35–36.

Bowers, B. B., & Burghardt, G. M. (1992). The scientist and the snake: Relationships with reptiles. In H. Davis & D. Balfour (eds.), *The Inevitable Bond: Examining Scientist-Animal Interactions* (pp. 250–263). Cambridge: Cambridge University Press.

Brattstrom, B. H. (1973). Social and maintenance behavior of the echidna, *Tachyglossus aculeatus*. *Journal of Mammalogy*, *54*, 50–71.

Breder, C. M. Jr. (1929). *Report on synentognath habits and development* Yearbook No. 28. Washington, D.C.: Carnegie Institution of Washington.

Breder, C. M. Jr. (1932a). On the habits and development of certain Atlantic Synentognathi. *Papers from Tortugas Laboratory of Carnegie Institution of Washington Vol. 28*. Washington, D.C.: Carnegie Institution of Washington.

Breder, C. M. Jr. (1932b). A record of *Sarda velox* and notes on other Block Island fishes. *Copeia*, *1932*, 31–32.

Brown, B. (1999). Optimizing expression of the common human genome for child development. *Current Directions in Psychological Science*, *8*, 37–41.

Brown, J. A. (1985). The adaptive significance of behavioural ontogeny in some centrarchid fishes. *Envionmental Biology of Fishes*, *13*, 25–34.

Brown, J. A., Wiseman, D., & Kean, P. (1997). The use of behavioural observations in the larviculture of cold-water marine fish. *Aquaculture, 155,* 297–306.

Brown, S. (1998). Play as an organizing principle: Clinical evidence and personal observations. In M. Bekoff & J. A. Byers (eds.), *Animal Play: Evolutionary, Comparative, and Ecological Perspectives* (pp. 243–259). Cambridge: Cambridge University Press.

Brownlee, A. (1954). Play in domestic cattle in Britain: An analysis of its nature. *British Veterinary Journal, 110,* 48–68.

Brunelli, S. A., & Hofer, M. A. (2001). Selective breeding for an infantile phenotype (isolation calling). In E. M. Blass (ed.), *Handbook of Behavioral Neurobiology* (Vol. 13, *Developmental Psychobiology,* pp. 433–482). New York: Plenum.

Bruner, J. S., Jolly, A., & Sylva, K. (eds.). (1976). *Play: Its role in development and evolution.* New York: Basic Books.

Bshary, R., Wickler, W., & Fricke, H. (2002). Fish cognition: A primate's eye view. *Animal Cognition, 5,* 1–13.

Büchner, L. (1880). *Mind in animals.* 3rd ed. (A. Besant, trans.). London: Freethought Publishing.

Budiansky, S. (1997). *The nature of horses.* New York: Free Press.

Bühler, K. (1930). *Die geistige Entwicklung des Kindes.* 6th ed. Jena, Germany: Gustav Fischer.

Bull, C. M. (1994). Population dynamics and pair fidelity in sleepy lizards. In L. J. Vitte & E. R. Pianka (eds.), *Lizard Ecology: Historical and Experimental Approaches* (pp. 159–174). Princeton, N.J.: Princeton University Press.

Bullock, T. H. (1977). *Introduction to nervous systems.* San Francisco: W. H. Freeman.

Burgdorf, J., & Panksepp, J. (2001). Tickling induces reward in adolescent rats. *Physiology and Behavior, 72,* 167–173.

Burggren, W. W. (1982). "Air gulping" improves blood oxygen transport during aquatic hypoxia in the goldfish, *Carassius auratus. Physiological Zoology, 55,* 327–334.

Burghardt, G. M. (1969). Effects of early experience on food preference in chicks. *Psychonomic Science, 14,* 7–8.

Burghardt, G. M. (1970). Defining "communication." In J. W. Johnston, Jr., D. G. Moulton, & A. Turk (eds.), *Communication by Chemical Signals* (pp. 5–18). New York: Appleton-Century-Crofts.

Burghardt, G. M. (1973). Instinct and innate behavior: Toward an ethological psychology. In J. A. Nevin & G. S. Reynolds (eds.), *The Study of Behavior: Learning, Motivation, Emotion, and Instinct* (pp. 322–400). Glenview, Ill.: Scott Foresman.

Burghardt, G. M. (1975). Behavioral research on common animals in small zoos. In *Research in Zoos and Aquariums* (pp. 103–133). Washington DC: National Academy of Sciences.

Burghardt, G. M. (1977a). Learning processes in reptiles. In C. Gans & D. Tinkle (eds.), *The Biology of Reptilia* (Vol. 7, *Ecology and Behavior,* pp. 555–681). New York: Academic Press.

Burghardt, G. M. (1977b). Of iguanas and dinosaurs: Social behavior and communication in neonate reptiles. *American Zoologist, 17,* 177–190.

Burghardt, G. M. (1977c). Ontogeny of communication. In T. Sebeok (ed.), *How Animals Communicate* (pp. 67–93). Bloomington: University of Indiana Press.

Burghardt, G. M. (1982). Comparison matters: Curiosity, bears, surplus energy and why reptiles don't play. *Behavioral and Brain Sciences, 5,* 159–160.

Burghardt, G. M. (1983). Aggregation and species discrimination in newborn snakes. *Zeitschrift für Tierpsychologie, 61,* 89–101.

Burghardt, G. M. (1984). On the origins of play. In P. K. Smith (ed.), *Play in Animals and Humans* (pp. 5–41). Oxford: Basil Blackwell.

Burghardt, G. M. (1985a). Animal awareness: Current perceptions and historical perspective. *American Psychologist, 40,* 905–919.

Burghardt, G. M. (ed.). (1985b). *Foundations of comparative ethology.* New York: Van Nostrand Reinhold.

Burghardt, G. M. (1988a). Anecdotes and critical anthromorphism. *Behavioral and Brain Sciences, 11,* 248–249.

Burghardt, G. M. (1988b). Precocity, play, and the ectotherm-endotherm transition: Superficial adaptation or profound reorganization? In E. M. Blass (ed.), *Handbook of Behavioral Neurobiology* (Vol. 9, *Developmental Psychobiology and Behavioral Ecology* pp. 107–148). New York: Plenum.

Burghardt, G. M. (1990). Chemically mediated predation in vertebrates: Diversity, ontogeny, and information. In D. W. McDonald, D. Müller-Schwarze, & S. E. Natynczuk (eds.), *Chemical Signals in Vertebrates* (Vol. 5, pp. 475–499). Oxford: Oxford University Press.

Burghardt, G. M. (1992). Human-bear bonding in research on black bear behavior. In H. Davis & D. Balfour (eds.), *The Inevitable Bond: Examining Scientist-animal Interactions* (pp. 365–382). Cambridge: Cambridge University Press.

Burghardt, G. M. (1996). Environmental enrichment or controlled deprivation? In G. M. Burghardt, J. T. Bielitski, J. R. Boyce, & D. O. Schaefer (eds.), *The Well-being of Animals in Zoo and Aquarium Sponsored Research* (pp. 91–101). Greenbelt, Md: Scientists Center for Animal Welfare.

Burghardt, G. M. (1997). Amending Tinbergen: A fifth aim for ethology. In R. W. Mitchell, N. S. Thompson, & H. L. Miles (eds.), *Anthropomorphism, Anecdotes, and Animals* (pp. 254–276). Albany: State University of New York Press.

Burghardt, G. M. (1998a). The evolutionary origins of play revisited: Lessons from turtles. In M. Bekoff & J. A. Byers (eds.), *Animal Play: Evolutionary, Comparative, and Ecological Perspectives* (pp. 1–26). Cambridge: Cambridge University Press.

Burghardt, G. M. (1998b). Play. In G. Greenberg & M. Haraway (eds.), *Comparative Psychology: A Handbook* (pp. 757–767). New York: Garland.

Burghardt, G. M. (1998c). Snake stories: From the additive model to ethology's fifth aim. In L. A. Hart (ed.), *Responsible Conduct with Animals in Research* (pp. 77–95). New York: Oxford University Press.

Burghardt, G. M. (1999). Conceptions of play and the evolution of animal minds. *Evolution and Cognition, 5*, 115–123.

Burghardt, G. M. (2001). Play: Attributes and neural substrates. In E. M. Blass (ed.), *Handbook of Behavioral Neurobiology* (Vol. 13, *Developmental Psychobiology*, pp. 327–366). New York: Plenum.

Burghardt, G. M. (2004). Play: How evolution can explain the most mysterious behavior of all. In A. Moya & E. Font (eds.), *Evolution: From Molecules to Ecosystems* (pp. 231–246). Oxford: Oxford University Press.

Burghardt, G. M., & Bekoff, M. (1978). *The development of behavior: Comparative and evolutionary aspects*. New York: Garland STPM Press.

Burghardt, G. M., & Burghardt, L. S. (1972). Notes on the behavioral development of two female black bear cubs: The first eight months. In S. Herrero (ed.), *Bears—Their Biology and Management* (Vol. 23, pp. 255–273). Morges, Switzerland: International Union for the Conservation of Nature and Natural Resources (I.U.C.N.).

Burghardt, G. M., & Herzog, H. A., Jr. (1980). Beyond conspecifics: Is brer rabbit our brother? *Bio-Science, 30*, 763–768.

Burghardt, G. M., & Herzog, H. A., Jr. (1989). Animals, evolution and ethics. In R. J. Hoage (ed.), *Perceptions of Animals in American Culture* (pp. 129–151). Washington, D.C.: Smithsonian Institution press.

Burghardt, G. M., & Krause, M. A. (1999). Plasticity of foraging behavior in garter snakes (*Thamnophis sirtalis*) reared on different diets. *Journal of Comparative Psychology, 113*, 277–285.

Burghardt, G. M., Chiszar, D., Murphy, J. B., Romano, J. Jr., Walsh, T., & Manrod, J. (2002). Behavioral complexity, behavioral development, and play. In J. B. Murphy, C. Ciofi, C. de la Panouse, & T. Walsh (eds.), *Komodo Dragons: Biology and Conservation* (pp. 78–117). Washington, D.C.: Smithsonian Institution Press.

Burghardt, G. M., Layne, D. G., & Konigsberg, L. (2000). The genetics of dietary experience in a restricted natural population. *Psychological Science, 11*, 69–72.

Burghardt, G. M., Ward, B., & Rosscoe, R. (1996). Problem of reptile play: Environmental enrichment and play behavior in a captive Nile soft-shelled turtle (*Trionyx triunguis*). *Zoo Biology, 15*, 223–238.

Burghardt, G. M., Bielitski, J. T., Boyce, J. R., & Schaefer, D. O. (eds.). (1996). *The well-being of animals in zoo and aquarium sponsored research*. Greenbelt, Md: Scientists Center for Animal Welfare.

Burrell, H. (1927). *The platypus*. Sydney: Angus & Robertson.

Burton, R. (1883). *The anatomy of melancholy*. 6th ed. Philadelphia: Claxton.

Buss, D. M. (1999). *Evolutionary psychology*. New York: Allyn and Bacon.

Buss, D. M. (2000). The evolution of happiness. *American Psychologist, 55*, 15–23.

Butler, A. B., & Hodos, W. (1996). *Comparative vertebrate neuroanatomy: Evolution and adaptation*. New York: Wiley-Liss.

Byers, J. A. (1984). Play in ungulates. In P. K. Smith (ed.), *Play in Animals and Humans* (pp. 43–65). Oxford: Basil Blackwell.

Byers, J. A. (1985). Olfaction related behavior in collared peccaries. *Zeitschrift für Tierpsychologie*, *70*, 201–210.

Byers, J. A. (1997). *American pronghorn. Social adaptations and the ghosts of predators past*. Chicago. Ill.: University of Chicago Press.

Byers, J. A. (1998). Biological effects of locomotor play: Getting into shape, or something more specific? In M. Bekoff & J. A. Byers (eds.), *Animal Play: Evolutionary, Comparative, and Ecological Perspectives* (pp. 205–220). Cambridge: Cambridge University Press.

Byers, J. A. (1999a). The distribution of play behaviour among Australian marsupials. *Journal of Zoology, London*, *247*, 349–356.

Byers, J. A. (1999b). Play's the thing. *Natural History*, *108*(6), 40–45.

Byers, J. A., & Walker, C. (1995). Refining the motor training hypothesis for the evolution of play. *American Naturalist*, *146*, 25–40.

Byrne, R. W., Corp, N., & Byrne, J. M. E. (2001). Estimating the complexity of animal behaviour: How mountain gorillas eat thistles. *Behaviour*, *138*, 525–557.

Bywater, I., & Patrick, G. T. W. (1969). *Heraclitus of Ephesus*. Chicago: Argonaut.

Cabanac, A., & Cabanac, M. (2000). Heart rate response to gentle handling of frog and lizard. *Behavioural Processes*, *52*, 89–95.

Cabanac, M. (1999). Emotion and phylogeny. *Journal of Consciousness Studies*, *6*, 176–190.

Cabanac, M., & Bernieri, C. (2000). Behavioural rise in body temperature and tachycardia by handling of a turtle (*Clemmys insculpta*). *Behavioural Processes*, *49*, 61–68.

Cabib, S., & Bonaventura, N. (1997). Parallel strain-dependent susceptibility to environmentally-induced stereotypies and stress-induced behavioral sensitization in mice. *Physiology and Behavior*, *61*, 499–506.

Cabib, S., Puglisi-Allegra, S., & Ventura, R. (2002). The contribution of comparative studies in inbred strains of mice to the understanding of the hyperactive phenotype. *Behavioural Brain Research*, *130*, 103–109.

Cain, P., Gerin, W., & Moller, P. (1994). Short-range navigation of the weakly electric fish, *Gnathonemus petersii* L. (Mormyridae, Teleostei), in novel and familiar environments. *Ethology*, *96*, 33–45.

Caldwell, R. L. (1985). A test of individual recognition in the stomatopod *Gonodactylus festae*. *Animal Behaviour*, *33*, 101–106.

Calvin, W. H. (1983). A stone's throw and its launch window: Timing precision and its implications for language and hominid brains. *Journal of Theoretical Biology*, *104*, 121–135.

Calvin, W. H. (1993). The unitary hypothesis: A common neural circuitry for novel manipulations, language, plan-ahead, and throwing. In K. R. Gibson & T. Ingold (eds.), *Tools, Language, and Cognition in Human Evolution* (pp. 230–250). Cambridge: Cambridge University Press.

Cacioppo, J. T., Semin, G. R., & Berntson, G. G. (2004). Realism, Instrumentalism, and scientific symbiosis. *American Psychologist, 59,* 214–223.

Cardinal, R. N., Parkinson, J. A., Hall, J., & Everitt, B. J. (2002). Emotion and motivation: The role of the amygdala, ventral striatum, and prefrontal cortex. *Neuroscience and Biobehavioral Reviews, 26,* 321–352.

Caro, T. M. (1980). Effects of the mother, object play and adult experience on predation in cats. *Behavioral and Neural Biology, 29,* 29–51.

Caro, T. M. (1988). Adaptive significance of play: Are we getting closer? *Trends in Ecology and Evolution, 3,* 50–54.

Caro, T. M. (1995). Short-term costs and correlates of play in cheetahs. *Animal Behaviour, 49,* 333–345.

Caro, T. M., & Alawi, R. M. (1985). Comparative aspects of behavioural development in two species of free-living hyrax. *Behaviour, 95,* 87–109.

Carpenter, C. R. (1934). A field study of the behavior and social relations of howling monkeys. *Comparative Psychology Monographs, 10,* 1–168.

Carr, H. A. (1902). The survival values of play. *Investigations of the Department of Psychology and Education of the University of Colorado, 1*(2), 1–47, Boulder, Colo.

Carroll, S. B., Grenier, J. K., & Weatherbee, S. D. (2001). *From DNA to diversity: Molecular genetics and the evolution of animal design.* Oxford: Blackwell.

Carruthers, P. (2002). Human creativity: Its cognitive basis, its evolution, and its connection to childhood pretence. *British Journal of Philosophy of Science, 53,* 225–249.

Case, T. J. (1978). Endothermy and parental care in terrestrial vertebrates. *American Naturalist, 112,* 861–874.

Case, T. J. (1982). Ecology and evolution of the insular gigantic Chuckawallas *Sauromalus hispidus* and *Sauromalus varius.* In G. M. Burghardt & A. S. Rand (eds.), *Iguanas of the World: Their Behavior, Ecology, and Conservation* (pp. 184–212). Park Ridge, N.J.: Noyes.

Cermak, M. (1996). Gripping feats of the weightlifter mouse. *Geo Australasia, 18*(1), 78–86.

Chalmers, N. R. (1980). The ontogeny of play in feral olive baboons. *Animal Behaviour, 28,* 570–585.

Changizi, M. A., McGehee, R. M. F., & Hall, W. G. (2002). Evidence that appetitive responses for dehydration and food-deprivation are learned. *Physiology and Behavior, 75,* 295–304.

Chepko, B. D. (1971). A preliminary study of the effects of play deprivation on young goats. *Zeitschrift für Tierpsychologie, 28,* 517–526.

Chick, G. (2001). What is play for? Sexual selection and the evolution of play. In S. Reifel (ed.), *Theory in Context and Out* (pp. 3–25). Westport, Conn.: Ablex.

Chinsamy, A., & Dodson, P. (1995). Inside a dinosaur bone. *American Scientist, 83,* 174–180.

Chiszar, D. (1985). Ontogeny of communicative behaviors. In E. S. Gollin (ed.), *The Comparative Development of Adaptive Skills: Evolutionary Implications* (pp. 207–238). Hillsdale, N.J.: Erlbaum.

Christian, K., & Weavers, B. (1994). Analysis of the activity and energetics of the lizard *Varanus rosenbergi*. *Copeia, 1994*, 289–295.

Christian, K. A., Corbett, L. K., Green, B., & Weavers, B. W. (1995). Seasonal activity and energetics of two species of varanid lizards in tropical Australia. *Oecologia, 103*, 349–357.

Christian, K., Green, B., Bedford, G., & Newgrain, K. (1996). Seasonal metabolism of a small arboreal monitor lizard, *Varanus scalaris*, in tropical Australia. *Journal of Zoology, London, 240*, 283–296.

Christian, K. A., Griffiths, A. D., Bedford, G., & Jenkin, G. (1999). Androgen concentrations and behavior of frillneck lizards (*Chlamydosaurus kingii*). *Journal of Herpetology, 33*, 12–17.

Ciali, S., Gordon, J., & Moller, P. (1997). Spectral sensitivity of the weakly discharging electric fish *Gnathonemus petersi* using its electric organ discharges as the response measure. *Journal of Fish Biology, 50*, 1074–1087.

Clark, C. D., & Miller, P. J. (1998). Play. In H. Friedman (ed.), *Encyclopedia of Mental Health* (Vol. 3, pp. 189–197). San Diego: Academic Press.

Clark, J. M., Norell, M. A., & Chiappe, L. M. (1999). An oviraptorid skeleton from the Late Cretaceous of Ukhaa Tolgod, Mongolia, preserved in an avianlike brooding position over an oviraptorid nest. *American Museum Novitates, 3265*, 1–36.

Clements, R. L. (ed.). (1995). *Games and great ideas*. Westport, Conn.: Greenwood Press.

Clemons, W. A. (1989). Diagnosis of the class Mammalia. In D. W. Walton & B. J. Richardson (eds.), *Fauna of Australia* (Vol. 1B, *Mammalia*, pp. 401–406). Canberra: Australian Government Publishing Service.

Clemons, W. A., Richardson, B. J., & Baverstock, P. R. (1989). Biogeography and phylogeny of the Metatheria. In D. W. Walton & B. J. Richardson (eds.), *Fauna of Australia* (Vol. 1B, *Mammalia*, pp. 527–548). Canberra: Australian Government Publishing Service.

Cloarec, A. (1982). Predatory success in the water stick insect: The role of visual and mechanical stimulations after molting. *Animal Behaviour, 30*, 549–556.

Cloninger, C. R. (1987). Neurogenetic adaptive mechanisms in alcoholism. *Science, 236*, 410–416.

Clutton-Brock, T. H. (1991). *The evolution of parental care*. Princeton, N.J.: Princeton University Press.

Cohen, D. (1987). *The development of play*. London: Croom Helm.

Colbert, E. H., Morales, M., & Minkoff, E. C. (2001). *Colbert's evolution of the vertebrates*. 5th ed. New York: Wiley-Liss.

Collis, K., & Borgia, G. (1993). The costs of male display and delayed plumage maturation in the satin bowerbird (*Ptilonorhynchus violaceus*). *Ethology, 94*, 59–71.

Colombo, J. (1993). *Infant cognition: Predicting later intellectual functioning*. London: Sage.

Coombs, W. P. (1989). Modern analogs for dinosaur nesting and parental behavior. In J. O. Farlow (ed.), *Paleobiology of the Dinosaurs* (pp. 21–53). Boulder, Col.: Geological Society of America.

Coppinger, R., & Coppinger, L. (1998). Differences in the behavior of dog breeds. In J. Serpell (ed.), *Genetics and the Behavior of Domestic Animals* (pp. 167–202). New York: Academic Press.

Coppinger, R., Glendinning, J., Torop, E., Matthay, C., Sutherland, M., & Smith, C. (1987). Degree of behavioral neoteny differentiates canid polymorphs. *Ethology*, *75*, 89–108.

Coppinger, R. P., & Smith, C. K. (1989). A model for understanding the evolution of mammalian behavior. In H. Genoways (ed.), *Current Mammalogy* (Vol. 2, pp. 335–374). New York: Plenum.

Coppolillo, H. P. (1991). The use of play in psychodynamic psychotherapy. In M. Lewis (ed.), *Child and Adolescent Psychiatry* (pp. 805–811). Baltimore: Williams and Wilkins.

Corballis, M. C. (2002). *From hand to mouth: The origins of language.* Princeton: Princeton University Press.

Coss, R. G. (1991). Evolutionary persistence of memory-like processes. *Concepts in Neuroscience, 2*, 129–168.

Coss, R. G. (1999). Effects of relaxed natural selection on the evolution of behavior. In S. A. Foster & J. A. Endler (eds.), *Geographic Variation in Behavior: Perspectives on Evolutionary Mechanisms* (pp. 180–208). New York: Oxford University Press.

Coss, R. G., & Goldthwaite, R. O. (1995). The persistence of old designs for perception. In N. S. Thompson (ed.), *Perspectives in Ethology* (Vol. 11, pp. 83–148). New York: Plenum.

Coss, R. G., & Perkel, D. H. (1985). The function of dendritic spines: A review of theoretical issues. *Behavioral and Neural Biology, 44*, 151–185.

Costabile, A., Smith, P. K., Matheson, L., Aston, J., Hunter, T., & Boulton, M. (1991). Cross-national comparison of how children distinguish serious from playful fighting. *Developmental Psychology, 27*, 881–887.

Coulson, G. (1996). Anti-predator behaviour in marsupials. In D. B. Croft & U. Ganslosser (eds.), *Comparison of Marsupial and Placental Behaviour* (pp. 158–186). Fürth, Germany: Filander Verlag.

Craig, W. (1918). Appetites and aversions as constituents of instincts. *Biological Bulletin, 34*, 91–107.

Crane, J. (1975). *Fiddler crabs of the world.* Princeton, N.J.: Princeton University Press.

Crews, D. J., & Landers, D. M. (1992). Electroencephalographic measures of attentional patterns prior to the golf putt. *Medicine and Science in Sports and Exercise, 24*, 116–126.

Croft, D. B. (1982). Communication in the Dasyuridae (Marsupialia): A review. In M. Archer (ed.), *Carnivorous Marsupials* (pp. 291–309). Sydney: Royal Society of New South Wales.

Croft, D. B. (1989). Social organization of the Macropodoidea. In G. Grigg, P. Jarman, & I. Hume (eds.), *Kangaroos, Wallabies and Rat-Kangaroos* (pp. 505–524). Kensington, New South Wales: Surrey Beatty and Sons.

Croft, D. B., & Ganslosser, U. (eds.). (1996). *Comparison of marsupial and placental behaviour.* Fürth, Germany: Filander Verlag.

Croft, D. B., & Snaith, F. (1991). Boxing in red kangaroos, *Macropus rufus*: Aggression or play? *International Journal of Comparative Psychology, 4*, 221–236.

Crowe, M. (1996). The verses of Heraclitus of Ephesus. *Computing and Information Systems*, *3*, 97–106.

Crump, M. L. (1996). Parental care among the Amphibia. In J. S. Rosenblatt & C. T. Snowdon (eds.), *Parental Care: Evolution, Mechanisms, and Adaptive Significance* (Vol. 25, pp. 109–144). San Diego: Academic Press.

Csikszentmihalyi, M. (1991). *Flow: The psychology of optimal experience*. New York: HarperCollins.

Csikszentmihalyi, M. (1996). *Creativity: Flow and the psychology of discovery and invention*. New York: HarperCollins.

Csikszentmihalyi, M. (1999). If we are so rich, why aren't we happy? *American Psychologist*, *54*, 821–827.

Cummings, J. W. (1979). Physiological and biochemical adaptations to training in *Rana pipiens*. *Journal of Comparative Physiology*, *134*, 345–350.

Daenen, E. W. P. M., Wolterink, G., Gerrits, M. A. F. M., & van Ree, J. M. (2002). The effects of neonatal lesions in the amygdala or ventral hippocampus on social behaviour later in life. *Behavioural Brain Research*, *136*, 571–582.

Damasio, A. R. (1999). *The feeling of what happens*. New York: Harcourt Brace.

Dao, J. (2003). Beady-eyed stinkers feast on urban fringes. *New York Times*, Aug. 6, 2003.

Darwin, C. (1871). *The descent of man and selection in relation to sex*. London: Murray.

Darwin, C. (1872). *The expression of the emotions in man and animals*. London: Murray.

Darwin, C. (1877). *The descent of man and selection in relation to sex*. 2nd revised and augmented ed. London: John Murray.

Darwin, C. (1888). Letter to Asa Gray dated May 22, 1860. In F. Darwin (ed.), *The Life and Letters of Charles Darwin* (Vol. 2, pp. 104–106). New York: Appleton.

Dave, A. S., & Margoliash, D. (2000). Song replay during sleep and computational rules for sensorimotor vocal learning. *Science*, *290*, 812–816.

Dave, A. S., Yu, A. C., & Margoliash, D. (1998). Behavioral state modulation of auditory activity in a vocal motor system. *Science*, *282*, 2250–2254.

Dawson, T. J., Finch, E., Freedman, L., Hume, I. D., Renfree, M. B., & Temple-Smith, P. D. (1989). Morphology and physiology of the Metatheria. In D. W. Walton & B. J. Richardson (eds.), *Fauna of Australia* (Vol. 1B, *Mammalia*, pp. 451–504). Canberra: Australian Government Publishing Service.

De Fazio, A. (1979). Object discrimination in a weakly electric fish, *Gnathonemus petersii* (Mormyriformes). Unpublished Ph.D. dissertation, City University of New York, New York.

Debelius, H., & Baensch, H. A. (1994). *Marine atlas*. Melle, Germany: Hans A. Baensch.

Delfour, F., & Aulagnier, S. (1997). Bubble blow in beluga whales (*Delphinapterous leucas*): A play activity? *Behavioural Processes*, *40*, 183–186.

Depue, R. A., & Collins, P. F. (1999). Neurobiology of the structure of personality: Dopamine, facilitation of incentive motivation, and extraversion. *Behavioral and Brain Sciences, 22,* 491–568.

Desmond, A. J. (1976). *The hot-blooded dinosaurs: A revolution in paleontology.* New York: Dial Press.

DeVoogd, T. J., & Lauay, C. (2001). Emerging psychobiology of the avian song system. In E. M. Blass (ed.), *Handbook of Behavioral Neurobiology* (Vol. 13, *Developmental Psychobiology,* pp. 357–392). New York: Plenum.

Dewsbury, D. A. (1994). On the utility of the proximate-ultimate distinction in the study of animal behavior. *Ethology, 96,* 63–68.

Diamond, J., & Bond, A. B. (1999). *Kea, bird of paradox.* Berkeley: University of California Press.

Diamond, J. & Bond, A. B. (2003). A comparative analysis of social play in birds. *Behaviour, 140,* 1091–1115.

Diener, A. (1985). Verhaltensanalysen zum Sozialspiel von Iltisfrettchen (*Mustela putorius furo*). *Zeitschrift für Tierpsychologie, 67,* 179–197.

Dimelow, E. J. (1963). The behaviour of the hedgehog (*Erinaceus europaeus*) in the routine of life in captivity. *Proceedings of Zoological Society of London, 141,* 281–289.

Dissanayake, E. (1992). *Homo aestheticus: Where art comes from and why.* New York: Free Press.

Dodd, A. T., Rogers, C. S., & Wilson, J. T. (2001). The effects of situational context on playful behaviors of young preschool children. In S. Reifel (ed.), *Theory in Context and Out* (pp. 367–389). Westport, Conn.: Ablex.

Doolan, S. P., & Macdonald, D. W. (1999). Co-operative rearing by slender meerkats (*Suricata suricatta*) in the Southern Kalahari. *Ethology, 105,* 851–866.

Drea, C. M., Hawk, J. E., & Glickman, S. E. (1996). Aggression decreases as play emerges in infant spotted hyaenas: Preparation for joining the clan. *Animal Behaviour, 51,* 1223–1236.

Drickamer, L. C., Vessey, S. H., & Meikle, D. (1996). *Animal behavior.* 4th ed. Dubuque, Iowa: William C. Brown.

Dücker, G., & Rensch, B. (1977). The solution of patterned string problems by birds. *Behaviour, 62,* 164–173.

Dugatkin, L. A. (ed.) (2001). *Model systems in behavioral ecology.* Princeton, N.J.: Princeton University Press.

Dugatkin, L. A. (2004). *Principles of animal behavior.* New York: Norton.

Dugatkin, L. A., & Bekoff, M. (2003). Play and the evolution of fairness: A game theory model. *Behavioural Processes, 60,* 209–214.

Dugatkin, L. A., & Sih, A. (1995). Behavioral ecology and the study of partner choice. *Ethology, 99,* 265–277.

Dumbacher, J. P., & Pruett-Jones, S. (1996). Avian chemical defenses. In V. Nolan, Jr. & E. D. Ketterson (eds.), *Current Ornithology* (Vol. 13, pp. 137–174). New York: Plenum.

Durier, V., & Rivault, C. (2001). Effects of spatial knowledge and feeding experience on foraging choices in German cockroaches. *Animal Behaviour, 62,* 681–688.

Ebinger, P. (1995). Domestication and plasticity of brain organization in mallards (*Anas platyrhynchos*). *Brain, Behavior and Evolution, 45,* 286–300.

Ecclesiastes, Book of (1993). *The complete parallel Bible.* New York: Oxford University Press.

Eibl-Eibesfeldt, I. (1970). *Ethology: The biology of behavior.* New York: Holt, Rinehart and Winston.

Eisenberg, J. F. (1981). *The mammalian radiations.* Chicago: University of Chicago Press.

Elias, J. A. (1973). Art and play. In P. P. Wiener (ed.), *Dictionary of the History of Ideas* (Vol. 1, pp. 99–107). New York: Scribner's.

Ellis, A. C., & Hall, G. S. (1921). A study of dolls. In G. S. Hall (ed.), *Aspects of Child life and Education* (pp. 157–204). New York: Appleton.

Emery, N. J. & Clayton, N. S. (2004). Comparing the complex cognition of birds and primates. In L. J. Rogers & G. Kaplan (eds.), *Comparative Vertebrate Cognition* (pp. 3–55). New York: Kluwer, Academic, Plenum.

Emerson, R. W. (1870). *Society and solitude.* Boston: Fields, Osgood.

Emshwiller, M. G., & Gleeson, T. T. (1997). Temperature effects on aerobic metabolism and terrestrial locomotion in American alligators. *Journal of Herpetology, 31,* 142–147.

Ernst, C. H. (1971). Observations of the painted turtle, *Chrysemys picta. Journal of Herpetology, 5,* 151–160.

Etnier, D. A., & Starnes, W. C. (1996). *The fishes of Tennessee.* Knoxville: University of Tennessee Press.

Ewer, R. F. (1968a). *Ethology of mammals.* New York: Plenum.

Ewer, R. F. (1968b). A preliminary survey of the behaviour in captivity of the dasyurid marsupial, *Sminthopsis crassicaudata* (Gould). *Zeitschrift für Tierpsychologie, 25,* 319–365.

Fadem, B. H., & Corbett, A. (1997). Sex differences and the development of social behavior in a marsupial, the gray short-tailed opossum (*Monodelphis domestica*). *Physiology and Behavior, 61,* 857–861.

Fadiga, L., Fogassi, L., Pavesi, G., & Rizzolatti, G. (1995). Motor facilitation during action observation: A magnetic stimulation study. *Journal of Neurophysiology, 73,* 2608–2611.

Fagen, R. M. (1974). Selective and evolutionary aspects of animal play. *American Naturalist, 108,* 850–858.

Fagen, R. M. (1976). Exercise, play, and physical training in animals. *Perspectives in Ethology, 2,* 189–219.

Fagen, R. M. (1977). Selection for optimal age-dependent schedules of play behavior. *American Naturalist, 111,* 395–414.

Fagen, R. (1978). Evolutionary biological models of animal play behavior. In G. M. Burghardt & M. Bekoff (eds.), *The Development of Behavior: Comparative and Evolutionary Aspects* (pp. 385–404). New York: Garland.

Fagen, R. (1981). *Animal play behavior*. New York: Oxford University Press.

Fagen, R. (1984). Play and behavioural flexibility. In P. K. Smith (ed.), *Play in Animals and Humans* (pp. 159–173). Oxford: Basil Blackwell.

Fagen, R. (1993). Primate juveniles and primate play. In M. E. Pereira & L. A. Fairbanks (eds.), *Juvenile Primates: Life History, Development, and Behavior* (pp. 182–196). New York: Oxford University Press.

Fagen, R. (1995). Animal play, games of angels, biology, and Brian. In A. D. Pellegrini (ed.), *The Future of Play Theory* (pp. 23–44). Albany: State University of New York Press.

Fagen, R. M., & George, T. K. (1977). Play behavior and exercise in young ponies (*Equus caballus* L.). *Behavioral Ecology and Sociobiology*, *2*, 267–269.

Fairbanks, L. A. (1993). Risk-taking by juvenile vervet monkeys. *Behaviour*, *124*, 57–72.

Fairbanks, L. A. (2000). The developmental timing of primate play: A neural selection model. In S. T. Parker, J. Langer, & M. L. McKinney (eds.), *Biology, Brains, and Behavior: The Evolution of Human Development* (pp. 131–158). Santa Fe, N.M.: School of American Research.

Fairbanks, L. A., & Pereira, M. E. (1993). Juvenile primates: Directions for future research. In L. A. Fairbanks (ed.), *Juvenile Primates: Life History, Development, and Behavior* (pp. 359–366). New York: Oxford University Press.

Fallows, C., & le Sueur, M. (2001). Depth chargers. *BBC Wildlife*, *19*(4), 48–55.

Felsenstein, J. (1985). Phylogenies and the comparative method. *American Naturalist*, *125*, 1–15.

Fentress, J. C., & Gadbois, S. (2001). The development of action sequences. In E. M. Blass (ed.), *Handbook of Behavioral Neurobiology* (Vol. 13, *Developmental Psychobiology*, pp. 393–431). New York: Plenum.

Ficken, M. S. (1977). Avian play. *Auk*, *94*, 573–582.

Finlay, B. L., Darlington, R. B., & Nicastro, N. (2001). Developmental structure in brain evolution. *Behavioral and Brain Evolution*, *24*, 263–308.

Fiorito, G., & Scotto, P. (1992). Observational learning in *Octopus vulgaris*. *Science*, *256*, 545–547.

Fisher, P. E., Russell, D. A., Stoskopf, M. K., Barrick, R. E., Hammer, M., & Kuzmitz, A. A. (2000). Cardiovascular evidence for an intermediate or higher metabolic rate in an ornithischian dinosaur. *Science*, *288*, 503–505.

Fleay, D. (1944). *We breed the platypus*. Melbourne: Robertson & Mullins.

Fodor, J. A. (1983). *The modularity of mind*. Cambridge, Mass.: MIT Press.

Font, E., Desfilis, E., Pérez-Cañellas, M. M., & Garcia-Verdugo, J. M. (2001). Neurogenesis and neuronal regeneration in the adult reptilian brain. *Brain, Behavior and Evolution*, *58*, 276–295.

Forel, A. (1929). *The social world of the ants compared with that of man*. (C. K. Ogden, trans.) 2 vol. New York: Albert & Charles Boni.

Forger, N. G. (2001). Development of sex differences in the nervous system. In E. M. Blass (ed.), *Handbook of Behavioral Neurobiology* (Vol. 13, *Developmental Psychobiology*, pp. 143–198). New York: Plenum.

Foreman, N., Stirk, J., Pohl, J., Mandelkow, L., Lehnung, M., Herzog, A., & Leplow, B. (2000). Spatial information transfer from virtual to real versions of the Kiel locomotor maze. *Behavioural Brain Research, 112*, 53–61.

Forencich, F. (2003). *Play as if your life depends on it: Functional exercise and living for Homo sapiens.* Seattle, WA: Go Animal.

Foroud, A., & Pellis, S. M. (2002). The development of 'anchoring' in the play fighting of rats: Evidence for an adaptive age-reversal in the juvenile phase. *International Journal of Comparative Psychology, 15*, 11–20.

Foroud, A., & Pellis, S. M. (2003). The development of "roughness" in the play fighting of rats: A Laban Movement Analysis perspective. *Developmental Psychobiology, 42*, 35–43.

Foster, S. A., & Endler, J. A. (eds.). (1999). *Geographic variation in behavior: Perspectives on evolutionary mechanisms.* Oxford: Oxford University Press.

Fowler, H. (1965). *Curiosity and exploratory behavior.* New York: Macmillan.

Fox, M. W., Halperin, S., Wise, A., & Kohn, E. (1976). Species and hybrid differences in frequencies of play and agonistic actions in canids. *Zeitschrift für Tierpsychologie, 40*, 194–209.

Fragaszy, D. M., & Adams-Curtis, L. E. (1997). Developmental changes in manipulation in tufted capuchins (*Cebus apella*) from birth through 2 years and their relation to foraging and weaning. *Journal of Comparative Psychology, 111*, 201–211.

Frank, H. (1980). Evolution of canine information processing under conditions of natural and artifical selection. *Zeitschrift für Tierpsychologie, 53*, 389–399.

Frank, H., Frank, M. G., Hasselbach, L. M., & Littleton, D. M. (1989). Motivation and insight in wolf (*Canis lupus*) and Alaskan malamute (*Canis familiaris*): Visual discrimination learning. *Bulletin of the Psychonomis Society, 27*, 455–458.

Franz, V. (1912). Das Mormyridenhirn. *Zoologische Jahrbücher. Abteilung für Anatomie und Ontogenie der Tiere, 32*, 465–491.

Fraser, A. F., & Broom, D. M. (1990). *Farm animal behaviour and welfare.* London: Bailliere-Tindall.

Freud, S. (1959). The relation of the poet to day-dreaming (I. F. Grant Duff, trans.). In J. Riviere (ed.), *Collected Papers by Sigmund Freud* (Vol. 4, pp. 173–183). New York: Basic Books.

Friedman, H. H. (2000). Humor in the Hebrew bible. *Humor: International Journal of Humor Research, 13*, 257–285.

Friend, J. A., & Burrows, R. G. (1983). Bringing up young numbats. *Swans, 13*(1), 3–9.

Frith, C. D., & Frith, U. (1999). Interacting minds—a biological basis. *Science, 286*, 1692–1695.

Fritz, U. (1999). Courtship behavior and systematics in the subtribe Nectemydina 2. A comparison above the species level and remarks on the evolution of behavior elements. *Bulletin of the Chicago Herpetological Society, 34*, 129–136.

Fromberg, D. P., & Bergen, D. (eds.). (1998). *Play from birth to twelve and beyond.* New York: Garland.

Frost, J. L., Wortham, S. C., & Reifel, S. (2001). *Play and child development.* Upper Saddle River, N.J.: Merrill Prentice Hall.

Galef, B. G. Jr. (1998). Tradition and imitation in animals. In G. Greenberg and Haraway, M. (eds.), *Comparative Psychology: A Handbook* (pp. 614–622). New York: Garland.

Gallese, V., Fadiga, L., Fogassi, L., & Rizzolatti, G. (1996). Action recognition in the premotor cortex. *Brain, 119,* 593–609.

Gamble, J. R., & Cristol, D. A. (2002). Drop-catch behaviour is play in herring gulls, *Larus argentatus. Animal Behaviour, 62,* 339–345.

Gandelman, R. (1992). *The psychobiology of behavioral development.* New York: Oxford University Press.

Gans, C. (1975). Amphisbaenian or worm lizards. In B. Grzimek (ed.), *Grzimek's Animal Life Encyclopedia* (Vol. 6, *Reptiles,* pp. 338–344). New York: Van Nostrand Reinhold.

Gans, C. (1996). An overview of parental care among the Reptilia. In J. S. Rosenblatt & C. T. Snowdon (eds.), *Parental Care: Evolution, Mechanisms, and Adaptive Significance* (Vol. 25, pp. 145–157). San Diego: Academic Press.

Garcia, J., Hankins, W. G., & Rusniak, K. W. (1976). Flavor aversion studies. *Science, 192,* 265–266.

Gariépy, J.-L., Bauer, D. J., & Cairns, R. B. (2001). Selective breeding for differential aggression in mice provides evidence for heterochrony in social behaviours. *Animal Behaviour, 62,* 933–947.

Garvey, C. (1990). *Play* (enlarged ed.). Cambridge, Mass.: Harvard University Press.

Gatten, R. E., Jr. (1974). Effects of temperature and activity on aerobic and anaerobic metabolism and heart rate in the turtles *Pseudemys scripta* and *Terrapene ornata. Comparative Biochemistry and Physiology, 48A,* 619–648.

Gauthier, J., Cannatella, D., de Queiroz, K., Kluge, A. G., & Rowe, T. (1989). Tetrapod phylogeny. In B. Fernholm, K. Bremer, & H. Jörnvall (eds.), *The Hierarchy of Life* (pp. 337–353). Amsterdam: Elsevier Science.

Gaylin, W. (1990). *Adam and Eve and Pinocchio: On being and becoming human.* New York: Viking.

Geist, V. (1978). *Life strategies, human evolution, and environmental design.* New York: Springer Verlag.

Gerrish, C. J., & Alberts, J. R. (1997). Postsuckling behavioral arousal in weanling rats (*Rattus norvegicus*). *Journal of Comparative Psychology, 111,* 37–49.

Gery, J. (1973). Order: Mormyrids. In B. Grzimek (ed.), *Grzimek's Animal Life Encyclopedia* (Vol. 4, *Fishes I,* pp. 205–212). New York: Van Nostrand Reinhold.

Ghiselin, M. T. (1974). *The economy of nature and the evolution of sex.* Berkeley: University of California Press.

Gibson, J. J. (1978). The theory of affordances. In R. Shaw & J. Bransford (eds.), *Perceiving, Acting, and Knowing* (pp. 67–82). Hillsdale, N.J.: Erlbaum.

Gibson, K. R. (1990). New perspectives on instincts and intelligence: Brain size and the emergence of hierarchical mental construction skills. In S. T. Parker & K. R. Gibson (eds.), *"Language" and Intelligence in Monkeys and Apes: Comparative Developmental Perspectives* (pp. 97–128). Cambridge: Cambridge University Press.

Gillette, J. R., Jaeger, R. G., & Peterson, M. G. (2000). Social monogamy in a territorial salamander. *Animal Behaviour, 59,* 1241–1250.

Gilmore, J. B. (1966). Play: A special behavior. In R. N. Haber (ed.), *Current Research in Motivation* (pp. 343–355). New York: Holt, Rinehart, and Winston.

Girard, I., Swallow, J. G., Carter, P. A., Koteja, P., Rhodes, J. S., & Garland, T., Jr. (2002). Maternal-care behavior and life-history traits in house mice (*Mus domesticus*) artificially selected for high voluntary wheel-running activity. *Behavioural Processes, 57,* 37–50.

Glickman, S. E., & Sroges, R. W. (1966). Curiosity in zoo animals. *Behaviour, 26,* 151–188.

Goldin-Meadow, S., Nusbaum, H., Kelly, S. D., & Wagner, S. (2001). Explaining math: Gesturing lightens the load. *Psychological Science, 12,* 516–522.

Goldstein, M. H., King, A. P., & West, M. J. (2003). Social interaction shapes babbling: Testing parallels between birdsong and speech. *Proceedings of the National Academy of Sciences, 100,* 8030–8035.

Gomendio, M. (1988). The development of different types of play in gazelles: Implications for the nature of the functions of play. *Animal Behaviour, 36,* 825–836.

Goodwin, B. (1994). *How the leopard changed its spots.* New York: Scribner's.

Goodwin, D., Bradshaw, J. W. S., & Wickens, S. M. (1997). Paedomorphosis affects agonistic visual signals of domestic dogs. *Animal Behaviour, 53,* 297–304.

Gordon, D. M. (1986). The dynamics of the daily round of the harvester ant colony (*Pogonomyrmex barbatus*). *Animal Behaviour, 34,* 1402–1419.

Gordon, N. S., Burke, S., Akil, H., Watson, S. J. & Panksepp, J. (2003). Socially-induced brain "fertilization": Play promotes brain derived neurotrophic factor transcription. *Neuroscience Letters 341,* 17–20.

Gordon, N. S., Kollack-Walker, S., Akil, H., & Panksepp, J. (2002). Expression of c-*fos* gene activation during rough and tumble play in juvenile rats. *Brain Research Bulletin, 57,* 651–659.

Görlitz, D., & Wohlwill, J. F. (eds.). (1987). *Curiosity, imagination, and play.* Hillsdale, N.J.: Erlbaum.

Gorton, R. E., Colliander, K. G., & Bell, W. J. (1983). Social behaviour as a function of context in a cockroach. *Animal Behaviour, 31,* 152–159.

Gould, J. L. (2002). Can honey bees create cognitive maps? In M. Bekoff, C. Allen, & G. M. Burghardt (eds.), *The Cognitive Animal: Empirical and Theoretical Perspectives on Animal Cognition* (pp. 41–46). Cambridge, Mass.: MIT Press.

Gove, D., & Burghardt, G. M. (1983). Context-correlated parameters of snake and lizard tongue-flicking. *Animal Behaviour, 13,* 718–723.

Govind, C. K. (1989). Asymmetry in lobster claws. *American Scientist, 77*, 468–474.

Gowaty, P. A. (1996). Field studies of parental behavior in birds: New data focus questions on variation among females. In J. S. Rosenblatt & C. T. Snowdon (eds.), *Parental Care: Evolution, Mechanisms, and Adaptive Significance* (Vol. 25, pp. 477–531). San Diego: Academic Press.

Graham, J. B., Dudley, R., Aguilar, N. M., & Gans, C. (1995). Implications of the late Palaeozoic oxygen pulse for physiology and evolution. *Nature, 375*, 117–210.

Grant, T. R. (1983). The behavioral ecology of monotremes. In J. F. Eisenberg & D. G. Kleiman (eds.), *Advances in the Study of Mammalian Behavior* (pp. 360–394): American Society of Mammalogists special publication No. 7.

Grant, T. R. (1989). Ornithorhynchidae. In D. W. Walton & B. J. Richardson (eds.), *Fauna of Australia* (Vol. 1B, Mammalia, pp. 436–450). Canberra: Australian Government Publishing Service.

Graybiel, A. M. (1995). Building action repertoires: Memory and learning functions of the basal ganglia. *Current Opinion in Neurobiology, 5*, 733–711.

Green, C. S., & Bavelier, D. (2003). Action video game modifies visual selective attention. *Nature, 423*, 534–537.

Greenberg, N. (2004). The beast at play: The neuroethology of creativity. In R. L. Clements & L. Fioentino (eds.), *The Child's Right to Play: A Global Approach* (pp. 309–327). Westport, Conn.: Greenwood Press.

Greenberg, R. (1992). Differences in neophobia between naive song and swamp sparrows. *Ethology, 91*, 17–24.

Greene, H. W. (1997). *Snakes: The evolution of mystery in nature.* Berkeley: University of California Press.

Greene, H. W. (2002). Vertebrates. In M. Pagel (ed.), *Encyclopedia of Evolution* (pp. 1127–1131). Oxford: Oxford University Press.

Grier, J. M. (1984). *Biology of animal behavior.* St. Louis, Mo.: Mosby Year Book.

Grier, J. M., & Burk, T. (1992). *Biology of animal behavior.* 2nd ed. St. Louis, Mo.: Mosby Year Book.

Griffin, D. (1976). *The question of animal awareness.* New York: Rockefeller University Press.

Griffin, D. R. (2001). *Animal minds.* Chicago: University of Chicago Press.

Griffiths, M. (1978). *The biology of the monotremes.* New York: Academic Press.

Griffiths, M. (1989). Tachyglossidae. In D. W. Walton & B. J. Richardson (eds.), *Fauna of Australia* (Vol. 1B, *Mammalia*, pp. 407–435). Canberra: Australian Government Publishing Service.

Griffiths, S. W., & Magurran, A. E. (1997). Familiarity in schooling fish: How long does it take to acquire? *Animal Behaviour, 53*, 945–949.

Groos, K. (1898). *The play of animals* (E. L. Baldwin, trans.). New York: Appleton.

Groos, K. (1901). *The play of man* (E. L. Baldwin, trans.). New York: Appleton.

Gross, C. G. (2000). Neurogenesis in the adult brain: Death of a dogma. *Nature Neuroscience, 1*, 67–73.

Grützner, F., Deakin, J., Rens, W., El-Mogharbel, N., Graves, J. A. M. (2003). The monotreme genome: A patchwork of reptile, mammal and unique features? *Comparative Biochemistry and Physiology Part A, 136,* 867–881.

Grzimek, B. (1972). The opossums. In B. Grzimek (ed.), *Grzimek's Animal Life Encyclopedia* (Vol. 10, *Mammals I,* pp. 66–69). New York: Van Nostrand Reinhold.

Gudger, E. W. (1944). Fishes that play "leapfrog." *American Naturalist, 78,* 451–463.

Gunter, G. (1953). Observations on fish turning flips over a line. *Copeia, 1953,* 188–190.

Hailman, J. P. (2001). Why the Piagetian A-not-B phenomenon is no error: A comparative perspective. *Behavioral and Brain Sciences, 24,* 44–45.

Hall, G. S. (1904). *Adolescence: Its psychology and its relations to physiology, anthropology, sociology, sex, crime, religion and education.* New York: Appleton.

Hall, S. L. (1998). Object play in adult animals. In M. Bekoff & J. A. Byers (eds.), *Animal Play: Evolutionary, Comparative, and Ecological Perspectives* (pp. 45–60). Cambridge: Cambridge University Press.

Hall, W. G., Arnold, H. M., & Myers, K. P. (2000). The acquisition of an appetite. *Psychological Science, 11,* 101–105.

Halloy, M., & Burghardt, G. M. (1990). Ontogeny of fish capture and ingestion in four species of garter snakes (*Thamnophis*). *Behaviour, 112,* 299–318.

Hancock, T. V., Adolph, S. C., & Gleeson, T. T. (2001). Effects of activity duration on recovery and metabolic costs in the desert iguana (*Dipsosaurus dorsalis*). *Comparative Biochemistry and Physiology Part A, 130,* 67–79.

Handler, L. (1999). Assessment of playfulness: Herman Rorschach meets D. W. Winnicott. *Journal of Personality Assessment, 72,* 208–217.

Hanlon, R. T., & Messenger, J. B. (1996). *Cephalopod behaviour.* Cambridge: Cambridge University Press.

Hansenne, M., Pinto, E., Pitchot, W., Reggers, J., Scantamburlo, G., Moor, M., & Ansseau, M. (2002). Further evidence on the relationship between dopamine and novelty seeking: A neuroendocrine study. *Personality and Individual Differences, 33,* 967–977.

Harcourt, R. (1991a). The development of play in the South American fur seal. *Ethology, 88,* 191–202.

Harcourt, R. (1991b). Survivorship costs of play in the South American fur seal. *Animal Behaviour, 42,* 509–511.

Harlow, H. F. (1950). Learning and satiation of response in intrinsically motivated complex puzzle performance by monkeys. *Journal of Comparative and Physiological Psychology, 43,* 289–294.

Harlow, H. F. (1964). Early social deprivation and later behavior in the monkey. In A. Abrams, H. H. Garner, & J. E. P. Toman (eds.), *Unfinished Tasks in the Behavioral Sciences* (pp. 154–173). Baltimore: Williams and Wilkins.

Harlow, H. F. (1971). *Learning to love.* San Francisco: Albion.

Harper, L. V., & Huie, K. S. (1978). The development of sex differences in human behavior: Cultural impositions, or a convergence of evolved response-tendencies and cultural adaptations. In G. M. Burghardt & M. Bekoff (eds.), *The Development of Behavior: Comparative and Evolutionary Aspects* (pp. 297–318). New York: Garland STPM Press.

Harrison, J. M. (1986). Caste-specific changes in honeybee flight capacity. *Physiological Zoology, 59,* 175–187.

Hartley, R. E., Frank, L. K., & Goldenson, R. M. (1952). *Understanding children's play.* New York: Columbia University Press.

Harvey, P. H., & Bennett, P. M. (1983). Brain size, energetics, ecology, and life history patterns. *Nature, 306,* 314–315.

Hatfield, J. W., III. (1996). *Green iguana: The ultimate owner's manual.* Portland, Ore.: Dunthrope Press.

Hauser, M. D. (1996). *The evolution of communication.* Cambridge, Mass.: MIT Press.

Hediger, H. (1950). *Wild animals in captivity.* London: Butterworths.

Heinbuch, B., & Weigman, T. (2000). Unusual behavior of dwarf caiman. *Crocodile Specialist Group Newsletter, 19,* 14–15.

Heinrich, B. (1995a). An experimental investigation of insight in common ravens (*Corvus corax*). *Auk, 112,* 994–1003.

Heinrich, B. (1995b). Neophilia and exploration in juvenile common ravens, *Corvus corax. Animal Behaviour, 50,* 695–704.

Heinrich, B., & Smolker, R. (1998). Play in common ravens (*Corvus corax*). In M. Bekoff & J. A. Byers (eds.), *Animal Play: Evolutionary, Comparative, and Ecological Perspectives* (pp. 27–44). Cambridge: Cambridge University Press.

Helfman, G. S., Collette, B. B., & Facey, D. E. (1997). *The Diversity of Fishes.* Oxford: Blackwell Science.

Helmuth, L. (2001). Beyond the pleasure principle. *Science, 294,* 983–984.

Hendrichs, H. (1996). Specific properties of metatherian and eutherian sociality. In D. B. Croft & U. Ganslosser (eds.), *Comparison of Marsupial and Placental Behaviour* (pp. 125–133). Fürth, Germany: Filander Verlag.

Henry, J. D. (1986). *Red fox: The catlike canine.* Washington D.C.: Smithsonian Institution Press.

Henry, J. D., & Herrero, S. M. (1974). Social play in the American black bear: Its similarity to canid social play and an examination of its identifying characteristics. *American Zoologist, 14,* 371–389.

Herrnstein, R. J. (1997). *The matching law: Papers in psychology and economics* (H. Rachlin & D. I. Laibson, eds.). Cambridge: Harvard University Press.

Hertz, P. E., Huey, R. B., & Garland, T. Jr. (1988). Time budgets, thermoregulation, and maximal locomotor performance: Are reptiles Olympians or boy scouts? *American Zoologist, 28,* 927–938.

Herzog, H. A., Jr., & Burghardt, G. M. (1977). Vocal communication signals in juvenile crocodilians. *Zeitschrift für Tierpsychologie, 44*, 294–304.

Herzog, T. R., & Anderson, M. R. (2000). Joke cruelty, emotional responsiveness, and joke appreciation. *Humor: International Journal of Humor Research, 13*, 333–351.

Hess, E. (1964). On anthropomorphism. In A. Abrams, H. H. Garner, & J. E. P. Toman (eds.), *Unfinished Tasks in the Behavioral Sciences* (pp. 174–180). Baltimore: Williams and Wilkins.

Hess, E. H. (1973). *Imprinting.* New York: Van Nostrand.

Hicks, J. W., & Farmer, C. G. (1998). Lung ventilation and gas exchange in theropod dinosaurs. *Science, 281*, 45–46.

Hill, C. (1946). Playtime at the zoo. *Zoo Life, 1*(1), 24–26.

Hirata, S., Yamakoshi, G., Fujita, S., Ohashi, G., & Matsuzawa, T. (2001). Capturing and toying with hyraxes (*Dendrohyrax dorsalis*) by wild chimpanzees (*Pan troglodytes*) at Bossou, Guinea. *American Journal of Primatology, 53*, 93–97.

Hirsch, H. V. B., Tieman, S. B., Barth, M., & Ghiradella, H. (2001). Tunable seers: Activity-dependent development of vision in the fly and the cat. In E. M. Blass (ed.), *Handbook of Behavioral Neurobiology* (Vol. 13, *Developmental Psychobiology*, pp. 81–142). New York: Plenum.

Hobson, J. A., Pace-Schott, E. F., & Stickgold, R. (2000). Dreaming and the brain: Toward a cognitive neuroscience of conscious states. *Behavioral and Brain Sciences, 23*, 793–842.

Hoese, H. D. (1985). Jumping mullet—the internal diving bell hypothesis. *Envionmental Biology of Fishes, 13*, 309–314.

Hoff, M. P., Forthman, D. L., & Maple, T. L. (1994). Dyadic interactions of infant lowland gorillas in an outdoor exhibit compared to an indoor holding area. *Zoo Biology, 13*, 245–256.

Hoffman, M. A. (1982). Encephalization in mammals in relation to the size of the cerebral cortex. *Brain, Behavior and Evolution, 20*, 84–96.

Hogan, J. A. (1988). Cause and function in the development of behavior systems. In E. M. Blass (ed.), *Handbook of Behavioral Neurobiology* (Vol. 9, *Developmental Psychobiology and Behavioral Ecology*, pp. 63–106). New York: Plenum.

Hogan, J. A. (2001). Development of motor systems. In E. M. Blass (ed.), *Handbook of Behavioral Neurobiology* (Vol. 13, *Developmental Psychobiology*, pp. 229–279). New York: Plenum.

Hol, T., van den Berg, J. M., van Ree, J. M., & Spruijt, B. M. (1999). Isolation during the play period in infancy decreases adult social interactions in rats. *Behavioural Brain Research, 100*, 91–97.

Holden, C. (2000). Researchers pained by effort to define distress precisely. *Science, 290*, 1474–1475.

Holden, C. (2001). "Behavioral" addictions: Do they exist? *Science, 294*, 980–981.

Holder, C. F. (1892). *Along the Florida reef.* New York: Appleton.

Holder, C. F. (1899). *Stories of animal life.* New York: American Book.

Holder, C. F. (1903). Why and how fishes leap. *Scientific American*, *88*, 151–152.

Hole, G. J., & Einon, D. F. (1984). Play in rodents. In P. K. Smith (ed.), *Play in Animals and Humans* (pp. 95–117). Oxford: Basil Blackwell.

Hölldobler, B., & Wilson, E. O. (1990). *The ants*. Cambridge: Harvard Universitty Press.

Holman, J. A. (2000). *Fossil snakes of North America*. Bloomington: Indiana University Press.

Holmes, W. G. (2001). The development and function of nepotism: Why kinship matters in social relationships. In E. M. Blass (ed.), *Handbook of Behavioral Neurobiology* (Vol. 13, *Developmental Psychobiology*, pp. 281–316). New York: Plenum.

Hornaday, W. T. (1922). *The minds and manners of wild animals*. New York: Scribner's.

Horner, J. R., & Gorman, J. (1988). *Digging dinosaurs*. New York: Workman.

Horwich, R. H. (1972). The ontogeny of social behavior in the gray squirrel (*Sciurus carolinensis*). *Advances in Ethology* (Paul Parey, Berlin), *8*, 1–103.

Hotchkiss, A. K., Ostby, J. S., Vandenbergh, J. G., & Gray, L. E. Jr. (2002). Androgens and environmental antiandrogens affect reproductive development and play behavior in the Sprague-Dawley rat. *Environmental Health Perspectives*, *110*, 435–439.

Hoyenga, K. B., & Hoyenga, K. T. (1984). *Motivational explanations of behavior: Evolutionary, physiological, and cognitive ideas*. Monterey, Calif.: Brooks/Cole.

Hubbs, C. L. (1948). "Leapfrogging" by topsmelt and shark. *Copeia*, *1948*, 298.

Huber, L., Rechberger, S., & Taborsky, M. (2001). Social learning affects object exploration and manipulation in keas, *Nestor notabilis*. *Animal Behaviour*, *62*, 945–954.

Huber, P. (1810). *Recherches sur les moeurs des fourmis indigenes*. Paris: J. J. Paschoud.

Huber-Eicher, B., & Wechsler, B. (1997). Feather pecking in domestic chicks: its relation to dustbathing and foraging. *Animal Behaviour*, *54*, 757–768.

Hudson, W. H. (1892). *The naturalist at La Plata*. London: J. M. Dent.

Hughes, R. N. (1997). Intrinsic exploration in animals: Motives and measurement. *Behavioural Processes*, *41*, 213–226.

Hughes, S., Zelus, D., & Mouchiroud, D. (1999). Warm-blooded isochore structure in Nile crocodile and turtle. *Molecular Biology and Evolution*, *11*, 1521–1527.

Huizinga, J. (1955). *Homo ludens: A study of the play element in culture* (R. F. C. Hull, trans.). Boston: Beacon.

Hull, D. L. (1990). *Science as a process*. Chicago: University of Chicago Press.

Hull, D. L. (2000). *Science and selection: Essays on biological evolution and the philosophy of science*. Cambridge: Cambridge University Press.

Hurme, K., Gonzalez, K., Halversen, M., Foster, B., Moore, M., & Chepko-Sade, B. D. (2003). Environmental enrichment for dendrobatid frogs. *Journal of Applied Animal Welfare Science*, *6*, 285–299.

Hutt, C. (1966). Exploration and play in children. *Symposium of the Zoological Society of London, 18*, 61–81.

Hutt, C., & Hutt, S. J. (1965). Effects of environmental complexity on stereotyped behaviours of children. *Animal Behaviour, 13*, 1–4.

Hutt, S. J., Tyler, S., Hutt, C., & Christopherson, H. (1989). *Play, exploration and learning: A natural history of the pre-school child*. London: Routledge.

Hyland, D. A. (1984). *The question of play*. Lanham, Md: University Press of America.

Ikemoto, S., & Panksepp, J. (1992). The effects of early social isolation on the motivation for social play in juvenile rats. *Developmental Psychobiology, 25*, 261–274.

Immelmann, K., & Beer, C. (1989). *A dictionary of ethology*. Cambridge, Mass.: Harvard University Press.

Ingle, D. (2004). Recreational fighting. In C. S. Cross (ed.), *Encyclopedia of Recreation and Leisure in America*, Vol. 2. Detroit: Charles Scribner's Sons.

Iwaniuk, A. N., Nelson, J. E., & Pellis, S. M. (2001). Do big-brained animals play more? Comparative analyses of play and relative brain size in mammals. *Journal of Comparative Psychology, 115*, 29–41.

Iwaniuk, A. N., Nelson, J. E., & Whishaw, I. Q. (2000). The relationships between brain regions and forelimb dexterity in marsupials (Marsupialia): A comparative test of the principle of proper mass. *Australian Journal of Zoology, 48*, 99–110.

Iwaniuk, A. N., & Whishaw, I. Q. (2000). On the origin of skilled limb movements. *Trends in Neuroscience, 23*, 372–376.

Jackson, C. G., Jr. (1972). A quantitative study of the courtship behavior of the red-eared turtle, *Chrysemys scripta elegans* (Wied). *Herpetologica, 28*, 58–64.

Jackson, D. C. (2000). Living without oxygen: Lessons from the freshwater turtle. *Comparative Biochemistry and Physiology* Part A, *125*, 299–315.

Jackson, D. C., & Prange, H. D. (1979). Ventilation and gas exchange during rest and exercise in adult green sea turtles. *Journal of Comparative Physiology, 134*, 315–319.

Jackson, R. R., & Wilcox, R. S. (1993a). Observations in nature of detouring behaviour by *Portia fimbriata*, a web-invading aggressive mimic jumping spider from Queensland. *Journal of Zoology, London, 230*, 135–139.

Jackson, R. R., & Wilcox, R. S. (1993b). Spider flexibly chooses aggressive mimicry signals for different prey by trial and error. *Behaviour, 127*, 21–36.

Jackson, R. R., & Wilcox, R. S. (1998). Spider-eating spiders. *American Scientist, 86*, 350–357.

Jaeger, R. G., Gillette, J. R., & Cooper, R. C. (2002). Sexual coercion: males punish socially polyandrous female partners. *Animal Behaviour, 63*, 871–877.

Jambor, T. (1998). Challenge and risk-taking in play. In D. P. Fromberg & D. Bergen (eds.), *Play from Birth to Twelve and Beyond* (pp. 319–323). New York: Garland.

James, W. (1890). *Principles of psychology*. New York: Holt.

Janssen, R. M., & Janssen, J. L. (1990). *Growing up in ancient Egypt*. Newington, Conn.: Rubicon Press.

Janvier, P. (1996). *Early vertebrates*. Oxford: Clarendon Press.

Jarman, P. J., & Kruuk, H. (1996). Phylogeny and spatial organization in mammals. In D. B. Croft & U. Ganslosser (eds.), *Comparison of Marsupial and Placental Behaviour* (pp. 80–101). Fürth, Germany: Filander Verlag.

Jarmer, K. (1928). *Das Seelenleben der Fische*. Munich: R. Oldenbourg.

Jayne, B. C., Voris, H. K., & Ng, P. K. L. (2002). Snake cirumvents constraints on prey size. *Nature, 418*, 143.

Jeannerod, M. (1994). The representing brain: Neural correlates of motor intention and imagery. *Behavioral and Brain Sciences, 17*, 187–245.

Jerison, H. J. (1973). *Evolution of brain and intelligence*. Orlando, Fla.: Academic Press.

Jerome, J. (1996). *Stone work: Reflections on serious play and other aspects of country life*. Hanover, N.H.: University Press of New England.

Johnson, F., Soderstrom, K., & Whitney, O. (2002). Quantifying song bout production during zebra finch sensory-motor learning suggests a sensitive period for vocal practice. *Behavioural Brain Research, 131*, 57–65.

Johnson, J. E., Christie, J. F., & Yawkey, T. D. (1999). *Play and early childhood development*. New York: Longman.

Johnston, I. A., & Moon, T. W. (1980). Endurance exercise training in the fast and slow muscles of a teleost fish (*Pollachius virens*). *Journal of Comparative Physiology, 135*, 147–156.

Joireman, J. A., Fick, C. S., & Anderson, J. W. (2002). Sensation seeking and involvement in chess. *Personality and Individual Differences, 32*, 509–515.

Judson, O. (2002). *Dr. Tatiana's sex advice to all creation*. New York: Metropolitan.

Kassem, M., Ridet, J. M., & Bauchot, R. (1989). Analyse volumétrique des principales subdivisions encéphaliques chez les *Gobioidei* (Téléostéens, Perciformes). *Journal für Hirnforschung, 30*, 59–67.

Katz, P. S., & Harris-Warrick, R. M. (1999). The evolution of neuonal circuits underlying species-specific behavior. *Current Opinion in Neurobiology, 9*, 628–633.

Kavanagh, K. (1998). Notes on the frequency and function of glancing behavior in juvenile *Acanthochromis* (Pomacentridae). *Copeia, 1998*, 493–496.

Kawata, K. (1980). Notes on comparative behavior in three primate species in captivity. *Zoologische Garten N.F., 50*, 209–224.

Kawata, K. (1990). "An ape in a bear costume"—Belle Isle Zoo's versatile spectacled bear. *International Zoo News, 37*(4), 11–15.

Kawata, K., & Elsen, K. (1994). Behavior of the Hoffmann's sloth, *Choloepus hoffmanni*, in captivity. *Zoologische Garten N.F., 64*, 9–24.

Keiper, R. R. (1969). Causal factors of stereotypies in caged birds. *Animal Behaviour, 17*, 114–119.

Keller, H., Schneider, K., & Henderson, B. (eds.). (1994). *Curiosity and exploration*. Berlin: Springer-Verlag.

Kilham, L. (1974). Play in hairy, downy, and other woodpeckers. *Wilson Bulletin, 86*, 35–42.

Killeen, P. R. (2001). The four causes of behavior. *Current Directions in Psychological Science, 10*, 136–140.

King, C. (1993). Environmental enrichment: Is it for the birds? *Zoo Biology, 12*, 509–512.

Kirchshofer, R. (1953). Actionsystem des Maulbrüters *Haplochromis desfontainesii*. *Zeitschrift für Tierpsychologie, 10*, 297–318.

Klausewitz, W. (1966). Ein bemerkenswerter Zähmungsversuch an freilebenden Fischen. *Natür und Volk, 90*, 91–96.

Klimley, A. P. (1994). The predatory behavior of the great white shark. *American Scientist, 82*, 122–133.

Koene, P., van Dijk, J., van Leeuwen, N., Tjemmes, L., & Huizen, E. T. (2000). Bear-wolf interactions in different contexts: Interspecific play behaviour? *Ethology Supplement, 35*, 38.

Kohler, W. (1925). *The mentality of apes*. New York: Harcourt Brace.

Kolb, B., Pellis, S. M., & Robinson, T. E. (2004). Plasticity and functions of the orbital frontal cortex. *Brain and Cognition* (in press).

Kolb, B., & Whishaw, I. Q. (1998). Brain plasticity and behavior. *Annual Review of Psychology, 49*, 43–64.

Kortmulder, K. (1998). *Play and evolution: Second thoughts on the behaviour of animals*. Utrecht: International Books.

Kosslyn, S. M., & Sussman, A. L. (1995). Role of imagery in perception: Or, there is no such thing as immaculate perception. In M. S. Gazzaniga (ed.), *The Cognitive Neurosciences* (pp. 1035–1042). Cambridge, Mass.: MIT Press.

Kramer, B. (1990). *Electro-communication in teleost fishes*. Berlin: Springer-Verlag.

Kramer, M., & Burghardt, G. M. (1998). Precocious courtship and play in emydid turtles. *Ethology, 104*, 38–56.

Kramer, M., & Fritz, U. (1989). Courtship behavior of the turtle, *Pseudemys nelsoni*. *Journal of Herpetology, 23*, 84–86.

Krause, M. A., Burghardt, G. M., & Lentini, A. (1999). Improving the lives of captive reptiles: Object provisioning in Nile soft-shelled turtles (*Trionyx triunguis*). *Lab Animal, 28*(7), 38–41.

Kruijt, J. P. (1964). Ontogeny of social behaviour in Burmese red jungle fowl (*Gallus gallus spadiceus*). *Behaviour Supplement, 12*, 1–201.

Kruska, D. (1987a). How fast can total brain size change in mammals? *Journal für Hirnforschung, 28*, 59–70.

Kruska, D. (1987b). Mammalian domestication and its effect on brain structure and behavior. In H. J. Jerison & I. Jerison (eds.), *Intelligence and Evolutionary Biology* (Vol. G17, NATO ASI Series, pp. 211–250). Berlin: Springer-Verlag.

Kuba, M. (2004). Exploration, habituation and play in *Octopus vulgaris*. Unpublished Ph.D. dissertation, University of Vienna (Austria).

Kuba, M., Meisel, D. V., Byrne, R. A., Griebel, U., & Mather, J. A. (2003). Looking at play in *Octopus vulgaris*. *Berliner Paläontologische Abhandlungen, 3*, 163–169.

Kucza, S. A., II (1983). *Crib speech and language play*. New York: Springer-Verlag.

Kühme, W. (1961). Verhaltensstudien am malubrütenden (*Beta anabatoides* Bleeker) und am nestbauenden Kampfisch (*Beta splendens* Regas). *Zeitschrift für Tierpsychologie, 18*, 33–55.

Ladiges, W. (1954). Der Sterlet im Aquarium. *Die Aquarien- und Terrarien Zeitschrift, 7*, 200–202.

Lafuma, L., Lambrechts, M. M., & Raymond, M. (2001). Aromatic plants in bird nests as a protection against blood-sucking insects? *Behavioural Processes, 56*, 113–120.

Lampard, K. (2002). The effects of movable novel objects, novel olfactory stimuli and novel auditory stimuli on the exploratory, play and stereotypical behaviour of captive species: A comparative study. Unpublished Ph.D. dissertation, University of Adelaide (Australia).

Lancy, D. F. (1996). *Playing on the mother-ground*. New York: Guilford Press.

Lang, C. D., & Jaeger, R. G. (2000). Defense of territories by male-female pairs in the red-backed salamander (*Plethodon cinereus*). *Copeia, 2000*, 169–177.

Lawrence, A. B., & Rushen, J. (eds.). (1993). *Stereotypic animal behaviour*. Wallingford, England: CAB International.

Lazar, J. W., & Beckhorn, G. D. (1974). Social play or the development of social behavior in ferrets (*Mustela putorius*). *American Zoologist, 14*, 405–414.

Lazell, J. D., Jr., & Spitzer, N. C. (1977). Apparent play behavior in an American alligator. *Copeia, 1977*, 188.

Lefebvre, L., Whittle, P., Lascaris, E., & Finkelstein, A. (1997). Feeding innovations and forebrain size in birds. *Animal Behaviour, 53*, 549–560.

Lefebvre, L., Gaxiola, A., Dawson, S., Timmerman, S., Rosza, L., & Kabai, P. (1998). Feeding innovations and forebrain size in Australasian birds. *Behaviour, 135*, 1077–1097.

Levine, J. A., Eberhardt, N. L., & Jensen, M. D. (1999). Role of nonexercise activity thermogenesis in resistance to fat gain in humans. *Science, 283*, 212–214.

Lewis, K. (2000). A comparative study of primate play behaviour: Implications for the study of cognition. *Folia Primatologica, 71*, 417–421.

Lewis, K. (2003). A comparative analysis of play behaviour in primates and carnivores. Unpublished Ph.D. Dissertation. Durham: University of Durham.

Lewis, K., & Barton, R. A. (2004). Playing for keeps: Evolutionary relationships between social play and the cerebellum in non human primates. *Human Nature, 15*, 5–21.

Lewontin, R. (1998). The evolution of cognition: Questions we will never answer. In D. Scarborough & S. Sternberg (eds.), *Invitation to Cognitive Science* (Vol. 4, Methods, models, and conceptual issues, pp. 110–132). Cambridge, Mass.: MIT Press.

Leyhausen, P. (1948). Beobachtungen an einen jungen Schwartzbaren. *Zeitschrift für Tierpsychologie, 6*, 433–444.

Leyhausen, P. (1979). *Cat behavior*. New York: Garland STPM Press.

Lillegraven, J. A., Thompson, S. D., McNab, B. K., & Patton, J. L. (1987). The origin of eutherian mammals. *Biological Journal of the Linnean Society, 32*, 281–336.

Lillywhite, H. B. (1989). Unusual shedding behaviors in an aquatic snake, *Acrocordus granulatus*. *Copeia, 1989*, 768–770.

Lindauer, M. (1961). *Communication among social bees*. Cambridge, Mass.: Harvard University Press.

Lindsay, W. L. (1879). *Mind in the lower animals in health and disease*. London: Kegan Paul.

Lipkind, D., Nottebohm, F., Rado, R., Barnea, A. (2002). Social change affects the survival of new neurons in the forebrain of adult songbirds. *Behavioural Brain Research, 133*, 31–43.

Lissowsky, M. (1996). The occurrence of play behaviour in marsupials. In D. B. Croft & U. Ganslosser (eds.), *Comparison of Marsupial and Placental Behaviour* (pp. 187–207). Fürth, Germany: Filander Verlag.

Loizos, C. (1967). Play behavior in higher primates: A review. In D. Morris (ed.), *Primate Ethology* (pp. 176–218). Chicago: Aldine.

Longley, W. H., & Hildebrand, S. F. (1941). Systematic catalogue of the fishes of Tortugas, Florida with observations on color, habits, and local distribution. *Papers from Tortugas Laboratory*, Vol. 34 (publication 535). Washington, D.C.: Carnegie Institution of Washington.

López-Calleja, M., & Bozinovic, F. (2003). Dynamic energy and time budgets in hummingbirds: A study in *Sephanoides sephaniodes* (Sig). *Comparative Biochemistry and Physiology Part A, 134*, 283–295.

Loranca, A., & Salas, M. (2001). Social play development in pre-weaning olfactory deprived or stimulated rats. *Brain Research, 921*, 150–159.

Loranca, A., Terrero, C., & Salas, M. (1999). Development of play in neonatally undernourished rats. *Physiology & Behavior, 66*, 3–10.

Lordi, B., Patin, V., Protais, P., Mellier, D., & Caston, J. (2000). Chronic stress in pregnant rats: Effects on growth rate, anxiety and memory capabilities of offspring. *International Journal of Psychophysiology, 37*, 195–205.

Lorenz, K. (1956). Play and vacuum activities. In M. Autuori (ed.), *L'instinct dans le comportement des animaux et de l'homme* (pp. 633–645). Paris: Masson.

Lorenz, K. (1969). Innate bases of learning. In K. Pribram (ed.), *On the Biology of Learning* (pp. 13–93). New York: Harcourt Brace Jovanovich.

Lorenz, K. Z. (1981). *The foundations of ethology*. New York: Springer-Verlag.

Lorenz, K. (1985). Preface. In G. M. Burghardt (ed.), *Foundations of Comparative Ethology* (pp. xiii–xiv). New York: Van Nostrand Reinhold.

Losey, G. S., Jr., & Margules, L. (1974). Cleaning symbiosis provides a positive reinforcer for fish. *Science, 184*, 179–180.

Lovejoy, N. R. (2000). Reinterpreting recapitulation: Systematics of needlefishes and their allies (Teleostei: Beloniformes). *Evolution, 54*, 1349–1362.

MacDonald, K. (ed.). (1993). *Parent-child play: Descriptions and implications*. Albany: State University of New York Press.

MacLean, P. (1985). Brain evolution relating to family, play and the separation call. *Archives of General Psychiatry, 42*, 405–417.

Macrí, S., Adriani, W., Chiarotti, F., & Laviola, G. (2002). Risk taking during exploration of a plus-maze is greater in adolescent than in juvenile or adult mice. *Animal Behaviour, 64*, 541–546.

Maier, N. R. F., & Schneirla, T. C. (1935). *Principles of animal psychology*. New York: McGraw-Hill.

Maier, R. (1998). *Comparative animal behavior: An evolutionary and ecological approach*. Boston: Allyn and Bacon.

Main, A. R., & Bull, C. M. (1996). Mother-offspring recognition in two Australian lizards, *Tiliqua rugosa* and *Egernia stokesii*. *Animal Behaviour, 52*, 193–200.

Malmkvist, J., & Hansen, S. W. (2002). Generalization of fear in farm mink, *Mustela vison*, genetically selected for behaviour towards humans. *Animal Behaviour, 64*, 487–501.

Mann, M. A., & Mellgren, R. L. (1998). Sea turtle interactions with inanimate objects: Autogrooming or play behavior? In R. Byles & Y. Fernandez (eds.), *Proceedings of the Sixteenth Annual Workshop on Sea Turtle Biology and Conservation* (pp. 93–94). Washington, D.C.: NOAA Technical Memorandum NMFS-SEFSC-412.

Manning, A., & Johnstone, G. (1970). The effects of early adult experience on the development of aggressiveness in males of the cockroach, (*Nauphoeta cinera*). *Review Comportemont Animal, 4*, 12–16.

Manrod, J. (2003). Object introduction, exploration, and play behavior in black-throated monitor ligards (*Varanus albigularis albigularis*). Unpublished M. S. thesis, University of Tennessee, Knoxville.

Marans, S., & Cohen, D. J. (1991). Child psychoanalytic theories of development. In M. Lewis (ed.), *Child and Adolescent Psychiatry* (pp. 129–145). Baltimore: Williams and Wilkins.

Marchetti, M. P., & Nevitt, G. A. (2003). Effects of hatchery rearing on brain structures of rainbow trout, *Oncorhynchus mykiss*. *Environmental Biology of Fishes, 66*, 9–14.

Marler, P. (1996). Social cognition: Are primates smarter than birds? In V. Nolan, Jr. & E. D. Ketterson (eds.), *Current Ornithology* (Vol. 13, pp. 1–32). New York: Plenum.

Marler, P., & Peters, S. (1982). Subsong and plastic song: Their role in the vocal learning process. In D. E. Kroodsma & E. H. Miller (eds.), *Acoustic Communication in Birds* (Vol. 2, Song learning and its consequences, pp. 25–50). New York: Academic Press.

Marriner, L. M., & Drickamer, L. C. (1994). Factors influencing stereotyped behavior of primates in zoos. *Zoo Biology, 13*, 267–275.

Martin, L. D., & Rothschild, B. M. (1989). Paleopathology and diving mosasaurs. *American Scientist, 77*, 460–467.

Martin, P. (1984a). The (four) whys and wherefores of play in cats: A review of functional, evolutionary, developmental, and causal issues. In P. K. Smith (ed.), *Play in Animals and Humans* (pp. 71–94). Oxford: Basil Blackwell.

Martin, P. (1984b). The time and energy costs of play behaviour in the cat. *Zeitschrift für Tierpsychologie, 64*, 298–312.

Martin, P., & Caro, T. M. (1985). On the function of play and its role in behavioral development. *Advances in the Study of Behavior, 15*, 59–103.

Martin, R. A. (2002). Is laughter the best medicine? Humor, laughter, and physical health. *Current Directions in Psychological Science, 11*, 216–220.

Martins, E. P. (ed.). (1996). *Phylogenies and the comparative method in animal behavior*. New York: Oxford University Press.

Mason, G. J. (1991). Stereotypies: A critical review. *Animal Behaviour, 41*, 1015–1037.

Mason, G. J. (1993). Forms of stereotypic behavior. In A. B. Lawrence & J. Rushen (eds.), *Stereotypic Animal Behaviour* (pp. 7–40). Wallingford, England: CAB International.

Mason, W. A. (1978). Social experience and primate cognitive development. In G. M. Burghardt & M. Bekoff (eds.), *The Development of Behavior: Comparative and Evolutionary Aspects* (pp. 233–251). New York: Garland STPM Press.

Masson, J. M. (1999). *The emperor's embrace: Reflections on animal families and fatherhood*. New York: Simon and Schuster.

Mather, J. (1982). Choice and competition: Their effects on occupancy of shell homes by *Octopus joubini*. *Marine Behavior and Physiology, 8*, 285–293.

Mather, J. (1994). "Home" choice and modification by juvenile *Octopus vulgaris* (Mollusca: Cephalopoda): Specialized intelligence and tool use? *Journal of Zoology, London, 233*, 359–368.

Mather, J. (1995). Cognition in cephalopods. *Advances in the Study of Behavior, 24*, 317–324.

Mather, J. (1998). How do octopuses use their arms? *Journal of Comparative Psychology, 112*, 306–316.

Mather, J., & Anderson, R. C. (1993). Personalities of octopuses (*Octopus rubescens*). *Journal of Comparative Psychology, 107*, 336–340.

Mather, J. A., & Anderson, R. C. (1999). Exploration, play, and habituation in octopuses (*Octopus dofleini*). *Journal of Comparative Psychology, 113*, 333–338.

Matsumoto, K., Suzuki, W., & Tanaka, K. (2003). Neuronal correlates of goal-based motor selection in the prefrontal cortex. *Science, 301*, 229–232.

Mayr, E. (1994). Recapitulation reconsidered: The somatic program. *Quarterly Review of Biology, 69,* 223–232.

McCowan, B., Marino, L., Vance, E., Walke, L., & Reiss, D. (2000). Bubble ring play of bottlenose dolphins (*Tursiops truncatus*): Implications for cognition. *Journal of Comparative Psychology, 114,* 98–106.

McCracken, G. F. (1984). Communal nursing in Mexican free-tailed bats. *Science, 223,* 1090–1091.

McCurdy, D. G., & Herman, T. B. (1997). Putative anting behavior in wood turtles. *Herpetological Monographs, 28,* 127–128.

McDiarmid, R. W., & Altig, R. (eds.). (1999). *Tadpoles: The biology of anuran larvae.* Chicago: University of Chicago Press.

McDonough, C. M. (1994). Determinants of aggression in nine-banded armadillos. *Journal of Mammalogy, 75,* 189–198.

McDougall, W. (1924). *An outline of psycholgy.* 2nd ed. London: Methuen.

McFarland, D. (ed.). (1981). *The Oxford companion to animal behavior.* Oxford: Oxford University Press.

McGraw, M. B. (1943). *The neuromuscular maturation of the human infant.* New York: Columbia University Press.

McManus, J. (2000). Fortune's smile: Betting big at the World's Series of poker. *Harper's Magazine* (12), 39–57.

McNab, B. K. (1980). Food habits, energetics, and the population biology of mammals. *American Naturalist, 116,* 106–124.

McNab, B. K. (1988). Complications inherent in scaling the basal rate of metabolism in mammals. *Quarterly Review of Biology, 63,* 25–54.

McNab, B. K. (2002). *The physiological ecology of vertebrates: A view from energetics.* Ithaca: Comstock Publishing Associates.

McNab, B. K., & Eisenberg, J. F. (1989). Brain size and its relation to the rate of metabolism in mammals. *American Naturalist, 133,* 157–167.

McNicol, R. E., Scherer, E., & Murkin, E. J. (1985). Quantitative field investigations of feeding and territorial behaviour of young-of-the-year brook charr, *Salvelinus fontinalis. Environmental Biology of Fishes, 12,* 219–229.

Meder, E. (1958). *Gnathonemus petersii* (Günter). *Zeitschrift für Vivaristik, 4,* 161–171.

Meer, A. L. H. v. d., Weel, F. R. v. d., & Lee, D. N. (1995). The functional significance of arm movements in infants. *Science, 267,* 693–695.

Meister, I. G., Krings, T., Foltys, H., Boroojerdi, B., Müller, M., Töpper, R. & Thron, A. (2004). Playing piano in the mind—an fMRI study on music imagery and performance in pianists. *Cognitive Brain Research, 19,* 219–228.

Melzack, R., & Thompson, W. R. (1956). Effects of early experience on social behavior. *Canadian Journal of Psychology, 10*, 82–90.

Mercer, J. G., & Speakman, J. R. (2001). Hypothalamic neuropeptide mechanisms for regulating energy balance: From rodent models to human obesity. *Neuroscience and Biobehavioral Reviews, 25*, 101–116.

Mergen, B. (1982). *Play and playthings: A reference guide.* Westport, Conn.: Greenwood Press.

Metcalfe, N. B., Taylor, A. C., & Thorpe, J. E. (1995). Metabolic rate, social status and life history strategies in Atlantic salmon. *Animal Behaviour, 49*, 431–436.

Mettke-Hoffman, C., Winkler, H., & Leisler, B. (2002). The significance of ecological factors for exploration and neophobia in parrots. *Ethology, 108*, 249–272.

Metzger, M. A. (1997). Applications of nonlinear dynamical systems theory in developmental psychology: Motor and cognitive development. *Nonlinear Dynamics, Psychology, and Life Sciences, 1*, 55–68.

Meyer-Holzapfel, M. (1960). Über das Spiel bei Fischen, insbesondere beim Tapirrüsselfisch (*Mormyrus kannume* Forskål). *Zoologische Garten, 25*, 189–202.

Meyer-Holzapfel, M. (1978). On the readiness for play and instinctive activities (C. Müller-Schwarze, trans.). In D. Müller-Schwarze (ed.), *Evolution of Play Behavior* (pp. 252–268). Stroudsburg, Pa: Dowden, Hutchinson & Ross.

Meylan, P. A. (1987). The phylogenetic relationships of soft-shelled turtles (Family Trionychidae). *Bulletin of the American Museum of Natural History, 186*, 1–101.

Meylan, P. (1996). Book review of *Turtles of the United States and Canada*. *Herpetological Reviews, 27*, 41–42.

Miklosi, A. (1999). The ethological analysis of imitiation. *Biological Review, 74*, 347–374.

Milinski, M., Külling, D., & Kettler, R. (1990). Tit for tat: Sticklebacks (*Gasterosteus aculeatus*) "trusting" a cooperating partner. *Behavioral Ecology, 1*, 7–11.

Millar, S. (1968). *The psychology of play.* London: Penguin.

Millar, S. (1981). Play. In D. McFarland (ed.), *The Oxford companion to animal behavior* (pp. 457–460). Oxford: Oxford University Press.

Miller, M. N., & Byers, J. A. (1991). Energetic cost of locomotor play in pronghorn fawns. *Animal Behaviour, 41*, 1007–1013.

Miller, M. N., & Byers, J. A. (1998). Sparring as play in young pronghorn males. In M. Bekoff & J. A. Byers (eds.), *Animal Play: Evolutionary, Comparative, and Ecological Perspectives* (pp. 141–160). Cambridge: Cambridge University Press.

Minogue, K. (2001). How civilizations fall. *The new criterion on line, 19*(8), http://www.newcriterion.com/archive19/apr01/minogue.htm.

Mitchell, E. D., & Mason, B. S. (1934). *The theory of play.* New York: A. S. Barnes.

Mitchell, R. W. (1990). A theory of play. In M. Bekoff & D. Jamieson (eds.), *Interpretation and Explanation in the Study of Animal Behavior* (Vol. 1: *Interpretation, Intentionality, and Communication*, pp. 197–227). Boulder, Col.: Westview Press.

Mitchell, R. W. (2002). A history of pretense in animals and children. In R. W. Mitchell (ed.), *Pretending and Imagination in Animals and Children* (pp. 23–42). Cambridge: Cambridge University Press.

Mitchell, R. W., & Thompson, N. S. (1986). Deception in play between dogs and people. In R. W. Mitchell & N. S. Thompson (eds.), *Deception: Perspectives on Human and Nonhuman Deceit* (pp. 193–204). Albany, NY: SUNY Press.

Mitchell, R. W., & Thompson, N. S. (1991). Projects, routines, and enticements in dog-human play. In P. P. G. Bateson & P. H. Klopfer (eds.), *Perspectives in Ethology* (Vol. 9, pp. 189–216). New York: Plenum.

Mitchell, R. W., Thompson, N. S., & Miles, H. L. (eds.). (1997). *Anthropomorphism, anecdotes, and animals*. Albany: State University of New York Press.

Mohr, E. (1952). *Der Stör*. Leipzig: Akademische Verlagsgesellschaft Geest & Portig K.-G.

Moller, P. (1995). *Electric fishes: History and behavior*. London: Chapman and Hall.

Mook, D. G. (1996). *Motivation*. 2nd ed. New York: W. W. Norton.

Morgan, C. L. (1920). *Animal behaviour*. 2nd ed. London: Edward Arnold.

Morris, P. H., Gale, A., & Duffy, K. (2002). Can judges agree on the personality of horses? *Personality and Individual Differences*, *33*, 67–81.

Morton, S. R., Dickman, C. R., & Fletcher, T. P. (1989). Dasyuridae. In D. W. Walton & B. J. Richardson (eds.), *Fauna of Australia* (Vol. 1B, *Mammalia*, pp. 560–582). Canberra: Australian Government Publishing Service.

Moyal, A. (2001). *Platypus: The extraordinary story of how a curious creature baffled the world*. Washington, D.C.: Smithsonion Institution Press.

Müller-Schwarze, D. (1968). Play deprivation in deer. *Behaviour*, *31*, 144–162.

Müller-Schwarze, D. (ed.). (1978). *Evolution of play behavior*. Stroudsburg, Pa: Dowden, Hutchinson & Ross.

Müller-Schwarze, D. (1984). Analysis of play behaviour: What do we measure and when? In P. K. Smith (ed.), *Play in Animals and Humans* (pp. 147–158). Oxford: Basil Blackwell.

Murphy, K. E., & Pitcher, T. J. (1991). Individual behavioural strategies associated with predator inspection in minnow shoals. *Ethology*, *88*, 307–319.

Musser, A. M. (2003). Review of monotreme fossil record and comparison of paleontological and molecular data. *Comparative Biochemistry and Physiology Part A*, *136*, 927–942.

Myrberg, A. A., Jr. (1965). A descriptive analysis of the behaviour of the African cichlid fish, *Pelmatochromis guentheri* (Savage). *Animal Behaviour*, *13*, 312–329.

Nagy, K. A. (1982). Energy requirements of free-living iguanid lizards. In G. M. Burghardt & A. S. Rand (eds.), *Iguanas of the World: Their Behavior, Ecology, and Conservation* (pp. 49–59). Park Ridge, N.J.: Noyes.

Nagy, K. A. (2000). Energy costs of growth in neonate reptiles. *Herpetological Monographs, 14*, 378–387.

Nair, D. G., Purcott, K. L., Fuchs, A., Steinberg, F., & Kelso, J. A. S. (2003). Cortical and cerebellar activity of the human brain during imagined and executed unimanual and bimanual action sequences: a functional MRI study. *Cognitive Brain Research, 15*, 250–260.

Nalepa, C. A. (1994). Nourishment and the origin of termite eusociality. In J. H. Hunt & C. A. Nalepa (eds.), *Nourishment and Evolution in Insect Societies* (pp. 57–104). Boulder, Col.: Westview Press.

Neill, W. T. (1971). *The last of the ruling reptiles. Alligators, crocodiles, and their kin.* New York: Columbia University Press.

Nell, V. (2002). Why young men drive dangerously: Implications for injury prevention. *Current Directions in Psychological Science, 11*, 75–82.

Nelson, C. A. (1999). Neural plasticity and human development. *Current Directions in Psychological Science, 8*, 42–45.

Nice, M. (1941). Studies in the life history of the song sparrow. II. *Transactions of the Linnean Society of New York, 6*, 1–238.

Nice, M. (1962). Development of behavior in precocial birds. *Transactions of the Linnean Society of New York, 8*, 1–211.

Nielsen, J. L. (1990). Environment and behavior affecting growth and development of juvenile coho salmon (*Oncorhynchus kisutch*). Unpublished M.S. thesis, University of California, Berkeley.

Niewiarowski, P. H., Balk, M. L., & Londraville, R. L. (2000). Phenotypic effects of leptin in an ectotherm: A new tool to study the evolution of life histories and endothermy? *Journal of Experimental Biology, 203*, 295–300.

Nijman, V., & Heuts, B. A. (2000). Effects of environmental enrichment upon resource holding power in fish in prior residence situations. *Behavioural Processes, 49*, 77–83.

Noakes, D. G. (1978). Ontogeny of behavior in fishes: A survey and suggestions. In G. M. Burghardt & M. Bekoff (eds.), *The Development of Behavior: Comparative and Evolutionary Aspects* (pp. 103–125). New York: Garland STPM Press.

Noakes, D. G., & Barlow, G. W. (1973). Ontogeny of parent-contacting in young *Cichlasoma citrinellum* (Pisces, Cichlidae). *Behaviour, 46*, 221–255.

Noble, G. K. (1926). *The biology of the Amphibia.* New York: McGraw-Hill.

Noble, G. K., & Zitrin, A. (1942). Induction of mating behavior in male and female chicks following injection of sex hormones. *Endocrinology, 30*, 327–334.

Novacek, M. J. (1992). Mammalian phylogeny: Shaking the tree. *Nature, 356*, 121–125.

Nowak, R. M. (1999). *Walker's mammals of the world*. 6th ed. Baltimore: Johns Hopkins University Press.

Nunes, S., Muecke, E. M., Anthony, J. A., & Batterbee, A. S. (1999). Endocrine and energetic mediation of play behavior in free-living Belding's ground squirrels. *Hormones and Behavior, 36*, 153–165.

Ohbayashi, M., Ohki, K., & Miyashita, Y. (2003). Conversion of working memory to motor sequence in the monkey premotor cortex. *Science, 301*, 233–236.

de Oliveira, C. R., Ruiz-Miranda, C. R., Kleiman, D. G., & Beck, B. B. (2003). Play behavior in juvenile golden lion tamarins (Callitrichidae: Primates): Organization in relation to costs. *Ethology, 109*, 593-609.

Olomon, C. M., Breed, M. D., & Bell, W. J. (1976). Ontogenetic and temporal aspects of agonistic behavior in a cockroach, *Periplaneta americana*. *Behavioral Biology, 17*, 243–248.

Ono, K. A., Boness, D. J., & Oftedal, O. T. (1987). The effect of a natural environmental disturbance on maternal investment and pup behavior in the California sea lion. *Behavioral Ecology and Sociobiology, 21*, 109–118.

Oppenheim, R. W. (2001). Early development of behavior and the nervous system, an embryological perspective: A postscript from the end of the millennium. In E. M. Blass (ed.), *Handbook of Behavioral Neurobiology* (Vol. 13, *Developmental Psychobiology*, pp. 15–52). New York: Plenum.

Orgeur, P. (1995). Sexual play behavior in lambs androgenized in utero. *Physiology & Behavior, 57*, 185–187.

Ortega, J. C., & Bekoff, M. (1987). Avian play: Comparative evolutionary and developmental trends. *Auk, 104*, 338–341.

Osborn, I. (1999). *Tormenting thoughts and secret rituals: The hidden epidemic of obsessive-compulsive disorder*. New York: Dell.

Osgood, C. E. (1953). *Method and theory in experimental psychology*. New York: Oxford University Press.

Osorio, D., Bacon, J. P., & Whitington, P. (1997). The evolution of arthropod nervous systems. *American Scientist, 85*, 244–253.

Pandolfi, M. (1996). Play activity in young Montagu's harriers (*Circus pygargus*). *Auk, 113*, 935–938.

Panksepp, J. (1980). The ontogeny of play in rats. *Developmental Psychobiology, 14*, 327–332.

Panksepp, J. (1998a). *Affective neuroscience*. New York: Oxford University Press.

Panksepp, J. (1998b). Attention deficit hyperactivity disorders, psychostimulants, and intolerance of childhood playfulness: A tragedy in the making? *Current Directions in Psychological Science, 7*, 91–98.

Panksepp, J. (2000). The riddle of laughter: Neural and psychoevolutionary underpinnings of joy. *Current Directions in Psychological Science, 9*, 183–186.

Panksepp, J., & Beatty, W. W. (1980). Social deprivation and play in rats. *Behavioral and Neural Biology*, *30*, 197–206.

Panksepp, J., Burgdorf, J., & Gordon, N. (2001). Towards a genetics of joy: Breeding rats for "laughter." In A. Kaszaiak (ed.), *Emotions, Qualia, and Consciousness* (pp. 124–136). Singapore: World Scientific.

Panksepp, J., & Panksepp, J. B. (2000). The seven sins of evolutionary psychology. *Evolution and Cognition*, *6*, 108–131.

Panksepp, J., Siviy, S., & Normansell, L. (1984). The psychobiology of play: Theoretical and methodological perspectives. *Neuroscience and Biobehavioral Reviews*, *8*, 465–492.

Paquette, D. (1994). Fighting and playfighting in captive chimpanzees. *Aggressive Behavior*, *20*, 49–65.

Pardini, A. T., Jones, C. S., Noble, L. R., Kreiser, B., Malcolm, H., Bruce, B. D., Stevens, J. D., Cliff, G., Scholl, M. C., Francis, M., Duffy, C. A. J., & Martin, A. P. (2001). Sex-biased dispersal of great white sharks. *Nature*, *412*, 139–140.

Parker, A. (1975). Young male peregrines passing vegetation fragments to each other. *British Birds*, *68*, 242–243.

Parker, S. T. (1977). Piaget's sensorimotor series in an infant macaque: A model for comparing unstereotyped behavior and intelligence in human and nonhuman primates. In S. Chevalier-Skolnikoff & F. E. Poirier (eds.), *Primate Biosocial Development: Biological, Social, and Ecological Determinants* (pp. 43–111). New York: Garland.

Parker, S. T. (1984). Playing for keeps: An evolutionary perspective on human games. In P. K. Smith (ed.), *Play in Animals and Humans* (pp. 271–293). Oxford: Basil Blackwell.

Parker, S. T. (1990). Why big brains are so rare: Energy costs of intelligence and brain size in anthropoid primates. In S. T. Parker & K. R. Gibson (eds.), *"Language" and Intelligence in Monkeys and Apes: Comparative Developmental Perspectives* (pp. 129–154). Cambridge: Cambridge University Press.

Parker, S. T. (1996). Using cladistic analysis of comparative data to reconstruct the evolution of cognitive development in hominids. In E. P. Martins (ed.), *Phylogenies and the Comparative Method in Animal Behavior* (pp. 361–398). New York: Oxford University Press.

Parker, S. T., & Gibson, K. R. (1979). A developmental model of the evolution of language and intelligence in early hominids. *Behavioral and Brain Sciences*, *2*, 367–407.

Parker, S. T., & Gibson, K. R. (eds.). (1990). *"Language" and intelligence in monkeys and apes: Comparative developmental perspectives*. Cambridge: Cambridge University Press.

Parker, S. T., & McKinney, M. L. (1999). *Origins of intelligence: The evolution of cognitive development in monkeys, apes, and humans*. Baltimore: Johns Hopkins University Press.

Parkes, K. C., Weldon, P. J., & Hoffman, R. L. (2003). Polydesmidan millipede used in self-anointing by a strong-billed woodcreeper (*Xiphocolaptes promeropirhyncus*) from Belize. *Ornitotologia Neotropical*, *14*, 285–286.

Parrott, W. G., & Gleitman, H. (1989). Infant's expectations in play: The joy of peek-a-boo. *Cognition and Emotion, 3,* 291–311.

Parten, M. (1932). Social participation among preschool children. *Journal of Abnormal and Social Psychology, 27,* 243–269.

Pasztor, T. J., Smith, L. K., MacDonald, N. L., Michener, G. R., & Pellis, S. M. (2001). Sexual and aggressive play fighting of sibling Richardson's ground squirrels. *Aggressive Behavior, 27,* 323–337.

Patenaude, F. (1984). The ontogeny of behavior of free-living beavers (*Castor canadensis*). *Zeitshrift für Tierpsychologie, 66,* 33–44.

Pearse, A. S. (1912). The habits of fiddler crabs. *Philippine Journal of Science, 7,* 113–133.

Pearson, M. P., Spriet, L. L., & Stevens, E. D. (1990). Effect of sprint training on swim performance and white muscle metabolism during exercise and recovery in rainbow trout (*Salmo gairdneri*). *Journal of Experimental Biology, 149,* 45–60.

Pedersen, J. M., Glickman, S. E., Frank, L. G., & Beach, F. A. (1990). Sex differences in the play behavior of immature spotted hyenas, *Crocuta crocuta. Hormones and Behavior, 24,* 403–420.

Pederson, B. H. (1997). The cost of growth in young fish larvae, a review of new hypotheses. *Aquaculture, 155,* 259–269.

Peiper, J. (1999). *Leisure: The basis of culture* (A. Dru, trans.). Indianapolis: Liberty Fund.

Pellegrini, A. D. (1989). What is a category? The case of rough-and-tumble play. *Ethology and Sociobiology, 10,* 331–341.

Pellegrini, A. D., & Boyd, B. (1993). The educational and developmental roles of play in early education. In B. Spodek (ed.), *Handbook of Research in Early Childhood Education* (pp. 105–121). New York: Macmillan.

Pelligrini, A. D., Horvat, M., & Huberty, P. (1998). The relative cost of children's physical play. *Animal Behaviour, 55,* 1053–1061.

Pellegrini, A. D., & Perlmutter, J. C. (1987). A reexamination of the Smilansky-Parten matrix of play behavior. *Journal of Research in Childhood Education, 2,* 89–96.

Pellegrini, A. D., & Smith, P. K. (1998). Physical activity play: The nature and function of a neglected aspect of play. *Child Development, 69,* 577–598.

Pellis, S. M. (1981). A description of social play by the Australian magpie *Gymnorhina tibicen* based on Eshkol-Wachman notation. *Bird Behaviour, 3,* 61–79.

Pellis, S. M. (1983). Development of head and foot coordination in the Australian magpie *Gymnorhina tibicen,* and the function of play. *Bird Behaviour, 4,* 57–62.

Pellis, S. M. (1991). How motivationally distinct is play? A preliminary case study. *Animal Behaviour, 42,* 851–853.

Pellis, S. M. (1993). Sex and the evolution of play fighting: A review and model based on the behavior of muroid rodents. *Play Theory and Research, 1,* 55–75.

Pellis, S. M. (2001). Sex differences in play fighting revisited: Traditional and nontraditional mechanisms of sexual differentiation in rats. *Archives of Sexual Behavior, 31*, 11–20.

Pellis, S. M., & Iwaniuk, A. N. (1999a). The problem of adult play fighting: A comparative analysis of play and courtship in primates. *Ethology, 105*, 783–806.

Pellis, S. M., & Iwaniuk, A. N. (1999b). The roles of phylogeny and sociality in the evolution of social play in muroid rodents. *Animal Behaviour, 58*, 361–373.

Pellis, S. M., & Iwaniuk, A. N. (2000a). Adult-adult play in primates: Comparative analyses of its origin, distribution, and evolution. *Ethology, 106*, 1083–1104.

Pellis, S. M., & Iwaniuk, A. N. (2000b). Comparative analyses of the role of postnatal development on the expression of play fighting. *Developmental Psychobiology, 36*, 136–147.

Pellis, S. M., & Iwaniuk, A. N. (2002). Brain stem size and adult-adult play in primates: A comparative analysis of the roles of the non-visual neocortex and the amygdala. *Behavioural Brain Research, 134*, 31–39.

Pellis, S. M., & Officer, R. C. E. (1987). An analysis of some predatory behaviour patterns in four species of carnivorous marsupials (Dasyuridae) with comparative notes on the eutherian cat *Felis catus. Ethology, 75*, 177–196.

Pellis, S. M., & Pellis, V. C. (1987). Play-fighting differs from serious fighting in both target of attack and tactics of fighting in the laboratory rat *Rattus norvegicus. Aggressive Behavior, 13*, 227–242.

Pellis, S. M., & Pellis, V. C. (1996). On knowing it's only play: The role of play signals in play fighting. *Aggression and Violent Behavior, 1*, 249–268.

Pellis, S. M., & Pellis, V. C. (1998a). Play fighting of rats in comparative perspective: A schema for neurobehavioral analysis. *Neuroscience and Biobehavioral Reviews, 23*, 87–101.

Pellis, S. M., & Pellis, V. C. (1998b). Structure–function interface in the analysis of play fighting. In M. Bekoff & J. A. Byers (eds.), *Animal Play: Evolutionary, Comparative, and Ecological Perspectives* (pp. 115–140). Cambridge: Cambridge University Press.

Pellis, S. M., O'Brien, D. P., Pellis, V. C., Teitlebaum, P., Wolgin, D. L., & Kennedy, S. (1988). Escalation of feline predation along a gradient from avoidance through "play" to killing. *Behavioral Neuroscience, 102*, 760–777.

Pellis, S. M., Pasztor, T. J., Pellis, V. C., & Dewsbury, D. A. (2000). The organization of play fighting in the grasshopper mouse (*Onychomys leucogaster*): Mixing predatory and sociosexual targets and tactics. *Aggressive Behavior, 26*, 319–334.

Pellis, S. M., Pellis, V. C., Manning, C. J., & Dewsbury, D. A. (1991). The paucity of social play in *Mus domesticus*: What is missing from the behavioural repertoire? *Animal Behaviour, 42*, 686–687.

Pepperberg, I. M. (1991). A communicative approach to animal cognition: A study of conceptual abilities of an African grey parrot. In C. A. Ristau (ed.), *Cognitive Ethology: The Minds of Other Animals* (pp. 153–186). Hillsdale, N.J.: Erlbaum.

Pepperberg, I. M. (2002). Cognitive and communicative abilities of grey parrots. *Current Directions in Psychological Science, 11*, 83–87.

Pepperberg, I. M., Brese, K. J., & Harris, B. J. (1991). Solitary sound play during acquisition of English vocalizations by an African grey parrot (*Psittacus erithacus*): Possible parallels with children's monologue speech. *Applied Psycholinguistics, 12*, 151–178.

Pereira, M. E., & Fairbanks, L. A. (eds.). (1993). *Juvenile primates: life history, development, and behavior*. New York: Oxford University Press.

Petersen, A. F. (1988). Why children and young animals play: A new theory of play and its role in problem solving. *Historisk-filosofiske Meddelelser (Royal Danish Academy of Science and Letters), 54*, 1–57.

Petitto, L. A., Holowka, S., Sergio, L. E., & Ostry, D. (2001). Language rhythms in baby hand movements. *Nature, 413*, 35–36.

Petroski, H. (2003). Early education. *American Scientist, 91*, 206–209.

Pfeffer, K., Fritz, J., & Kotrschal, K. (2002). Hormonal correlates of being an innovative graylag goose, *Anser anser*. *Animal Behaviour, 63*, 687–695.

Phillips, J. A., Alberts, A. C., & Pratt, N. C. (1993). Differential resource use, growth, and the ontogeny of social relationships in the green iguana. *Physiology and Behavior, 53*, 81–88.

Phillips, P. E. M., Stuber, G. D., Helen, M. L. A. V., Wightman, R. M., & Carelli, R. M. (2003). Subsecond dopamine release promotes cocaine seeking. *Nature, 422*, 614–618.

Piaget, J. (1962). *Play, dreams and imitation in childhood* (C. Gattegno & F. M. Hodgson, trans.). New York: W. W. Norton.

Piaget, J., & Inhelder, B. (1969). *The psychology of the child* (H. Weaver, trans.). New York: Basic Books.

Piccione, P. A. (1990). Mehen, mysteries, and resurrection from the coiled serpent. *Journal of the American Research Center in Egypt, 27*, 43–52.

Pigliucci, M. (2001). *Phenotypic plasticity: Beyond nature and nurture*. Baltimore: Johns Hopkins University Press.

Plato (1957). *The Republic of Plato* (A. D. Lindsay, trans.). New York: E. P. Dutton & Co.

Poirier, F. E., Bellisari, A., & Haines, L. (1978). Functions of primate play behavior. In E. O. Smith (ed.), *Social Play in Primates* (pp. 143–168). New York: Academic Press.

Poirier, F. E., & Field, M. (2000). Pavlovian perceptions and primate realities. *Behavioral and Brain Sciences, 23*, 262.

Poirier, F. E., & Smith, E. O. (1974). Socializing functions of primate play. *American Zoologist, 14*, 275–287.

Poole, T. B., & Fish, J. (1975). An investigation of playful behaviour in *Rattus norvegicus* and *Mus musculus* (Mammalia). *Journal of Zoology, London, 175*, 61–71.

Porter, C., & Bundy, A. C. (2001). Validity of three tests of playfulness with African American children and their parents and relationships among parental beliefs and values and children's observed playfulness. In S. Reifel (ed.), *Theory in Context and Out* (pp. 315–334). Westport, Conn.: Ablex.

Portmann, A. (1990). *A zoologist looks at humankind.* New York: Columbia University Press.

Post, N., & von der Emde, G. (1999). The "novelty response" in an electric fish: Response properties and habituation. *Physiology and Behavior, 68,* 115–128.

Pough, F. H. (1977). Ontogenetic change in blood oxygen-carrying capacity and maximum activity in garter snakes (*Thamnophis sirtalis*). *Journal of Comparative Physiology B, 166,* 337–345.

Pough, F. H. (1978). Ontogenetic changes in endurance in water snakes (*Nerodia sipedon*): Physiological correlates and ecological consequences. *Copeia, 1978,* 69–75.

Pough, F. H. (1980). The advantages of ectothermy for tetrapods. *American Naturalist, 115,* 92–112.

Pough, F. H. (1983). Amphibians and reptiles as low-energy systems. In W. P. Aspey & S. I. Lustick (eds.), *Behavioral Energetics: The Cost of Survival in Vertebrates* (pp. 141–188). Columbus: Ohio State University Press.

Pough, F. H., Janis, C. M., & Heiser, J. B. (eds.). (2002). *Vertebrate life.* 6th ed. Upper Saddle River, N.J.: Prentice-Hall.

Pough, F. H., Andrews, R. M., Cadle, J. E., Crump, M. L., Savitzky, A. H., & Wells, K. D. (eds.). (2001). *Herpetology.* 2nd ed. Upper Saddle River, N.J.: Prentice-Hall.

Pough, F. H., Magnusson, W. E., Ryan, M. J., Wells, K. D., & Taigen, T. L. (1992). Behavioral energetics. In M. E. Feder & W. W. Burggen (eds.), *Environmental Physiology of the Amphibians* (pp. 395–436). Chicago: University of Chicago Press.

Power, T. G. (2000). *Play and exploration in children and animals.* Mahwah, N.J.: Erlbaum.

Preyer, W. (1893). *Mental development in the child* (H. W. Brown, trans.). New York: Appleton.

Price, E. O. (1984). Behavioral aspects of domestication. *Quarterly Review of Biology, 59,* 1–32.

Proctor, J. B. (1928). On a living Komodo dragon *Varanus komodoensis* Ouwens, exhibited at the scientific meeting, October 23rd, 1928. *Proceedings of the Zoological Society London, 1928,* 1017–1019.

Proske, U., & Gregory, E. (2003). Electrolocation in the platypus—some speculations. *Comparative Biochemistry and Physiology Part A, 136,* 821–825.

Provine, R. R. (2001). *Laughter.* New York: Penguin.

Pruitt, C. H. (1974). Social behavior of young captive black bears. Unpublished Ph.D. dissertation, University of Tennessee, Knoxville.

Pruitt, C. H. (1976). Play and agonistic behavior in young captive black bears. *International Conference on Bear Research and Management, 3,* 79–86.

Punzo, F. (1985). Neurochemical correlates of learning and the role of the basal forebrain in the brown anole, *Anolis sagrei* (Lacertilia: Iguanidae). *Copeia, 1985,* 409–414.

Purvis, A. (1995). A composite estimate of primate phylogeny. *Philosophical Transactions of the Royal Society of London B, 348,* 405–421.

Rand, A. S., Gorman, G. C., & Rand, W. M. (1975). Natural history, behavior, and ecology of *Anolis agassizi.* In J. B. Graham (ed.), *The Biological Investigation of Malpelo Island, Colombia* (pp. 27–38). Washington, D.C.: Smithsonian Institution Press.

Rasa, O. A. E. (1984). A motivational analysis of object play in juvenile dwarf mongooses (*Helogale undulata rufula*). *Animal Behaviour, 32,* 579–589.

Reeve, H. K. (2001). In search of unified theories in sociobiology: Help from social wasps. In L. A. Dugatkin (ed.), *Model Systems in Behavioral Ecology* (pp. 57–71). Princeton, N.J.: Princeton University Press.

Rendell, L., & Whitehead, H. (2001). Culture in whales and dolphins. *Behavioral and Brain Sciences, 24,* 309–382.

Renfree, M. B., Holt, A. B., Green, S. W., Carr, J. P., & Cheek, D. B. (1982). Ontogeny of the brain in a marsupial (*Macropus eugenii*) throughout pouch life. I. brain growth. *Brain, Behavior and Evolution, 20,* 57–71.

Renner, M. J. (1998). Curiosity and exploratory behavior. In G. Greenberg & Haraway, M. (eds.), *Comparative Psychology: A Handbook* (pp. 649–652). New York: Garland.

Renner, M. J., & Seltzer, C. P. (1991). Molar characteristics of exploratory and investigatory behavior in the rat (*Rattus norvegicus*). *Journal of Comparative Psychology, 105,* 326–339.

Renouf, D. (1993). Play in a captive breeding colony of harbour seals (*Phoca vitulina*): Constrained by energy or time. *Journal of Zoology, London, 231,* 351–363.

Renouf, D., & Lawson, J. W. (1986). Play in harbour seals (*Phoca vitulina*). *Journal of Zoology, London, 208,* 73–82.

Restak, R. M. (1994). *The modular brain.* New York: Simon and Schuster.

Revonsuo, A. (2000). The reinterpretation of dreams: An evolutionary hypothesis of the function of dreaming. *Behavioral and Brain Sciences, 23,* 877–901.

Rheingold, H. L., & Hess, E. H. (1957). The chick's "preference" for some visual properties of water. *Journal of Comparative and Physiological Psychology, 50,* 417–421.

Richards, R. J. (1987). *Darwin and the emergence of evolutionary theories of mind and behavior.* Chicago: University of Chicago Press.

Richmond, B. J., Liu, Z., & Shidara, M. (2003). Predicting future rewards. *Science, 301,* 178–179.

Ridet, J. M., & Bauchot, R. (1990a). Analyse quantitative de l'encéphale des téléostéens: Caractères évolutifs et adaptatifs de l'encéphalisation. I. Généralitiés et analyse globale. *Journal für Hirnforschung, 31,* 51–63.

Ridet, J. M., & Bauchot, R. (1990b). Analyse quantitative de l'encéphale des téléostéens: Caractères évolutifs et adaptatifs de l'encéphalisation. II. Les grandes subdivisions encéphaliques. *Journal für Hirnforschung, 31,* 433–458.

Rieppel, O., & deBraga, M. (1996). Turtles as diaspid reptiles. *Nature, 384,* 453–455.

Rieppel, O., & Reisz, R. R. (1999). The origin and early evolution of turtles. *Annual Review of Ecology and Systematics, 30,* 1–22.

Rike, E. (1993). Guided symbolic dramatic play as the missing link to literacy. In J. Wilkinson (ed.), *The Symbolic Dramatic Play—Literacy Connection: Whole Brain, Whole Body, Whole Learning* (pp. 25–42). Needham Heights, MA: Ginn Press.

Ristau, C. A. (ed.). (1991). *Cognitive ethology: The minds of other animals*. Hillsdale, N.J.: Erlbaum.

Ritter, E. K. (2001). Food-related dominance between two carcharhinid shark species, the Caribbean reef shark, *Carcharinus perezi*, and the blacktip shark, *Carcharinus limbatus*. *Marine and Freshwater Behavior and Physiology*, *34*, 125–129.

Rivas, J., & Burghardt, G. M. (2002). Crotalomorphism: A metaphor for understanding anthropomorphism by omission. In M. Bekoff, C. Allen, & G. M. Burghardt (eds.), *The Cognitive Animal: Empirical and Theoretical Perspectives on Animal Cognition* (pp. 9–18). Cambridge, Mass.: MIT Press.

Rives, J. D., III. (1978). A comparative study of courtship related behavior in immature emydid turtles of two species. Unpublished M.S. thesis, University of Southwestern Louisiana, Lafayette.

Robbins, T. W., & Everitt, B. J. (1995). Arousal systems and attention. In M. S. Gazzaniga (ed.), *The Cognitive Neurosciences* (pp. 703–720). Cambridge, Mass.: MIT Press.

Robinson, J. G. (1986). Seasonal variation in use of time and space by wedge capped capuchins *Cebus olivaceus*: Implications for foraging theory. *Smithsonian Contributions to Zoology*, *431* (entire issue).

Robinson, M. (1992). *Touching the serpent's tail*. Keene, Ontario: Martin House.

Rogers, C. S., Impara, J. C., Frary, R. B., Harris, T., Meeks, A., Semanic-Lauth, S., & Reynolds, M. R. (1998). Measuring playfulness: Development of the child behaviors inventory of playfulness. In M. C. Duncan, G. Chick, & A. Aycock (eds.), *Diversions and Divergences in the Fields of Play* (pp. 121–135). Greenwich, Conn.: Ablex.

Roggenbuck, M. E., & Jenssen, T. A. (1986). The ontogeny of display behaviour in *Sceloporus undulatus* (Sauria: Iguanidae). *Ethology*, *71*, 153–165.

Rohlman, D. S., Anger, W. K., Tamulinas, A., Phillips, J., Bailey, S. R., & McCauley, L. (2001). Development of a neurobehavioral battery for children exposed to neurotoxic chemicals. *Neurotoxicology*, *22*, 657–665.

Roitblat, H. L. (1987). *Introduction to comparative cognition*. New York: Freeman.

Romanes, G. J. (1883). *Mental life of animals*. London: Kegan, Paul, Trench, Trübner.

Romanes, G. J. (1892). *Animal intelligence*. 5th ed. London: Kegan, Paul, Trench, Trübner.

Romanes, G. J. (1897). Recreation. In C. L. Morgan (ed.), *Essays by George John Romanes* (pp. 164–212). London: Longmans, Green.

Romeo, R. D., Richardson, H. N., & Sisk, C. L. (2002). Puberty and the maturation of the male brain and sexual behavior: Recasting a behavioral potential. *Neuroscience and Biobehavioral Reviews*, *26*, 381–391.

Rooney, N. J., Bradshaw, J. W. S., & Robinson, I. H. (2000). A comparison of dog-dog and dog-human play behaviour. *Applied Animal Behaviour Science*, *66*, 235–248.

Rose, M. R., & Lauder, G. V. (eds.). (1996). *Adaptation*. San Diego: Academic Press.

Rosenberg, A. (1990). Is there an evolutionary biology of play? In M. Bekoff & D. Jamieson (eds.), *Interpretation and Explanation in the Study of Animal Behavior* (Vol. 1, *Interpretation, Intentionality, and Communication*, pp. 180–197). Boulder, Col.: Westview Press.

Roth, G., Nishikawa, K. C., Naujoks-Manteuffel, C., Schmidt, A., & Wake, D. B. (1993). Paedomorphosis and simplification in the nervous system of salamanders. *Brain, Behavior and Evolution*, *42*, 137–170.

Rougier, G. W., Fuente, M. S. d. l., & Arcucci, A. B. (1995). Late Triassic turtles from South America. *Science*, *268*, 855–858.

Rowe, M. (1996). Sensorimotor cortical organization: How do marsupials compare with other mammals? In D. B. Croft & U. Ganslosser (eds.), *Comparison of Marsupial and Placental Behaviour* (pp. 3–45). Fürth, Germany: Filander Verlag.

Ruben, J. A., & Battalia, D. E. (1979). Aerobic and anaerobic metabolism during activity in small rodents. *Journal of Experimental Zoology*, *208*, 73–76.

Ruben, J. A., Jones, T. D., Geist, N. R., & Hillenius, W. J. (1997). Lung structure and ventilation in theropod dinosaurs and early birds. *Science*, *278*, 1267–1270.

Ruben, K. H., Fein, G. G., & Vandenberg, B. (1983). Play. In E. M. Hetherington (ed.), *Handbook of Child Psychology*. 4th ed. (Vol. 4, *Socialization, Personality, and Social Development*, pp. 693–744). New York: Wiley.

Russell, E. M. (1982). Patterns of reproductive investment in marsupials. *Biological Reviews of the Cambridge Philosophical Society*, *57*, 423–486.

Russell, E. M. (1986). Observations on the behaviour of the honey possum, *Tarsipes rostratus*, (Marsupialia: Tarsipedidae) in captivity. *Australian Journal of Zoology*, Supplement series, *121*, 1–63.

Russell, E. M., Lee, A. K., & Wilson, G. R. (1989). Natural history of the Metatheria. In D. W. Walton & B. J. Richardson (eds.), *Fauna of Australia* (Vol. 1B, *Mammalia*, pp. 505–526). Canberra: Australian Government Publishing Service.

Russon, A. E., Vasey, P. L., & Gauthier, C. (2002). Seeing with the mind's eye: Eye-covering play in orangutans and Japanese macaques. In R. W. Mitchell (ed.), *Pretending and Imagination in Animals and Children* (pp. 241–254). Cambridge: Cambridge University Press.

Ryan, B. C., & Vandenbergh, J. G. (2002). Intrauterine position effects. *Neuroscience and Biobehavioral Reviews*, *26*, 665–678.

Ryden, H. (1997). *Lily pond: Four years with a family of beavers*. London: Lyons & Burford.

Sander, K., & Scheich, H. (2001). Auditory perception of laughing and crying activates human amygdala regardless of attentional state. *Cognitive Brain Science*, *12*, 181–198.

Sanders, N. J., & Gordon, D. M. (2002). Resources and the flexible allocation of work in the desert ant, *Aphaenogaster cockerelli*. *Insectes sociaux*, *49*, 371–379.

Sanz, J. L., Chiappe, L. M., Pérez-Moreno, B. P., Moratalla, J. J., Hernández-Carrasquilla, F., Buscalioni, A. D., Ortega, F., Poyato-Ariza, F. J., Rasskin-Gutman, D., & Martínez-Delclòs, X. (1997). A nestling bird from the Lower Cretaceous of Spain: Implications for avian skull and neck evolution. *Science*, *276*, 1543–1546.

Schiller, F. (1967). *On the aesthetic education of man* (E. M. Wilkinson & L. A. Willoughby, trans.). Oxford: Oxford University Press.

Schiller, P. H. (1957). Innate motor action as a basis of learning: Manipulative patterns in the chimpanzee. In C. H. Schiller (ed.), *Instinctive Behavior* (pp. 269–287). New York: International Universities Press.

Schleidt, W. M. (1970). Precocial sexual behaviour in turkeys (*Meleagris gallopavo* L.) *Animal Behaviour, 18,* 760–761.

Schneirla, T. C. (1965). Aspects of stimulation and organization in approach/withdrawal processes underlying vertebrate behavioral development. In D. S. Lehrman, R. A. Hinde, & E. Shaw (eds.), *Advances in the Study of Behavior* (Vol. 1, pp. 1–74). New York: Academic Press.

Schubert, K. (1973). Order: Tarpons. In B. Grzimek (ed.), *Grzimek's Animal Life Encyclopedia* (Vol. 4 *Fishes I,* pp. 152–156). New York: Van Nostrand Reinhold.

Schütz, M., & Barlow, G. W. (1997). Young of the Midas cichlid get biologically active non-nutrients by eating mucus from the surface of their parents. *Fish Physiology and Biochemistry, 16,* 11–18.

Secor, S. M. (2001). Regulation of digestive performance: A proposed adaptive response. *Comparative Biochemistry and Physiology* Part A, *128,* 565–577.

Secor, S. M., & Phillips, J. A. (1997). Specific dynamic action of a large carnivorous lizard, *Varanus albigularis. Comparative and Biochemical Physiology, 117A,* 515–522.

Seeley, T. D. (2001). A feeling and a fondness for bees. In L. A. Dugatkin (ed.), *Model Systems in Behavioral Ecology* (pp. 27–40). Princeton, N.J.: Princeton University Press.

Serruya, D., & Eilam, D. (1996). Stereotypies, compulsions, and normal behavior in the context of motor routines in the rock hyrax (*Procavia capensis*). *Psychobiology, 24,* 235–246.

Settle, G. A. (1978). The quiddity of tiger quolls. *Australian Natural History, 19,* 164–169.

Shapiro, K. J. (1997). A phenomenological approach to the study of nonhuman animals. In R. W. Mitchell, N. S. Thompson, & H. L. Miles (eds.), *Anthropomorphism, Anecdotes, and Animals* (pp. 277–295). Albany: State University of New York Press.

Sharpe, L. L., Clutton-Brock, T. H., Brotherton, P. N. M., Cameron, E. Z., & Cherry, M. I. (2002). Experimental provisioning increases play in free-ranging meerkats. *Animal Behaviour, 64,* 113–121.

Sheets-Johnstone, M. (1999). *The primacy of movement.* New York: John Benjamins.

Sherwin, C. M. (1998). Voluntary wheel running: A review and novel interpretation. *Animal Behaviour, 56,* 11–27.

Shettleworth, S. J. (1998). *Cognition, evolution, and behavior.* New York: Oxford University Press.

Shine, R. (1988). Parental care in reptiles. In C. Gans & R. B. Huey (eds.), *Biology of the Reptilia* (Vol. 16, Ecology B, pp. 275–329). New York: Alan R. Liss.

Short, J., Kinnear, J. E., & Robley, A. (2002). Surplus killing by introduced predators in Australia—evidence for ineffective anti-predator adaptations in native prey species? *Biological Conservation, 103,* 283–301.

Sibley, C. G., & Ahlquist, J. E. (1990). *Phylogeny and classification of birds*. New Haven, Conn.: Yale University Press.

Sibley, C. G., & Monroe, B. L. J. (1990). *Distribution and taxonomy of birds of the world*. New Haven, Conn.: Yale University Press.

Siegel, M. A., & Jensen, R. A. (1986). The effects of naloxone and cage size on social play and activity in isolated young rats. *Behavioral and Neural Biology, 45*, 155–168.

Sih, A. (1992). Prey uncertainty and the balancing of antipredator and feeding needs. *American Naturalist, 139*, 1052–1069.

Sih, A., & Mateo, J. (2001). Punishment and persistence pay: A new model of territorial establishment and space use. *Trends in Ecology and Evolution, 16*, 477–479.

Simmons, K. E. L. (1966). Anting and the problem of self-stimulation. *Journal of Zoology, London, 149*, 145–162.

Singer, D. G., & Singer, J. L. (1990). *The house of make believe: Children's play and the development of imagination*. Cambridge, Mass.: Harvard University Press.

Singer, J. L. (1991). Cognitive and affective implications of imaginative play in childhood. In M. Lewis (ed.), *Child and Adolescent Psychiatry* (pp. 174–186). Baltimore: Williams and Wilkins.

Singer, J. L., & Lythcott, M. A. (2002). Fostering school achievement and creativity through sociodramatic play in the classroom. *Research in the Schools, 9*, 43–52.

Siviy, S. M. (1998). Neurobiological substrates of play behavior: Glimpses into the structure and function of mammalian playfulness. In M. Bekoff & J. A. Byers (eds.), *Animal Play: Evolutionary, Comparative, and Ecological Perspectives* (pp. 221–242). Cambridge: Cambridge University Press.

Siviy, S. M., Baliko, C. N., & Bowers, S. (1997). Rough-and-tumble play behavior in Fischer-344 and Buffalo rats: Effects of social isolation. *Physiology and Behavior, 61*, 597–602.

Siviy, S. M., Love, N. J., DeCicco, B. M., Giordana, S. B., & Seifert, T. L. (2003). The relative playfulness of juvenile Lewis and Fischer-344 rats. *Physiology and Behavior, 80*, 385–394.

Skeate, S. T. (1984). Courtship and reproductive behaviour of captive white-fronted Amazon parrots *Amozona albifrons*. *Bird Behaviour, 5*, 103–109.

Skeate, S. T. (1985). Social play behaviour in captive white-fronted Amazon parrots *Amazona albifrons*. *Bird Behaviour, 6*, 46–48.

Skutch, A. F. (1996). *The minds of birds*. College Station: Texas A&M University Press.

Slentz, K. L., & Krogh, S. L. (2001). *Teaching young children: Contexts for learning*. Mahwah, N.J.: Erlbaum.

Slobodchikoff, C. N. (2002). Cognition and communication in prairie dogs. In M. Bekoff, C. Allen, & G. M. Burghardt (eds.), *The Cognitive Animal: Empirical and Theoretical Perspectives on Animal Cognition* (pp. 257–266). Cambridge, Mass.: MIT Press.

Smilansky, S. (1968). *The effects of sociodramatic play on disavantaged children*. New York: Wiley.

Smith, D., Collins, D., & Holmes, P. (2003). Impact of mental practice on strength. *International Journal of Sport Psychology, 1*, 293–306.

Smith, E. N., Robertson, S. L., & Adams, S. R. (1981). Thermoregulation of the spiny soft-shelled turtle *Trionyx spinifer. Physiological Zoology, 54*, 74–80.

Smith, E. O. (ed.). (1978). *Social play in primates*. New York: Academic Press.

Smith, L. K., Fantella, S.-L. N., & Pellis, S. M. (1999). Playful defensive responses in adult male rats depends on the status of the unfamiliar opponent. *Aggressive Behavior, 25*, 141–152.

Smith, P. K. (1982). Does play matter? Functional and evolutionary aspects of animal and human play. *Behavioral and Brain Sciences, 5*, 139–184.

Smith, P. K. (1988). Children's play and its role in early development: A reevaluation of the "play ethos." In A. D. Pellegrini (ed.), *Psychological Bases for Early Education* (pp. 207–226). Chichester, England: Wiley.

Smith, P. K. (1996). Play, ethology, and education: A personal account. In A. D. Pellegrini (ed.), *The Future of Play Theory* (pp. 3–21). Albany: State University of New York Press.

Soares, D. (2002). An ancient sensory organ in crocodilians. *Nature, 417*, 241–242.

Sober, E., & Wilson, D. S. (1998). *Unto others: The evolution and psychology of unselfish behavior.* Cambridge, MA: Harvard University Press.

Sol, D., Timmermans, S., & Lefebvre, L. (2002). Behavioral flexibility and invasion success in birds. *Animal Behaviour, 63*, 495–502.

Somma, L. A. (2003). A few more additions to the literature on parental behavior in lizards and snakes. *Bulletin of the Chicago Herpetological Society, 38*, 217–220.

Sommer, V., & Mendoza-Granados, D. (1995). Play as indicator of habitat quality: A field study of langur monkeys (*Presbytis entellus*). *Ethology, 99*, 177–192.

Spear, L. P. (2000). Neurobehavioral changes in adolescence. *Current Directions in Psychological Science, 9*, 111–114.

Spencer, H. (1872). *Principles of psychology*. 2nd ed. (Vol. 2). New York: Appleton.

Spinka, M., Newberry, R. C., & Bekoff, M. (2001). Mammalian play: Training for the unexpected. *Quarterly Review of Biology, 76*, 141–168.

Stamps, J. A. (1995). Motor learning and the value of familiar space. *American Naturalist, 146*, 41–58.

Stephens, P. R. & Wiens, J. J. (2003). Ecological diversification and phylogeny of emydid turtles. *Biological Journal of the Linnean Society, 79*, 577–610.

Stephenson, W. (1967). *The play theory of mass communication*. Chicago: University of Chicago Press.

Stokstad, E. (2003). New attention to ADHD genes. *Science, 301*, 160–161.

Stone, P. A., Dobie, J. L., & Henry, R. P. (1992). The effect of aquatic oxygen levels on diving and ventilation behavior in soft-shelled *Trionyx spiniferus*, stinkpot *Sternotherus odoratus*, and mud turtles *Kinosternon subrubrum. Physiological Zoology, 65*, 331–345.

Stoner, E. A. (1947). Anna hummingbird at play. *Condor, 49*, 36.

Strahan, R. (ed.). (1995). *Mammals of Australia*. Washington, D.C.: Smithsonian Institution Press.

Stumper, R. (1921). Etudes sur les Fourmis. III. Recherches sur l'ethologie du *Formicoxenus nitidulus* Nyl. *Bulletin de la Société Entomologique de Belgique, 3*, 90–97.

Sullivan, J. P., Lavoué, S., & Hopkins, C. D. (2000). Molecular systematics of the African electric fishes (Mormyroidea: Teleostei) and a model for the evolution of their electric organs. *Journal of Experimental Biology, 203*, 665–683.

Sutton-Smith, B. (1997). *The ambiguity of play*. Cambridge, Mass.: Harvard University Press.

Sutton-Smith, B. (1999). Evolving a consilience of play definitions: Playfully. In S. Reifel (ed.), *Play and Culture Studies* (Vol. 2, pp. 239–256). Stamford, Conn.: Ablex.

Sutton-Smith, B. (2003a). Play as a parody of emotional vulnerability. In D. Lytle (ed.), *Play and Culture Studies* (Vol. 5, pp. 3–17). Westport, Conn.: Praeger.

Sutton-Smith, B. (2003b). Tertiary emotions and ludic nature—the ideologies and human nature. In M. Krüger (ed.), *Menschenbilder in Sport* (pp. 262–278). Schorndorf, Germany: Verlag Karl Hoffman.

Sutton-Smith, B., & Abrams, D. M. (1978). Psychosexual material in the stories told by children: The fucker. *Archives of Sexual Behavior, 7*, 521–543.

Sutton-Smith, B., & Kelly-Byrne, D. (1984). The idealization of play. In P. K. Smith (ed.), *Play in Animals and Humans* (pp. 305–321). Oxford: Basil Blackwell.

Swanson, P. L. (1949). "Hurdling" by the needlefish. *Copeia, 1949*, 219.

Symons, D. (1978). *Play and aggression: A study of rhesus monkeys*. New York: Columbia University Press.

Tchernov, E., Rieppel, O., Zaher, H., Polcyn, M. J., & Jacobs, L. L. (2000). A fossil snake with limbs. *Science, 287*, 2010–2012.

Tegano, D. W., Sawyers, J. K., & Moran, J. D., III. (1989). Problem-finding and solving in play: The teacher's role. *Childhood Education, 66*, 92–97.

Thelen, E. (1995). Motor development: A new synthesis. *American Psychologist, 50*, 79–95.

Thelen, E., Schöner, G., Schlier, C., & Smith, L. B. (2001). The dynamics of embodiment: A field theory of infant perserverative reaching. *Behavioral and Brain Sciences, 24*, 1–86.

Thierry, B., Iwaniuk, A. N., & Pellis, S. M. (2000). The influence of phylogeny on the social behaviour of macaques (Primates: Cercopithecidae, genus *Macaca*). *Ethology, 106*, 713–728.

Thomas, R. B. (2002). Conditional mating strategy in a long-lived vertebrate: Ontogenetic shifts in the mating tactics of male slider turtles (*Trachemys scripta*). *Copeia, 2002*, 456–461.

Thompson, E. P. (1851). *The passions of animals*. London: Chapman and Hall.

Thompson, K. V. (1996). Behavioral development and play. In D. Kleiman, M. E. Allen, K. V. Thompson, Lumpkin S., & Harris, H. (eds.), *Wild Mammals in Captivity: Principles and Techniques* (pp. 352–371). Chicago: University of Chicago Press.

Thompson, K. V. (1998). Self assessment in juvenile play. In M. Bekoff & J. A. Byers (eds.), *Animal Play: Evolutionary, Comparative, and Ecological Perspectives* (pp. 183–204). Cambridge: Cambridge University Press.

Thompson, R. A., & Nelson, C. A. (2001). Developmental science and the media. *American Psychologist, 56*, 5–15.

Thompson, S. D., Ono, K. A., Oftedal, O. T., & Boness, D. J. (1987). Thermoregulation and resting metabolic rate of California sea lion (*Zalophus californicus*) pups. *Physiological Zoology, 60*, 730–736.

Thorpe, W. H. (1956). *Learning and instinct in animals.* Cambridge, Mass.: Harvard University Press.

Thorpe, W. H. (1966). Ritualization in ontogeny: I. animal play. *Philosophical Transactions of the Royal Society of London B, 251*, 311–319.

Timberlake, W. (2001). Motivational modes in behavior systems. In R. R. Mowrer & S. B. Klein (eds.), *Handbook of Contemporary Learning Theories* (pp. 155–210). San Francisco: Erlbaum.

Timberlake, W., & Silva, K. (1995). Appetitive behavior in ethology, psychology, and behavior systems. In N. S. Thompson (ed.), *Perspectives in Ethology* (Vol. 11, Behavioral design, pp. 211–253). New York: Plenum.

Tinbergen, N. (1951). *The study of instinct.* Oxford: Clarendon Press.

Tinbergen, N. (1963). On aims and methods of ethology. *Zeitschrift für Tierpsychologie, 20*, 410–433.

Toerring, M. J., & Belbenoit, P. (1979). Motor programmes and electroreception in mormyrid fish. *Behavioral Ecology and Sociobiology, 4*, 369–379.

Tropp, J., & Markus, E. J. (2001). Sex differences in the dynamics of cue utilization and exploratory behavior. *Behavioural Brain Research, 119*, 143–154.

Trut, L. N. (1999). Early canid domestication: The farm-fox experiment. *American Scientist, 87*, 160–169.

Turner, V. (1982). *From ritual to theatre: the human seriousness of play.* New York: PAJ Publications.

Valerio, M., & Barlow, G. W. (1986). Ontogeny of young Midas cichlids: A study of feeding, filial cannibalism and agonism in relation to differences in size. *Biology of Behaviour, 11*, 16–35.

van den Berg, C. L., Hol, T., van Ree, J. M., Spruijt, B. M., Everts, H., & Koolhaas, J. M. (1999). Play is indispensable for an adequate development of coping with social challenges in the rat. *Developmental Psychobiology, 34*, 129–138.

Vaňková, D., & Bartoš, L. (2002). The function of mounting behaviour in farmed red deer calves. *Ethology, 108*, 473–482.

van Tienderen, P. H. (1997). Generalists, specialists, and the evolution of phenotypic plasticity in sympatric populations of distinct species. *Evolution, 51*, 1372–1380.

Vanderschuren, L. J. M. J., Niesink, R. J. M., & Van Ree, J. M. (1997). The neurobiology of social play behavior in rats. *Neuroscience and Biobehavioral Reviews, 21*, 309–326.

Veblen, T. (1899/1994). *The theory of the leisure class*. New York: Penguin.

Visser, E. K., van Reenen, C. G., van der Werf, J. T. N., Schilder, M. B. H., Knaap, J. H., Barneveld, A., & Blokhuis, H. J. (2002). Heart rate and heart rate variability during a novel object test and a handling test in young horses. *Physiology and Behavior, 76*, 289–296.

Vogt, R. C. (1978). Systematics and ecololgy of the false map turtle complex *Graptemys pseudogeographica*. Unpublished Ph.D. dissertation, University of Wisconsin, Madison.

von Uexküll, J. (1921). *Umwelt und Innenwelt der Tiere* (second edition). Springer, Berlin.

Vygotsky, L. S. (1967). Play and its role in the mental development of the child. *Soviet Psychology, 12*, 62–76.

Vygotsky, L. S., & Luria, A. R. (1993). *Studies on the history of behavior: Ape, primitive, and child* (V. I. Golod & J. E. Knox, trans.). Hillsdale, N.J.: Erlbaum.

Wagener, T. K. (1998). The ontogeny of red wolf (*Canis rufus*) social behavior: Implications for sociality and taxonomy. Unpublished M.S. thesis, University of Tennessee, Knoxville.

Wälder, R. (1978). The psychoanalytic theory of play. In D. Müller-Schwarze (ed.), *Evolution of Play Behavior* (pp. 36–52). Stroudsburg, Pa: Dowden, Hutchinson & Ross.

Walker, C., & Byers, J. A. (1991). Heritability of locomotor play in house mice, *Mus musculus*. *Animal Behaviour, 42*, 891–898.

Walker, L. (1996). Female mate-choice: Are marsupials really so different? In D. B. Croft & U. Ganslosser (eds.), *Comparison of Marsupial and Placental Behaviour* (pp. 208–225). Fürth, Germany: Filander Verlag.

Walton, D. W., & Richardson, B. J. (eds.). (1989). *Fauna of Australia* (Vol. 1B, Mammalia). Canberra: Australian Government Publishing Service.

Wang, T., Busk, M., & Overgaard, J. (2001). The respiratory consequences of feeding in amphibians and reptiles. *Comparative Biochemistry and Physiology* Part A, *128*, 535–549.

Ward, J. A., & Barlow, G. W. (1967). The maturation and regulation of glancing off the parents by young orange chromides (*Etroplus maculatus*: Pisces—Cichlidae. *Behaviour, 29*, 1–56.

Ward, R. E. Jr. (2002). Fan violence: Social problem or moral panic. *Aggression and Violent Behavior, 7*, 453–475.

Waring, G. H. (1983). *Horse behavior*. Park Ridge, N.J.: Noyes.

Washburn, M. F. (1908). *The animal mind*. New York: Macmillan.

Wasman, E. (1905). *Comparative studies in the psychology of ants and higher animals*. St. Louis: B. Herder.

Wasserman, E. A. (1997). The science of animal cognition: Past, present, and future. *Journal of Experimental Psychology: Animal Behavior Processes, 23*, 123–135.

Watson, D. M. (1992). Object play in a Laughing Kookaburra *Dacelo novaeguineae*. *Emu, 92*, 106–108.

Watson, D. M. (1993). The play associations of red-necked wallabies (*Macropus rufogriseus banksianus*) and relation to other social contexts. *Ethology, 94*, 1–20.

Watson, D. M. (1998). Kangaroos at play: Play behaviour in the Macropodoidea. In M. Bekoff & J. A. Byers (eds.), *Animal Play: Evolutionary, Comparative, and Ecological Perspectives* (pp. 61–95). Cambridge: Cambridge University Press.

Watson, D. M., & Croft, D. B. (1993). Playfighting in captive red-necked wallabies, *Macropus rufogriseus banksianus*. *Behaviour, 126*, 219–245.

Watson, D. M., & Croft, D. B. (1996). Age-related differences in playfighting strategies of captive male red-necked wallabies (*Macropus rufogriseus banksianus*). *Ethology, 102*, 336–346.

Webb, N. B. (ed.). (1991). *Play therapy with children in crisis*. New York: Guilford Press.

Weinstein, R. B., & Full, R. J. (1999). Intermittent locomotion increases endurance in a gecko. *Physiological and Biochemical Zoology, 72*, 732–739.

Weisfeld, G. (1999). *Evolutionary principles of human adolescence*. New York: Basic Books.

Weisler, A., & McCall, R. (1976). Exploration and play. *American Psychologist, 31*, 492–508.

Weiss, H., & Bradley, R. S. (2001). What drives societal collapse? *Science, 291*, 609–610.

Weldon, P. J., Aldrich, J. R., Klun, J. A., Oliver, J. E., & Debboun, M. (2003). Benzoquinones from millipedes deter mosquitoes and elicit self-anointing in capuchin monkeys (*Cebus* spp.). *Naturwissenschaften, 90*, 301–304.

Welker, W. I. (1971). Ontogeny of play and exploratory behaviors: A definition of problems and a search for new conceptual solutions. In H. Moltz (ed.), *The Ontogeny of Vertebrate Behavior* (pp. 171–210). New York: Academic Press.

Wells, H. G. (1934a). *Seven famous novels*. New York: Knopf.

Wells, H. G. (1934b). The time machine. In H. G. Wells (Ed.), *Seven Famous Novels* (pp. 3–66). New York: Knopf.

Wells, K. D. (1977). The social behaviour of anuran amphibians. *Animal Behaviour, 25*, 666–693.

Wells, M. J. (1978). *Octopus: Physiology and behavior of an advanced invertebrate*. London: Chapman and Hall.

Wells, R. T. (1989). Vombatidae. In D. W. Walton & B. J. Richardson (eds.), *Fauna of Australia* (Vol. 1B, *Mammalia*, pp. 755–768). Canberra: Australian Government Publishing Service.

West, M. (1974). Social play in the domestic cat. *American Zoologist, 14*, 427–436.

West, M. J., & King, A. P. (1985). Social guidance of vocal learning by female cowbirds: Validating its functional significance. *Zeitschrift für Tierpsychologie, 70*, 225–235.

Whishaw, I. Q., Metz, G. A. S., Kolb, B., & Pellis, S. M. (2001). Accelerated nervous system development contributes to behavioral efficiency in the laboratory mouse: A behavioral review and theoretical proposal. *Developmental Psychobiology, 39*, 151–170.

Whitaker, L. M. (1957). A résumé of anting, with particular reference to a captive orchard oriole. *Wilson Bulletin, 69*, 195–262.

Whiten, A., & Byrne, R. W. (1988). Tactical deception in primates. *Behavioral and Brain Sciences, 11*, 233–244.

Whitman, C. O. (1899). Myths in animal psychology. *Monist, 9*, 524–537.

Wickler, W., & Seibt, U. (1997). Aimed object-throwing by a wild African elephant in an interspecific encounter. *Ethology, 103*, 365–368.

Wilcox, R. S., & Jackson, R. R. (1998). Cognitive abilities of araneophagic jumping spiders. In R. P. Balda, I. Pepperberg, & A. C. Kamil (eds.), *Animal Cognition in Nature* (pp. 411–434). San Diego: Academic Press.

Wilcox, R. S., Jackson, R. R., & Gentile, K. (1996). Spiderweb smokescreens: Spider trickster uses background noise to mask stalking movements. *Animal Behaviour, 51*, 313–326.

Wilcoxon, H. C., Dragoin, W. B., & Kral, P. A. (1971). Illness-induced aversions in rat and quail: Relative salience of visual and gustatory cues. *Science, 171*, 826–828.

Wilkinson, R. G. (2000). *Mind the gap.* New Haven: Yale University Press.

Williams, G. C. (1991). *Natural selection.* Oxford: Oxford University Press.

Williams, R. W., Cavada, C., & Reinoso-Suárez, F. (1993). Rapid evolution of the visual system: A cellular assay of the retina and dorsal lateral geniculate nucleus of the Spanish wildcat and the domestic cat. *Journal of Neuroscience, 13*, 208–228.

Willingham, D. B. (1998). A neuropsychological theory of motor skill learning. *Psychological Review, 105*, 558–584.

Willingham, D. B. (1999). The neural basis of motor-skill learning. *Current Directions in Psychological Science, 6*, 178–182.

Wilson, D. S., Clark, A. B., Coleman, K., & Dearstyne, T. (1994). Shyness and boldness in humans and other animals. *Trends in Ecology and Evolution, 9*, 442–446.

Wilson, D. S., & Sober, E. (1994). Reintroducing group selection to the human behavioral sciences. *Behavioral and Brain Sciences, 17*, 585–654.

Wilson, E. O. (1975). *Sociobiology: the new synthesis.* Cambridge: Belknap Press.

Wilson, S. C., & Kleiman, D. G. (1974). Eliciting play: A comparative study (*Octodon, Octodontomys, Pediolagus, Choeropsis, Ailuropoda*). *American Zoologist, 14*, 341–370.

Wilsson, L. (1971). Observations and experiments on the ethology of the European beavor (*Castor fibor* L.). *Vilrevy Swedish Wildlife, 8*, 115–226.

Winnicott, D. W. (1971). *Playing and reality.* New York: Basic Books.

Winter, J. W. (1996). Australasian possums and Madagascan lemurs. In D. B. Croft & U. Ganslosser (eds.), *Comparison of Marsupial and Placental Behaviour* (pp. 262–292). Fürth, Germany: Filander Verlag.

Wolff, A., & Hausberger, M. (1994). Behaviour of foals before weaning may have some genetic basis. *Ethology, 96*, 1–10.

Wood, J. B., & Wood, D. A. (1999). Enrichment for an advanced invertebrate. *The Shape of Enrichment, 8,* 1–5.

Wray, G. A., Levinton, J. S., & Shapiro, L. H. (1996). Molecular evidence for deep precambrian divergences among metazoan phyla. *Science, 274,* 568–573.

Wyman, R. L., & Walters-Wyman, M. F. (1985). Chafing in fishes: Occurrence, ontogeny, function, and evolution. *Envionmental Biology of Fishes, 12,* 281–289.

Yágüez, L., Canavan, A. G. M., Lange, H. W., & Hömberg, V. (1999). Motor learning by imagery is differentially affected in Parkinson's and Huntington's diseases. *Behavioural Brain Research, 102,* 115–127.

Young, S. A. (2001). Edward T. Hall (1924–2001). *Nature, 413,* 588.

Zardoya, R., & Meyer, A. (2004). Molecular evidence on the origin of and the phylogenetic relationships among the major groups of vertebrates. In A. Moya & E. Font (eds.), *Evolution: From Molecules to Ecosystems* (pp. 209–217). Oxford: Oxford University Press.

Zentall, T. R. (2003). Imitation by animals: How do they do it? *Current Directions in Psychological Science, 12,* 91–95.

Zimmerman, A., Stauffacher, M., Langhans, W., & Würbel, H. (2001). Enrichment-dependent differences in novelty exploration in rats can be explained by habituation. *Behavioural Brain Research, 121,* 11–20.

Zito, M., Evans, S., & Weldon, P. J. (2003). Owl monkeys (*Aotus* spp.) self-anoint with plants and millipedes. *Folia Primatologica, 74,* 159–161.

Zlamal, A., & Wieczorek, M. (2002). Stereotypies in polar bears kept at Warsaw Zoological Garden *Advances in Ethology (Ethology Supplement), 37,* 96.

Zucker, E. L., & Clarke, M. R. (1992). Developmental and comparative aspects of social play of mantled howling monkeys in costa Rica. *Behaviour, 123,* 144–171.

Zuckerman, M. (1984). Sensation-seeking: A comparative approach to a human trait. *Behavioral and Brain Sciences, 7,* 413–471.

Zug, G. R. (1974). Crocodile galloping: An unique gait for reptiles. *Copeia, 1974,* 550–552.

Zug, G. R., Vitt, L. J., & Caldwell, J. P. (2001). *Herpetology.* 2nd ed. San Diego: Academic Press.

Zupanc, G. K. (1999). Neurogenesis, cell death and regeneration in the adult gymnotiform brain. *Journal of Experimental Biology, 202,* 1435–1446.

Animal Index

This index is organized primarily by common names as well as orders and families. Scientific names are given where specific species are meant rather than the generic term for a group of animals such as bears, bushbabies, or barnacles. The latter are also used for most groups for which data on play are not given in this book. For species lacking well-known or accepted common names the scientific names are listed under the major group (e.g., cockroaches)

Name Index

Subject Index